S0-ADD-154

RESOURCES, ENVIRONMENT, AND POPULATION: PRESENT KNOWLEDGE, FUTURE OPTIONS

RESOURCES, ENVIRONMENT, AND POPULATION: PRESENT KNOWLEDGE, FUTURE OPTIONS

Kingsley Davis
Mikhail S. Bernstam
Editors

Based on a conference held at the
Hoover Institution, Stanford University,
1–3 February 1989

POPULATION AND DEVELOPMENT REVIEW
A Supplement to Volume 16, 1990

THE POPULATION COUNCIL
New York

New York   Oxford
OXFORD UNIVERSITY PRESS
1991

Oxford University Press

Oxford   New York   Toronto
Delhi   Bombay   Calcutta   Madras   Karachi
Petaling Jaya   Singapore   Hong Kong   Tokyo
Nairobi   Dar es Salaam   Cape Town
Melbourne   Auckland
and associated companies in
Berlin   Ibadan

© 1991 by The Population Council, Inc.

Published in the United States
by Oxford University Press, Inc. and The Population Council, Inc.

FIRST PRINTING 1991

Oxford is a registered trademark of Oxford University Press

ISBN 0-19-507049-6 clothbound
ISBN 0-19-507050-X paperback

Library of Congress Cataloging-in-Publication Data

Resources, environment, and population: present knowledge, future
options / Kingsley Davis, Mikhail S. Bernstam, editors.
     p.   cm.
     "Based on a conference held at the Hoover Institution, Stanford
University, 1–3 February 1989."
     "Population and development review. A supplement to volume 16, 1990."
     Includes bibliographical references.
     ISBN 0-19-507049-6 (cloth). — ISBN 0-19-507050-X (paper)
     1. Population—Economic aspects—Congresses.
     2. Population—Environmental aspects—Congresses.
     3. Natural resources—Congresses.
     4. Economic development—Environmental aspects—Congresses.
     I. Davis, Kingsley, 1908–   .   II. Bernstam, Mikhail S.   III. Population
and development review. Vol. 16 (Supplement)
     HB849.41.R47   1991
     333.7—dc20   91-3939
                                                                          CIP

PRINTED IN THE UNITED STATES OF AMERICA

CONTENTS

ACKNOWLEDGMENTS

NATURALLY, MORE THAN two or four hands have made this volume possible. First honors go to our donors, among whom it is our pleasure to list, as follows: Bergstrom Foundation, Cowell Foundation, Hewlett Foundation, Hoover Institution, Population Council, Skaggs Foundation, and Henry McIntyre. Without their generosity it would have been impossible to hold the conference and to arrange for publication of the present book.

In the work of keeping the enterprise going, and going exceedingly well, we were extremely fortunate to have, at different times, two assistants—first, Helen M. Sellers and then, Lynn Noble. Without their dedication and numerous skills, we would have found the task too overwhelming to get done.

We also wish to extend our thanks to Ethel Churchill, Managing Editor, and Robert Heidel, Production Editor, of *Population and Development Review,* who were responsible for the editing that proved indispensable throughout the preparation of the book for publication.

KINGSLEY DAVIS

MIKHAIL S. BERNSTAM

PREFACE

THE ORIGINAL IDEA behind the present book was that interdisciplinary science, especially applied science, is facilitated by face-to-face contact, and that in no subject is this truer than in the study of population and resources. For centuries now "the population problem" has been debated without being solved. For their part, demographers live in their own discipline and seldom venture into related fields where their knowledge is usually no better than that of educated laymen. On the other side, natural scientists tend to have an oversimplified view of human demography. Their discussion of environmental issues often ignores the social context. Our immediate aim, therefore, was to hold a conference of distinguished scholars representing many branches of science but focusing on a topic few can match in importance in the world today—the relationships between human demography, resource use, and environmental change. The different contingents sitting around the table would, we thought, be strongly impelled to talk to one another.

The conference was held at the Hoover Institution, Stanford University, 1–3 February 1989, with some 26 invited participants. It brought together experts from a wide variety of fields and elicited from them highly informative questions and answers. Although dealing with very controversial and important issues, the participants exhibited remarkably little belligerency. Rather they seemed to enjoy transcending for a while the boundaries of their own specialties.

From the start, we hoped to publish a book based on the proceedings. This idea was strengthened by the success of the conference, reflected in the quality of the written contributions and in the spirited discussion the meeting generated. It was felt, however, that such a book should not be simply a collection of the papers given at the conference, but instead a genuine symposium of papers edited, revised, and, often, rewritten for publication, and including some invited papers written after the conference.

The outcome of the work of editing and revision is the present book. The content is wide ranging, representing the differing theoretical, ideological, and disciplinary orientations of the contributors. The seventeen articles are complemented by eight commentaries. Broadly, the organization proceeds from general principles to documentation of specific areas of human concern related to resources and environmental impacts and concludes with implications for policy.

The volume starts with an article that examines four major historical efforts to conceptualize the relationship between population and resources—the search for scientific laws linking population and resources, the idea of "carrying capacity" and the related notion of "limits to growth," and demographic transition theory. The last of these is endorsed as an organizing and stimulating principle in comprehending the broad sweep of population change in the context of development.

In the section "Estimating the Future," the first article identifies conceptual issues to guide thinking about the future course of economic development and the environment and sketches out the operational principles of sustainable development. The second considers standard forecasts of demographic trends in the twenty-first century in the broader intellectual context of theoretical and empirical studies of population dynamics. Forecasts that hypothesize levels and changes in vital rates without reference to the implied changes in population size are contrasted with those that reason in terms of Earth's carrying capacity and the responsiveness of population growth rates to feedback.

The sections on "Water, Energy, and Development," "The Rise of Global Pollution," and "World Deforestation and Its Consequences" explore specific dimensions of the interrelations between population, resources, and the environment, including localized and global effects, present and future constraints, and scope for remedial action.

Because ultimately interactions between population and resources are reflections of paths toward socioeconomic development, the final section, "Are There Limits to Growth?," offers a synthesis of theoretical approaches to population–development relationships and explores in international political contexts the effects of economic growth and demographic trends on the environment. The first article in the section examines reasons for intervention to modify population processes under the four headings resources, capital, employment, and Earth. The two following articles discuss the long-term relationship between economic growth and pollution under contrasting institutional arrangements—those of market and socialist economies. Beginning with the assumption that improvements in the environment are subordinate to improvements in human welfare at large, the final article considers tradeoffs that confront human societies between continuing population growth and gains in material progress.

Since virtually all advanced countries today have a fertility rate below that needed for population replacement, it is reasonable to expect that as the whole world becomes more highly developed, mankind's interest in growth in terms of sheer human numbers will diminish and, wisely, cease. In the meantime, however, the global population is still growing rapidly, and the world seems already crowded. The urgency of understanding the implications of the relationships examined in this volume can hardly be overstated.

Hoover Institution   KINGSLEY DAVIS
Stanford University   MIKHAIL S. BERNSTAM

Population and Resources: Fact and Interpretation

KINGSLEY DAVIS

THE INTERRELATION BETWEEN POPULATION AND RESOURCES is a difficult subject. For this there seem to be several reasons. First, the two interacting sets of phenomena (resources and population) come from different universes of discourse. To bring them together in a common frame of reference is not like comparing apples and oranges, which at least are both fruit, but more like comparing, say, houses and trees, or horses and bacteria. The category "resources" itself includes a huge and diverse miscellany of things having little in common. Copper and fresh water, for example, have nothing in common except that both are used by man. Further confusion arises from the fact that mankind's use of resources is not just a phenomenon to be observed and understood scientifically, but a matter of major political and economic significance and therefore of controversy and popular opinion (Teitelbaum and Winter, 1985).

Further, no one specializes in the study of population and resources as an integrated discipline. One is either a demographer or a natural scientist, but not both at once. Demographers are baffled by the encyclopedic knowledge they think the natural scientist must possess, and the environmental specialist often has only a sketchy view of human demography.

Demography itself is a peculiar subject. It has developed analytic tools that can be applied to nonhuman as well as to human entities—for instance, to telephone poles, rabbits, machines, and cells. Scholars in the social sciences, however, are not used to dealing with human beings in abstraction from ideas, motives, and, in general, subjective aspects of behavior. As a result, the demographer is often regarded in social science circles as a mere provider of statistical facts, while the economist, sociologist, and social psychologist provide the interpretation. It frequently turns out, however, that the best person to interpret the facts is the scholar who produced them in the first place.

On the environmental side, the wide array of disciplines that must somehow be drawn upon is intimidating. Since no one individual could

1

possibly master all the fields involved, the best course is to bring different specialists together. Specialization is a necessity, not a fault.

As things stand, despite the intense public interest in population and resources, the subject receives little direct attention from demographers. The reason is not that they regard it as unimportant, but rather that they take its importance for granted. For instance, during the last three decades, a field of study much favored by demographers has been fertility in Third World countries. The most expensive survey ever undertaken—the World Fertility Survey—was carried out during this period, as were countless other surveys and studies. The reason for this interest is not a preoccupation with human fertility per se, but rather an unquestioned belief that high fertility is causing too much population growth in the Third World, straining limited resources. But demographers have tended to rule themselves out of the direct study of environmental and ecological questions. They feel that mastering the voluminous literature on human demography is hard enough, without trying to cross the barrier separating social from natural sciences.

In the present article, I shall briefly examine four concepts that have been used in the field of population and resources. These are the search for scientific "laws" linking population and resources, the idea of "carrying capacity," the related notion of "limits to growth," and the concept of the "demographic transition." In considering these overlapping ideas, or principles, I shall be quite critical but not malicious because the subject is too important to be buried under needless controversy. My perspective is that of a demographer.

The search for laws linking population and resources

In view of the difficulties of focusing on the linkages between population and resources, it is not surprising that scholars have sought a way out. One way they have pursued is to find scientific "laws," or "principles," that can order and simplify an otherwise chaotic subject. This has been accomplished in what is variously called "formal demography," "mathematical demography," or "stable population theory."[1]

In fact, however, mathematical demography has little to do with resources. It has, so to speak, kept away from messy population–resource problems by dealing almost exclusively with "inside variables" rather than with "external" ones. In the meantime, those demographers willing to tackle resource questions have kept looking for helpful generalizations of one sort or another.

One demographer who was willing to state generalizations about population was Malthus. In his *Essay* (p.12), he says: (1) Population is necessarily limited by the means of subsistence. (2) Population invariably increases where the means of subsistence increase, unless prevented by some very powerful and obvious checks.

Unfortunately, these are two of the most confusing propositions in social science. If they are taken literally, as empirical findings, they are patently false. Population is not in fact "necessarily limited" by a scarcity of the means of subsistence. It is limited by whatever contributes to mortality, such as wars, epidemics, overeating, alcohol consumption, smoking, and so on. On the other hand, if Malthus's statements are taken as hypothetical, they are true only by definition. A "check" to population must be defined as whatever impedes population growth. The proposition in effect, therefore, is a simple tautology: population growth is impeded by whatever impedes it.

Another example of the search for laws is provided by two articles by E. G. Ravenstein in the *Journal of the Royal Statistical Society,* 1885 and 1889, on "The laws of migration." One rule is that people move no farther than they have to, and as a result there are more short-range than long-range migrants. A further rule is that a migratory stream always produces a counter-current of lesser strength. A third rule is that women predominate among short-range migrants. Finally, he maintains that migration tends to increase with the development of manufactures and commerce.

Under criticism for calling his rules "laws," Ravenstein admits they are not laws in the scientific sense. They are characterized by unexplained exceptions and are not logically connected with other propositions in a system of reasoning (Davis, 1989: 248).

Although Ravenstein searched for laws of migration in order to lay the foundations of a science of migration, and though he is often cited, there was no follow-up building upon his work.

One problem with the search for empirical regularities is that the regularity is viewed as operating mechanically, thus overlooking perhaps the most important trait of the human animal—namely, his possession of culture. We can ask why it is that the human organism requires very little material to subsist and yet, in fact, has transformed the world in its ceaseless search for material goods. It is mankind's possession of culture that has given him his accumulative technology and his language and social organization. It is this that has ultimately allowed an explosion of the Earth's human population. And it is this that now paradoxically gives mankind the ability to satisfy wants that have little to do with the simple needs of the human animal. Indeed, it is amazing how, starting only about 10,000 years ago with the spread of agriculture, this once-inconspicuous mammal, hunting and gathering for a living, was soon able to create nation-states with tens of millions of citizens and with social structures and procedures so complicated that a system of sciences (the social sciences) has evolved to try to understand them. It is equally amazing that this inconspicuous animal has been able to build huge cities and can make airplanes that fly faster and farther than any bird.

What drives the creation and maintenance of this complex civilization? Whatever it is, it is surely not the primary, or absolute needs of the species, but the secondary and tertiary needs that have been created. People have transformed goods into symbols of status, and symbols into material forms. Instead of using the powerful new engines of production to give themselves more leisure and freedom from drudgery, the citizens of today's industrialized nations admonish one another to work harder, to compete in an unremitting struggle to "get ahead," to "insure one's future," to "succeed." Yet, increasingly, new inventions and devices are made simply to overcome the noxious effects of inventions and devices already in place. We build cars, for instance, with antismog devices, but the manufacture of antismog equipment itself contributes to air pollution. The solution of one problem nearly always creates new problems or makes old problems worse. People become enmeshed in a complicated system of paperwork, regulatory requirements, bureaucratic rituals, escalating taxes, and countless other tasks. It seems that human beings had more leisure and were under less "pressure" when they were hunters and gatherers than is the case now in civilized societies (Lee, 1968; Howell, 1979).

But the story of man's unique reliance on culture has often been told. Why repeat it here?

The answer is clear. If I am right—if the main feature that most clearly distinguishes humans from other mammals is their ability to make and use tools, to exchange goods, and to organize groups—then certain conclusions must follow. Perhaps the most important of these, and certainly the most elementary, is the principle that any theory of population and resources that overlooks cultural phenomena is very likely to be deficient. Yet in much of the literature, this is exactly what is done. The role of cultural factors is either minimized or distorted, often by unconscious assumption.

This is not a demand that every study in demography somehow inject cultural considerations into its analysis. Far from it. I am not talking about demography in general but about the study of the relationships between population and resources. It is this particular subject that requires close study of cultural and motivational factors. It is this field that exhibits some of the most glaring illogicalities.

"Carrying capacity"

If the search for scientific laws linking population and resources has not succeeded, perhaps another kind of approach will serve better. Let us take the concept of "carrying capacity" as an effort to build a bridge between demography and the environment. The general idea is that by analysis of soil and other elements of the environment, one can estimate how many people can be supported on a given amount of land. A recent symposium (Lee et al.,

1988) provides us with an example of the reasoning. One of the chapters—by the economist T. N. Srinivasan—deals with the question of "carrying capacity" in the rural areas of currently developing countries. His analysis is thoroughgoing and thus provides a good basis for discussion.

Srinivasan defines carrying capacity as "the maximum population that can be sustained indefinitely into the future" (p. 13). The built-in, unconscious bias of such a definition is readily apparent. Why should we be concerned only with the "maximum" population? Why not consider the "minimum" population as well? In some counties of western Texas, for example, there are not enough people to man the existing infrastructure. The same individual may therefore have to occupy more than one post. Yet few would claim that this population is too small to be "sustained." An animal species may suffer extinction if its numbers fall below a certain critical level, but hardly anyone would maintain that this is true of the human species today. If the population of a region is extremely scarce in relation to resources, people adjust their institutions and behavior to the situation. Australians and Canadians, for example, do not find their sparse populations to be an obstacle to maintaining a high level of living. On the contrary, in today's world a high population density is generally associated with poverty while a low density is associated with prosperity.

As a matter of fact, considerable attention has been given to areas that have lost population. Such loss is characteristically viewed by the business community as a calamity rather than a blessing. For example, on 3 January 1990, the *New York Times* ran a long story under the headline: "With rural towns vanishing, states choose which to save." The article, by Isabel Wilkerson, focused on Sheridan County, North Dakota, and its county seat, McClusky, as prototypes of what is happening across the rural areas of the United States. In North Dakota alone, there are ten "deeply distressed" counties.

> Complicating the problems of these counties is that their populations are steadily shrinking and aging. . . . While the population in the United States has doubled since 1930, the population in Sheridan County has dropped by two-thirds, from a peak of 7,373 people in 1930 to about 2,500 last year spread out over nearly 1000 square miles.

The article does not blame the economic plight of the rural towns on their loss of people, but it clearly regards the exodus as making things worse. In the words of the mayor of McClusky, "Watching shops close and towns disappear is like sitting there dying and waiting for someone to set the date for your funeral."

The assumption is that the depressed rural counties would be better off if they had not lost population, but no evidence is offered. One can argue the opposite—given the slender and uncertain resources of the "distressed" counties, if the population had grown as fast as that of the nation at large, it would have been a disaster. The exodus of people from rural areas is clearly a demographic adjustment to economic change. For the people who stay, as well as for those who leave, it helps to restore the balance between people and resources. If observers find vacant houses and stores depressing, bull-dozers can quickly reduce these structures to rubble and green crops can be planted for profit and beauty.

Another bias of the definition reported by Srinivasan lies in the word "sustained." The quotation says "carrying capacity" is "the maximum population that can be *sustained* indefinitely. . . ." Evidently, the word refers to commodities wholly or partially necessary for the individual to live, but from the context one gathers that the commodity really being considered is food. That is why I call the usual "carrying capacity" reasoning the "bread-alone fallacy." As we saw above, humans do not live simply to sustain themselves. Instead, they have a cultural heritage, a set of beliefs, attitudes, and instilled desires, a cumulative technology, and an identity within a group structure.

What does the "carrying capacity" theorist, if we may call him that, do with the sociocultural aspects of human existence? The chances are that he will ignore them and concentrate on calculations presumably showing how many human beings could have enough to eat under the stipulated conditions. For instance, the following quotation describes the procedures and results of a major study of this type by FAO, UNFPA, and IIASA. It demonstrates the weaknesses of this kind of reasoning.

> The study "combines a climate map . . . with a soil map . . . and then divides the study area into grids of 100km² each . . . the 15 most widely grown food crops were considered. . . . Three alternative levels of farm technology were postulated." Given these estimates of potential production, along with the calorie and protein requirements of the human body as recommended by FAO and WHO, the investigators computed "the maximum population which can be supported." (Srinivasan, 1988: 14–15)

The findings were as follows (ibid.: 16–17):

	Billions of people	
Farm technology	**Carrying capacity**	**Projected in 2000**
Low	5.6	3.6
Intermediate	14.9	3.6
High	33.2	3.6

Bear in mind that these are not estimates for the whole population of the Earth, which is projected to be 6.12 billion by the year 2000. They are figures only for the currently developing countries, with the largest country of all, China, omitted. For this reason, the estimates of "carrying capacity" are even more extreme than they seem at first to be. If the developing countries were to concentrate all resources on food production, the calculation implies, they could possibly feed 40 or more billion people.

Such calculations are clearly mere exercises having little or no relation to reality. They appear to assume that the goal of mankind is to maximize the number of people, and that in order to do so, every available resource must be turned into food. Yet there is no country in the world in which people are satisfied with having barely enough to eat.

Why, then, do writers on population concentrate so single-mindedly on food? I am not sure I know the answer, but I can make some pertinent observations. Not only is food necessary for existence, but it is intimately, continuously, and appetitively involved with the individual organism. It is consumed two or more times each day and is tied to a plethora of rituals and cultural associations. It is therefore often unconsciously viewed as a surrogate, or proxy, for population itself. Thus, to explain why a given region is populous, an observer may simply point out that the soil there is unusually fertile. The special role of food in an individual's life thus makes it easy, in reasoning about population and resources, to confuse a necessary cause (food) with a sufficient one.

The food bias in "carrying capacity" reasoning leads to other distortions—for instance, unwarranted and largely unconscious assumptions concerning the nature of demographic change. The biggest mistake of this sort, in my opinion, is the automatic tendency to view mortality as the chief mechanism by which human numbers are adjusted to resources. If, for example, the discussion concerns contemporary sub-Saharan Africa, the usual reasoning goes as follows: If the production of food in Central Africa continues to fall, the result will be more famines. These will drive up the death rate and thus slow the rate of population increase.

The preoccupation with food gives rise to another distortion—the assumption that self-sufficiency in food production is desirable. Actually, and for good reason, international trade in foodstuffs has been gaining. Since people must eat every day and since most foodstuffs are perishable or seasonal, international trade in food may have more advantages than it does in many other commodities. If, instead of food, we were to talk about, say, gold watches, what would be the carrying capacity? Perhaps it should be set at two gold watches per capita. Next, one could take hats—three hats per capita, and so on through the hundreds of items involved in modern human consumption. Obviously, if a country has certain advantages in nonfood trade, it can use these to buy food. A policy of self-sufficiency in food makes no sense for countries like England and Wales, Japan, Taiwan, the United States, or any other country that has access to international trade. The Earth is becoming one large trading system; and so the "carrying capacity" must refer not just to what food could be raised within national borders, but to the total of what could be gained in all ways.

Frequently, "carrying capacity" is treated as a norm, or optimum that should be sought. To say, for instance, that the world could "support" 33 billion people is to imply that below that figure they would be all right because they would have enough to eat, but above the 33 billion they would starve. Apparently, the idea is that as the increase in population reaches a high level, it automatically stops itself—mainly through diseases caused principally by malnutrition. According to this view, people are automatons, passively waiting to be killed by their own reproductive success. Overlooked is the possibility that the increase in human numbers may be stopped by the people themselves at a point far below the theoretical "carrying capacity," not because of a scarcity of food and other necessities, but because of a love for the frills and foibles of advanced civilization and a distaste for the arduous tasks of bearing and rearing children.

In short, the notion is false that each region has a carrying capacity that can be calculated and used in making projections and formulating policies. This idea is more applicable to cattle grazing in a pasture than to human beings.

"Limits to growth"

Our next concept, commonly used but highly ambiguous, is "limits to growth." As with "carrying capacity," use of this term without specifying the frame of reference or the level of abstraction is confusing. For instance, there is often uncertainty as to whether an alleged "limit" refers to a potential (theoretical or hypothetical) constraint or to an actual one. It is also difficult to tell whether a supposed limit to population growth is a goal or a simple fact. If it is a simple fact, does it occur automatically or as a result of human volition?

Given these ambiguities, one should not be surprised to find that the idea of limits has for centuries given rise to acrimonious, confusing, and inconclusive debate. The confusion and acrimony occur despite the fact that, at bottom, both sides of the debate agree. They agree that in a finite world the human population cannot continue to grow forever, but they disagree sharply about the time and circumstances of an ultimate limit.

On the one side of this great debate are the alarmists—people who believe that the limits to population growth are rapidly being approached and therefore that action should be taken now to reduce or reverse world population growth and thereby prevent a catastrophe. On the other side are the skeptics—those who think the Earth is big enough to accommodate a much larger population than it now has and that there is no need to worry.

The first group—the worriers, or environmentalists—claim that the supply of several indispensable resources is already running low and will soon be insufficient to sustain the present population, much less the population projected for the future. They also claim that the addition of approximately 85 million persons to the Earth's population each year is resulting in ever more ruthless and shortsighted handling of the resources that remain. It therefore seems only a matter of time until some essential but scarce resource gives out and stops population growth by causing widespread disease, famine, war, or some other calamity. The particular resource whose scarcity in relation to population size might become critical could be any one of a number of possibilities—topsoil, fresh water, clean air, forests, sites for safe waste disposal, or a particular species.

There is thus, according to this view, a collision course between, on the one hand, an expanding population and rising per capita consumption and, on the other, a diminishing resource base. Given this impasse, say the concerned scientists and activists, population growth cannot continue much longer. One way or another it will be halted, perhaps quite suddenly and catastrophically, perhaps gradually, as the necessary resources disappear. In the meantime, the longer population growth continues, the more painful and drastic must be the manner by which the growth is finally stopped. Already there are signs of acute stress from the swelling numbers and poverty of the world's people. About 85 percent of all children live in the Third World, where they are least likely to learn the skills necessary for work in a modern economy. Further, a high proportion of the world's people live within a few feet of sea level, a zone likely to be inundated if the polar icecaps are melted by global warming. Finally, according to this view, the driving force behind the world's population explosion has been a cheap but essential resource—energy from fossil fuels. This magical gift has been available for only the cost of extraction and transportation, but the price seems likely to rise rapidly in the future. Already fossil energy is too costly for ordinary people in less developed countries, leading them to continue to burn another resource (wood) that is becoming scarce and costly too.

On the other side are those who think the alarmists are wrong and who either do not see or refuse to discuss the possible exhaustion of any essential resource. These skeptics point out that the very growth of the world's population proves that the necessities for human existence are being met, and in abundance. The skeptics also recall the predictions of disaster made in the 1940s to 1970s—disasters that were supposed to result from population growth but that never occurred. In addition, the skeptics are quick to note the irony of talking about limits and scarcities when we live in a technological wonderland. By its very nature, they say, technology has no inherent limits that can be known in advance. So there is no reason to think that the world will run out of some essential resource and thus reach a limit to population growth, at least not soon enough to affect the present or the next generation.

This debate over limits to population growth may never be resolved, except by facts as time goes along. It is also a debate over a metaphysical concept that is only potentially, or theoretically, defined, and that therefore has little value in understanding the real world. Most people, when they speak of a "limit to growth," have in mind a number that the actual population may approach but never quite reach. It is an upper asymptote, determined post hoc but not before.

In the early 1970s, it was widely believed that the alarmists had won the debate. At that time a book entitled *The Limits to Growth* (Meadows et al., 1972) reported the findings of a team of scholars connected with the Massachusetts Institute of Technology and working under the auspices of a loose group intriguingly called the Club of Rome. Essentially the team selected five major variables and, with the help of a computer (not as familiar a tool then as it is now), traced out how changes in one variable would affect changes in the others. The five basic variables were land, food, industrialization, nonrenewable resources, and pollution. To determine causal relationships among these and between them and other variables involved in development, they used the actual trends during the period from 1900 to 1970.

In the "standard run" the researchers assumed that the 1900–70 trends would continue as long as possible. The result was "overshoot and collapse," brought on by the scarcity of nonrenewable resources. With population and industrialization both growing, the drain on resources quickly becomes so large that within a century, rising mortality brings massive population decline. One of their most startling claims was the speed at which collapse would arrive. If 3.18 billion hectares (7.86 billion acres) is taken taken as the potentially arable land on Earth, and if per capita land requirements and population growth rates remain as they are today (Meadows et al., 1972: 51), there will be "a desperate land shortage before the year 2000." Quadrupling soil productivity would merely postpone the shortage by about 50 years.

In another computer run the researchers asked what would happen if, through technological advance, available resources were doubled and energy became limitless. Population decline, the model indicated, would start about ten years earlier than in the standard run, due not to depletion of resources but to pollution. Provisionally released from the resource restraint, the growth of population and industrialization would poison the environment and drive up the death rate sharply.

But suppose that new technology reduced pollution by a factor of four. What then? There would be no pollution crises before 2100 but there would be a loss of population, due this time to a shortage of food.

Now suppose both that agricultural yields were doubled and that pollution per unit of industrialization were reduced by a factor of four. The world's population would still reach a limit and decline, paradoxically because of pollution. Even though pollution per unit of industrialization was reduced by a factor of four, industrialization would be so enormous that it would overload the environment, raising the death rate.

Thus, all variants of the model, incorporating different assumptions, suggest that if population and industrialization continue to expand, population will rise temporarily above some limit and then collapse, probably in less than 130 years. The only way to avoid this outcome, the Club of Rome suggested, would be to pursue a deliberate policy of limiting growth before the population reaches a natural limit. If population growth were stabilized by 1975 and industrialization by 1985, resource depletion and pollution would be sufficiently reduced to avoid collapse before 2100.

Limits to Growth caught the world's imagination overnight. For the first time in intellectual history, science was being used to confirm a long-held instinctive fear that mindless demographic and economic increase is leading the world to disaster. Further, the book preached a sermon: the only way to avoid catastrophe was to pursue a deliberate policy of curtailing growth. If this is not done in time, the Earth will become choked with people and pollution.

Doubtless *Limits* made many new converts to the environmentalist side. Soon, however, the book was subjected to intense criticism. For instance, a group at the University of Sussex, England, published a symposium called *Models of Doom* (Cole et al., 1973) devoted to refuting the Club of Rome study. As time went by without a let-up in world population growth and without such consequences as "overshoot" and "collapse," it became fashionable to dismiss the study as being unsound in its methods, biased in its assumptions, and extreme in its conclusions. In general, its greatest weakness was not only that it dealt with the future, but that it dealt with future technology, which is notoriously unpredictable. For instance, if a fourfold improvement of land productivity is achieved, a food crisis will obviously be postponed. But why stop at quadrupling soil productivity? There is no proof that it could not be raised 20 times, or for that matter that food could not be manufactured rather than caught or grown. Although population can hardly grow forever, setting any particular time for its demise is a dubious enterprise.

It is now two decades since *The Limits to Growth* was published. This is too brief a period to test the accuracy of even the short-term theoretical predictions, much less the long-term ones that were the main focus of interest in the project. Nevertheless, one cannot ignore developments in the last two decades that tend to support the study's findings. For instance, the world's population has grown faster during these years than it did between 1900 and 1970, and (to a lesser extent) so has industrialization. According to the Club of Rome study, this continuation of business-as-usual would lead to massive and deadly pollution, and that is what is happening now. On a global scale the atmosphere is being contaminated by the products of combustion from automobiles, forests, and factories; acid rain is spreading from industrial regions to many other parts of the globe; the protective ozone layer of the upper atmosphere is gradually being depleted; the problem of waste disposal has not been solved, especially the problem of nuclear waste; cities are engulfed in smog; the world's climate is being altered, with potentially grave consequences; and death rates in some countries are rising. Thus the grizzly truth may turn out to be that *Limits* was more prophetic than its detractors and even some of its defenders thought possible. In fact, during the last three decades several basic developments have occurred that together amount to a revolution in environmental concerns. First, the sheer number of discoveries of environmental problems has increased precipitously; second, the long-term seriousness of the problems has been increasingly recognized as more of the consequences of growth are felt; third, many problems formerly thought to be local in character are in fact global or near-global in scope; fourth, the involvement of science in understanding the causes of environmental change has increased rapidly; and fifth, the international scope of environmental damages has led inevitably to strong demands for conservationist policies.

It seems doubtful whether the debate over limits to growth will be resolved any time soon. Not only is the disagreement about the future; it is also about a concept that is only potentially, or theoretically, defined and that therefore has little value in understanding the real world.

The literature on population is filled with hypothetical reasoning. "The ultimate check to population," wrote Malthus, "appears then to be a want of food, arising necessarily from the different ratios according to which population and food increase" (Malthus, 1888: 6). But a potential limit is not necessarily realizable in the actual world. It is an imaginary concept like the "lifespan" of a species or the "reproductive potential" of the human female. Its use fails to enlighten us. We do not learn much by speculating on the potential or ultimate check to population growth. We learn a great deal more by analyzing the historical trends and circumstances of actual populations. This is what the Club of Rome tried to do. If it was not wholly successful, the fault lay less in the method (some kind of global system analysis seems called for) than in the application.

Discussions of population often envision a limit created by scarcity. They overlook the possibility of a limit rooted instead in abundance, as the failure of city populations to replace themselves suggests. They also overlook another kind of "limit to growth"—namely, a limit set by political fiat. At first glance one might think it easy to set an arbitrary limit (the authorities simply decide what they want and enforce it); but in practice this has proven difficult to do.

All told, then, concepts like carrying capacity and limits to growth teach us little about population and resources. Neither concept gives us a vision of the future. Neither gives us analytic power, or foresight instead of hindsight. Although they and similar ideas have sometimes hinted at an "iron law" or "general principle" by which population and resources are related, the truth is that this branch of science (in contrast to, for example, stable population theory) has not advanced beyond description and explanation of empirical regularities. These are less rigorous than the theorems found, say, in physics and chemistry, but they are nonetheless helpful in understanding the population–resources field. To see why, we can turn to one of the most widely known and respected concepts—the "demographic transition."

The "demographic transition"

This particular regularity was first publicized in the 1930s by Warren Thompson, the foremost American demographer of his day. He and other experts noted that the transition was being repeated in country after country. This allowed observers to put together not only two or three, but a whole system of variables. Also, instead of winding up with an equilibrium model (in which change is a distortion), transition theory made change its central focus. Finally, transition theory could be used to suggest new questions about population and new lines of research. In any study of population and resources, then, the demographic transition cannot be ignored. It represents a powerful tool for connecting demography with "outside" factors in a process of change.

Stripped to its essentials, "demographic transition" refers to a shift from a regime of high mortality and fertility to one of low mortality and fertility. Because the decline of mortality precedes the decline in fertility, there is a period during which population grows rapidly. As time goes by, however, fertility declines faster than mortality, with the result that the country's population growth stabilizes at a low or negative level.

Table 1 shows the stylized pattern of change; Figure 1 presents an actual example of the demographic transition, that in Singapore.

On the fertility side, a noteworthy feature of the post–World War II era has been the enormous difference between the more advanced and the less advanced countries. The latter, comprising more than two-thirds of the globe, have had five to seven births per woman, while the highly advanced

TABLE 1 Vital rates in transition

Phase	Death rate	Birth rate	Rate of natural increase
Early	High	High	Low
Middle	Low	High	High
Late	Low	Low	Low

FIGURE 1   Crude birth and death rates: Singapore, 1930–88

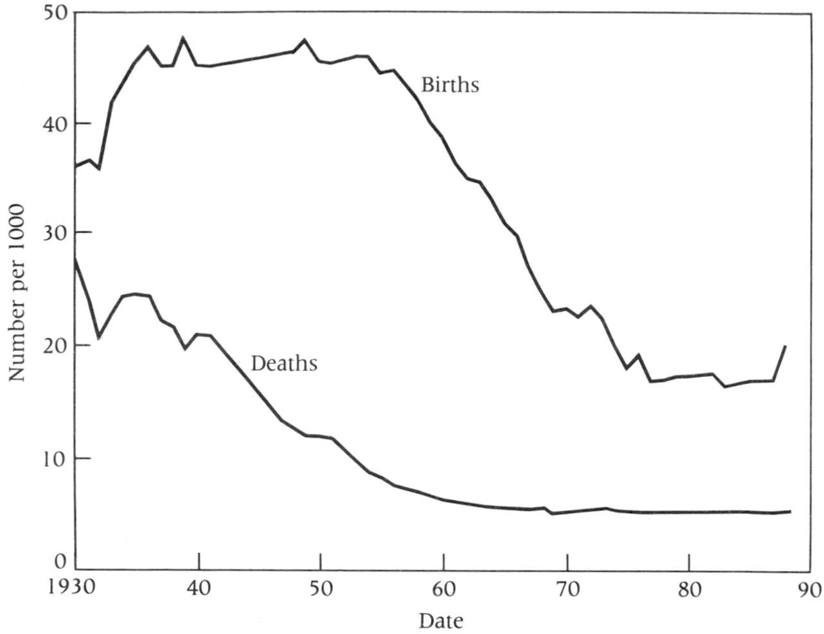

SOURCES: United Nations, *Demographic Yearbook* (issues for 1951, 1955, 1966, 1971, 1974, 1980, 1986, 1988); *Demographic Yearbook Historical Supplement*, 1978; *Population and Vital Statistics Report*, Series A, Vol. XL, No. 2, April 1988.

nations, despite their postwar baby boom, have had a drop in births so drastic as to portend reproductive failure.

Scientific interest in the transition is thus not confined to petty debates over whether a given country does or does not fit the pattern. Although no two countries behave exactly alike, none appears to have become urban-industrial without passing through, or at least entering the demographic transition.

But the more profound question is why the transition occurs in the first place. Why, with the process of economic and social modernization, does the demographic transition always occur? Why are there no real exceptions? Further, with respect to the dynamics of the transition, why does mortality decline first? Why does fertility eventually start down and then later stop falling? Does the drop in mortality somehow trigger mechanisms that reduce the birth rate? If so, are the mechanisms automatic or motivational? Finally, why does the demographic transition vary from one country or region to another? In particular, are there systematic and significant variations according to when, in history, the transition occurs? If these questions are answered, it may solve puzzles that have intrigued social scientists for some 200 years.

If the demographic transition always occurs as a country becomes more highly educated, urbanized, and economically developed, the cause must be nothing less than the Industrial Revolution, broadly conceived. Indeed, the theory of the demographic transition is part of a general theory of economic change. Beginning in the eighteenth century, continuing until today, and gradually spreading around the world, the Industrial Revolution has substantially raised the standard of living of people in the industrializing nations. Using ever more sophisticated machinery to harness stored-up fossil energy, the Revolution was so fundamental that it affected everything else. Its first demographic effect was to increase longevity. By raising the per capita consumption of goods and services, it probably had a greater impact on human life than the invention of agriculture. Indeed, it accomplished what human beings had been unsuccessfully trying to do for thousands of years: it dramatically extended the average length of life. It did this in two ways—first, by providing better and more reliable diets, clothing, shelter, and other elements of consumption; and second (after approximately 1850) by developing better sanitation and better medicine.

Why does mortality decline first? In some Northwest European countries the first sustained drop in the birth rate did not come until approximately a century after the first sustained fall in the death rate. Why such a long gap? The answer, I believe, is that longevity was what people wanted, whereas small families were not. Reproduction was governed by strong institutional controls that did not leave individuals free to do as they pleased. Furthermore, since the decline in mortality was sharpest in infancy and childhood, it had much the same effect as a rise in the birth rate. People responded by exercising their options. They migrated to towns and cities, moved to the New World, postponed marriage or never married at all, and relied on abortion and homemade contraceptive practices to reduce fertility within marriage (Davis, 1963). These adjustments took time, however, and while they were occurring Europe experienced a fairly rapid population growth.

Once the birth rate started downward, it fell faster than the death rate, with the result that eventually the population either ceased to grow or grew very slowly. As a further consequence, the proportion of the older population grew significantly. This was the demographic transition as it first occurred in Northwest Europe and in overseas nations of European settlement. Although the process differed in detail from one country to another, and although it was disturbed by two world wars, the Great Depression, the widespread adoption of pronatalist policies, and other political and economic interferences, the general outline of the transition in the older industrial countries matched the model remarkably well. For instance, in two countries as different as Norway and the United States the pattern of mortality change was much the same, except for the fact that the United States entered the cycle some 50 years after Norway did. As expected, then, the United States made the change more rapidly, as illustrated by levels of life expectancy shown in Table 2.

There were profound differences in the transition according to when in history it occurred. The classic model, which can be called "demographic transition A," was tightly linked to the rise and spread of the Industrial Revolution and was essentially completed by the end of World War II. Countries entering the transition after World War II followed a model that can be called "demographic transition B." These countries are moving through the entire trajectory much more rapidly than did the older industrial countries. As a consequence, the distortion among the phases of the transition is greater. The drop in mortality is more abrupt, and the fall in fertility, starting from a higher level, is sharper once it gets under way. As a result, the growth of population is two to three times what it was historically in transition "A."

This acceleration surprised most observers because the prevailing wisdom of the early postwar period was that economic development, not medicine or sanitation, determined the death rate. Only gradually was it recognized that public health measures could lower death rates independently of economic development. A typical case is that of Costa Rica. In 1950 that country had a life expectancy of 56 years. During the subsequent 35 years, it added 18 years to that figure. The rate of improvement was nearly three times that of the United States starting at a comparable level. Mexico's experience was similar. Its life expectancy improved at a rate nearly twice that of the United States from the same starting level.

The precipitous fall of death rates in the less developed world since World War II is perhaps the most profound change ever to occur in human population history. It was, for instance, the main cause of the unequalled world population growth in the postwar era. In the 40 years from 1950 to 1990, the Earth's inhabitants increased by 2.78 billion, or 110 percent, a far faster gain than ever before. It is often assumed that the acceleration in population growth was caused by high birth rates, but in fact the main cause was declining mortality.

The rapid fall in Third World death rates after 1945 was mainly due to the achievements of medical science in the advanced countries and to the

TABLE 2   Speed of trends from similar starting levels: Life expectancy at birth in Norway and the United States

	Start	Year	End	Year	Change per year
Norway	47.6	1855	76.3	1986	.22
United States	47.6	1900	75.4	1986	.32

SOURCES: Central Bureau of Statistics (Oslo): *Historical Statistics 1968*, p. 57; *Statistical Yearbook of Norway 1988*, p. 65; US Department of Health and Human Services, *Vital Statistics of the United States, 1986, Life Tables*, Vol. II, Section 6, p. 14.

unexpectedly low cost of applying these achievements in developing countries. The advanced countries made large investments in medical research, teaching, and application. By having access to the yield of these investments, the developing countries received a free ride, so to speak. The latest techniques were transferred to them quickly at low cost, and thus their death rates were dramatically reduced in a short time.

The rapid fall in mortality had the effect not only of multiplying the population but also of making families larger than they otherwise would have been. Reproduction in the developing world continued for some time to be governed by preindustrial mores. As a result, population growth in these countries was approximately double that of the now-industrialized nations when they were in the middle of their demographic transition. Countries like Sweden and Great Britain achieved at their peak a rate of natural increase of barely 15 per thousand population per year, whereas now, for countries like Kenya, Egypt, Mexico, Pakistan, and El Salvador the rate is between 25 and 40 per thousand.

The "demographic transition" and the future

As a model for predicting the future, the demographic transition has undeniable limitations. In a field where there are many variations from one time and place to another, the transitional model is too crude, and as a consequence it has a poor track record in clairvoyance. It did not enable the experts to predict the spectacular fall in death rates in developing countries after World War II, nor did it lead them to anticipate the baby boom in advanced nations. More recently, the transition model failed to predict the remarkable drop in fertility that has been occurring in much of Asia. For making projections the model is less satisfactory than relying on the particular history and idiosyncrasies of the country in question.

With such a record, one might wish to adopt other methods for projecting the population. One might, for instance, perform some mechanical extrapolation of recent trends. But for purposes of *understanding* what is going on, the theory of demographic transition still offers the best starting point.

According to stylized theory, the transition is finished when birth and death rates are both low and equal and zero population growth has been achieved. Most of the projections prepared by the United Nations, the US Bureau of the Census, and the World Bank, for example, seem to assume that the demographic transition will conform to this stylized pattern and, accordingly, the growth of world population will by and large cease sometime around the middle of the next century (United Nations, 1982; US Bureau of the Census, 1985; World Bank, 1984).

Actually, there is no compelling reason for equilibrium ever to be reached. For all we can tell, population growth may continue for a long time to come, and, as a result, the world may be teetering on the verge of the greatest calamity it has ever faced. The purpose of population projections is not simply to tell us how many people will be in the world according to present trends, but to tell us how many under various assumptions. In the literature, scant attention is given to catastrophic or other dire events. The reason for this inattention is easy to discern. In view of the many drastic, improbable, massive, and uncontrollable things that could happen to mankind, there is no way to pick the most likely. Also, anyone who pursues the question of what will actually happen gets branded as either a pessimist or an optimist and is shunned by those in the mainstream.

In speculating about the future world population, one should examine carefully those countries that appear to have recently completed the transition. A special group of nations, mostly Asian, demonstrate how rapidly a country can advance through the demographic transition despite adverse conditions. These countries, sometimes referred to as "miracle countries" due to their rapid development, include Hong Kong, Japan, Singapore, South Korea, and Taiwan. At the end of World War II these countries faced a bleak picture. Their economies had traditionally been heavily dependent on agriculture, yet their territory included little or no agricultural land. As a consequence, their population density on the land was extremely high, as tends to be the Asian pattern. To be sure, Japan had faced such conditions and moved through most of its demographic transition, but the other countries seemed to be mired in labor-intensive activity that supported high numbers of people at or near the subsistence level.

To the surprise of everyone, however, these countries recovered with incredible speed. On the demographic side, Figure 2 shows that in a mere 35 years, from 1950 to 1985, their total fertility rate dropped from around five to seven births per woman to below replacement. Figure 2 also shows how similar these countries are in their demographic behavior. If these countries were able to quickly reach a fertility rate below replacement, others can do it too, regardless of the starting conditions.

Naturally, there is keen interest in what the miracle countries will do next. Will they serve as a role model for the rest of the developing world— demographic transition "C," if you will—or will it prove impossible for many poor countries to travel that path? No one knows the answer, but from a demographic point of view the options are few. The prodigious growth of the Earth's population must soon stop somehow. It may stop because of a return to high mortality due to some catastrophe such as warfare, a worldwide epidemic, loss of an essential resource, or other disaster, perhaps induced by human crowding. Or, it may be stopped because of a birth rate continuously too low to replace the population, a condition possibly

FIGURE 2   Total fertility rates in selected countries, 1930–87

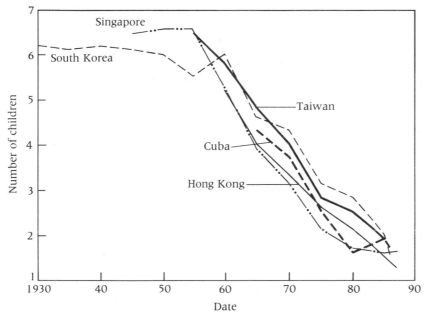

SOURCES: See note 2.

brought on by an increasing complexity of human society that makes child-bearing more costly in time and money and less rewarding.

If virtually all less developed countries acquire below-replacement fertility, will there be a strong effort to raise the birth rate by deliberate policy? Will governments provide positive incentives for childbearing? If the answer is yes, the policy will be dubious, owing to the changed conditions that prevail. In the first place, precisely because the highly advanced nations have now reached near-zero rates of population growth, their low fertility characterizes an ever smaller portion of the world's population. In 1950 approximately one-third of the human population lived in the advanced regions. By 1985, the proportion had fallen to just under a quarter. According to the medium variant of the UN projections, the proportion will be down to one-fifth in the year 2000 and to one-sixth in the year 2025 (United Nations, 1989). If the advanced nations want a higher birth rate merely to get a larger population, they can rely instead on immigration from the poor and crowded areas of the world. Admittedly, few advanced countries are currently willing to encourage immigration on a grand scale, but they may feel such extreme pressure from the Third World that mass migration occurs anyway. A relatively low rate of outmigration from the perspective of the Third World would be a major rate of immigration for the industrialized nations. Governments in the developed world might feel that acceptance of immigrants would be a small price to pay for temporary peace. At the moment, however, most of the advanced nations expect to continue to restrict rather than facilitate immigration.

These thoughts, I trust, demonstrate that simple or mechanical formulas do not exist for understanding the relation between population and resources. Formal demography has shown little interest in this relationship. The idea of carrying capacity is seriously biased, and conveys a grotesquely lopsided notion of human welfare. The idea of limits to growth knowable in advance is promising, but it requires more research than anyone now seems ready to undertake. As an organizing and stimulating principle, the demographic transition is virtually indispensable, for it brings "outside" and "inside" variables together in a creative fashion. Although it is too tied to historical and idiosyncratic factors to serve as a means of predicting future trends, it is nevertheless useful in comparative analysis and in comprehending the broad sweep of human demography. Such comprehension provides no comforting reassurance that a balance between population and resources can be trusted to come about through spontaneous convergence to a stabilized global population enjoying a high level of material affluence.

Notes

1 The foundation of these disciplines, laid early in the twentieth century by the mathematician and biologist Alfred J. Lotka, deals with mathematical relations among the elements of population and has been enormously successful. Indeed, Lotka's work and that of his colleagues and successors is the heart of demography as we know it today. Lotka's main work is contained in his treatise, *Théorie Analytique des Associations Biologiques*. One of the best accounts of his contribution to the field is contained in David V. Glass, *Population Policies and Movements in Europe* (Oxford: Clarendon Press, 1940). Other authors who have contributed significantly to the development of population theory are Brass, Coale, Das Gupta, Keyfitz, Pollard, and Schoen.

2 Sources for Figure 2 are as follows: Tai Hwan Kwon et al., *The Population of Korea*, Population and Development Studies Center, Seoul National University, 1975, p. 12; Ansley J., Coale, Lee-Jay Cho, and Noreen Goldman,

Estimation of Recent Trends in Fertility and Mortality in the Republic of Korea, Committee on Population and Demography, Report No. 1, National Academy of Sciences, Washington, D.C., 1980, p. 2; Saw Swee-Hock, *Population Control for Zero Growth in Singapore*, Oxford University Press, 1980, p. 161; Lee-Jay Cho, Fred Arnold, and Tai Hwan Kwon, *The Determinants of Fertility in the Republic of Korea*, Committee on Population and Demography, Report No. 14, National Academy Press, Washington, D.C., 1982, p. 38; Benjamin Mok, "Recent fertility trends in Hong Kong," in *Fertility Transition of the East Asian Populations*, ed. Lee-Jay Cho and Kasumasa Kobayashi, University Press of Hawaii, 1979, pp. 178–197; T. H. Sun and Y. L. Soong, "On its way to zero growth: Fertility transition in Taiwan, Republic of China," in Cho and Kobayashi, 1979, p. 120; Directorate of Budget, Accounting, and Statistics, Executive Yuan, *Statistical Yearbook of the Republic of China 1986*, p. 3; United Nations, *Demographic Yearbook*, 1986, pp. 554, 558–563.

References

Brass, W. 1971. *Biological Aspects of Demography.* Symposia of the Society for the Study of Human Biology, Vol. X. New York: Barnes and Noble.

Cole, H. S. D., et al. (eds.). 1973. *Models of Doom.* New York: Universe Books.

Davis, Kingsley. 1963. "The theory of change and response in modern demographic history," *Population Index* 29, no. 4: 345–366.

———. 1987. "The world's most expensive survey," *Sociological Forum* 2, no. 4: 829–834.

———. 1989. "Social science approaches to international migration," in Teitelbaum and Winter, 1989, pp. 245–261.

Glass, David V. 1940. *Population Policies and Movements in Europe.* Oxford: Clarendon Press.

Howell, Nancy. 1979. *Demography of the Dobe !Kung.* New York: Academic Press.

Keyfitz, Nathan, and Wilhelm Flieger. 1971. *Population: Facts and Methods of Demography.* San Francisco: W. H. Freeman.

Lee, Richard B. 1968. "What hunters do for a living," in *Man the Hunter,* ed. Richard B. Lee and Irven DeVore. Chicago: Aldine, pp. 30–48.

Lee, Ronald D., et al. 1988. *Population, Food and Rural Development.* Oxford: Clarendon Press.

Lotka, Alfred J. 1934–1939. *Théorie Analytique des Associations Biologiques: I, Principes; II, Analyse Démographique avec Application Particulière à L'Expece Humaine.* Paris: Hermann et Cie.

Malthus, Thomas Robert. 1888. *Essay on the Principle of Population,* 9th edition. London: Reeves and Turner.

Meadows, Donella H., et al. 1972. *The Limits to Growth.* New York: Universe Books.

Pollard, A. H., Farhat Yusaf, and G. N. Pollard. 1974. *Demographic Techniques.* Ruschcutters Bay, NSW: Pergamon Press.

Srinivasan, T. N. 1988. "Population growth and food—An assessment of issues, models, and projections," in Lee et al., 1988, pp. 11–39.

Teitelbaum, Michael S., and Jay M. Winter. 1985. *The Fear of Population Decline.* Orlando: Academic Press.

——— (eds.). 1989. *Population and Resources in Western Intellectual Traditions.* Cambridge: Cambridge University Press.

United Nations. 1982. *United Nations Demographic Indicators of Countries: Estimators and Projections as Assessed in 1980.* New York, pp. 3–28.

———. 1988. *World Population Prospects.* New York.

US Bureau of the Census. 1985. *Population Profile of the United States 1983/4,* Current Population Reports, Special Studies, Series P 23, No. 145. Washington, D.C.: US Government Printing Office, pp. 4–6.

World Bank. 1984. *World Development Report 1984.* New York: Oxford University Press.

ESTIMATING THE FUTURE

Sustainable Development: From Concept and Theory to Operational Principles

HERMAN E. DALY

THREE CONCEPTUAL ISSUES SEEM TO ME CRITICAL for clear thinking about economic development and the environment in the next decade. After stating the three issues briefly, I will elaborate each one in turn, along with the relations among them.

The first issue is whether the basic conceptual starting point of economic analysis should be the circular flow of exchange value, as it presently is, or the one-way entropic throughput of matter energy. The latter concept is virtually absent from economics today, yet without it it is impossible to relate the economy to the environment. It is as if biology tried to understand animals only in terms of their circulatory system, with no recognition of the fact that they also have digestive tracts. The metabolic flow is not circular. The digestive tract firmly ties the animal to its environment at both ends. Without digestive tracts animals would be self-contained perpetual-motion machines. Likewise for an economy without an entropic throughput.

The second issue is to distinguish two dimensions of the throughput: its scale and its allocation. The concept of optimal allocation among alternative uses of the total resource flow (throughput) must be clearly distinguished from the concept of an optimal scale of total resource flow relative to the environment. Under ideal conditions the market can find an optimal allocation in the sense of Pareto. But the market cannot find an optimal scale any more than it can find an optimal distribution. The latter requires the additon of ethical criteria; the former requires the further addition of ecological criteria. The independence of allocation from distribution is widely recognized; the independence of allocation from scale is not widely recognized, but is easily understood.[1] In theory whether we double the population and the per capita resource use rate, or cut them in half, the market will still grind out a Pareto optimal allocation for every scale. Yet the scale of the economy is certainly not a matter of indifference. A boat that tries to carry too much weight will still sink even if that weight is optimally allocated. Allocation is one thing, scale is something else. We must deal with both, lest even the efficiently allocated weight of the economy sink the environment. We need something like a Plimsoll line to keep the economic scale within the ecological carrying capacity. In trying to reduce scale issues to matters of allocation (just get the prices right), economics has greatly obscured the relation between the economy and the environment. While an optimal allocation can result from the individualistic marketplace, the attainment of an optimal scale will require collective action by the community.

The third issue, how to attain sustainable development, is already under intense discussion. Following the report of the World Commission on Environment and Development *(Our Common Future)* the concept has been endorsed by the United Nations and all its many development agencies, and urged upon all member countries. Nevertheless there remains considerable confusion as to the meaning of sustainable development. Underlying this confusion is the unresolved, indeed unaddressed, issue of steady state versus growth as the normal, healthy condition of an economy. Economists' growth-bound way of thinking makes it hard for them to admit the concept of throughput of matter-energy, because it brings with it the first and second laws of thermodynamics, which have implications that are unfriendly to the continuous growth ideology. The circular flow raises no such problems. The growth ideology is extremely attractive politically because it offers a solution to poverty without requiring the moral disciplines of sharing and population control. Also the obvious implication of recognizing an optimal scale is that growth should stop once the optimum is reached—that growth beyond the optimum scale is "anti-economic growth," that is, growth that makes us poorer rather than richer. Optimal allocation has no such growth-limiting implications.

The three issues I am raising are not difficult, arcane, or esoteric—they are no more than common sense—but it is hard for us to think clearly about them because doing so threatens the absolute priority of growth as the North Star of economic policy. Although the three issues are separable they are also clearly related. Once throughput is recognized as a fundamental and indispensable concept, then the question of its optimal scale within a finite ecosystem naturally arises, along with the recognition that the question is different from that of optimal allocation. Once we face the question of limiting scale, we recognize the collective or social nature of the task and the futility of leaving it up to the individualism of the market, which can only deal with allocation. We also confront the problem of criteria for optimal scale, the most obvious of which is sustainability. The discussion of sustainable development will not get far without the recognition of throughput and the problem of its scale.

Much confusion could be avoided if we would agree to use the word "growth" to refer only to the quantitative scale of the physical dimensions of the economy. Qualitative improvement could be labeled "development."[2] Then we could speak of a steady-state economy as one that develops without growing, just as the planet Earth, of which the economy is an open subsystem, develops without growing. Growth of the economic organism means larger jaws and a bigger digestive tract. Development means more complete digestion and wiser purposes. Limits to growth do not imply limits to development.

Entropic throughput of matter-energy versus the circular flow of exchange value

Nicholas Georgescu-Roegen (1971) has pointed to "the standard textbook representation of the economic process by a circular diagram, a pendulum movement between production and consumption within a completely closed system," as proof of the mechanistic epistemology of modern economics. There is only reversible motion, a circular flow, and no recognition of irreversible entropic change. There is only mechanical time, no historical time. This does not mean that economists deny historical time or the entropy law, but it does mean that they cannot deal with them at the most basic conceptual level of economics, and have to introduce them in ad hoc and unintegrated ways outside the structure of formal models—that is, as externalities.

In addition to the inability of the mechanistic epistemology to embrace irreversible phenomena, there was a practical reason for ignoring the entropic throughput. Economists are interested in scarcity, and during the formative years of economic theory the environment was considered an infinite source of raw materials and an infinite sink for waste materials. Therefore the throughput was not considered scarce and was naturally abstracted from. Only scarce items entered into exchange. Free goods were appropriated without need of a transaction. Since exchange value flowed in a circle, the circular flow became the paradigm within which the economic process was analyzed. Once the economy reached the scale at which throughput itself became scarce, then the circular flow vision became economically, as well as physically, misleading. It totally obscured the emerging scarcity of environmental services. The circular flow has no beginning and no end, no points of contact with anything outside itself. Therefore it cannot possibly register the costs of depletion and pollution, nor the irreversible historical effects induced by the entropic nature of the throughput.

The concept of throughput was introduced into economics by Kenneth Boulding (1966) and more fully elaborated and integrated into economic theory by Georgescu-Roegen (1971), who called it the "metabolic flow" and emphasized the manifold consequences of its entropic nature. Others (Kneese, Ayres, and d'Arge, 1970) have paid respect to the concept by emphasizing the importance of "material balances," thus recognizing the constraint on the economic process of the first law of thermodynamics, but neglecting that of the second law. The first law is consistent with the circular flow vision: the same indestructible building blocks of matter-energy could simply cycle faster and faster around the production–consumption loop. Nothing gets used up. But the second law says that something does indeed get used up—not matter-energy itself, but its capacity for rearrangement. Energy is conserved, but its capacity to do work is used up. To my knowledge no economics textbook has addressed any of these important contributions. Instead they perpetuate the circular flow vision without so much as a reference to the concept of throughput.[3] Naturally, if the very concept of throughput is not admitted, it will be impossible to consider the issue of its optimal scale, a theme to which we now turn.[4]

Optimal allocation versus optimal scale

Standard economics concerns the optimal allocation of resources, which in this broad sense includes labor and capital as well as natural resources. But natural resources are not viewed as the components of an entropic metabolic flow from and back to the environment. Rather they are seen as building blocks that are indestructible elements in the circular flow.[5] Allocation of these elements among competing uses is the only question raised for standard economics by its partial recognition of throughput. As mentioned earlier a Pareto optimal allocation can be achieved for any scale of population and per capita resource use. The concept of economic efficiency is indifferent to the scale of the economy's physical dimensions, just as it is indifferent to the distribution of income. Equity of income distribution and sustainability of scale are outside the concept of market efficiency. Yet the environment is sensitive to the physical scale of the economy, and human welfare is sensitive to how well the environment functions. To optimally allocate resources at a nonoptimal scale is simply to make the best of a bad situation. If the economy continues to grow beyond optimal scale, then optimal allocation means simply to make the best of an ever-worsening situation. This anomaly is absent from the circular flow vision: if the economy is an isolated system with no dependence on its environment, then it can never exceed the capacity of the environment. Its scale relative to the environment is a matter of complete indifference. But once we recognize the central importance of the throughput, we must concern ourselves with its optimal scale as well as its optimal allocation.

Optimal scale of a single activity is not a strange concept to economists. Indeed microeconomics is about little else. An activity is identified, be it producing shoes or consuming ice cream. A cost function and a benefit function for the activity in question are defined. Good reasons are given for believing that marginal costs increase and marginal benefits decline as the scale of the activity grows. The message of microeconomics is to expand the scale of the activity in question up to the point where marginal costs equal marginal benefits, a condition that defines the optimum scale. All of microeconomics is an extended variation on this theme.

When we move to macroeconomics, however, we no longer hear about optimal scale. There is no optimal scale for the macro economy, and no cost and benefit functions are defined for growth in scale of the economy as a whole. It simply does not matter how many people there are, or how much they consume. But if every micro activity has an optimal scale then why does the aggregate of all micro activities not have an optimal scale? If I am told in reply that the constraint on any one activity is the fixity of all the others and that when all economic activities increase proportionally the constraints cancel out, then I will invite the economist to increase the scale of the carbon cycle and the hydrologic cycle in proportion to the growth of industry and agriculture. I will admit that if the ecosystem can grow indefinitely then so can the aggregate economy. But until the surface of the Earth begins to grow at a rate equal to the rate of interest, one should not take this answer too seriously. The total absence in macroeconomics of the most basic concept of microeconomics is a glaring anomaly, and it is not resolved by appeals to the fallacy of composition. What is true of a part is not necessarily true for the whole, but it can be and usually is unless some aggregate identity or self-cancelling feedback is at work. (As in the classic example of all spectators standing on tiptoe to get a better view and each cancelling out the better view of the other; or in the observation that while any single country's exports can be greater than its imports, nevertheless the aggregate of all exports cannot be different from the aggregate of all imports.) But what analogous feedback or identity allows every economic activity to have an optimal scale while the aggregate economy remains indifferent to scale?

In the circular flow vision there is an aggregate identity: total expenditures equal total receipts; one person's expenditure is another person's income. Costs and benefits are conflated in transactions. In circular flow accounting we add up transactions rather than compare costs and benefits at the margin, so the question of an optimal scale of the circular flow never arises. It is the throughput that has an optimal scale. When growth pushes scale beyond the optimum, we experience generalized pervasive externalities, such as the greenhouse effect, ozone layer depletion, and acid rain, which are not correctable by internalization of localized external costs into a specific price.

Probably the best index of the scale of the human economy as a part of the biosphere is the percentage of human appropriation of the total world products of photosynthesis. Net primary production (NPP) is the amount of solar energy captured in photosynthesis by primary producers, less the energy used in their own growth and reproduction. NPP is thus the basic food resource for everything on Earth not capable of photosynthesis. Peter Vitousek et al. (1986) calculate that 25 percent of potential global (terrestrial and aquatic) NPP is now appropriated by human beings.[6] If only terrestrial NPP is considered the fraction rises to 40 percent. Taking the 25 percent figure for the entire world it is apparent that two more doublings of the human scale will give 100 percent. Since this would mean zero energy left for all nonhuman and nondomesticated species, and since humans cannot survive without the services of ecosystems, which are made up of other species, it is clear that two more doublings of the human scale is an ecological impossibility, although arithmetically possible. More than two doublings exceeds 100 percent. Furthermore the terrestrial figure of 40 percent is probably more relevant since we are unlikely to substantially increase our take from the oceans. Total appropriation of the terrestrial NPP is only slightly more than one doubling time in the future. Perhaps it is theoretically possible to increase the Earth's total photosynthetic capacity, but the actual trend of past economic growth is decidedly in the opposite direction.

Assuming a constant level of per capita resource consumption, the doubling time of the human scale would equal the doubling time of current world population, which is on the order of 40 years. Of course economic growth currently aims to increase average per capita resource consumption and consequently to reduce the doubling time of the scale of the human presence below that implicit in the demographic rate of growth.

As growth increasingly turns previously free goods into scarce goods, the standard solution is to impose positive prices on the newly scarce goods. Once a good has become scarce it is important that it have a positive price in order to be properly allocated. But there is a prior question: How do we know that we were not better off at the previous scale when the good was free and its proper price was zero? In both instances the prices were right. But that does not mean that the scale was right. Furthermore, the new exchange value created when previously free goods become scarce reflects a cost, not a benefit as currently reckoned. The classical economist Lauderdale recognized that private riches could expand while public wealth declined. This perversity will occur whenever formerly abundant objects with great use value, but no exchange value, become scarce and thus acquire exchange value. Although scarcity is necesssary for value in the sense of measurable exchange value, "the common sense of mankind would revolt at a proposal for augmenting wealth by creating a scarcity of any good generally useful and necessary to man."[7] The revolt has been slow in coming, but let us hope that Lauderdale was right.

Some economists argue that futures markets and present value maximization automatically deal with the scale issue because the costs of excessive scale are merely the future costs of the present use of resources. But even in a single-period analysis in which no future is assumed, there is still the possibility of exceeding optimal scale by sacrificing current ecosystem services that are worth more than the current extra economic product whose production required the sacrifice of those services. It is true that many of the costs of increasing scale do fall on the future. But neither present value maximization under assumptions of perfect knowledge and foresight, nor an imaginary futures market, is adequate for taking account of these future costs (Page, 1977).[8] If Archimedes had had a fulcrum and a long enough lever he could have moved the Earth. But an abstract principle is no substitute for an operational procedure.

Optimal allocation at least has a definition, however restrictive and limited its relevance may be. But how do we define optimal scale? This question demands not only much greater knowledge of carrying capacity and ecological relations, but also much clarification and deeper understanding of our own purposes. Many economists avoid the scale question by rejecting the concept of carrying capacity on the grounds that it is not clearly defined. But by that criterion they should also refuse to talk about "time," one of the most difficult concepts to define. Some say time is absolute, others say it is relative, still others insist that it is pure illusion. Even "money" should not be spoken of, since what is really money, M1 or M2? or M1A? One of the temptations of debate is to demand an unreasonable standard of precision for concepts that have troublesome implications for one's position, while being less demanding in the company of concepts known not to raise impolite questions. But there is one thing we know about the optimal scale: it must at least be sustainable. So for the time being we can devote our practical policies toward sustainability, while we puzzle over the deeper philosophical issues of optimal scale.

One further criterion for optimal scale, suggested indirectly by Perrings (1987), is that the economy be small enough to avoid generating feedbacks from the ecosystem that are so novel and surprising as to render economic calculation impossible. Perrings begins with the first law of thermodynamics, pointing out that an increasing throughput (exactions and insertions in his language) provokes ever greater feedbacks from the environment (external costs) as the scale of exactions and insertions grows. Since we do not understand the ecosystem very well, the feedbacks from it provoked by our actions come as surprises to us. These surprises are nearly always unpleasant ones, since random interference in a complex system nearly always disrupts the functioning of the system, and since our welfare depends on the proper functioning of the system. Novelty and surprise begin to outweigh the calculated projections of the costs and benefits of the increasing scale of our activities. We can react to this loss of predictability in two ways: (1) increase the sphere of control so as to internalize the "surprises" (Boulding's image of the spaceman economy in which the entire life support system is planned and controlled—that is, everything is economy and nothing is environment, leading to what we might call "full-world economics"); or (2) decrease the scale of human interference to such a level that the ecosystem can function on "automatic pilot" (Boulding's image of the cowboy economy in which nearly everything is environment, and sinks are automatically recycled into sources without any planning by the cowboy—"empty-world economics"). Our ability to centrally plan economies does not inspire optimism about the likelihood of our success in the vastly more difficult task of planning the ecosystem. One of the main criteria for an optimal scale, therefore, is that the economy be small enough to avoid unmanageable interference with the "ecological invisible hand" or automatic pilot. Ecological laissez faire requires social control of the scale of the economic subsystem.

Sustainable development

The value of sustainability is so basic that it is usually tacitly assumed in our economic thinking. Sustainability is built into the very concept of income. J. R. Hicks (1946: 172) defined income as the maximum amount that a person or a nation could consume over some time period and still be as well off at the end of the period as at the beginning. Hicks further argued that the practical reason for calculating income is to have a guide to how much we can consume year after year without eventually impoverishing ourselves. Income equals maximum sustainable consumption.

Lack of a precise definition of "sustainable development" is not without benefit. It has allowed a considerable consensus to evolve in support of the main idea that it is both morally and economically wrong to treat the world as a business in liquidation. If development is to be the major policy goal of nations, then it should mean something that is generalizable both to all members of the present generation and to many future generations. The popularity of the notion of sustainable development derives from the increasing recognition that present patterns of economic development are not generalizable. Present levels of per capita resource consumption underlying the economies of the United States and Western Europe (which is what is generally understood by development) cannot be generalized to all currently living people, much less to future generations, without destroying the ecological sources and sinks on which economic activity depends.[9] The Brundtland Commission Report (World Commission on Environment and Development, 1987) was wise not to foreclose the emergence of this vague but important consensus by insisting on a precise analytical definition from the outset.

But the term is now in danger of becoming an empty shibboleth. For example, many people in the development community who use the term cannot specify what is being sustained in sustainable development—whether a level of economic activity or a rate of growth of economic activity.

Some, therefore, have become impatient with the concept and want to abandon it. That would be a great mistake. After all we do not have a precise definition of money either, but we certainly cannot abandon the concept. Nor is income a precise concept, yet in practical affairs we can hardly do without it. Even though we must not expect analytical precision in reasoning with dialectical concepts, it is nevertheless possible and very necessary to clarify the notion of sustainability and to offer a few first principles of sustainable development.

Two terms are frequently used more or less synonymously: "sustainable growth" and "sustainable development." Earlier I suggested the following distinction: that "growth" refer to expansion in the scale of the physical dimensions of the economic system, while "development" refer to qualitative change of a physically nongrowing economic system in a state of dynamic equilibrium maintained by its environment. By this definition the Earth is not growing, but it is developing. Any physical subsystem of a finite and nongrowing Earth must itself also eventually become nongrowing. Therefore the term sustainable growth implies an eventual impossibility, while the term sustainable development does not. It is development that can have the attribute of sustainability, not growth. What is being sustained is a level, not a rate of growth, of physical resource use. What is being developed is the qualitative capacity to convert that constant level of physical resource use (throughput) into improved services for satisfying human wants.

The concept of sustainability is by no means new in economics, although the word is. As noted earlier, sustainability is implicit in Hicks's definition of income as the maximum amount that a person or community could consume over some time period and still be as well off at the end of the period as at the beginning. Remaining equally well off means maintaining capital intact, or maintaining the wealth and population of the community. Growth in Hicksian income is by definition sustainable. Any consumption that is not sustainable cannot be counted as income. Exploiting renewable resources at a profit-maximizing sustainable yield is an application of the Hicksian concept of income to resource management.

How, then, can there be a problem of lack of sustainability if that notion is implicit in the very concept of income? The problem is that the capital we have endeavored to maintain intact is manmade capital only. There is also the important but relatively unappreciated category of natural capital—natural stocks that yield flows of natural resources and services without which there can be no production.[10] In practice we do not maintain natural capital constant in the process of production, and consequently the net national product generated is not Hicksian income. The present System of National Accounts treats receipts from liquidating natural assets as income, thus giving countries the illusion that they are better off than they really are.

Why has natural capital been left out of our accounts? There are two main reasons.

First, the scale of the economy (population times per capita resource use) relative to the environment used to be negligible, and consequently natural capital regeneration was either automatic or perceived as unimportant because it was not a limiting factor. Between 1950 and 1986 the scale of the world population doubled (from 2.5 to 5.0 billion), while the scale of gross world product and fossil fuel consumption each quadrupled. The physical presence of the economy within the ecosystem was not negligible even in 1950 and is certainly not so now. The humanly directed flows of matter and energy through the economy rival in magnitude the flow rates of many natural cycles and fluxes. As previously noted human beings now appropriate 40 percent of terrestrial net primary productivity. In the past the limiting factor in economic development was the accumulation of manmade capital. We are now entering an era in which the limiting factor will be the remaining natural capital. The notion of limiting factors implies less than perfect substitutability between them—that is, that factors are to some extent complementary. This leads us to the second reason for the neglect of natural capital.

Neoclassical economic theory has taught that manmade capital is a near-perfect substitute for natural resources, and, consequently, for the stock of natural capital that yields the flow of these natural resources. Even if this assumed near-perfect substitutability were true, it would still be necessary to maintain total capital (manmade plus natural) intact in calculating Hicksian income—that is, the exhaustion of natural capital would still have to be offset by the accumulation of an equivalent value of manmade capital. Even this is not done. Moreover, substitution in economic theory is reversible, while the substitution of manmade for natural capital is frequently irreversible. Contrary to neoclassical assumptions, natural and manmade capital are more complements than substitutes, with natural capital increasingly replacing manmade as the limiting factor in development.

Maintaining total capital intact might be referred to as "weak sustainability," in that it is based on generous assumptions about substitutability of capital for natural resources in production. By contrast "strong sustainability" would require maintaining both manmade and natural capital intact separately, on the assumption that they are really not substitutes but complements in most production functions. For example, the manmade capital represented by a sawmill is worthless without the existence of the complementary natural capital of a forest. In the strong sustainability case, economic growth would require the increase of whichever type of capital is limiting at the margin. At the current margin in many countries, natural capital is limiting for sutainable development, yet it is routinely sacrificed for more manmade capital under the prevailing model of unsustainable development based on national accounts that treat consumption of natural capital as income.

We might distinguish a third concept of sustainability that I would label "very weak sustainability." Some authors (e.g., Pezzy, 1989) define sus-

tainability as the maintenance of a constant (or non-declining) level of
utility. What is being sustained in this instance is a psychic state rather than
a physical state. This subjectivist definition incorporates psychological substitution in the utility function as well as technological substitution in the
production function. In this view we can learn to enjoy more fully the services of manmade capital relative to the services of natural capital and remain equally happy as the former is continually substituted for the latter
(the "Disneyland effect"). The appeal to economists of the subjectivist view
is that it allows sustainability so defined to fit directly into the discounted
utility-maximizing theoretical framework of neoclassical economics. The
overwhelming operational disadvantage is that it defines one imprecise concept (sustainability) in terms of something even less definable—utility, nay,
discounted, future, aggregated utility.[11] It is better to aim at something more
operational by retaining the physical approach of the ecologist. It is impossible for the present to bequeath happiness or utility to the future. The only
thing that can be passed on is natural and manmade capital (also knowledge, although that has to be taught and learned, not just bequeathed). The
physical approach can provide a definition of sustainability that can be imposed as a constraint on the maximization of utility in neoclassical models.
Sustainability should not refer to a psychic state, but rather to a state of the
biophysical world, namely a condition of dynamic equilibrium between the
physical dimensions of the economy and the larger environment of which it
is an open subsystem. In this view the major determinant of sustainability is
likely to be the physical scale of the economic subsystem relative to the containing ecosystem.

   An operational approach to sustainability that does not hinge on resolution of the substitutability question is to adjust national accounts so as to
arrive at a closer apporoximation of Hicksian income than that given by net
national product. One way to do this is to subtract from net national product
two categories of expenditure that measure nonsustainable activities. First,
subtract an estimate of the value of natural capital depreciation. Second,
subtract an estimate of defensive or regrettably necessary expenditures
made to protect ourselves against the unwanted side effects of other production.[12]

   The main idea of Hicksian income is captured in the definition of sustainable development offered by the Brundtland Commission as development that "meets the needs of the present without compromising the ability
of future generations to meet their own needs."[13] Two questions will arise in
any attempt to make this definition operational. First, the "needs of the
present" requires some distinction between basic needs and extravagant
wants. If needs of the present include an automobile for each Chinese family
of three, then sustainable development is impossible. Sustainable development is about sufficiency as well as efficiency. Second, the "ability of the
future generations to meet their own needs" may be interpreted as requiring

either strong or weak sustainability—the pervasive issue of substitutability surfaces again.

At what level of community is sustainability to be sought? International trade allows one country to draw on the ecological carrying capacity of another country, yet both together might be sustainable in their symbiotic relationship. How does trade affect sustainability defined at the national level? This brings us again to the question of complementarity versus substitutability of natural and manmade capital. If we follow the path of strong sustainability (natural and manmade capital are more complements than substitutes) then this complementarity must be respected either at the national or at the international level. A single country may substitute manmade for natural capital to a very high degree if it can import the products of natural capital (i.e., the flows of natural resources and natural services) from other countries that have retained their natural capital to a greater degree. In other words, the demands of complementarity can be evaded at the national level, but only if they are respected at the international level. One country's ability to substitute manmade for natural capital depends on some other country's making the opposite (complementary) choice.

There are strong theoretical and commonsense reasons for believing that natural and manmade capital are complements. Natural resource stocks yield a flow of inputs that is physically transformed by stocks of manmade capital and labor into a flow of product outputs. A great deal of substitutability may exist between labor and manmade capital (the two agents of transformation), or between the various resource flows (that which is being transformed). But the main relation between what is being transformed and the agent of transformation must be one of complementarity, not substitutability. Otherwise we could build the same wooden house with, say, half the lumber and twice as many saws and carpenters. Of course one could substitute brick or fiberglass for lumber, but that is the substitution of one resource flow for another, not the substitution of manmade capital stock for a natural resource flow. The agent of transformation (efficient cause) and the substance being transformed by it (material cause) must be complements.[14] Also we should not forget the obvious fact that production of capital itself requires natural resources—the production of the "substitute" requires the very thing being substituted for. And finally, if capital really were a near-perfect substitute for natural resources, then natural resources must also be a near-perfect substitute for capital—but if that were true, why bother to accumulate capital in the first place? For these reasons strong sustainability is the fundamental concept. Weak sustainability is an option for a single country only in the context of a set of trading countries which taken together meet the conditions of strong sustainability. Consequently we must distinguish closed from open economy concepts of carrying capacity. In the former a country must draw only on its own ecosystem for everything. In the latter drawing on other ecosystems and economies is permitted as long as imports are paid for by current exports. Subsidies and continuing unpaid debts are excluded, though international trade is permitted.[15]

Sustainable development ultimately implies a stationary population. Penultimately, however, possibilities remain of substitution between population size and resource use per capita, since it is really the product of these two factors that is limited by biophysical constraints. Sustainability is compatible with a large population living at a low level of per capita resource use, or with a small population living at high levels of resource use per capita. For many countries resource consumption levels are below sufficiency, yet ecological carrying capacity has already been exceeded (e.g., in Haiti and El Salvador). In such cases population control is a precondition rather than an ultimate consequence of sustainable development.

Sustainable development does not imply constant technology, nor is the concept rendered unnecessary by technological progress. New technology can have positive or negative effects. Technologies that increase resource productivity will reduce the pressure on natural capital stocks to yield increasing flows of natural resources. Technologies that increase the productivity of manmade capital and labor frequently require processing a greater flow of resources, and thus tend to reduce resource productivity in the interests of raising capital and labor productivity. Historically, technological progress has favored capital and labor productivity at the expense of resource productivity (e.g., declining energy productivity in agriculture resulted from greater use of energy per unit of labor and capital, with a consequent increase in labor and capital productivities). Sustainable development implies a different direction of technical progress: one that squeezes more service per unit of resource, rather than one that just runs more resources through the system; one that is efficiency-increasing rather than throughput-increasing; one that does not sacrifice natural resource productivity, and, if necessary will sacrifice labor or capital productivity instead. This sort of progress will be politically difficult due to the tie between marginal productivity and income for all factors. In industrial society labor and capital are much stronger social classes than landlords (resource owners). Naturally each class prefers those technologies that increase its own marginal productivity and income. At one time the landlord was dominant and preferred labor-intensive technologies (and large populations) that increased the marginal product and rent of land. Today the political demise of the landlord has left land (resources) without a social class to champion its higher price and productivity. Resources tend to be used lavishly in the interests of labor and capital productivity. This works against sustainability.

The most obvious principle of sustainable development is that renewable resources should be exploited on a sustained-yield basis. The choice among many levels of sustained yield can be made on the criterion of profit maximization. In general the profit-maximizing level at which to maintain the exploited stocks will not correspond to the biologically maximum sustainable yield. For wild stocks it will be greater (assuming rising costs of capture); for cultivated stocks it will be less (assuming rising costs of maintenance). Only with constant costs will the maximum biological yield coincide with the maximum economic profit.

A major problem for sustainable development is how to treat nonrenewable resources, which by definition have no sustainable yield, at least on time scales relevant to human experience. A way of handling this problem is suggested in an ingenious article by Salah El Serafy (1989). He divides net receipts from a nonrenewable resource into an income component that can be consumed annually, and a capital component that must be invested annually in a renewable asset that yields a rate of return such that, at the end of the lifetime of the nonrenewable resource (reserves divided by rate of depletion), a new renewable asset will have been built up to the point at which it can yield a perpetual stream equal to the income component of the now-depleted nonrenewable resource. A somewhat similar principle was suggested by the economist John Ise in the 1920s, namely to use up the nonrenewable resource at such a rate that its price will be equal to the price of its nearest renewable substitute. In other words, resources should be priced according to their long-run replacement costs. El Serafy's rule is more closely oriented to the operational problems of proper income accounting rather than pricing, and does not require the identification of a specific long-run renewable substitute. It does implicitly assume, however, that something useful in the real world is capable of growing at a rate equal to the rate of discount used in calculating the income component. That something, it would seem, must be some renewable resource service, that is, the biological growth rate of renewable resources plus the technological rate of growth of the productivity of all resources (not the productivity of labor or capital, but of resources). Also the analysis assumes a chosen or given rate of depletion, which is often taken by economists as that which is to be determined. El Serafy's method does not answer the traditional question of what is the optimal rate of depletion, but rather tells us how much we can sustainably consume and how much we must invest of receipts from a nonrenewable resource under different discount rates, depletion rates, and reserves. It sets the guidelines for exploiting nonrenewable resources under a regime of sustainable development.

If we take sustainable development as our guiding principle, then the projects we finance should, ideally, each be sustainable. Whenever that is not possible (e.g., nonrenewable resource extraction) a complementary project should insure sustainability for the two taken together. A portion of the receipts from nonrenewable extraction should be invested in a renewable asset in an annual amount such that, given the renewable asset growth rate and the life expectancy of the nonrenewable asset, the former will provide a permanent income stream equal to the part of the receipts consumed annually from the latter. This is the basic principle underlying the El Serafy method, just discussed, only here it is applied at the project or micro level rather than at the macro level of national income accounting.

Also, if projects must be sustainable, then it is inappropriate to calculate the benefits of a sustainable project or policy alternative by comparing it with an unsustainable option—that is, by using a discount rate that reflects rates of return on alternative uses of capital that are themselves in the majority of cases unsustainable. For example, if a sustainably managed forest that can yield 4 percent is judged uneconomic in comparison with a discount rate of 6 percent, while on closer inspection the 6 percent discount rate turns out to be based on alternative uses of capital that are unsustainable (including perhaps the unsustainable use of that same forest), then clearly the decision boils down to sustainable versus unsustainable use. If we have a policy of sustainable development then we choose the sustainable alternative, and the fact that it has a negative present value at an unsustainable discount rate is irrelevant. The discount rate must reflect the rate of return on alternative sustainable uses of capital. The efficiency allocation rule (maximize present value) cannot be allowed to subvert the very goal of sustainable development by applying an unsustainable discount rate (i.e., a discount rate based on alternative uses of capital that are unsustainable).

Sustainability of an investment project is a benefit. In general an extra benefit usually requires an extra cost. A policy of sustainable development means that we are willing to pay that cost, at least within reason. The preceding discussion suggests two alternative ways of evaluating projects in a regime of sustainable development. The first is a halfway measure, the second is more complete. (1) When evaluating sustainable projects, use a discount rate that excludes nonsustainable projects from the alternative uses of capital. Likewise, investments in nonsustainable projects should be evaluated on the basis of a discount rate reflecting only alternative nonsustainable projects. Allocation between these two broad categories, not addressed by this splitting of the discount rate, remains undetermined. (2) A better way is to pair unsustainable projects with compensating sustainable ones and count only the income component of receipts in calculating rate of return on all projects. The single discount rate would then measure the rate of return on alternative projects, all of which (being paired) are sustainable.[16] Perhaps the "pairing" of projects need not be explicit. Counting only the income component in calculating the rate of return on unsustainable projects may be sufficient, on the assumption that the capital component is invested in a sustainable project with a growth rate equal to the discount rate used in separating the income and capital components.

Summary and conclusions

The major conceptual issue we must resolve in thinking about economic development and the environment over the next decade is to integrate the one-way throughput as the basic starting point of economic analysis, even more fundamental than the circular flow. Next we must distinguish clearly the problem of the optimal allocation of the throughput from that of its optimal scale. Our attention will then naturally become focused on limiting the scale to an optimal, or at least sustainable level, thereby giving the discussion of sustainable development a firmer theoretical foundation. From there we can begin to investigate operational principles of sustainability, such as those discussed here and summarized below.

(1) The main principle is to limit the human scale to a level which, if not optimal, is at least within carrying capacity and therefore sustainable. Once carrying capacity has been reached the simultaneous choice of a population level and an average "standard of living" (level of per capita resource consumption) becomes necessary. Sustainable development must deal with sufficiency as well as efficiency, and cannot avoid limiting scale. An optimal scale would be one at which the long-run marginal costs of expansion are equal to the long-run marginal benefits of expansion. Until we develop operational measures of the cost and benefit of scale expansion, the idea of an optimum scale remains a theoretical formalism, but a very important one. The following principles aim at translating this general macro-level constraint to the micro level.

(2) Technological progress for sustainable development should be efficiency-increasing rather than throughput-increasing. Limiting the scale of resource throughput would induce this technological shift.

(3) Renewable resources, in both their source and sink functions, should be exploited on a profit-maximizing sustained-yield basis and in general not be driven to extinction, since they will become ever more important as nonrenewable resources run out. Specifically this means that harvesting rates should not exceed regeneration rates, and that waste emission should not exceed the renewable assimilative capacity of the environment.

(4) Nonrenewable resources should be exploited at a rate equal to the creation of renewable substitutes. Nonrenewable investments should be paired with renewable investments, and their rates of return should be calculated on the basis of their income component only, since that is what is perpetually available for consumption in each future year. If occasionally a renewable resource is to be depleted in a nonrenewable fashion (partially divested), then the same pairing rule should apply to it as for a nonrenewable resource. Thus the mix of renewable resources would not be static; a compensating renewable investment would be made for every divestment.

Perhaps there are other principles of sustainable development as well, and certainly those listed above need to be refined, clarified, and made more consistent between the micro and macro levels. But these four are both an operational starting point and a sufficient political challenge to the present order. Will those nations seeking sustainable development be able to operationalize a concept from which such "radical" principles follow so logically?

Or will they, rather than face up to population control, wealth redistribution, and living on income, revert to the cornucopian myth of unlimited growth, rechristened as "sustainable growth"? It is easier to invent bad oxymorons than to resolve real contradictions.

Notes

The views expressed in this article are those of the author and should in no way be attributed to the World Bank or any other institution. The author is indebted for helpful comments to S. Davis, S. El Serafy, P. Ehrlich, R. Goodland, P. Knight, and R. Overby. Earlier versions of parts of this paper were presented at a conference on development and environment, sponsored by the Italian Ministry of the Environment, Milan, March 1988.

1 An example of the consequences of non-recognition of the distinction between scale and allocation can be found in Daly (1986). A similar distinction is made by D. W. Pearce (1987), who develops the idea of an ecologically bounded economy and argues that sustainability cannot be derived from the market mechanism.

2 This distinction is not the result of any idiosyncratic redefinition. It is explicit in the dictionary's first definition of each term. To *grow* means literally "to increase naturally in size by the addition of material through assimilation or accretion." To *develop* means "to expand or realize the potentialities of; bring gradually to a fuller, greater, or better state" (*The American Heritage Dictionary of the English Language*).

3 Some texts explicitly announce in bold print that "the flow of output is circular, self-renewing, and self-feeding." See Heilbroner and Thurow (1981).

4 A recent treatise by Charles Perrings (1987) is an important theoretical contribution toward integrating the concept of throughput and the laws of thermodynamics with standard economics.

5 For a more extended discussion, see Daly (1985).

6 The definition of human appropriation underlying the figures quoted includes direct use by human beings (food, fuel, fiber, timber), plus the reduction from the photosynthetic potential due to degradation of ecosystems caused by humans. The latter reflects deforestation, desertification, paving over, and human conversion to less productive systems (such as agriculture).

7 Lauderdale (1819:44). I am indebted to George Foy for this reference.

8 Present value maximization attempts to allocate resources efficiently over time. But once intergenerational time periods are encountered we escape the domain of allocation and must speak instead of distribution. Different generations are different people. Dividing the resource base among different people is distribution; dividing it among different uses for the same group of people is allocation. The former is a matter of justice, the latter of efficiency. Present value maximization (discounting) over intergenerational time conflates allocation and distribution.

9 This lack of generalizability can be seen from the following back-of-the-envelope calculation, based on the crude estimate that the United States currently uses 1/3 of annual world resource flows (National Commission on Materials Policy, 1973). If the United States, with 1/21 of the world's population, consumes 1/3 of the world's resources, then we would need to increase world resources sevenfold to provide everyone with the current US level of resource consumption. This is simple arithmetic since US per capita resource consumption is seven times higher (1/3 divided by 1/21) than that of the rest of the world.

But even the sevenfold increase is a gross underestimate of the increase in environmental impact, for two reasons. First, because the calculation is in terms of current flows only, with no allowance for the increase in accumulated stocks of capital goods necessary to process and transform the greater flow of resources into final products. Some notion of the magnitude of the extra stocks needed comes from Harrison Brown's (1970) estimate that the "standing crop" of industrial metals already embodied in the existing stock of artifacts in the ten richest nations would require more than 60 years' production of these metals at 1970 rates. Second, because the sevenfold increase of net, usable minerals and energy will require a much greater increase in gross resource flows, since we must mine ever less accessible deposits and lower grade ores. It is the gross flow that provokes environmental impact.

10 Natural capital may be divided into marketed and nonmarketed natural capital. The former yields the flow of priced natural resources; the latter yields the flux of unpriced natural life-support services. The term is a bit awkward because capital has traditionally been defined as produced (manmade) means of production. The term "land" in earlier times meant something equivalent to natural capital, but has now lost that meaning. The term natural capital is used to call attention to the fact that there is a stock of natural assets that yield a flow of resources and services and that require maintenance in the face of depreciation and whose consumption cannot be counted as income.

11 Discounting is an operational concept when applied to money in the bank that is growing at a rate of interest. By extension it can, within limits, be applied to trees in a forest or fish in a pond, as long as we remember that there is a limit to the number of trees in a forest and the number of fish in a pond—while there is no limit to how much money there can be in the bank. But to discount utility—a psychic experience that cannot be accumulated or saved, and which has no natural tendency to grow in any case—is to commit Whitehead's fallacy of misplaced concreteness. Furthermore, to aggregate this future psychic experience across individuals before discounting it by a nonexistent natural growth rate is to lose touch completely with any possibility of a real-world counterpart to the paper-and-pencil operation.

12 This and other ways of adjusting the national accounts are discussed in Ahmad, El Serafy, and Lutz (1989).

13 World Commission on Environment and Development (1987:8).

14 See N. Georgescu-Roegen (1971:224–244).

15 For a discussion of the conflicts between free trade and sustainable development see Chapter 11 of Daly and Cobb (1989).

16 This approach is in agreement with Markandya and Pearce's (1988:58) general principle that "where possible it is better to adjust the cost and benefit values than to adjust the discount rate."

References

Ahmad, Yusuf J., Salah El Serafy, and Ernst Lutz (eds.). 1989. *Environmental Accounting for Sustainable Development*. Washington, D.C.: World Bank.

Boulding, Kenneth. 1966. "The economics of the coming Spaceship Earth," in Henry Jarrett (ed.), *Environmental Quality in a Growing Economy*. Baltimore: Johns Hopkins University Press.

Brown, Harrison. 1970. "Human materials production as a process in the biosphere," *Scientific American* (September): 194–208.

Daly, H. E. 1985. "The circular flow of exchange value and the linear throughput of matter-energy: A case of misplaced concreteness," *Review of Social Economy* (December): 279–297.

———. 1986. Review of National Research Council, *Population Growth and Economic Development: Policy Questions*, in *Population and Development Review* 12, no. 3 (September): 582–585.

———, and John B. Cobb, Jr. 1989. *For the Common Good: Redirecting the Economy Toward Community, the Environment and a Sustainable Future*. Boston: Beacon Press.

El Serafy, Salah. 1989. "The proper calculation of income from depletable natural resources." in Ahmad, El Serafy, and Lutz (1989), pp. 10–18.

Georgescu-Roegen, Nicholas. 1971. *The Entropy Law and the Economic Process.* Cambridge, Mass.: Harvard University Press.

Heilbroner, Robert, and Lester Thurow. 1981. *The Economic Problem.* Englewood Cliffs, N.J.: Prentice-Hall.

Hicks, J. R. 1946. *Value and Capital.* Oxford: Oxford University Press.

Kneese, A. V., R. V. Ayres, and R. C. d'Arge. 1970. *Economics and the Environment: A Materials Balance Approach.* Washington, D.C.: Resources for the Future.

Lauderdale. 1819. *An Inquiry into the Nature and Origin of Public Wealth and into the Means and Causes of its Increase,* second edition. Edinburgh: Archibald Constant and Co.

Markandya, Anil, and David Pearce. 1988. "Environmental considerations and the choice of discount rate in developing countries," World Bank, Environmental Department Working Paper No. 3.

National Commission on Materials Policy. 1973. *Material Needs and the Environment Today and Tomorrow.* Washington, D.C.: US Government Printing Office.

Page, Talbot. 1977. *Conservation and Economic Efficiency.* Baltimore: Johns Hopkins University Press.

Pearce, D. W. 1987. "Foundations of an ecological economics," *Ecological Modelling* 38, nos. 1 and 2: 9–18.

Perrings, Charles. 1987. *Economy and Environment.* Cambridge: Cambridge University Press.

Pezzy, John. 1989. "Economic analysis of sustainable growth and sustainable development," World Bank, Environmental Department Working Paper No. 15.

Vitousek, Peter M., Paul R. Ehrlich, Anne H. Ehrlich, and Pamela A. Matson. 1986. "Human appropriation of the products of photosynthesis," *BioScience* 34, no. 6 (May): 368–373.

World Commission on Environment and Development (The Brundtland Commission). 1987. *Our Common Future.* Oxford: Oxford University Press.

Long-Run Global Population Forecasts: A Critical Appraisal

MAJOR FORECASTS OF DEMOGRAPHIC TRENDS in the twenty-first century are in reassuringly close agreement[1]: growth rates will decline steadily throughout the century, leading to a nearly stationary world population of 10 to 11 billion people, or roughly twice the current number.[2] Thus the next and final doubling of world population will take three times as long as the previous, and the population explosion will recede into history as a brief aberration.

This scenario may be comforting or appalling, depending on one's views of the economic and environmental consequences of population size and growth. But in any event, one might well wonder about how such a forecast is made, the nature of its conceptual underpinnings, and the degree of confidence it merits. This article considers standard demographic forecasts in the broader intellectual context of theoretical and empirical studies of population dynamics.

The article has four parts. First, I consider the insights to be gained from demographic analysis, with an emphasis on the declining influence of mortality change on growth rates. Second, I consider at some length the different approaches to forecasting: those that hypothesize levels and changes in the vital rates without reference to the implied changes in population size, and those that reason in terms of the Earth's carrying capacity and the responsiveness of population growth rates to feedback. Third, I consider the degree of uncertainty in population forecasts. Fourth, I review some recent long-run forecasts of global population.

Mechanical aspects of forecasting and demographic insights

Demography per se makes a number of useful contributions to the task of forecasting. Doubtless the most important is establishing the baseline numbers, distributions, and rates, and the historical depth necessary to perceive trends. Demography also contributes analytic techniques and insights. Two here merit particular attention. The first is the role of population age distribution as an influence on the future evolution of the population. This is particularly important in transitions from one regime of vital rates to another, where the age distribution is said to impart "momentum" to the growth process: a population with a history of growth will continue to grow even after the net reproduction rate (NRR) reaches unity. For example, in the World Bank forecasts to be discussed below, the NRR in sub-Saharan Africa reaches unity in 2045, but the population eventually grows a further 40 percent. The second demographic contribution is an appreciation of the different roles of fertility and mortality in the growth process, a point to which I will turn in more detail in a moment. Other demographic insights, such as the cohort view of demographic behavior, or subtle analyses of the influence of the changing timing of events, are of relatively little importance here. Nor are surveys of childbearing intentions, since these change over time roughly in parallel with fertility behavior (Lee, 1981).

Let us consider the relative importance of variations in fertility and mortality for future population trajectories. Some have taken the extreme view that parents adjust their planned fertility in response to their accurate expectations about mortality levels and trends, and thereby fully neutralize mortality's effects on growth rates. A more reasonable view is that although parents adjust their fertility to perceived mortality to some degree, rapid mortality change nonetheless leads to a disequilibrium situation in which many parents have more surviving children than anticipated. Indeed, it is the common view, and a reasonable view, that the exceptionally rapid population growth of the period since World War II is largely due to the rapid decline of mortality. Failure to appreciate the pace of mortality declines in the period after the war caused large errors in global demographic forecasts in the 1940s and 1950s (Demeny, 1989). Mortality in the less developed countries will surely decline further in the next few decades. Demographic analysis can illuminate the relative importance of such trends for future population trajectories.

In the long run, mortality affects the population size and age structure in two ways: first, by influencing the trajectory of births, through its effect on survival of women to childbearing ages (as reflected in the net reproduction rate); and second, by determining the number and distribution of person-years lived over the life cycle per birth, and therefore determining the size of the population surviving from a prior trajectory of births.

We can isolate the first effect by noting that the intrinsic rate of natural increase approximately equals the natural log of the NRR divided by the mean age of childbearing. Straightforward analysis of this relationship gives the result that, to a first approximation, the effect of mortality on the (steady-state) rate of population growth is independent of the level of fertility.[3] (A similar result can be derived for a non–steady-state birth trajectory.) It is a simple matter, then, to pick an arbitrary level of fertility—let us say a gross reproduction rate (GRR) of 1.0 or a total fertility rate (TFR) of 2.05—and calculate and plot the effect of a one-year improvement in life expectancy on the growth rate.

Figure 1, calculated from Coale–Demeny (1983) stable population models,[4] shows that at low life expectancy at birth (e_0)(that is, high mortality), a decline in mortality has a relatively large effect. For example, a one-year increase in e_0 from an initial level of 20 years causes an increase in the annual growth rate of about .16 percent. But as we move to higher and higher levels of e_0, the effect of further gains (or losses) in e_0 becomes negligibly small, so that at e_0 = 50, the growth rate increases by less than .06 percent, and at e_0 = 70, by only .03 percent. Of course, future mortality declines will still have an important influence on some population growth rates. For Africa, growth rates would rise by a full percentage point if life expectancy were now 80. My point here is rather that forecasting errors arising from mortality are likely to be very much smaller than those arising from fertility.

Further analysis reveals that the effect of a change in fertiliy on the population growth rate is also approximately independent of mortality, and is inversely proportional to the level of fertility.[5] When the GRR equals unity, as in the developed countries today, the effect of a variation will be three

FIGURE 1   Effect of a one-year increase in life expectancy at birth (e_0) on the population growth rate, by initial level of e_0, across stable populations

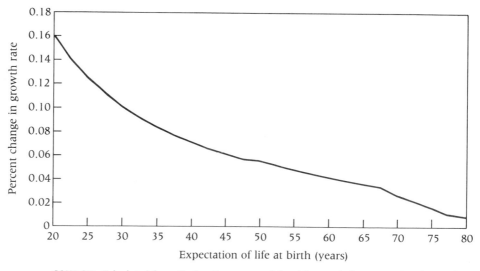

SOURCE: Calculated from Coale—Demeny model stable populations assuming the Model West Female family with the GRR held constant at 1.0.

times as great as when it equals 3, as in many pretransitional less developed countries.

We see, therefore, that over the course of the demographic transition, the influence of mortality change on the growth rate eventually becomes vanishingly small, while that of fertility becomes ever larger. Under conditions of high fertility and high mortality, a difference of one child in the TFR has the same effect on the population growth rate as a four-year difference in e_0. But under conditions of low fertility and low mortality, the same difference in fertility has an effect more that 25 times as great as this difference in mortality.[6]

The line of argument pursued above establishes that mortality variations, and errors in forecasting mortality, will have little effect on future birth trajectories. Nevertheless, the size of the resulting population will be affected, and over the transitional period during which mortality change is occurring, the growth rate of the population will also be affected. Mortality's impact on the size of a stationary population is easily stated: the population size equals the annual number of births times the life expectancy at birth. Given the same constant stream of births, an e_0 of 80 implies a population size 14 percent larger than an e_0 of 70 (80/70 = 1.14). Since, as we shall see below, most long-run population forecasts eventually reach demographic stationarity, the effect on them of further mortality decline is easily seen, and comparatively modest.

Now consider the influence of mortality on the age distribution. Starting from high to moderate levels, further mortality declines have little effect on the age distribution of the population, since the tendency of births to live longer is offset by the tendency of the population to grow more rapidly. But once relatively low mortality levels have been attained, further mortality declines strongly age the population, since the offsetting effect on growth rates disappears. For some purposes, the aging effect of mortality decline would be of capital importance, but it does not matter much for population–environment interactions.[7]

This discussion has shown that our energies can best be focused on understanding and forecasting fertility change. Mortality decline, which played the central role in accounting for the rapid population growth of the past four decades, will play only a secondary role in the future. I will now turn to the difficult problem of forecasting fertility and mortality.

Autonomous vital rates: Forecasting without feedback

Population forecasters typically begin by choosing plausible trajectories for the vital rates and then deriving the implications for population growth rates and size. This approach seems so natural as to need no defense; yet it can certainly be questioned, and will be, in a later section. Here I consider three approaches to forecasting vital rates or vital events. The first is extrapolation, in more or less sophisticated ways; the second is historical analogy; and the third is socioeconomic theory.

Extrapolation

The most primitive understanding of the growth process suggests that we reason in terms of proportional growth rates, or equivalently the time derivative of logarithms, rather than absolute changes. Joel Cohen (1986) has suggested using the long-term average growth rate to project population when an inspection of long time series does not reveal evidence of a trend in the growth rate. Since Third World growth rates do show strong secular trends, this method is not suitable for global forecasts.

For most of the world we know not only the rate of growth, but also the trend in the rate of growth over the past several decades, and so we can extrapolate future changes in the growth rate. The simplest version of such an approach replicates surprisingly well the forecasts of major agencies through the next century. Assume a linear trend in the growth rate, say $n(t) = a + bt$. Then, if $t = 0$ is the starting point of the projection, and population size is initially $P(0)$, future sizes are given by: $P(t) = P(0) \exp(at + bt^2/2)$. Let us choose July 1987 as our starting point, and select a and b to fit two growth rate observations: $n(1965–69) = .0206$ and $n(1985–89) = .0177$ (which are taken from United Nations Secretariat, 1988). Then the expression for $P(t)$ given above generates projections for as many years into the future as we like. Comparing the results with forecasts by the UN and the US Bureau of the Census (reported later) reveals discrepancies of less than 1.5 percent through 2050. The growth rate reaches zero in 2088, at which point the population peaks at about 13 billion—20 percent higher than the World Bank's projected size.

Of course, this is not literally the procedure of these agencies, but it is conceptually quite close to what they do—that is, they rely heavily on the assumption that trends will continue in a regular way.[8] Projections for sub-Saharan Africa deviate most strongly from this approach, since growth rates there have not yet begun to decline.

Such a mechanical extrapolative approach may work very well over a limited horizon, but eventually it must lead to implausible results, and it is of course incapable of dealing with turning points. Unlike such ad hoc procedures, formal time-series analysis systematically exploits the relation between the past history of a series and its future evolution, and has been used to forecast fertility, mortality, and population itself (e.g., Lee, 1974; McDonald, 1981; Lee and Lau, 1987). The US Census Bureau is now preparing US forecasts based on this method. Time-series methods may prove useful for post-transitional populations, but by their very nature they are ill suited for predicting the kind of structural change and long-run turning points that characterize the fertility transition.

Historical model

The demographic history of the developed countries is often viewed as a prototype for the developing countries, which are assumed to retrace the prior patterns of the developed countries at an accelerated pace. The experience of quite a number of developing countries in Asia and Latin America conforms to this view. Once fertility begins a secular decline, the process appears to follow a fairly regular monotonic form until a low level has been reached. The puzzling baby boom experienced by many of the developed countries following World War II presents the most serious challenge to this notion, although nowhere did it result in a sustained return to high fertility. Since the fertility of the developed countries has been relatively flat at a level somewhat below replacement over the past 15 years, it would be natural to take this as the endpoint of the decline for the less developed countries. Instead, forecasting agencies have preferred to assume that fertility in the developed countries will rise to replacement levels, while fertility in the less developed countries will decline until their net reproduction rates reach unity. I will return to this point later.

Behavioral theory

Another approach is to draw on social and economic theory for clues about the future evolution of population growth rates, or fertility. The basic messages from sociology and from economics are very similar. Broad social and economic changes of various sorts have eroded the traditional sexual division of labor and the economic role of the family and household, while increasing the desirability of investing heavily in the human capital of each child. These changes are expected to continue, and the theories and models, if taken at face value, predict continued decline in fertility. This approach leads us to expect population decline at an accelerating pace in the developed countries, and presumably the same would eventually be true of the less developed countries.

As an example of how estimated economic models could lead to fertility forecasts, consider the most widely accepted effort to explain fertility trends in a number of developed countries, using a version of the New Home Economics model (Butz and Ward, 1979). This approach posits two effects of growth in earning power: on the one hand, rising life cycle wealth would lead couples to choose to have more children; but on the other hand, rising wage rates increase the opportunity cost of time devoted to children, thereby making them more expensive. Empirical work identifies these two effects by assuming that children are costly only in women's time, so that men's wages exert a pure income effect, and women's a mixed income and price effect.

Increases in the husband's wage are expected to raise fertility, while increases in the wife's wage should lower it. The net effect of equiproportional increases in their wages is to alter fertility in proportion to the sum of the fertility–wage elasticities, call it E. The stability of the male–female wage differential suggests that we assume male and female wages grow at the same rate, let us say r. Then the predicted annual rate of change in fertility is simply rE. In their two studies, Butz and Ward (1979; Ward and Butz, 1980) found elasticities that sum to $-.54$ and $-.99$.[9] If the rate of wage growth were 2 percent per year (as recently forecast by the US Bureau of Labor Statistics), then fertility would decline by 1 to 2 percent per year, depending on the estimate chosen. After 30 years, it would have fallen by 25 to 45 percent. Thus the theory, as empirically implemented, predicts a rapid and unremitting downward trend in fertility as productivity increases.[10] Butz and Ward (1979) speculate that rising marginal utility of children would eventually halt the decline, but this notion is neither modeled nor quantified; it is a deus ex machina.

Malthus: Population change as equilibrating response

All of these approaches treat population growth independently of any feedback arising from population size in relation to the Earth's resources or reproducible capital. Yet historical populations were regulated by Malthusian feedback, or so many historians argue, and the acceleration of population growth over the past few centuries is sometimes viewed as a response to rising carrying capacity due to the industrial revolution. In this interpretation, we are currently in the midst of a transition to a new and higher global population equilibrium under industrial technology.

Although most demographers would hesitate to endorse such a view, something very much like it appears to underlie most contemporary long-run global forecasts, which take for granted that regional net reproduction rates will move smoothly to unity and remain there.[11] What is the support for this view, and what are its implications?

Does fertility respond to density?

Elsewhere (Lee, 1987) I have surveyed dozens of estimates of density-dependent fertility response in agrarian populations, historical and contemporary.[12] Figure 2 summarizes the results. It shows the distribution by size of nearly 50 estimated elasticities of fertility with respect to density.[13] These cluster in the range 0 to $-.3$, indicating that a 10 percent increase in density

FIGURE 2   Fertility and population density: Frequency distribution of estimated elasticities from studies of agricultural populations

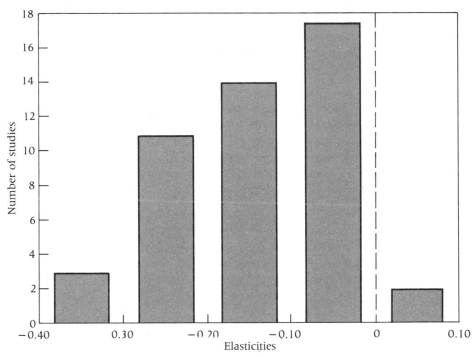

NOTE: Four kinds of studies are represented: long–run aggregate time series, short–run fluctuations in aggregate time series, aggregate cross–areal data, and household–level data.
SOURCES: Results are from 47 studies (cited in Lee, 1987) of agricultural populations in Africa, Latin America, Asia, Europe, and North America for various periods, mainly in the nineteenth and twentieth centuries.

would induce a 0 to 3 percent decline in fertility, and a doubling of density would induce a decline of up to 20 percent. Figure 2 provides strong evidence that Malthusian forces have been at work in many agricultural societies both in the now developed countries and in the contemporary Third World.[14] However, these homeostatic forces are far too weak to deal with the rapid dislocations of recent decades. For example, we may assume Third World mortality decline to be largely exogenous to the Malthusian system, a shock to which the system must respond and adjust. The probability that a female birth survives to childbearing age has more than doubled as mortality has fallen. To restore equilibrium, fertility must be halved. With a fertility–density elasticity of − .3, density would have to increase by a factor of ten to bring this about; with an elasticity of − .1, an increase by a factor of a thousand would be required. In practice, smaller increases would be necessary, because there would be some direct adjustment of fertility to declining child mortality.

Equilibration in the next century

Any attempt to apply the Malthusian perspective in the contemporary context must confront a number of difficult questions. First, will economic signals—prices, wages, and incomes—respond significantly to resource shortages arising from population growth over the next half century or century? Second, if the economy does signal resource scarcity, how will the population respond? Third, if the economy fails (at least in advance) to signal actual resource and environmental problems, because of externalities, nonlinearities, failures of intertemporal markets, and threshold effects, how will these problems impinge on the population? I raise these issues because they are important for long-run forecasting, and also central to issues related to population and the environment. My discussion will be brief.

A number of recent surveys by economists (World Bank, 1984: National Research Council, 1986; Kelley, 1988) agree that Third World economies are not currently sending clear signals of natural resource shortages or environmental problems induced by population growth. Rapid population growth is more frequently blamed for difficulties in raising human and physical capital per head. It is not clear, however, what assumptions should be made about institutions and government economic policies when assessing the role of population growth in, for example, the current abysmal economic performance of sub-Saharan Africa. In any event, economies are not now signaling current or impending resource scarcity, so a crucial part of the Malthusian system is doing nothing to induce demographic equilibration.

What of the future? Forecasts made in the early 1980s of global food supply through 2000 agree in foreseeing moderate growth in overall per capita food availability (as surveyed in Srinivasan, 1988). Local famines may occur, as always, and impoverished subpopulations will be unable to buy adequate nourishment, but no aggregate shortfall is foreseen (how far the more recent climatic trends, if they continue, would alter this generally favorable picture I do not know).

For the longer run, we must resort to theoretical calculations of the world's carrying capacity, with all their problems. The question could be posed in terms of various limiting factors, but most commonly upper limits on food production have been assessed. Over the past few decades, estimates of agricultural carrying capacity have ranged from less than a billion people to 147 billion. A joint project of the Food and Agriculture Organization (FAO), United Nations Population Fund (UNFPA), and the International Institute for Applied Systems Analysis (IIASA) has produced estimates of potential food production based on the most disaggregated analysis to date (Harrison, 1984). Their methods and results are briefly described in the Appendix. They conclude that the territories of most of the Third World excluding China could feed a population of 33 billion people with technology, investments, and inputs similar to those of Europe around 1980.[15] Africa alone could feed nearly 13 billion. However, a number of nations would encounter difficulties feeding their populations by 2000, even with advanced technology in place.[16]

These calculations can be criticized for their assumption of low per capita calorie requirements, their inattention to energy sources, their neglect of the role of forests in the global environment, and optimistic assumptions about the cultivability of tropical soils now forested (Gilland, 1983; Hendry, 1988). Furthermore, it must be remembered that this is a calculation of static theoretical upper limits, and not in any sense a forecast. Achieving the potential would require very costly investments and in many cases the import of fertilizer. The study has also been criticized as unduly pessimistic, particularly for ignoring possibilities of trade and of further technological progress (Repetto, 1987).

Nonetheless, this is the most detailed study available covering a substantial portion of the Earth's land surface, and in many respects it was executed with great care. It is a simple matter to allow for more calories per head; Gilland (1983) assumed three times as many, or 9,000. With this assumption, the FAO estimate drops from 33 to 11 billion. Allowing, as the FAO study suggests, for one-third of the area to be used for nonfood crops further reduces the estimate to 7.3 billion. This, as we shall see, is quite close to the eventual population forecast for these regions by the World Bank.

This brief review suggests that unyielding natural limitations on agricultural output will not soon be encountered at the global level. It also suggests that critical situations, submerged in regional potential surpluses, will quickly emerge at the national level. This point is brought out forcefully by Falkenmark (in this volume). Therefore one's view of the implications of these figures must depend strongly on one's assessment of the likelihood of substantial international trade in food or water or of substantial international migration.

Will clear economic signals of resource limitations emerge in the next century? This review of estimates of potential food production has been inconclusive. More will be said of this later. For the moment, let us consider what the demographic response might be to economic signals if these were to occur.

Suppose that global resource constraints caused food prices to rise sharply and per capita incomes to fall. Is there reason to believe that fertility would decline? There is ample evidence that fertility drops in response to economic adversity in the short run. This has been observed in every major Third World famine in recent decades (the shortfall of births roughly equals the increase in deaths). But long-run economic deterioration is quite a different matter. Most fertility theories were structured to explain why the poor have more children than the rich, and to account for the long-run decline of fertility during the course of economic growth and industrialization. If set in reverse, they would predict an increase in fertility as incomes fell. In a subtler interpretation, the outcome would depend on concurrent changes in society and on how these affect both the economic value of children and the relative rewards to quantity and quality in childbearing.

It appears, then, that the economic system might fail to signal the costs of approaching environmental limitations in the coming decades, and that even if it did, the demographic response might be perverse. One important reason that markets may fail to reflect serious environmental deterioration and resource scarcities is that ownership is public and access is free. Even adverse changes that will strongly affect future output may escape the market. In this case, population growth feedback may be delayed, but must occur eventually, perhaps in a catastrophic way. But some sorts of environmental change may affect humans directly, without the mediation of the market. Changes in air temperature, ozone depletion, or environmental pollution may be of this sort. Although there is strong evidence that short-run fluctuations in temperature (unusually cold winters or hot summers) affect mortality, it is unlikely that there is a comparable effect of long-run temperature change. Depletion of the ozone layer is expected to raise deaths from melanoma, but I have no idea how great the effects on aggregate mortality from this and other causes could be. Similarly, I cannot evaluate the direct effects of environmental pollution on human fertility and mortality. Therefore I have no basis for assessing feedback effects of population growth arising directly from environmental response, rather than mediated by agriculture or the economic system more generally. All this could change drastically in the future if institutions are altered so as to bring the full environmental costs of activities, including childbearing, to bear on individual decisionmaking.

Populations in the past did equilibrate, at least weakly, with their resource base. The brief review just completed suggests, however, that they no longer do, at least not within the contemporary range of densities and circumstances. On the one hand, the response of economic well-being to population growth is currently weak. On the other hand, even the sign of the response of fertility to income or wealth is problematic. Of course, there remains the positive check, that court of last resort. The threat of population-induced famine and war has been raised often by scholars. However, mortality is still declining in all regions of the world, and the famines since World War II (for example, in China and in Bangladesh) are generally attributed more to mistaken policy than to demographic pressure.

I now turn from the conceptual foundations of forecasting to a consideration of the past record of long-run global forecasts, and an assessment of the uncertainty inherent in the enterprise.

Uncertainty and confidence intervals

The UN record

Many notable failures have characterized postwar global population forecasts (Demeny, 1989). The record of the United Nations, however, in the nearly 40 years they have been preparing forecasts, is quite good. Table 1 shows UN forecasts for total population size in the years 1980, 1985, and 2000, with baseline dates ranging from 1951 to the present. The early forecasts of the 1980 population were not good, involving errors of about 1 percent per year in the average growth rate. Otherwise, errors and revisions over time are rather small. For example, the 1957 forecast of the 1985 population, over a horizon of 28 years, was off by only 4 percent on the size and by .13 percent on the average annual growth rate. The forecasts to the year 2000 show what is to me an extraordinary consistency.

Deeper examination of the errors in the forecasts by the United Nations has revealed that until those of 1968, the dominant source of error was in the data characterizing initial levels and rates of growth of the populations. Starting with the 1968 forecasts, however, after data sources and estimation methods had substantially improved, the major source of error was in the forecast assumptions (see Inoue and Yu, 1979). We can assume that this will remain the case in the future.

TABLE 1   UN projections of world population to 1980, 1985, and 2000 from various base years (billions)

Year of projection	Year projected to		
	1980	1985	2000
1951	3.277	—	—
1954	3.628	—	—
1957	4.220	4.660	6.280
1963	4.330	4.746	6.130
1968	4.457	4.933	6.494
1973	4.374	4.817	6.254
1978	4.415	4.829	6.199
1980	—	4.826	6.116
1982	—	4.842	6.127
1984	—	—	6.122
1988	—	—	6.250
Actual	4.450	4.853	—

SOURCES: Figures for forecasts made through 1982 are taken from El-Badry and Kono (1987) and from Frejka (1981b); figures for subsequent forecasts are taken from United Nations (1988).

It is common practice, when presenting demographic forecasts, to provide "high" and "low" variants that give a sense of the range of uncertainty associated with the enterprise. Typically no probabilistic interpretation is given to such forecast brackets, however. Two approaches have been taken to the problem of generating more objective confidence intervals for demographic forecasts: stochastic models and ex post analysis of performance.[17] For various reasons, the latter is more relevant here.[18]

Nathan Keyfitz (1981) and Michael Stoto (1983) have pioneered in the analysis of ex post errors in UN forecasts for individual countries, as a basis for attaching confidence intervals to current forecasts. They conclude that for horizons up to 30 years, the error in the growth rate forecast does not increase as the forecast horizon lengthens. Keyfitz also concludes that the forecast error has declined somewhat for more recent estimates. He finds that the standard deviation of growth rate forecast errors is .4 percent for all countries together. Stoto, considering developed and less developed countries separately, concludes that the standard deviation of errors for the former is .28 percent and for the latter is .51 percent. Most of this is due to across-all-region errors, rather than between-region error differences for a given forecast starting date. To illustrate what the Keyfitz estimate implies, for a 100-year forecast the 67 percent confidence interval would extend from two-thirds of the medium forecast to one and a half times it.

The United Nations (1983: 28) took note of Keyfitz's work in its long-run forecasts, suggesting that individual country errors would tend to cancel out in the global forecasts. They found a standard error of only .13 percent for forecasts from 1958 to 1973 of the 1980 population. But that calculation ignores the forecasts made in 1951 and 1954, which had large growth rate errors of 1.03 and .82 percent respectively. If they are included, then the standard error is four times as great, at .55 percent. It is not clear that these two early forecasts should be included, since errors in initial conditions due to poor data should be much smaller in the future. At the same time, because declining mortality had a strong effect on growth rates in the 1950s, the 1951 and 1954 estimates provide a better test of forecast accuracy during times of change.

Unfortunately, these analyses of ex post errors are necessarily limited to rather short horizons, relative to the 160-year span of the World Bank forecasts I examine below. To redress the imbalance, I have examined the longer run forecasts listed in Tomas Frejka's (1981b) survey of global population forecasts. I used the Keyfitz–Stoto method to evaluate the uncertainty of forecasts with horizons of 50 to 350 years, carried out by Gregory King, Raymond Pearl, Frank Notestein, and others. Frejka presents six such forecasts, which have a mean squared error of just over 1 percent.[19] Furthermore, the three longest forecasts have the smallest (by far) growth rate errors. All the forecasts underestimated future population, and the smallest average growth rate error is .46 percent. Although knowledge of baseline levels and trends was of course far inferior when these were done, I see nothing here to suggest that the Keyfitz–Stoto confidence bands are too pessimistic for long-run forecasts.

Review of current forecasts

Three organizations dominate the enterprise of generating medium- to long-term forecasts of national, regional, and global population: the United Nations, the World Bank, and the US Bureau of the Census. These three organizations cooperate in their work, so their forecasts cannot be viewed as entirely independent. The most widely used forecasts are those of the UN, with the World Bank, due to the frequency of their forecasts and their longer range, also cited often. The discussion below will concentrate on forecasts by the UN and the World Bank.

Assumptions underlying forecasts

None of the organizations explains what theory or conceptual model underlies its assumptions about the future course of fertility. When they speak of their fertility "assumptions," they mean the trajectory assumed for fertility. It is clear that the initial demographic, socioeconomic, and policy context is taken into account in some formal or informal way, but it is not clear exactly how. The United Nations and the World Bank share a distinctive approach, pioneered by Frejka (1973) and used again by Frejka in more recent long-run forecasts (1981a): fertility is assumed to decline to the replacement level, and the main effort is devoted to choosing a date at which this level will be reached.[20] Once the date of attaining a net reproduction rate (NRR) of unity is fixed, trajectories from the initial levels to that point are fit in ways that reflect recent trends. The result is that by 2025, the global NRR in the World Bank forecasts has fallen to 1.06, so that the intrinsic rate of natural increase is .2 percent per year. Because of population momentum, however, the actual rate of natural increase is still .9 percent per year. At that point, sub-Saharan Africa is the only world region with an NRR above 1.07. Figure 3 displays the World Bank's fertility forecasts for various regions of the world, up to 2050, after which changes are minor; before 1985, past fertility is taken from UN sources.

Mortality is forecast by noting the past association between the initial level of e_0 and its rate of increase.[21] As applied by the World Bank, this procedure gives a maximum rate of increase in e_0 of about .5 years per calendar year, declining to .03 per year when female e_0 reaches 82.5, a level not yet attained by any national population (although several are very close).

FIGURE 3   Projected total fertility rates by region

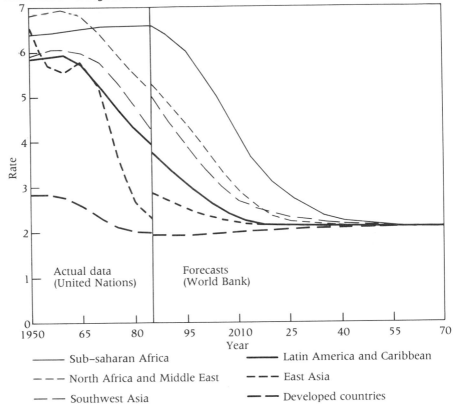

SOURCES: United Nations (1986); Vu et al. (1988).

Under these assumptions, the less developed countries as a whole, which in 1985 had a life expectancy of 61.5 years (according to World Bank data), would attain an e_0 of 70 in 2025, and of nearly 80 by 2150. Given that Hong Kong is reported to have a life expectancy of 79 in 1988, this appears a bit pessimistic. The developed countries, starting from a 1985 level of 74.3, would reach nearly 80 by 2100. The United Nations, in its latest forecasts to 2025, has raised the upper limit on e_0 to 85 years (Haub, 1988),[22] more than five years higher than the Bank's upper limit for 125 years later.

The forecasts

Under these assumptions, every national population will (barring migration) converge to a stationary population, as will the world as a whole. In the World Bank forecast, the stationary world population is 10.8 billion, or a bit more than twice its current level. Figure 4 plots the most recent available

FIGURE 4   World population projections

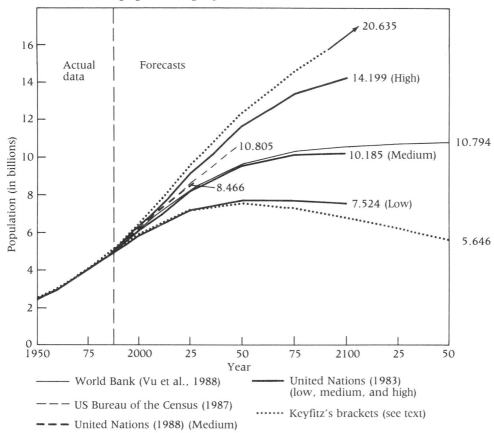

long-run forecasts of the United Nations, the World Bank, and the US Bureau of the Census; for the UN, the high and low variants are plotted as well. Also, because the UN forecast was done in 1982, I have included the most recent (1988) forecast, which goes only to 2025. As can be seen, the UN and World Bank long-run forecasts are in very close agreement; had there been space to show Frejka's (1981a) forecast, that would be seen to be very close as well. They are similar because all three use Frejka's approach and assume rather similar dates for attaining replacement-level fertility. The Census Bureau does not use this method, and its forecasts are substantially higher than the others, although still within the UN high–low range. Figure 4 also plots the 67 percent confidence intervals derived from Keyfitz. The high–low range for the long-run UN growth rate forecast to 2100 is .49 to .97 percent per year; this is only 60 percent of the confidence interval of plus or minus .4 suggested by Keyfitz (1981).[23] The range for 2025 (not shown on the graph) is very similar in size, and therefore also smaller than ex post analysis suggests is appropriate.

The world population is still growing at about 1.7 percent annually, a rate that is not expected to decline quickly. All the forecasts indicate a substantial amount of growth in the next few decades, no matter what the long-term outlook. The most recent UN forecast, for example, indicates that the population will increase by two-thirds up to 2025, a growth of 3.3 billion, equal to the entire population of the world in 1965. World population is currently growing by close to 90 million people per year, and by 2035 it will still be growing by about 75 million annually. Indeed, of the total population increase forecast over the next 160 years, about 60 percent will occur by 2025. Most of this growth will take place in the less developed regions, which will increase their size by three-fourths by 2025.

Figure 5 plots the regional World Bank forecasts. The more developed countries grow by only 14 percent up to 2150. Latin America and the Caribbean more than double, as does Asia as a whole. Africa increases by a factor of about 4.75. Within the broad Asian region, Eastern Asia, dominated by China, increases by only about 80 percent, while Southern and Western Asia increase by a factor of 2.3. The growth of Africa is particularly striking. While the global population growth rate is 1.7 percent and the developing world's is 2.1 percent, that of sub-Saharan Africa is 3.2 percent, highest of any region. Its population is forecast nearly to triple by 2025 and to quadruple by 2050, relative to 1985, so its future growth is heavily concentrated in the next half century.

FIGURE 5   Population projections based on World Bank forecasts, 1985–2150

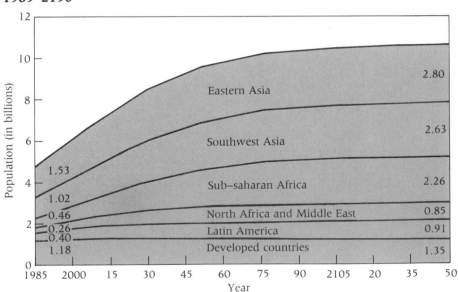

SOURCE: Calculated from numbers in Vu et al. (1988).

Of course, these differing regional growth paths during the overall doubling of the world population lead to important shifts in regional distribution. These changes are shown in Figure 6, which plots the regional
percentage shares of the total from 1985 to 2150. Clearly, the most dramatic
change is the decline in the share of the now developed countries from 24.1
to 12.5 percent, and the increase in the share of sub-Saharan Africa from 9.4
to 20.9 percent. Eastern Asia, moving rapidly through the demographic
transition, declines from 31.6 to 25.9 percent; Latin America remains the
same; and Southern and Western Asia, along with the Middle East and
North Africa, gains what East Asia loses.

Population growth in relation to FAO estimates of carrying capacity

It might be informative to consider the population densities implied by these
forecasts, but because the agro-climatic conditions differ so markedly
among regions and countries, a more refined measure is desirable. Despite
their shortcomings, the aforementioned FAO/UNFPA/IIASA calculations of

FIGURE 6   Population share of world regions (percent), based on World Bank forecasts

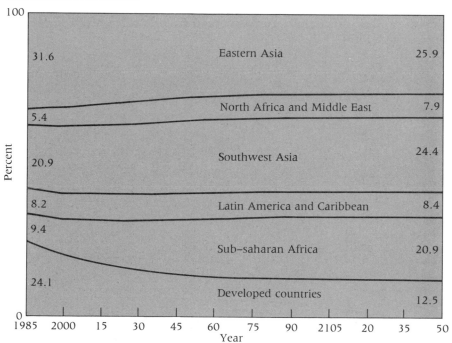

NOTE: Regional allocation of countries is standard, or can be inferred from the
definition of Southwest Asia, which includes Afghanistan, Bangladesh, Bhutan, India,
Nepal, Pakistan, and Sri Lanka.
SOURCE: Calculated from numbers in Vu et al. (1988).

carrying capacity provide a useful benchmark. While we should not attach significance to the absolute ratios given, because of the uncertainty over per capita caloric levels, nonfood needs, and global environmental concerns, the ratios do help us compare the situation across countries and regions. When examining the results, one should keep in mind that self-sufficiency in food production is not necessary for individual regions, countries, or sub-areas within countries. Trade, in principle, provides an alternative. Even areas that are now heavily agricultural, and with no obvious opportunities for exports, could begin to trade internationally during the next century.

Figure 7 shows the projected population/carrying capacity ratios by region. The carrying capacity is for "high inputs" in the year 2000, which means it assumes an extent of irrigation projected by FAO for 2000, and other inputs corresponding to European practices around 1980. This carrying capacity is in no sense an estimate of attainable agricultural output in 2000; rather, it is an estimate of what could be attained if appropriate costly investments were made. The carrying capacity figure used here does not change over time; only the population size varies in these figures. The regions in Figure 7 follow those of the FAO study, and require comment. Recall that China is not included. "Southwest Asia" is actually mainly the Middle East. What is commonly known as South Asia is included in Southeast Asia.

FIGURE 7 Ratio of actual and projected population to carrying capacity, by region

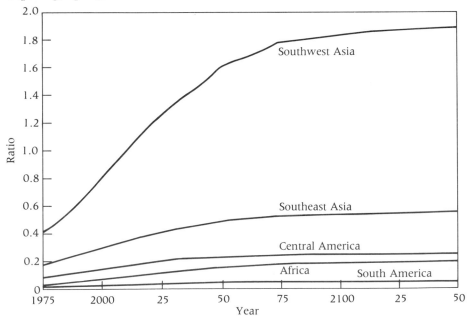

SOURCE: Population projections are taken from Vu et al. (1988). Carrying capacity figures, from FAO (1984), are for the year 2000 under the high–input assumption.

Figure 7 shows that the population of Southwest Asia will greatly exceed its maximum carrying capacity in the twenty-first century; indeed, the FAO calculates that its population is already above carrying capacity given its actual level of inputs. However, the populations involved are quite small. This is also true of the Central American region. Attention should be focused on the rest of Asia and Latin America and on Africa. It appears that the aggregate future populations of Africa and South America could in principle be fed from local production, even if we reduce the carrying capacity estimates by about 80 percent (to allow for higher caloric consumption and for nonfood output). However, it is not clear to what degree, and with what consequences, deforestation is assumed in order to reach this potential. In Southeast Asia (including such countries as India, Bangladesh, Pakistan, and Indonesia), the forecast shows far less leeway, since the dense populations of that region are already much closer to their upper limits.

Figure 8 takes a closer look at eight individual countries. For each country, there are up to three horizontal lines. The top line, corresponding to unity, indicates the high-input carrying capacity, as in Figure 7. The middle line indicates the carrying capacity with intermediate-level inputs as a pro-

FIGURE 8   Ratio of actual and projected population to carrying capacity, selected countries

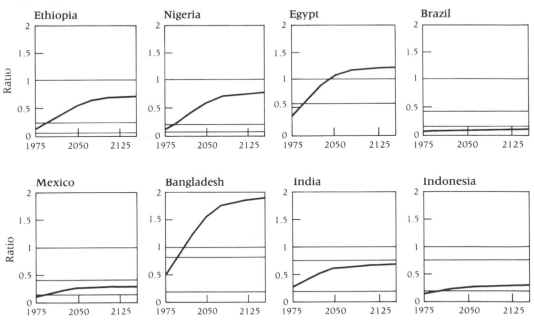

NOTE: The horizontal line at unity represents the carrying capacity under the FAO's high–input assumption. The middle horizontal line represents the carrying capacity under the intermediate–inputs assumption as a proportion of the high–input level. The lowest horizontal line represents the low–input carrying capacity as a proportion of the high–input level.
SOURCES: Carrying capacity data from Higgins et al. (1983). Population projections are taken from Vu et al. (1988).

portion of the high-input carrying capacity, and the bottom line indicates the low-input carrying capacity in the same way (see the Appendix for interpretations of these variants).

The figure confirms that Bangladesh and Egypt, everyone's favorite examples of countries with serious population problems, indeed face trouble that will get substantially worse. Surprisingly, after rapid growth from initially low density, the Nigerian population is projected to press as hard on the land base as is the Indian population. The same is true of Ethiopia. It is also perhaps surprising that Indonesia is expected to be relatively well off, and considerably more comfortable than Mexico. Brazil appears to be in a class by itself.

The FAO figures suggest that as far as soil, water, and climate are concerned, global agricultural output could in principle keep pace with World Bank forecasts of population growth. Some areas would need to develop exports to exchange for food imports. Questions remain, however, about limitations other than soil, water, and climate. Costly investments would be required to exploit the capacity. Energy would be needed to manufacture fertilizer, and the environmental consequences of clearing and cultivating additional land could affect agricultural productivity. In sum, comparison of population forecasts with potential agricultural productivity suggests that resource and environmental constraints may cause feedback effects on population growth in some areas. Forecasts of population should consider this possibility more seriously.

Why assume ultimate stationarity?

Why should it be assumed that fertility declines to replacement levels and therefore that population size eventually becomes stationary? The idea is taken from Frejka's work on long-term forecasts (1973, 1981a). I could find no explanation in Frejka's 1973 book, but in the 1981 article we find the following sentence: "Replacement level is selected as the value around which fertility will ultimately stabilize because that is the level of fertility that most populations tend to approximate in the long run" (1981a: 490). The United Nations, taking a slightly different tack, says, "This level is usually hypothesized in long-range projections . . . because any other level of fertility if maintained indefinitely, would eventually cause a population to expand to an improbable size or to decline to the point of disappearing" (UN Secretariat, 1983: 18).

Now, it is true that the average growth rate of the human population over the past million years has been essentially zero; but over the past thousand years, it has been .3 percent per year, and over the past four centuries, it has averaged nearly .6 percent per year. Table 2 shows the factor by which population multiplied and the average growth rate for global population by

**TABLE 2   World population growth since 1600
and forecasts to 2150**

Date	Global population (millions)	Growth factor (prev. 50 yrs.)	Growth rate (prev. 50 yrs.) (percent per year)
1600	545	—	—
1650	545	1.00	.00
1700	610	1.12	.23
1750	720	1.18	.33
1800	900	1.25	.45
1850	1,200	1.33	.57
1900	1,625	1.35	.60
1950	2,565	1.58	.91
2000	6,241	2.43	1.78
Forecasts			
2050	9,639	1.54	.86
2100	10,560	1.10	.19
2150	10,837	1.03	.06

SOURCES: The historical data are taken from McEvedy and Jones (1978). The forecasts are taken from Vu et al. (1988). The population figure for 2000 is the Vu et al. forecast from the 1988 base year, but is here treated as a known quantity.

50-year intervals since 1600, including figures forecast by the World Bank through 2150. The growth rate forecast for the first half of the twenty-first century is very similar to that for the first half of the twentieth century. However, to find a growth rate comparable to the forecast for the second half of the twenty-first century, we have to go as far back as the interval 1650 to 1700. To justify the forecast, as Frejka does, on the grounds that most populations tend to approximate replacement-level fertility in the long run is not to base it very solidly in history. One could with more reason say that the historical tendency has been for the pace of population growth to accelerate.

Why then would one want to assume a future growth rate of zero? I believe there are two strong conceptual influences. The first is Malthusian theory, broadly construed. While Malthusian theory would predict that population growth would continue in step with economic growth, a strong concern with environmental and natural resource limitations convinces many that growth cannot continue for long. The second influence is demographic transition theory, which attributes the rapid population growth of the past century to the fact that mortality declined before fertility, and asserts that socioeconomic changes accompanying development eventually lead to fertility decline. The theory itself does not provide grounds for picking stationarity as the natural endpoint of this process. Furthermore, the experience of the developed countries suggests that fertility may stabilize below replacement levels, and the basic economic theory of fertility, fit to the experience of several developed countries, suggests that continued economic growth will be accompanied by further declines.

But these two theories provide a weak rationale at best for assuming stationarity after 2100. If economic growth continues, even at a much reduced rate, the Malthusian approach would expect continued population growth; and transition theory does not really provide grounds for predicting why and where fertility decline will end. Moreover, if Malthusian concerns underlie the forecast, then the forecasts must surely take into account the long-run economic prospects of each country, rather than base the forecast exclusively on a closed demographic model. The experience of the developed countries suggests that below-replacement fertility may persist. Indeed the new (1988) UN assumption of continuing below-replacement fertility in developed countries undermines the assumption that the fertility of the less developed countries will cease declining at replacement level.

Conclusion

Current long-run population forecasts ignore economic, natural resource, and environmental constraints to growth. Yet they assume that populations are even now converging to stationarity at a global level about twice the current population. If the assumption derives from a Malthusian orientation, it must be based on unexpressed and, in this context, unexamined views about future growth prospects and reproductive response to economic or environmental change. If the stationary forecast reflects the belief that environmental resistance will halt population growth, then the forecasts should not be viewed optimistically—unless it is expected that institutions will change radically to internalize the environmental costs of childbearing.

If, instead, population convergence to stationarity has been inferred from some version of transition theory, such as modern socioeconomic fertility models, then again the forecasts rest on unexamined assumptions. They must assume that growth and development will proceed along global trend patterns without encountering serious Malthusian constraints, particularly in sub-Saharan Africa where population is expected nearly to quadruple in the next 60 years. For those who believe that population growth has already exceeded global carrying capacity, and consequently that economic growth cannot long continue, the implicit assumptions underlying the forecast should be viewed very skeptically. In any event, as I noted earlier, the assumption that the endpoint of the transition is at replacement-level fertility is supported neither by history nor by the logic of relevant social theory.

All this said, the long-run global forecasts of the United Nations and the World Bank are very well done and very useful, and the UN has an admirable record of success in the past. Their assumption that world population is converging to stationarity is a peculiar departure from their generally conservative, pragmatic, and historically informed approach. My main purpose in raising these issues is not to suggest that the forecasts are wrong and should be altered but rather to stimulate thought and speculation about world population growth and the principles governing it.

As long as we keep clearly in mind the great uncertainty of the forecasts, as reflected in the Keyfitz–Stoto confidence intervals, we shall not be badly misled. Their work suggests that 160 years from now, there is a two-to-one chance that population will be bracketed between half the forecast and twice the forecast, or between about 5 billion and 22 billion. A range such as this does not seem unnecessarily wide if we imagine ourselves placed in 1830, attempting to forecast population size in 1990, 160 years later!

Appendix: The FAO/UNFPA/IIASA carrying capacity estimates

Dividing the land surface into small sub-areas (Kenya alone had 1213), the project estimated potential production of 15 widely grown crops, based on soil type, topography, climate, and water availability. Calculations were made for three levels of inputs (fertilizer, pesticide, herbicide, crop varieties, cropping patterns, and soil conservation measures), ranging from "low" (current practice in sub-Saharan Africa) to "high" (current practice in Northwest Europe). Calculations were for rainfed agriculture, except where irrigation was actually practiced in 1975, or, where relevant, was projected by FAO to be practiced in 2000 (Harrison, 1984: 1–10; Higgins et al., 1983). Livestock production was also assessed under various assumptions, and calculations were carried out under the assumption that one-third of available land would be devoted to nonfood crops. An allowance was made for seed and for postharvest crop loss. Allowance was also made for land use for settlement, industry, and transportation. Fallowing was taken into account where appropriate.

Overall, for the developing world outside China, Mongolia, and the Koreas, the report concluded that the climate was suitable for rainfed agriculture in 37 percent of the area studied and too dry or cold in the remainder. Only 21 percent of the soils were classified as posing "no fertility limitation"; the remainder were "problematic" (Harrison, 1984: 5). Of the land judged suitable for rainfed agriculture, 81 percent is divided equally between Africa and Latin America, with only 19 percent for Asia (excluding China, Mongolia, and the Koreas).

To calculate carrying capacity, the food production calculations are combined with recommended diets from a 1973 study by FAO and the World Health Organization, to produce estimates of the maximum population that could be fed. Apparently the diet required production of only about 3,000 calories per person, which has been sharply criticized as too low (Gilland, 1984).

Notes

The research on which this article is based was funded by a grant from the US National Institute of Child Health and Human Development: R01-HD24982-01. The author is grateful to Magali Barbieri for research assistance.

1 In my view, almost all demographic projections are in fact forecasts, in that they present the author's best guess about the future.

2 I refer here to United Nations (1983), Vu et al. (1988), and Frejka (1981a). The forecasts of the United States Bureau of the Census (1987) do not share this feature as far as one can judge from their more limited horizon (up to 2050) and limited discussion of underlying assumptions.

3 The NRR is approximately the product of the probability of surviving to the mean age of childbearing, p_A, times the gross reproduction rate, or GRR. p_A, in turn, varies with the general level of mortality, which we can index by e_0. In symbols: $n = \ln(\text{NRR})/A = [\ln(p_A(e_0)) + \ln(\text{GRR})]/A$, where A is the mean age at childbearing. Clearly n depends on both the level of fertility and that of mortality. To find the effect of a change in mortality, indexed by e_0, we differentiate: $dn/de_0 = (dp_A/de_0)/(Ap_A)$. The effect is independent of the level of the GRR. The Coale–Demeny model tables illustrate this result. Moving from $e_0 = 20$ to $e_0 = 30$, first for GRR = 1.0, and then for GRR = 3.0, raises n by .00380 in the first case and by .00384 in the second.

4 Model West Female tables were used. The irregularity of the line apparently reflects a deficiency in the tables.

5 We can differentiate n with respect to the GRR in the earlier expression: $dn/d\text{GRR} = 1/(A^*\text{GRR})$. This shows the effect of fertility to be (approximately) independent of the mortality level, and inversely proportional to the initial level of fertility.

6 This was inferred from Coale–Demeny (1983) Model West Female Stable Populations. The difference in growth rates between GRR = 3.0 and 3.5 is slightly greater than that between $e_0 = 20$ and $e_0 = 24$. But the difference in growth rates between GRR = .80 and GRR = 1.25 is about 26 times as great as that between $e_0 = 76$ and $e_0 = 80$.

7 Since environmental impact probably depends more on the total consumption by a population than on the number of people consuming, it will matter a great deal whether the older segment of the population is economically active or inactive.

8 In all fairness, I should add that the United Nations forecasts anticipated the growth rate decline following the late 1960s, before it had begun.

9 In the 1979 study, the elasticity for wives was – 1.846 and for husbands, + 1.307. In the 1980 study, with a different model the corresponding figures were – 1.43 and + .44. A number of studies by others for the United States, England, and West Germany have found broadly similar figures.

10 The elasticities used for the calculation all depend on the female labor force participation rate. I assumed this would remain constant at values appropriate to the mid-1970s, values that have already been left far behind. Increasing participation rates would make female wage elasticities more negative and thereby hasten the pace of predicted fertility decline. Were the analysis enriched by consideration of the quantity-quality tradeoff, the decline would be still more rapid.

11 Raymond Pearl's forecasts based on fitted logistic curves were also justified by reference to a population equilibrium sustained by a given technology.

12 Of course, it is not density per se that matters, but rather productivity. Productivity depends on many factors besides natural resources, such as technology, social organization, and reproducible capital.

13 Some studies relate fertility to size of landholding; some relate fertility to aggregate density (e.g. of states, districts, or counties); and some relate fertility to real wages or incomes and were combined with an estimated response of real wages or incomes to population growth to derive the elasticity shown in Figure 2.

14 To be sure, the feedback is weak, and in the short run its influence is overwhelmed

by many other factors, as discussed in Lee (1987). It is one thing to argue that the estimated coefficients have the theoretically correct sign, another to argue that density explains an important component of the variance in fertility.

15 Other recent calculations yield much lower numbers. Gilland (1983), in a review of the subject, assumes caloric requirements about three times higher than the FAO study, at 9,000 calories per capita per day, or roughly one ton of grain equivalent per year. If we translate his numbers into the FAO requirements, they imply a global carrying capacity of 21 billion persons (three times the 7 billion he gives). His figure is based on a study by Revelle (1976), which implies 34 billion at FAO standards, and one by Buringh and van Heemst (1977) giving 30 billion (with Staring, they also published a more visionary study in 1975 that would imply 150 billion at FAO dietary standards).

16 The distribution of potential output is very different from that of current population. In Africa, most of the potential food production is located in Zaire.

17 On reflection, it is clear that the high–low intervals cannot even in principle be given a probabilistic interpretation. Or, put differently, if the brackets have a probabilistic meaning for population size, they cannot for the related quantities of vital rates, births, deaths, age distributions, and dependency ratios, which also come in high and low variants. In the standard method, the high and low forecasts are produced by choosing a high and low trajectory for fertility and mortality, and then tracing the implications for births, survival, and population size. But because errors average out, the survival-weighted sum of past births should have a much narrower confidence band than would be obtained by taking the upper and lower limits of the interval on vital rates (or births) for every year. Conversely, if the high and low forecasts of population size have a certain probability of containing the true size, then the high and low vital rate trajectories will have a far lower chance of containing the true vital rates. Similarly, the age distribution and dependency ratios are far more likely to fall outside the range derived from the high and low forecasts (see Lee, 1981 and Lee and Lau, 1987).

18 The other approach is to formulate a stochastic model of population renewal and to estimate the relevant parameters and variance-covariance structures from the population of interest. Forecasts and their confidence intervals can then be calculated directly from the fitted model. Some of the time-series methods mentioned earlier are of this sort (e.g. Lee, 1974), and produce confidence intervals that I have elsewhere argued are misleadingly wide (Lee and Lau, 1987). Another approach is taken by Cohen (1986). However, his method assumes statistical stationarity of stochastic vital rates, which is to say, no trend in the underlying mean values. He does not recommend using it when the population growth rate exhibits a trend, as it surely does for the global population, or for the developing countries as a group.

19 In some cases, I had to compare the forecast to UN forecasts of the population rather than to actual population; this is unlikely to have had much effect on the results. The calculated percent growth rate errors were .71, .46, 1.48, .66, 1.46, and 1.16.

20 See United Nations (1986: 10) and Vu et al. (1988) for descriptions of these procedures. In the UN forecasts, "replacement level" is defined in terms of the lowest attainable mortality; in the World Bank forecasts, it is defined in terms of the mortality of the moment. Therefore, in the UN forecast, once fertility has declined to "replacement" level, it is constant thereafter. In the World Bank forecasts, fertility continues to decline slightly after "replacement" is reached, so as to maintain an NRR of unity while mortality declines further. In practice, this difference in procedures is of very little consequence. The World Bank uses a formal regression analysis based on current levels of educational attainment, mortality, and contraceptive use to pick a terminal date. The UN uses informed judgment, but no equation. In the latest set of forecasts, the UN has dropped its previous assumption that the fertility of developed countries would rise to replacement levels, and instead adopts the assumed fertility trajectory of the developed countries' official forecasts (see Haub, 1988).

21 For example, the World Bank (see Vu et al., 1988) assumes that the patterns of mortality change observed for the decade 1965–

75 will continue for the next century, in the sense that the observed relationship of increases in e_0 to initial levels of e_0, calculated separately for populations with high and low initial levels of female enrollment in primary school, will be preserved.

22 That is, 82.5 for males and 87.5 for females.

23 In addition to the high–low variants, the UN (1983) also presented a growth and decline version that spans a wider range. In my view, the high and low variants should best reflect the author's assessment of the uncertainty of the forecasts.

References

Buringh, P., and H. D. J. van Meemst. 1977. "An estimation of world food production based on labour-oriented agriculture." Wageningen: Centre for World Food Market Research.

——, and G. J. Staring. 1975. "Computation of the absolute maximum food production of the World." University of Wageningen.

Butz, William, and Michael Ward. 1979. "The emergence of countercyclical U.S. fertility," *American Economic Review* 69, no. 3 (June): 318–328.

Coale, Ansley J., and Paul Demeny with Barbara Vaughan. 1983. *Regional Model Life Tables and Stable Populations*, Second Edition. New York: Academic Press.

Cohen, Joel. 1986. "Population forecasts and confidence intervals for Sweden: A comparison of model-based and empirical approaches," *Demography* 23, no. 1: 105–126.

Demeny, Paul. 1979. "On the end of the population explosion," *Population and Development Review* 5, no. 1 (March): 141–162.

——. 1984. "A perspective on long-term population growth," *Population and Development Review* 10, no. 1 (March): 103–126.

——. 1986. "The world demographic situation," in *World Population and U.S. Policy: The Choices Ahead*, ed. Jane Menken. New York: W. W. Norton, pp. 27–66.

——. 1989. "World population trends," *Current History* (January): 17–19, 58–59, 64–65.

El-Badry, M. A., and Shigemi Kono. 1987. "Demographic estimates and projections," in United Nations Secretariat, *Population Bulletin of the United Nations*, No. 19/20, pp. 35–43.

Frejka, Tomas. 1973. *The Future of Population Growth: Alternative Paths to Equilibrium*. New York: John Wiley and Sons.

——. 1981a. "Long-term prospects for world population growth," *Population and Development Review* 7, no. 3 (September): 489–511.

——. 1981b. "World population projections: A concise history," in *Proceedings of the IUSSP International Population Conference, Manila*, vol. 3, pp. 505–528.

Gilland, Bernard. 1983. "Considerations on world population and food supply," *Population and Development Review* 9, no. 2 (June): 203–211.

——. 1984. Review of P. Harrison, *Land, Food and People*, in *Population and Development Review* 10, no. 4 (December): 733–735.

Harrison, Paul. 1984. *Land, Food and People*. New York: Food and Agriculture Organization of the United Nations.

Haub, Carl. 1987. "Understanding population projections," *Population Bulletin* 42, no. 4.

——. 1988. "U.N. raises its global projections," *Population Today* 16, no. 12 (December): 3.

Hendry, Peter. 1988. "Food and population: Beyond five billion," *Population Bulletin* 43, no. 2.

Higgins, G. M., et al. 1983. "Potential population supporting capacities of lands in the developing world," Technical Report of FAO/UNFPA/IIASA.

Inoue, S., and Y.C. Yu. 1979. "United Nations new population projections and analysis of *ex post facto* errors," paper presented at the Annual Meeting of the Population Association of America, April.

Kelley, Allen C. 1988. "Economic consequences of population change in the Third World," *Journal of Economic Literature* 26, no. 4 (December): 1685–1728.

Keyfitz, Nathan. 1981. "The limits of population forecasting," *Population and Development Review* 7, no. 4 (December): 579–593.

Lee, Ronald. 1974. "Forecasting births in post-transitional populations: Stochastic renewal with serially correlated fertility," *Journal of the American Statistical Association* 69, no. 247 (September): 607–617.

———. 1980. "Aiming at a moving target: Period fertility and changing reproductive goals," *Population Studies* 34, no. 2 (July): 205–226.

———. 1981. "Comment on McDonald: Modeling demographic relationships: An analysis of forecast functions for Australian live births," *Journal of the American Statistical Association* 76, no. 376 (December): 793–795.

———. 1987. "Population dynamics of humans and other animals." *Demography* 24, no. 4 (November): 443–465.

———, and Joseph Lau. 1987. "The uncertainty of population forecasts: Insights from nonrecursive times series methods," unpublished manuscript of the Graduate Group in Demography, University of California at Berkeley.

McDonald, John. 1981. "Modeling demographic relationships: An analysis of forecast functions for Australian births," *Journal of the American Statistical Association* 76, no. 376 (December): 782–792.

McEvedy, C., and R. Jones. 1978. *Atlas of World Population History.* New York: Penguin Books.

National Research Council. 1986. *Population and Economic Development: Policy Questions.* Washington D.C.: National Academy of Sciences Press.

Repetto, Robert. 1987. "Population, resources, environment: An uncertain future," *Population Bulletin* 42, no. 2.

Revelle, Roger. 1976. "The resources available for agriculture," *Scientific American* (September): 164–178.

Smith Stanley. 1987. "Tests of forecast accuracy and bias for country population projections," *Journal of the American Statistical Association* 82, no. 400 (December): 991–1003.

Srinivasan, T.N. 1988. "Population–food projections," in *Population, Food and Rural Development*, ed. Ronald Lee, et al. Oxford: Clarendon Press, pp. 11–39.

Stoto, Michael. 1983. "The accuracy of population projections," *Journal of the American Statistical Association* 78, no. 381 (July): 13–20.

United Nations Secretariat. 1983. "Long-range global population projections, as assessed in 1980," *Population Bulletin of the United Nations*, No. 14, pp. 17–30.

———. 1986. *World Population Prospects: Estimates and Projections as Assessed in 1984.* Population Studies no. 98. New York.

———. 1988. "Population growth and structure in the less developed regions of the world according to the 1988 United Nations assessment," paper presented at the United Nations Expert Group Meeting on Consequences of Rapid Population Growth in Developing Countries, New York (August).

United States Bureau of the Census. 1987. "World population profile." Washington, D.C.: US Government Printing Office.

Vu, My T., Eduard Bos, and Rodolfo Bulatao. 1988. *Africa Region Population Projections (1988–89 edition)*, Working Papers of the Population and Human Resources Department of the World Bank (October), WPS 114. (Working papers for the other regions were also used.)

Ward, Michael, and William Butz. 1980. "Completed fertility and its timing," *Journal of Political Economy* 88, no. 3 (October): 917–940.

World Bank. 1984. *World Development Report 1984.* New York: Oxford University Press.

Comment: On the Uncertainty of Population Projections

GRIFFITH FEENEY

THE UNCERTAINTY OF LONG-RUN POPULATION PROJECTIONS, by which we mean projections extending 50 to 100 years or more, is great. Ronald Lee begins his interesting review of the subject by telling us that there is "reassuringly close agreement" on twenty-first century population trends. He ends with the observation that, although a world population between 10 and 11 billion is projected for 160 years hence, the chances are only two in three that the actual figure will lie between 5 and 22 billion. Or, to put it another way, there is one chance in three that world population at that distant time will be less than 5 billion or more than 22 billion.[1]

That is a remarkable devolution, from reassuring agreement to uncertainty bordering on total ignorance. What does this say about the relevance of such long-run projections for the discussion of population and resources? At one level, the relevance is clearly nil. At another, the projections are relevant precisely because their uncertainty conflicts with widely held convictions about world population.

Consider for example the long-run history of human population growth as it has frequently been portrayed in graphic form. The upper curve in Figure 1 shows world population growth between 1950 and 1985 (time scale above). The lower curve shows growth between the birth of Christ and 1985 (time scale below).[2] If we look at the upper curve for clues to the future, the conclusion is uncertain. It is both natural and appropriate to extrapolate the recent trend, suggesting continued population growth at recent rates. At the same time, nothing in the picture rules out a gradual leveling off of the numbers, or a renewed increase.

The lower curve is not so reticent. The growth in the recent past appears so great as to rule out anything but continued sharp increases. This plot really does suggest a "population explosion." The problem with this conclusion is that both plots show exactly the same data, as indicated by the dashed lines connecting the common points. The "explosion" suggested by the lower plot is an artifact of the choice of time scale.[3]

FIGURE 1   Two perspectives on world population growth

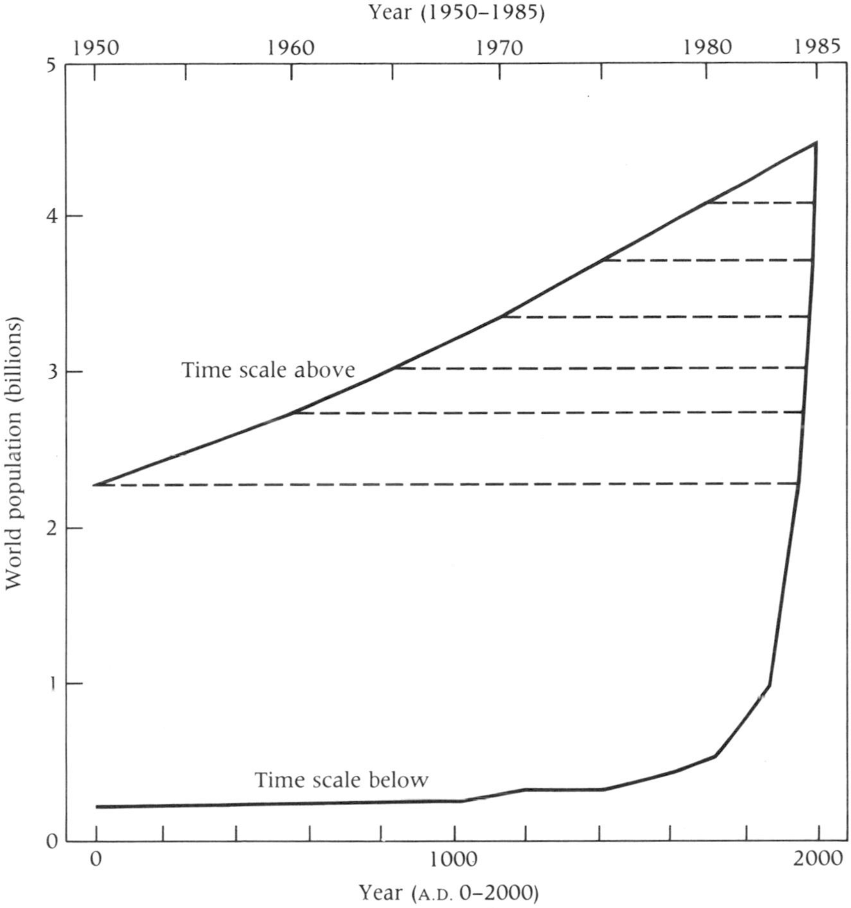

Year (1950–1985)

If data plotted by the upper curve in Figure 1 can be made to look explosive, so can virtually any other series that increases over time. A plot of doctoral degrees awarded over the past two thousand years would appear to argue for immediate closure of graduate schools. Similar plots might have been used at various points in history to suggest runaway growth of anything from papyrus to buggy whips.

The idea that rapid future population growth is a virtual certainty derives as well from the notion that the world is in the grip of a rapacious mathematical monster called "exponential growth." The purely mathematical statement here is that human population growth at any (positive) constant rate would eventually overwhelm the Earth. This is true, but the rate of human population growth, like everything else involving human action, is variable. The expectation is not that it will remain constant, but that it will change. Nor does a past increase in growth rates imply a continued increase in the long-term future. Population growth rates are useful in forecasting population for as many as several decades, and more importantly, for comparing growth in populations of different sizes. They contain no information whatever about population growth a century from now.

Short-term population projections are a different matter, for the simple reason that most of the persons whose numbers are forecast already exist and have high and relatively well-known chances of surviving into the future. This observation was made long ago by John Hajnal in a classic paper that anyone interested in the topic would do well to reread at intervals.[4] It is also true that the current age distribution of world population embodies a demographic momentum that makes substantial growth highly likely for the next several decades.[5] Whether this constitutes a problem is another matter. The population growth rate is not large in relation to past and present rates of economic growth.

Some will argue that the world is already overpopulated, that no further growth is required. It is of course every person's right to venture his own opinion of what world population should be, and to campaign as vigorously as he may wish on its behalf. If we are to recommend imposing our ideas on the rest of the world, however, something more is required. On what grounds is it claimed that the world is overpopulated? Few people doubt that population pressure exists in particular areas, or that local population crises, perhaps very severe ones, may develop. Lee's juxtaposition of data on population and agriculture suggests danger for "Bangladesh and Egypt, everyone's favorite examples of countries with serious population problems." The argument is inherently difficult to make for the world as a whole, however, because conditions in different parts of the world are so divergent.

Is there a biological measure that would neatly circumvent what Paul Demeny has called these "difficult and stubbornly unresolved" questions? One obvious candidate is human expectation of life at birth, arguably a significant indicator of human welfare, and a statistic widely known, understood, and available. It is, as we all know, higher in the world as a whole today than it has ever been, and by a substantial margin. On this evidence, the world is not overpopulated, whatever else may be wrong with it.

The pleasures and satisfactions of working in demography are many. One of the disappointments is the frequency with which one encounters flimsy arguments, often passionately advanced, that there is a world population problem, or that there are no population problems at all.

Notes

1 The 2-to-1 odds are based on systematic analysis of the errors in past projections. See Nathan Keyfitz, "The limits of population forecasting," *Population and Development Review* 7, no. 4 (December 1981): 579–593.

2 The data plotted in the upper curve are from Table 5, p. 19, of *World Population Trends and Policies: 1987 Monitoring Report* (New York: United Nations, 1988). The data for earlier years are from Tables II and III, pp. 10 and 12,

respectively, of Robert C. Cook, "How many people have ever lived on Earth?," *Population Bulletin* 18, no. 1 (February 1962): 1–19.

3 This tendentious representation has been displayed repeatedly over the years in articles and textbooks. See for example Figure 1, p. 111, of John D. Durand, "The modern expansion of world population," in *Population and Society*, ed. Charles B. Nam (Boston: Houghton Mifflin, 1968); Figure 5–1, p. 182, of Paul R. Ehrlich et al., *Ecoscience: Population, Resources, Environment* (San Francisco: W. H. Freeman, 1977); Figure 2.1, p. 24, of Robert H. Weller and Leon F. Bouvier *Population: Demography and Policy* (New York: St. Martin's Press, 1981); Figure 3–1, p. 38, of David Yaukey, *Demography: The Study of Human Population* (New York: St. Martin's Press, 1985); Figure 3.1, p. 53, of John R. Weeks, *Population: An Introduction to Concepts and Issues* (Belmont, Calif.: Wadsworth Publishing Company, 1986). Most recently it appeared in *Parade Magazine* in an article by Carl Sagan, "The secret of the Persian chessboard," *Honolulu Star-Bulletin*, Sunday, 5 February 1989, pp. 14–15. The only instance I have seen that clearly indicates the distorting effect of the time scale is Ansley J. Coale, "The history of human population," in *The Human Population*, A Scientific American Book (San Francisco: W. H. Freeman, 1974). I am grateful to Alice Harris of the East-West Population Institute for assistance in locating the citations in this note.

4 "The prospects for population forecasts," *Journal of the American Statistical Association* 50 (June 1955): 309–322.

5 The phenomenon of momentum may be illustrated with a few population numbers taken from recent United Nations projections (p. 141 in *World Population Prospects: Estimates and Projections as Assessed in 1982*, Population Studies No. 86, Department of International Economic and Social Affairs, New York,

1985). They are, for total world population in millions, as follows:

Age	1990	1995	2000	2005	2010
0–4	599	–	–	–	–
5–9	555	584	–	–	–
10–14	524	550	579	–	–
15–19	527	520	546	575	–
20–24	495	522	515	542	571
25–29	**435**	489	520	510	537
30–34	**393**	**430**	484	512	505
35–39	**341**	387	**424**	478	506
40–44	**278**	335	381	**418**	471
45–49	**230**	272	327	373	**410**

The number of persons aged 45–49 nearly doubles between 1990 and 2010, but this has nothing to do with fertility during these years. It reflects the shape of the 1990 age distribution. Because few persons die in adult ages, the decrease in numbers of persons as we move down the table from the 25–29 to the 45–49 age group in 1990 (boldfaced entries in first column) translates into a nearly corresponding increase in numbers of persons aged 45–49 as we move forward in time from 1990 to 2010 (boldfaced entries in last row; boldfaced diagonal entries indicate survivorship). The increasing numbers of persons aged 20–24 between 1990 and 2010 likewise reflect the numbers of persons in the age groups 0–4 to 20–24 in 1990. Increases in the reproductive ages mean larger numbers of births, and hence increases in younger age groups. Because the shape of the 1990 age distribution is primarily the result of rapid population growth in previous years (past growth means larger numbers of births in recent years and fewer in more distant years), we think of the age distribution as embodying a "momentum" that tends to make the population grow in the future.

Comment: Reflections on "Time Left Us"

KENNETH W. WACHTER

DEMOGRAPHERS OFTEN COMMUNICATE THE MEANING of a population growth rate by expressing it in terms of a doubling time. Resource scientists often communicate the limited amount of a resource or class of resources as a depletion time, or the "time left us," consuming and growing in numbers as we are. Sometimes the conversion from units of "amount" to units of "time" is just a quick vivid turn of style. Sometimes it is the outcome of a modeling and simulation exercise and is tantamount to a prediction. Estimates of "time left us," quick ones and careful ones alike, have not on the whole been shortening as time has been passing. They have been lengthening. It is tempting to see in such progressive postponement of the day of reckoning a cause for optimism.

"Time left us" may mean "time left us till the last chance to change our course" or it may mean "time left us till we are through." With the first meaning a portion of any nonrenewable resource has to be kept back from the calculation of depletion times: some nonrenewable resources will be required to build facilities dependent only on renewable resources. Some have to be classified not as consumables but as reserves required for the transition to an economy and society capable of long-term survival.

With the second meaning of "time left us," reserves can be added to consumables. A discount rate can be applied to all future consumption. Longer periods of continued population growth and larger total populations can be entertained. There is no doubt that much larger human populations can subsist on this planet in the short term if resources are not held back to assure a high probability of human survival over the long term.

The pilgrims in Massachusetts need not have gone hungry through their first winter if they had decided to eat their seed corn. Limits to growth are more lax if all resources are deemed consumable, or if the discounting of future consumption extends to the whole of the future itself. These points relate closely to the theory of sustainable development discussed by Herman Daly in this volume.

The distinction between consumables and reserves is like the familiar distinction between living off income and living off principal. Over the years since early estimates of "time left us" began to be offered, the tendency to live off principal and consume beyond the bounds of income has become pronounced in the public finances of many countries. It has become pronounced in the private finances of many people. It likely intrudes into the unspoken assumptions of many of those who prepare estimates of resource limits. It is worth wondering whether the lengthening estimates of "time left us" do not reflect some shift from the first meaning of time left us to the second, an implicit weakening of the reserve requirements and a toleration of the possibility of human nonsurvival.

A second interpretation of the lengthening estimates of "time left us" recognizes a process of feedback from experience to estimates. Extrapolating resource stocks is a relatively new and absolutely tricky business. It is not surprising that early judgments needed revision. The crux of the problem with which the forecasters, especially the simulators, have had to grapple is the interaction between material resources and time. The list of resources that are being measured to assess future opportunities itself changes rapidly with time. While some sources clearly face degradation, for others substitution has turned out to be easier than was once supposed.

Experience has been exerting pressure on early underestimates of the scope for substitution. Just enough feedback should help estimates converge toward truth. But feedback systems often overcompensate, driving matters from one extreme to the opposite. Views may cycle rather than converge, and views about the scope for resource substitution may be a case in point.

The green revolution, at first considered a lesson in the great potential for resource substitution, now begins to appear as a lesson in its limits. Understanding is emerging of how necessary it is to keep account of costs that are externalized over the course of the green revolution, such as insecticide resistance, soil erosion, water runoff, exacerbation of inequality, and the marginalization of members of the population. If only part of the costs of substituting one resource (e.g., pesticides, fertilizers) for another (e.g., land) has to be borne by those who can reap the benefits, there appears to be far greater scope for substitution than there truly is.

A third interpretation of the lengthening estimates of "time left us" gives the credit to technological innovation, but asks what the costs are. Technological innovation, as a possible route of escape from problems of world resource scarcity, has a "free-gift" component that comes on top of whatever benefits can be gained from efficient substitution. The "free-gift" part is the creative idea or scientific breakthrough. It is called free because the costs of research are not in any way a fixed proportion of the economic benefits derivable.

But here, too, hidden costs to the "free gift" emerge. Among these costs are those of sustaining an intellectual and scientific establishment in a form conducive to creative rather than routine innovation. There are aspects of critical mass and of long-term investment that seem to require a society rich beyond its immediate needs or organized to divert resources away from them. In a world of accelerating scarcity, such concentration of resources seems to entail inequalities, whose maintenance on an international scale and among classes within countries brings with it palpable costs.

Each of the issues mentioned here—reserves, substitution, technological innovation—brings to the fore overt or hidden "costs." Costs are not measured essentially in units of amount. They are measured essentially in units of value. They raise questions of value: What values? Whose values?

The tradeoff between current resource use and future availability is not a tradeoff decided by experts or by leaders. Most decisions that determine population growth and current and future consumption are made by individuals. The scope for affecting these decisions is in many respects limited. The same is true about many environmental policies. Individuals around the world, by their own reproductive, economic, and environmental behavior, reveal their true valuation of the future relative to the present. A balance is struck between the valuation of present well-being and the survival chances of future generations. Involved in any estimation of "time left us" is the problem of understanding and foreseeing these human choices about values.

WATER, ENERGY, AND

DEVELOPMENT

Rapid Population Growth and Water Scarcity: The Predicament of Tomorrow's Africa

MALIN FALKENMARK

POPULATION PROJECTIONS CUSTOMARILY EXAMINE rates of birth, death, and migration, and extrapolate from past trends or serial correlations in the data (Keyfitz, 1984). Current long-run population projections, which ignore economic, natural resource, and environmental constraints, assume that the populations of different world regions will converge to stationarity at various specified points in time. United Nations projections indicate, for example, that Africa is expected to more than quadruple its population before converging to stationarity by the end of the twenty-first century (World Resources Institute, 1986).

One question most projections leave open is the degree to which the level of population is resource-determined. The most basic of all resources—although often taken for granted—is water. The poorest of the world continents in terms of annual freshwater renewal is Africa (World Resources Institute, 1986). In a number of articles, I have drawn attention to the massive water shortages threatening many countries in Africa in the next few decades, should the projected increases in population materialize (Falkenmark, 1986, 1987, 1989). Accelerating water scarcity may well influence the time to population stabilization—for example, by significantly influencing birth rates, death rates, migration patterns, or all of these variables.

A large part of the African continent lies in the zone where at least part of the year is arid and where recurrent droughts severely disturb agricultural production. This implies a high risk of crop failure, which makes domestic food supplies insecure. These factors notwithstanding, African leaders are following the general tendency in developing countries to strive for food self-sufficiency as a means toward development, while reserving their import capacity for the purchase of capital goods (Keyfitz, 1984).

This article assesses the implications of growing water scarcity for living conditions in Africa, particularly food production. I will analyze the constraints that projected population increases would place on the potential for satisfying various categories of water demands and will try to quantify the water scarcity predicament in different parts of Africa as a function of time. In the final section I discuss the reasons this widespread water scarcity has escaped the attention of the international development community and even of such concerned organizations as the World Commission on Environment and Development (1987).

Water and civilization

Water is the basis for all life. Life is based on myriads of flows through every plant and animal form. The deep involvement of water in life processes makes living matter vulnerable to changes in the quantity and quality of the water.

Early civilizations developed in fertile river valleys in regions with warm climates where ample amounts of water were imported to compensate for a dry climate. Hyams (1976) has explained how the decline of some of those civilizations can be attributed to unbalanced interaction between man, soil, and water ("man as a soil disease"), resulting in eroded or salinized lands, reduced soil fertility, and decreasing crop yields.

Industrialization, by contrast, developed several millennia later in Europe, in the temperate zone, where the soils were fertile and the climate was humid without large annual fluctuations in rainfall. When population increased sufficiently to exceed the food supporting capacity, a massive emigration started to other continents, especially to North America, where the climate was broadly similar to that of Europe.

Today, the less developed countries are predominantly located in the tropical and subtropical zones. The newly industrialized of these countries are situated mainly in the humid tropics, where water is readily available. The cluster of drought-prone countries in semi-arid zones occupy the lowest step of the income ladder. In short, the problems of the arid tropics remain largely unsolved.

These observations support the hypothesis that easy access to water is a necessary condition not only for habitability in general but also for development. Where water is in short supply, and financial and technological resources do not exist for water transfer, development faces considerable obstacles. Today, these problems are generally discussed as those of "drought and desertification." Analysts have tended to discuss the problems under diffuse and largely effect-oriented concepts, for example, droughts, desertification, pollution, environmental stress.

These problems could instead be seen as a combination of natural and manmade water scarcity (see Falkenmark and Lundqvist, 1988). We have argued that the causes of water scarcity—aridity, intermittent droughts, desiccation of the landscape (often spoken of as desertification), and societal water stress—should be addressed as a totality, because these causes tend to be superimposed on one another, developing a population-fueled risk spiral.

Life is based on water flows from the micro scale of a single plant up to the global water cycle that distinguishes this planet from others. Disturbances of water flows, as already indicated, imply disturbances of life processes. Such disturbances exert an impact on four main functions and factors: the wetting of the soil; the recharge of freshwater systems (aquifers and rivers); the quality of freshwater; and the per capita availability of water for societal use.

Quantification of water shortages in Africa

In a recent article (Falkenmark, 1989) I have analyzed the water penury of semi-arid Africa, using proxy data available from the hydrological database of Lvovich (1979). The findings will be used below to develop a schematic presentation of projected water shortages. The reason for using these macro-scale data is that only a few countries in Africa have produced information on water availability. In fact, it is probable that many countries do not even possess the basic data needed to assess water availability.

Before I address the specifics of African conditions, I examine a theoretical relationship between water availability and population size. Figure 1 depicts various possible levels of water scarcity, expressed in terms of the population size per unit of water flow per year. In effect, it models various levels of population pressure per unit of available water. Our conclusions about the degree of scarcity depend on our knowledge of how much water is

FIGURE 1   Rising levels of water scarcity resulting from increasing pressure of population on available water

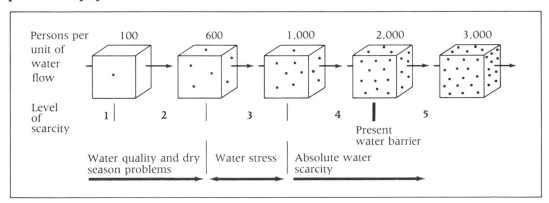

potentially available to serve a given number of people. The figure visualizes the progression of water scarcity. Each million cubic meters of water flow per year in a given area is depicted as a cube. Each 100 persons who live in this area and whose survival depends on this water are depicted as one dot on the surface of the cube.

The order of scarcity can be presented as follows:

(a) Water quality problem and dry season problem The population pressure is below some 600 persons per million cubic meters of water per year. This ratio is represented by levels 1 and 2, indicated as the space to the left of the second cube in the figure;

(b) Water stress The population pressure ranges from some 600 to 1,000 persons per million cubic meters of water per year. The space between the second and the third cube on the figure represents this ratio (level 3);

(c) Absolute water scarcity The population pressure exceeds 1,000 persons per million cubic meters of water per year. This is represented by the space to the right of the third cube in the figure. The fourth cube corresponds to about 2,000 persons per million cubic meters of water available per year. This can be seen as the maximum population pressure that a modern country can manage at present, given access to advanced technology, computer support, and administrative capability. This level will be referred to below as the "water barrier."

To examine country-specific conditions, a two-digit code was developed to express on the one hand the relative level of water scarcity (first digit), and on the other the need for increases in agricultural yield to secure self-reliance in food production on a subsistence level (second digit). The codes enable us to depict the dynamic of population growth, water scarcity, and the increase in agricultural yields that would be needed to sustain projected populations in African countries in the years 2000 and 2025. The maps in Figure 2 characterize African countries by the two digits for these two years.

The first digit, ranging from one to five, represents increasing levels of water scarcity as depicted in Figure 1. The second digit ranges from one to four, symbolizing the ascending level of agricultural yield required to cope with anticipated population growth: the higher the number, the higher the necessary yield increase. Level 1 in the first digit suggests that present yields would be enough, level 2 requires a medium increase in yields, level 3 requires a high increase, and level 4 implies that even a high increase in yields will not be enough, given the growth of population. High yield increase is possible only if water in the root zone can be secured.

A combination of low numbers in both first and second digits implies a tolerable water situation. High numbers in both first and second digits imply a severe water scarcity predicament and a high water dependence to reach the necessary increase in agricultural yields.

FIGURE 2   Water scarcity as compared with needed increase in agricultural yields in 2000 and 2025, expressed as two-digit country-level codes

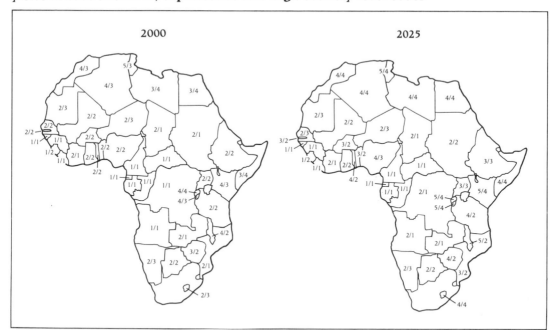

SOURCE: Water availability: Lvovich, 1979; population and yields: FAO, 1986.

Especially under drought-prone conditions an increase in agricultural yield is highly dependent on increasing root-zone water security, whether by stimulated infiltration of local rain or by irrigation with water available in aquifers and rivers. In both cases, the food-production system competes with other human needs for water.

The results in Figure 2 indicate widespread water stress in Africa within the coming decade. By the year 2000, 250 million people will be living in areas as highly water-stressed as the Lower Colorado Basin in the United States or worse. Out of these, 150 million people will be living in areas with chronic or absolute scarcity. By the year 2025, 1.1 billion people, representing two-thirds of the population of the continent, will be living in conditions with severe water scarcity.

Per capita availability of water

The importance of water for socioeconomic development implies that per capita demand will increase: improved agricultural yields depend on reducing the risk of root-zone water deficiency; improved health depends on increasing household water supplies; industrial development requires ample amounts of water. In addition to this rising demand, continued population growth implies that the actual ceiling of affordable water use would decrease to half its present level in about 25 years (assumed time for the population to double), and to a quarter of its actual value when the population had quadrupled. Population growth, in other words, consumes the water potential still available to meet an increasing water demand. There is a rapidly growing risk that it will not be possible to provide for future increases in the quality of life insofar as the latter depends on water. One important consequence is that large amounts of water would not be accessible to supply a rapidly growing industrial sector. In short, the need to appreciate water scarcity and to formulate realistic policies is urgent.

Table 1 indicates the maximum amount of water that a country can supply per year on a per capita basis, given the population pressure on available water (population size per unit of water flow) and the achievable level of use (the relative amount of the total availability possible to mobilize).

As described earlier, the degree of water scarcity may be measured by the number of persons per unit of water flow per year. (In another study, I refer to this as the "water competition level"; see Falkenmark, 1989.) Consider three levels of water availability in column 1 of Table 1, namely 600 persons per million cubic meters of water, 1,000 persons, and 2,000 persons. If it were possible to use 100 percent of all annual water flows, the inverse value of these levels would yield the maximum per capita water availability in cubic meters per year: 1,670, 1,000, and 500 cubic meters per capita per year, respectively (column 2). However, 100 percent of the total water flow is seldom possible to mobilize, especially in hot and flat countries. Where topographical constraints make water storage difficult, or where a hot climate causes large losses of stored water due to evaporation, it may be difficult to raise the water mobilization level above 20 or 30 percent. Column 3 reflects 20 percent use levels. and shows the maximum amount of

TABLE 1 Maximum availability of water per capita under given water, population, and utilization parameters (actual use in several countries is shown for comparison)

Population pressure on available water (persons per million cubic meters)	Maximum availability of water (cubic meters per capita per year) Achievable level of use:		Actual use in 1980 (cubic meters per capita per year)	
	100 percent	20 percent		
600	1,670	330	California	2,800
1,000	1,000	200	Sweden	600
2,000	500	100	Syria	1,150
			Egypt	1,200

SOURCE: Forkasiewicz and Margat (1980).

water per capita many developing countries can use, given their population size per unit of water flow. For comparison, consider the actual cubic meters of gross per capita water use in several regions and countries in 1980 (column 5).

It is important to grasp the regional implications of the maximum availability of water per capita as presented in Table 1. A further comparison with water demand levels in various parts of the world may help clarify the water scarcity dilemmas into which rapid population growth will force many arid and semi-arid countries.

Different environments are characterized by the following annual demand levels in cubic meters per capita (Forkasiewicz and Margat, 1980):

Irrigated agriculture in semi-arid areas of developed countries, such as the Southwestern United States	2,500–7,200
Irrigated agriculture in semi-arid developing countries	700–3,500
Irrigated agriculture in a water-efficient developed country such as Israel (which represents the lowest demand among developed semi-arid areas)	500
Temperate developed countries	150–1,100

According to Higgins et al. (1988), water requirements for a country with a food strategy based on irrigated agriculture would correspond to 500–2,500 cubic meters per capita per year. Thus we may conclude that a semi-arid African country would need at least 500 cubic meters of water per capita per year in order to be able to follow conventional development strategies of the past.

Figure 3 shows the relationship between present water demand levels and the projected population growth between 1975 and 2020 for a few Northern African countries (demand data are not available for most African countries). The vertical axis denotes water demand in cubic meters per capita per year. The horizontal axis denotes water availability in cubic meters per capita per year. It also indicates the level of water scarcity according to the code numbers in Figure 1. The diagonal lines denote ratios of demand-to-availability, that is, levels of water use. Ratios above 100 percent imply the existence of demands that cannot be met with renewable freshwater availability. Horizontal arrows exemplify how growing populations will push the countries into zones of more severe water scarcity. This reflects decreases in the per capita availability of water resulting from high population growth.

FIGURE 3   Relationship between water demand and availability, four Northern African countries, mid-1970s and 2025

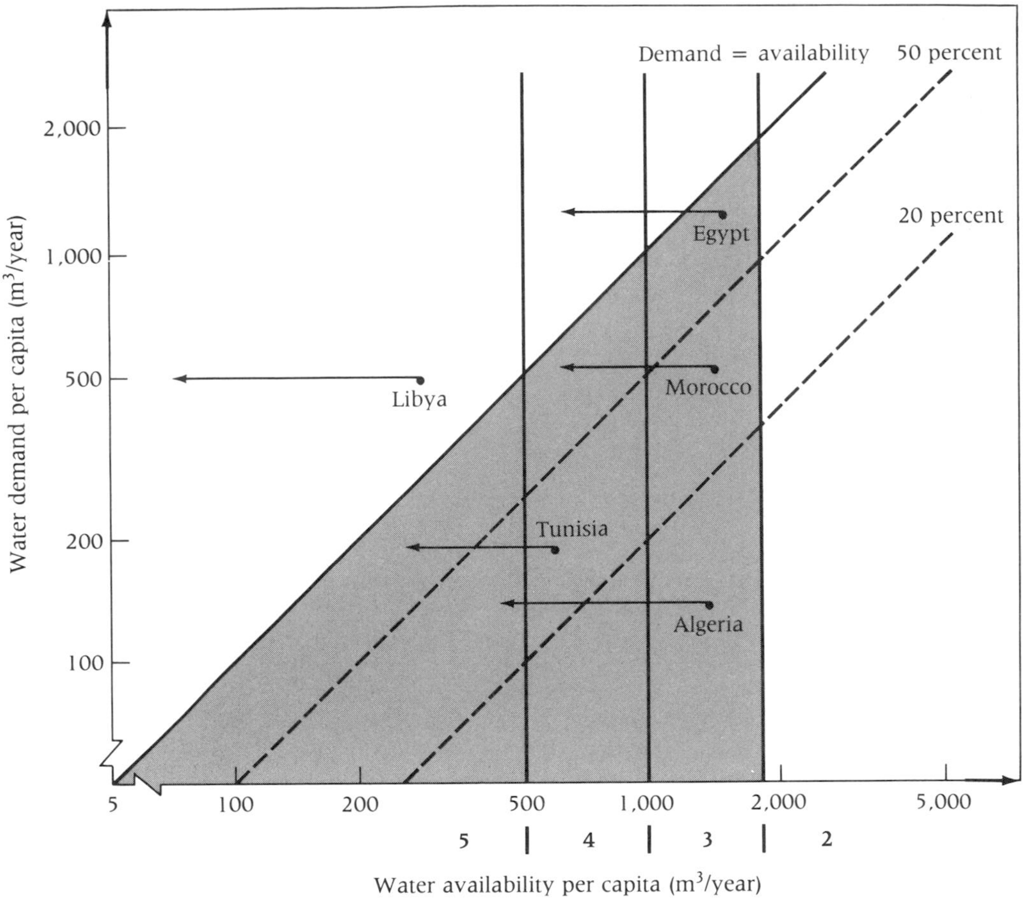

SOURCES: Government data on water availability and water demand from Forkasiewicz and Margat, 1980. Water demand per capita is assumed to remain at the level of the mid–1970s. Population in 1989 and 2025 from WRI, 1988–89.

The trends indicate how much larger a share of the available water has to be mobilized within a few decades simply to be able to satisfy the present demand level. The figure shows the particular dilemma of Egypt, which will be forced to reduce its general water demand level. The action needed is facilitated, however, by the fact that much water is now being wasted in large-scale, low-efficiency irrigation.

Let us now combine the information in Figure 2—according to which in around three decades 1.1 billion Africans will be living in countries experiencing severe water scarcity—with the water management problems facing countries of Europe. Major water management problems in Europe were generally encountered when water demand exceeded 20 percent of potential availability (Szesztay, 1972). We may therefore conclude that, as populations grow, the countries currently in scarcity category 3 will not be able to get much beyond 250 cubic meters per capita in a few decades, and the countries currently in category 4, that is, those with chronic water scarcity, not much beyond 130 cubic meters per capita.

Thus, should the population increase in Africa projected by conventional demographic methods materialize, rapid socioeconomic development will be possible only if a given society is able to develop fundamentally different attitudes toward water and water-dependent activities. This conclusion has far-reaching implications both for food self-sufficiency and for standards of living more broadly.

The threat of water scarcity may be well hidden today in situations where the gap between realized demand and potential availability remains quite large. What we are speaking about is a long-term issue planners should recognize: the maximum amount of water per capita that can be mobilized once the population has stabilized and the ceiling has decreased accordingly may be quite low.

Regional dilemmas

Given the evidence that the amount of water that could be made accessible to the projected populations in many African countries is severely limited, the next question is for what purposes water demand will be greatest. Generally, irrigated agriculture is the most water-consuming sector in a society. A crucial question is therefore how much water would be needed in order to secure self-reliance in food production. This question hinges on two factors: the length of the growing season under the given hydroclimate and the risk of crop failure in drought years.

In Figure 4 the water scarcity dilemma is set forth in a matrix comparing five African regions in 1982 and 2025. The horizontal axis shows the length of the growing season; the vertical axis depicts the levels of population pressure on water in terms of the number of persons per million cubic meters per year. A growing season of less than 75 days indicates that only pasture is possible unless there is recourse to irrigation. With such a short growing season, crop production would require special measures to secure adequate water in the root zone—in other words, dependence on a supply of extra water by regular irrigation, water harvesting, water concentration schemes, and the like. A growing season of 75–150 days indicates high vulnerability to droughts, so that water storage would be necessary to secure supplementary irrigation during drought periods and years. Drought problems, although less severe, also characterize a growing season of 150–210 days.

FIGURE 4   Population pressure on water (vertical scale) compared with length of growing season (horizontal scale) in 1982 and 2025, indicating areas of special concern

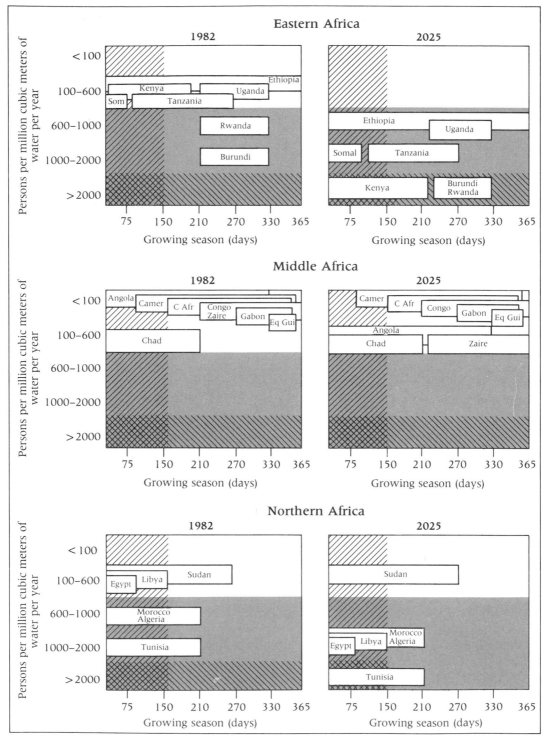

FIGURE 4   (continued)

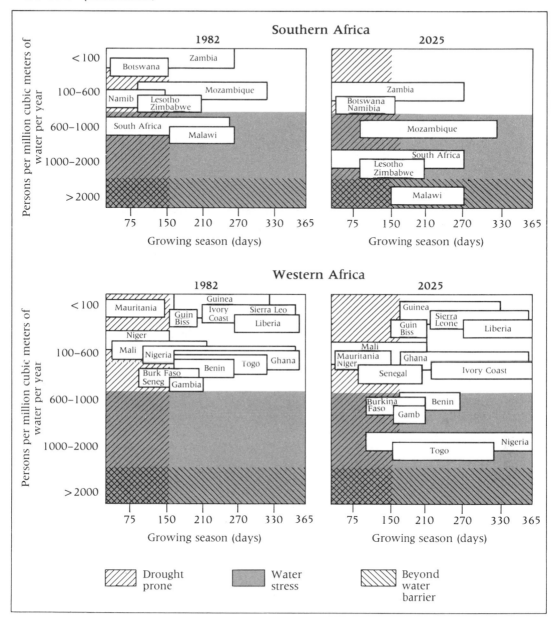

The diagrams highlight the differences between regions and the "water-strangling" effect of the projected population growth. The most water-stressed countries are Kenya and Tunisia, both highly water-dependent for food security. Severely water-stressed countries also include Egypt, Libya, Morocco, and Algeria in Northern Africa; Somalia and parts of Tanzania in Eastern Africa; Lesotho, Zimbabwe, and South Africa in Southern Africa; and parts of Nigeria in Western Africa. Water stress could also be predicted for parts of Ethiopia, Mozambique, and Burkina Faso. Burundi,

Rwanda, and Malawi are presumably less water-dependent because of longer growing seasons.

It is essential to add, of course, that this is the situation at the macro-level, treating whole countries as units. Countries heavily dependent on water for food security may well develop severe regional water stress, as illustrated by present conditions in Egypt, Libya, Sudan, Ethiopia, Kenya, and several of the Sahelian countries.

Reasons for the lack of attention to water shortage

The conventional approach to water as a natural resource, still adhered to in Northern development strategies—and when the North counsels Southern countries on their development options—is strongly technology-oriented. Studies typically start by estimating the future water demand, followed by the question: "Is that amount accessible, and where?" If the answer is "no" the next question is "How, then, would we get hold of it—by desalination, by water transfer from water-rich regions, by iceberg towing, or what other means?"

Donors and experts from the North generally display a surprisingly poor understanding of the implications of watercycle-related phenomena for livelihood in the semi-arid tropics. They tend to concentrate on techno-logical measures to obtain water supplies and irrigation on a project basis rather than confronting directly the problem of water scarcity and its implications. There is a corresponding lack of awareness among ecologists: they tend to see lack of water in the root zone as a soil fertility problem rather than a water problem. They often identify the concept "water" with "visible water" only, without considering the "invisible" water feeding the plants. Evidently, perceptions based on experience in the temperate zone, where water can generally be taken for granted, dominate present thinking. Even in the arid Southwestern United States, technological thinking has been dominant until quite recently.

The heavy emphasis on technology has caused engineers to spend decades exploring ways to induce more precipitation from the atmosphere. Expensive research studies have determined that occasionally, in some localities, it may be possible to make rain. The scientists involved, however, have been less interested in ascertaining who would otherwise have gotten that particular rainwater.

The technological approach was inherited from Europe. It was brought by immigrants across North America to the arid and sunny Southwest. The affluence of large oasis cities and their heavily subsidized cash crop irrigation schemes were made possible by large-scale water transfers across mountain ridges from better-endowed river basins in neighboring areas.

In the arid Southwestern United States this very simplistic approach—seeing nature as something to serve man by means of more and more advanced technology—is now giving way to a new philosophy: adaptation to the "safe yield" of regional fresh water systems (El-Ashry and Gibbons, 1986). One reason is the increasing number of competitive claims on the water diverted from the Colorado River. Another is the growing public interest in environmental issues and a new appreciation of aquatic ecosystems in the river valleys of northern Colorado. As a consequence, a new reluctance has developed to export water to water-scarce regions even for a profit. This general change in attitude has made imported water an unreliable resource. New legislation forces arid states to find ways to adapt to the constraints of the natural freshwater renewal in their areas.

In view of such developments in countries of the North, the approach in counseling the South should also be revised. Where water resources are limited, the right question to ask is: "How much water is available and how could we best benefit from it?"

Conclusion

This article has shown the potential for water scarcity to become a severe constraint on the quality of life in sub-Saharan Africa. Population growth is at the heart of the problem of semi-arid development. Development implies increasing water demands for improved health, quality of life, food security, and "lubrication" of industrial growth more broadly. Population growth places severe constraints on the water available to achieve these goals.

The fundamental importance of water both for habitability and for rural access to biomass for food, fodder, fuelwood, and timber makes water scarcity a crucial problem in the struggle for a higher quality of life for poor rural populations. Lack of water will contribute to environmental stress and threaten environmental security. It is highly probable that the water scarcity predicament discussed here will influence basic demographic variables in Africa, especially death rates and migration patterns. Two-thirds of the African population can expect to be living in severely water-stressed countries a few decades from now. Jacobson (1988) has discussed the flows of environmental refugees generated by water scarcity. Migration out of the area will inevitably occur if habitability is reduced by water shortages.

Awareness of the implications of water scarcity is greatly needed both among planners and political leaders in the arid and semi-arid developing countries and among donors and international organizations. Importation of food is one possible answer and a very effective one because irrigation is known to be extremely water-consuming. A recent roundtable discussion on this issue (Falkenmark et al., 1987) concluded that stable food prices on the international market would be the best support that industrialized countries could give to the poverty-stricken countries in the semi-arid tropics. This would make it possible for them to use their water for other, more economic, purposes. In other words, the present goal of self-reliance in food production is not necessarily realistic in the long term and might better be selectively abandoned.

In spite of its multiple functions both in the natural environment and in human society, the issue of availability of water has generally been addressed in a simplistic manner, mainly as a question of supply. A better understanding of the water-related constraints to African development calls for new perceptions and a broadened perspective. Problems due to water scarcity—whether in the soil or in terrestrial water systems—need to be addressed in a more integrated manner, taking account of the long run.

References

El-Ashry, M.T., and D.C. Gibbons. 1986. "Troubled waters: New policies for managing water in the American West," World Resources Institute, Study 6.

Falkenmark, M. 1986. "Fresh water—Time for a modified approach," *Ambio* 15, no. 4: 192–200.

———. 1987. "Water-related constraints to African development in the next few decades," in *Water for the Future: Hydrology in Perspective* (Proceedings of the Rome Symposium, April 1987), International Association of Hydrological Sciences Publ. No. 164, pp. 439–453.

———. 1989. "The massive water scarcity now threatening Africa—Why isn't it being addressed?," *Ambio* 18, no. 2: 112–118.

———, et al. 1987. "Water-related limitations to local development: Round table discussion," *Ambio* 16, no. 4: 191–200.

Falkenmark, M., and J. Lundqvist. 1988. "Land use for sustainable development: Strategies for crop production adapted to water availability," Proceedings of the International Water Resources Association Congress, Ottawa.

Food and Agriculture Organization (FAO). 1986. Need and justification of irrigation development. Consultation on Irrigation in Africa, Lomé, Togo, 21–25 April 1986. FAO, AGL: IA/86/Doc I-D.

Forkasiewicz, J., and J. Margat. 1980. "Tableau mondial de données nationales d'économie de l'eau, ressources et utilizations." Département Hydrogéologie, 79 SGN 784 HYD, Orléans.

Higgins, G.M., P.J. Dieleman, and C.L. Albernethy. 1988. "Trends in irrigation development, and their implications for hydrologists and water resources engineers," *Hydrological Sciences Journal* 22, no. 1–2: 43–59.

Hyams, E. 1976. *Soil and Civilisation*. New York: Harper and Row.

Jacobson, T. 1988. "Environmental refugees: A yardstick of habitability," *Worldwatch Paper* 86.

Keyfitz, N. 1984. "Impact of trends in resources, environment and development on demographic prospects," *Population Bulletin of the United Nations* 16: 1–5.

Lvovich, M.I. 1979. *World Water Resources and Their Future* (translation by the American Geophysical Union). Chelsea, Michigan: LithoCrafters Inc.

Szesztay, K. 1972. "The hydrosphere and the human environment," in *Results of Research on Representative and Experimental Basins: Studies and Reports in Hydrology*, no. 12. UNESCO, pp. 455–467.

World Commission on Environment and Development (the Brundtland Commission). 1987. *Our Common Future*. London: Oxford University Press.

World Resources Institute. 1986. *World Resources 1986*. New York: Basic Books.

Energy, People, and Industrialization

Amory B. Lovins

The round-earth theory poses ultimate limits to population growth and industrialization. Biotic and social carrying capacities, and some resource finitudes, constrain the scope for Los Angelizing the planet. However, even very large expansions in population and industrial activity need not be energy-constrained: if we apply what we know, energy can be among the weakest of the many reasons for concern about foreseeable levels of population and industrial growth. This essay first explains why energy need not limit traditional industrial expansion (at least not until very far beyond most other limits) and then explores why goals other than indiscriminate growth are worthier.

The product of five terms determines the total societal cost of providing energy services: population × stock of material artifacts[1] per capita × resource throughput to maintain each unit of stock[2] × energy consumption per unit of resource throughput × cost and impact per unit of energy consumption. The essay describes how modern improvements mainly in the fourth (energy-efficiency) term, and secondarily in the third (resource-efficiency) and fifth (clean-energy-technology) terms, can compensate for growth in the first two terms: not forever, but certainly long enough to sustain, with essentially no fossil or nuclear fuels, a fully industrialized world of 8–10 billion people, assuming that such a world were not earlier forestalled by more proximate problems.

Supporting evidence is adduced largely from experience in the United States, but the implications are readily generalizable.

If we simply pursue the narrowest of economic interests, the energy problem can be solved by available new technologies—primarily for more efficient end-use, secondarily for more efficient conversion and sustainable supply. In the United States, for example,

— full practical use, in existing buildings and equipment, of the best electricity-saving technologies already on the market would save at least

FIGURE 1 Preliminary supply curve of the technical potential to save US electricity (cumulative quantity in billion kW-h/y vs. marginal cost in ¢kW-h saved) by fully applying the best commercially available technologies for improving end-use efficiency while providing unchanged or improved services

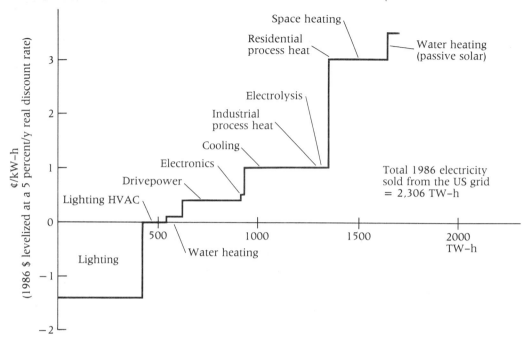

NOTE: One TW–h equals 1 million megawatt–hours or 1 billion kilowatt–hours.
SOURCE: See note 4.

three-fourths of all electricity now used, at an average cost[3] certainly below 1¢/kW-h and probably around 0.6¢/kW-h[4] (see Figure 1)—much less than the cost of simply running a coal or nuclear power station, even if building it cost nothing; and

    — full practical use of the best demonstrated oil- and gas-saving technologies (many already on the market and the rest ready for production within about four to five years) would save about four-fifths of all oil now used, at an average cost of approximately $2½/bbl[5] (see Figure 2)—less than the typical cost of just finding new domestic oil.

    These savings are of a purely technical character and would entail no loss—indeed, often a substantial improvement—in the quantity and quality of services provided.

    The magnitude of potential energy savings and their low cost may surprise many. But the findings summarized below are calculated by conventional methods from documented cost and performance data that have been independently measured for real, commercially available devices. There should be little dispute about empirical data. Disputes tend to arise, rather,

FIGURE 2   Preliminary supply curve of the technical potential to save US oil consumption (cumulative quantity vs. marginal cost) by fully applying the best demonstrated technologies for improving end-use efficiency while providing unchanged or improved services

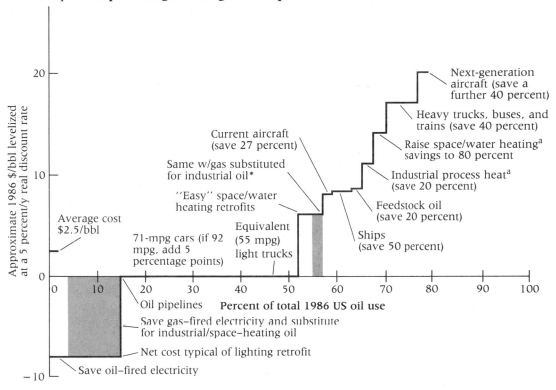

[a]Plus extra natural-gas savings equivalent to 20 percent of total oil use, at an average cost of $10/bbl.
SOURCE: See note 5.

from differences in the modernity of technologies assumed, in the thoroughness with which their performance is characterized, in the degree of disaggregation (most analysts omit many small savings that are collectively large[6]), and over whether important synergisms between technical measures are captured in the analysis.[7]

Efficiency technologies have already begun to sweep the market despite the many obstacles placed in their way—chiefly inadequate information, immature delivery mechanisms, and asymmetrical economic comparisons. There is now abundant evidence that efficiency's rapid rise to complete dominance of marginal investments would be a natural outcome of free-market competition among all ways to provide desired energy services.[8]

Unfortunately, however, most governments and many private-sector actors are less committed to market outcomes in energy policy than to lemon socialism—to bailing out their favorite technologies, many of which are now dying of an incurable attack of market forces. As long as this ideology continues to dominate public policy and the private investments that such policy influences, energy will continue to impose intractable economic, environmental, and security constraints on the type and degree of global development.

The secret success

In spite of persistent official obstructions summarized below, the genius of even a very imperfect market has been able to assert itself to a striking degree. Consider these facts:

— Since 1979, the United States has obtained more than seven times as much new energy from savings as from all net increases in energy supply.

— Of that new supply, more has come from renewables (now about 11–12 percent of total primary supply) than from nonrenewables.

— During 1979–86, energy savings expanded US energy availability by seven times as much as nuclear power did, and during 1984–86, by nearly 13 times as much.

— Because of the reductions in energy intensity achieved since 1973, the annual US energy bill has recently been about $430 billion instead of roughly $580 billion—a saving of some $150 billion per year (comparable to the federal budget deficit). However, if the United States were now as efficient as its competitors in Europe and Japan, it would be saving an additional $200 billion or so per year. And simply choosing the most cost-efficient energy for the rest of this century could yield a cumulative net saving of several trillion of today's dollars—more than the national debt.

— During 1977–85, the United States steadily and routinely saved oil four-fifths faster than it needed to in order to keep up with both economic growth and declining domestic oil output. This 5 percent per year increase in national oil productivity cut total oil imports in half. It was achieved largely with such simple measures as caulk guns, duct tape, insulation, plugged steam leaks, and a five-mile-per-gallon gain in the efficiency of the car fleet.

— By 1986 the US energy saving achieved since 1973—chiefly in oil and gas—was "producing" two-fifths more energy each year than the domestic oil industry, which took a century to build. Yet oil has rising costs, falling output, and dwindling reserves; efficiency has falling costs, rising output, and expanding reserves.

— The Electric Power Research Institute (EPRI, the research arm of the US utility industry) estimates that US electrical intensity reductions during 1973–83 cut construction needs by some 141 GW,[9] corresponding to a marginal capacity cost on the order of $200–500 billion. Yet EPRI now agrees that newly available, still cost-effective savings are many times larger than utilities are now planning to capture.

— Numerous utilities, by investing in more efficient use of electricity by their customers, are saving large amounts of electricity at low and falling real cost; in mature programs, the utilities' expenditures typically correspond to costs of saved energy on the order of 0.1–0.5¢ per kW-h saved. For example, if all Americans saved electricity at the same speed and cost at which the roughly 10 million people served by Southern California Edison Company actually saved electricity during 1983–85, then national forecast needs for long-run power supplies would decrease by about 40 GW per year (equivalent to an avoided capital cost, including its federal subsidy, of about $80 billion per year). Utilities' cost to achieve those savings would average about 0.1–0.2¢/kW-h—roughly 1 percent of the cost of new power plants.[10]

Similarly striking progress is evident on the supply side:

— Life extension of conventional plants, retrofitting of combustion turbines to combined-cycle operation, packaged combined-cycle plants, and steam-injected gas turbines have virtually supplanted central steam plants as utilities' marginal supply investments of choice. With good design and favorable local conditions, small hydro plants, hydro upgrading, windpower, some solar-thermal-electric plants, and geothermal power can also be highly competitive on the margin with standard steam plants even if the latter are subsidized while the former are not.[11] Other options, such as fuel cells and photovoltaics, are rapidly coming over the horizon of competitiveness. Even without demand-side competition, the era of the big steam plant would be over.

— As proof of this, during 1981–84, US orders and firm letters of intent, minus cancellations, totaled: − 65 net GW for fossil-fueled and nuclear central plants; + 25 GW for cogeneration (about 20 percent of it renewable); and + >20 GW for small hydro, windpower, etc. Thus over two-thirds of lost central-station capacity was made up by smaller, faster, cheaper options that enabled investors to manage financial risks so as to minimize regret.[12] The other third was far more than made up by improved end-use efficiency. Since 1984, the conditions that produced this extraordinary shift of private capital have only intensified: by some estimates, more new generating capacity was added to the US grid in 1990 by private, independent producers than by utilities.

An example of the power of competition: California, a tenth of the US economy, had around 1984 a 37-GW peak electric load, supplied by 10 GW of hydroelectricity and geothermal power plus 27 GW of fossil-fueled and nuclear plants. Around 1982, the state's utilities started offering to buy privately generated power at a fair price with roughly equalized subsidies (and to buy private savings on much less favorable terms). Within a few years of this approximation to fair competition:

— the utilities had firmly committed over 13 GW of long-term (ten-year) electrical savings, not including an additional 11 GW or so under serious discussion;

— private investors had firmly offered over 21 GW of new generating capacity, most of it renewable;

— over 13 GW of that offered capacity was already built or being built; and

— new offers for private generation were arriving at the rate of 9 GW, or one-fourth of total peak demand, per year.

Because of the resulting power glut, the state of California suspended new contracts in April 1985. If the market response had been allowed to continue for another year or two, it would already have displaced every thermal power plant in California. Yet utilities in at least two dozen other US states and Canadian provinces are still hoping to sell their surpluses to California simultaneously. Some California utilities, unhappy with competition from private generators, are also trying to prevent or defer much of the already-agreed-upon new private generating capacity from coming online—while they simultaneously complain that such capacity is "unreliable" because it is not always completed.

Around 1988–90, diverse US utilities in at least 27 states ran auctions to see which private investors might wish, at their own expense and risk, to generate power for sale to the grid. Those utilities were offered, at very competitive prices, eight times as much power as they wanted.[13] Presumably they would have been even more swamped with attractive bids had they offered a similar price for energy savings, as some are now starting to do (as is discussed below).

The energy efficiency revolution

These developments reflect rapid change on four related fronts:

Technology for extremely efficient end-use of energy

Most of the best electricity-saving technologies on the US market today were not available a year ago, and the same was true a year before that. Twice as much electricity can be saved now as could have been saved five years ago, and at only a third the real cost—a gain in aggregate cost-effectiveness by about a factor of 6 in five years, or nearly a factor of 30 in ten years. This technological revolution shows no sign of abating. The availability of negative-cost savings in both electricity[14] and oil[15] permits large savings, e.g., about 50 percent of electricity, at zero net cost, making the corresponding environmental benefits better than free.

New ways to finance and deliver energy-saving technologies to customers

The Natural Resources Defense Council, Lawrence Berkeley Laboratory, Rocky Mountain Institute, and some utilities have developed, and US utilities are now bringing into successful use, many techniques for implementing the least-cost investment strategies now demanded by the increasingly competitive energy-service market (and, in more than 20 states, by law).[16] Complementing the concessionary utility loans and rebates now available to most US electric customers, and other approaches such as information programs, gifts, and leases, these new methods include:

— competitive auctions for all ways to make or save electricity (such "all-source" bidding is beginning in at least eight states);

— secondary-marketable covenants to stabilize or cap facilities' electric demand;

— making electrical savings fungible ("wheelable") within and between utilities' service territories (the first two such transactions were negotiated in 1988, whereby a utility will invest in saving electricity in another utility's territory and buy back, at a discounted price, the power thereby rendered surplus);

— making spot, futures, and options markets in "negawatts" (saved electricity);

— sliding-scale hookup fees for new buildings—fees that are positive or negative depending on the efficiency of each building;

— sale of electric efficiency by electric utilities[17] in other utilities' terriories (as about a dozen utilities are now profitably doing), and also by gas utilities.

These and similar innovations make saved electricity a commodity subject to all the market mechanisms that pertain to other commodities— trading and fungibility in space and time, auctions, secondary markets, derivative instruments, arbitrage, and the like. Similar evolution now occurs in savings of other forms of energy, including oil, and in other resources such as water.

Such implementation methods are essential to overcome the "payback gap"—the tendency for customers' energy-saving investments to be assessed at a discount rate about ten times that used for evaluating the supply-side investments that utilities and other energy providers must otherwise make instead. (This means that a customer who can avoid energy priced at 10¢/kW-h will only buy, unaided, efficiency costing about 1¢/kW-h.) While consumers' requirements for payback in typically two years, and utilities' in more like 20, are both rational from those parties' own perspectives, their combination results in a huge misallocation of societal capital: consumers buy too little efficiency, so suppliers must buy too much supply. The new financing methods close this gap by effectively equalizing discount rates so as to compare all options symmetrically. In effect, the utilities' business opportunity here is arbitrage on the tenfold spread in discount rate between themselves and their customers. Moreover, utilities can and do play a key role in creating the new service institutions needed to design, manage, finance, and conveniently deliver well-designed, integrated packages of modern efficiency technologies.

Radical changes in utilities' mission and culture

These changes are returning utilities to the historic roots of their business.[18] A minority of American utilities is reinventing its mission as (in Georgia Power's phrase) "the profitable production of customer satisfaction." This minority is rapidly growing as these firms become noted as more profitable than their competitors. Utilities that begin to sell both electricity and electrical savings (the main intermediate goods for providing electrical services) as commodities are shifting their orientation from being vendors of a single commodity (kW-h) to being a service industry—that is, to delivering a different mix of efficiently provided commodities, including information and financing, in a way that ensures customer success. This means, among other things, learning to focus on the bottom line rather than the top line—learning that it is acceptable to sell less electricity and bring in less revenue, so long as costs fall even more.

Small but important shifts in regulatory policy

These shifts provide clear incentives that support and drive cultural change. The most important such development is the unanimous November 1989 agreement by the National Association of Regulatory Utility Commissioners that utilities' profits should be decoupled from their sales (so that they are at least indifferent to whether they sell more or less electricity), and that utilities should be rewarded for cost-minimizing behavior (e.g., by being allowed to keep as extra profit part of what they save their customers). This would radically transform current regulatory practice, which (a) except in five states, penalizes utilities for selling less electricity (or gas) and rewards them for selling more, and (b) passes on any cost savings entirely to the consumers, not to the utility investors.

This progress is most prominent in, but not confined to, electric utilities. Some major vendors of fuels, including one or two of the world's largest oil companies, are now becoming seriously interested in selling all forms of energy efficiency for profit.

Underlying all these developments is the post-1973 revolution in energy-policy methodology. This change is now so nearly complete that it is hard to remember the primitive methods used almost universally only a decade ago. In 1976, a memo by Herman Daly summarized how energy needs were then generally determined:

> Recent growth rates of population and per capita energy use [or of population, per capita GNP, and energy use per unit of GNP] are projected up to

some arbitrary, round-numbered date. Whatever technologies are required to produce the projected amount are automatically accepted, along with their social implications, and no thought is given to how long the system can last once the projected levels are attained. Trend is, in effect, elevated to destiny, and history either stops or starts afresh on the bi-millenial year, or the year 2050 or whatever.

This approach is unworthy of any organism with a central nervous system, much less a cerebral cortex. For those of us who also have souls, it is almost incomprehensible in its inversion of ends and means.

. . . [It says] that there is no such thing as enough[;] that growth in population and per capita energy use are either desirable or inevitable[;] that it is useless to worry about the future for more than 20 years, since all reasonably discounted costs and benefits become nil over that period[;] and that the increasing scale of technology is simply time's arrow of progress, and refusal to follow it represents a failure of nerve.

It is now widely accepted that the end-use/least-cost approach introduced in 1976[19]—asking what we want the energy for, and how much energy, of what quality, at what scale, from what source, will do each task at least cost—is the best way to understand likely market developments and to plan optimal investments. It is also widely accepted that future energy needs are not fate but choice. Only the handful of analysts who have carefully examined the new technologies and delivery methods, however, realize how flexibly that choice can now be exercised. Technology transfer is needed at least as much by policymakers, whose notion of the possible is long outdated, as by consumers.

High-energy futures, sometimes considered inherently plausible because their extrapolation from the past requires so little thought, are in fact internally inconsistent. Their massive and costly supply expansions would require high energy prices. But those prices would in turn elicit much more efficient end-use. High-energy futures also tend to be politically unattractive, implying greater dirigisme than most societies are likely to tolerate.

Continuing blunders

The achievements of energy efficiency are all the more startling in view of the powerful forces arrayed against it. For decades, efficiency has been greatly retarded by its opponents, and has often suffered grievously even at the hands of its friends. (President Carter's public equation of saving energy with privation, discomfort, and curtailment may have set back efficiency more than his other policies helped it.[20]) At the same time, wastefully used, depletable, environmentally damaging, and egregiously uncompetitive energy options have received government succor lavishly and continuously. The triumph of narrow-private-interest expedience over macroeconomic efficiency, especially in the United States, beggars description. For example,

— The lopsidedness of federal subsidies to the energy sector was already severe[21] when last fully assessed in fiscal year 1984 (see Figure 3).[22] The 1986 tax reform may have modestly reduced the total amount of subsidies, which was upwards of $50 billion in fiscal year 1984 alone, but has certainly increased their distortions of market choice.[23]

— The Interior Department has hastened to sell or lease public fuel resources into a glutted market at depressed prices, counting externalities as worth zero.

— The Federal Energy Regulatory Commission has sought to stifle state initiatives to introduce genuine competition into the electrical-services market.

— Federal monitoring and enforcement of existing environmental, health, safety, and antitrust laws awkward for the energy industries has been minimal.[24]

FIGURE 3   Energy supplied by, and direct federal subsidies to, US sources of energy services in 1984

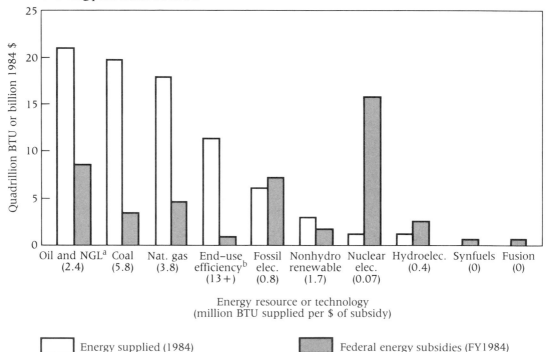

Energy resource or technology
(million BTU supplied per $ of subsidy)

☐ Energy supplied (1984)   ▥ Federal energy subsidies (FY1984)

[a]Natural gas liquids
[b]Conservatively assuming that improved end-use efficiency accounted for only half of the 1973–84 reduction in primary energy/real $ GNP.
SOURCE: See note 11.

— Building and appliance standards and a financing mechanism legislated to overcome well-known market failures have been opposed, weakened, or ignored.[25]

— The US Department of Energy, having cut real spending for efficiency research, design, and development by 71 percent, sought in fiscal year 1989 a further 50 percent cut and 96 percent in the state and local programs that deliver efficiency information to citizens—even though such investments in the past have consistently yielded returns of hundreds or thousands of percent to the national economy. Such further cuts will now reportedly not be made after fiscal year 1989, but rebuilding the capabilities already destroyed may take a decade.

— Remaining federal research, design, and development continues to be overwhelmingly (about 96–99 percent) biased toward roughly 0–7 percent of marginal energy needs (central-electric supply vs. generation at appropriate scale, nonelectric supply, and demand-side options).

Such interventions have serious, even absurd, consequences. For example,

— The energy wasted[26] in the United States today costs about twice as much as the federal budget deficit, or more than the entire $9,000-a-second military budget.

— The amount of crude oil wasted in 1986[27] by that year's rollback of US light-vehicle efficiency standards[28] equalled 1985 US imports from the Persian Gulf. It also equals the average annual oil output that the Department of the Interior hopes to achieve over 30 years from beneath the Arctic National Wildlife Refuge. In effect, the administration thereby *un*discovered one Refuge's worth of potential Arctic oil—even as it sought Congressional consent to lease for exploration in the Refuge, at great environmental cost and very probably at a financial net loss to the lessees.

— Shielding potentially hazardous industries from market and political accountability encourages sloppy operations that incur enormous future costs—viz., the roughly $100-billion cleanup bill starting to be presented by the military nuclear sector. This nasty surprise seems likely to be dwarfed by a similar bill, similarly created, from the civilian nuclear sector.[29]

— Electricity in fiscal year 1984 (the last reliable data available) got upwards of $35 billion in federal subsidies—two-thirds of all federal energy subsidies, going to only 14 percent of the delivered energy.[30] This distortion made electricity look a fifth cheaper than it really was, thereby artificially increasing demand, and, by effectively financing new power plants at approximately zero (or negative) interest rates, leveraged most or all of the roughly $30 billion of annual private investment in expanding electrical supply. (The impact on national capital allocation was large, because marginal central-electric systems are about a hundred times as capital-intensive as the traditional oil, gas, and coal systems on which today's American economy was built.) The total investments still being made for new US electric supply—some $60 billion a year, half private and half public—equal the total investment in US durable-goods manufacturing. Thus, electric savings only fast enough to keep up with growth in service demand and plant retirements would leave nearly twice as much capital to keep those manufactures competitive.

— The difference in energy intensity between the US and Japanese economies now creates an automatic cost advantage on the order of 5 percent for the typical Japanese export. This gap is widening, especially with regard to electrical productivity: the Japanese gross national product in 1986 was 36 percent less electricity-intensive than the US gross national product, and this gap is officially projected to become 45 percent by 2000. In particular major industries, such as cars, paper, and cement, electricity intensity per ton is falling in Japan—proof that such falling intensity can accompany, even increase, competitiveness—yet it is rising in the United States, following the official US dogma that rising electricity intensity is essential to economic health and must therefore be further subsidized.

— Large expenditures are being contemplated to mitigate or respond to such problems as acid rain, CO_2 emissions, and nuclear proliferation—all of which are an artifact of an economically inefficient energy policy and could be abated not at extra cost but at a profit (as is discussed below).

In 1973 and again in 1979 the US government responded to an oil shock by spurring supply and ignoring demand. Both times, the supply initiatives collapsed while the market rapidly produced efficiency, leaving the supply industries with unsaleable costly surpluses. In the late 1980s, and especially in 1991 while at war in the Persian Gulf, the federal government continued its efforts to repeat this mistake for a third time. To be sure, it has learned the lesson that "balance" is required between supply- and demand-side investments, albeit in roughly the proportions of the classic recipe for elephant-and-rabbit stew—one elephant, one rabbit. This "balance" rests not on the neoclassical calculus of marginal costs and benefits, but rather on the Chinese-restaurant-menu theory of energy policy—pick one option from Column A, one from Column B, and so on, to please the major constituencies—and on the hand-waving claim that more supply is needed as "insurance" in case efficiency somehow fails to work. The result of trying to buy both, of course, would be to stint both (since they compete for the same resources), and hence could be to get neither. Worse, as in the recent past, we could get both—and hence further bankrupt the supply industries, which need increased demand to pay for costly new supplies.

Environmental bonuses

It is at least conceivable that the confluence of environmental problems now stirring public anxiety may help to rebuild energy policy on a foundation of economic rationality. This is far from certain—virtually every newsmagazine except *Business Week,* for example, has fallen for the fallacious argument that nuclear power can help to abate global warming[31]—but it offers a new opportunity to reframe the basic arguments.

Fuels that are not mined and burned have no environmental impacts. It is generally cheaper today to give away efficiency[32] than to dig up and burn the fuels to do the same task. Most environmental impacts associated with obtaining, converting, and using energy can thus be abated at negative net internal cost to society.

For example, rather than raising people's electric bills to put diapers on dirty coal plants to reduce acid gas emissions, one can use well-established delivery methods to help the same customers to get superefficient lights, motors, appliances, and building components. They will then need less electricity to obtain the same services. The utility can burn less coal and emit less sulfur (preferably using "environmental dispatch" to back out the dirtiest plants first). But the main effect will be that the utility saves a great deal of money, because efficiency is cheaper than coal.[33] The utility can then use part of its saved operating cost to clean up the remaining plants by any method of its choice, part to reduce its tariffs, and part to reward its investors. On very conservative assumptions,[34] one analysis of this approach found that the Midwest region responsible for a third of all US power-plant sulfur emissions could achieve a 55 percent sulfur reduction at a net-present-valued 1985–2000 cost of about minus $4–7 billion, rather than the plus $4–7 billion of conventional abatement without end-use efficiency improvements—a net saving of some $11 billion.

Naturally, the same approach simultaneously abates other impacts of power generation, coal-mining, and so on. For example, an 18-watt compact fluorescent lamp, producing the same light as a 75-watt incandescent lamp for about 13 times as long, will over its lifetime save about one-ten-millionth as much electricity as a huge (1,000-megawatt) power station generates in a year. A single such lamp will thus avoid the emission from a typical US coal plant of a ton of CO_2, which adds to global warming,[35] and about 8 kg of SO_2, which contributes to acid rain, plus NO_x, heavy metals, and other pollutants; or avoid the production by a typical nuclear plant of half a curie of strontium-90 and cesium-137 (two major components of high-level waste) and about 25 milligrams of plutonium—about equivalent in explosive power to 385 kg of TNT, or in radiotoxicity, if uniformly distributed into human lungs, to at least 2,000 or so cancer-causing doses.

Yet far from costing extra, the lamp will save the cost of a dozen ordinary lamps and their installation labor (typically totaling about $20), plus the cost of generating about 610 kW-h of electricity (typically around $20–30 worth of fuel), and during its lifetime will defer approximately $200–300 worth of generating capacity, reserve capacity, grid, and fuel-cycle equipment.

Since the lamp's typical retail price is only about $12–18, and its real resource cost is about half or a third of that, its use generates for society at least tens of dollars of net wealth, not counting its avoided environmental costs. It is also noteworthy that in a country which (unlike the United States) still generates much electricity from oil, one such lamp will save enough oil (200 liters or 1.25 barrels) to run a family-size American car for a thousand miles or to run a superefficient prototype car entirely across the United States and back.

Similar economic considerations apply to the more complex issues of abating nuclear proliferation,[36] improving domestic energy security against accidental or deliberate disruption,[37] and reducing dependence on Middle Eastern oil.[38] Achieving these benefits by improved end-use efficiency makes all participants richer, even if the benefits prove illusory or worthless. This is, in a variant on Marv Goldberger's memorable phrase, "spherically sensible": energy efficiency makes sense no matter which way you look at it. It should be done to save money, even if we are not concerned about such issues as global warming.

In most cases, the environmental benefits of energy savings can be achieved most quickly and profitably by saving electricity, because this energy form uses several units of fuel at the power plant per unit delivered, the generation and delivery systems are extremely expensive, and electricity, for both these reasons, is by far the costliest form of energy.[39] This high environmental and economic leverage puts a premium on saving electricity, even though virtually all official and private effort has so far focused instead on saving directly used oil and gas. The leverage is highest in countries like the Soviet Union, where low-grade coal is inefficiently mined and burned, then about 30–40 percent of the power is lost in long-distance transmission to inefficient end-uses. From this perspective, among the most attractive ways to head off global warming would be to save electricity in the Soviet Union, China, and India.

International applicability

The substantial and little-noted progress in electric efficiency has been fastest in the United States because of its immensely diverse utility system. Among some 3,500 enterprises in about 50 major and hundreds of minor regulatory jurisdictions (along with substantial unregulated operations), a great many experiments have already been tried. This has occurred with little help—indeed despite overt and covert opposition—from the federal government; most of the initiative has come from the utilities themselves, from other private-sector actors, and from state and local governments.

Unfortunately, most other countries have a much more monolithic structure of their electric and energy industries[40]—often nationalized, usually centrally planned, generally devoid of market or political accountability, and hence with no incentive and little inclination to innovate. This discouraging picture is starting to change, however, as political (and, especially in developing countries, financial) constraints hamper traditional supply expansion and as public concern rises about acid rain, global warming, and nuclear safety. In country after country—even those previously most immune to innovation, such as Great Britain and the Soviet Union—new incentives are beginning to appeal to entrepreneurs.

Naturally, there are important differences between end-use structures, behavioral patterns, and capital stocks in various countries. Nonetheless, it is becoming apparent in the roughly 20 countries in which I am active in energy policy, and in others where my colleagues work, that the technical (and, usually, the institutional) opportunities for major savings are strikingly similar even in countries with quite different levels of overall energy efficiency. For example, Jørgen Nørgård at the Technical University of Denmark has recently found a potential to save about three-fourths of the electricity now used in Danish buildings, at an average cost of around 1.3¢/kW-h[41]—coincidentally very close to my best estimate for all sectors and end-uses in the United States. (Several other European analysts are converging on similar results.) To be sure, Europeans generally light their offices less intensively, and turn the lights off more, than Americans do, but that does not affect the *percentage* savings available in the lighting energy that *is* used— a function only of the lighting technology itself, which is similar on the two continents.

Contrary to the common but fallacious view that developing countries can save little energy because they use so little (at least in commercial forms), the same is true there too. Replacing an incandescent with a compact-fluorescent lamp will save about 70–85 percent of the energy per unit of delivered light regardless of whether the original lamp is in Belgium or Bihar. Superwindows[42] cut cooling loads by the same (or a greater) percentage in Bangkok[43] as in Bakersfield.

Indeed, both the end-use structure and the technological stock in developing countries generally imply a greater technical potential for efficiency gains than in industrialized countries. In aggregate, the energy efficiency of the typical rich country is nearly three times as great as that of the typical poor country. Since we already know how to make the typical rich country at least four times as energy-efficient as it now is, without coming anywhere near present limits of cost-effectiveness, one may infer a potential to fuel roughly tenfold economic growth in the typical poor country with no increase in its total energy use—and at the same time to maintain or improve rich countries' standard of living with a severalfold reduction in energy use.

Efficiency opportunities may well turn out to be smaller and costlier in Europe and Japan than in North America, but on current evidence the differences will probably be unimportant;[44] and they may well be offset, or more, by even bigger opportunities for savings in the socialist[45] and developing countries. (Table 1 summarizes one aggregated measure of how far many such countries have to go, and why.)

There is considerable room for argument about how much energy can be saved, both in theory and in practice. In round numbers, however, a four-to tenfold (or greater) aggregate efficiency gain, compared with 1973 levels, seems to represent the practical and cost-effective potential. The lower figure is broadly consistent with a careful, technically conservative analysis by Goldemberg et al.,[46] based on case studies for Brazil, India, Sweden, and the United States. The upper figure is consistent with an earlier analysis for the German Federal Environmental Agency,[47] based on 1980 end-use patterns, efficiency levels, technologies, and cost in West Germany, cross-checked against a variety of case studies from other countries and regions.

The latter study assumed a world of 8 billion people roughly a century hence, uniformly industrialized to the level of West Germany in 1973, when it was the most heavily industrialized country on Earth, and one of the most

TABLE 1   Some comparative energy intensities (primary megajoules per 1983 US$ of 1983 gross national product)

Market-oriented economies	
Sweden	8.6
France	8.6
Japan	9.7
Spain	11.8
West Germany	11.8
Italy	12.9
United Kingdom	17.2
United States	19.3
Centrally planned economies	
Yugoslavia	21.5
Poland	26.9
East Germany	29.0
Czechoslovakia	30.1
Soviet Union	32.3
Romania	37.6
China	40.9
Hungary	49.5

SOURCES: Worldwatch Institute, *State of the World 1987* (Washington, D.C.), p. 182. COMECON GNPs adjusted from 1980 dollar levels derived by Paul Marer, *Dollar GNPs of the USSR and Eastern Europe* (Baltimore: Johns Hopkins University Press, 1985).

energy-efficient. This assumed level of industrialization corresponds to global economic activity nearly five times that of 1975, and a tenfold increase in the developing countries. (Of course, this may well be impossible or undesirable for reasons other than energy.) If such a world used energy in a way that would have saved money under 1980 West German conditions, then its total primary energy use would have been approximately 3.5 TW, or less than half of the actual 1973 level, or about a third of the actual 1988 level. Moreover, except for one instance of modest interregional trade in biofuel, each of the world's major regions would be independently able to meet all or virtually all of its resulting needs for energy in each form using only renewable sources that were already available in 1980 and cost-effective on the long-run margin. In short, there would be no energy problem even under economic-growth assumptions that most would consider implausibly high. And complete implementation over some decades would require only a rate of efficiency improvement (and, for some countries like the United States, renewable-supply deployment) somewhat below that actually achieved since 1973.

The energy supply system required in such low-energy futures differs strikingly from that of conventional projections, and so do the corresponding costs and impacts. Even the low IIASA scenarios imply world energy use in 2030 some 2.5 times that of 1983. That projection is about two- to threefold lower than was in vogue in the late 1970s, but still requires thousands of reactors (with a new one commissioned roughly every four to six days), a three- to sixfold increase in the rate of coal mining, fossil-fuel supplies increased at a rate equivalent to about two million barrels per day (one Alaska) every one or two months, and hence largely depleted global conventional hydrocarbon resources. The resulting CO_2 concentration in 2030 would be around 450 parts per million by volume (ppmv), rising by 50 ppmv every decade or so.

In contrast, the "efficiency scenario" assuming the same economic and population growth, but using energy in a way that saves money (under 1980 conditions, which are probably less favorable than today's), uses 4–5 times less energy, costs much less, stretches oil and gas for centuries, dispenses with reliance on both the Middle East and the atom, and by 2030 has attained a CO_2 level barely above today's and rising by 5 ppmv every three decades or so, making this part (roughly 40 percent) of future global warming virtually vanish. Many other problems would also disappear, such as those associated with the million bombs' worth of plutonium proposed to be annually extracted and put into global commerce under the IIASA scenarios.

Another, more micro-scale, example: the Swedish State Power Board recently published a description of how electric end-use efficiency, some fuel-switching to gas and biofuels, and environmental dispatch (running the cleanest plants most and the dirtiest ones least) could simultaneously enable this cold, heavily industrialized, and already very efficient country to: expand its economy by roughly 50 percent from now to 2010; phase out, as required by law, the nuclear half of its electric supply; reduce the CO_2 output of providing heat and power by a third; and reduce the cost of electrical services by almost $1 billion per year. Interestingly, the Board's chief executive reportedly ordered the usual disclaimer—that the paper did not necessarily represent the Board's views—removed.[48]

In view of the well-known institutional barriers to using energy efficiently, especially in developing countries, some will ask whether this technical potential has any practical force. I believe the real issue is just the opposite: how can such countries develop without a high degree of efficiency? Consider these few examples:

— A colleague formerly in charge of Haitian energy policy estimated that giving away quadrupled-efficiency light bulbs throughout Haiti could increase the average household's disposable income by as much as a fifth—because so much of the cash economy goes to electricity, chiefly for lighting. (Southern California Edison Company has in fact given away more than half a million such lamps to its low-income residential customers and their neighborhood shops, because that is cheaper than operating the utility's existing power stations.)

— Ashok Gadgil at the Tata Energy Research Institute has shown by a Bombay case study that lighting is responsible for some 37 percent (or roughly 9 GW) of India's evening peak load, which overstresses the grid and is often responsible for rotating blackouts. The blackouts in turn greatly hamper economic output and competitiveness, both directly by shutting down production and indirectly by forcing factories to install very costly backup diesel generators. Again, giving away efficient lamps could largely solve the problem. (Such giveaways in an Alaskan village recently reduced the peak lighting load by a factor exceeding seven.)

— China recently decided it was time people had refrigerators, and built more than 100 refrigerator factories. The fraction of Beijing households owning a refrigerator rose from roughly 2 percent to 62 percent during 1981–86. Unfortunately, however, through mere inattention, an inefficient refrigerator design had been chosen—thereby committing China to billions of dollars' worth of electric capacity to serve those appliances.

These examples are especially striking when one recalls that at least a fourth of the world's total development capital goes to electrification; that a large, even dominant, fraction of many developing countries' debt service is energy-related; and that inadequate electric supplies now severely constrain the development of many countries which lack the capital to build (or the skills to operate reliably) more plants and grid.

In energy, as in water, minerals, and many other resources, it appears that developing countries can achieve their economic goals only by building comprehensive resource efficiency into their infrastructure from scratch. This is easier than the developed nations' task of having to retrofit trillions of dollars of obsolete stocks, and in principle could therefore give developing countries a comparative advantage. In practice, most developing countries lack the technical and commercial sophistication to ensure that they are buying and using the best options[49]—especially in the face of developed countries' often strenuous efforts to sell them equipment so inefficient that it is obsolete on their home markets (a dangerous and immoral export akin to that of deregistered pesticides, but not yet subject to any international constraints). The continued fixation of major international lenders on central generating plants, and the greater opportunity for decisionmakers to receive large "commissions" on such projects, also make it as difficult as in the industrialized countries for the political process to accommodate efficiency gains that would inconvenience the vendors of uncompetitive energy-supply technologies. Nor are most industrialized countries setting a laudable example of efficiency at home. But if developing countries hope to break the cycle of poverty in a capital-constrained world, they have extremely strong incentives to overcome these daunting barriers.

Another hidden advantage of energy efficiency in a technologically dynamic world is that it buys time. Time can be used to develop and deploy better technologies for both supply and demand. The former type of progress, of which we have lately seen dramatic examples (such as the 40 percent cost reduction in the technology used to bring in Royal Dutch/Shell's Kittiwake oilfield in the North Sea[50]), stretches supply curves, expands reserves, and slows depletion. This yields more time in which to deploy efficiency, which has similar effects. Both kinds of progress reduce real resource costs, freeing capital for more productive investment elsewhere, while demand-side efficiency gains reduce sensitivity to supply costs. Buying time and using it to advantage for developing and deploying better technologies, taken together, thus make many problems recede into the future, or disappear altogether.

Whose development path?

The deeper question of whether energy must, may, or should constrain development cannot be addressed in isolation from what kind of development is contemplated, by and for whom, chosen how and by whom. These questions in turn rest on still deeper questions of social purpose.

Consider, for example, the data shown in Table 2 on Danish patterns of primary energy use for heating and cooking over five centuries. If, looking at the last three lines, one made a facile identification of energy use with well-being, one would then have to conclude that Danes have only recently regained the standard of living that they enjoyed in the Middle Ages. What actually happened was that in 1500 and 1800, Danes burned a lot of wood

TABLE 2   Average per capita primary energy used in Denmark for heating and cooking

Year	kW
Ca. 1500	0.9–1.9
1800	0.9
1900	0.4
1950	0.9
1975	2.3

SOURCE: "Energy in Denmark 1990–2005: A case study," Report No. 7, Survey by the Work Group of the International Federation of Institutes for Advanced Study, c/o Sven Bjørnholm, Niels Bohr Institutet, København, September 1987; units converted from the original Ggcal/y.

and peat in very inefficient open fires, similar to the situation in many developing countries today;[51] by 1800, more Danes were burning wood in fairly efficient wood and ceramic stoves; by 1900, they burned mainly coal in very efficient stoves, and in 1950, mainly oil (incurring refinery losses) in fairly inefficient furnaces. By 1975, they had added the Carnot and grid losses of expanded electrification. This example shows that simply equating energy use with social benefits telescopes together several distinct relationships that are best kept separate, namely: how much primary fuel is fed into the energy system does not determine how much useful energy is supplied—the latter depends on the system's conversion efficiency; how much useful energy is supplied does not determine how much service is performed—the latter depends on end-use efficiency; and how much service is provided does not determine whether what was done with the energy was worth doing. This last question is a very important one, although it is normally considered to lie outside the scope of energy policy.

Mimicry of traditional development paths via normal industrialization ignores both industrialized countries' mistakes and developing countries' new opportunities. It is by no means clear that industrial countries' development path must, even if it can, be repeated by other countries striving for similar material wealth. Hong Kong and Singapore have parlayed skilled, well-educated, hardworking people into a global economic force without any significant heavy industry; they simply earn enough to buy materials and manufactures from abroad, much as do many American communities or states (e.g., Vermont) or even sizable "industrialized" countries (e.g., Denmark). To be sure, heavy industries no longer competitive or attractive in the "advanced" countries are moving offshore to other countries desperate for any kind of investment; but it is not at all obvious that such low-value-added enterprises are advantageous to those countries either.

The technologies that can create wealth today are very different, and generally far less materials- and more information-intensive, than they were when the industrialized countries built their infrastructure. No sensible country today, building an urban sanitary system from scratch, would build Western-style sewers and treatment plants; if it used flush toilets at all (rather than advanced composters), it would probably do better with ones five or more times as water-efficient,[52] feeding into relatively localized biological wastewater-treatment systems.[53] No sensible country would imitate Los Angeles's car dependence or its freeway system, together with their costs, fuel-intensity, and smog; instead, it would encourage people to live near where they want to be, work nearer home, telecommute more, and use sophisticated public transport.[54] No sensible country would try to extend electric grids into rural areas when, even competing with cheap US grid power, the breakeven distance to the grid, beyond which it is cheaper to use photovoltaics and superefficient appliances, is already typically less than 400 meters and falling fast. Such examples are almost endless. In short, much of the money- and resource-intensive infrastructure that is commonly thought of as central to development is in fact obsolete—unable to compete with newer, smarter ways to do the same thing better.

By a happy coincidence, at a time when many countries are seeking to develop on the strength of few resources other than people and sunlight, the combination of very efficient energy use with advances in many kinds of solar technologies is bringing modern energy services within economic reach.[55] This is a pattern of "ecodevelopment" that integrates energy, water, waste, food, and other services at a village scale, providing a sound alternative to migrating to urban slums.

The very assumption that development requires large increments of certain basic-materials industries' capacity (the most energy-intensive kind[56])—whether in one's own country or elsewhere—is itself up for review. US steel consumption per dollar of GNP is now below its 1860 level and falling; Americans still use steel, but much less of it,[57] and the same is true for virtually all basic materials. Does a country that builds with local materials[58] need many cement plants? Does one that jumps straight to advanced materials need much steel? Does one that "goes electronic" early need much paper? Does one that makes an *ab initio* commitment to product longevity, recycling, reuse, remanufacture, scrap recovery, near-net-shape processing, and limited packaging need so much of *any* kind of material to maintain an ample stock (not flow) of material artifacts? What are the industrial underpinnings required for systematic "ecodevelopment" on a national or regional scale? Nobody knows, but certainly the answer will be very different from what many industrialized countries require today.

The steady rise of the ethic of "voluntary simplicity" in the richest countries suggests that the heretical question—"How much is enough?"[59]—

will be asked with ever greater force as "economic growth and technical achievement, the greatest triumphs of our epoch of history, [show] . . . themselves to be inadequate sources for collective contentment and hope."[60] The frequently observed correlation between outward wealth and inner poverty[61] bespeaks what may prove to be an unexpected flexibility in rich countries' demand patterns as social values undergo rapid evolution. As global communications undercut solipsism and cultural arrogance, it is becoming easier to appreciate the wisdom of other cultures and of the lesson in Gandhiji's reply, when asked what he thought of American civilization: "I think it would be a very good idea." A renascence of religious values, too, is making many question an economy that treats means as ends and that places goods above people—one in which, as Lewis Mumford caustically observes,[62]

> All but one of [the seven deadly] . . . sins, sloth, was transformed into a positive virtue. Greed, avarice, envy, gluttony, luxury, and pride were the driving forces of the new economy. . . . Goals and ends capable of working an inner transformation were obsolete: mechanical expansion itself had become the supreme goal.

In short, the response to the morbid social conditions, the alienation and rootlessness, the lack of balance and rhythm that trouble so many thoughtful observers in the West will go far toward determining development patterns in industrialized countries in the decades ahead, and the patterns followed by their emulators. Should policymakers choose a path that measures success not by the rate of growth in consuming goods and services, but rather by the achievement of human satisfaction, joy, and inward growth with a minimum of consumption—the crux of E. F. Schumacher's classic essay on Buddhist economics—then the effect on the energy and the industrial activity needed to live a good life would probably far outweigh the structural and efficiency variations considered in most technical analyses. In short, we know next to nothing about the industrial structure of right livelihood, and it is long past time we started finding out.

As biological paradigms belatedly start to augment or supplant those based on physics and engineering, it is becoming more obvious that single-minded pursuit of efficiency generally sacrifices resilience—an attribute far more vital for survival. Most forms of "modern" development transfer risk to those who would be better off without it: traditional forms of "insurance," conservative decisional processes, diversity, buffer stocks, and safety margins are eroded in the name of more efficient production. The increasing fragility of overcentralized, overengineered, overspecialized economies[63] is leading many to look at more subtly sophisticated cultures with new respect. Two lessons stand out here. First, among the most critical issues of social, economic, and technical design (as Schumacher rightly emphasized) is appropriate scale.[64] Second, biological wisdom—the design experience reflected in whatever has survived several billion years of trial and error—is usually more valuable than the intuition of commercial expedience. Those prone to presume that a bird in the hand is worth two in the bush should remember, as Paul Sears reminds us, that birds come in pairs and nest in bushes.

In particular, the failure of what Marie Antoinette might have called the "Let them eat croissance" distributional theory of economic growth, contrasted with the expanding success of such societies as Costa Rica, compels a fresh look at the importance of developing *people*, not economies. In unpublished research to which I attach considerable importance, Royal Dutch/Shell's strategic planning group in London, and the late London human-rights barrister Paul Sieghart, have found three indicators that are virtually perfect predictors of economic success (conventionally measured) across the entire range of developing countries: the health and education of the people ten years earlier; absence of subsidies to basic commodities; and adherence to basic human rights. This suggests that the basic-human-needs approach (as opposed to the trickle-down, capital-intensive industrial approach) already works—and that in some sense social efficiency is advanced by functioning markets not only in goods but also in ideas.

Conclusion

Energy need not constrain global development. But it may well do so, much more widely than it is doing at present, if some of our major institutions do not start practicing the economic rationality they preach. Moreover, there exist many other, more ineluctable, constraints on traditional industrialization.[65] These can be greatly mitigated by reforms that can and doubtless will occur—resource efficiency, waste minimization, phasing out of biocides, chlorine-free chemistry, and so on—but on present knowledge it appears that environmental and social constraints will cap classical industrial activity if nothing else does first. (This has indeed already occurred in many heavily industrialized regions.) These reflections should therefore be construed, not as a Micawberish exclamation that everything will turn out all right, but as a plea for rethinking the fundamentals of industrialization, of the development process, and of economic growth itself.

I am originally a physicist, not an economist, and despite my neoclassical perspective have some sympathy with the view that economists lie awake at night worrying about whether what works in practice can possibly work in theory. But the biggest evolution in my thinking over the 18 years since the first modern oil shock has been an increased respect for how well even very imperfect markets can work. Efficiency and renewables have swept the US energy market despite a formidable array of officially erected obstacles meant to achieve the opposite result. How much more could be accomplished if governments were to truly take markets seriously? My main residual concern here, beyond helping the market to work better (via better information, fair access to capital, real competition, etc.), is that amidst the dramatic global shift now under way toward market mechanisms, we not forget that markets are meant to be efficient, not fair; that while they can be superb short-term allocators of scarce resources,[66] there are many other important things that they do badly or were never designed to do; and that if markets do something good for whales or wilderness, for God or grandchildren, it is purely accidental.

My conclusions here will already have suggested to many readers a charming historical irony. In the day of *Limits to Growth*—a prescient work still maligned by those who have not read it or who missed its central message of the importance of adaptation—there were those whom many called "cornucopians" (such as John Maddox and Wilfrid Beckerman, among the forerunners of Julian Simon). The cornucopians said not to worry about the problems of population, resources, and environment; these would be solved, they said, by the intelligent application of advanced technology. Some of us, however, pointed out that technology, though no doubt very powerful, was not omnipotent, had costs, and often had side effects—what Garrett Hardin called "consequences we didn't think of, the existence of which we will deny as long as possible." For this caveat, we were derided as "technological pessimists"—not in James Branch Cabell's sense ("The optimist proclaims we live in the best of all possible worlds; the pessimist fears this is true"), but as ignoramuses denying the reality of technological progress.

Today, however, the former "technological pessimists" are pointing out that new technologies—albeit of a more mundane, vernacular, and "transparent" kind than those anticipated by the cornucopians, such as insulation rather than fusion reactors, and microelectronic motor controls rather than solar power satellites—have indeed proven far more powerful than anyone thought possible. These relatively small, accessible, and cheap technologies even seem powerful enough to solve the energy problem, the water problem, many strategic-minerals problems, and probably a good many other thorny problems such as agriculture and national security.[67] For saying this, we are berated by the former cornucopians, now turned "technological pessimists," who successively assert that our proposed technological innovations do not exist, or will not work, or are not cost-effective, or will not sell, or will not remain popular in the long run.[68] Thus the role reversal is complete. But it reminds us born-again technological optimists not to overlook—as our partners in this debate long did—the limits of technical fixes, the restricted relevance of markets to achieving justice, the ever-shifting tapestry of social values, the importance of surprises, and the inherent frailty of the human design.

Notes

The author gratefully acknowledges the valuable suggestions on content and structure by Bill Freudenberg and L. Hunter Lovins.

1 "Artifacts" here includes physical circumstances such as the maintenance of comfort or illuminance or the provision of mobility.

2 Herman Daly and Nicholas Georgescu-Roegen make explicit this often overlooked concept that "throughput" measures only the negentropic *flow* of resources from depletion to pollution. For any desired level of the *stock* of material artifacts, this flow can be *minimized* by a further set of technological choices, including product longevity, materials efficiency in design and manufacturing, and resource recovery. We shall return to this important issue below.

3 Throughout this article costs of saved energy are calculated in 1986 US$ levelized at a real discount rate of 5 percent per year. They equal the installed capital cost of an efficiency improvement (adjusted for any concomitant change in its present-valued operating and maintenance costs), amortized over the discounted stream of energy savings resulting during the device's operating lifetime.

4 This potential is exhaustively documented by the technical reports of Rocky Mountain Institute's COMPETITEK update service, currently provided to more than 190 subscribers (chiefly electric utilities and governments) in 31 countries. The application of those technical and economic data to a practical case is illustrated by RMI's June 1988 analysis *Negawatts for Arkansas* (Publication #U88-30, Vol. I). No interfuel substitution (e.g., of gas for electricity) is assumed here, although it is often worthwhile. See also A. Fickett, C. Gellings, and A. Lovins, "Efficient use of electricity," *Scientific American* (September 1990): 64–74.

5 Amory B. Lovins, "Drill rigs and battleships are the answer! (but what was the question?)," in Robert G. Reed III and Feridun Fesharaki (eds.), *The Oil Market in the 1990s: Challenges for the New Era* (Boulder: Westview, 1989), pp. 83–138. Modest gas-for-oil substitution is assumed here, but only where the gas has also been saved; indeed, saved gas equivalent to 20 percent of total oil consumption is left over. No interfuel or intermodal substitution is assumed in the transport sector, nor any light-vehicle efficiency improvements with marginal costs exceeding zero.

6 Saving energy is like eating a lobster: if, having eaten the big, obvious chunks of meat in the tail and front claws, one discards the rest, one is losing a roughly equal quantity of tasty morsels that must be dug out of individual crevices.

7 E.g., in RMI's 1989 analysis of motor systems (see note 4), of the 35 main classes of measures analyzed, only seven need to be paid for; the other 28 are free side effects of those seven, if one understands the whole system well enough to capture and take credit for them.

8 Throughout this article, I adopt the motives, methods, and criteria of orthodox neoclassical economics, and conclude that saving energy will generally be desirable because it is Pareto-optimal. One could, but I do not, reach the same conclusion by many other routes, such as ethical concern about people (and other beings) in other times and places, or a desire to achieve social goals with an elegant frugality of effort. For present purposes, my approach is that of a pure free-marketeer shopping for "technical fixes." In effect, I assume a goal of fueling indiscriminate industrialization at minimum private internal cost, with no changes in where or how we live or how we run our society. Readers who prefer other goals, or who feel that prevalent values or institutions are in any way imperfect, are welcome to assume instead some mixture of technical and social change; this would only make a low-energy future easier to achieve.

9 One GW, or 1,000 megawatts, or 1 million kilowatts, is the nominal electric output capacity of a single giant power station.

10 Specifically, when its peak load was 14 GW, Southern California Edison (SCE) was reducing its long-term forecast peak by nearly 1.2 GW/y—about 45 percent through its own programs, costing 0.3¢/kW-h for efficiency and $30-odd/peak kW for load management, and about 55 percent through state programs, such as the Title 24 building code, which cost

the utility nothing. Absent that state action, SCE could have achieved similar results at costs ranging from zero (for sliding-scale hookup fees replacing building codes) to roughly 0.6¢/kW-h (for seller rebates replacing appliance standards). The average of these costs to the utility would have been approximately 0.1–0.2¢/kW-h. The corresponding cost to society, including participating customers' contributions, would have been severalfold larger, but still less than 1¢/kW-h.

11 During 1979–85, more new US capacity was ordered from small hydro plants and windpower than from coal and nuclear plants, not counting their cancellations, which collectively exceeded 100 GW. At the time, all these options enjoyed significant subsidies, though those to the renewables were probably smaller per unit of energy supplied: see H. Richard Heede, "A preliminary analysis of federal energy subsidies in FY 1984," Rocky Mountain Institute (RMI) Publication #CS85-7, 1985, summarized in H.R. Heede and A.B. Lovins, "Hiding the true cost of energy sources," *Wall Street Journal*, p. 28, 17 September 1985, RMI Publication #CS85-22.

12 Because the dispersed investments are small, modular, and relatively cheap, and have very short lead times, fast paybacks, and high velocity of cashflow. They thus avoid playing "You Bet Your Company" that demand forecasts a decade ahead will be accurate enough to ensure amortization of a multi-billion-dollar central station.

13 Most, though not all, of the proposals could be relied upon to produce actual, reliable capacity if accepted; many utilities have also found that private cogeneration is typically more reliable than their own central plants.

14 The first step in the supply curve—the roughly 92 percent potential saving in lighting energy, displacing about 120 GW of US generating capacity—has a negative cost (which balances the positive cost of subsequent steps up to around 50 percent total savings). This is because the efficient new lighting equipment often lasts longer (or less of it is needed) than the inefficient equipment which it replaces— to the extent that the new equipment more than pays for itself by avoided customer maintenance cost, making its electrical savings bet-

ter than free (by about $30 billion a year). See Amory B. Lovins and Robert Sardinsky, *The State of the Art: Lighting*, RMI/COMPETITEK, March 1988. Indeed, the horizontal axis of Figure One therein should be labeled sales, not consumption; Amory B. Lovins, *The State of the Art: Drive-power*, RMI/COMPETITEK, May 1989, found additional off-the-grid consumption by utilities and self-generators, but it was nearly all for drivepower and, if shown, would be roughly half offset by an increase in the drivepower savings potential shown.

15 The initial increment of savings is the displacement of oil- and gas-fired electricity by efficient lighting equipment (see note 14).

16 These methods are described in detail in RMI's COMPETITEK series of Implementation Papers, and briefly summarized in the paper cited in note 66.

17 In the form of any combination of financing, information, design services, project management, equipment, installation, operation, and monitoring. A utility that sells such elements can, but need not, bill the results according to the energy services delivered.

18 Thomas Edison sold light, not kW-h; New York Edison Company wished to do the opposite. Edison was overruled in 1892, and the industry has been making the same mistake ever since.

19 Amory B. Lovins, "Energy strategy: The road not taken?," *Foreign Affairs* 55, no. 1 (October 1976): 65–96; the concept was later clarified, and the term "least-cost" introduced, in a series of pioneering quantitative analyses by my colleague Roger Sant. Interestingly, while the "soft path" diagram in the *Foreign Affairs* article was meant to be illustrative, not a forecast, it accurately represents actual renewable supply in 1988 (a fourth of the way through the half-century shown), and shows total energy demand 12–14 percent above actual.

20 Similarly, President Carter's solar tax credits rewarded effort rather than success— they rewarded people for spending money, not for saving or supplying energy—and most of the rent was captured by the vendors. The credits therefore produced charlatans, preserved the uncompetitive at the expense of

the honest and clever, and removed incentives to cut costs. Waiting for the credits to be implemented destroyed roughly half the solar industry; their removal eliminated most of the other half by drying up distribution channels for many viable products. Unfortunately, Congress scrapped the credits rather than fixing them—even though it retained, and even increased, most of the larger subsidies given throughout to competing energy forms, leaving the playing field even less level than before.

21 For example, electricity was 11 times more heavily subsidized per unit of energy supplied than were direct fuels; nuclear power was about 80 times more heavily subsidized than were efficiency improvements and nonhydroelectric renewable sources; and the subsidies per unit of energy supplied were at least 200 times as great for nuclear power as for efficiency.

22 See note 11. Heede's far more detailed final report is to be published by RMI in 1991–92.

23 Chiefly by removing most subsidies for efficiency and renewables. But other policy actions are expanding the damage. In 1988, e.g., nuclear power was offered a new, roughly $9 billion, subsidy in the form of a writeoff of enrichment debts. The US Department of Energy had ignored warnings—among others, by me when I served on the Department's senior advisory board in 1980–81—that those debts would prove unpayable.

24 Among the most recent examples are the dismantling of most enforcement of coal-stripping restoration rules, the pervasive lack of monitoring of Arctic oil operations (especially with regard to pollution, e.g. by drilling muds), and numerous nuclear problems, such as the late-1988 removal of promised funding for Nevada's independent assessment of nuclear waste-disposal operations. The major national environmental groups have thoroughly documented dozens of such issues.

25 This is still going on, e.g., in the Department of Energy's proposed rules on appliance standards. The proposed Building Energy Performance Standards (a national energy building code) was made voluntary rather than mandatory, and even the voluntary residential standards were never issued.

Congress established in 1980 a Conservation and Solar Bank to finance the best buys, but abandoned it after seven years of administration stonewalling.

26 "Wasted" in the sense that it is used, instead of being displaced by cheaper efficiency options now commercially available and practically applicable and deliverable for doing the same task.

27 The equivalent waste in each subsequent year is probably even larger.

28 Together, in unknown degree, with the simultaneous 70 percent cutback in the print run of the government's *Gas Mileage Guide,* so that two-thirds of new-car buyers could not get a copy.

29 The pervasive self-deception involved in promoting the latter sector is discussed in Amory B. Lovins, "The origins of the nuclear power fiasco," *Energy Policy Studies* 3 (1986): 7–34, RMI Publication #E86-29.

30 Heede, cited in note 11.

31 This is fallacious because of the opportunity cost of buying any option costlier than efficiency. Because nuclear power (for example) costs much more on the margin than efficiency does, it can displace proportionately less coal-fired electricity per dollar invested. Buying nuclear power instead of efficiency thus makes global warming worse. It is not very practical in any case: William N. Keepin and Gregory Kats, "Greenhouse warming: Comparative analysis of nuclear and efficiency abatement strategies," *Energy Policy* 16, no. 6 (December 1988): 538–561 and "Global warning," *Science* 241 (1988): 1027; A.B. Lovins, "Energy options," *Science* 242 (6 January 1989): 348.

32 And cheaper still to deliver efficiency by the many proven methods that share the cost between the energy vendor and the customer: electric utilities' rebates, for example, typically pay about 15 percent of the cost, while the customer puts up the remaining 85 percent in the expectation of avoiding the retail tariff.

33 For example, *Negawatts for Arkansas* (cited in note 4) found in that state a full technical potential to save roughly $5–7 billion (1986 net present value) against an avoidable short-run marginal cost of only 2¢/kW-h.

34 Including electric savings a third as big (26 percent) and several times as costly as RMI has estimated as being presently available. The study is H. Geller et al., *Acid Rain and Electricity Conservation*, American Council for an Energy-Efficient Economy, Washington D.C., 1987.

35 The oxygen, of course, is already in the air; the carbon released weighs 2/7 as much as the CO_2. For a full explication of this thesis, see A.B. and L.H. Lovins, *Least-Cost Climatic Stabilization*, RMI, 1991.

36 Amory B. Lovins, L. Hunter Lovins, and L. Ross, "Nuclear power and nuclear bombs," *Foreign Affairs* 58, no. 5 (Summer 1980): 1137–1177; A.B. and L.H. Lovins, *Energy/War: Breaking the Nuclear Link* (New York: Harper and Row Colophon, 1980); Patrick O'Heffernan, L.H. and A.B. Lovins, *The First Nuclear World War* (New York: W.W. Norton, 1983), RMI Publication #S83-14.

37 A.B. and L.H. Lovins, *Brittle Power: Energy Strategy for National Security* (originally written for the US Defense Civil Preparedness Agency), Brick House, Andover MA, 1982, summarized in "The fragility of domestic energy," *The Atlantic* 252, no. 5 (November 1983): 118–126, RMI Publication #S83-8. See also more broadly RMI's *Energy Security Reader*, 2nd ed. (an anthology including many papers cited here), Publication #S88-45, October 1988.

38 See note 5; A.B. and L.H. Lovins, "The avoidable oil crisis," *The Atlantic* 260, no. 6 (December 1987): 22–30, RMI Publication #S87-25, and letters, id. 261, no. 4 (April 1988): 10–11 and 261, no. 6 (June 1988): 10–12, RMI Publication #S88-15; and "Oil-risk insurance: Choosing the best buy," *GAO Journal* (US General Accounting Office, Washington, D.C.) (Summer 1988): 52–60, RMI Publication #S88-26.

39 Each cent per kilowatt-hour is equivalent in heat content to oil at $17 per barrel; so typical US retail electricity costs about seven times as much per unit of heat contained as does current world-market oil.

40 At least in function if not in outward appearance: Switzerland, for example, has some 1,200 utilities, mostly very small distribution companies, but capital allocation to the Swiss electric industry is chiefly made by a few people in a handful of large generating companies.

41 Niels I. Meyer, personal communication, 23 November 1988. Nørgård's calculation does not include space heating or commercial lighting. Including them should make his result similar or more favorable, since space heating, though a relatively costly saving, is a small term, while commercial lighting savings are a large term with a strongly negative net cost.

42 An important new class of technologies. Their spectrally selective thin-film coatings and special gas fillings make them insulate 2–4 times as well as triple glazing; they cost about the same, passively keep buildings cooler in summer and warmer in winter, and pay back in about 2–3 years. They are equivalent just in US oil- and gas-saving potential to one Alaska (at the lower insulating value, namely twice triple glazing, or twice that much at the higher value). Simple versions recently captured most of the US insulated-glass market within just a few years.

43 Because the cooling equipment is probably less efficient and less well maintained to start with, and Thailand's climate and average building size are more favorable for such shell measures.

44 For further references, see Amory B. Lovins, "End-use/least-cost energy strategies," invited paper, World Energy Conference (Montreal), September 1989, Paper 2.3.1.

45 A Soviet energy economist who has recently launched a for-profit cooperative selling energy-efficiency services in Moscow reports that energy prices are about a third of actual cost, but that efficiency is also roughly three times worse than in the West, so the economics of saving energy work out about the same.

46 José Goldemberg, Thomas B. Johansson, Amulya K.N Reddy, and Robert H. Williams, *Energy for a Sustainable World* (Washington, D.C.: World Resources Institute, 1987).

47 Amory B. and L. Hunter Lovins, Florentin Krause, and Wilfrid Bach, *Least-Cost Energy: Solving the CO_2 Problem* (Andover, Mass.: Brick House, 1981) and 2nd ed., Rocky Mountain Institute, April 1989; summarized

in *Climatic Change* 4 (1982): 217–220, RMI Publication #E82-2. Recalculating the results with today's efficiency technologies would yield more favorable results, i.e., slightly larger savings at much lower costs—lower by a factor greater than the concomitant decline in real energy prices.

48 Birgit Bodlund, Evan Mills, Tomas Karlsson, and Thomas B. Johansson, "The challenge of choices: Technology options for the Swedish electricity sector," pp. 883–947 in Thomas B. Johansson, Birgit Bodlund, and Robert H. Williams (eds.), *Electricity: Efficient End-Use and New Generation Technologies, and Their Planning Implications* (Lund University Press, 1989).

49 The International Foundation for the Survival and Development of Humanity (Moscow and Washington, D.C.) has recently proposed, however, an ambitious effort to establish a global network of developing country centers of excellence in energy efficiency.

50 When it was sought to bring in the field at costs implying a retail crude-oil price of around $20/bbl, Shell planners, seeing the 1986 crash coming, said the project would not be pursued unless the price could be cut to $12/bbl. The engineers at first said this would be impossible. It took them a year to do. Apparently they had previously been told only to bring in new fields as quickly as possible, with cost as no object. This time, they were asked to bring in a field as cheaply as possible, even if it took a little longer—so they invented a completely different design approach. In how many other supply technologies have we gotten the wrong answer by assigning the wrong task?

51 This, the real energy crisis for approximately one billion people, is conceptually similar to the energy problems of industrialized countries, but overlain by a different set of cultural complications, many related to the role of women in traditional societies. Some "technical fixes" are available (better stoves and cooking-pots, fuel crops, etc.), but a more comprehensive approach can address the fuelwood *and* oil problems rather than substituting one for another; Amulya K.N. Reddy (Indian Institute of Science, Bangalore) does this with a multistage fuel-substitution program for India, summarized in Jim Harding et al., *Tools for the Soft Path* (San Francisco: Friends of the Earth, 1982), pp. 232–233.

52 See RMI's *Catalog of Water-Efficient Technologies for the Urban/Residential Sector,* Publication #W87-30, 1988, or 2nd ed., in press, 1991.

53 Such as those now being commercialized by John Todd and colleagues at Four Elements Corporation (Falmouth, MA), which use a sophisticated greenhouse-enclosed "swamp" to turn raw sewage into ultrapure polished drinking water, crops, and flowers, with no hazard, no odor, and a third the capital cost of a chemical-based plant.

54 Perhaps such as the brilliant bus-system innovations developed by Jaime Lerner in Brazil. These include, for example, a curbside "boarding pod"—a transparent plastic cyclinder closed at one end. It fills up with passengers who pay their fare as they enter the other end. A bus pulls up alongside; large matching doors open in bus and pod, both of which have the same floor level; and *once a minute* (at rush hour) this cycle is repeated. This system alone nearly trebled density, to an astonishing 12,000–18,000 passengers per corridor per hour, at an unsubsidized cost of 10¢/ride.

55 Surprisingly, this is also true even in the most industrialized, densely populated, cold, and cloudy countries. In terms of renewable energy, as my analyses have found since 1972, Japan probably has the most—and the most clearly ample—supply options of any major OECD country.

56 Table 1's exegesis. But this too is a function of technology. As Ernie Robertson (then at the Biomass Institute in Winnipeg) once remarked, there are three ways to make limestone into a structural material: (a) Cut it into blocks. This is not very interesting. (b) Bake it at thousands of degress into Portland cement. That is inelegant. (c) Feed chips of it to a chicken. Twelve hours later it emerges as eggshell, several times stronger than Portland cement. Evidently the chicken knows something we don't about ambient-temperature technology.

57 This is also true per capita: during 1975–84 alone, per-capita consumption of steel fell by 11.5 percent, paralleling a trend in many other countries, both industrialized

(U.K.–32 percent, Sweden–43 percent, etc.) and developing (Brazil–40 percent, Argentina–46 percent, Philippines–50 percent, etc.). This is partly because of increased net imports of steel-intensive products such as cars, but also in substantial part because of, e.g., lighter-weight cars. The US National Academy of Engineering published analyses of the "dematerialization" of the US economy as a shift to services combines with more materials-efficient design, manufacturing, and resource recovery.

58 The many advantages of adobe, rammed earth, caliche, and so forth are now being rediscovered in even the most advanced countries—e.g., through the work of Pliny Fisk in Austin and Hassan Fathy in Egypt, and by Indian and Iranian pioneers of fired-ceramic buildings.

59 Or, more formally, "Is the net marginal utility of increased GNP positive, and if so, to whom and for how long?"

60 Robert Heilbroner.

61 This is hardly a new theme. *Ecclesiastes* 5:9–12 remarks: "Moreover the profit of the earth is for all: the king himself is served by the field. He that loveth silver shall not be satisfied with silver, nor he that loveth abundance with increase: this is also vanity. When goods increase, they are increased that eat them: and what good is there to the owners thereof, saving the beholding of them with their eyes? The sleep of a laboring man is sweet, whether he eat little or much; but the abundance of the rich will not suffer him to sleep."

62 In *The Transformations of Man* (New York: Harper, 1956).

63 See *Brittle Power*, cited in note 37, esp. Chapter 13, on the design principles of resilience.

64 *Id.* at Appendix One, which analyzes roughly 50 effects of scale on the economics of energy systems.

65 For an early but still largely applicable survey, see Amory B. Lovins, "Long-term constraints on human activity," *Environmental Conservation* (Geneva) 3, no. 1 (Spring 1976): 3–14.

66 So long as we bear clearly in mind that market costs and prices are neither revealed truth nor, per se, a meaningful test of desirable behavior, because they depend largely on tacit accounting and philosophical conventions—such as whether depletable resources are valued at extraction cost or at long-run replacement cost. For a discussion of new ways to enable consumers to act upon proper price signals for depletion and pollution, by converting their potential loss into another actor's profit, see Amory B. Lovins, "Making markets in resource efficiency," RMI Publication #E89-27, June 1989.

67 See M. Shuman, H. Harvey, and D. Arbess, *Alternative Security: Beyond the Controlled Arms Race* (New York: Hill and Wang, in press).

68 The last of these responses—the only one left now that the others have proven groundless—is essentially a theological argument that cannot be settled on its technical merits. It dominates much of today's energy policy debate, in the superficially plausible form, "We must buy more power plants in case people don't go on buying efficiency as consistently as they have so far." Of course, buying the plants creates strong economic incentives (at least for top-line thinkers) to sell more energy, not less.

Land Use, Migration, and Natural Resource Deterioration: The Experience of Guatemala and the Sudan

RICHARD E. BILSBORROW
PAMELA F. DeLARGY

MANY ENVIRONMENTAL PROBLEMS, INCLUDING ELIMINATION of tropical forests, desertification, and reductions in biodiversity, are most clearly evident in the Third World. While rapid population growth is often considered an important factor in this environmental degradation, solid empirical evidence on its role is almost nonexistent. Understanding the effects of population on the environment requires careful consideration of the full range of factors responsible for environmental deterioration and of how they interact with demographic factors. The nature of this relationship is heavily determined by land use patterns and agricultural policies adopted by governments. This essay describes some of the relationships between population growth, migration, and natural resources with reference to agricultural practices in two very different less developed countries, Guatemala and the Sudan.

Migration and the environment

Most studies linking population factors and the environment focus on the impact of population growth on resource use. While population size and growth rates are important determinants of resource use, population movements also affect, and are affected by, the natural environment.

There is little research directly linking migration to environmental degradation.[1] While international migration is also important, the focus of the discussion below is on internal rural-to-urban migration and its significant impact on the environment in developing countries. Migration is defined here as a change of residence involving movement both across an administrative border (as defined in the country) and simultaneously from a rural to an urban area (again, as defined in the country). It must be noted, however, that rural-to-rural population movements continue to be extremely important (particularly in countries where most of the population lives in rural areas, as throughout sub-Saharan Africa), albeit neglected in the literature, and that urban-to-urban population movements are increasingly dominant where most of the population already resides in urban areas, as in most of Latin America.

Table 1 shows that the proportion of the world's population living in urban areas is expected to continue to increase and to exceed 50 percent around the year 2000. Shortly thereafter, urbanization in the Third World will also surpass 50 percent. Already the proportion urban in Latin America is well beyond that and, indeed, comparable to levels in the more developed regions (two-thirds urban). The pace or rate of urbanization has already passed its peak and is declining in much of Latin America, the Middle East, and parts of Asia, simply because the cities themselves have become large relative to the rural populations from which net migrants can be drawn. On the other hand, in most of sub-Saharan Africa and South Asia, the pace of urbanization is accelerating, a trend that is likely to exacerbate the urban environmental problems already existing in those parts of the world characterized by especially low per capita incomes and urban poverty.

In the most simplistic sense, internal migration is a redistribution of inhabitants that alters the population density of different areas within a country. In the present context, migration is seen as a fundamental factor determining population distribution and, hence, resource use.[2] Population redistribution has important benefits in many situations, including creating a more efficient distribution of human capital and facilitating economies of scale in the provision of public services and infrastructure. Increasing rural population density, whether from natural population increase or inmigration, may also promote agricultural intensification (Boserup, 1965; Bilsborrow, 1987). Whether this is sufficient to increase agricultural production per capita depends on the circumstances, but it is hard to conceive of this as being generally likely in most contemporary Third World areas, given both prevailing high population density (as in much of Asia) and low levels of income, which make the adoption of new agricultural methods (embodying expensive inputs) difficult to achieve and far from automatic.

The argument of classical economists is that higher population density with fixed technology results in diminishing returns to labor. Increasing application of labor on a fixed amount of land eventually leads to decreasing levels of output per unit of input. The net effects of the struggle between diminishing returns to labor, Boserupian intensification, and changes in the natural productivity of the fixed resource (land) due to any environmental degradation (e.g., soil erosion) determine farm incomes and, hence, influence rural outmigration. Thus, if the net effects are negative, outmigration is likely to occur—to the extent conditions allow it. Moreover, such a re-

TABLE 1 Proportion of population urban, average rates of growth of rural and urban population, and rate of urbanization: Selected world regions and time periods

	1970–80				1990–2000				2010–20			
	Proportion urban	Rate of growth Rural	Rate of growth Urban	Rate of urbanization	Proportion urban	Rate of growth Rural	Rate of growth Urban	Rate of urbanization	Proportion urban	Rate of growth Rural	Rate of growth Urban	Rate of urbanization
World total	38	1.5	2.5	0.7	44	0.8	2.4	0.9	55	−0.1	2.1	1.1
More developed regions	69	−0.3	1.3	0.5	74	−0.2	0.8	0.3	77	−0.2	0.5	0.2
Less developed regions	27	1.8	3.6	1.4	36	0.9	3.4	1.6	50	−0.1	2.7	1.4
Africa	24	2.2	4.6	1.8	36	2.0	4.8	1.8	49	1.1	3.7	1.4
East Africa	12	2.5	6.8	3.8	25	2.3	6.1	2.8	39	1.5	4.4	1.8
Latin America	61	0.3	3.7	1.3	75	0.1	2.6	0.7	82	−0.1	1.7	0.3
Central America	57	1.5	4.1	1.2	68	0.7	2.9	0.7	76	0.0	2.0	0.5
Asia	25	1.8	3.2	1.0	32	0.7	3.0	1.6	46	−0.4	2.5	1.6
South Asia	23	1.8	4.1	1.7	33	0.8	3.7	1.9	48	−0.3	2.8	1.5

NOTES: Rates of growth are in percent per year. Rate of urbanization is the percentage rate of change in the proportion of population urban.
SOURCE: United Nations, 1988: Tables 74–75.

sponse is likely even if per capita incomes are maintained or increased, to the extent income levels per person in other areas of the country rise faster, widening the typical rural–urban gap in income and living levels. The extent of rural-to-urban migration also depends on the degree to which rural families are aware of differences in opportunities; on the availability, accessibility, and size of urban areas that can absorb potential migrants; and on the extent to which urban areas grow economically, providing increasing employment opportunities.

But there are other ways to look at the process. With more people, the increased demand for food results in increased competition for arable land, tending to change land prices. In the common situation in which farmers with small plots have much less access to credit and new technology than those with large plots, this may result over time in a smaller proportion of the rural population owning land, smaller average size of plots for the majority of small farmers who continue to own land, and an increase in the average size of large farms. This process of increasing socioeconomic differentiation has been well documented in Latin America and may be occurring in Africa and Asia as well. In addition to such an indirect process working through economic factors, demographic factors are also important. An increase in population in a closed community with privatized landholdings often causes average plot sizes to decline over time because of subdivision among heirs, making an increasing proportion of the small plots too small to sustain larger families. As a result, some sell off their land to survive, resulting in increasing landlessness.[3] Intensification of land use and changing landownership patterns may precipitate a number of responses at the household level. One is a shift from traditional to nontraditional crops on small plots (such as shifting from food grains to cash crops).[4] A second response is a shift from crops to livestock, which has been observed on larger plots, both in traditional areas of population concentration and in new areas of tropical forest lowlands, particularly in Latin America. In forest lowlands, the sequence has often been for small farmers to move into an area, clear part of the forest, plant crops for a few years until the soil is depleted, and then abandon the land or switch to raising animals, which requires a much larger cleared area to sustain a family. Alternatively, the land is cleared and (ironically) increased in value; wealthier farmers move in and buy up the land. (Regarding the Brazilian Amazon, see Goodland, 1988.)

A third response is recourse to local off-farm employment. If available, such employment can provide a supplemental source of income while the family continues to grow food for its basic needs. The land provides a form of basic security or insurance, while off-farm employment provides cash for additional consumption needs.

A fourth response is for one or more members of the household, often an older son or male household head, to migrate seasonally to earn income to help sustain the family in the community of origin. Seasonal employment may be rural, such as work on a sugar or cotton plantation at the time of planting or harvest, or urban, such as construction work. This pattern is very common in parts of Africa.

A fifth response, which is more disruptive to the traditional way of life of the household and therefore may be a last resort, is for the whole family to move, either to new agricultural lands or to urban areas, both of which have environmental effects. Rural-to-rural migration generally involves clearing and deforestation of new (usually marginal) areas, drainage of wetlands, or use of steep slopes to expand agricultural production.[5]

Collectively, these alternative responses of small farmers constitute a peasant "household survival strategy." Which response or combinations of responses occur is a function of natural conditions and the existing socioeconomic and institutional structure. Government policies play a critical role in determining which type of response is likely. For example, if food prices are kept low by price-fixing and subsidies, then rural outmigration is likely to occur. But if food prices are allowed to increase as a result of growing demands for food, rural incomes rise, the rural–urban income gap declines, and rural-to-urban migration declines. Some governments attempt to control migration (through such programs as Indonesia's transmigration scheme or Tanzania's *ujamaa* program), but few are successful (exceptions include socialist countries using direct controls, such as ration cards and employment assignments).

The nature of the relationship between migration and the environment varies greatly across developing countries, as countries differ in natural resources and climate, level of development, government policies, social institutions, and customs. But the two country examples described below—Guatemala and Sudan—show that similar patterns occur in very different settings.

Deforestation in Guatemala

In the past two decades, population growth in Guatemala (as elsewhere in Latin America) has been close to 3 percent per year. The total population now surpasses 9 million. Despite rapid rural-to-urban migration, impelled by insurgency in the countryside and by the more general factors of wide rural–urban income gaps and land inequality, the proportion of the population urban is still only one-third, relatively low for Latin America (see Table 1). Rural population density increased from 1.8 to 2.3 persons per hectare of agricultural land, while land in agriculture grew by only 1.2 percent per year between the last two agricultural censuses in 1964 and 1979. Labor productivity (value added per agricultural worker) remained constant between

1970 and 1985 (SEGEPLAN, 1987). Total agricultural production grew by 4.6 percent in the 1970s but not at all in the 1980s. This was also true of food production, with the result that per capita food production fell by nearly one-fifth during the 1980s. The consequences are increased food imports and food insecurity.

Government policies stimulating the production of export cash crops to provide foreign exchange to service the growing foreign debt have undoubtedly contributed to the food production problem. Additionally, extremely inegalitarian land distribution is a direct cause of rural poverty (Brockett, 1988). If poverty is defined as not having sufficient family income to meet minimum needs for food, shelter, and clothing, then 84 percent of the rural population of Guatemala lived in poverty in 1980. While this was the highest percentage in Central America, over 66 percent of the rural population in all countries of the region except Costa Rica were estimated to be living in poverty in that year (Peek, 1986).

We examined past population trends and prepared population projections for Guatemala to assess the extent to which major problems of the rural population, including environmental stress, are likely to be exacerbated by population growth and migration patterns. We made two projections, starting from a total fertility rate (TFR) of 6.0 in 1980 (observed rate), falling slowly to 4.8 in the year 2030 in the high projection and to 2.0 (essentially replacement fertility) in the low projection (details in Stupp and Bilsborrow, 1989). Life expectancy and the proportion urban were assumed to rise equally in the two scenarios, with the latter rising from 33 percent in 1980 to 45 percent in the year 2000 and 68 percent by 2030. The total population rises rapidly in either case, reaching 24 million in the low run and 37 million in the high. We now consider the likely effects of these two alternative future population growth scenarios on the size of landholdings, land distribution, rural labor demand, rural outmigration, and the environment.

Land distribution and land fragmentation

Out of a total national territory of 10.8 million hectares in Guatemala, some 5.2 million hectares, or 48 percent, is classified as suitable for agriculture. Of this, 4.4 million, or 85 percent, was already in farms in 1979, although only about half of that was actually in use. Land is distributed extremely unequally in Guatemala, probably more so than anywhere else in Latin America. For example, in 1979 farms with less than 1.5 hectares accounted for 60 percent of all farms[6] but had less than 4 percent of the land, while 2 percent of the farms with over 35 hectares had 67 percent of the land. We now examine briefly what happened between the two agricultural census years of 1964 and 1979. First, in all regions most new farmland was concentrated in the largest (35+ hectare) size category. Furthermore, such land was mainly in the northern, semitropical forest region of the Petén (by far the largest of the three *departamentos* comprising the Norte region), which accounted for 76 percent of new farmland. At the same time, most new farms that came into existence between 1964 and 1979 were concentrated in the smallest (less than 1.5 hectare) size category: below-subsistence farms accounted for 60 percent of all farms in Guatemala in 1979, up from 44 percent in 1964. Also, the average size of the under–1.5 hectare holdings nationwide declined from 0.7 to 0.45 hectare between 1964 and 1979. This suggests increasing fragmentation of land by subdivision among heirs.[7] Continuing population growth is likely to continue to swell the number of below-subsistence farms, leading to increasing impoverishment of the rural population. This in turn contributes to rural outmigration.

Rural employment adequacy

The rural employment problem in Guatemala is severe. We know from studies by SEGEPLAN (1986) and Banco de Guatemala that the intensity of labor use per unit of land is much greater on smaller farms. On farms of less than 1.5 hectares, 0.48 full-time-equivalent persons were employed per ha. per year ("full-time" defined as working 150 days/yr). In the 1.5–3.5 hectare category, 0.25 full-time persons were employed per ha. The 3.5–35 and 35 + hectare farms employed considerably less labor per unit of land in use, specifically 0.13 and 0.10 persons/ha./yr.

The number of full-time farm workers that could be absorbed at the intensities of labor use prevailing in 1979 was 690,000. That there was already considerable underemployment in agriculture is seen by comparing this with the estimated agricultural labor force in 1980 (1.12 million). The ratio of these two figures provides an "employment adequacy ratio" (a better term than underemployment, we feel) of only 0.62.

We now compare the projected size of the future agricultural labor force with the employment that would be provided under two scenarios of labor intensity. We first project employment by expanding land in use at a rate of 1.2 percent per year (the rate prevailing between 1964 and 1979), but keeping the average intensity of labor use per unit of land constant at the 1979 national average of 0.15 persons/ha. All potential agricultural land is then in use by 2030.[8] In the second scenario, we again assume land in use increases, but also that average labor intensity grows over time to a level of 0.25 persons per ha., the labor intensity on 1.5–3.5 ha. farms in 1979. Under this latter scenario (a possible government goal, if the seriousness of the rural employment problem were recognized), the gap between available employment and labor force size under the low fertility assumption narrows after 2010, with the employment adequacy ratio rising to 0.86. But with high fertility, the employment adequacy ratio rises only to 0.66, even with the substantially increased labor intensity.

The implication is that bringing more land into production (including tropical forest land) will not alleviate the rural employment problem unless land is used at significantly higher levels of labor intensity and labor force growth is slowed by lower (rural) fertility. Regarding the first point, most agricultural research has focused on increasing yields through technologies that require *less* labor per unit of land, not more. The continuing substantial rate of growth of tractorization in Guatemala (and most other developing countries) in recent decades also suggests that rural employment absorption will become an increasing problem, contributing to even higher rates of rural outmigration in the future.

Environmental deterioration

We have seen that rural population growth is resulting in growing land fragmentation, rural underemployment, and outmigration. What impact do these trends have on the environment? The major forms of environmental deterioration associated with population growth and urbanization in Guatemala include deforestation, soil degradation, watershed destruction, and urban encroachment on prime agricultural land. Figure 1 shows the areas of Guatemala with heavy forest cover in 1950 and 1985. By comparing *munici-*

FIGURE 1   Forest cover in Guatemala, 1950 and 1985

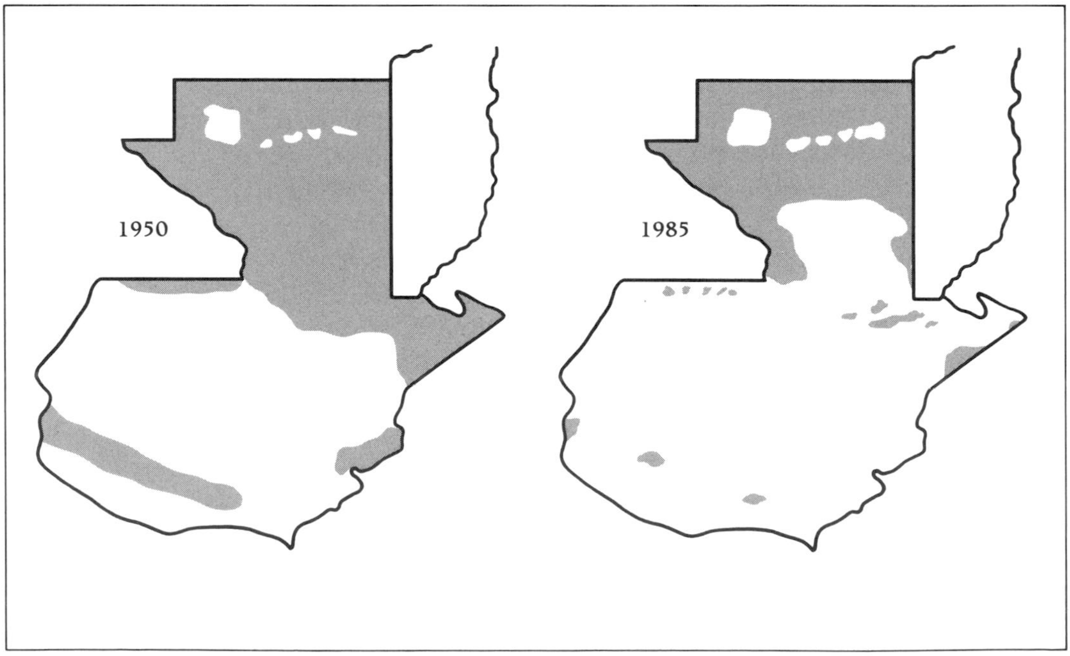

SOURCE: Leonard, 1987.

pio (district) data on population density and percent of land area in forests
from population and agricultural censuses between 1950 and 1981 (the latest population census), and on the basis of field visits to a sample of 40 rural
municipios, Mendez (1988) finds forest cover strongly inversely correlated
with population density.

Between 1960 and 1981, some 43 percent of Guatemala's 1950 forested
area was lost. Practically no forests exist now except in the northern Petén,
where the agricultural frontier is pushing further north each year (SEGE-
PLAN, 1986: 214). While some of the larger, mature trees are floated (generally illegally) downriver westward into Mexico from the northern Petén and
sold commercially, the main cause of deforestation is not the timber industry but clearing of land for agriculture, cattle ranching, and fuelwood.
(Wood provides over 90 percent of the energy of rural households.) The ad-
vancement of the agricultural frontier into the northern semitropical forest
has been aided by the penetration of roads and the lack of enforcement of
government laws forbidding the felling of trees on the vast public forest
lands.[9]

It is illuminating to compare this process of deforestation with data on
migration flows by region and *departamento* (state) since the first modern
population census in Guatemala in 1950. As the population of Guatemala
has grown at about 3 percent for over 30 years, it is now about 250 percent
greater than its 1950 level. Particularly during 1950–70 population distribution shifted from the densely populated rural highlands toward Guatemala
City, the eastern lowlands, and the Pacific coast. Of the three *departamentos* in
the sparsely populated, forested northern region, only the northernmost
and largest, the Petén, experienced net inmigration during this period. But
inmigration to the Petén accelerated starting in the late 1960s. The percentage of (lifetime) inmigrants was one-fourth in 1950 and over half by 1973.
The absolute number of net inmigrants in 1973 was 32,000, seven times that
of 1964, and this doubled again by 1981. The net intercensal inmigration
rate to the Petén was only 17 percent in 1950–64, but 47 percent in 1964–73
and 49 percent in 1973–81 (SEGEPLAN, 1986: 36), and the annual rate of
population growth varied from 4.3 to 18.7 percent during 1973–81. This
process appears to have continued throughout the 1980s. (The next census
will not be carried out until at least 1992.)

The clearing of new land for agricultural use is a response to pressures
on the land, increasing land fragmentation, and the lack of adequate off-
farm rural employment opportunities, especially in the densely populated
highlands and the eastern lowlands. Indeed, in the latter, inappropriate
marginal land is being used increasingly for agriculture as population pressure rises and the agricultural frontier advances (USAID, 1987). Figure 2
identifies regions of the country where it is likely that marginal land is being
used for agriculture, with resulting environmental destruction. It shows that
the proportion of land classified as "appropriate for agriculture" already

FIGURE 2   Percent of land appropriate for agriculture already in farms: Guatemala, 1979

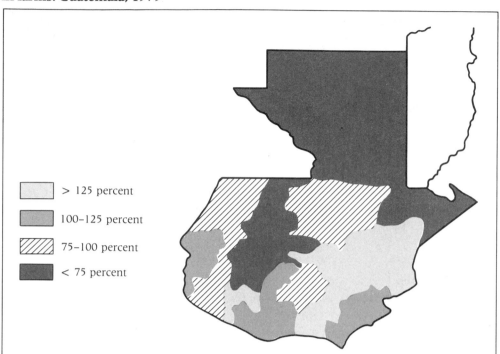

> 125 percent

100–125 percent

75–100 percent

< 75 percent

SOURCE: USAID, 1987.

used in farming in 1979 was well over 100 percent in each department in the eastern region, as well as along the Pacific coast, where together about half the total rural population lives. As we indicated earlier, only 48 percent of the total land area is appropriate for agriculture. Therefore, whenever the proportion of land in farms exceeds 100 percent, it is likely that inappropriate marginal land is used in farms. One consequence may be that the eastern region and Pacific coast are the two areas providing the largest numbers of direct migrants to the Petén—26 percent and 39 percent, respectively, according to the 1981 census (SEGEPLAN, 1986: 56).

In Figure 3, we consider four other forms of rural environmental degradation and depletion of renewable natural resources. Each is related to the pressure of population growth and distribution on resources, whether through exploitation of areas characterized by fragile soils and low carrying capacity or through diversion to other uses of land appropriate for agriculture. The loss of agricultural land to urban areas is primarily an issue in the region surrounding Guatemala City, about two-thirds of whose growth in recent decades has been due to high rates of natural increase and one-third to net inmigration (United Nations, 1980). In every decade since 1950, the

**FIGURE 3   Location of four types of environmental damage:
Guatemala, 1981**

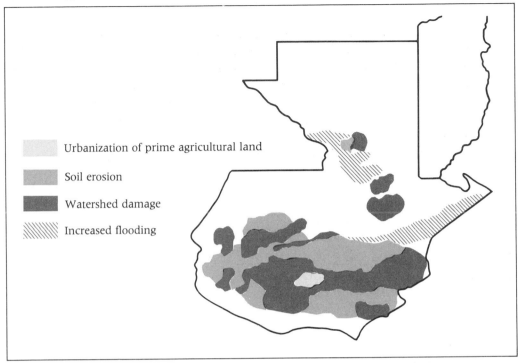

SOURCE: Leonard, 1987.

municipio in which Guatemala City is located received the largest number of inmigrants.

Soil erosion is a much more widespread problem. Deforestation reduces moisture retention, especially in highland areas, leading to erosion. The problem is greatest on the Pacific slopes because the topsoil is thin and there are concentrated periods of rainfall. Nevertheless, extensive erosion also occurs in the western highlands, with topsoil losses of 5–35 tons/hectare per year in some places (Leonard, 1987). Another cause of soil loss is the abandonment of ancient Indian practices of terracing and contour planting. Exploitation of lowland areas of inferior quality, characterized by shallow, lateritic soils that can sustain agriculture for only a few years, also results in soil degradation, as in the Petén.

Two additional environmental problems are water-related—watershed damage and increased flooding. Both occur widely on the Pacific slopes and in large areas of the Caribbean basin (Motagua River), and are now even seen in the Petén. Every major watershed on the Pacific side of the country has been denuded of vegetation and now suffers from erosion, flooding, and sedimentation of rivers (Leonard, 1987). Sedimentation is also occurring in major rivers and dams supplying water for Guatemala City. Rapid river runoff has reduced replenishment of groundwater, the major water source for Guatemala City.

To confront the increasingly serious environmental problems in Guatemala, a variety of policy interventions appear warranted, including the provision of family planning services (particularly in underserved rural areas), land redistribution, and price and technology policies to stimulate agricultural production and raise rural family incomes and labor absorption. Finally, policies are also necessary to deal more directly with increasing deforestation and soil erosion, including farmer education programs and stricter enforcement of existing legislation banning unauthorized tree cutting.

Desertification in the Sudan

Perhaps the only positive result of the recent famines in the Sudan and elsewhere in sub-Saharan Africa has been to shock donors and governments into paying greater attention to the role of renewable resources in development. Much has been published on the causes and consequences of these droughts and famines. Sindiga (1984) and Talbot (1986) found that rapid population growth of the pastoralist Maasai and inmigration of sedentary farmers increased land conflicts between the two groups and led to overgrazing and soil and water exhaustion of Maasai lands. Government policies of restricting rangelands to create tourist-attracting national parks exacerbated the problem. In studies spanning two decades in Meru district, Kenya, Bernard (1988) observed that increasing population density in fertile highland areas, road construction, and government policies promoting privatization led to (a) deforestation and resulting soil erosion on the rich, volcanic soil slopes and (b) a decrease in fallow periods on nearby poor-soil lowland areas that traditionally had been used for grazing, resulting in soil degradation and desertification. In this section, we look at interrelationships between population growth, environmental degradation, and migration in the Sudan, the largest country in Africa.

Sudan, roughly the size of the United States east of the Mississippi, had a population of about 21 million at the 1983 census, resulting in one of the lowest average population densities in the world—6 persons per km². This number is deceptive, though, since much of the country is arid, and population distribution is largely determined by availability of water. The area between the White and Blue Nile Rivers near their junction is the Gezira—which contains the world's largest agricultural project, an irrigated cotton scheme begun in the 1920s that remains the heart of the Sudanese economy. Modern agricultural development is heavily concentrated near the Nile and its tributaries, but there is increasing investment in mechanized agriculture on the wide plains of the savanna belt, where rainfed production is possible. It is in these latter areas, however—in Darfur and Kordofan in the west and the Eastern and Red Sea provinces in the east—that the recent famine was most severe and environmental degradation appears most pronounced. There are clear patterns of desertification, deforestation, and erosion due to increasing human and animal populations and to agricultural practices—both traditional and modern—that "mine" the vulnerable sandy and clay soils for short-term gain, leaving them unable to regenerate (Ibrahim, 1984).

The Sudanese population is largely rural and settled, but an estimated 11 percent is nomadic, and about 20 percent reside in urban areas. Urbanization has been increasing rapidly, particularly since the 1984–85 famine, and the primacy of the three-city capital area, with over 3 million people, is pronounced. Population growth exceeds 3 percent annually, the total fertility rate is around 7, and life expectancy at birth is below 50 years. Literacy is very low: 28 percent for men and 6 percent for women, with great regional disparities (e.g., 58 percent in Khartoum province versus 4 percent in the southern province of Bahr El Ghazal).

Besides nomadism, other forms of migration are significant: seasonal labor migrants number over one million—predominantly male migrants from subsistence farms in the west, who travel to the large agricultural schemes in the east.[10] A large proportion of the population is seminomadic, engaging in shifting cultivation and herding. Rural-to-urban migration is also high, with most families having one or more members working in a city.[11] Environmental degradation and drought have made it impossible for many rural families to survive by animal husbandry and cultivation alone, so it is common for some family members to engage in wage employment, either in urban areas or on large farms, at some point during the year (El Sammani et al., 1986). A high rate of emigration of semiskilled, skilled, and professional workers to the Persian Gulf and other Arab states is producing serious shortages of educated labor in some sectors, but remittances—over US$3 billion in 1984–85, equivalent to 40 percent of official GDP—are crucial to the economy. Finally, Sudan is host to a million political refugees from Ethiopia, Uganda, and Chad, which further contributes to fuelwood depletion.

Sudan provides a sharp contrast to Guatemala culturally, economically, and geographically, but patterns of natural resource degradation are depressingly similar. Sudan has a variety of ecological settings—from desert to tropical rainforest—with a concomitant variety of land use patterns and problems. Geographically (and culturally), the country can be seen as a microcosm of Africa. Sudan has some distinctive problems, but the major economic and environmental ones are found in most other African countries as well.

First, although extremely good rains led to an excellent year for agriculture in 1988, there has been a general decline in agricultural (especially food) production per capita over the past 15 years despite large increases in land used for agriculture. Many factors have contributed: climate change, increasing inability of farmers to purchase agricultural inputs, declines in soil productivity, and expansion of cropping onto marginal lands. The 1984–85 famine resulted not only from the well-publicized failure of rains but also from environmental degradation. Government attempts to increase cash crop production have included clearing land for huge mechanized schemes to grow millet, sorghum, or groundnuts; and expanding the irrigated sector to increase cotton exports. Both strategies have proved harmful to the environment, partly due to poor planning and management.

Second, increasing numbers of people and animals and the expansion of agriculture have placed stress on rangelands. The development of new water sources has altered nomadic patterns and resulted in concentrated areas of land degradation.

Third, deforestation has become a serious problem, because energy demands for wood and charcoal have increased and land has been cleared for agriculture and settlement. The decline in tree and bush cover reduced soil productivity and promoted erosion.

Finally, desertification has resulted from deforestation and removal of ground cover. In areas nearest the desert, this has involved expansion of dunes; in other regions, it resulted in denuded land and declining soil fertility. Deforestation is driven by both clearing of land for agriculture and use of wood for fuel. Expansion of cultivation onto marginal land is partly due to population growth and declining yields in existing fields (owing to soil depletion, erosion, and salinization). But a critical factor has been agricultural policy. Cultivators and pastoralists have been pushed onto marginal lands by the expansion of rainfed, mechanized, and irrigated agriculture designed to increase food and export crop production.

One region where these patterns have been well documented is Darfur, the country's westernmost province, an arid area of highly variable rainfall and traditional mixed subsistence cultivation and pastoralism. Pastoralism is well suited to areas of variable rainfall because grazing routes make efficient use of scarce water and vegetation. Herds follow rains at calculated intervals, allowing vegetation to replenish itself each year. Sedentary animal husbandry, in contrast, by using the same land year-round, does not allow for soil replenishment. As the population has grown in Darfur, palatable grasses have virtually disappeared in areas of sedentary livestock-raising (Ibrahim, 1984). Settlements are always built around secure sources of water, and the many boreholes dug in the 1960s and 1970s during the national campaign to provide water to all became centers of settlement. From the air, one now sees desertification rings around each of them.

Previous patterns of shifting cultivation are also giving way to large agricultural projects, which involve completely clearing large areas of all trees and vegetation, leaving bare, vulnerable soil. Topsoil is scratched and loosened during planting and weeding and then exposed for 8–10 months between rains. Some of this soil is blown into the atmosphere, contributing to the increased levels of atmospheric dust.[12] Many of the large agricultural projects in Darfur, as well as farmers on smallholdings who have gone into cash cropping, raise millet. Recent studies have shown that productivity of many fields has declined significantly in the past 30 years.

Traditionally, local farmers planted a variety of crops that responded to different rain and temperature conditions to insure that, no matter what the rainfall level, some crops would survive. This pattern of risk aversion does not produce the highest yields in good rain years but does provide some food in dry years. Since over the past two decades half of the years were dry, multicropping—even if yields are low—seems a reasonable practice. The move toward "modern" agriculture—monocropping of millet—in the region has resulted in less food security for many farmers. It is estimated that a family of six consumes about 1500 kg of grain per year and so must cultivate at least 15 hectares to guarantee subsistence. The population of the region has grown tenfold since the beginning of the century, and the animal population has increased dramatically over the last 40 years as well. This, combined with the expansion of commercial farms, has put stress on the cultivable land. A family rarely has access to 15 hectares for growing millet (most have to use some land for animals, vegetables, etc.). The result is chronic undernourishment. In dry years, cultivated areas are expanded to try to meet food needs, resulting in even greater competition between farmers and nomads. Fallow periods have shortened as pressures to produce crops have increased. Indeed, the majority of farmers engage in permanent cultivation without any fallow. The traditional system of rotating crops and fallowing has thus been abandoned and a chain of land degradation has begun. Population increase and the entry of farmers into the cash market have led to excessive cultivation, which, in turn, has led to soil erosion and impoverishment. Millet yields decreased by 50 percent from 1965 to 1980. At the same time, the area cultivated with millet increased from 392,000 hectares in 1960 to 1,055,000 in 1975, bringing fresh waves of desertification and pushing the pastoralists ever northward, where they have overgrazed the grasslands (Ibrahim, 1984).

Overgrazing is a problem in the whole of northern Sudan. Because of improved veterinary care and increasing demand for meat, herds expanded dramatically from the 1940s to the 1980s. The number of livestock (cattle, goats, sheep, and camels) quadrupled from 1956 to 1966, and by 1974 there were over 40 million head. Although herds were increasing, the amount of grazing land did not expand, so the carrying capacity of rangelands decreased due to overgrazing and replacement of perennial grasses by less palatable annuals. The annuals are more conducive to brush fires, which consume about 15 percent of the natural fodder in the savanna belt each year.[13] These patterns set the stage for disaster when the rains failed in 1983, 1984, and 1985. Large numbers of livestock died in the 1984 drought. Thousands of pastoralists and rural farmers subsequently migrated to urban areas, where food was more plentiful. As a first response, men went to work as wage laborers, leaving families behind. The first waves of migrants to regional towns placed burdens on the local resources, such as fuelwood, water, and food. Relief supplies of food eventually arrived, but there was no relief for the natural environment. Deforestation intensified during the drought, and rapidly growing towns began to experience fuel shortages and increased prices as food and fuel had to come from further and further away. Later, as conditions in rural areas became more desperate, wage earners increasingly tried their luck in the capital. As livestock was sold to buy grain or died off, and crops failed, women and children eventually were also forced to migrate to regional towns and the capital where food was available. Many have not returned to rural areas, so the capital has grown enormously since the drought. The expansion of squatter settlements and crowding of other neighborhoods have put such stress on transport networks and municipal services that city services have virtually collapsed. Pollution and sanitation problems are ubiquitous. The government is encouraging people to return to rural areas, which have improved due to a few years of good rains, but many poorer farmers have already given up their land and have little to return to.

A study by Tully (1985) of the Masalit in western Darfur documents the increasing difficulties of maintaining families and communities. Traditionally, the Masalit would farm an area of land until productivity declined and then move on to establish a new community. A mix of herding and farming provided flexibility and resilience in case of drought. During a period of good rainfall beginning in the 1930s, herds expanded and the population grew through natural increase and inmigration. Farmers began to grow crops for the market. When the drought began in the 1970s, the area under cultivation was increased, and people consumed their savings. They also began to overexploit the forests through intensive hunting and gathering. To save their animals, they concentrated around secure water sources. Those who had to moved to towns to seek wage income. These were "normal" responses and had occurred in the past for brief periods. But the survival strategies that had worked in the past—expanding cultivation and forest use—had now been exhausted. Many went to towns, and, as the rains failed again and again, the degradation of land around towns and waterholes intensified. The consumption of wood for cooking and other uses led to the destruction of forests near towns. Game and wild fruit became scarce. The larger area cultivated and grazed, and the reduced forest cover, increased wind erosion. Lack of vegetation caused rains to run off the land

and increased gullying. Family members migrated to other agricultural areas to seek work, but this alleviated the problem only temporarily.

The pressures of market production, higher urban consumption levels, and rural population densities resulted in the more intense use of land and the expansion of cultivation onto unsuitable lands—both of which resulted in degradation.

Temporary male migration to seek work has long been common among the Masalit, but Galal-el-Din (1978) documents that net outmigration quadrupled from the 1950s to the 1970s. In the sample villages in Dar Masalit, Tully (1985) finds that among men aged 31–40, 100 percent had emigrated at least once, many citing land shortages as a motivating factor. The migrants, most of whom went to work on mechanized farms in eastern Sudan, normally were unable to help their families with remittances but sometimes brought clothing or tools back with them. Although traditionally only men had migrated, in the late 1970s women and families began to move, too. Some went to nearby richer agricultural areas—Kordofan or Southern Darfur—and others crossed the country to eastern Sudan, where prices were higher for crops and lower for consumer goods. There are few firm data on the fate of the Masalit during the drought and famine of the early 1980s, but it seems clear that outmigration increased tremendously—first to other agricultural areas in search of employment, and then to towns and cities in search of food.

The eastern savanna is also experiencing environmental degradation because of both population growth and inappropriate agricultural practices associated with mechanization. Rainfed mechanized farming was once considered the hope of development for the Sudan. It began in the 1940s when the British were concerned with feeding their troops in east Africa and increased at an annual compound growth rate of 21 percent from 1946 to 1976 (Affan, 1982). Millions of dollars were invested by the wealthy Arab states in sorghum, groundnut, and sesame schemes across the savanna belt, but particularly in the eastern region, in the 1960s and 1970s. Sudan was intended to become the "breadbasket of the Middle East," providing food security to the Arab world. This money was followed by large loans to local investors by the World Bank and other lenders, and the area under cultivation in this region expanded dramatically to cover 4 million acres by 1976—or 27 percent of the total land under cultivation in the country. Mechanization seemed a useful way to expand production and increase yields on the broad plains. Tractors could break up the heavy, clay soil, and wage laborers could do the planting, weeding, and harvesting. In the short term, this provided employment for many workers at good wages and increased production of crops dramatically. The planning of the farms led to problems, however. Low-interest loans were given to owners (who actually only rented the land at very low cost from the government), and the use of machinery was subsidized. Owners, often urban merchants, exploited the lands for maximum production (and profits), leaving no fallow time and providing no modern inputs. The result was rapidly declining yields and land degradation. So much land was available that owners found it easier to "use up" one area and then rent another rather than to conserve the land. One OXFAM report on mechanized farming in the area calls it "environmental hit-and-run."

The social implications of mechanized farming were negative as well. Family farmers were forced off their land to make way for the mechanized farms, and though some found wage employment the living standards of many others declined. Modern farms were primarily owned by urbanites, and the profits from them went back to the city, so the infrastructure and services of the region were not improved. The farms also blocked traditional nomadic grazing paths and increased conflicts between nomads and farmers. The use of savanna land for cultivation meant that herders were forced to intensify grazing in the marginal areas because they had to stay there year-round. This, in combination with the increase in human and animal populations, led to desertification patterns in the east similar to those in Darfur and Kordofan in the west.

Landless farmers settled in towns that grew at a rapid rate and that also serve as centers for Ethiopian refugee settlement, since they are near the border. The population of Gedaref, a major town in the east, grew from 17,537 in 1956 to 70,355 in 1970, 122,000 in 1976, and over 200,000 people in the late 1980s. In a study of wage workers in Gedaref in 1982, only 11 percent reported being born in the region (ILO/UNHCR, 1984). Gedaref is a crowded town with little sanitation, erratic electricity, and chronic water shortages. Social conflict between refugees and the various Sudanese ethnic groups is high, in part because of competition for employment on the large farms, which has depressed wages.

An accompanying problem throughout northern Sudan is deforestation due in part to the cutting of trees for fuel and building materials for the growing population. Nearly all rural households depend on wood for fuel. In Darfur, for example, the average consumption of wood per family is 50–70 kg a week. Over a year, it is estimated that a family uses about 195 trees and shrubs, but replanting is virtually nonexistent.

The implications of this wood use are severe. In 1980 the country consumed the energy equivalent of 7 million tons of oil. Eighty-five percent of this was in the form of wood and charcoal, 93 percent of which was consumed by households for cooking. Nine million tons of wood were cut and used directly; 16 million tons were made into charcoal. This means 70 million m^3 of wood were cut for energy use. In the north, 52 million m^3 were cut and only 15 million m^3 regenerated. Because of the scarcity and high cost of other energy sources, wood use is not expected to decrease. The country's National Energy Administration predicts that within ten years all of northern Sudan will lack wood for energy if forests are not actively regenerated. Thus, the cost of wood is expected to continue to increase, leaving the poorest without fuel.

Mukhtar (1982) estimated the average per capita consumption of fuelwood at 1.62m³ in 1962 and 2.00m³ in 1976. Estimates of urban consumption are as high as 2.8m³. With an increasing population and consumption per capita also rising due to urbanization, shortages of fuelwood will grow more serious. The average distance traveled to obtain wood increases constantly, adding additional burdens to already overworked women in rural areas and raising transport costs of fuelwood to urban areas. For example, the distance for transport of wood to Khartoum has increased from 5–10 km to as much as 200 km in the past two decades. The price of wood and charcoal has skyrocketed over the past ten years due largely to rising transport costs.

The rapid growth of Khartoum, although exacerbated by war displacement, is still largely fueled by migration from rural areas. Landless farmers have also settled in secondary towns, which are growing at about 7 percent per year.[14] This urbanization contributes to deforestation since urban industrial and service sectors use wood or coal as fuel. In 1984 total industrial fuelwood consumption in Khartoum province was almost 200,000 tons, double that of 1980 (Abdel Salaam, 1985).

Sudanese people have always been mobile, but most movement has been of pastoralists and seasonal migrants. The dramatic increase in "permanent" migration over the past 10–15 years is due to a number of factors—war, drought, poverty—but environmental degradation clearly plays an increasingly important role. The degradation is a result of both development policies and population growth. And, as in Guatemala, migration, especially to urban areas and marginal lands, has negative indirect and direct effects on the environment.

Conclusions

The increasing severity of environmental problems in the Third World is now widely recognized. Its causes are not well known, although continuing population growth and the nature of development are widely considered responsible. Clearly, far more and better data—and analyses of data to sort out underlying causes in particular ecological contexts—are needed.

In principle, the major forms of environmental damage now so widespread in the Third World—deforestation of tropical forests, desertification, and soil degradation—could be greatly alleviated by appropriate government policies and private practices. The literature is replete with recommendations to this effect, which often purport to show that neither population growth nor development (increased production) per se is a serious problem for the environment, since it is *possible* to improve standards of living while maintaining the environment. Ideally, political systems *could* be changed. But these are dreamers' "wish lists." While policy changes are desirable, one must consider realistically what is technically and financially feasible in most countries of the Third World. How can such countries implement policies to achieve permanent, "sustainable development," or increase production while maintaining the natural productive capacity and beauty of the world for future generations? Lowering population growth rates in the Third World would surely be beneficial for both the environment and the people, but wouldn't a slower expansion of per capita incomes and consumption in the industrialized countries make an even greater difference to the global environment? Over a quarter of the cultivable land in the Third World is currently used to grow crops for markets of the industrialized countries. Indeed, Third World agricultural exports have been increasing by 17 percent annually since the 1970s (often at low prices), while food imports have increased by about 20 percent per year (Vergopoulous, 1984). In the United States, fertilizer use per capita has increased fivefold since 1950. Most Third World countries do not have the economic resources to purchase fertilizer to restore the fertility of overused soils. Could not increased resource transfers to the Third World or even a restructuring of the global economy reduce the degradation of the environment associated with extreme poverty and ignorance?

Development and environmental protection policies need to change soon to reduce damage. Moreover, some forms of environmental degradation are irreversible: While some damaged land can be reforested or irrigated and fertilized to be agriculturally productive again, losses of topsoil and of species diversity are essentially permanent. Long-run policy changes are also needed. Policies to slow population growth, like other human resource development policies, have little effect in the short run but powerful effects in the long run on reducing the potential for environmental deterioration. Migration policies, particularly those regulating access to and exploitation of fragile lands, are important even in the short run. Slowing rural-to-urban migration is also critical to alleviating urban environmental problems.

The need to develop, to increase incomes and consumption, will continue to have priority over environmental protection because of massive poverty. Because this poverty is concentrated in the rural areas where most of the environmental damage in the Third World is occurring, assurance of development will continue to outweigh environmental considerations. With a clearer understanding of the environmental problems and their underlying causes, we can learn to recognize that environmental protection and economic development *can* be reconciled. But the concept that embodies both—sustainable development—should be linked to a slower-growing population.

Notes

1 In 1983 the United Nations organized two conferences, one on migration and the other on population and the environment, in preparation for the 1984 International Conference on Population in Mexico City. In neither volume are the linkages between migration and environmental degradation considered.

2 The inherent role of migration in development processes is widely recognized and embodied in economic models, such as Lewis (1954), and in empirical studies, such as Rodgers et al. (1978).

3 Brockett (1988) documents that the proportion landless of rural households in most countries of Central America, including Guatemala, is approximately one-fourth, and that this has increased in recent decades because of the combination of demographic pressures, increasing fragmentation, and export-oriented agricultural policies. Increasing landlessness is also occurring in parts of Asia and Africa.

4 The downside of such a shift from traditional food crops to horticulture in some highland communities in Guatemala is a decrease in the food security of small farmers, since they no longer produce their own food. While the value of the vegetables they produce is currently much higher than that of the corn and beans previously produced, they are now subject to the vagaries of the international market for their basic food needs and to exploitation by intermediaries. In Sudan, the shift to cash crops has also led to nutritional problems. Whereas farmers previously would have planted a mix of crops to ensure the harvest of some regardless of climate patterns during the growing season, dependence on one crop has increased their vulnerability to weather conditions.

5 Other induced responses neglected in this essay include (long-run) reductions in fertility and postponement of marriage (Davis, 1963; Bilsborrow, 1987). Our feeling, however, is that such purely demographic responses are less likely to occur in the usual Third World situation unless there are strong government policy efforts. Such efforts, of course, have been made in a number of countries—e.g., Mexico, Colombia, Tunisia, China.

6 Farms in the category of < 1.5 hectares are considered by the national planning organization (SEGEPLAN) as insufficient to support an average rural family.

7 Land inheritance practices apparently vary from one Indian/Ladino region/subculture of Guatemala to another, but land is usually divided either among all sons or among all children, ensuring fragmentation of existing farm plots unless children migrate away.

8 Thus, land reform/redistribution, as crucial as it would be for redistributing control over resources, reducing poverty and "buying time," is ultimately not sufficient in itself: fertility must also fall dramatically by 2030.

9 The National Forestry Institute was placed under the Ministry of Agriculture in 1988 in an attempt to improve the situation.

10 The return migration of workers from central agricultural and urban areas back to their homes in the west has introduced a number of nonindigenous diseases to the region, including tuberculosis, meningitis, malaria, and hepatitis.

11 In 1984–85 about a million persons—"environmental refugees"—migrated permanently from the west to the Khartoum area because of the drought. Also, about a million persons have migrated from the war-torn south to the Khartoum area. The rapid growth of the capital has resulted in large squatter settlements with few services, increasing strain on transportation systems and health services, high unemployment, and increasing crime. There are an estimated 20,000 "street children"—a phenomenon unheard of in Sudanese society ten years ago.

12 Thick dust storms, called "haboob," are common in the spring in northern Sudan; an estimated 200 million tons of fertile topsoil are blown from the Sahel into the atmosphere each year.

13 Another example of this occurs in the central region. In 1978 the Sudan Environment Conservation Society estimated the carrying capacity of the central region's grazing lands at 12 hectares per unit per year, which would mean that 800,000 animals could survive by grazing. If feed were augmented by

crop residues, an additional 1 million could be supported, totaling 1.8 million. That same year there were 5 million animals in the region. This is probably due to high demand for beef and lamb in urban areas in and near the region; urban consumption of beef per person is ten times that of rural consumption.

14 Barnes (1986) notes the effect of urban firewood demand on creating rings of deforestation of up to 100 km radius around many cities in sub-Saharan Africa.

References

Abdel Salaam, A. A. 1985. "Use of firewood in traditional industries: Khartoum province," *Energy News* (June).

Affan, Khalid. 1982. "Effects on aggregate peasant labour supply of rural–urban migration to mechanized farming. . . . " Ph.D. thesis, University of Sussex.

Barnes, Douglas. 1986. "Population growth and household energy in sub-Saharan Africa," PHN Technical Note 86-17. Washington, D.C.: World Bank.

Bernard, F. E. 1988. "Population growth and agricultural change in Meru district, Kenya," paper prepared for Population Growth and Agricultural Change in Africa Conference, University of Florida, Gainesville, 1–3 May.

Bilsborrow, Richard E. 1987. "Population pressures and agricultural development in developing countries: A conceptual framework and recent evidence," *World Development* 15, no. 2: 183–203.

———, Amarjit Oberai, and Guy Standing. 1984. *Migration Surveys in Low-Income Countries: Guidelines for Survey and Questionnaire Design.* London and Sydney: Croom-Helm, for the International Labour Office.

Boserup, Ester. 1965. *Conditions of Agricultural Growth: The Economics of Agrarian Change Under Population Pressure.* Chicago: Aldine.

Brockett, Charles D. 1988. *Land, Power, and Poverty: Agrarian Transformation and Political Conflict in Central America.* Boston, Mass.: Unwin Hyman.

Davis, Kingsley. 1963. "The theory of change and response in modern demographic history," *Population Index* 29, no. 4: 345–366.

DeJong, Gordon F., and Robert W. Gardner (eds.). 1981. *Migration Decision Making: Multidisciplinary Approaches to Microlevel Studies in Developed and Developing Countries.* New York: Pergamon Press.

El Sammani, M. O., et al. 1986. *Management Problems of Greater Khartoum.* Sudan: Institute of Environmental Studies, University of Khartoum.

Galal-el-Din, Mohamed. 1978. *Population Dynamics and Socioeconomic Development in Rural Sudan.* Sudan: Development Studies and Research Centre, University of Khartoum.

Goodland, R. J. A. 1988. "Environmental sustainability in economic development—with emphasis on Amazonia." Washington, D.C.: Biology Department and the Graduate Students' Committee on Human Values, the World Bank.

Ibrahim, Fouad. 1984. *Ecological Imbalance in the Republic of the Sudan—With Reference to Desertification in Darfur.* Bayreuther Geowissenschaftliche Arbeiten, Vol. 6, Bayreuth, Federal Republic of Germany.

ILO/UNHCR. 1984. *Labour Markets in the Sudan.* Geneva: International Labour Office.

Leonard, H. Jeffrey. 1987. *Natural Resources and Economic Development in Central America.* International Institute for Environment and Development. New Brunswick, N.J.: Transaction Books.

Lewis, W. A. 1954. "Development with unlimited supplies of labor," *The Manchester School of Economic and Social Studies* 22: 139–191.

Mendez Dominguez, Alfredo. 1988. *Population Growth, Land Scarcity, and Environmental Deterioration in Rural Guatemala.* Guatemala City: Universidad del Valle de Guatemala (unpublished manuscript).

Mukhtar, M. E. 1982. *Wood Fuel as a Source of Energy in Sudan.* Sudan: Forestry Administration, Government of Sudan.

Peek, Peter (ed.). 1986. *Rural Poverty in Central America: Causes and Policy Alternatives.* Geneva: International Labour Office (mimeograph).

Rodgers, Gerry, Mike Hopkins, and Rene Wery. 1978. *Population, Employment and Inequality: BACHUE-Philippines.* Saxon House, for the Interational Labour Office.

Secretaria General del Consejo Nacional de Planificación Económica (SEGEPLAN). 1986. *Migración interna y distribución geográfica de la población,* Serie Resultados No. 13. Guatemala.

———. 1987. *Agricultura, población y empleo en Guatemala,* Serie Resultados No. 5. Guatemala.

Sindiga, I. 1984. "Land and population problems in Kajiado and Narok, Kenya," *African Studies Review* 2, no. 1: 23–39.

Stupp, Paul W., and Richard E. Bilsborrow. 1989. "The effects of population growth on agriculture in Guatemala," paper presented at the Annual Meeting of the Population Association of America, Baltimore, 29 March–1 April.

Talbot, Lee M. 1986. "Demographic factors in resource depletion and environmental degradation in East African rangeland," *Population and Development Review* 12, no. 3 (September): 441–451.

Tully, Dennis. 1985. *Culture and Context in Sudan.* Albany: State University of New York Press.

United Nations. 1980. *Patterns of Urban and Rural Population Growth,* Population Studies No. 68. New York: United Nations Department of International Economic and Social Affairs.

———. 1988. *World Population Trends and Policies: 1987 Monitoring Report.* New York.

USAID/Guatemala. 1987. *Guatemala Agriculture Sector Review.* Guatemala City: US Agency for International Development.

Vergopoulous, K. 1984. "La crise alimentiere dans le tiers-monde," *Les temps modernes* (October).

World Urbanization in Perspective

IRA S. LOWRY

THE DISTINCTION BETWEEN URBAN AND RURAL COMMUNITIES and their ways of life is deeply imbedded in the world's folklore, literature, and social science. The scientific view of the difference is that urban populations cluster in larger groups and live at higher densities than rural populations, pursue different occupations, and develop a different outlook on life. Although urban/rural differences actually range along a continuum, the dichotomy is so convenient that it has been adopted as a statistical concept throughout the world. Rules of classification vary between nations, but it will do for now to define an "urban place" as any permanent settlement containing at least 2,000 people who are not engaged in agriculture and who live within easy walking distance of one another;[1] and a city as a similarly dense settlement with at least 100,000 inhabitants.

Cultural attitudes toward cities and urban life have been highly ambivalent. Although cities are often represented as the centers of civilization and the engines of economic progress, folklore and literature reveal a deep skepticism about urban values and the amenities of urban life. In our own time, urbanization is often represented as a vicious trend in human society, by both students of economic development and students of the environment. Thus, Michael Lipton, a British development economist, says:

> The most important class conflict in the poor countries of the world today is not between labour and capital. Nor is it between foreign and national interests. It is between the rural classes and the urban classes. The rural sector contains most of the poverty, and most of the low-cost sources of potential advance; but the urban sector contains most of the articulateness, organisation and power. So the urban classes have been able to "win" most of the rounds of the struggle with the countryside; but in doing so they have made the development process needlessly slow and unfair. (1977: 13)

And Lester Brown, Director of Worldwatch Institute, laments:

City dwellers—currently some 43 percent of the world's population—command a disproportionate share of society's fiscal and natural resources and create a disproportionate share of its wastes. Land and water scarcity, inefficient energy use and waste disposal, and the resulting problems of pollution all contribute to the escalating ecological and economic costs of supporting modern cities. (Brown and Jacobson, 1987: 6)

In this essay, I will argue that casting cities (or city dwellers) as the villains of the global morality play is at best a convenient shorthand, at worst seriously misleading. Most of the ills that are blamed on urbanization can be more accurately attributed to population growth, industrialization, and prosperity. Although these factors have in different ways encouraged urbanization, they would continue to cause economic dislocation and ecological disasters even if global urbanization were to halt or reverse.

Following this introduction, I offer a brief history of world urbanization since 1850, a convenient summary of the salient facts that provides a foundation for subsequent discussion. It particularly emphasizes three dimensions of urbanization: the growth of very large cities, the absolute increase in the urban population, and the balance between urban and rural inhabitants. Finally, it summarizes the prospects for the near future.

The third section of the essay reviews the demographic processes entailed in urbanization and urban growth—mainly natural increase and rural-to-urban migration. The lesson from this section is that, after a period of transition from a rural to an urban society, the rate of urban growth approaches the general rate of natural increase in that society. For the industrialized nations of Europe (including the Soviet Union), North America, and East Asia (e.g., Japan), the rates of both natural increase and urban growth are declining and will probably approach zero during the first half of the twenty-first century. The outcome for the rest of the world is less clear.

The fourth section of the essay investigates the factors affecting the distribution of population between rural and urban residence: the "degree of urbanization" or the "urban/rural balance." The sustainable degree of urbanization in a country is limited by the fact that some part of its population must produce food for all, and agriculture is essentially a rural activity. The national endowment of arable land, the size of the total population, and the available farming technology jointly determine how much of an agricultural surplus is available to support city dwellers. Some countries feed their urban populations with imported food, a durable arrangement only for those that are able to pay for the imports by exporting urban manufactures or services.

The fifth section considers the prospects of very large cities. Already, the world has at least six urbanized areas with over 10 million inhabitants, and the United Nations projects the emergence of at least another 24 places of that size by the year 2000. Some observers believe that economic and ecological limits to urban size will forestall this outcome. A review of the evidence reveals no substantial barriers to massive conurbations of 30 million inhabitants or more.

The last section explores the factual and logical connections between urbanization and (a) energy consumption and (b) environmental degradation. This section is rather speculative, because I only superficially understand the chemical and physical processes involved. It seems to me, however, that in an industrialized world, farmers are as profligate as city dwellers. The difficulty is not urbanization per se but the high-energy technology that supports high standards of living. Arcadian rustication is hardly the answer to our problems; technological progress may be.

World urbanization in modern times

Evidence of urban life can be found in the Near East as far back as 3,500 BC, but the world's population remained overwhelmingly rural and agricultural until the twentieth century. A review of the sparse and often ambiguous archeological and historical record (Grauman, 1976) indicates that the urban population fluctuated between 4 and 7 percent of total population from the beginning of the Christian era until about 1850. In that year, out of a world population of between 1.2 and 1.3 billion persons, about 80 million or 6.5 percent lived in urban places.

Although 80 million is a large number of people, they were dispersed over hundreds of urban places worldwide. In 1850, only three cities, London, Beijing, and Paris, had more than a million inhabitants; perhaps 110 cities had more than 100,000 inhabitants (Golden, 1981). Of the 25 largest cities, 11 were in Europe, 8 in East Asia, 4 in South Asia, and 2 in North America.

Over the next century, 1850–1950, the number of large cities in the world increased from 110 to 946, and the largest city's population increased from 2.3 million (London, 1850) to 12.3 million (New York, 1950). Moreover, for the first time in history there was a decided shift in the urban/rural balance; by 1950, 29 percent of the world's population lived in urban places and about 16 percent lived in cities of 100,000 or more.

Since 1950, world urbanization has been extremely rapid. Thanks to the efforts of the UN statistical agencies, the process is also well documented, despite problems of international comparability for statistical concepts and irregular or incomplete national censuses in various countries. Table 1 shows that the number of urban areas containing at least 100,000 inhabitants grew from 946 in 1950 to 1,773 in 1975. By the year 2000, the number of such places will probably double again, and about 400 of them will have at least one million inhabitants. Altogether, nearly half of the world's population in the year 2000 will probably live in urban areas and a fifth will live in places with more than a million inhabitants.

TABLE 1   Number of urban areas and total urban population by size of area: World, 1950–2000

Size of urban area (thousands)	Number of urban areas			Total urban population (millions)		
	1950	1975	2000	1950	1975	2000
16,000+	—	2	5	—	32.4	106.5
8,000–15,999	3	12	25	33.1	113.8	279.3
4,000–7,999	10	16	37	54.7	84.1	195.2
2,000–3,999	17	47	122	47.0	129.2	335.5
1,000–1,999	48	102	209	65.5	141.8	298.5
500–999	101	224	(a)	69.6	156.7	(b)
250–499	192	445	(a)	66.1	153.0	(b)
100–249	575	925	(a)	86.7	148.2	(b)
Other urban	(a)	(a)	(a)	312.7	602.0	1,638.7
Total, 1,000+	78	179	398	200.3	501.3	1,215.0
Total, all urban	946	1,773	—	735.4	1,561.2	2,853.7

NOTES: The urban places listed above are areas of dense contiguous settlement whose boundaries do not necessarily coincide with administrative boundaries; they usually include one or more cities and an urbanized fringe. Nations differ in their definitions of "urban"; those differences are reflected principally in the residual category, "Other urban." For the year 2000, the UN independently projected the total urban population of each country and the population of each city that had reached 500,000 inhabitants by 1980. Entries for the year 2000 thus do not include smaller places that might grow to a million or more by that year.
(a) Not separately enumerated. See Notes, above.
(b) Included in "Other urban."
SOURCES: UN-ESA, 1985a; UN-CHS, 1987. Entries for 1950 and 1975 are based on the UN's 1982 assessment; projections for the year 2000 are based on the 1984 assessment.

Table 2 provides detail for some 22 regions of the world at 25-year intervals between 1950 and 2025. Using each country's own definition of "urban" population, the United Nations expects 4.9 billion urban residents in the year 2025, or 60 percent of the projected world population. Only in Eastern Africa, China, and certain South Pacific islands do demographers expect a majority of the regional population to live in rural areas. At the other extreme, over 85 percent of the populations of Northern and Western Europe, South America, South Korea, and Australia-New Zealand are expected to live in urban places.

The projected levels of urbanization are, of course, speculative. They are essentially extrapolations of relative rates of urban and rural population growth in the recent past that do not consider the special circumstances of individual countries (UN-ESA, 1987: ch. 4). However, the UN's 1984 assessment of recent national censuses and other systematic population data indicated that in all regions of the western hemisphere and Europe, and also in Japan and Australia-New Zealand, urban residents were already a majority. Tropical Africa, China, and most of Asia were still predominantly rural. The already urbanized countries will surely remain so, but the future of coun-

TABLE 2   Estimates and projections of total and urban populations, by world region: 1950–2025

Population (millions) or percent

World region	1950 Total	1950 Urban	1950 Percent urban	1975 Total	1975 Urban	1975 Percent urban	2000 Total	2000 Urban	2000 Percent urban	2025 Total	2025 Urban	2025 Percent urban
Northern America	166	106	64	239	176	74	297	223	75	345	267	77
Caribbean	17	6	35	27	14	52	41	27	66	58	43	74
Central America	37	15	41	80	46	58	149	105	70	223	178	80
Tropical South America	86	31	36	175	107	61	301	239	79	429	370	86
Temperate South America	25	17	68	39	31	79	55	49	89	70	64	91
Northern and Western Europe	195	135	69	234	188	80	240	201	84	234	201	86
Eastern Europe	88	37	42	106	60	57	120	80	67	131	94	72
Soviet Union	180	71	39	253	152	60	315	222	70	368	273	74
Southern Europe	109	48	44	134	78	58	152	104	68	159	122	77
Western Asia	42	10	24	85	41	48	168	107	64	271	205	76
Northern Africa	52	15	29	94	36	38	176	89	51	261	172	66
Western Africa	65	7	11	123	24	20	277	97	35	558	300	54
Middle Africa	27	4	15	45	13	29	92	44	48	170	110	65
Eastern Africa	63	3	5	122	15	12	272	77	28	537	246	46
Southern Africa	17	7	41	29	14	48	55	33	60	91	67	74
China	555	61	11	927	187	20	1,256	315	25	1,475	645	44
Japan	84	42	50	112	84	75	130	101	78	132	106	80
Other East Asia	33	9	27	57	31	54	89	70	79	114	98	86
Southeastern Asia	182	27	15	324	71	22	520	184	35	688	374	54
Southern Asia	480	76	16	849	181	21	1,387	466	34	1,855	968	52
Australia–New Zealand	10	8	80	17	14	82	22	19	86	27	24	89
Melanesia–Micronesia–Polynesia	3	0	0	5	1	20	8	3	38	11	5	45
World total	2,516	734	29	4,076	1,564	38	6,122	2,844	46	8,206	4,932	60

NOTE: A list of countries composing each region is given in each source publication. Estimates and projections of urban population for each country are based on that country's definition of "urban."
SOURCES: UN-CHS, 1987: Annex Table 1; UN-ESA, 1987: Table 2. Entries are based on the UN's 1984 assessment.

tries that are still predominantly rural is cloudy. Their economic and political instability has in many cases resulted and could again result in civil war, mass starvation, or genocide.

The pace of urban growth

The acceleration of world urbanization since 1850 partly reflects a corresponding acceleration of world population growth; but urbanization is not merely an increase in the average density of human settlement. If the world's 5.2 billion people were evenly distributed over the global landmass, the uniform density would be only 0.4 person per hectare, a distinctly rural density as compared with 14 persons per hectare for large US cities and 160 for large Asian cities.

I know of no large area of human settlement where population density is nearly uniform. From earliest times, hunters, farmers, and fishermen have clustered at places particularly suitable for making a living or for protecting themselves against marauders. By comparative advantage, some of these clusters grew more than others, and a system of urban places gradually emerged. The distribution of cities by size and over space is patterned but irregular. The patterns, described by central place theory (W. Christaller, A. Losch) and the rank-size rule (G. K. Zipf), seem to reflect a hierarchy of the economic, social, and political functions in which cities specialize. The irregularities reflect variable topography and microclimates, locations of natural transport channels, and historical accidents (Isard, 1956: ch. 3).

Although the impetus for urban growth is primarily economic or political, the pace of growth and the transitional characteristics of the urban population are governed by demographic processes—rates of natural increase (an excess of births over deaths) and net inmigration. In the past, rural-to-urban migration (including international rural-to-urban migration) was the main mode of urban growth. In the future, natural increase will be the leading growth factor.

Throughout most of human history, urban places have been less healthy than the countryside because in dense settlements with shared water supplies disease was easily transmitted. Today that disadvantage of high-density life can be, and in many regions of the world has been, remedied by investment in urban infrastructure and by systematic public health measures. Recent urban death rates, especially rates of infant mortality, are generally somewhat lower than those of the same region's rural areas (see Table 3).

Within a given region, however, birth rates are also usually lower among urban than among rural populations. The reasons are not biological or medical, but social and economic: under urban conditions, a large family is usually a handicap to its members, rather than, as in peasant agriculture,

TABLE 3 Decomposition of population growth rates for urban and rural populations, by world region: 1960

Annual rate per 1,000 population

World region	Urban				Rural			
	Growth	Birth	Death	Net migration[a]	Growth	Birth	Death	Net migration[a]
Northern America	24.3	24.2	8.9	9.0	−1.2	24.8	9.3	−16.7
Caribbean	34.2	30.8	11.3	14.7	15.1	41.9	12.9	−13.9
Central America	47.0	42.7	11.5	15.8	21.1	47.0	13.0	−12.9
Tropical South America	49.6	31.1	11.2	29.7	11.7	45.0	12.8	−20.5
Temperate South America	30.2	24.3	9.1	15.0	−9.1	34.3	9.5	−33.9
Northern Europe	11.2	17.4	11.0	4.8	−6.4	17.6	11.1	−12.9
Western Europe	19.5	17.4	10.6	12.7	−6.5	20.9	11.2	−16.2
Eastern Europe	19.2	17.3	9.6	11.5	−3.8	22.6	9.3	−17.1
Soviet Union	34.5	20.8	6.5	20.2	−1.4	26.5	8.4	−19.5
Southern Europe	21.0	19.3	9.1	10.8	−2.2	23.0	9.4	−15.8
Western Asia	46.4	38.0	15.1	23.5	18.6	48.9	19.5	−10.8
Northern Africa	42.3	43.8	17.1	15.6	18.5	47.4	22.1	−6.8
Western Africa	49.9	41.1	20.0	28.8	17.9	50.2	27.1	−5.2
Middle Africa	58.6	47.2	20.6	32.0	13.0	44.8	27.7	−4.1
Eastern Africa	49.9	44.6	18.9	24.2	20.1	46.9	24.8	−2.0
Southern Africa	32.9	32.1	15.1	15.9	16.3	47.6	20.1	−11.2

China	50.3	33.9	15.4	31.8	9.7	38.2	20.7	−7.8
Japan	29.2	15.8	6.6	20.0	−5.9	18.5	8.6	−15.8
Other East Asia	56.2	35.8	9.0	29.4	14.9	43.3	13.6	−14.8
Southeastern Asia	43.3	42.2	16.2	17.3	21.9	46.7	21.1	−3.7
Southern Asia	32.6	39.6	17.9	10.9	21.1	47.2	23.9	−2.2
Australia–New Zealand	25.8	22.2	8.9	12.5	1.8	29.0	7.5	−19.7
Melanesia	47.9	45.8	13.8	15.9	22.4	42.7	19.8	−0.5
Micronesia–Polynesia	47.6	35.5	9.1	21.2	25.8	42.6	12.9	−3.9
World total	33.0	27.7	11.6	16.9	12.5	39.8	19.1	−8.2
More developed regions	23.5	20.1	8.9	12.3	−2.6	23.3	9.3	−16.6
Less developed regions	45.5	37.9	15.4	23.0	16.5	44.1	21.7	−5.9

NOTE: The assignment of countries to regions is the same as in Table 2. Vital rates c. 1960 were estimated from a detailed analysis of urban and rural age structures in each country.
[a] I calculated the migration rate as a residual: Net migration rate = growth rate − birth rate + death rate; negative values indicate net outmigration. However, the growth rate given in the source includes some reclassification of civil divisions from rural to urban, so the rates of urban immigration and rural outmigration are both overstated.
SOURCES: UN-CHS, 1976: Vol. 2, Table 2; Rogers, 1982: Table 4.

an advantage. In modern times, the rural/urban fertility differential has diminished, but is still quite large in South America and South Africa (see Table 3).[2]

In the past, the rate of natural increase for large cities was never high and was often negative (low birth rate, high death rate). Only continual rural-to-urban migration enabled such cities as London to grow rapidly in the eighteenth and nineteenth centuries. Public health measures have now altered the balance between urban births and deaths to the point where even in less developed regions cities can grow rapidly by natural increase alone—by as much as 2 to 3 percent annually. The combination of urban natural increase and net inmigration is explosive.

In a predominantly rural nation, a few urban centers attract all the rural outmigrants. Although the rate of rural outmigration may be quite modest—say, 1 percent per annum—the rate of urban inmigration (whose base is the small urban, not the large rural, population) can easily reach 5 to 10 percent per annum for a decade or two. But such a growth regime cannot continue indefinitely. As urbanization proceeds, the pool of rural population on which rural-to-urban migration draws becomes relatively smaller and the urban population becomes relatively larger, so that rural-to-urban migration becomes less important to cities than natural increase.[3] The overall rate of urban growth diminishes, approaching the national rate of natural increase.

Variations on these themes can be generated by considering typical changes in rural and urban rates of natural increase as urbanization proceeds (Rogers, 1982). In particular, rural-to-urban migration tends to raise urban birth rates temporarily because most migrants are of childbearing age, and they retain the rural preference for large families until they have learned urban ways. Nevertheless, the general lesson is clear and, I think, important: although rural-to-urban migration tends to drive urban growth in the early stages of urbanization, urban natural increase governs in the later stages.

In 1960, nearly all less developed (less urbanized) regions of the world had low rates of rural outmigration—under 1 percent annually—and high rates of urban inmigration—1.5 to 3.2 percent annually (see Table 3). With a few exceptions, urban and rural rates of natural increase were about the same. Yet urban growth rates were two to five times above rural growth rates, reflecting the focused effect of rural-to-urban migration in regions with relatively small urban sectors.

The more developed (more urbanized) regions had high rates of rural outmigration—1.5 to 3.4 percent annually; yet the rates of urban inmigration averaged only half those experienced by the less developed regions: 1.2 as compared with 2.3 percent annually (see the last two rows of Table 3). The urban populations of some developed regions were growing rapidly

from natural increase—for example, Northern America and temperate
South America. In other developed regions, particularly Northern and Western Europe, both urban and rural rates of natural increase were low (because of low birth rates). Consequently, urban growth was modest and rural
populations were decreasing.

I have not located any global account of births, deaths, and migration
by urban/rural residence subsequent to the 1960 data in Table 3.[4] However,
the UN regularly estimates urban and rural population growth rates for individual countries (UN-ESA, 1988a), so we can compare recent rates to those
prevailing in 1960:

| | Annual growth rate per 1,000 inhabitants | | | |
| | Urban | | Rural | |
	1960	1985	1960	1985
More developed regions	23.5	10.0	-2.6	-2.1
Less developed regions	45.5	34.4	16.5	12.4
World total	33.0	23.6	12.5	12.2

In both developed and developing regions, the rate of growth of urban populations slowed considerably during the 25-year period, 1960–85, reflecting a
modest worldwide decline in rates of natural increase as well as the declining influence of rural-to-urban migration as the level of urbanization increased. The combined effect was most striking for the developed regions,
whose urban growth rate of 10 per thousand urban population was only
slightly above the same regions' overall growth rate of 6.5 per thousand. For
the less developed regions, however, the dramatic and probably spurious
drop in China's urban growth rate (down from 50.3 in 1960 to 14.3 in 1985)
is partly offset by a modest increase in urban growth rates for Southern Asia
(primarily India and Pakistan).[5]

The urban/rural balance

The rapid growth of urban population in developing countries, described in
the preceding section, has raised grave concerns about "overurbanization,"
concerns reflected in the publications of development economists, the policies of national governments, and the proceedings of international commissions (Todaro and Stilkind, 1981; Beier, 1984; OECD, 1984; FAO, 1985; Salas,
1986). Although these concerns sometimes focus on the problems of managing very large cities, generally they address the question of "balance" between the numbers of urban and rural residents.

The cited symptoms of overurbanization include substandard living
conditions for urban residents, the failure of municipal governments to pro-

vide the infrastructure and services that make urban life more efficient and comfortable, urban unemployment and low wages, and the need to import food from abroad in order to sustain the urban population. Less often cited but probably salient in the deliberations of governments are the political consequences of urbanization: population clustered on a scale that facilitates mass demonstrations and mob violence against unpopular national policies or privileged groups.

Those who think that developing countries are overurbanized often blame an urban bias in national policy, resulting in more job creation in urban areas, better wages, and better education and health care than are available in rural areas. In almost the same breath, they worry about urban unemployment, low wages, inadequate housing, the high cost of food, and the lack of public services (OECD, 1984; Salas, 1986). But the facts seem clear enough: cities are more attractive to rural folk than rural places are to city folk, so that the net flow of voluntary migration in developing countries is invariably from rural to urban places. Furthermore, objective indexes of welfare seem to confirm the judgment of those who have voted with their feet: real wages are higher in cities, urban schools and health care are better than their rural counterparts, and those who seek upward mobility will find the best opportunities in the cities.

Although critics of "overurbanization" treat it as a problem for developing countries, it seems at the same time almost a goal of development. Those nations called "developed" by virtue of their high standards of living include nearly all the highly urbanized countries. More than three-fourths (and up to 96 percent) of the populations of the United Kingdom, Belgium, the Netherlands, West Germany, Denmark, Japan, Canada, Sweden, Norway, and the United States are classified as urban by their respective statistical bureaus.

However, two fundamental facts support the notion of a desirable "balance" between a country's urban and rural populations. One is that agriculture is land-intensive, and so is intrinsically a rural activity. The other is that urban dwellers cannot get along without food. In a closed national economy, the limit to urbanization is set by the size of the agricultural surplus produced by the rural population.

Table 4 shows the world situation in 1982 with respect to agricultural productivity, and suggests how we may account for the interregional variation. As measured by the value of agricultural production (using world-market prices) the Food and Agriculture Organization's list of developed countries averages nearly 15 times the output per agricultural worker reported by the developing countries. North American (US and Canadian) agriculture yields nearly 120 times the output per worker reported for Asian planned economies (mostly China, but including Vietnam and North Korea).

TABLE 4 Value of agricultural output and factor inputs per worker, by world region: 1982

World region	Value per agricultural worker			Distribution of agricultural energy by application (percent)			
	Value of product (US$, 1974–76)	Arable or cropland (ha.)	Energy used (kg. oil equiv.)	Farm machinery	Ferti- lizer	Irriga- tion	Pesti- cides
North America	36,791	91.98	25,744	66.8	29.7	1.4	2.1
Oceania	24,133	99.72	7,786	72.2	26.4	1.0	0.4
Western Europe	7,708	6.13	4,387	66.4	31.6	0.6	1.3
Eastern Europe and USSR	3,766	7.65	1,557	44.9	52.7	0.8	1.6
Other developed economies [a]	3,243	2.08	1,789	na	na	na	na
Latin America	1,547	4.50	286	40.3	56.2	1.4	2.1
Near East	958	2.37	235	42.9	49.1	6.8	1.1
Other developing economies	609	0.67	33	na	na	na	na
Africa	393	1.44	26	41.0	49.2	4.2	5.5
Far East	322	0.93	72	21.9	71.4	6.9	0.7
Asian planned economies [b]	309	0.38	106	15.7	79.3	3.0	2.0
Developed market economies	9,227	14.37	5,581	68.4	29.1	1.0	1.5
Eastern Europe and USSR	3,766	7.65	1,557	44.9	52.7	0.8	1.6
Total, developed countries	6,123	10.56	3,294	62.1	35.5	0.9	1.5
Developing market economies	488	1.45	95	32.4	61.3	4.9	1.4
Asian planned economies [b]	309	0.38	106	15.7	79.3	3.0	2.0
Total, developing countries	418	1.03	99	25.5	68.8	4.1	1.7
Total, world	854	1.76	344	52.3	44.3	1.8	1.6

NOTES: Country groupings differ from those in Tables 2 and 3. Western Europe includes Yugoslavia. The Near East extends from Cyprus and Turkey in the Northwest to Afghanistan in the east, and includes Egypt, Libya, and the Sudan, but not Israel. Africa excludes Egypt, Libya, the Sudan, and South Africa. The Far East excludes Asian planned economies (listed below) and Japan. Totals for developed and developing market economies include countries not elsewhere specified by region.
[a] Japan, Israel, and South Africa
[b] Mainly China, Vietnam, and North Korea.
na = not available.
SOURCE: FAO, 1986.

The high productivity of agricultural workers in developed countries rests on two fundamental advantages: relatively large expanses of arable land that can be worked with modern machinery, and access to large quantities of commercial energy in the form of tractors, combines, fuel, and fertilizer. North America is blessed in both respects, with nearly 92 hectares of arable land and over 25 metric tons of commercial energy per agricultural worker. Two-thirds of the energy is applied in the form of agricultural machinery (roughly, a tractor, a motor truck, and a harvesting machine for each agricultural worker) and nearly one-third in the form of commercial fertilizer.

At the other end of the scale, the low agricultural productivity of Asian planned economies reflects relative scarcity of both arable land and commercial energy. The nations in this group average less than 0.4 hectare of arable land and about 100 kilograms of commercial energy, mostly in the form of fertilizer, per worker. If cropland is naturally fertile or is well fertilized, labor-intensive farming methods produce high yields per hectare, about twice as much as tractor-based agriculture,[6] but low yields per worker.

Generally, a farmworker has between one and three dependents living with him; if for convenience we accept an average of two, and suppose that one hectare of intensively cultivated cropland will provide food for ten people, then an Asian farmer with .38 hectare can support himself, two dependents, and one other person. For a closed economy, this calculation indicates that the maximum supportable level of urbanization would be one out of four persons, or 25 percent—about the level of China today.

Aided by heavy applications of fertilizer, the style of agriculture practiced in North America yields about as much food per hectare as an Asian rice-paddy. But with the help of a tractor and combine, the North American farmer can plow, plant, and harvest 90 hectares, enough to feed about 450 people. That is why North America can prosper with only one farmworker per 80 persons of total population, and still export about a third of its grain harvest. That also is why more than three out of four inhabitants of North America can live in urban places.

Where agricultural resources are limited because of climate, poor soil, or lack of open space for farming, population growth entails urbanization but depends on imported food. Some crowded countries have been long accustomed to importing much of their sustenance. For example, Japan (76 percent urban) has only .04 hectare of cropland per capita, about half of which is used to grow rice. The annual rice crop amounts to about 120 kilograms per inhabitant; to fill out their diet, the Japanese import 220 kilograms of other cereals per inhabitant, and pay for the imported food by exporting manufactures. Belgium (96 percent urban) has about .08 hectare of cropland per capita, of which a fourth is used to grow wheat. The yield is about 134 kilograms per inhabitant, which the Belgians supplement with 300 kilograms per capita of imported cereals. The imports are mostly corn, and over half the total is re-exported as cattle feed, dairy products, or meat. Belgium's exports of steel and machinery pay for the rest of the imported food (WRI-IIED, 1988: Tables 17.1 and 17.2; US-BC, 1986: Tables 1464 and 1465).

China, India, and Indonesia—together accounting for 40 percent of the world's population—have recently achieved a precarious self-sufficiency in food crops. Most developing countries, however, import a substantial share of their food. Only a few have exports that are adequate to pay for both food and the capital equipment they need for industrial development. The imported food goes mostly to urban populations and is often subsidized. To critics of over-urbanization, this allocation of public funds and foreign exchange seems misguided.

In these cases, however, the problem does not really seem to be urbanization, except in the sense that mobs take to the streets whenever the government announces an increase in the price of foodstuffs (Brown and Jacobson, 1987: Table 8). If the same number of people were distributed evenly throughout the land, they would still have to eat, and it is not usually the case in developing nations that their labor in agriculture would add much to total product. For example, about 46 percent of Egypt's population lives in urban places, and Egypt imported 10.6 million metric tons of cereals annually, 1984–86—about 490 kilograms for each urban resident. However, Egypt's agricultural population is already dense—about 8.9 persons, including 2.5 workers, per hectare of arable land (FAO, 1986: Annex Table 12B). Rusticating Egypt's urban population would do little to increase agricultural output unless new land could be brought into cultivation.[7]

Before 1980, China pursued a deliberate policy of restricting urban growth, refusing residence permits and ration cards to would-be rural-to-urban migrants; in addition, some 14 to 17 million young urban residents were forcibly rusticated during the Cultural Revolution (1966–1976). Consequently, rural population growth far outstripped the availability of arable land. The commune system of agricultural production offered little incentive for using labor efficiently, but calculations based on technical estimates of farm labor requirements indicate an enormous surplus. Taylor and Banister estimate that the surplus of rural workers peaked in 1983 at 133 million persons, about 42 percent of the agricultural labor force (1988: Tables 2 and 4).

On the other hand, it seems that urbanization in developing countries often leads to counterproductive food policies. To accommodate the demands of a poor urban population, some national governments either regulate the prices at which the country's farmers can sell their crops, or sell imported food to urban residents at prices below the domestic cost of production. Both practices discourage farmers from expanding production, guaranteeing continued dependence on imports. Especially in sub-Saharan Africa, resources exist for increasing agricultural production, but the institutions are lacking.[8]

How big can cities get?

The growth of very large cities in both the developed and developing world has disturbed students of human society as well as those with broader ecological concerns. In the developed world, problems of traffic congestion, air pollution, and social disorder seem to increase with city size, threatening the livability of urban environments. In the developing world,

> The weak economic base of most third world cities has put their urban managers in a desperate race to cope with uncontrolled squatter settlements, to mount an increasingly expensive search for water, and to adjust to growing dependence on imported food and energy. The desperation of this search leaves little time for consideration of the long-term effects of these decisions on the physical environment and, hence, on the resilience of a city itself as an ecosystem. (White, 1983: 1568)

Certainly, the number of very large urban agglomerations has grown rapidly in our lifetime, especially in the world's developing countries (see Table 5). In 1950, the world contained only eight urbanized areas with more than 5 million inhabitants, and only three (New York, London, and Shanghai) with more than 10 million. In 1975, 22 urbanized areas had more than 5 million inhabitants and 6 had more than 10 million. Between 1950 and 1975, Mexico City grew from 3.0 million to 11.6 million; São Paulo grew from 2.8 million to 10.3 million; and Seoul grew from 1.1 million to 7.0 million. Jakarta and Delhi tripled in size.

Is there any limit to the population size that a city can attain and still function? UN projections suggest that by the year 2000, the world will contain 24 urban agglomerations with more than 10 million inhabitants, the largest of which (Mexico City) might contain nearly 26 million people. Can that possibly work?

Although cities have often been founded by government fiat, something more is usually needed to nourish their growth. Urban historians solidly agree that a strategic location is the basic ingredient of a city's success. A good location provides access to food and fuel for the city's inhabitants, raw materials for its manufactures, and markets for its output; in earlier times the site also had to be defensible against armed attack. The intersection of natural transportation channels has always been advantageous; seaports with rich agricultural hinterlands are especially favored. Those places whose locational advantages endured are the ones that grew to very large size. Others, indifferently located to begin with or deprived of their advan-

TABLE 5 Populations of the 30 largest urbanized areas: World, 1950–2000

Rank in year 2000	Country	Urbanized area	Thousands of inhabitants		
			1950	1975	2000
1	Mexico	Mexico City	3,050	11,610	25,820
2	Japan	Tokyo–Yokohama	6,736	17,668	24,172
3	Brazil	São Paulo	2,760	10,290	23,970
4	India	Calcutta	4,520	8,250	16,530
5	India	Bombay	2,950	7,170	16,000
6	United States	New York–NE New Jersey	12,410	15,940	15,780
7	Rep. of Korea	Seoul	1,113	6,950	13,770
8	Brazil	Rio de Janeiro	3,480	8,150	13,260
9	China	Shanghai	10,420	11,590	13,260
10	Indonesia	Jakarta	1,820	5,530	13,250
11	India	Delhi	1,410	4,630	13,240
12	Argentina	Buenos Aires	5,251	9,290	13,180
13	Pakistan	Karachi	1,040	4,030	12,000
14	Iran	Teheran	1,126	4,267	11,329
15	Bangladesh	Dhaka	430	2,350	11,160
16	Egypt	Cairo–Ginza–Imbaba	3,500	6,250	11,130
17	Iraq	Baghdad	579	3,830	11,125
18	Japan	Osaka–Kobe	3,828	8,649	11,109
19	Philippines	Manila	1,570	5,040	11,070
20	United States	Los Angeles–Long Beach	4,070	8,960	10,990
21	Thailand	Bangkok–Thonburi	1,440	4,050	10,710
22	United Kingdom	London	10,369	10,310	10,510
23	USSR	Moscow	4,841	7,600	10,400
24	China	Beijing	6,740	8,910	10,360
25	Germany	Rhein–Ruhr	6,853	9,311	9,151
26	Peru	Lima–Callao	1,050	3,700	9,140
27	France	Paris	5,525	8,620	8,720
28	Nigeria	Lagos	360	2,100	8,340
29	Italy	Milan	3,637	6,150	8,150
30	India	Madras	1,420	3,770	8,150

NOTE: The urban places listed above are areas of dense contiguous settlement whose boundaries do not necessarily coincide with administrative boundaries; they usually include one or more cities and an urbanized fringe. The list includes all such places projected to contain at least 8 million inhabitants in the year 2000.
SOURCE: UN-CHS, 1987: Annex Table 6. Based on the UN's 1984 assessment.

tages by shifts in regional population, changes in production or transport technology, or resource depletion, faded from prominence.

In time, the locational advantages that set a place on the path of growth may be reinforced by "agglomeration economies," an infelicitous term economists use to suggest that economic enterprise benefits in various ways from proximity to other enterprises and to population concentrations.

A number of studies have shown that manufacturing productivity (e.g., output per unit of capital or labor) increases with metropolitan population or labor force size, and others have shown that real wages rise with metropolitan size, even within narrowly defined occupational groups (Carlino, 1985; Henderson, 1986; Montgomery, 1988).

Although the statistical procedures of most such studies leave the results open to various interpretations, both common experience and informed reasoning support the idea that cities are efficient places to carry on enterprises that are capital- or labor-intensive; and that large cities offer more than small ones in the way of specialized technical and professional services, skilled labor, inventories of parts or commodities needed in production, and access to financial capital.

No small part of the urban advantage for production comes from the existence of a massive, publicly financed infrastructure—streets and highways, gas, water, and sewer mains, power grids, fire and police stations. The users of this infrastructure usually pay for it in one way or another,[9] but they reap the benefits of economies of scale in the production of vertically integrated urban services, and of economies of distribution where users are densely spaced (UN-ESA, 1980: 38–40). However, local geophysical conditions are often critically important in determining whether scale effects for these services are positive or negative within a given range (Linn, 1982).

Residents of cities benefit from urban scale as consumers of the public goods mentioned above, and also because large cities offer a wider range of employment opportunities, a wider selection of consumer goods and services, and a greater variety of social micro-environments from which to choose.

Some agglomeration effects are negative, however. One, clearly, is congestion in transportation and communication systems. Another is that the inhabitants must go farther and farther afield for food, fuel, water, and raw materials as a city grows. And waste disposal overwhelms natural recycling processes, resulting in polluted air and water and in massive rubbish piles or landfills (Brown and Jacobson, 1987).

The pattern of urban growth in developing countries is a matter of particular concern. Characteristically, one city, usually the seat of government, becomes very large relative to other urban places in that nation. In 1980, at least a fifth of the total populations of Argentina, Iraq, Peru, Chile, Egypt, South Korea, Mexico, and Venezuela lived in such a "primate city." These places accumulate a large share both of the population and of economic and cultural activity.

The case of Mexico City is particularly striking because Mexico is territorially a large and largely habitable nation—unlike, say, Iraq or Egypt. Around 1980, Mexico City had 14.5 million inhabitants out of an urban total of 46 million and a national total of 69 million (UN-CHS, 1987: Annex Tables 1 and 6). The city accounted for 46 percent of the country's gross domestic product, contained 53 percent of the manufacturing workforce, 42 percent of the institutions of higher education, 52 percent of the theaters, 76 percent of the radio stations, and all five television stations (FAO, 1985: ch.2).

The city's rapid growth, from only 3 million in 1950 to 14.5 million in 1980, clearly owes much to its special status as the seat of government, where those affected by government policies have access to the decisionmakers. The city is the prime beneficiary of the so-called urban bias in national policy that seems characteristic of developing nations: credit and price policies and publicly funded investment in infrastructure favor urban industrial development over rural agricultural development. The subsistence farmers of rural Mexico, barely surviving on small plots of infertile land, imagine life in Mexico City, harsh though it may be, as the better alternative for employment, health care, and education. In 1977, it was estimated that over half the adult population of Mexico City were inmigrants.

Many of the problems of very large cities in the developing world reflect their rapid growth rather than size per se. The most pervasive failings are those of overloaded urban infrastructure—streets, public transportation, water treatment plants and distribution systems, sewage collection and disposal, electrical power generation, and telephone service. In principle, all these services can be expanded, often without encountering rising marginal costs. But planning, financing, and building new capacity take more time than municipal authorities have been vouchsafed by rapid population growth—in the case of Mexico City averaging 5.3 percent annually for more than 30 years running.

From a rather sophisticated simulation of a composite developing economy, Kelley and Williamson (1984) concluded that the period 1960–73 was unusually favorable to the growth of Third World cities because of the international structure of relative prices for food, manufactures, and fuel. The post-OPEC price structures have been decidedly less favorable to urban growth, but under either price regime Kelley and Williamson predict that about 90 percent of the Third World urban transition will be completed by the year 2000:

> Based on the model, urban problems will be far less severe by the end of the century, even though there will be no serious diminution of Malthusian population pressure in the Third World over the remainder of the century. Presumably, we will hear fewer complaints from urban planners, the term "over-urbanization" will disappear from our lexicon, and pessimists' stress on urban environmental decay will lose its urgency. By the year 2000, it will be easier to cope with the far lower city growth rates. (p. 152)

Although simulation models are more likely to illustrate conclusions reached in advance of the modeling than they are to discover unexpected outcomes, this one deserves at least respectful attention as an antidote to the trend extrapolations of urban growth offered by the United Nations.

Over the long run, however, I see no particular limit to the size of urban agglomerations. Although living and working in a very large urbanized area certainly entails problems and costs not encountered in smaller places, larger places also offer compensating opportunities and benefits. When growth leads eventually to scale diseconomies—for example, traffic congestion—polynucleation follows. What was a functionally centralized urban place breaks up into cells, each containing a nearly self-sufficient subcity. Although the cell boundaries are permeable to traffic, those who live in such a subcity usually also work and shop there (Lowry, 1988: Table 9).

In fact, we seem to be on the verge of a dramatic escalation in our concept of urban scale. Some evidence of the coming change appears in the frequent revision of official statistics for urbanized areas. Successive reports by the same UN agency describe the 1980 population of the New York–Northeastern New Jersey urbanized area as 20.4 and 15.6 million; and similarly for Tokyo–Yokohama and São Paulo. These inconsistencies reflect shifting judgments about the proper boundaries of the multinucleated conurbation that forms as nearby urbanized areas expand peripherally until they collide, or as former suburbs grow into major urban centers with suburbs of their own.

Urbanization and the environment

Because urbanization historically accompanies rapid population growth, rural-to-urban migration, industrialization, and rising standards of living, cities are sometimes blamed for problems that would persist even if urban growth stopped or reversed. In this section I will try to sort out the effects of alternative patterns of human settlement on the natural environment, specifically with respect to resource depletion and pollution. Because my understanding of the physical and chemical processes entailed in environmental degradation is superficial, I could easily miss subtle connections that ought to qualify my conclusions; but I will be content if I persuade my readers to attend to the issues I raise even though they resolve the issues otherwise.

On the time scale of human history, urban settlements are novelties. The species' evolutionary adaptation to its environment occurred first in the context of hunting-and-gathering economies, then herding and primitive agriculture. These modes of subsistence relied rather directly on the annual harvest of solar energy, converted by photosynthesis to edible starches, proteins, and oils; or else to forage for animals that in turn supplied (or became) human food.

Converting solar energy to food by using plants and animals found in nature as intermediaries was not very energy-efficient.[10] For this reason, and because the available solar energy is proportional to surface area (land or water), low-density settlement was the rule for our species through all of prehistory and most of recorded history. Even so, resource depletion was a recurrent problem for primitive communities: when they overhunted, overgrazed, or overcropped their environs—as they often did—they had to move on or starve.

Waste disposal was generally less troublesome. Although primitive peoples produced abundant waste, most of it was biodegradable, and the rest, though durable, was not especially toxic. The remains of food plants, animals, and fish were left to rot at the edge of the village or were thrown in the river. The disposal of human excrement was not much more careful, though some primitive communities dug latrines. Bones and mussel-shells accumulated (along with potsherds and flint chippings) in midden heaps that have lasted for thousands of years, but without harming subsequent inhabitants of the area. Other wastes were recycled into the soil and water in a season or two; most of them quickly broke down into substances beneficial to plant growth.

This casual treatment of wastes worked for two reasons. First, many primitive peoples were seminomadic, seasonally moving to new encampments and leaving their trash behind. Second, even settled communities were small and widely spaced, so that trash left to decompose at the edge of the village was not much under foot, and trash thrown in streams was oxidized and diluted before reaching the next village's water supply.

The gradual transformation of human communities from low- to high-energy living entailed finding ways to concentrate and store the annual harvest of solar energy and to tap natural concentrations of kinetic or chemical energy. A fundamental step was the cultivation of cereal crops, whose abundant yield under favorable conditions provided a surplus above immediate subsistence needs, and whose physical and chemical characteristics allowed that surplus to be compactly stored and easily moved about. The main sequence of fuel improvement was from gathering twigs to harvesting forest logs to making charcoal, a compact and relatively clean fuel.

Large cities become feasible only when a society learns some way to produce a surplus of portable energy—that is, more than the producers need for their own subsistence. Cities live on imported food and fuel, making little use of locally incident solar energy. The available technology limits the size and spacing of urban settlements by limiting the amounts and forms of energy a city can draw from its hinterland. To support a population that never exceeded 800,000, Rome had to raid the granaries of the entire Mediterranean basin.

Today, we can manage larger cities and closer spacing by importing enormously concentrated energy resources, not just to the cities themselves but to their agricultural hinterlands. In 1982, the United States and Canada jointly consumed commercial fuels (coal, oil, gas, primary electricity) with an energy equivalent of 1,668 billion kilograms of oil (FAO, 1986: Table 1-28). Urban and rural nonfarm populations consumed about 96 percent of that energy, averaging a little less than 6,500 kg. per capita. By way of comparison, the food consumed by a typical North American in a year's time has a caloric value equal to about 126 kg. of oil.[11] In other words, only about a fiftieth of the total nonfarm energy consumption is in the form of food.

Although the nonfarm population, about three-fourths of which is urban, consumed 96 percent of the total commercial energy, farmers used energy much more lavishly than the nonfarm population. According to the FAO, North American farmers used the energy-equivalent of 25,744 kg. of oil per worker in 1982 (see Table 4, above). Allocated among the entire farm population, this amounts to about 11,700 kg. per capita—nearly twice the average consumption of the nonfarm population.

In short, the whole population, not just its urban part, uses energy lavishly. Moreover, such high levels of energy consumption are not necessary to high levels of urbanization or to the existence of large cities. Other countries, including advanced industrial nations, manage urbanization more economically. In 1985, about 74 percent of the US population was classified as urban, and its largest urbanized area (New York–NE New Jersey) had about 15.6 million inhabitants. By way of comparison, 76 percent of Japan's population was classified as urban and Tokyo–Yokohama was the world's largest urbanized area, with more than 20 million inhabitants. Yet in that year the Japanese consumed only two-fifths as much energy per capita as did the US population.

One factor that might account for this difference in energy consumption is a difference in urban densities. It is often argued that the US style of urban sprawl is particularly inefficient both from the point of view of its requirements for infrastructure—roads, power lines, and water, sewer, and gas mains—and with respect to the amount of energy required to travel between home and work. Although the inefficiency of sprawl is easily demonstrated by engineering calculations for each item of infrastructure taken separately, urban density, infrastructure design, travel patterns, and lifestyle are intricately interconnected, both historically and behaviorally.

Newman and Kenworthy (1989) have compiled data on gasoline consumption by residents of 32 large urbanized areas around the world, which they compare to various indicators of urban form and infrastructure, some of which are shown in Table 6. Their data indicate that residents of US cities use twice as much gasoline per capita as those of Australian cities, 4 times as much as those of European cities, and 10 times as much as those of Asian cities, a pattern that inversely reflects densities of population and employment. Fitting an inverse exponential function to the relationship between gasoline consumption and population density indicates "a strong increase in

TABLE 6 Factors affecting gasoline use and local travel patterns: Selected world cities, 1980

| City group | Gasoline used (gal/yr/person) | | Activity density (persons/acre) | | Average worktrip length (miles) | Modal split (Percent of all worktrips) | | |
	Actual	Adjusted	Population	Employment		Private automobile	Public transit	Bicycle or walking
10 US cities	446	446	5.7	2.8	8.1	83	12	5
5 Australian cities	227	333	5.7	2.4	7.5	76	19	5
Toronto, Canada	265	199	16.2	8.1	8.1	63	31	6
12 European cities	101	237	21.9	12.6	5.0	44	35	21
3 Asian cities	42	94	64.8	28.8	2.5	15	60	25
Moscow, USSR	3	na	56.2	na	na	2	74	24

NOTES: Adjusted gasoline consumption standardized at US levels for gasoline prices, per capita income, and vehicular fuel efficiency, allowing 20 years for consumption to adapt to the changed circumstances. However, the adjustment is not logically comprehensive: urban densities, trip lengths, alternative transportation facilities, and modal splits would undoubtedly change along with prices, income, and vehicles. The adjusted figures standardize for the real costs per mile of automobile travel, showing the residual differences in consumption associated with urban form (and other unidentified variables).

na = not available.

SOURCE: Newman and Kenworthy, 1989.

gasoline consumption where population density is under 12 people per acre. This relationship is conceptually quite possible, as low density appears to have a multiplicative effect, not only ensuring longer distances for all kinds of travel but making all nonautomobile modes virtually impossible, since many people live too far from a transit line and walking and biking become impossible" (p. 29).

Newman and Kenworthy seek to persuade Australian planners that their country would be better off with high-density cities featuring mass transit, bicycle, and pedestrian travel as opposed to low-density cities based on private automobile transportation. Without firm guidance from above, they fear, Sydney and Melbourne will rival Los Angeles in sprawl and automobile dependence (Newman, 1988).

For the residents of a city, minimizing travel or fuel consumption is not an end in itself, but only part of a broader calculation that reveals strong preferences for pleasant residential and workplace environments even at the cost of additional travel. The general prosperity that has accompanied high-energy technologies gives consumers more choices, and those choices are reflected in urban sprawl—not just in the United States, but also on the fringes of European and Asian cities.

Rather than lobbying fruitlessly for higher density land use, more compact cities, and public transit as ways to save energy, it would be more practical to encourage the dispersion of workplaces as well as residences. To the degree that homes and workplaces collocate, low-density development carries no penalty of transport costs. In the United States, such collocation is more common than is generally realized. Among residents of urban fringes (urban places outside central cities) of the nation's 119 urbanized areas in 1980, two-thirds also worked in fringe communities, although not necessarily in the neighborhood of their homes. The median length of usual home-to-work trips for all urban workers has been under 6 miles in three national surveys, 1969 to 1983 (Lowry, 1988: Tables 9 and 11).

In addition to the energy used in local travel, cities consume great quantities of fuel for space-heating, lighting, and operating industrial machinery and home appliances. Not much of this consumption is a consequence of urbanization itself; the same activities dispersed through the open countryside would probably use more fuel, because the combustion devices would be smaller and less efficient.[12]

Because nearly everything a city consumes must be imported, the energy cost of each item implicitly includes the cost of transporting it from where it is mined, grown, gathered, or manufactured. As a city grows, the hinterland from which it draws supplies must expand, so that the average energy cost of transportation for each item increases. Environmental anti-urbanism has made much of this point. Brown and Jacobson (1987: 36) point out, for example, that

Transporting water can involve enormous energy costs. Mexico City's elevated site means water must be lifted from progressively lower catchments. In 1982, Mexico City began pumping water from Cutzamala, a site 100 kilometers away and 1,000 meters lower than the city. British geographer Ian Douglas reports that "augmentation of the Mexico City supply in the 1990s will be from Tecolutla, which is some 200 kilometers away and 2,000 meters lower." Pumping water this far will require some 125 trillion kilojoules of electrical energy annually, the output of six 1,000-megawatt power plants.

A similar situation exists in sub-Saharan Africa and South Asia with respect to domestic fuel:

> Rising fuel prices and a scarcity of foreign exchange to import oil for kerosene have forced residents in hundreds of Third World cities to turn to the surrounding countryside for cooking fuel. As a result, forests are being devastated in ever-widening circles around cities, particularly in the Indian subcontinent and Africa. . . .
>
> As forests recede from fuelwood-dependent Third World cities, the cost of hauling wood rises. Eventually it becomes more profitable to convert the wood into charcoal, a more concentrated form of energy, before transporting it. This conserves transport fuel, but charcoal typically has less than half of the energy contained in the wood used in its manufacture. Not surprisingly, as urban fuel markets reach farther afield for wood supplies, village residents also suffer from depleted supplies and rising costs.
>
> If firewood harvesting was properly managed and evenly distributed throughout a country's forests, this renewable resource could sustain far larger harvests. But because the demand is often heavily concentrated around cities, nearby forests are decimated while more distant ones are left untouched. (ibid.: 20–21)

Although I find these arguments generally persuasive, they lack balance. If large urban concentrations of people use energy inefficiently, it must be so relative to some other spatial arrangement of those people. Suppose that Mexico City's 15 million inhabitants were evenly spread over a 200-kilometer radius surrounding the present center, or locally concentrated in towns of 150,000 inhabitants each. Would the total energy costs of water supply, including catchment management, purification, and distribution, really be substantially less?

Similarly, suppose the towns of India and Africa sent their residents to live in the countryside. There might be per capita savings in fuel consumption from using firewood instead of charcoal, and lower transport costs to supply a dispersed population. But wouldn't the exiles, deprived of urban occupations, have to clear the forest in order to grow crops?

The other side of the ecological balance sheet for cities is waste production. Brown and Jacobson note that the average urban resident of the United

States daily uses about 568 liters of water, 1.5 kilograms of food, and 7.1 kilograms of fossil fuels, and generates about 454 liters of sewage, 1.5 kilograms of refuse, and 0.6 kilograms of air pollutants:

> Cities require concentrations of food, water, and fuel on a scale not found in nature. Just as nature cannot concentrate the resources needed to support urban life, neither can it disperse the waste produced in cities. The waste output of even a small city can quickly overtax the absorptive capacity of local terrestrial and aquatic ecosystems. (1987: 35)

Without questioning the wasteful ways of some urbanized countries with respect to water, food, and fuel, I do not see why it is thought to be an urban problem, when it is more aptly a problem of affluence: what North Americans and Europeans discard or use carelessly, the poorer peoples of Asia and Africa would treasure, whether they lived in urban or rural settings.

The suggestion that the same amount of waste would be less offensive if generated by a dispersed population is not persuasive. It should be much easier to monitor, regulate, and detoxify effluent emissions in an urban than in a rural setting. A centralized city water supply can be kept potable and safe more cheaply than 50,000 domestic wells. I can remember when Californians were encouraged to dispose of their rubbish in backyard incinerators and rural dumps, and am sure that this technology was more polluting than high-temperature incineration and sanitary landfills.

In any event, both urbanization and high-energy economies are here to stay. Only a romantic could seriously entertain the idea that highly urbanized developed nations might be willing to rusticate their urban populations or return to modes of production that rely primarily on human musclepower. Only a romantic could propose to the people of developing countries that they should hold to subsistence farming as a means of livelihood.

To succeed, the environmental movement must ride the tide of history instead of opposing it. Practically speaking, this means higher rather than lower technology: finding energy sources whose byproducts are less toxic, conversion engines with higher thermal efficiencies, distribution systems with less leakage, and market mechanisms that impose full social costs on those who waste energy or pollute their environs. In forwarding these endeavors, I suspect that cities are, on balance, allies rather than adversaries.

Notes

The author thanks Peter A. Morrison of the Rand Corporation for help in assembling materials used in preparing this essay.

1 This definition allows urban places to include some people employed in agriculture and is intentionally vague about residential

density. In practice, most national statistical agencies classify populations as urban or rural according to the type of minor civil division they inhabit, without directly testing for density, size, or occupational structure (UN-ESA, 1980: 121–124).

2 The crude birth and death rates in Table 3 may also reflect compositional differences in the urban and rural population, especially differences in age structure. Nevertheless, controlled comparisons such as those in (UN-ESA, 1985b: Vol. 1, pp. 58–66) support my generalizations.

3 In 1980, the United Nations incorporated this principle into its projections of urban and rural populations, which basically operate by extrapolating into the future the most recently observed urban/rural growth differences. The extrapolation is now modified by a factor reflecting the proportion urban at the start of each projection period. The weight assigned to this factor increases as the projection horizon is extended. (For details, see UN-ESA, 1980: 9–11.)

4 Although the United Nations Population Division regularly publishes tables formatted to distinguish urban and rural vital rates, very few developing countries report such data. The experts who constructed Table 3 must have filled in enormous data gaps by estimation. Even today, the data are sparse: the 1986 *Demographic Yearbook* (UN-ESA, 1988b) contains birth rates by urban and rural residence for only 25 nations for any year, 1982–86; and urban/rural death rates for 22 nations for any year, 1982–86. Those entries generally support the broad generalizations offered in the text above.

5 Sorting out Chinese statistics pertaining to urbanization is a major analytical enterprise. Rapid changes in actual residence patterns due to internal migration are confounded with the effects of a recent reclassification of small settlements that shifted about 70 million people from officially rural to officially urban; and they are further confused by the official reluctance to acknowledge in census enumerations common but unsanctioned changes of residence. Banister estimates China's 1985 urban population (after reclassification) at 351 million (v. the UN's 218 million), and sets the "real" annual growth

rate at about 50 per 1,000 urban residents, nearly all due to net migration (1988: Tables 6 and 7).

6 Only the Japanese seem to have figured out how to use tractors to advantage in wet rice cultivation: FAO statistics credit the Japanese with 330 tractors per thousand hectares of arable land, or about one tractor for every three agricultural workers. Despite the use of tractors, Japanese farmers harvest about 5,900 kilos of rice per hectare, as compared with 6,360 kilos of corn or 2,440 kilos of wheat per hectare in the United States. (US crop yields are adapted from US-BC,1986: Table 1136.)

7 This point would not be worth emphasis except that it does not seem to be appreciated in high places. For example, the then Executive Director of the United Nations Fund for Population Activities wrote that "Urban population increase means that rural populations and the agricultural labour force will grow more slowly. But to meet urban needs, agricultural productivity should be increasing, by 17 percent for each agricultural worker in developing countries between 1980 and the year 2000" (Salas, 1986: 11). Salas seems to think that a more rapid growth in the agricultural labor force would increase output per worker. The opposite effect is virtually certain.

8 One very detailed study of the agricultural potential of developing countries (Higgins et al., 1982) concluded that the developing world (i.e., Africa, Asia, and Latin America) as a whole could feed twice its 1975 population using only manual labor with hand tools, suitable local cultivars, and no fertilizer or chemical pest, disease, or weed controls, simply by farming the existing irrigated and available rainfed land. However, in 42 of 117 nations, agricultural self-sufficiency would require more irrigation or modest improvements in farming methods. Only for 13 nations of the developing world, nearly all of them Southwest Asian desert lands, was agricultural self-sufficiency out of the question.

9 When municipal infrastructure or public services are supported by property taxes (common in developed countries) or by subventions from the national government (common in developing countries) rather than

by user fees, they tend to be overused unless rationed by scarcity, congestion, or queues. Most scholars from developed countries are struck by the irrationality of municipal finance in developing countries, with respect to both tax base and the pricing of public services.

10 Even modern, high-yield crops capture little of the solar energy needed to grow them. According to Pimentel (1980: 3), over 5 billion kilocalories of solar energy reach each hectare of a cornfield during the growing season. About 1.2 percent of this energy is converted into corn biomass, and only 0.4 percent into grain. Even so, the yield of 19 million kilocalories of grain per hectare could maintain about 15 people for a year.

11 This calculation is based on an estimate of 3,450 kilocalories of food consumed per day, and a standard value for oil energy of $(10)^4$ kcal. per kilogram of oil. A year's food supply is (365) $(3,450) = 1,259,250$ kcal., equivalent to 126 kg. of oil.

12 The point is sometimes made that the combination of heat-absorbing urban pavement and fuel combustion raises ambient temperatures in cities, and the higher temperatures in turn increase demand for energy-expensive air conditioning. This vicious cycle is apparent to anyone who has ever traversed the canyons of Manhattan in August; on the other hand, I suppose it becomes a beneficent cycle during the winter heating season. Note also that urban sprawl mitigates this particular problem.

References

Text citations of institutional publications are abbreviated as follows: FAO = Food and Agriculture Organization of the United Nations; UN-CHS = United Nations Center for Human Settlements (and its predecessor, the Centre for Housing, Building, and Planning); UN-ESA = United Nations Department of International Economic and Social Affairs; UN-FPA = United Nations Fund for Population Activities; US-BC = United States Bureau of the Census; WRI-IIED = World Resources Institute and International Institute for Environment and Development.

Banister, Judith. 1988. "Urban-rural population projections for China," CIR Staff Paper No. 15. Center for International Research. Washington, D.C.: US Bureau of the Census.
Beier, George J. 1984. "Can third world cities cope?" in *Urban Development in the Third World*, ed. P. K. Ghosh. Westport, Conn.: Greenwood Press.
Brown, Lester R., and Jodi L. Jacobson. 1987. "The future of urbanization: Facing the ecological and economic constraints," *Worldwatch Paper* No. 77. Washington, D.C.: Worldwatch Institute.
Carlino, G. A. 1985. "Declining city productivity and the growth of rural regions: A test of alternative explanations," *Journal of Urban Economics* 18, no. 1: 11–27.
Food and Agriculture Organization of the United Nations. 1985. *The State of Food and Agriculture 1984*. FAO Agriculture Series No. 18. Rome: FAO.
———. 1986. *The State of Food and Agriculture 1985*. FAO Agriculture Series No. 19. Rome: FAO.
Golden, Hilda H. 1981. *Urbanization and Cities: Historical and Comparative Perspectives on Our Urbanizing World*. Lexington, Mass.: D.C. Heath.
Grauman, John V. 1976. "Orders of magnitude of the world's urban population in history," *Population Bulletin of the United Nations* 8: 16–33.
Henderson, J. Vernon. 1986. "Efficiency of resource usage and city size," *Journal of Urban Economics* 19, no. 1: 47–70.
Higgins, Graham M., Amir Kassam et al. 1982. *Potential Population Supporting Capacities of Lands in the Developing World*. Technical Report of Project INT/75/P13. Rome: FAO, IIASA, and UNFPA.

Isard, Walter. 1956. *Location and Space-Economy.* Cambridge, Mass. and New York: Technology Press of M.I.T. and John Wiley and Sons.

Kelley, Allen C., and Jeffrey G. Williamson. 1984. *What Drives Third World City Growth? A Dynamic General Equilibrium Approach.* Princeton: Princeton University Press.

Linn, Johannes F. 1982. "The costs of urbanization in developing countries," *Economic Development and Cultural Change* 30, no. 3: 625–648.

Lipton, Michael. 1977. *Why Poor People Stay Poor: Urban Bias in World Development.* Cambridge, Mass.: Harvard University Press.

Lowry, Ira S. 1988. "Planning for urban sprawl," in *A Look Ahead: Year 2000.* Washington, D.C.: Transportation Research Board, National Research Council, pp. 275-312.

Montgomery, Mark R. 1988. "How large is too large? Implications of the city size literature for population policy and research," *Economic Development and Cultural Change* 36, no. 4: 691–720.

Organization for Economic Cooperation and Development. 1984. "The search for a rural-urban balance," in *Urban Development in the Third World,* ed. P. K. Ghosh. Westport, Conn.: Greenwood Press.

Newman, Peter W. G. 1988. "Australian cities at the crossroads," *Current Affairs Bulletin* 65, no. 7: 4-15. Published by the Workers' Educational Association of New South Wales, Australia, and the University of Sydney.

———, and Jeffrey R. Kenworthy. 1989. "Gasoline consumption and cities: A comparison of U.S. cities with a global survey," *Journal of the American Planning Association* 55, no. 1: 24-37.

Pimentel, David. 1980. *Handbook of Energy Utilization in Agriculture.* Boca Raton, Fla.: CRC Press.

Rogers, Andrei. 1982. "Sources of urban population growth and urbanization, 1950–2000: A demographic accounting," *Economic Development and Cultural Change* 30, no. 3: 483–506.

Salas, Rafael M. 1986. *The State of World Population 1986.* New York: United Nations Fund for Population Activities.

Taylor, Jeffrey R., and Judith Banister. 1988. *China: The Problem of Employing Surplus Rural Labor.* Washington, D.C.: Center for International Research, US Bureau of the Census.

Todaro, Michael P., with Jerry Stilkind. 1981. *City Bias and Rural Neglect: The Dilemma of Urban Development.* New York: The Population Council.

United Nations, Centre for Housing, Building, and Planning. Global Review of Human Settlements. 1976. *A Support Paper for Habitat: United Nations Conference on Human Settlements* (2 vols.). Oxford: Pergamon Press.

United Nations, Center for Human Settlements. 1987. *Global Report on Human Settlements 1986.* New York: Oxford University Press.

United Nations, Department of International Economic and Social Affairs. 1980. *Patterns of Urban and Rural Population Growth.* Population Studies No. 68. New York.

United Nations, Department of International Economic and Social Affairs. 1985a. *Estimates and Projections of Urban, Rural and City Populations, 1950–2025: The 1982 Assessment.* New York.

United Nations, Department of International Economic and Social Affairs. 1985b. *World Population Trends, Population and Development Interrelations, and Population Policies* (2 vols.). New York.

United Nations, Department of International Economic and Social Affairs. 1986. *World Population Prospects: Estimates and Projections as Assessed in 1984.* Population Studies No. 98. New York.

United Nations, Department of International Economic and Social Affairs. 1987. *The Prospects of World Urbanization, Revised as of 1984-85.* Population Studies No. 101. New York.

United Nations, Department of International Economic and Social Affairs. 1988a. *World Demographic Estimates and Projections, 1950–2025.* New York.

United Nations, Department of International Economic and Social Affairs. 1988b. *1986 Demographic Yearbook* (thirty-eighth issue). New York.

United States Bureau of the Census. 1986. *Statistical Abstract of the United States: 1987* (107th edition). Washington, D.C.: US Government Printing Office.

White, R. R. 1983. "Third-world urbanization and the environmental crisis," *Environment and Planning A* 15, no. 12: 1567–1569.

World Resources Institute and International Institute for Environment and Development. 1988. *World Resources 1988–89*. A report by WRI and IIED in collaboration with the UN Environment Programme. New York: Basic Books.

Additional readings

Chandler, Tertius, and Gerald Fox. 1974. *3000 Years of Urban Growth*. New York and London: Academic Press.

Davis, Kingsley. 1984. "Asia's cities: Problems and options," in *Urban Development in the Third World*, ed. P. K. Ghosh. Westport, Conn.: Greenwood Press.

Gilbert, Alan, and Josef Gugler, 1982. *Cities, Poverty, and Development: Urbanization in the Third World*. Oxford: Oxford University Press.

Hendry, Peter. 1988. "Food and population: Beyond five billion," *Population Bulletin* 43, no. 2

Renaud, Bertrand. 1981. *National Urbanization Policy in Developing Countries*. Published for the World Bank by Oxford University Press.

Tolley, George S., and Vinod Thomas (eds.). 1987. *The Economics of Urbanization and Urban Policies in Developing Countries*. Washington, D.C.: The World Bank.

United Nations, Department of International Economic and Social Affairs. 1988. *1986 Energy Statistics Yearbook*. New York.

THE RISE OF GLOBAL

POLLUTION

On the Interactions
Between Climate
and Society

MICHAEL H. GLANTZ

ALL COUNTRIES, REGARDLESS OF THEIR LEVEL OF DEVELOPMENT or type of political system, are subject to the adverse effects of climate variability (e.g., droughts, floods, severe storms). Recent studies have shown that industrialized countries are no more immune to the impacts of climate (in the form of extreme meteorological events) than are developing countries (Burton et al., 1978). Similar findings emerge from comparison of capitalist and socialist systems (e.g., Antal and Glantz, 1988).

Considerable discussion regarding climatic impacts has been generated by such occurrences as the devastating droughts throughout sub-Saharan Africa in the past two decades, exacerbating existing problems of access to food by large segments of the African population (Sen, 1981). El Niño events—the recurrent warming of sea surface temperatures off the western coast of South America—have been directly associated with devastating impacts on South American societies, and to varying degrees on other societies around the globe, and have also heightened interest in the effects of climate variability on society. The disruptive consequences of droughts and record-setting high temperatures in 1988 on North American agricultural production, navigation, and urban populations served as yet another stimulus for concern about climate variability and climate change.

The current belief within the atmospheric science community specifically and among scientists in general is that the Earth's atmosphere is heating up due to increasing amounts of carbon dioxide and other trace gases being produced by human activities, a process popularly referred to as the "greenhouse effect." In mid-1988, the American scientist James Hansen implied during congressional hearings on global warming that the North American droughts and high temperatures were early signs that such a warming was in progress (Hansen, 1988; Begley et al., 1988). Such changes in the global climate would have major implications for the economic development prospects of all nations. In fact, climate change may prove to be one of the most important problems of our time.

These examples and the ones to follow underscore the need for social scientists to become more active in the assessment of the interrelationships among atmospheric, environmental, and societal processes. In this article several issues related to the environmental and societal aspects of climate variability and change are briefly addressed: the past use of the concept of climate in development literature; the impacts of climate variability on society; the linkages between drought, seasonality, and development; the notion that "drought follows the plow"; the global warming issue; regional scenarios for global climate change; and the emergence of widespread interest in global environmental change. While these topics do indeed overlap, each has its own specific message for the reader.

Climate and economic development

Climate has been a neglected aspect of social science research for many decades. In part this neglect of the climatic aspects of the environment stems from an adverse reaction to the controversial works of Yale professor Ellsworth Huntington (1915), among others. Huntington's works on civilization and climate have come to symbolize the use of climate information to support the view that there is a "natural" cleavage between the work ethics of populations in the temperate climatic zones and those in the tropics. At the risk of oversimplification, Huntington's argument could be summarized as follows: tropical climates lack the marked seasonal changes of the temperate zones that serve to stimulate the energies of populations. Inhabitants of the tropics, according to Huntington, had been dealt an oppressive climate (hot and dry or hot and wet) and that was their fate. He contended that:

> [A] certain type of climate, now found mainly in Britain, France, and neighbouring parts of Europe, and in the Eastern United States is favourable to a high level of civilisation. This climate is characterized by a moderate temperature, and by the passage of frequent barometric depressions, which give a sufficient rainfall and changeable stimulating weather. (quoted in Brooks, 1926: 292)

Only against great odds might the leaders of a tropical country bring about economic, social, and political development similar to that generally found in the temperate regions. Huntington's views generated a reluctance to discuss climate and development issues in a scholarly context because they have been used to reinforce the belief in a climate–civilization connection. Only recently have researchers been able to circumvent the pejorative connotation of climate and development issues. Nevertheless, variations on

Huntington's theme of climate determinism have appeared in the literature throughout the last several decades, right up to the present. In the 1940s, for example, one author identified a "way out" for inhabitants of the tropics when he wrote about the potential benefits of the "air conditioning revolution" for economic development (Markham, 1944). He suggested that with this technological breakthrough islands of temperate zone climate could be artificially created in the tropics to serve as enclaves of development in the midst of an otherwise oppressive setting.

In the 1950s some authors continued to consider climate as a boundary constraint to economic development about which little could be done. One such report, produced by the US Council of Foreign Relations (Lee, 1957), sought to address the following concerns:

> Why is an underdeveloped country underdeveloped? ... By any rational definition of "underdeveloped country" most of them lie entirely or partially in the tropics. Is climate the common factor that keeps them underdeveloped? ... [A] hot tropical climate seems to be the common factor amongst the underdeveloped countries, and a temperate climate characteristic of the higher developed countries. (p.vii)

Since the 1970s there have been some attempts to reassess the role of climate in economic development processes in the tropical areas (Oury, 1969; Kamarck, 1976). In his report for the World Bank, Kamarck briefly hinted at the impacts of climate variability (as opposed to climate as a boundary condition) as a factor in development in the tropics. In the early 1980s an Indian social scientist assessed the potential effects of a climate change on the boundary constraints to economic development in the tropics. Bandyopadhyaya (1983: 158) believed that

> [T]he global climate dichotomy is ... responsible for the wide and widening economic gap between the North and the South and the neo-imperialistic economic exploitation of the latter by the former. ... It is evident that the amelioration of the tropical climate is one of the necessary conditions for the total emancipation of the South from the economic and political control of the North.

He concluded that a climate change (e.g., a global warming) could benefit Third World countries in the tropics and would reduce the development gap between North and South.

While discussions about the interrelationship of climate and economic development usually raise the name of Ellsworth Huntington and often evolve into a debate about the shortcomings (if not racial connotations) of climate determinism, there is some validity to the linkage of climate and development. To bypass the legacy of Huntington, the concept of climate (itself a construct) is best treated in terms of its disaggregated components. By breaking down the concept of climate into such key components as temperature, rainfall, range of variability, seasonality, and extreme meteorological events, one can more easily identify ways that climate affects society and ways that those societal effects can be mitigated or adapted to, if not prevented by, human action. Recent studies have suggested how specific characteristics of climate interact with the development process (e.g., Glantz, 1987,1989; Chambers et al., 1981; Spitz, 1981).

Climate-related impact assessment

1972: The year of climate anomalies

The first in a series of recent peaks in interest for undertaking climate impact studies came in the early 1970s. Before 1972, with an overabundance of wheat and corn in storage and with prices falling below the cost of production, major cereal-producing countries (e.g., the United States, Canada, Australia) were faced with a "grain crisis," one of surplus, not one of scarcity. American farmers were paid by the federal government not to grow crops already in surplus and to take agricultural land out of production. The Canadian government embarked on a similar program in the late 1960s called LIFT (Lower Inventory for Tomorrow), whose objective was to reduce the production of certain grains by 50 percent (Canadian Task Force on Agriculture, 1970).

The Canadian Task Force on Agriculture issued a report (1970) that typified the then-current thinking in both Canada and the United States about the impacts of climate on food production. That thinking can be generalized as follows: society had developed the technologies needed to buffer agricultural production from the vagaries of climate, and, as a result, the world was about to enter an era of cereal grain sufficiency, if not overabundance. In time, technological developments (e.g., high-yield varieties, new irrigation techniques and facilities) would be transferred to the developing countries, where major food production problems would largely disappear. Hopes were high that a "green revolution" was under way, with India, at the time, taking the lead.

In 1972 these perceptions changed abruptly. Droughts occurred simultaneously around the globe, adversely affecting food production in the Soviet Union, China, India, Central America, Australia, Indonesia, Argentina, Brazil, West Africa, Ethiopia, and elsewhere (see Figure 1).

The failure of agricultural production on such a large geographical scale led to a rapid drawdown of global grain reserves. In 1972 the Soviet Union consummated the largest grain (corn and wheat) purchase in history from the United States at low prices subsidized by the US government—a

FIGURE 1 Map of worldwide droughts, 1972–73

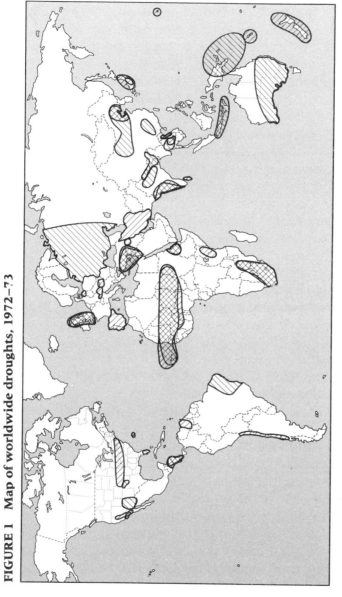

1972 droughts (March–December)

1972–73 droughts

1973 droughts (January–August)

transaction characterized by one American author as the "Great Grain Robbery" (Trager, 1974). Much of the grain that remained in the international marketplace commanded higher prices, the highest since World War II. Many countries in need of grain could not afford to buy it, losing out to countries that could pay the higher prices.

The 1972–73 climate anomalies drew attention to just how vulnerable societies were to climate variability. Climate impact studies suggested that technology had not necessarily made societies less vulnerable to weather and in some instances may have made them even more vulnerable. Complacency about coping with climate variability, as a result of high levels of agricultural productivity in the 1950s and 1960s, had minimized industrialized societies' capabilities to respond to the rapid, sharp downturn in agricultural production that occurred in the early 1970s. For example, US Secretary of Agriculture Earl Butz, testifying before Congress in December 1973, noted that the climate anomalies of 1972–73 had changed the perceptions about the resilience of global agriculture. He stated that, "In the last 18 months, we have shifted from concern over too much farm production to the question of potential food and fiber shortages both here and abroad. . . . Farmers now plant for markets—not Government storage" (US Senate, 1974: 20).

Yet, the droughts that received major attention were not those in the grain-producing regions. Humanitarian concerns focused (albeit belatedly) on the devastating droughts in sub-Saharan Africa. The large losses of human and animal populations and the destruction of the fragile environments in these areas were at first blamed on a succession of drought years in the West African Sahel (1968–73) and in Ethiopia (1972–74). Retrospective studies have since appropriately identified the major role that decisionmaking processes at all levels of social organization played in the hundreds of thousands of deaths and in the widespread destruction of the environment that occurred in these areas (Morentz, 1980; Shepherd, 1975).

The societal impacts of the worldwide anomalies of 1972–73 led to the convening of a world food conference in Rome in 1974 as well as a world population conference in Bucharest later that year. These global conferences sparked the convening of related United Nations conferences throughout the rest of the decade—on human settlements (1976), water (1977), desertification (1977), technology (1979), and even climate (1979).

In the search for causes of these simultaneous worldwide droughts, attention shifted to the Pacific Ocean, where another climate anomaly, El Niño, was making its way into the headlines. At the time of its occurrence, the 1972–73 El Niño was considered one of the "largest" in a century and has since been "blamed" for many of the climate anomalies which occurred that year. Once viewed as a local occurrence that primarily plagued Peruvian guano production and, later, regional fisheries, El Niño is now considered a regional phenomenon with worldwide environmental and societal implications.

El Niño is the name given to an oceanic-atmospheric phenomenon that can generally be defined as an invasion of warm surface water from the western part of the Pacific Basin into the eastern equatorial Pacific (primarily off the coasts of Peru and Ecuador). This "pool" of warm water heats the atmosphere above it, causing cloud formation, instability in the atmosphere, and, ultimately, rain. As the systems of rain-bearing clouds shift, following the location of higher sea surface temperatures, excessive rainfall patterns also shift. Thus, regions that are usually arid receive excessive rainfall (e.g., the arid coast of western South America), while regions that usually receive abundant rainfall (e.g., parts of Indonesia and the Philippines) are plagued by droughts. A schematic of the process is shown in Figure 2.

In addition to the reductions in agricultural productivity in 1972–73 discussed earlier, commercial fish landings also declined for the first time in decades. As one important example, the El Niño–related collapse of the Peruvian anchoveta fishery led to a sharp decline in the worldwide availability of fishmeal (a preferred livestock feed supplement), a sharp increase in the price of its preferred substitute, soymeal, and a shift by US farmers from growing wheat (for food) to soybeans, in order to take advantage of higher

FIGURE 2   Schematic of the mean atmospheric circulation along the equator during El Niño and non–El Niño years

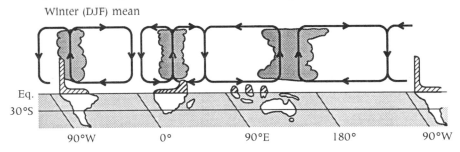

Winter (DJF) mean

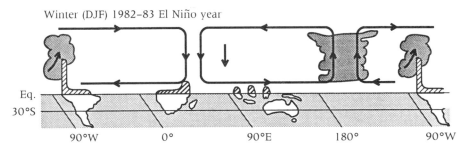

Winter (DJF) 1982–83 El Niño year

NOTE: Ascending motion creates clouds, descending motion deters cloud formation. There is a shift eastward of the rain–producing mechanisms. Locations that normally get rain have droughts, while normally dry areas are subjected to high levels of precipitation. (DJF = December, January, February.)

SOURCE: Adapted from Tourre, cited in WMO (1984).

prices and expanded demand for this commodity. All this occurred at a time when demand for food grains had sharply increased. In addition, the shortage of fishmeal and the consequent rise in soymeal prices stimulated Brazilian entrepreneurs to undertake a major expansion of soybean production. Soymeal has since become one of Brazil's major agricultural exports.

Recently, scientists have focused on the concept of teleconnections, or the linkages between El Niño events in the eastern equatorial Pacific and climate anomalies worldwide. Sometimes these anomalies precede the El Niño event, sometimes they lag it, and sometimes they are concurrent. There is widespread hope that forecasting such events may provide a major scientific tool for forecasting climate anomalies far from the Pacific region, enabling governments as well as individuals to take "evasive" actions to mitigate the impacts of such anomalies (Flohn and Fleer, 1975; Glantz et al., 1987).

With the El Niño–related worldwide climate anomalies of 1972–73 and those of 1982–83, which proved to be even larger, and the highly visible impacts of these anomalies on both industrialized and developing societies, attention was once again drawn by scientists, the media, and some US policymakers to the effects of climate variability on human activities and the environment.

Drought, seasonality, and development

While drought has received considerable attention in the past two decades because of its links to food production problems and shortages, drought alone seldom results in famine. In fact, drought's contribution to recent food (and agrarian) crises can properly be evaluated only in conjunction with consideration of internal political, economic, fiscal, military, and demographic factors as well as such external factors as the mounting international debt burden, worsening terms of trade, and foreign involvement in military conflicts such as in Ethiopia, Mozambique, and Angola.

An often overlooked factor implicated in generating food shortages (and famines) that may be almost as important as the direct effects of drought and other known factors is how drought affects (and most often exacerbates) the existing linkages between the natural rhythm of the seasons, food production, and various aspects of rural poverty. Consideration of the annual progression of the seasons and its effects on rural poverty, while addressed by a few researchers (e.g., Chambers et al., 1981; Watts, 1983), has not yet been integrated into assessments of drought, famine, and development. While drought and its direct impacts are highly visible and often spectacular, most often they only worsen the socioeconomic effects of an already existing, less spectacular, but potentially equally devastating climatic process, the changing of the seasons.

Some members of society benefit from the natural rhythm of the seasons (e.g., rich peasants, grain merchants, speculators) at the expense of the larger fraction of rural poor, especially during periods of cultivation when work demands are at a peak and the nutritional status of peasant workers, especially women and children, is at its lowest level. Droughts tend to intensify seasonal hunger and to spread it across other seasons. Depending on the political and economic setting in which it occurs, drought can eventually convert widespread chronic malnutrition and seasonal hunger into full-fledged famine conditions. For example, preharvest shortages are common in many African societies. Such shortages have been referred to as periods of seasonal hunger, during which the nutritional levels of a large segment of the rural population decline. Such periods of decline frequently occur during the wet season.

For a variety of reasons (including technological factors), some societies are clearly less vulnerable to climate anomalies than are others. A drought in the US Great Plains, for example, no longer leads to widespread malnutrition, migration, food shortages, and famine, as was the case in the 1930s and earlier, whereas droughts in such countries as Ethiopia and Mozambique continue to have devastating effects on their populations. Moreover, not all segments of society are equally affected. Prolonged drought at first adversely affects the poorest inhabitants of rural society, and, as it continues, its effects spread to the relatively more affluent members of society. On this point, Sen (1981: 43) noted:

> Indeed it is by no means clear that there has ever occurred a famine in which all groups in a country have suffered from starvation, since different groups typically do have very different commanding powers over food, and an overall shortage brings out the contrasting powers in stark clarity.

The impact of drought on society will vary in part according to its timing. If it occurs at the onset of the growing season, for example, those farmers in a position to do so might replant several times, thereby using up their seed reserves. If drought occurs in midseason, the number of options available to farmers, such as the planting of varieties that require shorter growing seasons, would be fewer, as the growing season would already have been considerably shortened.

There is little one can do about the seasons; they seemingly serve as a boundary constraint to agricultural activities. However, the way in which the inevitable recurrence of a single drought year or prolonged runs of drought years further distort the societal effects of seasonality on the livelihood and welfare of rural populations is of extreme importance for the improved understanding of how societies might best prepare for or mitigate the impacts of droughts. By assessing seasonality and its effects on human activities, we can more properly determine the role that droughts have played in the agrarian crisis in sub-Saharan Africa (Glantz, 1989).

Drought follows the plow

Today the scientific literature abounds with articles and studies about how land use can enhance or reduce rainfall in a region. Almost a century ago, the popular belief that "rain follows the plow" was a direct catalyst to accelerated population movements into the US Great Plains. The concept, fostered by land speculators and railroad companies as well as geographers and foresters, was centered on the belief that a region's atmospheric circulation is positively affected by increases in the sources of evaporation. These derive from breaking the ground with the plow, creating open bodies of water (ponds and reservoirs), and planting trees (e.g., Smith, 1950: 201–213). This notion still lives, although the number of people who hold such a view seems to vary from one decade to the next, and the opposite view has also been expressed, specifically for the Sahel (e.g., Charney et al., 1977).

Suggesting a belief in the notion that rain follows the plow, the United Nations and ALESCO (the Arab League Economic, Scientific, and Cultural Organization) some years ago proposed that tree belts be developed along the northern and southern edges of the Sahara desert to arrest sand dune encroachment and to return moisture to the air, thereby bringing rainfall back to desiccated areas. At least one knowledgeable and reputable scientist has pejoratively referred to these activities as a search for the Loch Ness Monster of the Sahara (Le Houérou, 1973, private correspondence).

Most of the world's best rainfed agricultural land is already in production or unavailable to production for political or other reasons. Increasing the amount of land available for agriculture frequently involves the destruction of forested areas that border agricultural lands, the introduction or expanded use of irrigation in arid areas, and the movement of people into areas that are agriculturally marginal in terms of soil (low fertility, or highly erodable in the absence of vegetative cover), climate (erratic rainfall within and between years), vegetation (rangeland grasses removed in order to grow crops), and topography (steep, deforested slopes of hillsides that are highly erodable). It can be effectively argued that as agriculture moves into increasingly marginal areas, drought, not rain, often follows the plow.

The notion that drought follows the plow is based on the view that, with increasing pressure to cultivate marginal areas, drought episodes will become more prevalent. This can result from the fact that crops grown in the more reliably watered areas are not well suited to environmental conditions in the margins. Whereas climate often is blamed for a crop failure, that failure may prove to be more the result, for example, of poor land-management practices unadapted to these margins. The following two examples illustrate this notion.

Thirty years ago, Nikita Khrushchev, then Secretary General of the Communist Party of the Soviet Union, launched his virgin lands scheme in an attempt to surpass US grain production. If successful, the scheme would have demonstrated to the developing world that the Soviet Union was as much an agricultural force as an industrial power. The plan "encouraged" people from various parts of the Soviet Union to move into Soviet Central Asia and Kazakhstan in order to put arid and semiarid land into mechanized agricultural production (Brezhnev, 1979). Stories about the failure of this approach soon reached the public, as lack of rainfall and dust storms prompted people to abandon the virgin lands and return home. Drought conditions and highly variable rainfall continue to plague these lands. Since that time, however, rainfed agriculture has been supplanted by irrigated farming, and the region has become quite productive. Nevertheless, the architects of the virgin lands strategy failed at the outset to take seriously the marginal nature of the climate for sustained agricultural production. For many marginal areas in the Third World, irrigation is a very costly option and most probably not a universal solution to resolving food shortages.

The West African Sahel provides a second example of drought following the plow. Briefly, in the 1950s and 1960s, rainfall in this region had increased above its long-term average. Increased rainfall sharply improved the vegetative growth in areas normally used as rangelands for the intermittent grazing of pastoral herds. Eyeing the lush green vegetation during this period of above-average rainfall, governments in the region encouraged their farmers to move northward toward the southern edge of the Sahara in order to cultivate these seemingly productive areas. In turn, indigenous pastoralists were pushed further north. With the return to prolonged multiyear drought conditions in the early 1970s, cultivators abandoned their farms and pastoralists lost their herds only to end up in refugee camps or as beggars in urban areas. The geographic and climatic reality of the region was that agricultural activities could not be sustained in the Sahelian margins because of the high degree of rainfall variability over the long term. Not only were cultivators unable to maintain crop production in the area, but the land that they cleared became further degraded as a result of wind and water erosion, giving rise in the mid-1970s to concern about the process of desertification, or the creation of desert-like conditions where none had existed in the recent past. The people and governments claimed that they had been the victims of a "natural disaster" when in fact they had sought to grow crops in areas where the long-term climatic conditions in the region are unsuited (Glantz, 1976).

Attempts to cultivate marginal lands tend to marginalize both land (reducing fertility) and people (pauperizing them). Most often, either a push or a pull into these areas initiates the process. Push factors include population pressure, environmental degradation, and government policies. If the best rainfed agricultural land is already in production, while populations continue to grow and the resource base continues to deteriorate at present rates, new farmers must move into increasingly marginal areas, which then become further impoverished by overuse and misuse.

The pull factors are relatively few. As mentioned earlier, climates fluctuate, sometimes with long wet or dry spells alternating. During wet periods in arid and semiarid areas, the normally dry areas appear to be capable of sustaining agricultural production. Thus encouraged to move there (by nature as well as by government), farmers often displace pastoral herders who have traditionally used these areas as rangelands for their livestock, an activity that is more closely suited to the highly variable nature of rainfall in the region.

The notion that drought follows the plow is based on the belief that increased pressures (whatever the source) on currently used agricultural areas cause populations to move into less productive, often marginal, areas. Consequently, we can expect to hear even more in the future about droughts and their impacts on humankind. The reason will not necessarily be that the climate has changed but rather that people have moved into areas that will prove to be unsuited in the long term to agricultural practices. Clearly, future generations will find it increasingly difficult to support themselves from the continued cultivation of marginal lands.

Climate change: Global cooling, global warming

In addition to issues raised by the impacts of climate variability on society and the environment, concern has been growing about the possibility of global climate change and its potential environmental and societal effects. Can human activities alter the chemical composition of the atmosphere, atmospheric processes, and, ultimately, the climate?

In the early 1970s scientists raised the possibility of an impending climate change of major proportions. More specifically, concern was expressed about the possible return of an ice age. Convincing (but eclectic and circumstantial) evidence was cited to support such a hypothesis: for example, between 1940 and 1970, the British growing season had been reduced by two weeks, fish populations normally caught off the northern coast of Iceland were found off its southern coast, hay production in Iceland declined due to cooler temperatures, and so forth. The US Central Intelligence Agency, among other government agencies, prepared reports on the strategic implications for Soviet and American agriculture of a cooling (US CIA, 1974). Several books and scores of articles appeared in the mid-1970s on this topic: *The Cooling* (Ponte, 1976), *The Weather Conspiracy: The Coming Ice Age*

(The Impact Team, 1977), "When the Sahel freezes over" (Ponte, 1977), "Ominous changes in the weather" (Alexander, 1974), and so forth. Congressional subcommittees also convened hearings on the prospects of a global cooling and its implications (US House of Representatives, 1976).

By the mid-1970s, however, it had become increasingly clear that some of the scientific theories and empirical evidence behind the global cooling hypothesis were misleading. At the same time, increasing scientific evidence began to suggest that a global warming was in progress: the continued burning of fossil fuels (coal, petroleum, natural gas) coupled with tropical deforestation was adding unprecedented amounts of carbon dioxide to the atmosphere. Increased atmospheric CO_2 was intercepting outgoing longwave radiation, thereby heating up the lower atmosphere—the effect being somewhat analogous to that observed in a greenhouse. A few decades of measurements of atmospheric CO_2 content, begun in 1957 during the International Geophysical Year and illustrated in Figure 3, indicated a steady rise in atmospheric CO_2 concentrations (Keeling, cited in Hoffman, 1987).

Speculation on possible future trends of CO_2 production abounds, as scientists and policymakers consider various energy options and policies. A sample of such speculation is shown in Figure 4.

FIGURE 3   Monthly measurement of atmospheric carbon dioxide concentration at Mauna Loa, Hawaii, 1958–85

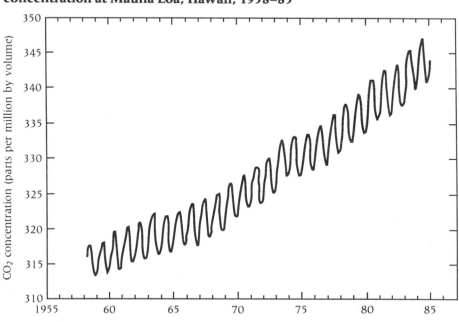

NOTE: The intra–annual variations in CO_2 concentration result from seasonal variations in photosynthetic activity.

**FIGURE 4   Past concentration of atmospheric carbon dioxide and
two possible scenarios of future concentrations**

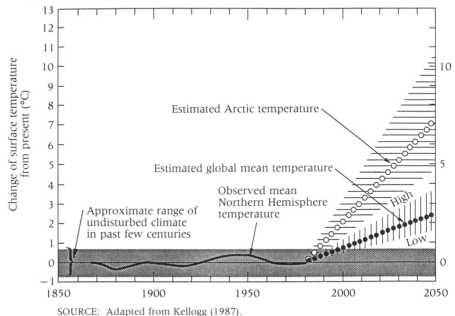

SOURCE: Adapted from Kellogg (1987).

Interest in the global warming issue is quite high today, reinforced by
its possible (but unproven) linkage with the occurrence of the five warmest
years on record, all in the 1980s. Although conclusive detection of a CO_2
warming signal or a "fingerprint" has not yet occurred, scientists respond
by noting that the recent droughts throughout North America are at least
consistent with what researchers think might be the impacts on climate of a
CO_2–induced global warming.

As of today, there appears to be a relatively firm scientific consensus
that CO_2, being added to the atmosphere by human activities and by natural
processes, is causing a global warming of the Earth's atmosphere. In addition, the production of other trace gases (chlorofluorocarbons for aerosol
sprays, refrigerants, and foam propellants; methane from rice paddies and
livestock; nitrous oxides from fertilizer use) is also contributing to the global
warming. Their combined future effects on global temperatures are projected to be equal to or greater than that of CO_2 early in the next century
(Ramanathan et al., 1985).

Much of the early interest in global warming was generated by the
scientific community. However, serious and growing concern about global
warming as a policy issue has emerged in the last few years (Mintzer, 1987).
Some US Senators and Representatives have become involved in the issue by
promoting, at first, scientific research programs (e.g., Department of Energy

state-of-the-art reports, from 1980 to present, such as DOE, 1980, 1985, 1988), and now studies of the policy implications of those research findings (e.g., the project carried out by the US Environmental Protection Agency to assess the effects of global warming, submitted to Congress in 1989).

In June 1988, a major international meeting was convened in Toronto by Canadian Prime Minister Brian Mulroney on "The changing atmosphere: Implications for global security." This was essentially a political conference about a scientific issue. In his opening remarks, the Prime Minister called for a "Law of the Atmosphere" along the lines of the Law of the Sea. Such a proposal was not well received by participants from the United States and some other nations.

For decisionmakers at all levels of social organization it is difficult to base decisions on changes in average global temperature. What they need to know is how an average global change of a few degrees Celsius will translate into changes that might affect temperature and precipitation variations and the frequency, intensity, and duration of extreme meteorological events at regional and local levels. Such information cannot yet be provided by atmospheric general circulation models. Considerable attention has focused recently on how to generate credible, plausible regional scenarios about future states of the atmosphere (e.g., Wigley et al., 1986; Pearman, 1988).

Societal responses to regional climatic change

One approach to assessing societal responses to climate-related environmental change (whether abrupt or long-term) has been to evaluate current responses to environmental changes as an indicator of how well societies might be prepared to cope with similar changes in the future. A recent study focusing on contemporary climate-related environmental stresses in North America was completed for the US Environmental Protection Agency (Glantz, 1988). The case studies evaluated are shown on the map in Figure 5.

The effects of a series of hard freezes on Florida's citrus production provide one example of this approach, referred to as "forecasting by analogy." For decades Florida had been viewed as the "king of citrus," not just in the United States but in other countries as well. Citrus production, especially for frozen concentrate of orange juice, is an $8 billion industry in Florida, although it accounts for only a small percentage of the state's total annual agricultural earnings. Perhaps until 1980 the claim of King Citrus was a valid one. In the early 1980s, however, Florida's citrus-growing regions were plagued by recurring hard freezes that decimated some of the state's major citrus-producing groves in four out of five years. Such a run of freeze years had not previously occurred this century.

FIGURE 5 Case studies of recent climate-related environmental stresses

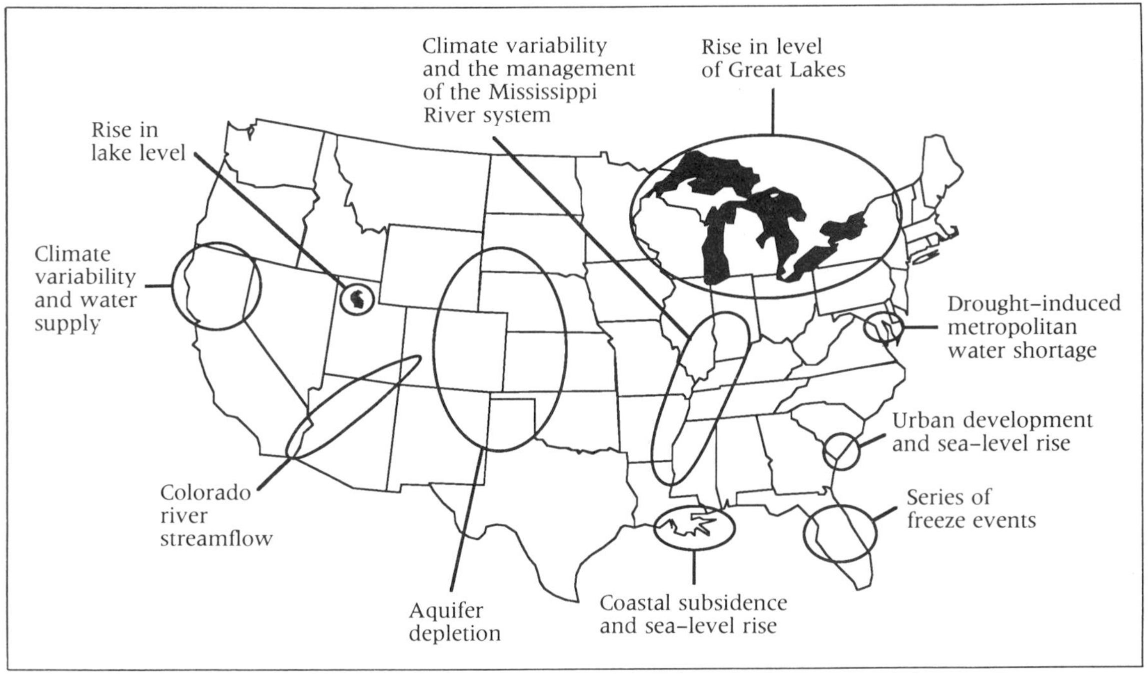

Rise in level
of Great Lakes

Climate variability
and the management
of the Mississippi
River system

Drought-induced
metropolitan
water shortage

Urban development
and sea-level rise

Series of
freeze events

Coastal subsidence
and sea-level rise

Aquifer
depletion

Colorado
river
streamflow

Rise in
lake level

Climate
variability
and water
supply

Following the first freeze, citrus growers believed that they had been hit by a not-unexpected occasional freeze. The second freeze year was considered unusual but not improbable. The third freeze year, however, perplexed grove owners and raised questions about whether the climate was in fact changing. Was this increase in the frequency of freezes a consequence of the greenhouse effect that was regularly being described in the media? The fourth freeze year was devastating, prompting some citrus owners to give up their business. Some sold their land to developers, an irreversible change in land use in central Florida. Others considered planting groves at the southern edge of the citrus-producing region, where climate is more certain but soil is less favorable. For their part, researchers intensified their efforts to develop hardier citrus species that might withstand mild freezes. They also developed new techniques to protect trees from cold temperatures (Miller, in preparation).

The winters of 1986 and 1987 were favorable ones for citrus production. The situation in 1987, however, was not the same as it had been in 1980, before the onset of the run of freezes. One new factor was that Brazilian entrepreneurs were in a position to capitalize on the decrease in frozen concentrate production in Florida. In the past, when freezes occurred in Florida the price for the undamaged citrus crop rose sharply because of reduced supplies. With Brazilian stocks available to fill in for losses due to the Florida freezes, prices failed to rise as sharply as before. Because of favorable climatic conditions in Brazil, the inexpensive labor supply, and large stocks of frozen concentrate, Brazil has managed to capture a large share of the North American market.

The Florida case study suggests that although we are constantly concerned about a "global" warming, the impacts of that warming will be felt at regional and local levels, and decisions to cope with those impacts will most likely be made at those levels. The situation also shows that grove owners are basically risk takers. Despite the adverse effects of this recent series of freezes, many of them have remained in the business. In fact, it seems that the grove owners tend to weigh in their minds the most recent climatic events more heavily than earlier ones. The recent mild winters have led many growers to believe that there has been a return to what they would like to consider "normal" climate.

Freezes in Florida also underscore the role of climate variability in the ability of countries (or states or industries) to compete economically. It was a severe freeze in Florida in 1962 that prompted Brazilian businessmen to consider developing a citrus industry for export markets. Thus, changes in climate in the future can alter the economic competitiveness of countries involved in the export of crops that are sensitive to climatic factors (for a detailed analysis of the Florida citrus case study, see Miller, 1988).

Forecasting by analogy also provides lessons about how societies might improve the ways they cope with climate variability today, independent of whether the global climate changes over the next several decades. Speculation about future states of the atmosphere and what those states mean for society is an important activity. The approach described here provides some insight into our understanding of the kinds of decisions that societies must make in the event of a future change in climate. In fact, a warming of the atmosphere by a few degrees does not mean that all temperatures will increase by that amount. Regional and seasonal changes could include a cooling as well. At this time no one can present decisionmakers with credible or reliable scenarios of the future. What forecasting by analogy does is to provide them with examples of how well societies (local, regional, and national) are prepared to deal with today's climate variability. After all, a climate change will most likely be felt through regional changes in the frequency, intensity, duration, and even location of extreme meteorological events. Having information about how well we deal with these factors today can help society to maintain flexibility to respond to unknown climate extremes of the future.

Concluding comments

Weather and climate have fascinated people through the ages. For the most part these phenomena were events that happened to individuals, settlements, societies, and nations. Most impacts of climate variability on society were seen as acts of God and were accepted as such, with societies in general resigned to their fate, ready to pick up the pieces and rebuild.

Today, a new view about climate is emerging. While countries have come to realize that technology alone is not sufficient protection against the vagaries of weather and climate, there is also a growing awareness that information about climate can be used to improve their ability to mitigate its societal and environmental impacts.

There is also a growing awareness that human activities—such as the burning of fossil fuels, deforestation, land-use practices, the manufacture of certain types of trace gases, rice production, and fertilizer applications—can alter atmospheric processes to varying degrees on all space and time scales. The examples cited in this article reinforce such awareness. Much research needs to be done to improve our understanding of how society affects atmospheric processes and how these processes affect society.

In order to understand atmospheric processes and their impacts on the environment and society, and in turn their feedback into atmospheric processes, scientists are increasingly being required to consider other elements of the Earth in addition to the atmosphere as a system. A recent report of the

National Aeronautics and Space Administration noted that "global connections among the Earth's components began to be recognized in the last century. However, it is only relatively recently that scientists in one discipline have had to confront the need for major contributions from other disciplines in order to achieve substantial research advances" (NASA, 1988: 12).

Several international programs are now being developed to focus on global change. The International Geosphere-Biosphere Programme (IGBP), subtitled "Global Change," is one such major effort (NRC, 1986; Malone and Roederer, 1985; IGBP, 1988). The various goals, activities, funding sources, and participants of these efforts are now identified and developed nationally and internationally (e.g., IGBP, 1988). Global change provides the latest challenge to researchers interested in the societal and humanistic aspects of environmental changes on the global, national, and local scales. Activities related to global change provide an opportunity for undertaking multidisciplinary research on climate-related impact assessment.

Natural scientists have, until recently, been reluctant to integrate into their global change program a meaningful social science and humanist component. However, to understand the factors affecting those rates of change and how to develop policies to control them, the underlying human forces must be identified and assessed. Many of the environmental changes that governments are most concerned about today are directly linked to human activities: population growth rates, fossil fuel consumption, deforestation, desertification, soil erosion, land use practices, atmospheric pollution, and so forth. Population growth (absolute numbers as well as rate) is clearly at the heart of these environmental changes. Thus, social science research must be integrated into national and international efforts toward research on global change.

Many social scientists are already directly involved in various aspects of research on environmental change. In many instances their efforts can be modified to fit into the context of a global change research program, once these scientists have been made aware that such a program exists.

While the consideration of climatic factors is important for the well-being of societies worldwide, this essay should not be taken as an effort to reduce all ills and good fortunes of society to climate-related factors. I do believe, however, that such factors are important, sometimes crucial, considerations that have generally been ignored in social science research. It is time to reconsider the interactions of climate variability and climate change with human activities and the environment.

Note

The National Center for Atmospheric Research is sponsored by the National Science Foundation.

References

Alexander, T. 1974. "Ominous changes in the weather, " *Fortune* (February): 90–152.

Antal, E., and M. H. Glantz. 1988. *Identifying and Coping with Extreme Meteorological Events.* Budapest, Hungary: Hungarian Meteorological Service.

Bandyopadhyaya, J. 1983. *Climate and World Order: An Inquiry into the Natural Cause of Underdevelopment.* New Delhi: South Asian.

Begley, S. with M. Miller and M. Hager. 1988. "The endless summer?," *Newsweek,* 11 July: 18–20.

Brooks, C. E. P. 1926. *Climate Through the Ages.* Revised 1949; present edition 1970. New York: Dover Publications.

Braybrooke, D., and G. Paquet. 1987. "Human dimensions of global change: The challenge to the humanities and the social sciences," *Transactions of the Royal Society of Canada* 5, no. 2: 271–291.

Brezhnev, L. 1979. *The Virgin Lands.* Moscow: Progress Publishers.

Burton, I., R. W. Kates, and G. F. White. 1978. *The Environment As Hazard.* New York: Oxford University Press.

Canadian Task Force on Agriculture. 1970. *Canadian Agriculture in the Seventies.* Ottawa: Information Canada.

Chamber, R., R. Longhurst, and A. Pacey (eds.). 1981. *Seasonal Dimensions to Rural Poverty.* Totowa, N.J.: Allenheld, Osmun and Co.

Charney, W. J., S. H. Quick, and J. Kornfield. 1977. "A comparative study of the effects of albedo change on drought in semiarid regions," *Journal of Atmospheric Science* 34: 1366–1385.

DOE (Department of Energy). 1980. *The Role of Tropical Forests on the World Carbon Cycle,* CONF-800350. Springfield, Virginia: National Technical Information Service.

———. 1985. *Detecting the Climatic Effects of Increasing Carbon Dioxide,* DOE/ER-0235. Springfield, Virginia: NTIS.

———. 1988. *A Primer on Greenhouse Gases,* DOE/NBB0083. Springfield, Virginia: NTIS.

Flohn, H., and H. Fleer. 1975. "Climatic teleconnections with the equatorial Pacific and the role of ocean/atmosphere coupling," *Atmosphere* 13, no. 3: 96–109.

Glantz, M. H. (ed.). 1976. *The Politics of Natural Disaster.* New York: Praeger.

———. 1987. "Drought and economic development in sub-Saharan Africa," in *Drought and Hunger in Africa,* ed. M. H. Glantz. Cambridge: Cambridge University Press, pp. 37–58.

———. (ed.) 1988: *Societal Responses to Regional Climatic Change: Forecasting by Analogy.* Boulder, Colo.: Westview Press.

———. 1989. "Drought, famine, and the seasons in sub-Saharan Africa," in *African Food Systems in Crisis,* ed. R. Huss-Ashmore and S. Katz. New York: Gordon and Breach Science Publishers, pp. 45–71.

———, R. Katz, and M. Krenz (eds.). 1987. *The Societal Impacts Associated with the 1982–83 Worldwide Climate Anomalies.* Boulder, Colo.: National Center for Atmospheric Research.

Hansen, J. E. 1988. "The greenhouse effect: Impacts on current global temperature and regional heat waves," paper presented to the US House of Representatives, Committee on Energy and Commerce, Subcommittee on Energy and Power, 7 July.

Hoffman, J. S. 1987. *Assessing the Risks of Trace Gases That Can Modify the Stratosphere.* EPA Report 400/1-87/001B. Washington, DC: US EPA, 2–16.

Huntington, E. 1915. *Civilization and Climate.* Reprinted 1971. Hamden, Conn.: The Shoe String Press.

IFIAS (International Federation of Institutes of Advanced Study). 1988. *Human Responses to Global Change: Prospectus for an International Programme,* draft, April. Toronto: IFIAS.

———, International Social Science Council, and United Nations University. 1988. *Human Responses to Global Change.* Progress report no. 2. Toronto: IFIAS.

IGBP (International Geosphere-Biosphere Programme). 1988. *A Plan of Action.* Report prepared by the Special Committee for the IGBP for discussion at the first meeting of the Scientific Advisory Council for the IGBP, Stockholm, Sweden, 24–28 October. Stockholm: IGBP Secretariat, Royal Swedish Academy of Sciences.

The Impact Team. 1977. *The Weather Conspiracy: The Coming of the New Ice Age.* New York: Ballantine Books.

Jacobson, H. K., and C. Shanks. 1987. *Report on the Ann Arbor Workshop on an International Social Science Research Program on Global Change.* Ann Arbor: Institute for Social Research, University of Michigan.

Kamarck. A. M. 1976. *The Tropics and Economic Development: A Provocative Inquiry into the Poverty of Nations.* Baltimore: The John Hopkins University Press, for The World Bank.

Kellogg, W. W. 1987. "Man's impact on climate: The evolution of an awareness," *Climatic Change* 10: 113–136.

Lee, D. H. K. 1957. *Climate and Economic Development in the Tropics.* New York: Harper & Brothers.

Malone, T. F., and J. G. Roederer (eds.). 1985. *Global Change.* Proceedings of a Symposium sponsored by the International Council of Scientific Unions. Cambridge: Cambridge University Press.

Markham, S. F. 1944. *Climate and the Energy of Nations.* London: Oxford University Press.

Miller, K. A. 1988. "Public and private sector responses to Florida citrus freezes," in Glantz, 1988, pp. 375–405.

——. (in preparation). "Economic adjustments to a changing climate: Evidence from Florida's orange groves."

Mintzer, I. M. 1987. *A Matter of Degrees: The Potential for Controlling the Greenhouse Effect.* Washington, D.C.: World Resources Institute.

Morentz, J. W. 1980. "Communications in the Sahel drought: Comparing the mass media with other channels of international communications," in *Disasters and the Mass Media,* Proceedings of the Committee on Disasters and the Mass Media Workshop, February 1979. Washington, D.C.: National Academy of Sciences

NASA (National Aeronautics and Space Administration). 1988. *Earth System Science: A Program for Global Change.* Washington, D.C.: NASA.

NRC (National Research Council). 1986. *Global Change in the Geosphere-Biosphere: Initial Priorities for an IGBP.* Washington, D.C.: National Academy Press.

Oury, B. 1969. "Weather and economic development," *Finance and Development* 6: 24–29.

Pearman, G. I. (ed.). 1988. *Greenhouse: Planning for Climate Change.* Melbourne, Australia: CSIRO Publications.

Ponte, L. 1976. *The Cooling.* Englewood Cliffs, N.J.: Prentice-Hall.

——. 1977. "When the Sahel freezes over," *Skeptic:* 37–38 and 55–58.

Ramanathan, V., R. J. Cicerone, H. B. Singh, and J. T. Kiehl. 1985. "Trace gas trends and their potential role in climate change," *Journal of Geophysical Research* 90: 5547–5566.

Sen, A. 1981. *Poverty and Famines: An Essay on Entitlement and Deprivation.* Oxford: Clarendon Press.

Shepherd, J. 1975. *The Politics of Starvation.* Washington, D.C.: Carnegie Endowment for International Peace.

Smith, H. N. 1950. *Virgin Land.* New York: Vintage Books.

Spitz, P. 1981. *The Economic Consequences of Food/Climate Variability.* Geneva: UN Research Institute for Social Development.

Trager, J. 1974. *The Great Grain Robbery.* New York: Ballantine Books.

US CIA (Central Intelligence Agency). 1974. *A Study of Climatological Research as it Pertains to Intelligence Problems.* Washington, D.C.: Library of Congress.

US House of Representatives. 1976. *A Primer on Climatic Variation and Change.* Subcommittee on the Environment and the Atmosphere of the Committee on Science and Technology. Washington, D.C.: US Government Printing Office.

US Senate. 1974. *US Agricultural Outlook.* Prepared for the Committee on Agriculture and Forestry, US Senate, 17–19 December 1973. Washington, D.C.: US Government Printing Office.

Watts, M. 1983. *Silent Violence: Food, Famine and Peasantry in Northern Nigeria.* Berkeley: University of California Press.

Wigley, T. M. L., P. D. Jones, and P. M. Kelly. 1986. "Warm world scenarios and the detection of climate change induced by radiatively active gases," in *The Greenhouse Effect, Climatic Change and Ecosystems,* ed. B. Bolin, B. R. Döös, J. Jäger, and R. A. Warrick. Chichester, England: John Wiley & Sons, pp. 271–322.

WMO (World Meteorological Organization). 1984. *The Global Climate System: A Critical Review of the Climate System during 1982–1984.* Geneva: WMO.

Comment: Environmental Risk and Policy Response

RICHARD ELLIOT BENEDICK

MODERN POLICYMAKERS HAVE A TENDENCY TO TEMPORIZE when confronted by situations with clear near-term costs but far less certain future implications. A fundamental issue before governments today is whether and how to act when faced with a new generation of environmental dangers combined with an absence of scientific certitude. These problems include global warming, ozone layer depletion, acid rain, tropical deforestation, desertification, ocean and groundwater pollution, hazardous substances, and extinction of species. Underlying them are pressures from burgeoning populations and consumer demand, translated into industrial, energy, and agricultural practices that threaten to overburden the natural balances on which life depends. This uniquely modern situation poses a serious question for public policy: under what circumstances is it desirable to impose near-term economic and social costs in order to avoid potentially grave—but uncertain—long-term dangers?

While it is true that technology has generally been able to come up with solutions to human dilemmas, there is no guarantee that ingenuity will always rise to the task. Policymakers must contend with a nagging thought: what if it does not, or what if it is too late?

Scarcity of minerals, for instance, leads to higher prices, which in turn should justify deeper mining and stimulate new technology. But what if there are simply insufficient minerals, even at lower depths, and what if inventiveness fails? Markets may be imperfect, information may be lacking or not factored in. It seems reasonably clear, for example, that contemporary fossil fuel and water prices do not adequately reflect long-term ecological costs; they cannot, therefore, be expected to stimulate either more efficient use of resources or the development of alternative technologies. The economists' tautological long-term equilibrium between supply and demand may eventually be reached via laissez-faire, but policymakers must ask themselves whether the costs en route for generations struggling with the adjustment process may be unacceptably high.

A major characteristic of this new generation of environmental issues is the paramount role of science. Science is essential for monitoring developments via satellites and other advanced technology; for constructing sophisticated computer models to project trends and effects; and for designing strategies and technologies to mitigate or adapt to environmental changes. The well-intentioned intuition of ecologists is not a sufficient basis for governments to undertake far-reaching and costly actions. What is required is international scientific consensus, a process of developing empirical data and reasoned projections, of appraising the risks, and of narrowing the bands of uncertainty.

This new situation imposes a burden on governments that transcends their normal political time horizon. How long should they wait for more evidence from a continually evolving science? How can they confront the objections of economic interests—business, labor, consumers—that may have to bear substantial near-term costs for the sake of avoiding uncertain future dangers?

Some answers to these questions—and some guidelines for the future—were provided, for the first time, in the negotiations leading up to the Montreal Protocol on protection of the stratospheric ozone layer, which was adopted in September 1987 by representatives of governments from every region of the world.

The treaty eschewed prescribing a "best available technology" to control the chemicals in question—a traditional concession to ease discomfort for economic interest groups. Rather, the negotiators established firm target dates for reductions in production and use of chlorofluorocarbons (CFCs), in full knowledge that the technology for substitute products or processes did not yet exist.

Significantly, as late as 1986, an executive of DuPont—the world's largest producer of CFCs—had publicly stated that "neither the marketplace nor regulatory policy . . . has provided the needed incentives" to invest in substitutes for CFCs.[1] In fact, DuPont had ceased research in this area in 1980. The Montreal Protocol provided industry with fixed dates for cutbacks in these otherwise rapidly proliferating chemicals, and thus "improved" the effectiveness of the market for the benefit of the environment. Industry now had the incentive to develop the necessary new technology.

During negotiations, while some ideologues in Washington vehemently argued against government intervention because of remaining gaps in scientific knowledge, the chemical industry on both sides of the Atlantic quietly resumed research, as they rationally faced up to the prospect of additional controls under the emerging treaty. Following the signing of the protocol, there has been a ferment of research activity in the chemical industry, and hardly a week goes by without press reports of a promising new lead.

The Montreal treaty was designed to unleash the creative energies of the private sector, and it is succeeding in focusing industry in directions that two years earlier had been considered impossible. Weighing future risks against near-term costs, governments intervened to make the market work toward solutions for a complicated environmental problem.

Some observers have criticized the treaty for being too timid and have even denied its relevance to other global issues. But memories are short: peer-reviewed scientific data did not incontestably link chlorofluorocarbons with ozone-layer depletion and the Antarctic "ozone hole" until several months *after* the treaty was negotiated.[2] In 1987, there was neither "corpse" nor "smoking gun." There were only scientific theories and computer models to implicate a family of chemicals that was synonymous with modern standards of living—chemicals with a wide variety of uses across a range of industries and products, involving billions of dollars in investments and hundreds of thousands of jobs.

At the time, the Montreal Protocol was hailed as a "monumental achievement"[3] and the "most significant environmental agreement in history."[4] It represented the first time that the community of nations was able to agree to severely curtail use of an important chemical before there was measurable evidence of any ecological damage or of harmful effects to life. The protocol was, therefore, not a response to an environmental disaster, like Chernobyl, but rather a conscious attempt at preventive action on a global scale. It was a prudent global insurance policy—a model for international decisionmaking under conditions of uncertainty.[5]

A similar answer to the policymakers' dilemma was provided by US Secretary of State James Baker, in his first diplomatic speech on 30 January 1989—significantly, before a meeting of international experts assembled in Washington to consider strategies for the even more complex issue of global warming. "The political ecology is now ripe for action," Baker said. "We face more than simply a scientific problem. It is also a diplomatic problem of when and how we take action." He continued: "We can probably not afford to wait until all of the [scientific] uncertainties have been resolved before we do act. Time will not make the problems go away." Baker concluded by recommending international actions on several fronts to mitigate the greenhouse effect, actions that are beneficial in their own right but that take on added urgency in light of their potential for moderating climate change: greater energy efficiency to reduce carbon dioxide emissions, phasing out CFCs, and reforestation.[6]

In sum, the Montreal Protocol on the ozone layer and Baker's prescription on global warming share a propensity to err on the side of caution when faced with extraordinarily large, if uncertain, dangers. The Montreal Protocol is in many ways an important precedent for addressing the greenhouse effect and other global environmental issues. It offers hope that the international community is capable of undertaking complicated cooperative actions in a world of ambiguity and imperfect knowledge.

Notes

1 "DuPont position statement on the chlorofluorocarbon-ozone-greenhouse issues," *Environmental Conservation* 13, no. 4 (Winter 1986): 363–364.

2 R.T. Watson, F. S. Rowland, and J. Gillie, *Ozone Trends Panel, Executive Summary* (Washington, D.C.: National Aeronautics and Space Administration, 15 March 1988).

3 "President signs protocol on ozone-depleting substances," text of statement by President Ronald Reagan, 5 April 1988, reported in *Department of State Bulletin* (June 1988): 30.

4 US Senate, Committee on Foreign Relations, *Ozone Protocol*, Statement of Lee M. Thomas, Administrator, US Environmental Protection Agency, Executive Report 100–14, 19 February 1988, p. 61.

5 For further discussion of the Montreal Protocol, see the author's *Ozone Diplomacy: The Montreal Protocol and New Directions in International Cooperation* (Washington, D.C.: The Conservation Foundation and Georgetown University Institute for the Study of Diplomacy, 1990).

6 Department of State, Remarks by the Honorable James A. Baker III before the Response Strategies Working Group, Intergovernmental Panel on Climate Change, Washington, D.C., 30 January 1989.

Acid Rain and Other Airborne Pollutants: Their Human Causes and Consequences

ELLIS B. COWLING

SINCE THE INDUSTRIAL REVOLUTION GATHERED MOMENTUM in the middle of the nineteenth century, human activities have added more and more substances to those that circulate naturally among the air, water, soil, and all living things (Smith, 1872). Almost everything human beings do on a large scale influences the chemistry of the atmosphere.

Some of the airborne substances introduced by human activity are beneficial for life in general and human life in particular. They provide oxygen and other nutrients that are essential for humans and for the growth of crops and forests. Other substances are inert biologically. Still others are detrimental because they cause stress in plants, animals, and microorganisms. They also alter surface and ground water quality, aggravate nutrient deficiencies in soils, or accelerate the soiling, weathering, or corrosion of engineering and cultural materials.

In recent decades, the term "acid rain" has captured the imagination of the public in much the same way and for substantially the same reasons that Rachel Carson's *Silent Spring* (1962) captured our imagination in the early 1960s. But "acid rain" must be recognized as only one special feature of a series of processes. These include emission, transport, transformation, deposition, uptake, and exchange of natural and manmade chemicals between the atmosphere and terrestrial and aquatic ecosystems (Altshuller and Linthurst, 1983).

During the past few years, a series of major shifts has been taking place in both scientific and public debates about "acid rain," "air pollution," and "global climate change" (Comptroller General, 1984; OTA, 1981). These issues are related because all three are manifestations of change in the chemical climate of the Earth, involve many of the same chemical emissions from

combustion of fossil fuels, involve many of the same photochemical trans-
formations that occur during short-distance and long-distance transport of
air pollutants, and are known or suspected to increase stress in terrestrial
and aquatic ecosystems.

This article summarizes the evidence that human activities are changing the chemical climate of the Earth and that many of these changes are
adversely affecting the health of human beings, the productivity of crops
and forests, the stability of engineering materials and cultural resources, the
quality of the atmosphere, and the stability of terrestrial and aquatic ecosystems in many parts of the world.

Recent changes in the chemical climate

Three general types of airborne chemicals are known or projected to affect
human beings and the terrestrial and aquatic ecosystems on which human
life depends. These substances include essential nutrients; toxic or growth-
altering substances that injure or inhibit the normal development of living
organisms; and radiatively active ("greenhouse") gases, which can lead to
general warming and other changes in the Earth's physical climate.

Airborne chemicals

The airborne chemicals that help living things grow include oxygen, water
vapor, carbon dioxide, nitric acid, ammonia, and sulfur dioxide. They also
include several nutritionally important aerosols and dissolved and suspended substances in precipitation, fog, and cloud water.[1] All of these essential nutrients are dispersed in the atmosphere and can be taken up readily
through leaves and green shoots as well as through roots of plants. They are
also ingested in food materials and thus assimilated by human beings, other
animals, and microorganisms.

The air pollutants of major concern to society are listed in the Appendix. They include two major types of pollutants (primary and secondary)
and eight specific chemical or physical groups of substances. Primary air
pollutants are gases or other volatile waste products emitted directly from
stationary or mobile sources.[2] Secondary pollutants include a wide variety
of substances formed in the atmosphere by chemical transformation of primary pollutants.

The six most important primary air pollutants are sulfur dioxide, nitrogen oxides, toxic elements such as lead and fluorine, a wide variety of
volatile organic compounds, carbon monoxide, and particulate matter. The
two most important secondary pollutants are photochemical oxidants (espe-

cially ozone) and acid deposition. Airborne acids and particulate matter can occur as both primary and secondary pollutants.

Climate-altering airborne chemicals

The most important climate-altering airborne chemicals include water vapor, carbon dioxide, certain nitrogen oxides (N_2O, NO_2), sulfur dioxide, methane, chlorofluorocarbons, and ozone. All are energy-absorbing gases that alter the radiative energy balance of the Earth. Warming of the Earth's surface is a result of a "blanketing" effect: water vapor, carbon dioxide, and the other trace gases listed above absorb infrared radiation from the Earth's surface and the atmosphere, and re-radiate a portion of that energy back to the Earth. This causes the "greenhouse effect" (McDonald, 1985). These changes in energy budget are also expected to increase the frequency and severity of droughts, wind-, rain-, snow-, and icestorms, and other extremes of hot and cold weather.

Some climate-altering chemicals such as chlorofluorocarbons are produced only by human activity; but all the other radiatively active gases listed above are both natural constituents and volatile waste products of human activity. For example, greatly increased amounts of carbon dioxide and methane are accumulating in the global atmosphere because of increased use of fossil fuels, increased agricultural production, biomass burning, deforestation leading to destruction of forests to make way for agriculture or human settlement, and decomposition, volatilization, or incineration of municipal and agricultural wastes (McDonald, 1985).

Natural versus human sources of airborne chemicals

All of these airborne substances—beneficial, injurious, and climate-altering—are released from a wide variety of natural and human sources. The natural sources include volatile emissions from living plants, animals, and microorganisms, decomposing plant and animal remains, volcanoes, wild fires, sea spray from oceans and large lakes, wind-blown dust from arid regions, and such biogenic particles as spores and pollen.

The largest of all human influences on the chemical climate include volatile waste products from combustion of fossil fuels in power plants, metal smelters, industrial boilers, transportation vehicles, and domestic and commercial space- and water-heating installations. They also include volatile emissions from decomposition or incineration of domestic, commercial, and industrial wastes, controlled burning of agricultural and forest residues, evaporation of solvents, liquid fuels, refrigerants, pesticides, and other volatile chemicals, and detonation of explosives in peace and war. Other human sources of airborne chemicals include refining and use of petroleum and pet-rochemical products, industrial processes of many sorts, and launching of space vehicles.

Operation of power plants, metal smelters, and motor vehicles illus-trates a human dilemma. Electricity, metals, and transport vehicles are used for many worthwhile purposes in society. Fossil fuels (mainly coal, oil, and natural gas) and sulfide metal ores are available near the Earth's surface. The fuels can be burned to generate electricity or to propel motor vehicles; the metal ores can be roasted to separate the "metal" from the sulfur and other "impurities." During these combustion and heating processes, certain waste products are produced—sulfur and carbon oxides formed from the fuels and sulfide ores; nitrogen oxides formed mainly from nitrogen in the air; and noncombustible materials including various toxic metals. These waste materials either accumulate as a solid (ash) or are released into the atmos-phere in a rapidly moving stream of exhaust gases, fine aerosols, and coarse particles.

Various engineering systems are available for decreasing emissions of these air pollutants. Sulfur, for example, can be removed from coal and oil in three ways—prior to combustion by desulfurizing the fuel, during com-bustion by modifying the combustion process, or after combustion by desul-furizing the flue gases. Use of lead-free gasoline together with catalytic converters and modified combustion systems in automobile engines can greatly decrease vehicle emissions of lead, carbon monoxide, and nitrogen oxides. Unfortunately, these engineering systems have not been installed or are not properly maintained in all power plants, metal smelters, and motor vehicles.

Earlier it was believed that most airborne waste products emitted from these stationary and mobile sources fell out of the atmosphere near the point of emission. Now it is recognized, particularly with increasing use of tall smokestacks at power plants and metal smelters, that meteorological pro-cesses can lead to extensive mixing and to both chemical and physical trans-formations of millions of tons of gases, fine aerosol particles, and coarse particles that are released into the atmosphere each year (Altshuller and Linthurst, 1983).

All airborne chemicals and their reaction products are carried by wind and clouds and then are deposited on vegetation, soils, surface waters, and engineering or cultural materials at short or long distances from the original sources of emission. Thus, the chemical composition of the air and of the rain, snow, dew, hail, fog, and cloud water within any region is a mixture of all the airborne substances dispersed, mixed, transformed, and transported into the atmosphere of that region and then deposited and taken up by the plants, animals, and microorganisms in terrestrial and aquatic ecosystems.

Recently, fog in industrial regions and cloud water high in the atmos-phere were discovered to be much richer in acids and other air pollutants than rain or snow. This discovery greatly increased concern about possible effects of airborne chemicals on high mountain forests and on such cultural resources as the Parthenon in Greece, the Taj Mahal in India, and the Statue of Liberty in New York.

A quantitative comparison of natural and human emissions

Some scientists argue that natural emissions of airborne chemicals are just as important in altering the atmosphere as emissions from human activities. There is a measure of truth in this contention so long as the whole Earth is used as the basis for reference rather than just the industrial regions. A Russian soil scientist, V. A. Kovda (1975), was among the first to compare the amounts of substances involved in natural processes and in human activities. His data, shown in Table 1, permit three major generalizations about the relative magnitudes of natural (biogeochemical) and human (anthropogenic) processes. First, the total amount of emissions produced by human activities is on the same order of magnitude as that produced by natural processes, namely 26.6 x 10^9 and 43 x 10^9 tons per year, respectively. Biogeochemical processes still create 1.6 times as much emission as anthropogenic forces. Second, garbage, urban wastes, and byproducts are now produced at about twice the rate at which photosynthesis occurs over the whole Earth. Third, industrial dusts, aerosols, and gases are now discharged into the at-

TABLE 1   Total emissions produced by natural processes and by human activities

Biosphere component	Tons per year
Biogeochemical processes	
Yield of photomass	1 × 10^{10}
Cycle of inorganic elements	1 × 10^{10}
River discharges	
Dissolved substances	3 × 10^9
Suspended substances	2 × 10^{10}
	43 × 10^9
Anthropogenic sources	
Output of fertilizers	3 × 10^8
Industrial dusts	3 × 10^8
Garbage, urban wastes, and byproducts	2 × 10^{10}
Mine refuse	5 × 10^9
Aerosols and gas discharges	1 × 10^9
	26.6 × 10^9

SOURCE: Kovda (1975).

mosphere at about one-half the rate at which dissolved chemicals drain from all the rivers of the world (1.3×10^9 tons per year and 3×10^9 tons per year, respectively).

When the question of the relative magnitude of human and natural sources of airborne chemicals is restricted to the industrial regions of the world, a stronger contrast emerges. Galloway and Whelpdale (1980) and Husar (NAS, 1986) have estimated that human activity in North America releases about 20 times more sulfur oxides and about 10 times more nitrogen oxides than are produced by all natural sources in this same continental area.

The remarkable increase in emissions of sulfur dioxide and nitrogen oxides in the northern and southern United States during the past century is shown in Figures 1 and 2: both have increased approximately tenfold since 1890. The southern states are rapidly catching up with the heavily industrialized northeastern states in terms of emissions (NAS, 1986). Volatile organic compound emissions are estimated to be of about the same order of magnitude (NAPAP, 1988). Human activity has indeed become a major force in the biogeochemical circulation of matter on the Earth.

FIGURE 1   Changes in emissions of sulfur dioxide per unit of land in the areas north and south of the Ohio River in the eastern United States, 1890–1980

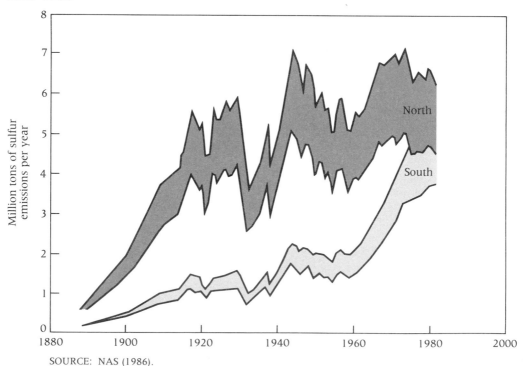

SOURCE: NAS (1986).

FIGURE 2   Changes in emissions of nitrogen oxides per unit of land in the areas north and south of the Ohio River, 1890–1980

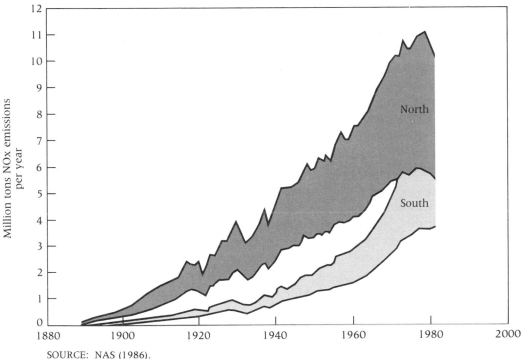

SOURCE: NAS (1986).

The ratio of natural to human sources also varies greatly with the particular chemical and by region of the world. In North America and Europe, for example, natural sources of ammonia and ammonium ion in the atmosphere are believed to be larger than human sources. As I noted earlier, however, in these same continental areas human sources are about 20 times larger than natural sources in the case of sulfur oxides and about 10 times larger in the case of nitrogen oxides.

Ozone and some other photochemical oxidants (e.g., formaldehyde) are natural constituents of the Earth's atmosphere, but are present in comparatively low concentrations (up to about 30 parts per billion, ppb). Urban-industrial areas register concentrations of ozone of 80–200 or more ppb. These high concentrations accumulate in the atmosphere as a result of photochemical transformations of natural and anthropogenic volatile organic compounds and nitrogen oxides released by human activity.

Time period of change in the chemical climate

Prior to the industrial era the concentrations of beneficial, injurious, and climate-altering chemicals in the atmosphere were relatively low. Forest trees, herbaceous plants, microorganisms, and animals all adapted their habits of growth and nutrition to this very diluted chemical environment (Bolin et al., 1972). The industrial revolution added many toxic substances produced by human activity.

Two of the three primary pollutants listed in the Appendix (sulfur dioxide and nitrogen oxides) are toxic in their own right, as has been demonstrated by numerous field studies around major industrial and urban sources of sulfur dioxide and by controlled-exposure experiments in the case of nitrogen oxides. Also, all three primary pollutants are the principal precursors of regionally dispersed secondary pollutants—ozone and acid deposition, the former rigorously proven and the latter widely suspected to be harmful to plants, animals, and microorganisms.

In the early days of industrialization, injuries to forests and other vegetation (and even to public health) were accepted as unavoidable side effects of primitive metal-smelting and combustion technologies. In time, as these adverse effects became better understood, methods were devised to minimize them. Control technologies are now required by law in most of Europe, North America, and Japan. As a result, the known adverse effects of gaseous sulfur dioxide, nitrogen oxides, and fluoride are now confined almost exclusively to the vicinity of large sources of air pollution such as metal smelters, power plants, and industrial complexes. Thus, the center of gravity in research on the human health and ecological effects of air pollution in most industrial countries has shifted from intensive studies of the acute effects of primary pollutants near large pollution sources, to extensive studies of chronic exposure to regionally dispersed secondary pollutants (such as acid deposition and ozone, hydrogen peroxide, and other photochemical oxidants), and to model calculations of the probable effects of radiatively active gases that may alter the physical climate of the Earth.

Current knowledge about the effects of airborne chemicals

Table 2 characterizes eight kinds of effects of airborne chemicals on society. All except the last of these eight effects—fertilization of crops, forests, and surface waters—are detrimental to the interests of society (NAS, 1981, 1983, 1985). In fact, even the last has proven to be detrimental in the case of some surface water systems such as Lake Erie and Lake Ontario in North America (NAS-RSC, 1985).

In examining the summary information in Table 2, note especially that:

— Sulfur dioxide (SO_2) emissions are involved in all eight effects;

— Nitrogen oxides (NO and NO_2) or their photochemical derivatives are involved in seven of the eight effects;

— Volatile organic compounds (VOC) or their photochemical derivatives such as ozone (O_3) are involved in five of the eight effects;

— All three of these primary pollutants (SO_2, NO_x, and VOC) are produced during combustion of fossil fuels in power plants, metal smelters, transportation vehicles, and other industrial, commercial, and domestic uses of energy; and

— SO_2, NO_x, and VOC are also the most important chemical precursors of photochemical oxidants, acid deposition, atmospheric haze, and certain types of particulate matter that have a range of detrimental effects on society. For this reason, these three primary pollutants are major keys to the proper management of air quality in most industrial regions of the world (NRC, 1977; NAS, 1983, 1986).

Responses of ecosystems to climate changes

Continuing processes of evolutionary change and adaptation have led to the development of the marvelously diverse communities of living organisms over the land and in the surface waters of the Earth (Woodwell, 1970). When human beings first appeared on the Earth and the development of civilization began, our collective impact on the processes of natural selection and evolution was hardly perceptible. But as we increased in numbers and particularly after we learned to harness the energy stored in fossil fuels and apply this energy to the processes of urbanization, industrialization, and intensive agriculture and forestry, our impact became progressively stronger (Cowling, 1982). Most peoples have considered that the diverse flora and fauna of the Earth are ours to use as we see fit—to manage carefully within the sustainable productive capacity of the ecosystems in question, or to exploit carelessly with only limited regard for the long-term stability of the ecosystems themselves.

As Hepting (1963) points out in his classic paper on "Climate and tree diseases," both annual and perennial plants are subject to stresses induced by natural variability in weather events (physical meteorology). But long-lived perennial plants and forest ecosystems that persist for decades or even centuries are also subject to natural stresses induced by long-term changes in the physical climate. Chemical stresses in forests induced by short-term or long-term exposure to airborne pollutants (chemical meteorology or chemical climatology) are, of course, superimposed on the physical stresses induced by natural changes in physical meteorology and physical climatology and by man-induced change in the physical climate.

Today, aquatic and terrestrial ecosystems are exposed to much heavier loadings of airborne nutrient chemicals, acidic substances, toxic substances, growth-altering chemicals, and climate-altering chemicals than were present during the preindustrial period. In some locations, essentially all the

TABLE 2   Major effects of air pollutants on society

Type of effect	Nature of effect	Pollutants involved
On human health, due to inhalation of airborne chemicals	Pulmonary dysfunction, respiratory disease, and mental retardation (especially in children)	Ozone Sulfur dioxide Nitrogen oxides Particulate matter Carbon monoxide Toxic elements
On human health, due to atmospheric deposition or leaching and later ingestion of airborne or soilborne chemicals via drinking water, fish, or other food products	Diarrhea and mental retardation in children and poisoning of adults by lead, mercury, copper, cadmium, or other toxic elements	Toxic elements Acid deposition resulting from emissions of sulfur dioxide and nitrogen oxides
Damage to engineering materials, statuary, monuments, and other cultural resources	Increased corrosion of metals; accelerated weathering of stone and masonry; soiling of textiles, glass, paints, and other materials; deterioration of paints, plastics, and rubber	Sulfur dioxide Nitrogen oxides Particulate matter Ozone Acid deposition
Increased haze in the atmosphere	Decreased visibility in urban and rural areas, with attendant decreases in safety of air transport and enjoyment of scenic vistas from aircraft and in parks	Particulate matter Sulfur dioxide Nitrogen oxides Volatile organic compounds Photochemical oxidants
Acidification of lakes, streams, ground waters, and soils	Death and reproductive failure in fresh-water fish; decreased fertility of soils	Sulfur dioxide Nitrogen oxides Acid deposition
Fumigation of crops and forests near point sources of pollutants	Decreased growth and yield of crops and forests	Ozone Sulfur dioxide Nitrogen oxides Toxic elements

nutrients needed to sustain some of these ecosystems are now provided from atmospheric sources (Schutt and Cowling, 1985; Ulrich, 1987). Never before in their evolutionary history have the natural and managed ecosystems of North America and Europe been "fed from above" to the extent that they are today.

TABLE 2   (continued)

Type of effect	Nature of effect	Pollutants involved
Regional changes in the health and productivity of forests	Decreased growth, increased mortality, and predisposition of forest trees to biotic and abiotic stress factors	Ozone Nitrogen oxides (?)[a] Ammonia and ammonium nitrogen (?) Sulfur dioxide (?) Acid deposition (?) Toxic elements (?)
Fertilization of crops, forests, and surface waters	Increased productivity of crops, forests, and surface waters	Nitrogen oxides Ammonia and ammonium nitrogen Sulfur dioxide Acid deposition Particulate matter

[a] Question marks indicate continuing uncertainty about the role of specific pollutants other than ozone, even though the involvement of air pollutants generally is widely assumed.

SOURCE: Cowling (1985).

Under these conditions of continuing change in the chemical and physical climate, additional pressures for further adaptation of plants, animals, and microorganisms are applied. At present we have only limited experience and even less scientific evidence with which to identify regions where the rates of continuing change in the chemical climate may exceed the elastic limits of ecosystem resiliency and adaptability. Nowhere are these uncertainties more evident than in the forests of central Europe and in the lakes, streams, and forests of northern Europe and certain parts of eastern North America (Woodman and Cowling, 1987).

In theory, airborne chemicals could cause several types of detrimental effects on aquatic or terrestrial ecosystems, either alone or in combination with other stress factors. These effects could include visible symptoms of injury, decreased growth and alteration of physiological processes such as photosynthesis or respiration (with or without other visible symptoms), changes in susceptibility or resistance to other stress factors, and interference with normal reproductive processes. Effects on whole ecosystems could include decreased productivity, changes in age-class distribution, changes in normal patterns of competition and mortality, changes in normal patterns of succession, changes in species composition, changes in patterns of nutrient cycling, and changes in hydrologic behavior, quality of wildlife habitat, or watershed functions. Effects on regional and social values could include changes in regional productivity, geographic distribution, or economic value of ecosystems, and changes in aesthetic quality or other ecosystem values for humans.

Many of these theoretical effects have been confirmed by observation and experiment in case studies of various aquatic or terrestrial ecosystems. In Europe and North America, most studies of the detrimental effects of air pollutants on forests and agricultural ecosystems have been made in the vicinity of strong point sources of sulfur dioxide and fluoride (Woodwell, 1970; Postel, 1984). Much less is known about the effects of regionally dispersed airborne chemicals such as ozone or acid deposition (Woodman and Cowling, 1987). Although nitrogen oxides have been demonstrated in controlled exposure tests to cause injury to many species of crop plants and forest trees, neither economic damage nor even visible injury by nitrogen oxides has been proven to occur in agricultural fields or forests (NRC, 1977).

Conclusions

All living organisms are subjected to a wide variety of natural stresses during their growth and development—including competition with other organisms, diseases and insects, and the normal vagaries of both the physical and the chemical climate. In many industrial and developing regions of the world, organisms are also subjected to additional stresses by airborne chemicals that include toxic gases, excess nutrient substances, and acidic and growth-altering substances. They may also be subjected to chemically induced change in the physical climate of the Earth.

It is usually not too difficult to determine cause-and-effect relationships in the case of locally dispersed primary pollutant chemicals in the vicinity of strong point sources. It is often much more difficult to determine these relationships in the case of regionally dispersed secondary pollutants such as acid deposition and ozone and other photochemical oxidants.

Rigorous scientific methods must be employed to distinguish the individual and combined effects of airborne pollutant chemicals from the individual and combined effects of many natural stress factors in both terrestrial and aquatic ecosystems.

In North America, ozone and other photochemical oxidants are the only regionally dispersed airborne pollutant chemicals that have been rigorously proven to cause detrimental effects on crops or forests. Hydrogen peroxide, excess nitrogen, and acid deposition leading to leaching of essential nutrients from foliage and from soils are hypothetical sources of stress that are currently being tested in the research programs of government and industry in the United States, Canada, and many countries in Europe.

Many government and some industry groups in North America and Europe are expanding their research on the responses of ecosystems to air pollutants to include the effects of chemically induced change in the physical climate.

Scientific uncertainty about cause-and-effect relationships between airborne pollutant chemicals and forests and agricultural crops is leading to some hesitancy on the part of industry and government to increase pollution control efforts despite the far better known effects of many of the same pollutants on public health, atmospheric haze, materials damage, and acidification of aquatic ecosystems. In many countries an integrated national program for management of air quality would have many advantages over the present single-pollutant and state-by-state and province-by-province methods of implementation. Cooperation, consultation, and statesmanship are likely to produce more economically and scientifically sound management plans than legislatively mandated solutions.

Appendix: Air pollutants of major concern to society

Sulfur dioxide (SO$_2$)   A colorless gas produced during combustion of sulfur-containing materials such as coal, oil, and biomass, and during smelting of sulfide metal ores. SO$_2$ is emitted mainly by large stationary sources such as fossil-fueled power plants, metal smelters, and other industrial and commercial installations. Biomass burning is an important source of sulfur oxides in tropical regions of the world.

Nitrogen oxides (NO$_x$)   Two colorless gases (NO and NO$_2$) produced in any high-temperature process such as combustion of coal, oil, gasoline, and natural gas. Nitrogen oxides are emitted by both stationary sources and transportation vehicles. In tropical countries, burning of biomass is also an important source of NO$_x$.

Toxic elements   Heavy metals and other toxic elements such as lead, cadmium, nickel, mercury, and fluorine are released mainly by large metal smelters and by transportation vehicles using leaded gasoline.

Volatile organic compounds (VOC)   A wide variety of carbon compounds ranging from such simple molecules as ethylene, gasoline, and cleaning and painting solvents to very complex molecules such as pesticides. VOC are emitted by many (usually small) stationary and mobile sources.

Carbon monoxide (CO)   A colorless and odorless but highly toxic gas produced during incomplete combustion of coal, oil, and natural gas and incineration of garbage and other solid and liquid wastes. Carbon monoxide inhibits respiration in humans and other animals. It is of concern to society mostly in urban areas, where it accumulates in stagnant air mainly from transportation vehicles.

Particulate matter (PM)   A catch-all category of pollutants ranging from very coarse "fugitive dust" particles that cause soiling of textiles, windows, paints, etc., to very fine aerosol particles that cause atmospheric haze or are drawn into the lungs, where they induce respiratory disease. These substances are extremely diverse both chemically and physically. The larger particles range from almost pure carbon in the case of soot from oil burners to mineral dusts in the case of manufacturing facilities that process cement, asbestos, clay, ceramics, glass, textiles, and other materials. The fine particles range from smoke to all sorts of sulfate, ammonium, organic, metallic, and other particles formed by condensation of gases, vapors, and other volatile substances in the atmosphere. Some of these particles have very remarkable and complex structures that are characteristic of the original sources of the emissions.

Ozone (O_3) *and other photochemical oxidants*   These substances include formaldehyde, hydrogen peroxide, peroxyacetyl nitrate (PAN), and peroxyproprionyl nitrate (PPN). They occur mainly as secondary pollutants that are produced when NO_x and VOC from various natural and human sources interact with atmospheric oxygen in the presence of sunlight. Ozone is the most important of these three pollutants because it is much more abundant even though somewhat less toxic than PAN or PPN. These compounds are among the most toxic gases to which plants, animals, and humans are exposed.

Acid deposition   A variety of acidic and acidifying substances produced when gaseous SO_2, NO_x, HCl, and certain other airborne chemicals interact with oxygen, ammonia, and moisture to give aqueous solutions or aerosols of sulfuric, nitric, and hydrochloric acids. Wet deposition of these substances occurs during all rain, snow, hail, dew, fog, cloud, or rime-ice events; dry deposition occurs at all times—by absorption or adsorption of gaseous SO_2, NO_x, HNO_3, and HCl and by impaction of sulfate, nitrate, and chloride aerosols on the surfaces of plants, soils, animals, microorganisms, surface waters, and materials. The acidic and acidifying substances in wet and dry deposition may be partially or completely neutralized by alkaline earth elements such as calcium, potassium, sodium, or ammonium ions. Acidification of ecosystems also occurs when ammonia or ammonium sulfate aerosol and certain other ammonium compounds are taken up by plants, animals, or microorganisms after deposition into ecosystems.

"Greenhouse" gases   A variety of energy-absorbing gases that alter the radiative energy balance of the Earth and thus induce a general warming of the atmosphere. The most important of these climate-altering gases include carbon dioxide, water vapor, certain oxides of nitrogen (nitrous oxides and nitrogen dioxide), sulfur dioxide, methane, chlorofluorocarbons, and ozone. These substances are released from a wide variety of natural and human sources that include burning of fossil fuels and deforestation in the case of carbon dioxide, cattle and termites in the case of methane, rice paddies in the case of nitrous oxide, refrigerants and plastics in the case of chlorofluorocarbons, etc. These gases warm the Earth's climate by forming a "blanket" within the atmosphere that absorbs infrared radiation from the Earth's surface and by re-radiating a portion of that energy back to Earth. This causes the so-called greenhouse effect. These changes in the Earth's energy budget are also expected to increase the severity of droughts, wind, rain, snow, and ice storms, and other extremes of hot and cold weather in many parts of the world.

Notes

This article is dedicated to the memory of Svante Oden, a remarkable man whose audacious ideas about our natural environment greatly changed my life in science. Preparation of this article was supported in part by a joint program of the US Forest Service, the Environmental Protection Agency, and the National Council of the Paper Industry for Air and Stream Improvement (NCASI) in the United States.

1 The latter substances include liquid water and nitrate, ammonium, phosphate, potassium, sulfate, magnesium, calcium, iron, copper, zinc, molybdenum, boron, and chlorine ions. These substances include all 16 of the essential elements required by plants for normal growth and development. Nine other micronutrient elements are required for normal growth and development of animals (including humans) and some microorganisms. These include cadmium, chromium, fluorine, iodine, nickel, selenium, silicon, tin, and vanadium.

2 Stationary sources include power plants, metal smelters, and other industrial or commercial installations, as well as domestic and commercial space- and water-heating units. Mobile sources are mainly cars, trucks, trains, aircraft, and ships.

References

Altshuller, A. P., and R. A. Linthurst (eds.). 1983. *The Acidic Deposition Phenomenon and Its Effects: Critical Assessment Review Papers.* Volume I: *Atmospheric Sciences;* Volume II: *Effects Sciences.* Washington, D.C.: Office of Research and Development, Environmental Protection Agency.

Bennett, D. A., R. L. Goble, and R. A. Linthurst. 1985. *The Acidic Deposition Phenomenon and Its Effects: Critical Assessment Document.* EPA/600/8-85/001. Washington, D.C.: Environmental Protection Agency.

Bolin, B., et al. 1972. *Sweden's Case Study for the United Nations Conference on the Human Environment: Air Pollution Across National Boundaries. The Impact on the Environment of Sulfur in Air and Precipitation.* Stockholm: Norstedt and Sons.

Carson, R. 1962. *Silent Spring.* Boston: Houghton Mifflin.

Comptroller General. 1984. *An Analysis of Issues Concerning "Acid Rain."* Report to the Congress of the United States. Washington, D.C.: General Accounting Office.

Cowling, E. B. 1982. "Acid precipitation in historical perspective," *Environmental Science and Technology* 16: 110A–123A.

_____. 1985. "Pollutants in the air and acids in the rain: Influences on our natural environment and a challenge for every industrial society," 25th Horace M. Albright Lectureship in Conservation, College of Natural Resources, University of California, Berkeley.

Galloway, J. N., and D. M. Whelpdale. 1980. "An atmospheric sulfur budget for eastern North America," *Atmospheric Environment* 14: 409–417.

Hepting, G. H. 1963. "Climate and tree diseases," *Annual Review of Phytopathology* 1: 31–50.

Kovda, V. A. 1975. *Biogeochemical Cycles in Nature, Their Disturbance and Study* (in Russian). Moscow: Nauka Publishing House.

McDonald, G. J. 1985. *Climate Change and Acid Rain.* McLean, Virginia: Mitre Corp.

Office of Technology Assessment (OTA). 1981. *Acid Rain and Transported Air Pollutants: Implications for Public Policy.* Office of Technology Assessment, United States Congress, Washington, D.C.

National Academy of Sciences (NAS). 1981. *Atmosphere–Biosphere Interactions: Toward a Better Understanding of the Consequences of Fossil Fuel Combustion.* Washington, D.C.: National Academy Press.

_____. 1983. *Acid Deposition: Atmospheric Processes in Eastern North America.* Washington, D.C.: National Academy Press.

_____. 1985. *Acid Deposition: Effects on Geochemical Cycling and Biological Availability of Trace Elements.* Washington, D.C.: National Academy Press.

_____. 1986. *Acid Deposition: Long-Term Trends.* Washington, D.C.: National Academy Press.

_____, Royal Society of Canada (NAS-RSC). 1985. *The Great Lakes Water Quality Agreement: An Evolving Instrument for Ecosystem Management.* Washington, D.C.: National Academy Press.

National Acid Precipitation Assessment Program (NAPAP). 1988. *1987 Annual Report.* Washington, D.C.: NAPAP Office of the Director.

National Research Council. 1977. "Effects of nitrogen oxides on vegetation," in *Nitrogen Oxides.* Washington, D.C.: National Academy of Sciences, pp. 197–214.

Postel, S. 1984. "Air pollution, acid rain, and the future of forests," Worldwatch Institute Paper No. 58, Washington, D.C.

Schutt, P., and E. B. Cowling. 1985. "Waldsterben, a general decline of forests in central Europe: Symptoms, development, and possible causes," *Plant Disease* 69: 548–558.

Smith, R. A. 1872. *Air and Rain: The Beginnings of a Chemical Climatology.* London: Longmans-Green.

Ulrich, B. 1987. "Stability, elasticity, and resilience of terrestrial ecosystems with respect to matter balance," in *Ecological Studies,* Vol. 61, ed. E. D. Schulze and H. Zwolfer. Berlin: Springer-Verlag, pp. 11–49.

Woodman, J. N., and E. B. Cowling. 1987. "Airborne chemicals and forest health," *Environmental Science and Technology* 21: 120–126.

Woodwell, G. M. 1970. "Effects of pollution on the structure and physiology of ecosystems," *Science* 168: 429–433.

Ocean Space: Use and Protection

Edward D. Goldberg

Over the coming decades the oceans will provide many resources for higher living standards—waste disposal sites, transportation, recreation, and food. Economic considerations to a large extent will govern how various parts of the marine environment are used, because ocean space, like land, has a spectrum of values. Coastal areas can be compared with land in central Tokyo: both are very costly. On the other hand, some deep ocean waters are more similar to the Sahara desert, clearly of lesser worth. To much of the world's populace, the beaches of the marine shorelines are the most desirable resource, providing a site for a variety of social activities, including recreation and aesthetic pleasures. Industrial and maricultural activities enhance the economic value of the coastal region.

In this article I will consider some possible changes and problems in the use of ocean space over the next several decades. I will suggest potential developments in the disposal of societal wastes, transportation, recreation, and marine farming and ranching. Such activities involve renewable resources. (I will not consider the nonrenewable resources such as gas, oil, and ferromanganese minerals that can be mined from the sea.) I will emphasize the issue of waste management since this is the area in which the ocean will probably provide the greatest economic and social benefits.

Two caveats guide this presentation. First, since each of these uses can affect another, the protection of ocean space depends upon the identification of any insulting forces. Further, the resolution of conflicts of use is the key to successful exploitation of renewable ocean resources.

Space for waste disposal

Space in the ocean for waste disposal is treated by much of the developed world's populace in an Orwellian way. Following the rise of environmental movements in the 1970s, a sense evolved that all space, be it open ocean or coastal, is equal in value and should remain inviolate with respect to receiving societal discards. The marine scientific and engineering communities, on the other hand, have in general a different view. They argue that multifaceted assessments of waste disposal processes must be carried out to make an optimal choice among land, air, and sea options (NAS, 1984). For example, a US workshop concluded that the waste capacity of that country's coastal waters is not fully exploited (NOAA, 1979). A consensus emerged that a scientific basis exists for regulating pollutant discharges to both coastal and open ocean waters. But further, foreclosure of the marine option for waste disposal can jeopardize the quality of the environment, especially within the terrestrial fresh waters, through leakages of toxic substances from waste disposal sites on land. As a consequence, underground waters, which furnish about 50 percent of US drinking water, are showing increased levels of pollutants that can adversely affect public health. To minimize pollutant entry, ocean disposal appears in some instances to be an attractive option.

Domestic and industrial waste

Domestic and industrial waste management is a growing problem to the populations of the developed countries. Land disposal sites are becoming increasingly scarce, yet the production of solid municipal waste continues to rise; at present it is about 140 million tons per year in the United States (O'Leary et al., 1988). Because of increasing distances between sites of generation and sites of disposal, the costs of moving the wastes become higher and higher. Pleas are continually made to recycle or to reduce domestic wastes. Only in a few countries are such actions effective.

Recent technological assessments of the problem (O'Leary et al., 1988) ignore the ocean disposal option. Incineration is also often slighted. Since over 50 percent of most domestic wastes (paper, food and yard waste, leather, textiles, etc.) can be incinerated, waste reduction by burning continues to be attractive. In spite of its successful practice in many cities of the world, incineration is opposed by many environmental groups, however, because of toxic emissions. Further, the ash, which often constitutes 25 percent of the bulk waste, must be disposed of in some way.

The estuarine and other coastal waters today receive the greatest amount of domestic and industrial wastes introduced to the marine environment. Negative impacts of such waste disposal include increasing areas of anoxia, human morbidities from exposure to microbial pathogens in beach areas and from the consumption of tainted fish and shellfish, and coastal zones littered with plastics, metals, and paper. A recent US survey of the role of the oceans in waste management predicts further degradation of coastal waters (OTA, 1987). On a global basis the principal problem from the discharge of domestic wastes is eutrophication, the overfertilization of waters through the entry of such plant nutrients as nitrate and phosphate.

The study by the Office of Technology Assessment found little degradation of the open ocean, primarily because little waste disposal today takes place there. In principle, open ocean sites offer the promise of waste space. The last remaining US open ocean site, Deepwater Dumpsite-106, is located over the continental slope off New Jersey. The impact of industrial and domestic disposals there over the last two decades has been little researched. Still, using conventional wisdom, the site's assimilative capacity for wastes can be roughly calculated (NOAA, 1979). The limiting factor for industrial waste discharge is the impact upon the biota in surface waters. Some preliminary data suggest that the effects of typical wastes discharged at the site (wastes from titanium dioxide production and from the manufacture of organic chemicals) upon zooplankton are not serious (Capuzzo and Lancaster, 1985). Sublethal effects were noted in the waste plumes at the site; they appeared to involve only a very small percentage of the organisms in the water mass. At the rates of dumping in the early 1980s, long-term consequences are expected to be minimal according to these investigators. Dumpsite-106 is being phased out by the US Congress in 1991 for both domestic and industrial wastes. In addition, Congress has voted to end all marine dumping of sewage sludge by 1 January 1992. This action seems to be a political response to a public disturbed by reports from environmental groups and from the news media, reports often more perceptual than substantial.

Comparison of land, air, and sea disposal options can be made rationally. A group of 55 social and natural scientists applied a variety of criteria to compare land and sea disposal (NAS, 1984), with biological effects providing the focus of concern. The participants recognized that a single index of impact would be most desirable for political decisionmakers; it appears that no such parameter exists nor can one be devised. A matrix of land, freshwater, and marine environments and the associated ecosystem responses to contaminants was prepared (Table 1). Semi-quantitative estimates of the potential impacts were made to provide a guide for judgment.

The crucial effect to be avoided is species extinction, most critical in streams, wetlands, and estuaries. Habitat loss through waste disposal is closely related to species extinction. The increases in nutrient levels, which can lead to eutrophication, are most serious in estuarine, freshwater and marine wetlands, and various terrestrial waters.

The ability of an aqueous environment to recapture a normal community structure following a large waste discharge episode, that is, the recoverability, is most tenuous for Arctic lands, open ocean, and ground waters, domains where pollutants can remain for centuries to millennia. The study also compared the ability of water and land to contain pollutants. The waters uniformly were less able to restrict the spread of inputs than was solid earth. Similarly, the ecosystems on land were deemed much easier to repair, following damage, than were aqueous systems. Finally, toxicants and

TABLE 1 Comparison of ecosystem responses to waste inputs according to a scale (0–5) of increasing severity or concern

Type of environment	Species extinction	Habitat loss	Elevated nutrients	Recoverability	Containment	Remedial action	Uncertainty	Visibility	Pathogen routes to society	Toxicant routes to society
Land										
Disturbed lands[a]	1	0	1	0	1	0	1	5	5	5
Remnants[b]	0	5	1	1	1	1	1	5	5	5
Temperate forest	1	1	1	2	1	1	1	3	2	2
Temperate grassland	1	1	1	1	1	1	1	3	3	3
Pasture	0	0	0	1	2	1	1	5	5	5
Agricultural land	0	1	0	2	2	1	1	5	5	5
Arid land	3	2	1	3	1	3	2	2	1	1
Arctic land	0	1	1	5	1	5	4	1	1	1
Freshwater										
Lake	1	5	5	3	5	4	2	5	4	4
Stream	5	5	3	2	5	4	3	3	5	5
Wetland	5	5	5	3	5	5	4	2	3	3
Groundwater	3	1	5	5	5	5	5	0	5	5
Marine										
Wetlands (US East Coast)	1	4	3	3	5	5	3	5	5	5
Wetlands (US West Coast)	5	5	3	3	5	5	2	5	5	5
Estuaries	5	5	3	3	5	5	2	5	5	5
Coastal areas	1	3	1	1	5	5	3	1	3	4
Open ocean	1	1	0	5	5	5	5	0	1	1

Interpretation of scale

Species extinction: 5 = greatest concern.
Habitat loss—loss of a significant portion of a habitat type: 5 = greatest concern.
Elevated nutrients: 5 = highest probability of change to ecosystem.
Recoverability—ability of system to repair itself after input ceases: 5 = slowest recovery, decades to centuries; 1 = rapid recovery, years.
Containment—ability of unmodified system to restrict spread of inputs: 5 = greatest difficulty.
Remedial action—ease with which we can repair damage to ecosystem: 5 = greatest difficulty.
Visibility: 5 = most visible.
Pathogen routes to society: 5 = highest probability of reaching society.
Toxicant routes to society: 5 = highest probability of reaching society.
a Land highly modified by human activity.
b Isolated natural spots within developed or otherwise highly modified areas.
SOURCE: NAS (1984).

pathogens generally were returned to society more easily through aqueous systems than through land.

Proceeding from these general concepts, two specific disposal problems were considered: industrial acid wastes from titanium dioxide production and municipal sewage sludge (NAS, 1984).

The former case involved options of (1) ocean disposal and (2) acid neutralization of the wastes with limestone, followed by disposal of the resultant iron sludge to land and the effluents to a stream. The assessment of the alternatives required data about potential impacts on human health, property, ecosystems, aesthetics, recreation, noise, and odors. Institutional considerations involved community attitudes, services, economy, and safety. The environmental and economic factors favored ocean discharge whereas the other institutional parameters were less inclined toward this alternative.

In the case of sewage sludge disposal, public perceptions, regulatory considerations, available technology, environmental risks, and economics did not produce a consensus in favor of either option. But the assembled group of scholars concluded that ocean disposal was at least as attractive as land disposal.

Hazardous waste

A simple definition of a hazardous waste is a disposable material that can jeopardize the vitality of living organisms. The production of hazardous wastes throughout the world is startling. In the United States about one ton per capita is generated annually, most of it coming from industry—chemical plants, petroleum refineries, and manufacturers. The global picture is far more alarming. A recent article in *Conservation Exchange* (1988) states, "In many underdeveloped countries, no facilities exist to handle hazardous waste—whether the waste comes from U.S. multinationals or domestic firms. . . . [S]ome [hazardous waste-generating] plants are located in countries without even sewage treatment facilities, much less sophisticated hazardous waste disposal facilities."

Seawaters in the past have successfully accommodated deliberately introduced hazardous wastes. A case in point is the 1970 disposal by the United States of some 67 tons of nerve agents held in projectiles (Linnenbom, 1971). The munitions were placed in steel-encased concrete vaults, which were loaded aboard an obsolete World War II Liberty ship. The vessel was towed to a site about 400 kilometers east of Cape Canaveral, Florida, and sunk in 5,000 meters of water. The ship did not break up upon hitting the bottom. Subsequent monitoring of the vessel provided no evidence that the marine biota were affected by any leakages of the nerve agents. The nerve gas, isopropyl methylphosphono-fluoridate (GB), rapidly decomposes in water with an estimated half-life of 30 minutes (Epstein, 1970). An effective discharge of the wastes was carried out.

Although today unlike in 1970 there may be preferable techniques for disposing of this type of military weaponry (freezing the projectiles, cutting them up into smaller pieces and incinerating the toxic materials), still a combination of environmental, technological, and economic concerns may in the future direct some such hazardous wastes to the sea.

Radioactive wastes constitute another collective of materials that have posed great disposal problems. The fine-grained sediments of the deep sea floor have been proposed as a site in which radioactive wastes might be placed (Hollister et al., 1981). Such deposits cover about 20 percent of the Earth's surface. The radioactive wastes, placed into a chemically stable solid form, would be encased in canisters and introduced into the sediments either gravitationally or by a boosting system that would be activated when the wastes were just above the sediment/water interface. Many scientific and technological considerations must be faced when evaluating the feasibility of such strategies. The barriers to the return of the radioactivity to living organisms once the canisters are in place must be investigated using chemical, physical, biological, and geological oceanography. In addition, economic and social considerations will weigh heavily in the potential use of such systems. Still, the feasibility of ocean disposal of radioactive wastes merits continued discussion in the face of tremendous problems associated with the identification of acceptable terrestrial sites.

Waste exportation

The inability of developed countries to absorb domestic and industrial wastes within their own confines has led to some exportation to the developing world. For example, notifications of intent to export filed with the US Environmental Protection Agency rose from 12 in 1980 to 465 in 1987 (French, 1988). Moreover, hundreds of tons of hazardous waste have been exported without notification (Conservation Exchange, 1988). While most of these shipments are to other developed countries, developing countries are receiving an increasing share.

Some leaders in developing countries have opposed this practice. For example, Sidiki Kone (1988), Chief of the Division for the Preservation of Nature and Human Environment of the Ministry of Natural Resources and the Environment of Guinea, states: "[Developing countries] must refuse to import foreign wastes no matter how much money we are offered, otherwise we risk turning our continent into the garbage dump of the world."

As such resistance grows, using scientifically and economically justifiable ocean space for waste disposal offers an increasingly attractive solution.

Transportation

Over recorded history the oceans have been used to transport goods from one place to another. The varying ability of countries to generate products of commerce—agricultural, industrial, medical, and so on—makes trade essential. The increasing world population is demanding more materials and energy to achieve higher standards of living. For those countries producing or importing high-volume, low-cost commodities such as coal, oil, timber, and wheat, large ocean-traversing carriers (150,000 dead weight tons or more) appear essential. At present such vessels primarily transport petroleum and petroleum products.

Increasing vessel movement across oceans can adversely affect the coastal environment. Loading and offloading of vessels can introduce over-the-side materials to the waters. Where port dredging is necessary, the disposal of the spoils, especially if contaminated, may pose environmental problems, as may changes in the geometry of the port area.

Deep-water ports

Nearly all deep-water ports in the world are involved in the petroleum trade (see Table 2). As recently as 1981 the United States had only three ports that could receive large bulk carriers (that is, ports with authorized depths of 47 feet or more), all of them in California. There are no such ports in the developing countries of Asia or Africa. Yet these countries without deep-water ports may be in need of large quantities of low-bulk imports in the near future.

A report by the US National Academy of Sciences (1985) poses the problem facing the United States: Is the expense of altering harbor space through dredging a rational path to take? To answer this question requires herculean assumptions as to the mix of materials the United States will import and export and the future role of the United States in the world economy.

The development of deep ports through dredging operations and the disposal of the spoils can have unacceptable environmental impacts. Changes in the geometry of a harbor can affect its hydraulic regime. Circulation patterns can be modified, causing disturbances to the prevailing composition of the seawater. In particular, the biological productivity of the harbor area can be altered with possible adverse impacts on recreational and commercial fishing. Channel deepening can result in the intrusion of saline waters into ground and surface waters, jeopardizing terrestrial resources

TABLE 2   **World ports capable of handling vessels of at least 150,000 dead weight tons**

Region	Port
North Pacific	
Japan	Niigata, Mizushima, Kure, Kashima, Kimitsu, Chiba, Oita, Kiire, Tsurusaki, Okinawa, Tokyo Bay, Kawasaki, Yokkaichi
South Pacific	
Australia	Port Hedlund, Dampier, Hay Point, Sydney Caves Beach, Clutha, Kembla, Bonython
North America (excluding USA)	
Canada	Seven Island, Come-by-Chance, St. John, Point Tupper, Roberts Bank
South America	
Venezuela	Puerto La Cruz
Brazil	Sepetiba, Tubarao
Chile	Huasco
Peru	San Nicolas
Argentina	Bolivar
North Atlantic	
Norway	Narvik
West Germany	Heligoland, Hamburg
United Kingdom	Clyde Port, Glasgow, Tees-Port, Liverpool, Milford Haven, Port Talbot, Foulness
Ireland	Bantry Bay
Spain	Bilbao, Gijon, Algeciras
Sweden	Gothenburg
France	Dunkirk, Le Havre
Netherlands	Rotterdam/Europoort
Belgium	Zeebrugge, Antwerp
Mediterranean	
France	Marseilles
Italy	Trieste, Genoa, Taranto
Libya	Marsa el Brega
Egypt	Port Said
Persian Gulf	
Iran	Kharg Island
Saudi Arabia	Ras-al-Khafji, Ras Tanura
United Arab Emirates	Das Island
Kuwait	Mina-al-Ahmadi
Africa	
South Africa	Richards Bay, Port Elizabeth, Algoa Bay, Saldanha Bay

SOURCE: NAS (1985).

(NAS, 1985). Most of these impacts are as yet only anticipated, not documented in actual cases. Still, they do provide guidance in considering the impacts of any proposed deep-water port constructions.

Problems with the disposal of dredged materials are generally small. If they contain toxic materials, there is the potential for adverse effects; however, there are few case studies on toxic materials in dredged spoils.

On the other hand, the dredged materials can be considered a resource for use as construction aggregate, sanitary landfill, beach replenishment, and the creation or enhancement of wetlands in those cases where they do not contain unacceptable levels of toxic substances.

Recreation

Increasing time for leisure activities is making public beaches more and more attractive to tourists and to residents of coastal regions. Yet, their use is being jeopardized in both the developed and developing world by the increasing entry of enteric bacteria and viruses into coastal waters through domestic waste disposal. There are both economic and social facets to the problem. For countries seeking a more secure financial footing the loss of tourist revenue in the short term must be weighed against the output of revenue for improved sanitation facilities. For the developed countries, the recreational amenity must be broached in the political arena.

Two challenges to public health arise from the disposition of the pathogens in the coastal zone. First is the risk of disease through exposure in the waters or on the beaches. Swimmers swallow water; they also take it up through body cavities other than the mouth. However, most information about morbidity from such exposures is anecdotal rather than epidemiological. Still, there are many reports to concerned international agencies strongly relating ear, nose, and throat disorders, respiratory infections, and gastrointestinal infections to microorganisms of the coastal zone.

On the other hand there is a substantial data base relating illness and even mortality to the consumption of seafoods contaminated with toxic viruses and bacteria. Most diseases are related to the consumption of mollusks; fish and crabs are less frequently the carriers of these microorganisms. Viruses are dominant over bacteria in inducing illnesses. Both cholera and viral hepatitis have been associated with the consumption of uncooked or poorly cooked seafoods taken from contaminated areas.

The more extensive use of coastal ocean space for recreation will clearly depend upon improved domestic waste management practices. The costs of upgrading will appear high in the eyes of developing countries. Whether one chooses pipe disposal of primary treated waters to the coastal ocean or advanced water treatment (such as secondary treatment), with subsequent disposal of sewage sludge, the costs may seem inordinately high with respect to short-term economic gains.

Farming and ranching

Farming and ranching the organisms of the sea are rapidly expanding industries. Aquaculture, including the cultivation of seaweeds, is estimated to have accounted for 10 percent of the world's fishery landings in 1985 (Rhodes, 1988) in the amount of some 12.5 million metric tons (see Table 3). Over the ten-year period 1975–85, finfish mariculture more than doubled, while the crustacean crop increased by nearly 900 percent. A smaller jump in production was achieved with mollusks. Inshore salmon farming, for example, now greatly exceeds the high-seas catch in Japan (see Figure 1). The inshore catch now exceeds 80 percent of the total.

In marine farming, the organisms are maintained in enclosures of one type or another, whereas in marine ranching the young fish or shellfish are introduced into rivers or estuaries. The fish, after spending time in the open ocean, return to the coastal waters for spawning. As Lowe (1988) points out, the difference in techniques depends upon who feeds the fish. In ranching, naturally existing prey provide the food; in farming, the farmer does.

Shrimp (crustaceans) have become one of the most valuable of the aquacultured organisms. Twenty-two percent of the world supply is farmed, with a value of $6 billion (Puzo, 1989). The major producing countries are China, Ecuador, Taiwan, Indonesia, Thailand, and the Philippines. As a result of the high level of activity, the price of medium-sized shrimp throughout the world has declined. As yet, larger shrimp have not been successfully raised. In time, it is felt, aquacultured shrimp will totally displace wild shrimp as articles of commerce (Puzo, 1989).

Lowe (1988) provides some statistics on the economics of salmon farming and ranching (together referred to as herding). In the latter, a return of

TABLE 3   Estimated aquaculture production in 1985, in metric tons

Region	Finfish	Crustaceans	Mollusks	Seaweeds	Others	Total
Africa	46,200	100	400			46,700
North America	300,900	39,000	176,800	200		516,900
South America	83,500	32,400	1,600	5,300		122,800
Asia and Oceania	4,599,700	209,800	2,115,400	3,515,700	39,400	10,480,000
Europe	370,900	300	591,500	4,500		967,200
USSR	296,000					296,000
Totals						
1985	5,697,200	281,600	2,885,700	3,527,700	39,400	12,429,600
1980	3,206,800	75,000	3,299,700			
1975	2,628,800	29,700	1,961,200			
Percent change, 1975–85	117	848	47			

SOURCE: Rhodes (1988).

**FIGURE 1   Salmon farming and wild catches:
Japan, 1974–84 (in metric tons)**

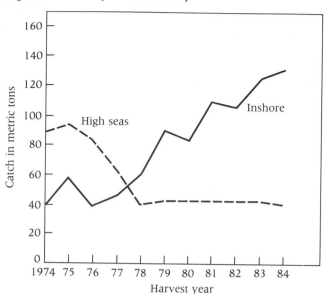

SOURCE: Isaksson (1988).

1 percent represents the break-even point, while 1 or 2 percent, or more, is usually found. On the other hand, farming offers the product protection from threats of the open ocean, as farmed species are maintained from hatching to harvest. Herding activities accounted in 1985 for over one-third of the world salmon production (see Table 4).

Knowledge is slowly accumulating as to the effects of farming and ranching of marine organisms on other members of ecosystems. In the case of farming, problems arise from the entry of organic materials, fecal pellets, and unconsumed food, as well as of ammonia, which can fertilize the growth of planktonic organisms in undesirable ways, the so-called eutrophication response. Toxic byproducts of eutrophication are methane and hydrogen sulfide. These substances have been detected as far as 60 meters from the farming sites (MPB, 1988). The farms can overload the coastal system, causing decreased water quality even to the point of jeopardizing the farming stock.

In the case of ranching large numbers of fish, there is the troubling, but as yet unestablished, problem of competition for food between herded organisms and wild species. Fish ranchers clearly wish to utilize the carrying capacity of the oceans for their organisms. How to ascertain whether this capacity is being exceeded is a difficult task. Increasing salmon releases in the Columbia River are associated with declining adult returns (Isaksson,

TABLE 4   Sources of market-place salmon

Source	Quantity (metric tons)	Percent of total
Wild catch	561,000	63
Ranching	281,000	32
Farming	45,300	5
Total	887,000	100

SOURCE: Lowe (1988).

1988). Also, the Atlantic Ocean may be supporting a smaller salmon population today than it did in the 1700s. Whether these phenomena are related to exceeding the carrying capacity (i.e., the abundance of food) of the open oceans is not yet known (Isaksson, 1988).

Maricultural activities are already depleting natural resources. For example, the depletion of mangrove forests, a valuable but declining marine ecosystem, is associated with shrimp farming in the southeast Pacific (Escobar, 1988). In Panama, the apparent loss rate is 1 percent per year. In Colombia, 5,000 hectares of mangroves are already dedicated to shrimp farming. Of the 177,000 hectares of mangroves in Ecuador, 60,000 have already been turned over to saltwater shrimp farming.

On the other hand, the intense culture of mussels in northwest Spain (about 0.1 million tons per year) has an overall positive effect on the associated food chains (Tenore et al., 1985). The fecal wastes of the mussels provide sustenance to demersal fish and crabs.

Conclusion

The increased exploitation of ocean space through the remainder of this century will clearly enhance the quality of life of a growing world population. It will primarily be driven by economic factors, although environmental concerns will regulate some activities. One may hope that these developments will be guided by the early identification and resolution of conflicts of use and the minimization of environmental degradation.

Note

The author is indebted to Judy Capuzzo, Charles Hollister, and John Ryther of the Woods Hole Oceanographic Institution, Warren Wooster of the University of Washington, Arne Jernelev of the Swedish Environmental Research Institute, and Kenneth R. Tenore of the University of Maryland for guidance to various parts of the literature. Kathe Bertine of San Diego State University and Justin Lancaster of the Scripps Institution of Oceanography provided critical assessments of the manuscript.

References

Brown, L. R. 1988. "The changing world food prospect: The nineties and beyond," *Worldwatch Paper* No. 85.

Capuzzo, J. M., and B. A. Lancaster. 1985. "Zooplankton population response to industrial wastes discharged at Deepwater Dumpsite-106," in *Wastes in the Ocean*, Vol. 5: *Deep Sea Waste Disposal*, ed. Kester et al. New York: John Wiley and Sons, pp. 209–226.

Conservation Exchange (National Wildlife Federation). 1988. "Beyond our borders," *Conservation Exchange* 6, no. 1.

Epstein, J. 1970. "Rate of decomposition of GB in seawater," *Science* 170: 1396–1398.

Escobar, J. 1988. "The South-east Pacific," *The Siren*, No. 36: 28–29.

French, H. F. 1988. "Combating toxic terrorism," *World Watch* 1: 6–7.

Hollister, C. D., D. R. Anderson, and G. R. Heath. 1981. "Subseabed disposal of nuclear wastes," *Science* 213: 1321–1326.

Isaksson, A. 1988. "Salmon ranching: A world review," *Aquaculture* 75: 1–33.

Kone, S. 1988. "Viewpoint," *The Siren*, No. 37: 2–3.

Linnenbom, V. J. 1971. *Final Report on First Post-Dump Survey of the Chase X Disposal Site.* Washington, D.C.: Naval Research Laboratory Memorandum Report 2273.

Lowe, M. D. 1988. "Salmon ranching and farming net growing harvest," *World Watch* 1: 28–32.

MPB. (1988). "Fish farming pollutes," *Marine Pollution Bulletin* 19: 501.

NAS (National Academy of Sciences). 1984. *Disposal of Industrial and Domestic Wastes: Land and Sea Alternatives.* Washington, D.C.: National Academy Press.

———. 1985. *Dredging Coastal Ports.* Washington, D.C.: National Academy Press.

NOAA (National Oceanographic and Atmospheric Administration). 1979. *Assimilative Capacity of U. S. Coastal Waters for Pollutants.* Boulder, Colo.: Environmental Research Laboratories.

O'Leary, P. R., P. W. Walsh, and K. Ham. 1988. "Managing solid waste," *Scientific American* 259: 36–42.

OTA. 1987. *Wastes in Marine Environments.* Congress of the United States, Office of Technology Assessment.

Puzo, D. P. 1989. "Shrimp farming booms," *Los Angeles Times*, 19 January.

Rhodes, R. J. 1988. "Status of world aquaculture: 1987," *Aquaculture Magazine Buyer's Guide*: 4–18.

Tenore, K. R., et al. 1985. "Effects of intense mussel culture on food chain patterns and production in coastal Galacia, NW Spain," in *Proceedings of the International Symposium on Utilization of Coastal Ecosystems: Planning, Pollution and Productivity*, ed. Ning Labbish Chao and W. Kirby Smith. Rio Grande, Brazil.

WORLD DEFORESTATION AND

ITS CONSEQUENCES

.

The World's Forests
and Human Populations:
The Environmental
Interconnections

NORMAN MYERS

THE WORLD'S FORESTS HAVE TRADITIONALLY BEEN SEEN as sources of timber and fuelwood. More recently, tropical forests in particular have come to be perceived as sites for agricultural expansion—a consequence, in part, of the rise in human numbers and human technology. But like the longstanding timber-and-fuelwood approach, this new approach overlooks the many other goods and services that forests have to offer. For instance, there has been scant recognition of the role played by forests in climate regulation, though it is now coming to be realized that forests, by virtue of their carbon stocks alone, act as giant flywheels stabilizing climate regimes. Forests also provide a host of other outputs that support human welfare—for instance, foods, beverages, nonwood fibers, medicinals, and gums and exudates among industrial materials.

This article has several aims. First, it seeks to describe, analyze, and appraise the multiple ways in which population growth often proves a major factor in deforestation of the tropics—especially at a time of unprecedented economic activity and material demands. Second, the article reviews and evaluates the diverse consequences of deforestation for human welfare. Finally, it describes a major proposal for reforestation that could be undertaken to offset the negative climatic and other consequences of environmental destruction.

Population growth and the environmental outlook

Let us establish a rough analytic framework within which to evaluate the impact of population growth on natural resources and the environment, notably on forests (for further analysis, see Benedick, 1988; Hinrichsen, 1988;

and Repetto, 1987). Since 1960 the world's population has expanded from 3 billion to just over 5 billion persons. This sudden surge in human numbers has often exacted a toll in terms of renewable natural resources and environmental quality, as exemplified by tropical deforestation, the spread of deserts, soil erosion, and the like. But population growth has not been the only factor at work. Soil erosion is as severe in Iowa as in much of India, even though Iowa's population pressures are only a fraction of those of India. One of the countries where desertification is occurring most rapidly is Botswana, with only 1.3 million people in a territory roughly the size of Texas or Spain—and a country where the bulk of desertifying processes are attributable to the activities of a few hundred large-scale cattle ranchers who make up a mere 5 percent of the livestock-owning industry.

Apparently, then, certain environmental problems have less to do with population growth than with other factors. This applies primarily of course in developed countries, where population growth rates are generally well below 1 percent per year. A leading pollution problem in North America and Western Europe is acid rain—not so much a population problem as a problem of inappropriate technology. So too, the over-harvesting of fisheries by affluent countries is not a reflection of growth in human numbers but of growth in human consumerism (the amount of fish consumed in Western Europe, whether directly or in the form of livestock feed, more than doubled during the period 1948–76; Food and Agriculture Organization, 1981). The so-called greenhouse effect and the depletion of the ozone layer are almost entirely the consequences of economic activity in the developed world. Clearly, then, population growth is just one among many variables (though it can sometimes rank as primus inter pares): important too are such factors as technology types, energy inputs, property rights, trade relations, economic systems, and political persuasions that either reduce or aggravate the impact of population growth.

At the same time, very rapid population growth can be a pronounced problem when it exceeds the capacity of a country's natural resource base to sustain it and exceeds the capacity of development planners to accommodate it. Kenya, for example, could conceivably support 50 million people some distant day, if it could build its manufacturing base and develop export markets to enable it to buy sufficient food overseas (Shah and Fischer, 1981). But Kenya, with a rate of natural increase of 4.1 percent per year, is projected to expand from its present 23 million people to 50 million in less than 20 years (Frank and McNicoll, 1987)—a prospect that would be daunting to even the most richly endowed and best governed nation. We must surely anticipate that Kenya will soon face burgeoning numbers of impoverished peasants, who will pursue whatever means are available to gain their subsistence livelihoods. If that means cutting down forests, ploughing up grasslands, and cultivating steep slopes (the phenomenon of marginal people in marginal environments), they will wreak havoc on Kenya's natural resource base in short order. Kenya's forests covered 12 percent of national territory in 1960, when the population was only 6 million. Since the forests often occupy fertile lands where property rights are vague at best, they have been a prime focus for agricultural settlement by landless peasants. Today forests occupy only a little over 2 percent of Kenya's land area.

Let us consider the question of property rights in Kenya's forest lands in more detail. Such rights are indeed "vague at best." In my 24 years of work in Kenya, I have seen virtually no methodical and comprehensive system for allocating property rights in discrete areas of land within forested sectors of the country. In the great majority of cases I have found that local people and officials are surprised that anyone should suppose there are any definable rights in forest lands, whether rights of *res nullius* or *res communis*. In Kenya, forest lands almost always belong to the government as part of the national estate; as such, property rights ultimately reside in the government's gift (to cite the official terminology), though in practice they are usually assigned to forest concessionaires. Moreover, the situation varies greatly from area to area and from one tribal culture to another. All this notwithstanding, large numbers of individual squatters, slash-and-burn cultivators, and an assortment of other farmers feel at liberty to enter and occupy forest lands for the purpose of small-scale cultivation. In principle the government objects to this form of occupation and exploitation; but the government proclaims that it is bound to meet the basic needs of landless peasants, if necessary by turning a blind eye to their invasion of forest lands. None of this is to be construed in terms of the government extending property rights, or even usufruct rights, to forest land farmers. In sum, the situation works itself out through default rather than design; there is nothing resembling an officially recognized, legally sanctioned, or codified response to the situation.

The present world with its 5 billion inhabitants is showing many ecological stresses and environmental strains. What will happen within another few decades when there are twice as many people, demanding three times as much food and fiber, seeking perhaps four times as much energy, and engaging in five to ten times as much economic activity (if the Third World is to leave behind its pervasive poverty) (World Commission on Environment and Development, 1987)? What will be the expanding impact of population growth, plus the associated factors of consumerism, technology, poverty, and so forth, upon the global environment—and particularly upon the world's forests? Before considering the main processes and causes of tropical deforestation, let us briefly review the extent of this loss.

Extent and rates of tropical deforestation

The original expanse of tropical forests, some 16 million square kilometers, has already been reduced to 8 million square kilometers, mainly within the past four decades (Food and Agriculture Organization, 1982; Myers, 1980), and the rate of deforestation is accelerating (Myers, 1989a). Until the late 1970s the rate of outright destruction of forest cover (not counting gross degradation of forests that still leaves some trees standing) was estimated at a minimum of 76,000–92,000 square kilometers a year, the divergence of estimates accounted for by questions of definitions and criteria (Houghton et al., 1985; Melillo et al., 1985). The Food and Agriculture Organization recently asserted (Singh, 1988) that there is no evidence of any increase in deforestation rates. Yet the widespread burning in the Brazilian Amazonia alone during the past few years (Malingreau and Tucker, 1988; Setzer and Pereira, 1989)—involving a total of 50,000 square kilometers in the dry season of 1987, for example—means that the deforestation rate biome-wide has surely increased 90 percent above its late-1970s level.

Causes of deforestation

By far the most significant agent of deforestation is the slash-and-burn cultivator, operating not so much as a shifting cultivator but as a shifted cultivator: to wit, the peasant who finds himself landless in traditional farming areas and migrates to the forests, the last unoccupied public lands available on which he can practice cultivation. Current population growth rates of selected tropical regions, proportions of the population living in rural areas, and projected population totals in the year 2000 are shown in Table 1. Of course many factors other than population growth are at work in the shifted cultivator phenomenon, notably maldistribution of farmlands and inequitable land-use practices. But population growth in itself is a prominent factor in the likely progressive expansion of numbers of shifted cultivators, and hence in the accelerating rates of deforestation.

The shifted cultivator phenomenon is most prominent in the two Brazilian states of Rondonia and Acre in southern Amazonia, with a combined area of 400,000 square kilometers. Deforestation there is proceeding with exceptional speed (Malingreau and Tucker, 1988; Setzer and Pereira, 1989). In the mid-1970s the Brazilian government began to sponsor smallholder settlements in Rondonia, and by the early 1980s in Acre as well. The population of Rondonia, which stood at 111,000 in 1975, soared to well over 1 million by 1986, for an almost tenfold increase in only 11 years. In 1975 only 1,200 square kilometers of forest had been cleared, but by 1982 the total had grown to well over 10,000 square kilometers, and by 1985 to almost 28,000 square kilometers. During the dry season of 1987 some 50,000 square kilometers of forest were burned in these two states alone.

This migratory surge into Rondonia and Acre is due in large part to population growth in Brazil. With 53 million people in 1950, Brazil today has 147 million, and the total is growing at a rate of 2.0 percent per year. The projected total for the year 2100 is almost 300 million people.

TABLE 1   Populations, present and projected, in selected tropical-forest countries

Country	Population in 1950 (millions)	Population in 1990 (millions)	Average annual growth of population (percent), 1980–86	Percent of labor force in agriculture (1980)	Population in 2000 (millions)	Assumed year of reaching net reproduction rate of 1	Hypothetical size of stationary population (millions)
Latin America							
Brazil	53	144	2.0	31	180	2015	306
Colombia	12	31	2.1	34	38	2010	59
Ecuador	3	10	2.8	39	14	2015	26
Peru	8	21	2.5	40	28	2015	48
Venezuela	5	19	2.4	16	25	2005	40
Southern/Southeast Asia							
Bangladesh	44	110	2.7	75	146	2030	342
Burma	18	41	2.1	53	52	2020	102
India	362	817	2.0	70	1013	2010	1698
Indonesia	77	177	1.7	57	214	2005	335
Malaysia	6	17	2.4	42	21	2005	33
Papua New Guinea	2	3.7	2.4	76	5	2025	10
Philippines	20	63	2.8	52	86	2015	137
Thailand	20	55	2.1	71	66	2000	99
Vietnam	24	65	2.6	68	86	2015	168
Africa							
Cameroon	5	11	2.6	70	15	2030	51
Congo	0.8	2.2	3.4	62	3	2030	10
Gabon	NA	1.3	1.6	75	1.6	2035	NA
Ivory Coast	3	11	3.1	65	17	2030	51
Madagascar	5	11	2.8	81	16	2035	52
Nigeria	41	112	2.9	68	161	2035	529
Zaire	14	33	3.0	72	48	2035	142

NA = not available.
SOURCES: McNamara, 1984; Population Reference Bureau, 1988; World Bank, 1988.

This is not to ignore the other factors involved in the recent migratory surge into Rondonia and Acre. The maldistribution of farmland in the main agricultural territories of southern Brazil is contributing to growing numbers of landless farmers. A response to the deforestation problem lies not only with population planning throughout Brazil, but with agrarian reform in the agricultural sector. In addition to factors of poorly defined property rights and ownership regimes, the problems of externalities are scarcely addressed by existing patterns and practices of forest land exploitation. The Brazilian government has directed inadequate policy emphasis toward improving agro-technologies, credit supplies, marketing networks, and rural infrastructure generally with respect to the small-scale farmer in traditional farmlands of southern Brazil. This deficiency is compounded by an overall policy orientation that favors industry over agriculture, urban concerns over rural interests, capital-intensive over employment-creating activities, and ultimately the rich over the poor (Binswanger, 1987; Mahar, 1989).

A similar situation with respect to the shifted cultivator arises in a number of other tropical forest countries. Driven significantly by population growth and sheer pressure of human numbers on existing farmlands (albeit often cultivated with only low or medium levels of agro-technology, hence cultivated in extensive rather than intensive fashion), slash-and-burn farming by smallholders is the principal factor in deforestation in the Philippines, Indonesia, Thailand, India, Madagascar, Tanzania, Kenya, Nigeria, Ivory Coast, Colombia, Peru, Ecuador, and Bolivia, plus other countries with smaller amounts of forest cover remaining (Myers, 1989a). Of course one must be careful not to over-simplify the situation. In many areas other factors are at work, notably inequitable land-tenure systems, inefficient agricultural techniques, and faulty development policies overall. But population growth appears at present to be the predominant pressure on forests.

Given the "demographic momentum" built into population-growth processes in developing countries, and even allowing for expanded family planning programs, population projections (Table 1) suggest that in those countries where economies are likely to remain primarily agrarian there will surely be progressive pressure on remaining forests for decades to come. Unless there is a resolution of the landless-peasant phenomenon (a prospect that appears less than promising; Salmi, 1988), most of the forest cover is likely to be destroyed within 30–50 years in such major tropical-forest countries as Indonesia, Thailand, Peru, and Colombia, and also in a major portion of Brazilian Amazonia.

As for other agents of deforestation, cattle raising, almost entirely confined to Latin America, eliminated some 20,000 square kilometers of forest per year in the late 1970s. Fuelwood gatherers, together with charcoal manufacturers, accounted for roughly 25,000 square kilometers per year. Commercial loggers affected around 45,000 square kilometers of forest per year; their selective logging has left a grossly degraded forest in their wake. Moreover, loggers, by establishing a network of long-truck tracks, opened up forest areas that had hitherto remained inaccessible to the small-scale cultivator, and thus strongly catalyzed the impact of the principal agents of deforestation, the slash-and-burn cultivators. While on the one hand the annual amount of deforestation due to cattle ranchers has declined somewhat in the late 1980s, the amount due to fuelwood gatherers has hardly expanded, and the amount of forest affected by commercial loggers has scarcely increased, on the other hand the numbers of shifted cultivators—those who have induced the great bulk of accelerated deforestation from the early 1980s onward—have grown greatly.

Exogenous demand for tropical forest resources

While the small-scale cultivator is the principal agent of deforestation, developed country exploitation of cheap food sources is exerting major pressure on tropical forests at the other end of the spectrum. Many tropical forests are being depleted owing to a rise in human consumption rather than a rise in human numbers. A notable case in point is the forests of Central America, which covered roughly two-thirds of the region as recently as 1950 but today are reduced to less than one-third and may all but disappear before the year 2000. The principal cause has been the "hamburger connection," driven by the demand for "cheap" beef in North America (Myers, 1981; Nations and Komer, 1982). From the late 1950s to the early 1980s, citizens of the United States displayed an ever-growing appetite for beef, especially in the form of fast foods such as hamburgers and frankfurters. Yet beef was proving to be one of the most inflationary items in Americans' shopping baskets. So the US government authorized expanded imports of beef from Central America, which cost much less than beef produced in Montana or Texas and was raised on pasturelands established through clearing of tropical forests. By seeking to trim a nickel off the price of a hamburger, the United States contributed—unwittingly, but effectively and increasingly—to progressive loss of forest cover from Mexico to Panama. In recent years, the linkage has been somewhat weakened, due largely to declining beef consumption in the United States as a result of health concerns.

No doubt the situation is more complex than represented above. Additional factors are at work besides the exogenous pressure of demand for cheap beef in the United States (Myers, 1984). Within most Central American countries the legal framework for forest exploitation fosters unnecessary and unproductive use of forest lands. An occupier of a patch of forest can gain property rights through whatever form of exploitation he chooses to engage in (including burning the forest and using it for a few years for cattle raising before repeating the process in another patch of forest). Equally to the point, the rancher is not obliged to take account of any environmental externalities (loss of species and their genetic resources, decline of watershed functions, climatic disruptions whether local or more widespread) that arise as a result of his deforestation: there are no policy prescriptions, land-use requirements, or economic inducements to persuade him to internalize the adverse spillover effects. Conversely if the forest occupier engages in no form of exploitation but leaves the forest intact, he incurs a penalty through increased taxation (Parsons, 1976).

A parallel with the US demand for cheap beef is the "cassava connection" between the European Economic Community and forests in parts of Southeast Asia. Manufacturers of livestock feed in Europe have been importing growing amounts of calorie-rich cassava from Thailand and other Southeast Asian countries, to be fed to cattle, pigs, and poultry (Phantumvanit and Sathisathai, 1988). The cassava has been grown almost entirely on croplands established at the expense of forests. As in the case of the hamburger connection, the cassava-fed beef, pork, and chicken amount to a sort of "free lunch" for Europeans, since the price paid does not cover all costs of production, notably in terms of deforestation.

A similar link can be invoked with respect to the international timber trade (World Resources Institute and World Bank, 1985; for substantiated detail and authoritative analysis, see Nectoux and Dudley, 1987). Roughly half of all hardwood timber cut in tropical forests is exported to the developed world. This trade with the developed world arises through marketplace demand for specialist hardwoods from tropical forests, supplied at artificially cheap prices because of unduly negligent logging practices that deplete tropical-forest resources and whose costs are not required to be internalized by the commercial logger. To this extent, of course, the responsibility for deforestation cannot justly be laid at the door of the logger; rather it belongs with the tropical-forest governments in question, as well as with the international trading system and its inadequate pricing structures.

Still further linkages can be demonstrated between economic activity in the developed world and deforestation in developing countries. Consider, for instance, the role of international debt (Bramble, 1986). Tropical-forest countries owe some $800 billion to banks both public and private, a situation that encourages certain countries to liquidate undue amounts of their forest capital. A good part of the responsibility lies with faulty development policies and investment decisions on the part of tropical-forest governments. But a sizable measure of responsibility too lies with major creditors, who seem unaware that their debt-recall practices serve, albeit indirectly, to induce additional and unsustainable exploitation of tropical forests (Binswanger, 1987; Maher, 1989).

Thus the developed countries, with their low population growth rates, play a central role in depletion of tropical forests. To reiterate, the linkages at work do not generally amount to a direct cause-and-effect connection, let alone an exclusively causative connection. Rather, a plethora of additional factors are operating. But this is not to ignore the factor of population growth in developed countries: with growth rates that often average only 0.5 percent per year, they are still adding many millions of people annually—and each person consumes on average many times more tropical hardwood per year than does an average person in a developing country. The situation with regard to the hamburger connection is even more revealing: while beef production in Central America expanded more than threefold between 1955 and 1980 (Myers, 1984), beef consumption among Central American citizens actually declined.

A further example of deforestation related to economic practices—rather than to sheer numbers of people—is provided by the decline of certain temperate-zone forests through the impact of "acid rain." Until recently temperate-zone forests were actually expanding a little through reforestation and afforestation. But today large expanses of forest in Western Europe and North America are declining, principally as a consequence of airborne pollutants (McCormick, 1985; Myers, 1988b). In Europe alone, acid rain is thought to have caused gross injury to almost 200,000 square kilometers of forests, a large proportion of which are dying or dead—a total that, equivalent in aggregate area to the whole of Great Britain, amounts to some 13 percent of all forest cover in the region. Similar extensive damage to forests is documented in North America, not only in the more industrialized Northeast but in the Western states as well.

Acid rain is starting to manifest itself, too, in certain sectors of the tropics, notably in southcentral Thailand, southern Peninsular Malaysia, southwestern India, southeastern China, southern Brazil, and northern Venezuela (Rodhe and Herrera, 1988). Moreover, in extensive tracts of tropical forests, naturally acid soils are likely to prove highly sensitive to the additional ecological burden of acid rain.

Of course we must be careful not to overstate the case. In much of the island of New Guinea, population pressures are slight and appear unlikely to become predominant within the near future. Much the same applies to the countries of the Zaire Basin in central Africa; in the countries of the Guyana shield, viz. Guyana, Suriname, and French Guyana; and in the western sector of Brazilian Amazonia.

Consequences of deforestation

Diverse consequences of deforestation will adversely affect human welfare. In the tropical-forest zone, deforestation leads not only to loss of hardwood stocks. It also causes, as a major externality, a decline of watershed functions in at least 1.4 million square kilometers of catchment systems and in valleylands of the humid tropics where some 2 billion people live (World Resources Institute and World Bank, 1985). In the Ganges Valley, deforestation in the Himalayan foothills contributes to disruption of river flows, leading to flood-and-drought regimes that levy costs on some 400 million downstream people amounting to an average of $1 billion a year in India alone (Myers, 1986). And the floodplains of other major rivers such as the Salween, Irrawaddy, Mekong, and Niger are already suffering from deforestation in upland catchments.

Even more important in the long term could be the mass extinction of tropical-forest species, with elimination of their genetic resources. It is now believed (Erwin, 1988) that tropical forests harbor at least 80 percent of Earth's 35 million species. The extinction rate in these forests is estimated at a minimum of one thousand, and possibly as many as several thousand, species per year (Wilson, 1988). Hundreds of products owe their existence, in one way or another, to species of tropical forests (Myers, 1983; Oldfield, 1989). At least half of all fruits originated in tropical forests; and in New Guinea alone, more than 250 tree species bear edible fruits, only three of which reach the supermarkets of the world. In addition, tropical forests supply germ plasm for genetic improvement of such major crops as rice, corn, coffee, and bananas. A few years ago, green revolution rice in eastern Asia was struck by disease, and rice geneticists searched in vain through their gene-bank collections of rice varieties to find a strain with resistance. Eventually they turned to wild relatives of rice, that is, plants which are close associates of cultivated rice; after much searching they came across a variety in a small threatened patch of tropical forest in India (Chang, 1984). A similar story applies to corn, and the remarkable wild teosinte (a relative of corn with commercial potential via multiple disease resistance and environmental adaptability) found in a montane forest of southcentral Mexico.

Tropical-forest species are also important in the field of medicine (Plotkin, 1988). One in four drug or pharmaceutical purchases derives, in one way or another, from startpoint materials of tropical-forest plants. The product may be an analgesic, antibiotic, laxative, diuretic, or tranquilizer, among many other materials. The contraceptive pill was originally manufactured from a wild yam growing in forests of Central America; today it is produced from plant materials from forests of West Africa. In the field of cancer therapies Madagascar's rosy periwinkle is the source of two potent drugs for use against leukemia and other blood cancers. The US National Cancer Institute believes that tropical forests could well contain at least ten other plants with similar potential against cancers. Commercial sales worldwide of plant-derived drugs and pharmaceuticals of tropical-forest origin are estimated at around $15 billion a year (Myers, 1983). Yet pharmacologists have intensively screened only one plant species in a hundred to assess their economic potential.

A still more important repercussion of tropical deforestation could lie with climatic change. Linkages between the world's forests and climate patterns exist at local, regional, and global levels (Myers, 1989b). By far the most important connection lies with the emergent greenhouse effect (Houghton and Woodwell, 1989; Myers, 1989c; Prance, 1986). Terrestrial vegetation and soils, within forest ecosystems for the most part, contain at least 2,000 gigatons of carbon, or roughly three times the amount in the atmosphere. The build-up of carbon dioxide in the atmosphere stems primarily from combustion of fossil fuels, which are emitted to the extent of some 5.6 gigatons a year. There is also a sizable contribution from the burning of tropical forests: a realistic figure to date is 1.9 gigatons a year (Houghton et al., 1987); and by the year 2000 the tropical-forest source could rise to almost 5 gigatons (because of increased forest burning by slash-and-burn cultivators), as compared with somewhere between 6 and 8 gigatons for fossil fuels. As the number of slash-and-burn farmers continues to increase in tropical forests, this source could contribute as much as 8 gigatons a year by 2025—but then decline sharply thereafter, because there will not be much more tropical forest left to burn.

In addition to carbon dioxide, there are several trace gases that, molecule for molecule, are far more efficient in absorbing infrared radiation from the planetary surface. These gases include nitrous oxide and methane, some of the main sources of which are in tropical forests (Goreau and de Mello, 1988).

The greenhouse effect is expected to exert a marked impact on forests of all kinds (Bolin et al., 1986). Increasing temperatures (together possibly with moisture and soil factors) are theoretically projected to expand tropical forests somewhat, from roughly 8 million square kilometers today to almost 10 million square kilometers over the next century, provided the forests have not been widely eliminated meantime, and provided too that there are unoccupied lands into which they can expand. Warm temperate forests may well expand from 21 percent of all forests today to 25 percent, and cool temperate forests from 15 percent to 20 percent (the same reservations apply). But the most pervasive changes are projected to occur at high latitudes, where the predicted temperature increases are largest. Boreal forests may well decline from 23 percent of all forests today to a mere 1 percent by 2070 or thereafter.

A measure to counter the greenhouse effect: Grand-scale reforestation in the tropics

A potential counter to the greenhouse effect could be provided by a grand-scale reforestation effort in the humid tropics. A tree is half carbon, which it absorbs from the atmosphere through photosynthesis. Thus tree planting across a sufficiently large area could serve to "soak up" large amounts of carbon dioxide and sequester it in tree tissues. Of course an effort of this sort would serve little purpose if deforestation, especially through burning, continues unchecked. But were an anti-deforestation program to be undertaken with appropriate policies and programs (as is not at all impossible—see World Resources Institute and World Bank, 1985), it might slow and even halt deforestation in large parts of the biome. A reforestation-grounded counter to the greenhouse effect would serve as a substantial boost for measures to stem and eventually stop deforestation (Myers, 1989c; see also Marland, 1988). (The humid tropics, with their year-round warmth and moisture, are by far the best place for fast-growing tree plantations.)

The net amount of carbon to be absorbed is currently about 3 billion tons (gigatons) per year; that is, the amount of carbon released through combustion of fossil fuels and from (reduced) burning of tropical forests, less the amount absorbed annually by the oceans and other carbon sinks (Houghton and Woodwell, 1989). One hectare of fast-growing trees can take up an average of 10 tons of carbon per year. To absorb 3 gigatons would require 3 million square kilometers of tree plantations. While this is no small area, equivalent to three times the size of California, Oregon, and Washington combined, it is available in the humid tropics in the form of lands that have already been deforested and are little used for human purposes. The cost is estimated, as a preliminary calculation, at $120 billion, or $12 billion a year spread over ten years. Large as this sum sounds, it is to be compared with the cost of re-jigging the world's irrigation and hydropower systems in the wake of the greenhouse effect, a cost that could reach $200 billion, apart from many other costs to agriculture and costs in terms of coastal flooding and other gross dislocations.

A key point here is that a reforestation effort of this sort, already receiving much attention from the US Congress and the World Bank, among others, would surely serve to transform the tropical-forestry situation. With funding of the order cited, there would be strong incentive for tropical-forest countries to take the necessary steps to curtail present processes of deforestation.

Conclusion

In this article we have briefly reviewed some interconnections between the world's forests and human communities. Until about 10,000 years ago and the start of agriculture, the Earth was mantled with roughly 62 million square kilometers of forests, covering about half the ice-free land area. Today at most 41 million square kilometers remain. Tropical forests could be all but eliminated within a few more decades—due primarily to the impact of impoverished populations of slash-and-burn farmers with their rapidly growing numbers, as well as to such other factors as development policies generally, agriculture planning and programs, and aid, trade, and debt relations between tropical-forest countries and the developed world.

Recent research reveals, however, that a major effort could be undertaken to slow or even halt tropical deforestation, and to markedly increase the expanse of tropical forests as a counter-measure to the greenhouse effect.

As for temperate-zone forests, they may continue to decline under the impact of acid rain and other broad-scope pollutants in the atmosphere—though they could conceivably expand as a consequence of the greenhouse effect. Boreal forests, by contrast, while little affected to date, may virtually disappear by the end of the next century in the wake of the greenhouse effect.

The changes in temperate-zone and boreal forests will not so much reflect population growth as stem from the pollutant impacts of human communities in industrialized countries. This contrasts with tropical forests, which will decline primarily as a consequence of mounting pressures of human numbers.

References

Benedick, R. E. 1988. "Population–environment linkages and sustainable development," *Populi* 15: 14–21.

Binswanger, H. 1987. *Fiscal and Legal Incentives With Environmental Effects on the Brazilian Amazon.* Agricultural and Rural Development Center, World Bank, Washington, D.C.

Bolin, B., et al. (eds.). 1986. *The Greenhouse Effect: Climatic Change and Ecosystems.* New York: John Wiley and Sons.

Bramble, B. J. 1986. *Third World Debt and Natural Resources Conservation.* Washington, D.C.: National Wildlife Federation.

Chang, T.T. 1984. "Conservation of rice genetic resources: Luxury or necessity?" *Science* 224: 251–256.

DeMontalembert, M. R., and J. Clement. 1983. *Fuelwood Supplies in the Developing Countries.* Rome: Food and Agriculture Organization.

DeWalt, B. R. 1983. "The cattle are eating the forest," *Bulletin of the Atomic Scientists* 39: 18–23.

Erwin, T. L. 1988. "The tropical forest canopy: The heart of biotic diversity," in Wilson (1988).

Food and Agriculture Organization. 1981. *Agriculture: Toward 2000.* Rome: FAO.

———. 1982. *Tropical Forest Resources.* Rome: FAO.

Frank, O., and G. McNicoll. 1987. "An interpretation of fertility and population policy in Kenya," *Population and Development Review* 13: 209–243.

Goreau, T. J., and W. Z. de Mello. 1988. "Tropical deforestation: Some effects on atmospheric chemistry," *Ambio* 17: 275–281.

Hinrichsen, D. 1988. *State of the World Population Report, 1988.* New York: United Nations Population Fund.

Houghton, R. A., et al. 1985. "Net flux of carbon from tropical forests in 1980," *Nature* 316: 617–620.

Houghton, R. A., et al. 1987. "The flux of carbon from terrestrial ecosystems to the atmosphere in 1980 due to changes in land use: Geographic distribution of the global flux," *Tellus* 39B: 122–139.

Houghton, R. A., and G.M. Woodwell. 1989. "Global climatic change," *Scientific American* 260: 18–26.

Leonard, H. J. 1987. *Natural Resources and Economic Development in Central America*. New Brunswick, N.J.: Transaction Books.

McCormick, J. 1985. *Acid Earth: The Global Threat of Acid Pollution*. London: Earthscan Publications.

McNamara, R. S. 1984. "The population problem: Time bomb or myth," *Foreign Affairs* 62: 1107–1131.

Mahar, D. 1989. *Government Policies and Deforestation in Brazil's Amazon Region*. Washington, D.C.: The World Bank.

Malingreau, J.-P., and C. J. Tucker. 1988. "Large-scale deforestation in the southeastern Amazon Basin of Brazil," *Ambio* 17: 49–55.

Marland, G. 1988. *The Prospect of Solving the CO$_2$ Problem Through Global Reforestation*. Washington, D.C.: US Department of Energy.

Melillo, J. M., et al. 1985. "A comparison of recent estimates of disturbance in tropical forests," *Environmental Conservation* 12: 37–40.

Myers, N. 1980. *Conversion of Tropical Moist Forests*. Washington, D.C.: National Research Council.

––––––. 1981. "The hamburger connection," *Ambio* 10: 3–8.

––––––. 1983. *A Wealth of Wild Species: Storehouse for Human Welfare*. Boulder, Colo.: Westview Press.

––––––. 1984. *The Primary Source: Tropical Forests and Our Future*. New York: W.W. Norton.

––––––. 1986. "Environmental repercussions of deforestation in the Himalayas," *Journal of World Forest Resource Management* 2: 63–72.

––––––. 1988a. "Tropical deforestation and remote sensing," *Forest Ecology and Management* 23: 215–225.

––––––. 1988b. "The future of forests," in L. Friday and R. A. Laskey (eds.), *The Fragile Environment*. Cambridge: Cambridge University Press, pp. 22–40.

––––––. 1989a. "Tropical deforestation: Rates and causes," Friends of the Earth, London.

––––––. 1989b. "Tropical deforestation and climatic change," *Environmental Conservation* 15: 293–298.

––––––. 1989c. "The greenhouse effect: A tropical forestry response," *Biomass* 18: 73–78.

Nations, J. D., and D. I. Komer. 1982. *Rainforests, Cattle and the Hamburger Society*. Austin, Texas: Center for Human Ecology.

Nectoux, F., and N. Dudley. 1987. *A Hardwood Story*. London: Friends of the Earth.

Oldfield, M. L. 1989. *The Value of Conserving Genetic Resources*. Sunderland, Mass.: Sinauer Associates.

Parsons, J. J. 1976. "Forest to pasture: Development or destruction?," *Revista Biologica Tropicale* 24: 121–138.

Phantumvanit, D., and K. Sathisathai. 1988. "Thailand: Degradation and development in a resource-rich land," *Environment* 30: 11–15, 30–32.

Plotkin, M. J. 1988. "The outlook for new agricultural and industrial products from the tropics," in Wilson (1988).

Population Reference Bureau. 1988. *World Population Data Sheet*. Washington, D.C.

Prance, G. T. (ed.). 1986. *Tropical Rain Forests and the World Atmosphere*. Boulder, Colo.: Westview Press.

Repetto, R. 1987. "Population, resources, environment: An uncertain future," *Population Bulletin* 42. Washington, D.C.: Population Reference Bureau.

Rodhe, H., and R. Herrera (eds.). 1988. *Acidification in Tropical Countries*. Chichester, U.K.: John Wiley and Sons.

Salmi, J. 1988. "Land reform—a weapon against tropical deforestation?," in M. Palo and J. Salmi (eds.), *Deforestation or Development in the Third World*. Helsinki: Division of Social Economics of Forestry, Finnish Forest Research Institure, Vol. 2, pp. 159–180.

Setzer, A. W., and M. C. Pereira. 1989. *Amazon Biomass Burnings in 1987 and Their Tropospheric Emissions*. Sao Jose dos Campos, Brazil: Instituto de Pesquisas Espaciais.

Shah, M. M., and G. Fischer. 1981. *Assessment of Food Production Potential, Resources, Technology and Environment—a Case Study of Kenya.* Laxenburg, Austria: International Institute for Applied Systems Analysis.

Shane, D. R. 1980. *Hoofprints on the Forest: An Inquiry into the Beef Cattle Industry in the Tropical Forest Areas of Latin America.* Report to the Office of Environmental Affairs, Department of State, Washington, D.C.

Singh, K. D. 1988. Comments on "Tropical deforestation and remote sensing, " *Forest Ecology and Management* 24: 312–313.

Wilson, E. O. (ed.). 1988. *Biodiversity.* Washington, D.C.: National Academy Press.

World Bank. 1988. *World Development Report 1988.* New York: Oxford University Press.

World Commission on Environment and Development. 1987. *Our Common Future.* London: Oxford University Press.

World Resources Institute and World Bank. 1985 *Tropical Forests: A Call for Action.* Washington, D.C.: World Resources Institute and World Bank.

Comment: On the Medicinal Value of Tropical Ecosystems

EUGENE ZAVARIN

TROPICAL FORESTS, SUCH AS THOSE of Western and Central Africa and the Amazon region, are an extremely valuable source of chemotherapeutically active agents. Their importance is twofold.

First, all plants contain a large number of chemical substances, some of which can be used as chemotherapeutic agents either directly or after modification. Some examples are quinine, salicylic acid, colchicine, morphine, atropine, and various steroids. Because the tropics are host to a much greater number of plant species than the temperate regions, tropical flora are more likely to yield substances of medicinal value. This is simply a matter of statistical probability; there is nothing peculiar to the tropical climate that would make plants there particularly likely to produce chemotherapeutic agents.

All natural chemotherapeutic agents, with the exception of extremely complicated chemical structures, can be synthesized from petroleum-based chemicals. The rationale for extracting the active agents from tropical plants—whether wild or cultivated—turns on economics: production of some artificial substances is more labor-intensive than extraction; in other cases, however, artificial synthesis is more expedient. Moreover, chemically related synthetic materials often prove to have a much higher potency and exhibit fewer undesirable side effects than their natural counterparts.

The second reason for the importance of tropical forests as a source of medically useful plants is found in the information that is already available about them. People have been living in tropical regions for thousands of years and have accumulated a body of folk knowledge about the usefulness of these plants for curing various diseases. The oral transmission of this cultural information is now being jeopardized through the influence of civilization, with its disruption of tribal unity and continuity. As a result, "prescientific" medical information is being lost at an alarming rate in spite of many efforts to preserve it. True, the relationship between various diseases and the chemical structure of curative agents can in principle be deduced by independent scientific research, but our knowledge about that relationship is poor, and folk knowledge can contribute to it.

Therefore, it is not merely the tropical plants themselves that are valuable to modern medicine, since active agents can be chemically synthesized. In addition, an extremely valuable resource is the traditional folk knowledge of how to use such naturally occurring agents.

Comment: Population Effects on Deforestation and Soil Erosion in China

JING-NENG LI

CHINA'S LARGE AND RAPIDLY GROWING POPULATION is widely viewed as a major cause of the country's existing social and economic problems. Population growth in China is held to have interfered with the process of modernization and to be responsible for the degradation of the environment and the growing scarcity of natural resources.

The imperfections of the communist socioeconomic system, as practiced in China, however, may be at the root of much environmental degradation there. Like all communist countries, China has recently been facing a series of social problems. Its serious challenge is in trying to find effective solutions to break the economic deadlock—to raise productivity and economic efficiency, which have lagged farther and farther behind levels in Western developed countries, but, at the same time, to keep Chinese economic development within the fundamental economic doctrines of Marxism. Doubtless, many factors result in the decline of economic efficiency, the waste of natural resources, and the degradation of the environment within the communist countries. Among these factors are the insufficient introduction of the market price mechanism, the lack of free mobility of labor, capital, and commodities, the negation of real private ownership, galloping inflation, the weakening of worker discipline and responsibility, and the lack of personal motivation, initiative, and innovation.

Nevertheless, China's population growth poses a major problem for economic development and the exploitation of natural resources. Since 1949, China's total population has increased continuously and often rapidly. In the period from 1949 to 1987, the population has nearly doubled, from 541.7 million in 1949 to 1080.7 million in 1987. Table 1 illustrates this growth.

TABLE 1   Total population and growth rate of China

Year	Total population (millions)	Annual growth rate (percent)
1949	541.7	
1950	552.0	1.9
1955	614.7	2.0
1960	662.1	− 1.5
1965	725.4	2.9
1970	829.9	2.9
1975	924.2	1.7
1980	987.1	1.2
1985	1045.3	1.4
1987	1080.7	2.2

NOTE: Growth rates of the total population have been recalculated.
SOURCES: State Statistical Bureau, *Statistical Yearbook of China*, various years.

More than 20 million births occur in China annually—more than 54,000 per day and more than 38 per minute (data from State Family Planning Commission). As a result of such rapid growth, China now contains more than one-fifth of the world's population.

Although the total population doubled during 1949–87, China's total arable land area remained almost unchanged, at about 100 million hectares. New lands are brought into cultivation yearly, but an almost equal amount of arable land is lost to housing and urban construction, factories, city infrastructure, roads and highways, and the like. As a result, cultivated land area per capita decreased from 0.2 hectare in 1949 to 0.1 hectare in 1987. This is less than one-third the world average on a per capita basis. Of the 26 most populous countries in the world, China ranks 24th in arable land availability. Moreover, according to my estimates, the proportion of arable land in China's total area is only about 10 percent, and few areas remain for further exploitation and cultivation.

The continuous growth of China's population requires increasing quantities of food. China is still in substance a traditionally agricultural society, with some 70 percent of the population living in rural areas. Agricultural technology, moreover, has remained almost fixed throughout China's long history. The peasant has always cleared and burned forest tracts in order to enlarge land area for cultivation. Such slash-and-burn techniques not only waste forest resources but also result in the rapid and permanent loss of forest cover.

A vicious circle appears to characterize the relationship between population growth and deforestation in China. Such a relationship might be diagramed as follows:

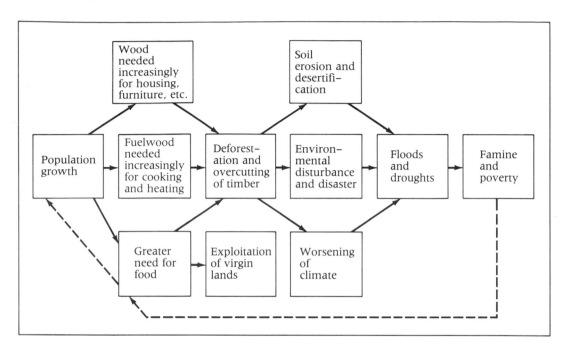

The scarcity of woodland and forest resources has reached serious proportions in China, as can be seen in Table 2.

The rate of deforestation in China is very high—approximately 1.2 percent per year. According to the State Statistical Bureau's data, the area that is forested land changed from about 8 percent of the total in 1949 to 12.0 percent in 1984 and to 8.4 percent in 1988. Forest area per capita in 1984 was only one-eighth the world average. In terms of forest area as a percentage of total area, China ranks 120th in the world. Moreover, the spatial distribution of Chinese forest resources is uneven. Half of its forests are concentrated in the northeast provinces of Heilongjiang and Jilin and in the southwest provinces of Sichuan and Yunnan. Because of this uneven distribution, the area of forest cover in many provinces and municipalities is less than 10 percent.

The most frequently cited cause of deforestation in China, especially in rural areas, is the need for cooking and heating fuel. Because rural energy sources consist mainly of fuelwood and hay (in southwest and northeast

TABLE 2   China's forest resources in 1984

Total forest area	115.25 million hectares
Forest area per capita	0.12 hectare (World: 1.04 hectares)
Percent of total area under forest cover	12.0 (World: 22.0)
Timber reserves	10,260 million cubic meters

SOURCE: SSB Statistics Yearbook, 1984.

China these two sources provide about 80 percent of the total energy used), a great deal of forest and woodland is lost in everyday household use. According to the statistics of Jingdong and Shipin counties of Yunnan Province, the average fuelwood use is one cubic meter per capita per year, and in the region of Xishuang-Bana each household uses 3.4 cubic meters per year. On the basis of the most conservative estimates, each year at least 60 million cubic meters of wood are burned as fuel for cooking and heating in China's rural areas.

China's most extensive forests are located in the northeast provinces, where deforestation is the most serious. Residents of Heilongjiang burn 3 million cubic meters of wood a year. Since the annual wood harvest amounts to only 6.9 million cubic meters, the proportion of total output that is burned is nearly 45 percent. The worst situation in 1987, however, was observed in the northern part of the Daxinan mountain forest in Heilongjiang Province, where more than 1.3 million hectares of forest were intentionally burned and another 1.4 million hectares damaged by fires. Deforestation is also occurring in the Changbai mountains of Jilin Province, where the forest area and wood stocks decline annually at a rate of 35,000 hectares and 5 million cubic meters respectively. In Guanxi Province the forest area declined from 12.5 million hectares in the early 1950s to only 5.5 million hectares in 1984. The loss of forest cover approaches 200,000 hectares a year. At this rate, the forests of Guanxi Province will disappear by the year 2011.

The problem of deforestation in the southwest provinces is also severe. In the province of Sichuan, the rate of deforestation to reforestation is currently about ten to one. This amounts to a decrease in forest cover from 20 percent to 13 percent of total area in the last 35 years.

Due to the loss of forest cover, soil erosion in China is also an extremely serious problem. Almost 5 billion tons of soil are washed away every year, wasting a soil-fertility equivalent of 40 million tons of chemical fertilizer. The areas affected by soil erosion grew from 1.1 million square kilometers in 1949 to 1.5 million square kilometers in 1984—or almost one-sixth of the entire land area of China (Li, 1987).

Annually, 1,600 million tons of soil and sand are swept away from the upper and central basins of the Yellow River, causing the riverbed to rise by more than 10 centimeters per year. In fact, the riverbed in some parts of the lower basin exceeds the elevation of the land along its banks by 10 meters or more. Hence, the lower basin of the river is under continual danger of flooding.

Indeed, the soil erosion and deforestation in the loess plateau located in the upper basin of the Yellow River may be the most grave in all of China. Although some 2,500 years ago the area was covered over with forest, it now has almost no primary forest. In the northern part of Shaanxi Province and the Haixi area of Gansu Province, only treeless mountains are left. Under such a long history of deforestation and soil erosion, the environment has been damaged, the climate has changed for the worse, and the lands and people suffer from drought because of the dried-up rivers.

The soil erosion in the loess plateau area has made the fertility of the soil very poor. Because peasant farmers continue to rely on low-technology agricultural techniques, they have to exploit more and more virgin land in order to sustain a continually growing population. To make matters worse, traditional agricultural methods rely heavily on human labor, and the expansion of land under cultivation induces people to have more children. Thus, famine and poverty bring forth more people. This vicious circle of overpopulation and deforestation has made those areas of Gansu and Shaanxi Provinces among the poorest in China.

Since 1949 the Chinese government has attempted to break the vicious circle tying population growth to deforestation, to solve the problems of erosion, and to improve the natural environment. Success has been limited, however, due to the effects of continuing population growth coupled with political and socioeconomic factors (e.g., during the so-called Steel-Melting Movement in 1958, woods in many rural regions were cut and used as fuel). From 1949 to 1981, more than 67 million hectares of forest were leveled (not including those destroyed by fire). According to the most conservative estimates, China currently uses 200 million cubic meters of forest products per year, two-thirds of which is a result of wood take in excess of the government's plan. Although the government has sponsored a great many reforestation projects, in recent years the rate of deforestation has been one and a half times faster than the rate of reforestation.

Despite its many policies and regulations to preserve the forest and woodlands, and thereby to maintain soil fertility and freshwater supplies, in the final analysis the most important thing the Chinese government can do to break the vicious circle of overpopulation and deforestation is to promote the practice of family planning and to strictly control population growth.

References

China's Economics Yearbook 1987.

China's Statistics Yearbook, 1984 and 1987.

Editorial Department of the PRC Yearbook in Beijing. 1987. *People's Republic of China Yearbook 1987.* Beijing: Xinhua Publishing House.

Li, Rangxi. 1987. "Population and natural resources," in *Population Almanac 1985.* Beijing: Social Sciences Publishing House.

Qu, Geping, and Woyen Lee (eds.) 1984. *Managing the Environment in China.* Dublin: Tycooly International.

Shaanxi Economy. 1985. Taiyuan: Shaanxi People's Publishing House.

Situations of Sichuan Province. 1984.

Tang, Yongluan (ed.) 1987. *Introduction to Environology.* Beijing: High Education Publishing House.

Winners and Losers in the Twentieth-Century Struggle to Survive

PETER H. RAVEN

THE MASSIVE LOSS OF SPECIES of plants, animals, and microorganisms that is taking place during our lifetime will seriously limit the ability of our descendants to construct stable and productive ecosystems and to provide for themselves in sound and substainable ways. Because of the scope and intensity of human activities, extinction is currently taking place at a rate unprecedented since the close of the Cretaceous Period, 65 million years ago. Thus the roughly 5.2 billion people who populate the Earth, double the number of the early 1950s, are estimated to be using directly, diverting, or wasting some 40 percent of total net photosynthetic productivity—the total available biological output—on land (Vitousek et al., 1986). Since humans are only one of between several million and several tens of millions of organisms that live on Earth, such a level of consumption is clearly extraordinary: its destructive consequences can be seen everywhere. Among these are the much-discussed atmospheric changes that are taking place so rapidly, widespread social instability, the loss of thousands of square kilometers of forests each year, and the extinction of species. Most serious are the prospects for the future. With the human population projected not to stabilize until it reaches a level of 10–14 billion during the twenty-first century (Sadik, 1989), it is clear that new modes of using the Earth's productivity on a sustainable basis must be developed rapidly.

Although the relationship between human population size and environmental effects is not linear, it is highly significant (e.g., Ehrlich and Holdren, 1971; Holdren and Ehrlich, 1974; Ehrlich et al., 1977). In the rich industrial countries, each individual consumes a relatively high proportion of the world's productivity; in the poor developing countries, on the other hand, population growth is especially rapid. Thus the proportion of people in each area is shifting rapidly. About 35 years ago, some 45 percent of the world's 2.5 billion inhabitants lived in mainly tropical, developing countries excluding China; by 2020, the developing world proportion will be about two-thirds.

The very poor people who make up the bulk of the population in most developing countries often use natural resources very destructively, having no practical alternatives. The inhabitants of these countries, now including China, constitute some 75 percent of the total world population, but have access to only about 15 percent of the world's wealth. In addition, they are home to no more than about 6 percent of the world's scientists and technologists. The industrial countries also consume 80–90 percent or more of virtually all commodities that contribute to the standard of living, such as industrial energy, metals, and other materials, while resources are being transferred rapidly out of poor, unstable regions into rich ones.

The exploitative use of natural resources in the tropics, which denies possibilities for the future and leads directly to biological extinction, has many causes. For example, the export of timber, beef, fruits, spices, tea, coffee, and other tropical crops has led to the cultivation of vast areas, often in such a way that productivity cannot be sustained for more than a few years. In Latin America, the often-subsidized production of beef for export in areas where long-term productivity is not attainable has been an ecological disaster for many areas. In most of the warmer regions of the world, the production of export crops, discussed by Norman Myers elsewhere in this volume, has tended to decrease the medium-term carrying capacity of these areas for the people who live there. Deforestation associated with these activities and with poverty in general is decimating the forests over many regions, with a consequent rapid loss of the species that might be used to create stable productive systems. More than half of the nearly 3 billion people in the tropics and subtropics depend on firewood as their primary source of fuel and rarely allow cutover forests to recover. With about a billion people in the tropics—more than a third of the population—living in absolute poverty, and half of them malnourished according to the latest UNICEF statistics, the pressures on the biological diversity of the ecosystem are obvious. In addition, little effort is being made to put in place stable agricultural systems, either for poor people or on a wider scale.

We do not, unfortunately, know how to manage most tropical soils, which are often highly infertile, for sustainable productivity (National Research Council, 1982). If these soils are fertilized and managed carefully, they may be productive, but this has been the case relatively rarely, owing to the conditions just outlined. So far it has been simpler to move on to previously unexploited areas of virgin forest, a "strategy" that it will soon be impossible to continue.

Forest and other habitat loss

The destruction of natural communities and the loss of species of plants, animals, and microorganisms is much more extensive in the tropics than in temperate regions. Moreover, it is precisely in the tropics that the species being lost have the greatest potential for the development of new kinds of productive systems in the future. For these reasons, I shall focus my attention on the tropics.

In 1981, the Food and Agriculture Organization (FAO) estimated that 44 percent of tropical, lowland, evergreen forests—rainforests—had been cut by the late 1970s and that more than 1 percent of the remainder was being cleared each year. In 1989 the area of remaining tropical rainforest is probably about 3.5 million square kilometers, roughly half of the original total; for comparison, the continental United States covers 5.8 million square km. Extrapolating from estimates made a decade ago, about 65,000 sq. km. of the remaining forest are being cut per year, a rate that would wipe out all of the tropical rainforest before the middle of the next century. Since the population of the areas where rainforest occurs is projected to at least triple in this period—the current growth rate is about 2.4 percent per year—we can assume that the actual rate of deforestation will be much greater. About half of the area of tropical forests is logged, and another quarter is cleared for cattle pastures (Myers, 1984). To the clearcutting studied by FAO experts in the late 1970s must be added the effects of shifting cultivation and fuelwood gathering, which together seriously disturb an area roughly equal to that being clearcut (Myers, 1984; Melillo et al., 1985). Given pressures of this magnitude, the forests do not have time to return to their original condition.

In the late 1980s, it became evident that even these dramatic estimates were too low. Brazilian scientists, studying satellite imagery, estimate that fires in 1987 in the Brazilian Amazon—two-thirds of the Amazon Basin—covered about 124,000 sq. km. Of these, at least 48,000 sq. km. were newly felled forest that had not been cleared before. More than 170,000 individual fires were detected, with the smoke often rising 12,000 feet or more. These fires attracted widespread attention because their scale indicated that the burning forest contributed substantially to global atmospheric changes.

There are a few areas of tropical rainforest that, because of their size and relatively low population density, may outlast the rest. The primary ones are in the northern and western Amazon, in the interior of the Guyanas in South America, and in the Central Zaire (Congo) Basin of Africa. Elsewhere, the pace of destruction is proceeding much more rapidly, so that one is justified in concluding that little rainforest will persist beyond the early years of the twenty-first century, and what little remains will consist of small patches or badly degraded remnants on land that is too wet, rocky, or steep to cultivate even temporarily.

Outside of the rainforests, the destruction of tropical forests in many regions is already nearly complete, because most of these forests occupy lands that are more fertile and thus suitable for cultivation, and the forests are also primary sources of fuelwood for 1.5 billion people (World Resources Institute and International Institute for Environment and Development, 1986).

262 THE TWENTIETH-CENTURY STRUGGLE TO SURVIVE

Extinction rates of species

It is impossible to determine current rates of extinction with certainty because we do not know how many species exist on Earth, even to an order of
magnitude (May, 1988). With about 1.4 million species of plants, animals,
and microorganisms having been named (Wilson, 1988), estimates of the
total range from 4–5 million (National Research Council, 1980) to as many
as 30 million (Erwin, 1982, 1983) or even to 80 million species of insects
alone (Stork, 1988). For the world's temperate regions, however, which are
much better known biologically than the tropics, the total number of species
is unlikely to exceed 1.5 million; thus, between 2.5 and 50 million species
inhabit the tropics.

Since no more than 500,000 tropical organisms have been named and
classified, we have recognized between a fifth and a fiftieth of the total species that are present. New species of all groups of vertebrates are being discovered each year, especially in the western Amazonia, together with
hundreds of species of plants, many of them large trees. Nonetheless, the
better-known groups can be used as a basis for estimating the extent of extinction overall, as I shall now outline.

Flowering plants, economically very important, and the largest group
of organisms for which reasonable estimates exist, consist of about 250,000
species worldwide, of which at least 165,000 are tropical. Half of the total
are estimated to occur in Latin America; about 40,000 in tropical Africa and
Madagascar; and probably at least 45,000 in tropical and subtropical Asia.
Using these figures, one can calculate that no more than 35,000 species occur in the three tropical rainforest areas that can be expected to survive past
the first years of the next century; thus some 130,000 tropical species do not
occur in these regions. These species, constituting more than half the total
number of flowering plants in the world, occur only in areas that will be
largely deforested or substantially disturbed over the next 30 years. What
does this relationship indicate in terms of probable extinction rates?

Extinction rates would clearly be reduced if substantial areas could be
protected, but economic factors will generally run against this, absent a substantial change in policy on the part of industrialized nations. Said another
way, only an explicit coupling of development with conservation, as outlined in the *World Conservation Strategy* issued jointly in 1980 by the International Union for the Conservation of Nature and Natural Resources, the
World Wildlife Fund, and the United Nations Environmental Programme,
will make conservation possible, even over the medium term. In addition,
the narrow ecological requirements of many tropical organisms make them
especially susceptible to extinction when their ranges are reduced and the
characteristics of the forests and other habitats in which they occur are altered. Hunting and other forms of harvesting of natural products are acceler-

ated in relatively small patches of vegetation, and the future of many kinds of organisms in them is becoming increasingly uncertain. Small populations of organisms are liable to extinction by chance alone, even if they are not genetically depleted.

The theory of island biogeography (summarized in MacArthur and Wilson, 1967) provides a basis for making projections about extinction rates. Such projections are based on the relationship between species number and area, which is a logarithmic one: a tenfold increase in area is associated with a doubling in the number of species of a given group. The reciprocal relationship, and one that has been verified empirically in a number of experiments throughout the world (e.g., Lovejoy et al., 1986), is that a reduction in area to one-tenth or less of its original size should place half or more of the kinds of organisms that occurred in the larger area at risk (review by Wilcox, 1986). In addition, the global climatic changes that are accompanying human population growth present an ultimate threat to the survival of organisms in remaining patches of vegetation (Pain, 1988); and regional alterations in precipitation and temperature, resulting from clearing of forests, have similar effects locally.

Local rates of extinction may be especially high. In 1980, it was pointed out that certain areas particularly rich in species were being altered so rapidly that they deserved special attention (National Research Council, 1980). More recently, Norman Myers (1988) has identified areas such as the Atlantic forests of Brazil, the eastern Himalayas, northwestern Borneo, and the rainforests of Madagascar—an island in which less than 10 percent of the original vegetation is left—as localities that feature remarkable concentrations of species with exceptional levels of endemism and exceptional degrees of threat. In these relatively small areas, which total just over 177,000 sq. km. and constitute only about 3.5 percent of the remaining primary forest, a major spasm of extinction seems to be impending. The large areas that I identified above, which may last in a relatively unaltered form for some 40 years to come, do not have nearly as high a proportion of extremely local species. For conservation purposes, therefore, the identification and preservation of the "hotspots" discussed by Myers is of special importance.

Generalizing from these considerations, we may observe that more than half the world's total diversity of plant species occurs in areas of the tropics where deforestation and destruction are expected to be relatively complete over the next 20 years. Making the minimum assumption, however, we could assert that perhaps 2.4 million species of a world total—almost certainly unrealistically low—of 5 million species occur only in the regions at greatest risk. For half of these species to become extinct would mean the disappearance of more than a million kinds of plants, animals, and microorganisms during the next 20 years—a rate of extinction that has not been matched for at least 65 million years (D. M. Raup, personal communication). As far as we can calculate, many fewer species of organisms were in existence at that time (e.g., Niklas et al., 1985), so that the absolute numbers of species that are expected to become extinct around the last years of this century and the beginning of the next are far greater than have ever vanished during any comparable period in the past. This amounts to the disappearance of more than a quarter of the biological diversity that exists today, with a much higher proportion of the total following by the middle of the twenty-first century. The great majority of these species will never be represented in any scientific collection or preserved in any way.

A loss of this magnitude represents a catastrophe for the future of the human race, and for a sustainable use of the global ecosystem. It is based on a rate of extinction a thousand times more than the background rate, and on the loss of hundreds of species per day over the coming decades. Since humans base their livelihood to a greater or lesser extent on their ability to manipulate the properties of other organisms, it stands to reason that their potential to help themselves, especially in those parts of the world where the need is most severe, will be substantially curtailed in the future. Many new kinds of crops and domestic animals might be used for the full exploitation of the available sites and in the search for self-sufficiency throughout the warmer parts of the globe. Among plants, just three species—rice, wheat, and corn—supply over half of all human energy requirements; only about 150 kinds of food plants are used extensively; and only about 5,000 have ever been used (National Research Council, 1982). Tens of thousands of additional possibilities exist (for a recent discussion see Tudge, 1988), but we may lose as many as 60,000 of them during our lifetime unless we take effective steps to learn about them and secure them for posterity (Hoyt, 1988). The general economic utility of a single tropical plant family, palms (scarcely appreciated outside the areas where they are native), is clearly shown by a recent outstanding symposium volume (Balick, 1988). Traditional Andean root crops other than the potato have likewise been emphasized in recent investigations by the US National Research Council and others (Sattaur, 1988).

In addition to their uses as food, many plants offer possibilities as sources of medicines, oils, waxes, fibers, and other commodities of interest to modern industrial society (Myers, 1983; Oldfield, 1984). Plants are natural biochemical factories, much of their diversity owing to their ability to deter the herbivores that attack them continuously; the chemical compounds that they produce are often of value, especially since they are, in general, obtainable without heavy investments of energy.

What can be done?

The global ecological crisis is so extensive, multidimensional, and threatening that we risk falling into inertia and failing to take prudent action. Imaginative plans, however, are being conceived to deal with the problem (e.g., Lovejoy, 1988).

The massive loss of biological diversity is directly related to an inability and general unwillingness to create sustainable, productive, ecologically sound systems of agriculture and forestry throughout the world. In developing such systems, nothing is more important than attaining a stationary level of human population throughout the world. There is no evidence that the world can sustain its present population, much less a larger one. Much scientific knowledge is necessary, and intensive programs need to be designed to chart the dimensions of life on Earth. Regional planning, including the sound use of those extensive areas that are already deforested, is the key to the maintenance of biological diversity as well as the key to human prosperity. Ecological information and environmental considerations ought to be integral parts of development planning, and projects ought to be conducted and monitored in such a way as to add to the information base for subsequent development plans. Increased development assistance is a necessary component of such efforts, and effective, cooperative plans must be developed to increase the efficacy of such aid. If development assistance is coupled with the strengthening of institutions in Third World countries, the outcomes are likely to be positive and lasting.

Industrial countries may be led to support such efforts in the future, because the economic deterioration and political disintegration that characterize many tropical countries constitute a threat to global security (Brown et al., 1986). Partly for this reason, the World Bank and other international lending and development agencies are paying increasing attention to environmental considerations in making loans available. There is a growing realization that the pursuit of short-term economic growth at the environment's expense will exact a lasting price (Brown et al., 1987).

Direct conservation actions likewise should be pursued to the extent possible. These should include setting aside a comprehensive network of protected areas, to preserve biological diversity. In order to accomplish this, international agreements like the Montreal Protocol will be required. Operational plans such as those of the International Timber Agreement and the Tropical Forest Action Plan should continue to be promoted. The recent study conducted by the US Congressional Office of Technology Assessment reflects a welcome interest in biological diversity and a desire to address the issue.

Clearly, the choices that mankind makes now and in the immediate future will largely determine the fate of biological diversity in the twenty-first century. If the world population does in fact stabilize at a level of 10 to 11 billion people around the middle of the next century, the remaining biological diversity should be increasingly viewed as important in realizing the human potential. As scientific knowledge grows, it will become possible to use the organisms that we have saved to reconstitute productive biological communities of many kinds, and to produce an array of products of use to us.

A number of people who have thought seriously about global environmental problems have concluded that we may be on the verge of crossing a number of important ecological thresholds, with uncertain but threatening effects (e.g., Brown et al., 1987; Lovejoy, 1988). It is increasingly evident that a strong, collective human effort must be made in response to these trends. We have already profoundly modified the global biosphere and have called into question its continued ability to function; the question now is what we will do to increase its stability and maintain its diversity for the future. Economists, ecologists, investors, foresters—all have a clear, common interest in promoting sustainability on a global scale.

References

Balick, M. J. (ed.). 1988. "The palm—tree of life: Biology, utilization and conservation," *Advances in Economic Botany* 6: 1-282.

Bickerstaff, G. 1988. "Hidden properties of the pineapple," *New Scientist* 118: 46-48.

Brown, L. R., et al. 1986. *State of the World 1986.* New York: W. W. Norton.

Brown, L. R., et al. 1987. *State of the World 1987.* New York: W. W. Norton.

Ehrlich, P. R., and J. P. Holdren. 1971. "Impact of population growth," *Science* 171: 1212-1217.

Ehrlich, P. R., A. H. Ehrlich, and J. P. Holdren. 1977. *Ecoscience: Population, Resources, Environment.* San Francisco: Freeman and Co.

Ehrlich, P. R., and A. H. Ehrlich. 1981. *Extinction: The Causes and Consequences of the Disappearance of Species.* New York: Random House.

Erwin, T. L. 1982. "Tropical forests: Their richness in Coleoptera and other arthropod species," *Coleoptera Bulletin* 36: 74-75.

————. 1983. "Beetles and other insects of tropical forest canopies at Manaus, Brazil, sampled by insecticidal fogging," in S. L. Sutton, T. C. Whitmore, and A. C. Chadwick (eds.), *Tropical Rain Forest: Ecology and Management.* Edinburgh: Blackwell, pp. 59-75.

Holdren, J. P., and P. R. Ehrlich. 1974. "Human population and the global environment," *American Scientist* 62: 282-292.

Hoyt, E. 1988. *Conserving the Wild Relatives of Crops.* Rome and Gland: International Board for Plant Genetic Resources, International Union for the Conservation of Nature and Natural Resources, and World Wide Fund for Nature.

Lovejoy, T. E. 1988. "Will unexpectedly the top blow off?," *BioScience* 38: 722-726.

————, et al. 1986. "Edge and other effects of isolation on Amazon forest fragments," in M. E. Soule (ed.), *Conservation Biology: The Science of Scarcity and Diversity.* Sunderland, Mass.: Sinauer Associates, pp. 257-285.

MacArthur, R. M., and E. O. Wilson. 1967. *The Theory of Island Biogeography.* Monographs in Population Biology 1. Princeton, N. J.: Princeton University Press.

May, R. M. 1988. "How many species are there on Earth?," *Science* 241: 1441-1449.

Melillo, J. M., et al. 1985. "A comparison of two recent estimates of disturbance in tropical forests," *Environmental Conservation* 12: 37-40.

Myers, N. 1983. *A Wealth of Wild Species: Storehouse for Human Welfare.* Boulder, Colo.: Westview Press.

————. 1984. *The Primary Source: Tropical Forests and Our Future.* New York: W. W. Norton.

————. 1988. "Threatened biotas: 'Hotspots' in tropical forests," *The Environmentalist* 8: 1-20.

National Research Council, Committee on Research Priorities in Tropical Biology. 1980. *Research Priorities in Tropical Biology.* Washington, D.C.: National Academy of Sciences.

National Research Council, Committee on Selected Biological Problems in the Humid Tropics. 1982. *Ecological Aspects of Development in the Humid Tropics.* Washington, D.C.: National Academy Press.

Niklas, K. J., B. H. Tiffney, and A. H. Knoll. 1985. "Patterns in vascular land plant diversification: An analysis at the species level," in J. W. Valentine (ed.), *Phanerozoic Diversity Patterns: Profiles in Macroevolution.* Princeton, N.J.: Princeton University Press, pp. 97–128.

Oldfield, M. L. 1984. *The Value of Conserving Genetic Resources.* Washington, D.C.: US Department of the Interior, National Park Service.

Pain, S. 1988. "No escape from the global greenhouse," *New Scientist* 120: 38–43.

Sadik, N. 1989. *The State of World Population 1989.* New York: United Nations Population Fund.

Sattaur, O. 1988. "Native is beautiful," *New Scientist* 118: 54–57.

Shen, S. "Biological diversity and public policy," *BioScience* 37: 709–712.

Stork, N. E. 1988. "Insect diversity: Facts, fiction and speculation," *Biological Journal of the Linnean Society* 35: 321–337.

Tudge, C. 1988. *Food Crops for the Future: The Development of Plant Resources.* Oxford: Blackwell Scientific Publications.

Vitousek, P. M., et al. 1986. "Human appropriation of the products of photosynthesis," *BioScience* 36: 368–373.

Wilcox, B. A. 1986. "Extinction models and conservation," *Trends in Ecology and Evolution* 1: 46–48.

Wilson, E. O. 1985. "The biological diversity crisis: A challenge to science," *Issues in Science and Technology* 2: 20–29.

———. 1988. "The current state of biological diversity," in E. O. Wilson (ed.), *Biodiversity.* Washington, D.C.: National Academy Press, pp. 3–18.

World Resources Institute and International Institute for Environment and Development. 1986. *World Resources 1986.* New York: Basic Books.

Biomass Burning in the Tropics: Impact on Environmental Quality and Global Climate

MEINRAT O. ANDREAE

THE ENVIRONMENTAL IMPACT OF FOSSIL FUEL BURNING is felt throughout the world. Concerns about its consequences are prominent in the public's mind, and its effects have been thoroughly investigated and quantified. Biomass burning, on the other hand, is not perceived as a comparable threat to the well-being of people and their environment. Its extent and effects are not well documented, mostly because it takes place largely in the developing countries, at the hands of individual farmers, ranchers, and housewives, for whom recordkeeping of amounts burned is not an issue.

Yet, pollution from biomass burning must have been one of the first occupational hazards: early humans must have been exposed to large amounts of carcinogenic compounds from the smoke of open fires in caves, huts, and tents. Today, we are frequently confronted with the evidence of pollution from biomass burning in our daily activities. In winter in North America, many communities have ordinances regulating domestic burning in fireplaces and wood-burning stoves. In the tropics, airports like Santarém, in the middle of the Amazon Basin, are forced to close frequently during the burning season because of poor visibility resulting from the smoke of gigantic fires hundreds to thousands of kilometers away. Such large fires and the resulting smoke plumes are a common sight to air travelers in the tropics, and even to the crews of the space shuttle.

Forest and savanna clearing for agriculture

The permanent removal of rainforest for agricultural use is progressing at a rapid rate. This process is driven not only by expanding populations requiring additional food and living space, but also by large-scale resettlement programs and land speculation tactics. Slash-and-burn, or shifting, agriculture is currently practiced by some 200 million people worldwide. It is not expected to grow much beyond its present extent, covering some 300–500 million ha, because virgin forest land that could be brought into this type of cultivation is becoming more scarce. Instead, land presently under shifting agriculture is likely to be used for permanent agriculture. Often, however, attempts to do this fail due to poor soil conditions or land management, and the areas turn into wasteland unsuitable for any type of agriculture.

The global rate of deforestation is subject to a significant degree of uncertainty. Based on earlier work by several groups of investigators, Hao et al. (1990) estimated a rate of about 22 million ha/yr. It must be emphasized that this rate applies to the 1970s, and is likely to have increased during the last decade. Of these 22 million ha, about 7.5 million ha/yr are cleared in virgin rainforest, amounting to an annual destruction of about 0.6 percent of the remaining area of some 1200 million ha. Estimates of the amounts of cleared land that go to shifting agriculture and to permanent land use range from 1.9 to 3.4 million and 4.1 to 5.1 million ha/yr, respectively. The discrepancies between the estimates of the fate of land cleared in secondary tropical forests are even greater. Detwiler et al. (1985) estimated that 18 million ha/yr are cleared, all for shifting cultivation. Houghton et al. (1985), on the other hand, calculated that 13.5 million ha/yr were cleared in second-growth forest, of which 10.1 million ha were cleared permanently.

Tropical savannas cover an area (1530 million ha) roughly similar to that of the tropical forests (1440 million ha). These savannas are burned periodically, at intervals ranging from one to three years. This frequency may be increasing in some regions as a result of growing population and more intensive use of rangeland. While lightning may start some fires in savannas, most investigators are convinced that almost all savanna fires are set by humans. Without burning, the grassy vegetation would tend to be overgrown rapidly by shrubs and brush, and under many conditions would progress to a chaparral or forest, unsuitable for grazing, which is the predominant agricultural use of the grassy savannas. Only the grass and small plants are consumed in the fires; the larger trees are fire-adapted species that suffer little damage and actually thrive under conditions of periodic burning. Other reasons for burning include pest control, nutrient regeneration, and hunting. The savanna area burned each year is substantial: Hao et al. (1990) estimate ca. 750 million ha, much more than the area burned in tropical rainforests. This applies especially to Africa, where about one-half of the global amount of savanna biomass burning is concentrated.

Burning of fuelwood, charcoal, and agricultural wastes

The annual amount of wood burning is difficult to estimate. The number given by the Food and Agriculture Organization (FAO) for 1987, 1050 Tg dm/

yr (teragram dry matter per year; one teragram = 10^{12} grams = one million tons) is probably an underestimate because it does not cover the use of wood that is not marketed. In Table 1, we present an estimate based on population and per capita use statistics, which may be more reliable than the FAO estimate. For the tropical regions, we have multiplied the 1985 population numbers by an annual fuelwood consumption of 475 kg per person, based on the discussion in Seiler and Crutzen (1980). These population-based estimates and the FAO statistics agree reasonably well for all continents except Asia, where the domestic use of coal in China may be replacing some fuelwood use. Throughout the developing world, population growth is causing an increasing demand for fuelwood, which is becoming progressively difficult to satisfy in some regions. For the ensuing calculations, we have adopted a "best guess" estimate, based on the mean between the FAO and population-based estimates for the developing countries in the tropics and on the FAO data for the developed countries (Table 1).

Charcoal production for domestic and industrial use has become an important alternative to the direct use of wood as fuel. Charcoal has a higher energy density and is thus cheaper to transport. In recent years, large charcoal production plants have been established in countries like Brazil in order to supply charcoal for industrial use, especially the smelting of pig iron. Often, the wood used in this type of charcoal manufacture is derived from fast-growing pine plantations. In some of the large projects in the Amazon, on the other hand (e.g., the Grande Carajás Program in the eastern part of the Basin), it is anticipated that the wood required for charcoal production will

TABLE 1 Burning of fuelwood, charcoal, and agricultural waste in tropical and extratropical regions (expressed as Tg dm/yr)

Region	Population 1985 (millions)	Fuelwood (a)	(b)	(c)	Charcoal (b)	Agricultural waste (d)
Tropical America	430	180	150	170	7.5	200
Tropical Africa	550	240	240	240	9.3	160
Tropical Asia	2820	1200	490	850	3.3	990
Oceania	25	11	6	8	0	17
Total tropics	3830	1640	890	1260	20	1360
USA and Canada	260	—	80	80	0.5	250
Western Europe	380	—	40	40	0.2	170
USSR and Eastern Europe	390	—	50	50	0.2	230
World total	4840	—	1050	1430	21	2020

(a) Based on population, a fuelwood consumption of 475 kg per person per year, and a burning efficiency of 90 percent.
(b) FAO, 1989.
(c) Best guess: mean of population-based and FAO estimates.
(d) Based on total production of crops (see text).

be obtained by clear-cutting the surrounding rainforest. A precedent exists in the state of Minas Gerais, where pig-iron production consumed nearly two-thirds of the state's forests. Depending on the efficiency of the kiln used in charcoal production, the ratio of carbon input (in the form of wood) to carbon output (in the form of charcoal) varies between about 2.0 and 1.2. For the purpose of our estimates of the amount of carbon released to the atmosphere due to charcoal production and use, we have multiplied in Table 1 the amount of charcoal burned by a factor of 1.4 to account for losses during production. These losses are mostly in the form of a mixture of water, carbon monoxide, tar, and other volatile products, which is distilled off from the kilns and represents a major pollution source.

In many tropical regions, a conspicuous source of air pollution is the burning of sugar cane fields before harvesting to facilitate the processing of the canes. Based on an extrapolation from waste burning practices in the United States and reasonable assumptions about the fraction of agricultural waste burned in developing countries, Seiler and Crutzen (1980) derive a global estimate for agricultural waste burning of 1700–2100 Tg dm/yr. In Table 1 we present a new estimate for this source of emissions, based on FAO crop production statistics for 1985. We assume that the amount of agricultural waste is the same as the amount of crops produced, which appears to be reasonable according to the discussion in Seiler and Crutzen. We then assume that 80 percent of the waste in developing countries and 50 percent in developed countries is burned, and that the combustion efficiency is 90 percent. The resulting global estimate is 2020 Tg dm/yr, near the high end of the range suggested by Seiler and Crutzen. In any case, this source appears to be one of the major contributors to atmospheric emissions from biomass burning. Fortunately, it has the potential of being reduced substantially by alternative agricultural practices.

Geographic distribution of biomass burning and its atmospheric emissions

The geographic distribution of biomass burning is discussed in some detail in the review by Seiler and Crutzen (1980). For the tropics, Hao et al. (1990) provide more recent estimates. Their results are summarized in Tables 2 and 3. Most biomass burning takes place in the developing countries of the tropics (Tables 1 and 3): adding an emission of 28 Tg C/yr (from Table 1: 20 Tg × 1.4) from charcoal production and combustion to the tropical emissions of 3410 Tg C/yr from forest and savanna burning, fuelwood use, and the incineration of agricultural waste, we obtain a total emission of 3440 Tg C from the tropics. This represents 87 percent of the global emissions from biomass burning (3940 Tg C/yr; Table 2). As we discuss below, this is consistent with the observation that the impact of burning on the atmospheric environment appears to be concentrated in the tropics.

TABLE 2   Global estimates of annual amounts of biomass burning and of the resulting release of carbon to the atmosphere

Source	Biomass burned (Tg dm/yr)			Carbon released (Tg/yr)
	(a)	(b)	(c)	(d)
Tropical forest	2420	1260	1260	570
Savanna	1190	3690	3690	1660
Temperate and boreal forests	280	—	280	130
Fuelwood	1050	620	1430	640
Charcoal	—	—	21	30
Agricultural waste	1900	660	2020	910
World total	6840	6230	8700	3940

(a) Seiler and Crutzen, 1980.
(b) Hao et al., 1990.
(c) Tropical forest and savanna from (b); temperate and boreal forests from (a); fuelwood, charcoal, and agricultural waste from Table 1.
(d) Based on a carbon content of 45 percent in dry biomass. For charcoal, the rate of burning (based on FAO production statistics) has been multiplied by 1.4 to account for losses in the production process (see text).

An interesting difference between the estimates of Seiler and Crutzen (1980) and Hao et al. (1990) is the relative importance of tropical forests and savannas with respect to biomass burning. In the older study, forest burning was predominant, whereas the more recent work suggests that savanna burning releases to the atmosphere about three times as much carbon as forest burning. This is especially evident in Africa (Table 3), where savanna fires account for almost 90 percent of the emissions from savanna and forest burning, and for almost one-third of the global emissions from biomass burning. In tropical America, forest burning is concentrated in the Brazilian states of Pará, Maranhão, Goiás, Mato Grosso, and Rondônia. Relatively little forest and savanna burning occurs in tropical Asia, with the exception of Indonesia, Thailand, Malaysia, and India, where rapid deforestation is ongoing.

TABLE 3   Biomass burning in tropical regions

Region	Forest (a)	Savanna (Tg dm/yr) (a)	Fuelwood (b)	Agricultural waste (b)	Regional total (Tg dm/yr)	(Tg C/yr)
America	590	770	170	200	1730	780
Africa	390	2430	240	160	3210	1450
Asia	280	70	850	990	2190	980
Oceania	—	420	8	17	450	200
Total tropics	1260	3690	1260	1360	7580	3410

(a) From Hao et al., 1990.
(b) From Table 1.

The impact of biomass burning is magnified by its concentration in both time and space: a large fraction of the burning of forests and savannas takes place during the dry season, and therefore burning is most intensive in the northern hemisphere from December to March and in the southern hemisphere from June to September. Even so, experience in tropical countries shows that burning is not limited to these burning seasons, and that some fires can be observed throughout the year. This applies especially to cooking and heating fires, and the burning of garden and agricultural wastes.

Carbon dioxide emission from biomass burning

On a long enough time scale, biomass burning does not influence the atmospheric carbon dioxide (CO_2) budget, but merely returns to the atmosphere CO_2 that had been removed by plants some time before. However, when biomass is burned but not rapidly replaced by regrowth, CO_2 is added to the atmosphere and will remain there until it is removed by some other process. It can then contribute to the CO_2 greenhouse effect in the atmosphere and to global climate change.

We must therefore distinguish between gross CO_2 emission from the burning of savannas and forests, and the net CO_2 released from deforestation. While prominent in the emission of trace gases to the atmosphere, the periodic burning of savannas has almost no influence on the CO_2 greenhouse effect, because the CO_2 released by burning is re-incorporated into savanna vegetation during the next growth cycle (i.e., within about one year). In contrast, the clearing of tropical forests by burning contributes directly to the CO_2 greenhouse effect, since the CO_2 emitted from the oxidation of large amounts of biomass stored in a rainforest (as much as 600 tons dm/ha) cannot be taken up again by the vegetation that will grow on the same site, usually grass or an agricultural crop, which has a much lower standing biomass (5–50 tons dm/ha). Furthermore, in the case of deforestation, not only does the CO_2 emitted directly by burning contribute to the atmospheric burden, but also that released during the decay of the unburned above-ground and below-ground biomass. Because the clearing burns in tropical rainforests typically affect mostly the branches and leaves and leave the trunks largely unburned, the CO_2 emissions from decaying biomass will usually be greater than from the burning itself.

The various estimates of the net amount of CO_2 added to the atmosphere from deforestation fall into a relatively narrow range: Houghton et al. (1985) give an estimate of 900–2500 Tg C/yr; Detwiler and Hall (1988) suggest a range of 400–1600 Tg C/yr; and Hao et al. (1990) calculate 700–2000 Tg C/yr. This agreement should not instill undue confidence in the accuracy of these estimates, however; it mostly reflects the fact that all authors base their estimates on the same data on biomass densities and land use conversion estimates. Hao et al. conclude that almost half of the net CO_2 released comes from the conversion of forest to permanent agriculture and cattle holdings. Detwiler and Hall propose that an additional net CO_2 release of about 25 percent may result from the oxidation of organic matter in cleared forest soils due to intensive cultivation. Incorporation of this component results in an estimate of 1800 ± 800 Tg C/yr for the release of CO_2 from land clearing in the tropics. This is a significant amount compared with the present annual emission of CO_2 from fossil fuel burning, 5200 Tg C/yr. We can therefore conclude that the destruction of tropical forests results in about 25 percent of the global CO_2 greenhouse effect.

Emission of other trace gases

In addition to CO_2, a large variety of gases and particles is emitted from the fires (Table 4)—the products of incomplete combustion of carbon compounds (e.g., carbon monoxide [CO], hydrogen [H_2], methane [CH_4], and other hydrocarbons) and of compounds containing other nutrient elements (e.g., nitric oxide [NO], ammonia [NH_3], and sulfur dioxide [SO_2] from the

TABLE 4 Emission ratios for trace gases and aerosols from biomass burning, based on field and laboratory studies

Species	Field studies (range of means)	Laboratory studies (range) (a)	Best guess (b)
Gases (c)			
CO	65–140	59–105	100
Methane	6.2–16	11–16	11
Non-methane hydrocarbons	6.6–11.0	3.4–6.8	7
Nitrous oxide	0.18–2.2	0.01–0.05	0.1
NO_x	2–8	0.7–1.6	2.1
Ammonia	0.9–1.9	0.08–2.5	1.3
Nitriles	–	0.24–0.93	0.6
SO_2 and aerosol sulfate	0.1–0.34		0.3
Carbonyl sulfide	0.005–0.016		0.01
Hydrogen	33		33
Ozone (c,d)	4.8–40		30
Aerosols (e)			
Total particulate matter	12–82		20
POC (f)	7.9–54		13
Elemental carbon	2.2–16		3.7
Potassium	0.24–0.58		0.4

(a) Results of individual burns of different types of biomass (savanna grasses, pine straw).
(b) Based on a subjective evaluation of field and laboratory results.
(c) Results expressed as moles of substance emitted per 1000 moles of CO_2 emitted.
(d) Photochemically produced ozone in the burning plumes.
(e) All data in g/kg $C(CO_2)$.
(f) Particulate organic carbon, including elemental carbon.

nitrogen and sulfur in amino acids and proteins). CO and the hydrocarbons are emitted especially strongly from smoldering fires, whereas CO_2 emission dominates from hot, flaming fires. Among the nitrogen gases emitted, NO is the single most abundant species, but it represents only some 10–20 percent of the nitrogen initially contained in the fuel. Other nitrogen compounds (NO_2, N_2O, NH_3, HCN, organic nitriles, and nitrates) account for an additional 10–20 percent of the fuel nitrogen, but some 60–70 percent of nitrogen gases are released in as yet unknown forms, possibly as molecular nitrogen (Crutzen et al., 1990). This may result in a substantial loss of nitrogen from ecosystems frequently subjected to burning. The emission ratios in Table 4 are the molar ratio between the species of interest and CO_2 in the smoke, with the exception of the aerosol emission ratios, which are expressed as g/kg $C(CO_2)$. (The ratios have been multiplied by 1000 to make the numbers easier to read.)

In Table 5, we combine the estimates of regional and global biomass burning rates (Tables 2 and 3) with our best estimate of the emission ratios

TABLE 5 Estimates of tropical and global emissions from biomass burning (Tg element/yr)

Species	Emission ratio (a)	Tropical America	Tropical Africa	Tropical Asia	Tropical Australia	Tropics total	World total
Carbon burned		780	1450	980	200	3410	3940
Gases							
CO_2 (b)		690	1270	860	180	3000	3460
CO	100	70	130	90	20	300	350
Methane	11	8	14	10	2	33	38
Non-methane hydrocarbons	7	5	9	6	1	21	24
Nitrous oxide	0.1	0.16	0.30	0.20	0.04	0.70	0.81
NO_x	2.1	1.7	3.1	2.1	0.4	7.4	8.5
Ammonia	1.3	1.0	1.9	1.3	0.3	4.6	5.3
Nitriles	0.6	0.4	0.9	0.6	0.1	2.1	2.4
SO_2 and aerosol sulfate	0.3	0.6	1.0	0.7	0.1	2.4	2.8
Carbonyl sulfide	0.01	0.02	0.03	0.02	0.00	0.08	0.09
Hydrogen	33	4	7	5	1	16	19
Ozone	30	80	150	100	20	360	420
Aerosols							
TPM (c)	20	14	25	17	4	60	70
POC	13	9	17	11	2	39	45
Elemental carbon	3.7	2.5	4.7	3.2	0.7	11	13
Potassium	0.4	0.9	1.7	1.1	0.2	3.9	4.5

(a) See Table 4.
(b) These values represent the actual amount of CO_2 emitted from the fires. They are 88 percent of the amount of carbon burned, since ca. 12 percent is emitted as CO, methane, and non-methane hydrocarbons. These compounds will eventually be converted to CO_2, however, by photochemical oxidation in the atmosphere.
(c) Total particulate matter (emission rate in Tg/yr).

(Table 4) to derive regional and global rates of pyrogenic emissions. The uncertainty of these estimates is about 50 percent in the case of CO_2, where the emission amount is relatively well constrained, and about a factor of two for most of the other gases, where additional uncertainty is contributed by the limited data base on emission ratios.

In spite of these uncertainties in our quantitative estimates, it is quite evident from this compilation that biomass burning results in globally important contributions to the atmospheric budget of several of these pollutant gases (Table 6). When we consider that much of the burning is concentrated in relatively limited regions (e.g., the African savannas) and occurs over a limited time, it is not surprising that it results in levels of atmospheric pollution that rival and sometimes exceed those in the industrialized regions of the developed countries. This applies especially to a group of gases that constitute the main ingredients of "classical" smog chemistry in the atmosphere: hydrocarbons, carbon monoxide, and nitrogen oxides (NO_x). These species react with one another to form other pollutants, particularly ozone (O_3). About 20–30 percent of the global emissions of these compounds is attributable to biomass burning (Table 6). Since only about half of the total

TABLE 6   Comparison between global emissions from biomass burning and emissions from all sources (including biomass burning, Tg element/yr)

Species	Biomass burning	All sources	Biomass burning percent
CO_2 (gross from combustion)	3500	8700(a)	40
CO_2 (net from deforestation)	1800	7000(b)	26
CO	350	1100	32
Methane	38	380	10
Non-methane hydrocarbons	24	100	24
Nitrous oxide	0.8	13	6
NO_x	8.5	40	21
Ammonia	5.3	13	40
Sulfur gases	2.8	150	2
Carbonyl sulfide	0.09	1.4	6
Hydrogen	19	75	25
Ozone	420	1100	38
TPM (c)	70	1530	5
Particulate organic carbon	45	180	25
Elemental carbon	13	<22	>50

(a) Biomass burning plus fossil fuel burning.
(b) Deforestation plus fossil fuel burning.
(c) Total particulate matter (Tg/yr).

source flux of these species is from anthropogenic emissions (the rest from natural sources), we find that biomass burning accounts for roughly one-half of the anthropogenic source of atmospheric hydrocarbons, CO, NO_x, and tropospheric ozone.

Methane (CH_4) and nitrous oxide (N_2O) contribute to the atmospheric greenhouse effect and are long-lived enough to enter the stratosphere and contribute to the ozone cycle there. Their pyrogenic emissions are on the order of 10 percent of the global source flux. The emission ratios for both of these gases are uncertain, however, and it is quite possible that the pyrogenic fraction could be as high as 15 percent for methane and 20 percent for N_2O. Additional information on both the pyrogenic and the other sources of N_2O is needed before the budget of this species can be assessed with reasonable accuracy.

The global atmospheric budget of ammonia is not well known. It has been suggested that the emissions are dominated by microbial release from animal excreta, with a total flux of about 6–16 Tg N/yr. The pyrogenic source estimate in Table 5 is of the same magnitude, making biomass burning a potentially very important source of ammonia.

In contrast to the nitrogen species, for which pyrogenic emissions are very important, only relatively small amounts of sulfur dioxide, carbonyl sulfide (COS), and aerosol sulfate are emitted. Biomass burning contributes only about 1.3 percent to the total atmospheric sulfur budget, and represents about 3 percent of the anthropogenic emissions. Still, since most of the natural emissions are from the oceans and most of the anthropogenic emissions are concentrated in the industrialized regions of the temperate latitudes, biomass burning does make a pronounced impact on the sulfur budget over remote continental regions (e.g., the Amazon and Congo Basins). Here, sulfur fluxes to the vegetation may be enhanced by as much as a factor of five due to tropical biomass burning.

Emission of aerosol particles (smoke)

Even though the smoke from biomass fires is one of the most obvious emissions, often visible in the tropics as a continuous pall hanging in the air for days or weeks, quantitative estimates on the amounts of particulate matter released are still highly uncertain. Particulate matter (aerosol) in the smoke consists of organic matter, black elemental carbon (soot and charcoal particles), and inorganic materials (e.g., potassium carbonate and silica). In fact, the element potassium derives its name from having been isolated from wood-burning ash (potash), where it is present in the form of potassium carbonate. In Table 5, the emission of total particulate matter (TPM) is estimated as 70 Tg/yr, most of which is organic matter (45 Tg/yr). Based on these estimates, particulate organic carbon from biomass burning would account for about one-third of the organic carbon aerosol released globally. Still, our estimates are much lower than those of Seiler and Crutzen (1980), who suggested an emission rate of 200–450 Tg/yr for TPM, of which about 90 percent is assumed to be carbon compounds, and 90–180 Tg/yr for elemental carbon. This discrepancy results from the large difference in the emission ratios used: Seiler and Crutzen's estimate is based on early work by D. E. Ward (1979, pers. comm. to Seiler and Crutzen), who had suggested emission ratios of 24–180 g TPM/kg $C(CO_2)$. Our value of 20 g TPM/kg $C(CO_2)$ is based on our own work in Amazonia (Andreae et al., 1988) and work by Ward reported in 1986. Sampling plumes that were quite "old" and had traveled for about one day following the burn, we obtained apparent emission ratios of 6–25 g/kg $C(CO_2)$. Due to the delay between emission and sampling in our work, it is likely that a substantial amount of the aerosol in particles larger than a few micrometers in diameter had already fallen out. The emission measurements of Ward were conducted in the immediate vicinity of the fires, on the other hand. He reported TPM emission ratios in the range of 2–46 g/kg $C(CO_2)$, with average values of 22 and 37 g/kg $C(CO_2)$ for flaming and smoldering conditions, respectively. Because some of the particles sampled very closely above the fire (as was done in Ward's experiments) are large enough to fall out almost immediately, it appears that a value of 20 g/kg $C(CO_2)$ is a reasonable estimate for the emission of particulate matter that may become subject to atmospheric transport. Our measurements in Amazonia showed that the carbon content of this aerosol is about 66 percent, which is consistent with the aerosol particles consisting mostly of partially oxygenated organic matter. The content of black elemental carbon in smoke particles from biomass burning is highly variable. In smoldering fires it is as low as 4 percent (weight percent carbon in TPM), while in intensively flaming fires it can reach 40 percent. We use a value of 18 percent, based on our work in Amazonia. From this and the estimate for global TPM emissions in Table 5 (70 Tg/yr), we obtain a source estimate for black carbon aerosol of 13 Tg/yr. This accounts for a very large fraction of the global emissions, which have been estimated to fall into the range of 3–22 Tg/yr.

Charcoal formation and carbon storage

In their 1980 paper, Seiler and Crutzen drew attention to an unexpected consequence of biomass burning: they argued that the formation of charcoal during burning and its consequent burial in soils and sediments would lead to a long-term sequestering of reduced carbon, and therefore provide a sink for atmospheric CO_2. In the absence of burning, photosynthesis and respiration in terrestrial ecosystems form a closed cycle where just as much CO_2 is released to the atmosphere during the biochemical oxidation of plant matter as was taken up during its production by photosynthesis; thus there is no net flux of CO_2 to or from the atmosphere. During combustion, however, some of the plant matter is turned into charcoal, which may either remain on the ground after the burn or be transported in the smoke. Once formed, charcoal and soot carbon do not appear to be reoxidized back to CO_2, even over geological time scales. This process therefore provides a long-term sink for atmospheric CO_2, and incidentally a net source of oxygen to the atmosphere. While this mechanism appears very plausible on a qualitative basis, its quantitative importance remains controversial.

To estimate the amount of charcoal and soot that becomes airborne during biomass fires, we can use the data on the elemental carbon component of the smoke aerosol given in Tables 4 and 5. The emission ratio estimate of 3.7×10^{-3} corresponds to about 1.4 g C per kg of burned biomass. Since only a fraction of the above-ground biomass is burned (20–80 percent, depending on vegetation type), the final fraction of biomass that becomes airborne as charcoal or soot particles is very small, probably less than 0.1 percent. This is consistent with the results of a recent study on the cycle of charcoal from biomass burning, which estimated that only 5 percent of the charcoal produced in a coastal watershed reached sediments in the adjacent Gulf of Panama. Most of this charcoal is transported by rivers, only about 3 percent by wind.

The main mechanism for charcoal storage must therefore be its incorporation into terrestrial soils and sediments. Seiler and Crutzen's (1980) review of the literature shows that charcoal layers do indeed occur frequently in tropical and temperate soils. They estimate that 20–30 percent of the carbon present on the ground after a biomass fire is in the form of charcoal. At the burning efficiency of 25 percent assumed by Seiler and Crutzen, this would correspond to conversion of 15–22 percent of the pre-burn biomass into charcoal. Recent measurements of the amount of charcoal produced in clearing fires in Amazonia found a much lower rate of charcoal production (3.6 percent of pre-burn above-ground carbon), about 20 percent of the value estimated by Seiler and Crutzen. As a result of these uncertainties, the range of estimates for the global rate of charcoal formation and the resulting sequestering of CO_2 is rather large, ca. 200–1700 Tg C/yr. If the actual value falls near the high end of this range, as much as 20 percent of the roughly 7000 Tg C added per year to the Earth's atmosphere may be removed by charcoal formation.

Outstanding uncertainties

One of the most puzzling aspects concerning emissions from biomass burning is the fate of fuel nitrogen. It is well established from both field and laboratory studies that most of the nitrogen contained in the biomass fuel is volatilized. Yet, only some 30 percent of the amount released has so far been identified (as NO, NO_2, N_2O, NH_3, HCN, and small amounts of other species). If the "missing nitrogen" turns out to be molecular nitrogen, biomass burning represents a substantial loss of nitrogen from tropical ecosystems. The pyrogenic emission rate of N_2O, a trace gas whose atmospheric budget is inadequately understood, also needs to be better defined. This is especially important since N_2O contributes to the greenhouse effect and is a precursor of stratospheric NO_x, which in turn regulates stratospheric ozone.

Another critical issue is the production rate of charcoal during biomass combustion. Given the wide range of estimates, this process may be either a trivial sink of atmospheric CO_2 or large enough to compensate for the amount of CO_2 released due to deforestation.

Finally, much uncertainty persists regarding the rate of particulate emissions from biomass burning. Since aerosols can be observed and measured from satellites, they provide a potentially useful tool for the estimation of global rates of pyrogenic emission. It is therefore essential to have accurate data on the emission ratios and optical characteristics of smoke aerosols from biomass burning.

Long-range transport of smoke plumes

Hot gases from fires, being lighter than the surrounding air, rise through the atmosphere. The turbulence created in this buoyant airmass entrains ambient air, which mixes with the flame gases. The rising air expands and cools, in many cases reaching a level where it becomes supersaturated with water vapor, and a cloud begins to form at the top of the smoke plume. If this cloud produces rain, some particulate matter and soluble gases may already be scavenged and removed at this stage. Like most other clouds, however, those formed on top of the smoke plumes will dissolve again, and the plume will start to drift horizontally with the prevailing winds. The height to which the smoke plumes can rise is usually limited in the tropics by the trade wind inversion, a layer where the density of the ambient air decreases sharply and which thus prevents the further buoyant rise of air from below. This inversion occurs at an altitude of some 3–5 km in the tropics. Only in the so-called Intertropical Convergence Zone (ITCZ), the meteorological equator, are conditions favorable for the injection of air and smoke into the upper layers of the troposphere.

When the rising smoke plumes have become trapped at an inversion layer and start spreading horizontally, they tend to become stretched out into relatively thin layers of great horizontal extent. Such thin haze layers can travel far from their point of origin without losing their identity. As most of the burning is within the tropical, rather than the equatorial region, the plumes will usually travel in a westerly direction, and toward the equator. As they approach the ITCZ, vertical convection in the troposphere intensifies, destroying the layered structure and distributing the pyrogenic emissions throughout the lower troposphere. Finally, in the ITCZ region, smoke and gases from biomass burning may be injected into the upper atmosphere and even into the stratosphere.

Evidence for the efficiency of these transport mechanisms is abundant. The smoke plumes from the fires in South America and Africa are easily seen from space and have been the subject of investigations from the space shuttle. They have been mapped using various space-borne sensors, in particular the Advanced-Very-High-Resolution-Radiometer (AVHRR) instruments on the NOAA series satellites. On the ground, haze and smoke from fires some thousand kilometers away are often dense enough to close airports in the middle of the Amazon Basin.

Less obvious than the visible smoke, but even more indicative of the extent to which the emissions from burning are transported around the globe, are the results of chemical measurements from satellites, aircraft, and research vessels. Soot carbon and other pyrogenic aerosol constituents have been measured during research cruises over the remote Atlantic and Pacific Oceans; and carbon monoxide and ozone originating from fires in Africa were consistently observed during the NASA/CITE-3 flights off the coast of Brazil. On an even larger scale, high levels of ozone and CO are seen from satellites over tropical Africa and South America and over large areas of the surrounding oceans.

Environmental impacts

Ozone pollution of the troposphere

In view of the large amounts of hydrocarbons and NO_x emitted in the biomass fires, it is not surprising that very high concentrations of ozone are produced in the plumes by essentially the same photochemical reactions that are responsible for urban smog. The highest concentrations, typically in the range of 50 to 100 ppb and often exceeding values found in the polluted regions of the northern hemisphere, are usually found in discrete layers at altitudes of 1–5 km, in accordance with the transport mechanisms of the burning plumes described above (see Figure 1). Depending on the rates of vertical exchange and on the efficiency of the vegetation in destroying ozone, the concentrations at ground level are substantially lower. They typically show a pronounced daily cycle, with a minimum at night and a maximum near mid-day. This cycle is controlled by the balance of O_3 sources and sinks: at night, O_3 consumption by deposition to vegetation and by the reaction with NO emitted from soils reduces the concentration of ozone near the Earth's surface. During the day, it is replenished by photochemical ozone formation and downward mixing of ozone-rich air from higher

FIGURE 1   Vertical profiles of ozone in the tropical troposphere

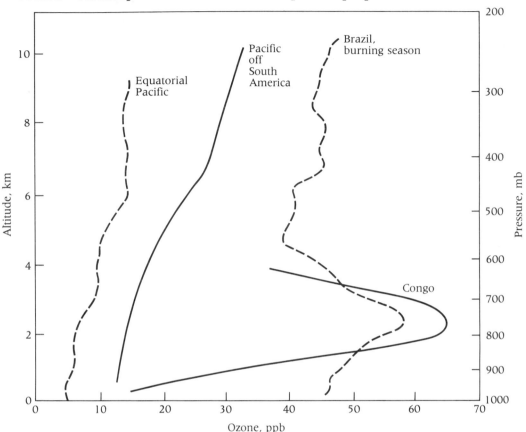

SOURCE: Modified from Fishman (1988).

altitudes. Over an unpolluted tropical rainforest (e.g., in the central Amazon Basin during the wet season), O_3 levels are very low: below 10 ppb at midday and below 3 ppb at night. Under somewhat more polluted conditions (e.g., in central Amazonia during the dry season), nighttime values are still very low, but daytime O_3 concentrations reach 10–30 ppb at the level of tree crowns. Finally, in tropical Africa, where biomass burning currently has the strongest impact, surface ozone concentrations in excess of 40 ppb are frequently measured, especially during the dry season. These values are similar to those observed in the highly polluted regions of the Eastern United States and of Central Europe. Studies in temperate forest regions have linked such levels of ozone pollution to the damage to trees and vegetation that has become widespread in Europe and North America. In view of the sharp increase of O_3 with altitude frequently observed in the tropics, the likelihood of vegetation damage by ozone is especially high in mountainous regions, where the ground surface intersects the levels where ozone concentrations above 70 ppb are encountered. Ozone episodes with ground-level concentrations of 80–120 ppb must be expected to occur in the tropics particularly during the dry season, when photochemically reactive air becomes trapped under a subsiding inversion layer.

The increase of tropospheric ozone concentrations is a cause for concern even beyond the likelihood of plant damage by this gas: ozone is also an efficient absorber of infrared radiation and thus acts as a "greenhouse gas" in the same way as CO_2. In fact, the global increase in tropospheric O_3 concentrations contributes about 15 percent to the overall greenhouse warming. The increase of O_3 over the tropics contributes strongly to this effect: photochemical ozone production from pyrogenic emissions accounts for about one-third of the total input of ozone into the troposphere (Table 6), about the same amount as produced from fossil-fuel emissions in the industrialized regions of the northern hemisphere (the rest is due to stratospheric inputs). Consequently, biomass burning is responsible for as much as one-half of the greenhouse warming attributable to increasing tropospheric ozone (see Figure 2).

FIGURE 2   Cumulative equilibrium surface temperature warming (greenhouse effect) due to increasing trace gas concentrations, 1980–2030, as computed by a one-dimensional climate model

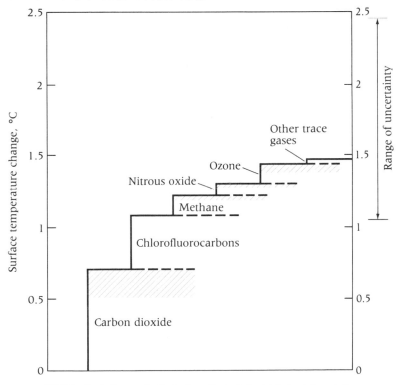

NOTE: Shaded areas indicate the effect attributable to deforestation and biomass burning.
SOURCE: After Ramanathan et al. (1985).

Perturbation of oxidant cycles in the troposphere

The large-scale increase in tropospheric ozone levels already being observed in the tropics indicates a fundamental change in the way the troposphere behaves chemically. Many gases, particularly hydrocarbons, are continuously emitted into the atmosphere from natural and anthropogenic sources. A buildup of these gases in the atmosphere is prevented by a self-cleaning mechanism, whereby these substances are slowly "combusted" photochemically to CO_2. The key molecule responsible for this oxidation process is the hydroxyl radical (OH). The reaction chains involved are such that ozone and OH are consumed when the concentration of NO_x is low. This is the "normal" condition of the unpolluted troposphere. On the basis of the observed increase of methane and CO in the atmosphere, Crutzen (1987) suggested the possibility of a global decrease in OH and O_3, leading through a feedback mechanism to further increase in CH_4 and CO, and a possibly unstable condition of the atmosphere. Injection of large amounts of NO_x from biomass burning may reverse this process, since hydrocarbon oxidation in the presence of elevated amounts of NO_x produces additional amounts of O_3 and OH. The model calculations of Keller et al. (1990) predict a tenfold increase in regional OH concentrations to result from deforestation and biomass burning in the tropics. The consequences of driving a large fraction of the world's atmosphere from its "natural" O_3-consuming mode of operation into the opposing, O_3-producing one are unforeseeable at this time.

Climate change

We have already noted that the clearing of tropical rainforests is responsible for about 25 percent of the greenhouse warming attributable to increasing CO_2, and that increasing tropospheric ozone adds further to the greenhouse effect. But biomass burning releases other gases that contribute to greenhouse warming, particularly methane and nitrous oxide. In the case of the latter two gases, biomass burning accounts for only about 10 percent of the global sources, but probably for a much greater fraction of the increase in global emissions, since many of the other sources (e.g., natural wetlands) are constant or shrinking. From estimates of the temporal trends of methane source strengths from 1940 to 1980 we can derive a pyrogenic contribution of 21 percent to the increase in methane emissions over that period. The current uncertainty about the atmospheric mass balance of N_2O makes it very difficult to estimate the contribution of biomass burning to its increasing tropospheric concentration: a fraction of 20–50 percent appears reasonable. The fraction of greenhouse warming attributable to biomass burning and deforestation is indicated as shaded areas in Figure 2.

The climatic effect of the smoke aerosols is beyond current understanding, due to the complex nature of the interactions involved. Because of the limited lifetime of aerosol particles (on the order of days) compared with the lifetime of most of the "greenhouse gases," their climatic effects act initially more on a regional than a global scale. Since the equatorial regions, particularly the Amazon Basin, the Congo Basin, and the area around Borneo, are extremely important in receiving solar energy and in redistributing this heat vertically through the atmosphere, any change affecting the operation of these "heat engines of the atmosphere" must be viewed with great concern. Aerosols can influence climate directly by changing the Earth's radiation balance. They can reflect sunlight back into space, thereby reducing the amount of heat the Earth receives. Black soot aerosol, on the other hand, may absorb sunlight and thus heat the atmosphere. There appears to be a weak consensus among climatologists that these direct effects are not large at this time relative to other agents of climate change. Indirect effects are a greater source of concern, especially the influence of pyrogenic particles on the behavior of clouds. Cloud droplets require the presence of aerosol particles, called cloud condensation nuclei (CCN), for their formation. The properties of the clouds depend on the number of available CCN: the more CCN, the more droplets form, which results in a smaller droplet size, given a constant amount of available water. Clouds made up of smaller droplets are whiter and reflect more sunlight back into space, but are less likely to produce rain. Since clouds are one of the most important controls on the Earth's heat balance, any large-scale modification of cloud properties is likely to have a strong impact on global climate. Preliminary work done on the efficiency of pyrogenic smoke aerosols as CCN suggests that their efficiency as CCN changes dramatically as they age in the atmosphere.

The potential changes in precipitation efficiency add to the perturbation of the hydrological cycle in the tropics caused by changes in the characteristics of the land surface brought about by deforestation and desertification. Tropical forests are extremely efficient in returning rainwater back to the atmosphere in the form of water vapor. There it can form clouds and rain again, and the cycle can repeat itself many times. A region like the Amazon Basin can thus retain water (which ultimately comes from the ocean and will return there) for a long time, and maintain a large "standing stock" of water. If the forest is replaced by grassland or, as often happens, is converted into an essentially unvegetated surface by erosion and loss of topsoil, water runs off quickly and returns through streams and rivers to the ocean without much chance of recycling. Beyond the unfavorable consequences that such large-scale changes in the availability of water will have on human activities, such a modification of the hydrological cycle may itself perturb climate. This is because the atmosphere makes use of the potential for storing energy in the form of water vapor and releasing this energy again when the vapor condenses into cloud droplets as an important mechanism for the redistribution of heat. If less water is available for this purpose, the heat absorbed at the ground has to be moved away by radiation and dry convection, leading to higher surface temperatures and a change in the vertical distribution of heat. Such perturbations of the atmospheric heat and water balance must be viewed with great concern.

Acid deposition

After acid rain became a notorious environmental problem in Europe and North America, scientists were surprised to learn that it is widespread in the tropics (see Table 7). Organic acids (especially formic and acetic acids) and nitric acid were shown to account for a large part of the acidity, in contrast to the situation in the industrialized temperate regions, where sulfuric and nitric acid predominate. It was originally thought that the organic acids were largely derived from natural, biogenic emissions, probably from plants. However, more recent evidence shows that they may be largely derived from direct emission of acetic acid from biomass burning and from the photochemical formation of formic and probably acetic acid in the plumes. In

TABLE 7   Rainwater pH and acid deposition at some continental tropical sites and in the Eastern United States

	pH Mean (a)	Range	Rainfall (cm)	Acid deposition (kg/ha/yr)
Venezuela				
San Eusebio	4.6	3.8–6.2	158	0.39
San Carlos	4.8	4.4–5.2	—	—
La Paragua	4.7	4.0–5.0	—	—
Brazil				
Manaus, dry season	4.6	3.8–5.0	240 (b)	0.29 (b)
Manaus, wet season	5.2	4.3–6.1		
Australia				
Groote Eylandt	4.3		—	—
Katherine	4.8	4.2–5.4	—	—
Jabiru	4.3		—	—
Ivory Coast				
Ayame	4.6	4.0–6.5	179	0.41
Congo				
Boyele	4.4		185	0.74
Eastern USA	4.3	3.0–5.9	130	0.67

(a) Volume weighted.
(b) Annual average.

regions affected by biomass burning, pyrogenic NO_x emissions overwhelm by far the natural sources of NO_x (e.g., soil emissions and NO formation in lightning bolts). Nitric acid is formed photochemically from the NO_x emitted in the fires. A model simulating the effects of biomass burning and a moderate amount of additional pollution, mostly connected with activities related to logging, suggests that rainwater pH values of ca. 4.2 can be expected in the tropics due to the formation of nitric acid alone (Keller et al., 1990). When the simultaneous production of organic acids and their incorporation into rainwater are considered, pH values well below 4 must be expected. Such values have indeed been frequently observed in Africa. For comparison, the mean pH measured during the period 1963–82 at the Hubbard Brook site in New Hampshire, an established site for the study of acid rain, was 4.2 and the mean pH in rain sampled throughout the Eastern United States in 1980 was 4.3 (Table 7).

Acidic substances in the atmosphere can be deposited to plants and soils either by rain and fog (wet deposition) or by direct removal of aerosols and gases at the surface (dry deposition). In the humid tropics, wet deposition accounts for most of the deposition flux, whereas in the savanna regions, especially during the dry season, dry deposition dominates. Acid deposition has been linked to forest damage in Europe and the Eastern United States. It is thought that such damage is usually caused by a combination of factors, including acid deposition, ozone damage, and the concurrent exposure to other sources of stress (e.g., drought or insect infestation). Acid deposition can act on an ecosystem by two major pathways: direct damage through the deposition of acidic aerosols and gases on leaves; and soil acidification. The danger of leaf injury is serious only at pH levels below 3.5, which is rarely encountered in the tropics. However, in the presence of highly soluble gaseous nitric and organic acids from biomass burning, it is quite likely that fog and dew can reach such pH levels during the dry season in many regions. Tropical forests may be inherently more sensitive to foliar damage than temperate forests due to the longer average leaf life in the tropics, where the leaves of many trees are shed only after two or more years. The resulting longer exposure of individual leaves may make cumulative damage more pronounced.

Many tropical soils are likely to be relatively resistant to rapid acidification due to their high sulfate adsorption capacity. However, there are also large areas where soils are quite susceptible to acidification (e.g., in Venezuela). Furthermore, even in relatively resistant soils, chronic exposure to acid deposition will eventually lead to soil acidification and such associated problems as leaching of aluminum, manganese, and other cations. Microbial processes in the soils are also at risk of being perturbed. Nitrogen cycling is likely to be influenced, both by decreasing pH and by the addition of nitrate and ammonium ions from wet and dry deposition.

Many species of tropical animals spend part of their lives in rainwater collected in bromeliads or similar plants. Other species, like frogs and salamanders, depend on water collected between dead leaves or mosses to keep their skin moist. Acid deposition poses a serious risk to these animals, which are essential components of the forest ecosystem. This applies particularly to insects, which are essential to many rainforest species for pollination.

Disruption of nutrient cycles and soil degradation

Tropical ecosystems, both natural and agricultural, are frequently deficient in nitrogen, sulfur, or both. When an area is burned, a substantial part of the nitrogen and sulfur present in the ecosystem is volatilized. As long as these elements are redeposited nearby, no net gain or loss would occur. In the case of nitrogen, however, only some 30 percent of the fuel nitrogen can be accounted for in the emissions. If the remainder is in fact emitted as molecular nitrogen, a significant overall loss of nutrient nitrogen results. This possibility needs to be investigated further. On the other hand, ecosystems that are not burned (e.g., remaining areas of intact rainforest) will receive an increased nutrient input. Indeed, studies of rainwater chemistry in the central Amazon Basin suggest that as much as 90 percent of the sulfur and nitrogen deposited there is from sources outside the forest ecosystem, with long-range transport of emissions from biomass burning playing a major role. The effects of such increasing inputs of nutrients to rainforests are not known. It must be remembered, however, that these increased nutrient inputs are accompanied by an increase in acid deposition and ozone concentration. The effect of this complex impact of environmental perturbations on tropical forest ecosystems will be difficult to analyze.

Besides the immediate volatilization of nitrogen during the burns, long-term changes in the microbial cycling of nitrogen in soils appear to result from the use of burning in agriculture. NO and N_2O emissions from soils at experimental sites where the vegetation had been burned were about twice as high as from soils at unburned sites. This effect persisted for at least six months following the burn. Studies have also shown enhanced fluxes of nitrogen oxides from soils following clearing of forest and conversion to grazing land, but in these studies the effect of burning was not isolated explicitly. It is clear that much research still needs to be done to elucidate the effects of biomass burning on nutrient cycling and especially on nitrogen volatilization. The few studies available already do suggest, however, that deforestation and biomass burning contribute to the inputs of nitrogen oxides and to the resulting perturbations of air quality and climate well beyond the direct emissions from the fires.

Perturbation of stratospheric chemistry and the ozone layer

Many of the trace gases released by biomass burning are involved in the chemical reaction cycles that maintain the stratospheric ozone layer. N_2O, for which biomass burning is a significant source, is sufficiently long-lived to diffuse into the stratosphere, where it is broken down to reactive nitrogen species. Methane and hydrogen gas are oxidized in the stratosphere, forming CO_2 and H_2O. The fact that some biomass burning occurs in close vicinity to the Intertropical Convergence Zone is particularly relevant: in this region of intensive vertical convection, even relatively short-lived gases (e.g., non-methane hydrocarbons) may be injected into the stratosphere. Carbonyl sulfide is the only sulfur gas that can escape tropospheric oxidation and diffuse to the stratosphere. Here it is oxidized to form sulfuric acid aerosol particles, which scatter sunlight and participate in the reaction cycles leading to the formation of the Antarctic ozone hole. It is impossible at this time to predict the nature of the overall effect of biomass burning on the fluxes of all of these species into the stratosphere and on the chemical reactions. But the potential for significant disruption of stratospheric chemical cycles is considerable enough to warrant future investigation by modeling and experiment.

Alternatives to biomass burning and deforestation: A challenge

In the preceding sections we have described the serious environmental problems caused by biomass burning and deforestation. We have not discussed the related ecological damage resulting from species extinction and habitat loss. We have also not addressed the grave social and economic consequences of the misguided agricultural practices and development policies responsible for much of the land clearing and burning in the tropics. These matters are of great concern and have become a focus of public and political attention and of wide-ranging media coverage. In discussions on the environmental damage caused by burning and land clearing in the tropics, it is often asked how we can deny local farmers the right to make a living. This question makes two assumptions: first, that the conversion of forest to agricultural or grazing land is in the best interest of the local population; second, that burning is the most appropriate agricultural tool for tropical farming and ranching. There is ample evidence accumulating that both assumptions may be false. Most of the land cleared in Amazonia becomes useless to small landholders within a period of one to three years. It then becomes the object of land speculation and lumber and agricultural development by large corporations. Even where land is used to feed the people, burning is likely to be a wasteful practice. As we have discussed above, it leads to a net loss of nutrients from the burned region. By reducing the amount of organic matter that can be incorporated into the soil, burning adversely influences soil texture and water retention capability. It removes plant cover from the soil, making it more prone to erosion by rainfall and runoff. From these considerations comes a challenge to agricultural science, development organizations, and the governments of tropical countries: land use practices must be developed to eliminate the need for clearing additional forest regions and to reduce the need for burning on agricultural lands and savannas. The local populations should be educated in the use of such alternative techniques, where appropriate. Often such knowledge already exists in indigenous populations, as pointed out by Peters et al. (1989), who show that the exploitation of fruit, latex, and other non-wood products from an Amazonian forest can provide a higher sustained rate of return than logging. In view of the potential for serious and irreversible damage to global climate, ecology, and human welfare, preservation of the wet and dry tropics as a functioning human and natural environment may well be the most important environmental issue of our time.

References

Andreae, Meinrat O., et al. 1988. "Biomass-burning and associated haze layers over Amazonia," *Journal of Geophysical Research* 93: 1509–1527.

Crutzen, Paul J. 1987. "The role of the tropics in atmospheric chemistry," in *The Geophysiology of Amazonia*, ed. Robert E. Dickinson. New York: John Wiley, pp. 107–130.

———, et al. 1990. "Emissions of CO_2 and other trace gases to the atmosphere from fires in the tropics," in *Our Changing Atmosphere. Proceedings of the 28th Liège International Astrophysical Colloquium*, ed. Paul J. Crutzen, J. C. Gerard, and R. Zander. Cointe-Ougree, Belgium: University of Liège, pp. 449–472.

Detwiler, R. P., Charles A. S. Hall, and P. Bogdonoff. 1985. "Land use change and carbon exchange in the tropics: II. Estimates for the entire region," *Environmental Management* 9: 335–344.

Detwiler, R. P., and Charles A. S. Hall. 1988. "Tropical forests and the global carbon cycle," *Science* 239: 42–47.

Food and Agriculture Organization. 1989. *Yearbook of Forest Products 1987 (1976–1987)*. Rome: FAO.

Fishman, Jack. 1988. "Tropospheric ozone from satellite total ozone measurements," in *Tropospheric Ozone: Regional and Global Scale Interactions*, ed. Ivar S. A. Isaksen. Dordrecht: Reidel, pp. 111–123.

Hao, Wei-Min, Mey-Huey Liu, and Paul J. Crutzen. 1990. "Estimates of annual and regional releases of CO_2 and other trace gases to the atmosphere from fires in the tropics, based on the FAO statistics for the period 1975–1980," in *Fire in the Tropical Biota: Ecosystem Processes and Global Challenges*, ed. Johannes G. Goldammer. Berlin: Springer-Verlag, in press.

Houghton, Richard A., et al. 1985. "Net flux of carbon dioxide from tropical forests in 1980," *Nature* 316: 617–620.

Keller, Michael, Daniel J. Jacob, Steven C. Wofsy, and Robert C. Harriss. 1990. "Effects of tropical deforestation on global and regional atmospheric chemistry," *Climatic Change*, in press.

Peters, Charles M., Alwyn H. Gentry, and Robert O. Mendelsohn. 1989. "Valuation of an Amazonian rainforest," *Nature* 339: 655–656.

Ramanathan, V., Ralph J. Cicerone, Hanwant B. Singh, and Jeffrey T. Kiehl. 1985. "Trace gas trends and their potential role in climate change," *Journal of Geophysical Research* 90: 5547–5566.

Seiler, Wolfgang, and Paul J. Crutzen. 1980. "Estimates of gross and net fluxes of carbon between the biosphere and the atmosphere from biomass burning," *Climatic Change* 2: 207–247.

ARE THERE LIMITS TO GROWTH?

Toward a Theory
of Population–Development
Interaction

NATHAN KEYFITZ

THIS ARTICLE JUXTAPOSES THE DIVERGENT VIEWPOINTS of scholars on population and development, in the hope of contributing to a synthesis of what the several disciplines have to say about the effects of population increase.

Economics has had the most to say. For its first 170 years of existence as a science, say from soon after Adam Smith to Myrdal, Coale, Lewis, and others writing up to the 1960s, it showed how large and growing populations handicap development. During this time there was no major disagreement by others who examined population. Sociologists took over the field after World War II, resting especially on the increasing mass of statistical data, and they also found rapid population increase a major handicap to development. Biologists had always been interested in the subject, seeing man as an element in the ecology of the planet and being familiar with instances of species, for instance locusts, that escape their natural checks and increase to the point of destroying their habitat. The several disciplines quoted one another approvingly, beginning with Darwin's report that Malthus had given him the idea with which he could start his work.

This unanimity has been disturbed in recent decades, as some economists claim that after all development is not much hindered by rapid growth (Kuznets, 1967; Simon, 1981; NRC, 1986). In this view the case for birth control rests mostly on the right of individuals to decide how many children they wish to have, a moral rather than an economic argument, and as such necessarily without any relation to evidence (NRC, 1986). The administrator who asks a neoclassical economist whether he should give high priority to birth control programs is told no; he then asks a biologist and is told yes. He is left to resolve a clash between disciplines that is too difficult for the experts in those disciplines to resolve.

A population, whether of humans or other species, exists in some kind of setting. Even a population of automobiles cannot be considered separately from the road network, repair facilities, gasoline stations, and other elements of the environment in which they have their usefulness and continue to operate; less developed countries, in which much more investment goes into the vehicles than into other elements of the system, demonstrate this strikingly. The setting for man is a habitat or environment to biologists, the complementary factors of production to economists. Different views of the setting will give rise to different conclusions on the need for population control.

I classify the reasons for population control under four heads, and find each one subject to its own special considerations. In four words they are resources, capital, employment, and Earth, and they constitute the four main sections of this essay.

Land and other resources

For Malthus, writing at the dawn of the industrial revolution, and not entirely accepting the changes it was making, let alone foreseeing the expansion that was imminent, the setting was principally land. There was only so much of it and once this was full the further increase of population would have to share it, and hence would have to share the fixed amount of product. Of course this is too simple; the land is never full; it varies in quality from the most fertile to the downright uncultivable, and the more fertile is naturally settled and exploited first. As the population increases it has to settle less productive land, so with everything else fixed it becomes poorer and poorer. Even with the settlement of America, which was prominent in the minds of English theorists at the turn of the nineteenth century, the limits still applied, though they were farther in the future than in England.

Malthus produced a simple and clearcut, essentially biological theory in 1798. Social aspects entered only with the preventive checks of later editions. His argument was further elaborated over the next few decades by himself, Ricardo, Mill, and others; and most secular thinkers—all writers who were not bound to an earlier religious or mercantilist view—could agree on it for the next 150 years.

As the industrial revolution advanced and the agricultural economy of England gave way to factories, the same concept of limits and scarcity came to be applied to natural resources other than land, and especially to coal. The most accessible seams were being exploited first, so coal would become more expensive, and England's manufacturing preeminence would sooner or later come to an end. Stanley Jevons saw this as posing a grave threat to the descendants of those then living, and advised that at least the national debt be paid off. What now seems ridiculous (who pays off debts?) made a good deal of sense in the simple world of those times: after borrowing to build a factory one must take out of each year's sales the depreciation, that is, one must set aside a due part for the repayment of the loan on which the factory was built. It was as though the coal was borrowed and posterity had to be compensated for its use, or at least not left in debt to continue paying for it after it was exhausted. Jevons was an early believer in sustainable development.

But ultimately new sources of energy were developed that had various advantages, and coal mines were abandoned long before their content gave out. The succession of fuels—oil, gas, nuclear—along with greater efficiency in their use and a shift to less energy-intensive industries, produced a strong impression that the classical economists had focused on the wrong problem. It was now the inventive process itself that was the resource—the vision that each kind of fuel would give place to some better fuel, even before the first was exhausted. Invention is no longer an accident attributable to genius; it is an established and continuing institution. In all fields of science, but especially in chemistry and biology, the computer so facilitates and automates research that it seems as though progress will henceforth be automatic; now discoveries can be made to order.

That perspective was applied to every part of the setting in which people lived and gained their living. We do not need more land, just improved yields on the existing stock. Copper, nickel, and other mines will be emptied out, but new sites will be discovered, and at the same time less scarce substitutes will be found. Glass fibers or microwaves will be used in place of copper, being more effective for transmission of signals, as well as less expensive. At an extreme it is said that there is no use going to the expense of conserving the forests, for wood is being replaced with plastic for many uses, and paper is better made with cultivated fast-growing trees.

Every week the press carries the news of an impending invention that will dispense with some other material, or at least use it more economically. The substitution is always in one direction—toward the lower cost, more generally available, material: acrylic for wool, corn oil in the form of margarine for butter. And often the substitute is better as well as cheaper. Thus, more people require more goods, and so more raw materials of every kind, and while this might disturb engineers who live in a world of fixed proportions, economists bet on flexibility; they show how substitution under the impulse of the price system can adapt to any shortcoming of nature.

Even without substitution, a small rise in price will cause more of most raw materials to appear on the market. Higher prices cause people to look more diligently, and they find unsuspected sources—oil in the Arctic Ocean and the North Sea, nickel in a dozen countries where once it was exploited in Canada only. And with higher prices existing materials are used more sparingly: thinner coatings on tin cans, less gasoline per mile of travel, less land per ton of wheat. Now that safety and comfort are taken for granted, the locus of competition among the world's aircraft manufacturers centers on fuel economy.

The euphoria of technical progress

News items on technical wonders are the stuff that fills the press. At the end of 1988, it was widely reported that a new transatlantic cable, using optical glass fibers rather than copper, will now be able to carry 40,000 simultaneous conversations in clear and reliable transmission, and that other such cables are under construction, across both the Atlantic and the Pacific. Glass is certainly more available than copper. And as for paper, the need for which contributes to the destruction of the world's forests, we learned in 1988 that *kenaf* is coming into commercial production; it produces a whiter, tougher, more durable paper that is easier on the eyes than newsprint made from trees. Kenaf makes much more efficient use of earth and sunlight than do the wild tree species for which it substitutes.

We are back to the euphoric view of the eighteenth century Enlightenment. Adam Smith was of the eighteenth century and an optimist—population was self-regulating. But after him economics became known as the dismal science because it said that each increase in production would be nullified by a corresponding increase in population, so the average welfare could not in the long run increase. Malthus, Ricardo, the Mills saw population as setting the limit to progress, though they differed in their estimates of the capacity of people to restrain their fertility. With a different rationale neoclassical economics is now back to Adam Smith, even to the mercantilists; Jean Bodin's "there is no wealth but men" (*De la République*, 1577) is what Julian Simon (1981) is now telling us.

Underlying the neoclassical view is confidence in the ability to innovate—to create new marvels and bring them into economic production. In a competitive economy the enterprising innovators who exploit new science will always be forthcoming.

This intoxication with the process of invention became widespread by the 1950s and 1960s. The word "Malthusian" came to mean a narrow, short-sighted niggardliness, a meaning it had always had in France, whose lands were more ample than those of Britain. A Malthusian, as Alfred Sauvy uses the term, is an over-cautious person fearful of apparent limits to resources, lacking confidence in future inventiveness and adaptation. He shows personal timidity in his fear of marrying and having a family.

It is in the realm of food supplies, the original Malthusian check, that limits are now least believable for Europeans and Americans. Bitter contentions arise among nations on how to dispose of surpluses of grain, chickens, wine, and other foodstuffs without causing a price collapse. With their attention mainly on the developed countries, and certainly disregarding Africa, economists can indeed say that the shortage of food has been definitively overcome. Similarly with other materials. In the eighteenth century, when Britain was running short of firewood, the crisis was overcome with coal. Nuclear energy from fission will supply stationary power; for automobiles, fusion and the hydrogen economy are waiting in the wings, with assurances that they will be ready for use long before oil and gas are exhausted.

Capital and skilled labor seem indefinitely substitutable for land. Hence it looks right to drop the classical "land" as a factor out of the production equation. I argue that this applies at most to the developed countries that are concerned about population decline, that inventions which increase their carrying capacity (however defined) simultaneously decrease the carrying capacity of the less developed countries. The sequence of inventions provides a solution to the problem of overpopulation appropriate to those countries where the problem is already solved by birth control practiced by couples who find children inconvenient.

The matter is summed up in the *World Development Report* of 1984: "The difficulties caused by rapid population growth are not primarily due to finite natural resources, at least not for the world as a whole" (World Bank, 1984: 80). The last clause is important; in a well-managed world the sequence of inventions and their application would provide for any population that is likely to come into existence.

No overall management is in sight. Moreover, each of the less developed countries has its own problems. For most the current stream of inventions has brought grave drawbacks; they have felt the bad side of the substitution process, the devaluation of their traditional exports. With a few conspicuous exceptions they do not have the capacity to switch over to modern technology on the scale required. Each one needs to be studied to judge how much benefit it would obtain from population restraint.

The perspective of less developed countries

The sequence of substitutions, starting with fertilizer for land in food production and of synthetics for land in the production of natural fibers, seems endless. The evidence of abundance is seen in the market prices of minerals as well as of farm products. The colonial period came to an end just as many of the goods that Europeans sought in the tropics—rubber, sisal, jute, kapok—were replaced by synthetics. Britain, the most farseeing of the colonial powers, made only token attempts to hold its colonies after World War II, sensing that their products could be replaced. Let the former colonial subjects be independent, Britain in effect said, so that they can have the troubles of managing economies based on rubber, tin, and jute. Why hold on to an economy based on tea when Coca Cola is cheaper to produce and more in demand? Sugar is in glut worldwide, and tropical cane has no advantage over beets. The Netherlands did not foresee this immediately, but after

forced decolonization they have replaced many of the products of the In-
dies—rubber, hemp, quinine—with more satisfactory products turned out
by modern factories.

President Sukarno once proposed a ten-year worldwide halt to all science and invention. One can imagine such a proposal greeted with enthusi-
asm in some circles, but hardly in the developed countries. We should try to
understand why many officials of less developed countries do not share the
industrialized world's confidence in technology.

If research is a competitive process among countries, each will try to
find substitutes for what it buys, not for what it produces. In the struggle to
determine the direction of science, the less developed countries come out
badly. Scientists everywhere follow where the track of discovery leads them,
but not independently of the national authorities who provide funding. The
science of the advanced countries is available to the less developed countries, but the application of science requires knowledge, organization, and
capital. In a time when capital is flowing from the poor to the rich countries
(for the years 1983–87 in the net amount of $93 billion—World Bank, 1988:
30), investment funds in the less developed countries are very tight.

Later I will discuss the limits capital sets on the capacity of countries
to grow economically at the same time as they grow demographically,
and then I will take up the matter of organization, specifically in relation to
employment.

A reversal in a fundamental principle
of economics

An outsider can well be surprised that a proposition so basic to all economics up to about 1960 has since then not only been qualified but has been
reversed, virtually replaced by its opposite. Those of us who have been looking for some cumulation in social science—especially in economics, which
has been the most hopeful—cannot but be discouraged by the sudden turn.
Were Ricardo, Malthus, and their successors down to Gunnar Myrdal dull-
witted, incapable of observing what was going on in the world?

It is the world that has changed. Communication, the conquest of
space, computing, the new cellular biology, atomic physics, were indeed
changing the world at exactly the time when economists discovered human
capital.

Nonlinearity

The population of Africa is expected to grow about three times from now to
2025. We do not live in a linear world, and extrapolation to the future that
tells us that Africa's problems will be multiplied by three could be deceptive;
they could be multiplied by 27, the third power of the population.

For an example of nonlinearity as well as nonsubstitutability, consider water. Arid regions depend on fossil water, and in some parts of the world it is necessary to descend 100 meters or more to reach the deposits. There comes a point at which the underground reservoir is used up, and at that point linear extrapolation fails. One need not be a science fiction devotee to accept that the stream of invention will continue. But somewhere there are limits to what invention can do: just as it cannot make space, so it cannot produce fresh water on an economic scale. Finding food plants that can thrive on sea water is more hopeful than finding enough energy to duplicate the sun's work of distilling the oceans, but we do not know how feasible that will be. So far, turning deserts into tillable land has been possible on a very small scale only, and even that will be limited in time by shortage of underground water. But let us overlook, as part of the unfinished business of science, the uncertainty that nonlinearities introduce.

Capital sets limits to growth

The turn from the dark pessimism of the classical economists to neoclassical optimism was not yet complete by the 1960s. Following the work of Coale and Hoover (1958), it became customary to say that resources set no limit on absolute population numbers, but shortage of capital does. Capital was no longer the loom constructed by the village carpenter, on which the village wives and daughters could weave cloth for local consumption; that kind of homemade capital could not survive in the face of automated looms abroad. Less developed countries could no longer convert without limit their simple, largely rural labor into capital; capital was something purchased from the city, in great part brought from overseas. And the amount that could be bought depended on savings, which could be greater for a couple with two children than for a couple with five or more. The cost of feeding, clothing, and educating children reduced the family's and the community's savings.

More important than this, the grown child had to be equipped with capital if he was to earn a living; the more additional workers who had to be so equipped the less capital for buying the new kinds of equipment that would transform and modernize the economy. So it was still important for less developed countries to restrain their reproduction, even if science could produce unlimited resources.

That opinion held for a decade or two, but then neoclassical economics took a further turn that largely nullified even this reason for controlling population. Savings of households were not important; what counted was undistributed profits of enterprises, and these did not depend on how many children people had. Moreover, invention would not only dispense with any limits set by land and natural resources, it would also make capital cheaper. More reliable and more durable equipment, insofar as it lasted longer, could not only save labor but could also be cheaper per year of service. Besides that, many of the gains in productivity in the advanced countries were found to depend little on capital, and much on the operation on the shop floor. Whole warehouses of spare parts could be eliminated by the Japanese system of "just-in-time" delivery from the parts plant to the assembly plant.

In the 1950s and 1960s we read much about ICOR (the Incremental Capital–Output Ratio), in effect a production function hinging on capital alone. In this adaptation of the Harrod–Domar model (Lewis, 1954), each three dollars (or some similar amount) of capital invested would produce a stream of income equal to one dollar per year. That supposed indefinite amounts of labor waiting only for capital to summon it into the modern sector. It almost seemed as though the development process could be ignited only with capital (in practice, capital from abroad). But this model has not been durable, and in Kelley's (1988) detailed review article it receives no mention. The stress on financial and physical capital fitted a period of heavy borrowing by less developed countries, a period that came to a sudden end in the early 1980s. Human rather than physical capital now dominates development thinking.

Such considerations influenced not only public thinking about economics, but also the technical models. Where production functions used to contain land, labor, and capital in symmetrical array, they now emphasize labor. The skill of labor has been increasingly important, as the term "human capital" implies. One implication of this expression is that people can substitute for physical capital. (Yet as Herman Daly points out, a house-builder lacking saws cannot make up for this by hiring more carpenters.)

That step seemed to remove the last of the limits to growth. If people—human capital—are the dominant agent of production, then there can be no such thing as too many people. With each added person there is the same addition to product as for the previous person. So much for John Stuart Mill's declining productivity as population grows beyond a certain optimum.

Of course the matter is not so simple. As Hicks (1946) told us long ago, the growth of population occurred simultaneously with the economic development of the West, and could have been part of its cause. Mikhail Bernstam reminds us that population growth did produce a cheap and mobile labor force and strong demand for industrial goods. The division of labor depends on the size of the market, of which population is one factor. Given the institutions that will take advantage of these circumstances, the capital-diluting effect of larger populations could be more than offset. This offsetting occurs especially when investment is directed into physical capital that embodies more efficient industrial technology. Human capital not only means more productive labor but also has an effect in directing investment toward the technological growing points.

What is important is that financial capital does not come easily to the less developed countries. Most have already stretched their credit beyond all caution. What is the debt crisis in such countries all about if not that capital is truly scarce? American and German banks counted on the development process to make the less developed countries rich enough to be able to repay their loans with ease. (They also counted on net imports of manufactured goods from those countries to service the debt—without reflecting that that would ruin many manufacturing industries in advanced economies. What they did not count on was that the rhythm of development is of a lower order of speed than the rhythm of debt accumulation.) It was the internal political pressure to make employment for the growing labor forces of less developed countries that as much as anything impelled the overborrowing. That will be the third of my four kinds of limit.

I leave the resources question with mild optimism, and the capital issue with serious doubts, and go on to two other points that constitute obstacles to population and welfare. These apply even if the succession of mechanical marvels was unlimited and the less developed countries could make all their own physical capital or buy it with current exports. One is the capacity of countries to share the work and the product under rapid population increase, the other is the capacity of the planet to absorb the effluents of progress.

Economic participation of a growing population

According to the classical economists there can be no unemployment. Just as the market will reach equilibrium prices that will clear all goods, so it will clear all labor. This law was put in its most unqualified form by Jean-Baptiste Say in 1803 and reiterated by virtually every economist up to the 1930s. Thus Alfred Marshall (1879: 34), "The whole of a man's income is expended in the purchase of services and commodities . . . [A] man purchases labor and commodities with that portion of his income which he saves just as much as he does with that which he is said to spend." Each person is creating employment with the whole of his earnings, and the recipient of these likewise; the circulation of goods and money leaves no room for unemployment. In Taussig's (1917) words, "The money which is put by . . . leads equally to the employment of labor [with the money that is directly spent on goods]." Commodity markets look after the disposal of goods, capital markets reconcile savings and investment, labor markets get everyone who wants work into a job.

Just the same there was long an underground in economics that doubted the capacity of markets to do all these things. J. A. Hobson declared that oversaving results in underconsumption, a thought that is also to be found in Malthus and Marx. This underground emerged to orthodoxy in the work of Keynes (1936) and suddenly underconsumption was no longer an *idée fixe* of cranks. Because liquidity is desired, the market-clearing rate of interest is set higher than the marginal productivity of capital, so people will try to save more than entrepreneurs want to invest.

Yet in discovering the cause Keynes could point to the remedy: suitable monetary and especially fiscal policies would create demand, raise the marginal productivity of capital, and get the unemployed back to work. For the first time respectable economics assigned governments an active role, far beyond the maintenance of order. By the prosperous 1960s this idea had so taken that economists spoke of "fine-tuning" the economy. With this condition the optimism of Say and Marshall could be restored. Under no circumstances was unemployment ever a sign of too many people, but only of bad policies.

Yet in fact persisting mechanisms seem to be keeping some people out of the economy. In Italy unemployment of the younger age groups reaches 30 percent, and does not decline even amid the general prosperity. It is true that in Italy there is unexampled rigidity in the labor market. It is so expensive for an employer to dismiss a worker that he will go to great lengths to hold down hiring new employees. Italians talk about the difficulty that youth has to insert itself (*inserirse* is the usual word) into the labor force, somehow to come to participate in the economy. Once inside the person is employed for life at an above-equilibrium wage, so it is almost as though there were two kinds of people—the permanently employed and the permanently unemployed. To an observer the unemployment of the young is a simple consequence of the old hanging onto their jobs and their high wages, irrespective of competence and diligence, in which they are protected both by the law and by unions. Governments listen to those who are safely in employment, not to those who are trying to get in. Does that prove there are too many people? I will try to answer this question.

The wall that protects the jobholders

Imagine a city with plenty of land, capital, and jobs, and full employment, surrounded by a high wall. Outside the wall are many young people, with no chance of access to the economy within the city because it is the preserve of those already in place. A policy analyst must say in this situation that either the wall should be broken down or the young people should go away. Either one of these is the solution to the employment problem.

The wall that I speak of is the set of laws, regulations, and practices that include minimum (and more generally above-equilibrium) wages, tenure, and requirements of admission to professions that have nothing to do with personal performance. In milder form they exist in the United States, but because they are milder the amount of unemployment they cause is less. They exist in less developed as well as in more developed countries, in rich countries like Sweden as well as in poor ones like Indonesia. Even where the advantages of a free market are most clearly understood, no one wants his own labor to be disposed by the market (Polanyi, 1944), and people agree to secure the benefit of commodity markets without subjecting themselves to the discomfort of labor markets.

In rich countries the unemployed are well supported by the working community, which pays its taxes because it is at least half aware that its own restrictive practices are the cause of the others being unemployed. In West Germany the unemployed are a substantial fraction of the labor force and receive for long periods state incomes that are 80 percent of what they would earn if they were working. The community apparently prefers to arrange things so that a part of it is working and supporting the other part, rather than all of it working shorter hours. (The unions place impossible conditions on any proposal to share the work; their condition for a 35–hour week is in effect an immediate increase of 15 percent in the already above-equilibrium hourly wage.)

It is also argued that the consumption of the unemployed is needed to keep up demand. If the unemployed all emigrated to another country, some of those presently employed would lose their jobs. This argument is incorrect. The taxes levied for the support of the unemployed could simply be paid to those working, who would increase their consumption accordingly. The unemployed have indeed a function as consumers as things now stand, but this function would willingly be taken over by those who are working. In fact everything would be much simpler; the taxes to support the unemployed would simply not be collected but spent by the taxpayers themselves.

If nothing can tear down that wall protecting the jobs of the people who are in the labor force, then is the excluded population not in excess of the needs of the walled-in city? And would the people in the city not be better off if they did not have those people on their conscience and on their welfare rolls? And is this not a case for birth control? I submit that the sight of the unemployed, of what looks like superfluous population, is one of many factors that have a bearing on the willingness of parents to have children. It certainly makes the state tolerant of low birth rates and intolerant of immigration.

Employment in the less developed countries

It is in poor countries that the employment problem takes on a grim aspect that hardly applies in the advanced welfare state just described. Powerful political forces make laws that give the employed a permanent hold on their jobs. Once a young man or woman is appointed assistant in an Indonesian university (that can happen before the bachelor's degree) and holds on for one year, he or she has the job for life. There is no force or accident that can remove him—no amount of incompetence or failure to perform makes an acceptable case for dismissal. One dean I know attempted to install a rule that a teacher had to show up on the campus at least once a month or he would lose his tenure; the attempt failed.

Everywhere the concern for those who have jobs takes precedence over using the abilities of those who are unemployed. The unwillingness to allow an untrammeled labor market in the formal sector does not lead to the comfortable leisure that is unemployment in Europe, but to an informal sector in which a high percentage of the labor force maintains itself—that is a truly competitive labor market. Above it is a formal sector that is even more distant from the competitive ideal than is West Germany. That the countries which are prospering—the newly industrializing countries, or NICs—set the example of free markets does not influence their poorer neighbors. Deregulation is now fashionable everywhere, but is has not so far greatly affected employment.

The result is a pervasive hopelessness of youth in less developed countries everywhere from Egypt to Mexico to Indonesia. Not a day passes but one sees in the press the political pressures that this engenders. Speaking of North Africa, *The Economist* (26 Nov.–2 Dec. 1988) says, "Runaway growth of population, and of cities, has placed time-bombs all along the southern coast of the Mediterranean. The streets are filling with unemployed, frustrated youngsters. To keep them quiet, governments cling to subsidies and price-controls, which make things worse and prevent job-creating growth."

What sorts of institutional pressures result from rapidly growing population? One possibility (NRC, 1986) is that population growth forces the abandonment of regulation and the privatization of common property. Another is that population pressure and food shortages force price-fixing that makes the shortages worse; examples of this latter are much easier to find than of real deregulation and privatization.

One has to believe the unanimous judgments along the same lines of observers from 30 or 40 countries. What is reported is a dangerous interaction between the new generation, produced by the high fertility and low mortality of the last 20 years, on the one side, and the rigidity of the labor market on the other, with its consequences for economic policy and ultimately for political stability.

Young people attend university in the hope of qualifying themselves for entry into the protected job market, and when they finish they cannot be placed. They go back to school with the thought that a further diploma will enable them to scale the heights of the formal sector, and moreover the time they lose by further schooling is not worth much anyway.

In this situation social order becomes a national preoccupation. It is this as much as anything that makes authoritarian rule an apparently unavoidable stage of development. Those countries that lack firm rule are upset by riots and threatened riots.

When the existing jobholders are protected, the private sector is reluctant to take on more people than it absolutely needs, so recruitment in the entry occupations falls off, affecting mostly the young. In countries where there was a huge increase in births surviving past infancy starting in the 1950s and 1960s, that is, in practically all of the less developed countries, the number of youth so affected is overwhelming. Add to that the rapid expansion of education in the 1970s, so that the young people left out are better qualified than their elders who have jobs, and one starts to have an idea of the potentially unsettling consequences of recent population growth.

Try to tell the administrator of a country which has extended its credit to the limit that physical capital is not important for employment, that human capital alone is what counts! He sees the shortage of real capital as an absolute barrier to employment, to income, and ultimately to social stability. The Indonesian Minister for Economic Affairs, Radius Prawiro, put the matter simply: "At home," he says, "our biggest problem is to create jobs for the steadily increasing labor force." And then, "Jobs can be created only by increasing investments" (quoted in *Jakarta Post*, 16 December 1988, p. 1).

The less developed countries want birth control: Are they ignorant of their own needs?

Some have said that the authorities in less developed countries are pursuing birth control only because Westerners have urged them to do so. That gives far too much credit to the Westerners—I personally can provide assurance that they do not have that degree of influence. The drive for birth control comes from within the less developed countries, and the employment problem is mentioned far more than any other as the reason. Next to that comes natural resources. The arguments cited above showing that resources set no limit to population apply to the industrialized countries and at most to the world as a whole. Poor countries that lack financial capital by no means see their salvation in a chain of inventions that will overcome their limits of land and minerals.

I have discussed three aspects of the need for a limit on population. Resource substitution depends on technological capacity that is much harder for poor countries to achieve than for rich ones. Physical capital is available in rich countries; it is desperately short in poor ones. Young people lacking access to the jobs for which they have been trained are increasingly a problem in the poor countries and make further additions to the population dangerous for civil order.

If these three problems were overcome, could a larger population than now exists flourish in the less developed countries? No. To see why not, we come to a fourth problem that no likely technical advance and no amount of capital in sight can dispose of—a universal national problem that is also a global problem.

Humans as a large-scale geologic force

The title of this final section is due to V. I. Vernadsky, the Russian geographer writing in the 1920s, as quoted in SSRC (1988). Thus, "human activities are now inducing change on a scale comparable to the natural cycles of the earth." The Social Science Research Council speaks of "the erosion of soils, the pollution of the air of cities, the hazards of earthquakes in builtup areas, the genetic dangers of biochemical control of weeds and pests, and the longterm menace of rising global mean temperatures" and complains that these concerns have not sufficed to bring social scientists into the needed research endeavors.

The economy exists within a larger setting

Certain future events now coming into view are not provided for in any economic or social science model. The economy is set within the ecology, is surrounded as it were by the ecology, influences the ecology, and is limited by the ecology. Perhaps because they were closer to nature than contemporary social scientists, the early economists never forgot the habitat within which the economy sits. Alfred Marshall considered biology the natural science to which economics ought to be closest, but since his time that has not often been heard.

Nonacademic observers of today come closer to this theme than do social scientists. *The New Yorker* (28 August 1988) speaks of "the decimation by air pollution and acid rain of the forests along the crest of the Appalachians; the presence of so much floating sewage (some of it medical) on the edge of the Eastern Seaboard that long stretches of public beaches have had to be closed; a drought so far-ranging and sustained as to qualify 40 percent of the counties in the United States as disaster areas; and, worldwide, the hottest temperatures in the hundred and thirty years that anyone has been counting." (Four of the hottest years of the century have come in the 1980s.) More-extended accounts of such limits of the capacity to sustain population can be found in Barney (1981), Ehrlich and Ehrlich (1970), Meadows et al. (1972), Clark (1988), and Clark and Munn (1986).

Warming of the biosphere

At any given level of living and with given technology, the amount of automobile emissions, the amount of water used, the amount of oil consumed, will be proportional to the population. As Kingsley Davis has reminded us, it is people that produce and consume these things.

And it appears that the planet can stand only so much of these products of the economy. James Hansen, head of NASA's Goddard Institute for Space Studies, testifying to a Senate committee on the hottest summer in the past 130 years, said that "it is time to stop waffling ... and say that the evidence is pretty strong that the greenhouse effect is here."

Others have expanded on the effects of the warming trend, some positive, some negative. If it is sustained, the strongest negative effects would be on rainfed agriculture in the less developed countries (Gleick, 1988). Many existing agricultural lands in the United States and the Soviet Union could become desert, while the more northerly parts of these two countries and of Canada will benefit. The Arctic could become open sea for at least part of each year. The oceans would rise, both because their waters would expand on warming and because of the melting of the polar ice caps. Flat coastal lands would become dangerously vulnerable to storms, in the way that Bangladesh already is. Many of the international river basins would suffer reduced flow, and this would contribute to disputes among the riparian states on the division of the smaller amount of water.

On an optimistic assessment there would be no net effect—the good results of warming would be just equal to the bad. Even in this unlikely case the world still faces an enormous problem. For the distribution of population over the face of the Earth has evolved in some sort of rough relation to the productivity of soil and climate in the various parts. Over most of human time those parts of the planet whose soil was more fertile tended to have more people. We need not exaggerate the correspondence, for many other factors entered, and there are many cases, as Ester Boserup tells us, when it was not the fertility of the soil that created the people, but the exceptional effort of people that made the soil fertile. Still, starting from the present baseline, one can imagine the dislocation if the grain output of the Soviet Union were to double at the same time as that of India and Africa were to drop by 50 percent.

Sustainable development and ecological borrowing

That the economy is set within the ecology is recognized in the concept of sustainable development, vague and undefined perhaps, but now so respectable that the United Nations has a book on it, with others coming. In the titles of these books appear such phrases as "Waste Water Management," "Airborne Sulfur Pollution," "Potentially Toxic Chemicals."

These and other hazards are charges against the economy, though not calculated as such. To exorcise them will require effort and expense, and much of that future expense will pay for income that we have already enjoyed. In short, some of our past income was borrowed; we were not and are not as rich as we thought. Whether it is damage to the ozone layer that we must seek to repair (though no one knows quite how) or poisoned streams, or dying forests, some sacrifice will be required in the future—either we will have to pay to clean or repair them, or else the damage to them will make production more costly (as in the loss of forests), or else there will be sacrifice of amenities.

In the words of the Brundtland Commission (World Commission on Environment and Development, 1987) "sustainable development is that development that meets present needs without compromising the ability of future generations to meet their needs." We are not borrowing any less because we are ignorant of the amount of the loan. For some kinds of borrowing, estimates can be made. Malcolm Slesser and Jane King (1988) have published estimates for energy.

Perhaps a calculation can be made of the cost of cleaning up rivers, because such cleanups have actually been undertaken in various parts of Europe. But the cost of forest dieback will depend on success in finding substitutes for wood. Nothing can replace the forests in their function of absorbing carbon dioxide. Nor is there any way to reconstruct the varieties of cultivated plants that have been abandoned, nor the wild plant and animal species that human activities have rendered extinct. It would be an anticlimax to discuss the general untidiness that goes with progress. Americans have a high tolerance of beer cans, bottles, and old newspapers on the streets, and abandoned refrigerators and automobiles in the woods. Europeans have less tolerance for these things.

The point is relevant to the present argument in that it is people who produce carbon dioxide and destroy the forests of the Amazon to gain (not very long-lasting) farmland. At present the number of those who drive automobiles and otherwise live a middle-class existence is about one billion of the 5 billion on the planet, and it is this billion who do more than their share to threaten the biosphere. What will be the "geological forces" unleashed on the planet under present development trends with the 8 billion middle-class people that economic planners expect by 2025?

No one knows for sure whether the greenhouse effect is here or whether it will be offset by something else. We do know that increased carbon dioxide is in the atmosphere, and it will not be absorbed into the oceans for thousands of years. But it is also possible that the contrails of jet planes and other human activity increase the cloud cover and so have a cooling effect that will just save us from the warming due to carbon dioxide. If that miraculous coincidence gets us out of the greenhouse effect, we will still have all the other problems of the global environment to deal with.

What makes these intractable is that the problems are created by activities that benefit individuals, corporations, or nations, while their costs are global. A trader or a country can risk shipping dangerous chemicals for use as insecticides; if the ship arrives he or it gets the benefit; if it sinks the ocean is contaminated, and the cost is spread among many countries. Where benefits are concentrated within a nation, and costs are supranational, national sovereignty makes effective action virtually impossible. In principle a package of environmental measures might be assembled, including matters ranging from acid rain to nuclear waste from which every country would derive net benefit. The difficulty of negotiating such a package is daunting, and even if it were agreed on, how does one prevent sovereign nations from cheating?

Conclusion

After more than a century and a half in which generation after generation of economists proved that a large population was deleterious to development, the discipline has gone into reverse and argued that population does not make much difference. Whatever the overt argument for this, its real justification is that the march of science and resulting economic innovation permit a substitution of common resources for scarce ones, so that resource limits to population have largely disappeared.

This reversal of economic theory corresponds to the reversal of the population problem for the developed countries—the one-fifth of the world that is facing population decline. The French, the English, the German, and the American publics readily agree—they have been saying it themselves since the 1960s—that the issue raised by Malthus is decreasingly applicable to them. Neoclassical economics has indeed indicated the solution to the problem of too many people—applicable to the countries where the problem no longer exists. (I optimistically disregard polluted streams, forest dieback, and a corrosive atmosphere, supposing that the wealth of Europe and America can clean these up at the present levels of population.)

The less developed countries contain four-fifths of the world population, are responsible for nine-tenths of present population growth, and can expect 100 percent of the world's population growth in the coming century. They do not have the spare land, or the capital, to accommodate their burgeoning citizenry. The demand for their raw materials constituted the economic basis on which they started their upward course, and now the science of the developed countries has invented substitutes that undercut even that basis.

One could say that the less developed countries are in the position that the developed ones were in when Malthus, Ricardo, Mill, and the other classical economists lived, except that the position of many is much worse. Not only do they face resource limits as Europe did, but their populations are orders of magnitude greater, and they have installed systems of mass education that give their young people expectations incompatible with available resources and capital. Recall how the contemporaries of Malthus, though not Malthus himself, feared the spread of education as socially unsettling. Contemporary students do not obtain from college the skills of the best Western engineers and scientists, but one thing they do get from college: the highest of expectations. The poor countries could not fully employ their young people when their net borrowing was at its peak; what about now when they are paying back?

The last thing they want or need is the prospective further growth in their unemployed youth. They see a birth today as a young man or woman with a high school or college diploma in 2010, unable to get the job for which he or she was supposedly trained.

Modern science, which has produced the substitutes (for rubber, sisal, cane sugar) from which the poor economies are suffering, affects them very differently from the way it affects the industrialized countries. They do not have the high-level scientific manpower to understand, import, and apply it, let alone to discover new science that will be appropriate to their particular problems. And even if their educational systems produced young people with the knowledge and skill that was consonant with their expectations, as their debt service increases they have less of the capital that would enable them to put that knowledge and skill to work. That is why they see the neo-classical view that the population problem is essentially solved as a monumental ethnocentrism.

So much for the first three points of my argument. Let me offer a scenario that will clarify the fourth point. It is improbable but not inconceivable, the possible endpoint within the first quarter of the twenty-first century of a trend that is already visible today.

A final scenario for Planet Earth

Suppose that by 2025 the economic problem is everywhere solved (Keynes's [1932] expression) in the sense that gross national product per capita is growing at more than 3 percent per year and either there is full employment or the unemployed are comfortably supported on social security. All of the standard statistical indexes indicate unprecedented prosperity.

Meanwhile the atmosphere is warming and rainfall patterns are changing, deserts are continuing to spread at the same rate as in the 1980s and have come to cover the larger part of the planet, water tables everywhere are falling, holes in the ozone layer are rapidly increasing cancer deaths, locust and other pest outbreaks are more and more frequent, all the tropical forests have disappeared, and the last of the boreal forests are threatened. Among other irreversible changes half of the plant and animal species existing 50 years earlier have become extinct.

As has always been the convention, gross national product can continue to rise because it is calculated gross of all depreciation; for national income the depreciation of plant and equipment is netted out, but not the deterioration of nature. The greater part of the very high national incomes has to be spent on disposing of wastes, on replanting of trees, on transporting water, on making dikes against the incursions of the oceans, on fighting pests, on restoring soils. These are all entered on the plus side of the national income, but the deterioration that they are (partially) correcting is nowhere subtracted. National accounts measure the sustainability of our activities insofar as they depend on plant and equipment, but make no pretense of measuring sustainability insofar as they depend on nature. (See the excellent review of national income and product accounts by Eisner, 1988.)

In this scenario people would feel poorer and poorer despite the assurance offered by steadily rising income per capita. And with other things fixed, every one of the unmeasured negative elements mentioned above is related to population.

References

Barney, Gerald O. (ed.). 1981. *The Global Two Thousand: Report to the President.* New York: Pergamon.

Boserup, Ester. 1987. "Population and technology in preindustrial Europe," *Population and Development Review* 13, no. 4: 691–701.

Clark, William C. 1988. "The human dimensions of global environmental change," unpublished manuscript.

———, and R. E. Munn. 1986. *Sustainable Development of the Biosphere.* Cambridge: Cambridge University Press.

Coale, Ansley J. and Edgar M. Hoover. 1958. *Population Growth and Economic Development in Low-Income Countries.* Princeton, N.J.: Princeton University Press.

Daly, Herman E. 1986. Review of *Population Growth and Economic Development: Policy Questions,"* in *Population and Development Review* 12, no. 3: 582–585.

———. 1988. "On sustainable development and national accounts," in D. Collard, D. Pierce, and D. Ulph (eds), *Economics and Sustainable Environments: Essays in Honor of Richard Lecomber.* New York: Macmillan.

Ehrlich, Paul R., and Anne H. Ehrlich. 1970. *Population, Resources, Environment.* San Francisco: W. H. Freeman.

Eisner, Robert. 1988. "Extended accounts for national income and product," *Journal of Economic Literature* 24, no. 4: 1611–1684.

Geertz, Clifford. 1963. *Agricultural Involution: The Processes of Ecological Change in Indonesia.* Berkeley: University of California Press.

Gleick, Paul H. 1988. "Global climatic changes and geopolitics: Pressures on developed and developing countries," unpublished manuscript.

Hicks, John R. 1946. *Value and Capital.* Oxford University Press.

Kelley, Allen C. 1988. "Economic consequences of population change in the Third World," *Journal of Economic Literature* 24, no 4: 1685–1728.

Keyfitz, Nathan. 1972. "Population theory and doctrine: A historical survey," in William Petersen (ed.), *Readings in Population.* New York: Macmillan, pp. 41–69.

———. 1984. "World population growth: Demographic and economic realities," *Issues in Science and Technology.*

Keynes, John Maynard. 1963. "Prospects for our grandchildren," In *Essays in Persuasion.* New York: W. W. Norton (first published 1932).

———. 1973. *The General Theory of Employment, Interest, and Money.* London and New York: Macmillan (first published 1936).

Kuznets, Simon. 1967. "Population and economic growth," *Proceedings of the American Philosophical Society 3,* no. 3: 170–193.

Leibenstein, Harvey. 1954. *Theory of Economic-Demographic Development.* Westport, Conn.: Greenwood Press.

———. 1971. "The impact of population growth on economic welfare—nontraditional elements," in National Academy of Sciences, *Rapid Population Growth: Consequences and Policy Implications.* Baltimore, Md.: Johns Hopkins University Press, pp. 175–198.

Lewis, W. Arthur. 1954. "Economic development with unlimited supplies of labor," *Manchester School of Economics and Social Studies 22,* no. 2: 139–192.

———. 1955. *Theory of Economic Growth.* Homewood, Ill.: R. D. Irwing.

Marshall, Alfred. 1879. *The Pure Theory of Domestic Values.* London School of Economics, Reprints of Source Tracts.

Meadows, Donella H., et al. 1972. *The Limits to Growth.* New York: Universe Books.

Myrdal, Gunnar. 1968. *Asian Drama.* New York: Pantheon Books.

National Research Council (NRC), Working Group on Population Growth and Economic Development, Committee on Population. 1986. *Population Growth and Economic Development: Policy Questions.* Washington, D.C.: National Academy Press.

Polanyi, Karl. 1944. *The Great Transformation.* New York: Reinhart & Co. Inc.

Repetto, Robert. 1986. *World Enough and Time: Successful Strategies for Resource Management.* New Haven, Conn.: Yale University Press.

———, et al. (eds). 1985. *The Global Possible: Resources, Development, and the New Century.* New Haven, Conn.: Yale University Press.

Rockwell, Richard C. 1988. "Human processes in earth transformation," Social Science Research Council, *Items 42,* no. 1/2.

Rosenbluth, Gideon. 1976. "Economists and the growth controversy," *Canadian Public Policy 11,* no. 2: 225–239.

Simon, Julian L. 1981. *The Ultimate Resource.* Princeton, N.J.: Princeton University Press.

Slesser, Malcolm, and Jane King. 1988. "Resource accounting: An application to development planning," *World Development 16,* no. 2: 293–303.

Social Science Research Council (SSRC). 1988. *Items.*

Taussig, Frank W. 1917. *Principles of Economics.* New York: Macmillan.

Woodwell, George M. 1985. "On the limits of nature," in Repetto et al. (1985).

World Bank. 1984. *World Development Report 1984.* New York: Oxford University Press.

———. 1988. *World Development Report 1988.* New York: Oxford University Press.

World Commission on Environment and Development (The Brundtland Commission). 1987. *Our Common Future.* London: Oxford University Press.

Comment: The Second Tragedy of the Commons

RONALD D. LEE

SOME PEOPLE JUSTIFY POPULATION CONTROL POLICIES on the grounds that population growth reduces economic well-being. It is not clear, however, whether population growth strongly affects such economic variables as prices, incomes, unemployment, balance of trade, saving and investment, and economic growth. Recent assessments find the evidence weak and conflicting (World Bank, 1984; National Research Council, 1986; Kelley, 1988). Of course, many potential consequences of population growth would not be caught in the net of economic statistics, which mainly reflect the goods and services passing through markets. The most serious consequences of population growth may well be those afflicting nonmarket resources, particularly environmental resources and amenities. While pressure on such resources, if unabated, must eventually affect production and the economy, it need not do so discernibly for a considerable time. Analysis is further complicated because many environmental consequences are global and therefore are not evident in international comparisons of performance.

In any event, even if population growth were known to reduce the well-being of future generations, it would not automatically follow that such growth should be slowed. After all, individual couples choose their family size with full knowledge that children are costly, and that more children mean fewer parental resources available for each, and lower per capita income in the household. Is the societal view of the tradeoff between numbers and well-being, now and in the future, anything beyond the sum total of the parental views, which are implicitly represented in their individual decisionmaking about fertility? Some may argue "yes," that society should take a better-informed, less selfish, intergenerationally more egalitarian, and longer run view than individual parents. Perhaps this is so. But we will see that laissez faire in family size can lead to a socially undesirable outcome even when social goals are no different from those of parents.

The discrepancy between the laissez faire outcome and the socially optimal outcome arises because of "externalities to childbearing," that is, costs and benefits of children that are passed on by the parents to society at large. When all assets are privately owned and there are no public sector and no public goods, then such externalities do not arise.[1] In the real world there are many exceptions to these conditions (see Lee, 1988a), and externalities to childbearing are pervasive. Among the most important are environmental externalities, since many enjoyable and productive aspects of the environment are not privately owned: air shed, water shed, ozone layer, parks, climate, freedom from noise, and so on.

What are the connections among future well-being, family size externalities, and the environment? Garrett Hardin sketched them in a seminal 1969 article, writing eloquently of the "tragedy of the commons" as a metaphor for the population problem. At one time, he suggested, all villagers could freely graze their cattle on the commons. Self-interest led each villager to add more cattle until the incremental private gain to doing so fell to zero. Although each additional cow reduced the food for all other cows and thereby diminished their value, this total reduction was spread thinly over the many individual villagers, so that those adding cows bore only a small fraction of the cost. In this way, the social gains from adding cows were always less than the individual gains, and they turned negative well before the individual gains did. Consequently, the commons was overused and degraded, and each villager fared worse than he or she could have, if use had been generally lower. In this case, even if the social goal is nothing other than maximization of individual welfare, rational individual behavior will not lead to the social optimum, which can be reached only by collective regulation of use.

"Common property resources" are often taken to be those for which markets are absent or poorly developed, as in Hardin's parable. In fact, in the past such resources have typically been efficiently managed by the communities that shared their use (Runge, 1981). The problems described by Hardin arise primarily after traditional management has been weakened by modernization or after increasing intensity of use, often due to population growth, makes previously abundant resources scarce, or innocuous behaviors harmful. Such is the case today for many resources shared by communities at the local, national, and global level, including water sheds and air sheds. Common property resources have special significance, for when they are present (and ineffectively managed), social and individual interests diverge, and a laissez faire policy does not lead to socially or individually optimal outcomes.[2] Thus Hardin's metaphor of too many cows on the commons could provide a powerful rationale for an interventionist population policy.

Crowding of cities, highways, and parks, pollution of air and water, overfishing, deterioration of the ozone layer, global warming from the greenhouse effect—these problems, which are certainly exacerbated by population growth, testify to Hardin's insight. For many, they appear sufficient reason for policies to limit fertility and population. Yet the logic is not entirely clear, and this view is open to a straightforward rebuttal: that the problems are not caused by population growth per se, but rather are due to faulty institutional arrangements. They arise because many common property resources are anachronistically treated as free access, with the predictable consequence that they are overused and degraded. Rather than tackle these problems indirectly and inefficiently through population policy, which is highly uncertain and at best brings change only in the long run, we should tackle them directly through optimal resource management. This might take the form of privatization, or imposition of user fees, or rationing and licensing, taxes and subsidies for users, or outright legislated levels of use. According to this view, once the common property resources are optimally managed, they pose no greater problem for laissez faire reproduction than do privately owned resources.[3] Why not, then, adopt policies of the sort just listed and allow people to make their own fertility decisions unhindered?

In fact, though, there are two distinct problems, two tragedies of the commons. The first problem is that with a given population size, a free-access resource is subject to overuse and degradation, such that the existing population could be made better off on its own terms if use of the resource were limited.[4] This problem arises because of the institutional arrangements and can best be addressed by altering these arrangements to establish the optimal level of use. Once this is done, however, a second problem remains, for even if the level of use is regulated for the existing population, there is still free access to the resource through reproduction. The optimal level of use per person depends on the number of people. Under optimal management, when the population is larger each person will be entitled to use the resource less—to visit Yosemite less often, to turn up the volume on his stereo less high, to burn less firewood, to discharge less waste. Furthermore, with a larger population, the optimal level of total use will generally be slightly higher (although less than proportionately so) and so each person will have to live with slightly more congestion, pollution, and degradation. Because each additional person is born with a birthright to public resource use, each birth inflicts costs on all others by reducing the value of their environmental birthright. Free access through reproduction is the second tragedy of the commons.

I have said that the first tragedy of the commons is appropriately remedied by direct policies restricting access, such as user fees or regulation. What of the second? We must pause here to consider how we may evaluate the tradeoff between numbers of people and quality of life, for pointing out that a tradeoff exists does not establish that smaller populations are better than larger ones. Much has been written on this issue, but one appealing approach is to view the tradeoff through the eyes of the parents (see Nerlove et al., 1987). This approach also permits the problem to be formulated in much the way in which Hardin originally formulated the tragedy of the commons. We assume that parents care about both the number of children they have and the future welfare of their children. Thus parents, in deciding how many children to have, take into account the consequences for the future welfare of their children, and strike a balance between conflicting aims, a balance reflecting their own values and circumstances. The societal goal is taken to be nothing other than to benefit the current generation of parents on the parents' own terms, and therefore to care about future welfare exactly to the extent to which they do. Under certain circumstances, including private ownership of all resources, it can be shown that no divergence of social and private interests occurs in this case; that is, individuals cannot, through collective decisionmaking, improve on the laissez faire outcome. When there are common property or free-access resources, however, the laissez faire outcome is suboptimal, and collective decisionmaking about reproduction will enable all parents to achieve a higher level of satisfaction by restricting fertility, just as the cattle owners in the original tragedy of the commons could all do better by collectively agreeing to reduce their herds.

Some economists have argued that the problem of free access through reproduction is effectively remedied by optimal resource management policies for the existing population, say user fees. A stiff charge for the use of Yosemite National Park, for example, would convey to all potential parents a message about the constraints their children would face, and this message would provide the optimal disincentive to reproduce.[5] But this argument is fallacious. The user fees provide no childbearing disincentive, since they are a fee on use and not on procreation. The prospective child's net wealth is not reduced by the fee he or she will pay in the future, for the fees, once collected, must be used to defray park management costs or general governmental costs, or be returned to the public in one way or another. These fees simply substitute for taxes that would otherwise be raised by some other means. This point is developed in more detail in the appendix.

If the optimal management policy does not also constitute an optimal fertility policy, then some other policy must be found. Many kinds are possible, but if a financial disincentive is chosen, it must be applied directly to the fertility decision; that is, it must be a tax of some sort on births. The appropriate level of the tax would depend on how much an additional birth reduces the satisfaction of all other persons through their use of nonprivate resources, and on the number of people so affected. This point is also developed in more detail in the appendix.

So many problems pertain to a heavy tax on childbearing that I believe it is useful only as a conceptual tool, and not as a practical policy. Yet the idea might provide a useful guide to thinking about alternative, more practical policies. Here are a few of the problems raised: Would such a tax leave the rich free to have as many children as they wished, and deter only the poor? Would it be applied globally? Should the same tax be levied on a birth in Bangladesh as in the United States?

Certainly the environmental impact of a birth would depend on the wealth of the parents to whom it was born, and therefore the tax should vary with social class and nationality. Also, while the appropriate tax might make children very costly indeed, it would also lead to a disbursement of funds to the population. Other things equal (including fertility), the poor would gain at the expense of the rich, for the tax and transfer system should recognize that the children of the rich would consume a disproportionate share of the environmental birthright of the poor.[6] Within each income stratum of each nation, income would be redistributed from those with many children to those with few; and across strata and across nations, income would be redistributed from the rich to the poor.

Herman Daly (in this volume) asserts that "the market cannot find an optimal scale any more than it can find an optimal distribution"[7] and suggests that in a finite world, public policy should recognize explicitly the limits of resources and the environment and choose an optimal sustainable scale for the global economy. It is not clear what "optimal" would mean in this context. Given any sustainable level of aggregate consumption, one would still have to choose the appropriate population size and corresponding per capita level of consumption. Such decisions would be very difficult to make, defend, and enforce. But setting aside the question of optimality, it is certainly not true that the market economy is indifferent to scale. The classical economists described the convergence of the economic system to the stationary state, at which population, capital, and incomes would all cease to grow. This convergence depended on assumptions about the behavior of parents and capitalists. Many neoclassical theoretical systems likewise converge to stationary states when they include natural resources, although in fact they often ignore such resources.[8] Assumptions about the reproductive behavior of parents would determine the qualities of the endpoint of economic growth, and under the assumption of inclusive markets and altruistic parental choice, the endpoint could indeed be claimed to be an optimal scale. In this view, parents vote on the optimal scale through reproductive choice, and we, unlike Malthus in his early writings, may hope that this decision is governed by rational minds, concerned about the future welfare of their children. However, in the presence of environmental (or other) externalities, the outcome of the vote would *not* have optimal properties—and this is the thrust of Hardin's story of the commons, and of the argument I have advanced here.

Imagine, now, a policy equivalent to the hypothetical system of taxes on births, with taxes chosen to internalize the environmental costs of childbearing. Individual couples could choose a number of children consistent with their individual tastes, values, and circumstances. No particular sus-

tainable population size or individual level of fertility would be imposed by
central authorities. It is not immediately clear to what kind of equilibrium
size and level of economic activity such a policy would steer the population.
For that matter, it is not clear that the long-run outcome would be a stationary state at all. Whatever its nature, the evolution of the system would ultimately reflect the preferences of the people in it. Whatever the tradeoff
implicitly chosen between numbers and environmental quality of life, it
would be theirs. This much cannot be said of the current situation, in which
we are ineluctably driven to an environmental standard lower than we
would choose for our descendants if we were able.

Appendix: Fertility choice and policy with a congestible free-access resource

Consider the following example of a collective externality, based loosely on
Willis, 1987, pp. 666–668. Suppose a fixed homogeneous population of N people has free access to a resource. Each derives satisfaction, u, from a level of
use, e, but satisfaction is diminished by the amount of aggregate use of the
resource by others, $Z = Ne$. Thus individual utility is given by $u(e,Z)$ with $u_e >
0$, $u_Z < 0$. In the laissez faire outcome, each individual uses the resource to such
an extent that its marginal utility falls to 0 (the price of use) and accepts whatever level of Z the behavior of others imposes. (A small congestive effect on
individuals arising from their own use can be ignored here when N is large.)

The optimal level of use of the resource, however, will be less. A planner
would maximize the individual utilities by choosing e such that $U_e = -U_Z N
> 0$, thus taking into account that each unit of additional consumption of e by
an individual imposes a cost U_Z on each of the N members of the population.
The planner could appropriately regulate use by establishing a user fee (for
each unit of e) equal to $-U_Z N$. In any case, with or without optimal management, population growth worsens the problem, since Z, which yields disutil-
ity, increases monotonically with the population size. The overuse of the
resource under laissez faire is the first tragedy of the commons, and its remedy
is appropriate management.

The second tragedy of the commons arises when the population size is
not fixed, but rather depends on the fertility decisions of the current generation. Suppose the utility of potential parents is given by $u(c_1, c_2, n, e_2, Z_2)$, where
c_1 is their consumption now, c_2 is consumption by their average child in the
future, n is the number of children, and e_2 and Z_2 are defined as before, and
refer to the children's future use of the free-access resource. (The current population's use is irrelevant and is ignored.) The current generation seeks maximum utility subject to the constraint that consumption is limited by $W = c_1 +
nc_2$ (W is the wealth available for both generations and can be stored without
interest for the next generation).

The first-order condition on parent's fertility under laissez faire is $u_n/u_{c_1}
= c_2$; that is, the private cost of a child equals the child's future consumption,

which must come out of W. But the planner will also take into account that an incremental child imposes congestion costs on all others. The planner's first-order condition would be: $u_n/u_{cl} = c_2 - (u_Z/u_{cl})Ne$. The difference between the two, $(u_Z/u_{cl})(N - 1)e$, is the cost imposed (u_Z/u_{cl}) on all other parents $(N - 1)$ by the future resource use of each additional child (e). To provide the correct incentive for optimal fertility, the planner may impose a tax on each birth equal to $(u_Z/u_{cl})(N - 1)e$, where these quantities should be evaluated at their optimal levels. Now this tax is quite similar to the optimal user fee (ignoring the denominator, u_{cl}, which converts the amount from utiles to consumption units), and indeed it is the same if we multiply the expected level of use of the next generation's children, e, by the user fee. It might appear, therefore, that the optimal user fee would also provide the optimal fertility disincentive.

The problem is that the user fees which are collected must also be disbursed, and each child should receive a share precisely equal to the amount the child has to pay in user fees (since all children are identical in tastes and income). Therefore, while the user fee does provide a disincentive for use of the resource, it does not provide any disincentive whatsoever for fertility, since it cancels out of the budget constraint of current parents. An optimal user fee will not suffice to avoid the second tragedy of the commons, and it is necessary to alter childbearing incentives directly by imposing a birth tax.

Notes

1 Actually, even in this case externalities may arise because the birth rate alters the population growth rate and age distribution, which influence the rate of interest. See Lee, 1980 and 1988b and Eckstein and Wolpin, 1985. However, when a recursive altruistic utility function is assumed, as in Willis, 1987 and Nerlove et al., 1987, externalities do not occur in this case.

2 That is, to a Pareto optimal outcome, in which no one can be made better off without making someone else worse off. This sort of optimality leaves aside the question of income distribution and focuses instead on efficiency.

3 A number of economic analyses have concluded that externalities to childbearing do not occur when all resources are privately owned (Ng, 1986; Willis, 1987; Nerlove et al., 1987; Lee, 1988a). Of course, externalities transcending national borders require international cooperation on policymaking and enforcement.

4 Historically, it appears that common property resources were communally managed in one way or another, to avoid such problems. In other words, common property resources were not free-access resources.

5 See, for example, Willis, 1987, p. 671 and Ng, 1986.

6 Of course, the environmental cost of childbearing is only one of many costs, both positive and negative, that are not borne by the parents. In a recent paper I have attempted to address more generally the issue of externalities to childbearing (Lee, 1988a).

7 Daly goes on: "The latter requires the addition of ethical criteria; the former requires the further addition of ecological criteria. . . . In theory whether we double the population and the per capita resource use rate, or cut them in half, the market will still grind out a Pareto optimal allocation for every scale. Yet the scale of the economy is certainly not a matter of indifference."

8 See Pitchford, 1974 for a detailed discussion of these issues.

References

Eckstein, Zvi, and Kenneth I. Wolpin. 1985. "Endogenous fertility and optimal population size," *Journal of Public Economics* 27 (June): 93–106.

Hardin, Garrett. 1968. "The tragedy of the commons," *Science* 162 (13 December): 1243-1248.

Kelley, Allen C. 1988. "Economic consequences of population change in the Third World," *Journal of Economic Literature* 26, no.4 (December): 1685-1728.

Lee, Ronald D. 1980. "Age structure, intergenerational transfers and economic growth: An overview," *Review Économique* 31, no.6 (November): 1129–1156.

———. 1988a. "Evaluating externalities to childbearing in developing countries: The case of India," forthcoming in a volume of collected papers from the UN-INED Conference on Population and Development, New York, August 1988.

———. 1988b. "Declining fertility and aging population: Consequences for intergenerational transfers within and between households," manuscript of the Graduate Group in Demography, University of California, Berkeley.

National Research Council. 1986. *Population Growth and Economic Development: Policy Questions.* Washington, D.C.: National Academy Press.

Nerlove, Marc, Assaf Razin, and Efraim Sadka. 1987. *Household and Economy: Welfare Economics of Endogenous Fertility.* Orlando, Florida: Academic Press.

Ng, Yew-Kwang. 1986. "On the welfare economics of population control," *Population and Development Review* 12, no.2 (June): 247–266.

Pitchford, J. D. 1974. *Population in Economic Growth.* New York: American Elsevier.

Ridker, Ronald G. 1972. "Resource and environmental consequences of population growth in the United States: A summary," in US Commission on Population Growth and the American Future, *Population, Resources, and the Environment*, ed. Ronald G. Ridker. Washington, D.C.: US Government Printing Office, pp. 17–33.

Runge, Carlisle Ford. 1981. "Common property externalities: Isolation, assurance, and resource depletion in a traditional grazing context," *American Journal of Agricultural Economics* 63, no.4 (November): 595–606.

Willis, Robert. 1987. "Externalities and population," in *Population Growth and Economic Development: Issues and Evidence*, ed. D. Gale Johnson and Ronald D. Lee. Madison: University of Wisconsin Press, pp. 661–700.

World Bank. 1984. *World Development Report 1984.* New York: Oxford University Press.

Comment: The "One World" Thesis as an Obstacle to Environmental Preservation

VIRGINIA ABERNETHY

IN ITS MODERN FORM, THE ETHIC of international redistribution is expressed in such terms as "one world." Although one world has primarily an ecological meaning, the phrase also calls upon industrialized countries to assist countries of the Third World; in some contexts, one world implies an attack on the legitimacy of unevenly distributed wealth. So construed, it may in fact be incompatible with conservation goals.

The idea that conservation depends upon appropriate incentives is not new. Garrett Hardin (1968), in "The tragedy of the commons," develops the insight that a scarce resource is inevitably consumed when those who use it most intensively get the largest share. In an unregulated commons, the admonition to "use it or lose it" takes on new meaning.

Any idea or practice that treats a resource as belonging to all or as claimable on the basis of need would appear to create a commons, and thus, except perhaps under conditions of low population density, creates the possibility if not the probability of a tragedy of the commons. An ethic of equity that entails involuntary redistribution undermines the legitimacy of ownership and undercuts the incentive to save. Since saving entails self-denial and postponement of consumption to some future date, it must overcome an initial handicap. A further burden, insecurity over rights to enjoy future benefits, can be overwhelming. A resource must, therefore, be conveyed with as much certainty as social institutions can muster, namely through ownership. When tenure is not secure, individual strategies of rapid consumption defeat efforts at conservation.

Nations, like individuals, have less motivation to forgo present benefits if they doubt they will reap future rewards from their saving. One-world ideology, which implies a commitment to sustaining the needy wherever they may be, creates ambiguity over the ownership of resources. As with most "commons," it fosters a preference for short-term consumption over long-term saving.

The redistribution ethic not only undercuts incentives to conserve, but in a vastly overpopulated world may be impracticable. Uneven distribution seems a requisite of conservation under conditions where many are absolutely destitute and cannot afford to forgo consumption of their capital stock.

With respect to land, continuing redistribution produces smaller and smaller units to the point where subsistence needs overwhelm all possibility of protecting long-term viability. The threat of famine is a quite sufficient inducement for a family to plant every last hectare in food crops, which in many instances results in deforestation and the degradation of marginal lands.

Thus, ethicists need to reexamine equity issues in terms of a system that encompasses global conservation. A conservation ethic may require a renewed acceptance of uneven distribution. Conservation in the sense of future-oriented protection of the carrying capacity is preferred by those who anticipate long-term tenure and is affordable only by those nations, institutions, and individuals who are not compelled to consume their wealth, including natural capital, as a last-ditch survival strategy.

No simple formula for conservation can be drawn, however, from such observations, which suggest only that the prospect for environmental preservation depends upon characteristics of the entity that owns, uses, or otherwise controls a resource. In other words, destruction of resources may result not only from entitlements and unregulated use of those that are held in a commons, but also from numerous functional equivalents.

Affluent individuals or entities will be motivated to protect the Earth's natural resources only insofar as it is in their interest to do so. The wealthy should be prevented from despoiling one niche and moving on to another: for example, lumbering off the Brazilian rain forest, selling the denuded land, and depositing profits in a foreign bank (Cohen, 1989). In the first quarter of 1989, nationals of the Third World's 15 largest debtor nations were holding US$340 billion in foreign banks, up from less than $100 billion in 1980 (*Business Week*, 1989). Given the mobility of monetized capital, it is difficult to envision a sufficient incentive, or workable enforcement mechanism, to tie wealthy individuals to land or any particular natural resource so that they would have a stake in conserving its long-term productivity. Yet, this must eventually be part of a solution.

Nor is government a reliable repository of resources. The Brazilian government regards international efforts to protect the rain forest as intrusive; conservation is secondary to its seeing forest lands as "resources to be exploited and as space for its fast-growing population" (Cohen, 1989: A6). Government control of the entire productive enterprise can be similarly wasteful of natural resources and long-term carrying capacity and without corresponding benefit to those governed in terms of useful outputs (see Carlson and Bernstam in this volume).

The factor lacking in each of these situations is the irrevocable linkage of individual long-term benefit to a particular piece of land, resource, community, or nation. The key appears to be accountability to one's own future and that of one's children in terms of preserving carrying capacity within a niche that one can control. Without control, or with the possibility of moving on, conservation becomes unlikely if not impossible.

The variety of tenure arrangements congruent with conservation of trees could become a model for policy research. Bruce and Fortmann (in press) confirm that the expectation of enjoying a long-term benefit is a common factor in all successful conservation efforts. They show that maintaining secure, private ownership of land on which trees grow and establishing rights to land by planting trees are both conducive to conservation. Under very limited circumstances they find that a commons may be a workable arrangement; but commons seem virtually impossible to establish programmatically, and they function only if use is regulated by strong conservation traditions. Moreover, conservation traditions governing use of forest products do not survive pressure from growing populations (ibid.). The gradual movement toward more intensive and ultimately destructive use resembles the shortening of fallow periods in shifting agriculture economies beset by overpopulation (see Russell, 1988).

A final criticism of the redistributive aspect of one-world ideology is that it may undermine population-control efforts within the very countries that could most benefit from such efforts. Forty countries are estimated to rely on foreign aid for at least a quarter of their national budget (Harper's Index, 1989), no doubt reinforcing both belief in the one-world rhetoric and felt entitlement to a share in the world's resources. The resulting sense of security, although false, can only neutralize signals of local scarcity that should be warnings against further population growth.

Local scarcity within a global, one-world frame of reference, when others are richer, must seem both unfair and artificial. Any shortfalls in supply tend to be interpreted as a problem of distribution and equity rather than as a signal of limits that inevitably impinge on all. Scarcity does not act as an inducement to curtail demand if one feels entitled to a share of someone else's property. This response is especially pernicious when those others (because of their generosity) are perceived to have unlimited and renewable wealth. One-world thinking, I suggest, is a stimulus to increase, not reduce, demands. It is probably a deterrent as well to decreasing desired family size.

Diversion of international development capital to support Third World consumption has been common (Brooks, 1989) and, unfortunately, probably confirms the widespread sense of entitlement and global wealth. Moreover, even if international aid results, as intended, in economic development, recent research suggests that the fertility reduction predicted by demographic transition theory may not materialize.

I have suggested elsewhere (Abernethy, 1979) that expectations of scarcity or of unfulfilled wants may facilitate demographic change. Consider, for example, China's 1958 famine that preceded a decade of fertility-control measures as severe as any recorded in modern times. Famine would probably not have inspired such draconian measures had China been linked with the world community at the time. By its own choice, China remained isolated. News of famine barely penetrated to the Western world. Certainly no assistance was asked for or proferred. One-world thinking did not blur reality: appreciation of the scarcity of China's own resources could not have been more stark.

By contrast, one-world redistributive ideology obscures the reality that resources are finite. By encouraging overpopulated countries to tolerate further growth, it may seal their fate.

There is a similar effect when one nation is perceived to have open borders, welcoming all migrants. A country that allows itself to be used as a safety valve for others' excess population gives a counter-productive signal. If people who cannot find jobs in their own country are welcome to migrate across national boundaries, a reasonable interpretation is that resources at the destination are abundant. Such, of course, is the message sent by the very open, kinship-driven immigration policy of the United States (McConnell, 1988). This policy probably contributes to neutralizing what would otherwise be alarming signals of scarcity and overpopulation in Central America (Willis, 1984) and elsewhere (Haub, 1988). The incorrect reading defeats many other inducements to reduce fertility.

Thus, much-reduced, time-limited international aid and restrictive immigration policies in wealthier countries may be responsible and ethical approaches on several grounds. Not only would correct signals about scarcity and population growth be sent to high-fertility regions, but also the dissipation of wealth and the impact of population growth on a wealthier nation's natural resources would be avoided (costs that almost always are disproportionately borne by their own poor).

Most Western countries now adhere to restrictive immigration policies. France, known as the refugee capital of Europe, rejects 67 percent of asylum applications: "French officials claim these are economic refugees rather than victims of political persecution" (Marlow, 1989: 19). The United States alone has raised both immigration and refugee admissions in response to advocacy group pressures. For example, recent legislation waives the usual test for refugee status—"having a well-founded fear of persecution"—for nationals of the Soviet Union and Indochina; if fully funded, the program would admit such persons in unlimited numbers on the basis of being "presumed" to be refugees. This legislation traveled at high speed despite its potential billion dollar annual cost: introduced by Congressmen Morrison, Frank, Schumer, Berman, and Fish on 18 April 1989, it passed both the House of Representatives and Senate before the summer recess.

Although a restrictive immigration policy has not yet been adopted by either the executive branch or the US Congress, it may be one of the stronger means available in the short run for impressing upon Third World countries the unsustainability of their population growth rates. Moreover, limiting immigration into the United States to "replacement level" would both help protect the domestic environment and accurately reflect the average American's concern over world population growth and immigration (*Pittsburgh Press*, 1988; Hernandez and Braun, 1988). Replacement-level immigration, an all-inclusive inflow of about 200,000 annually, would slightly more than balance those entering with the number estimated to be voluntarily leaving. Complementing the below-replacement fertility level already achieved in the United States, it would lead eventually to a stationary population and at a much lower level of population than is currently assumed with, say, 600,000 immigrants per year.

I have suggested that unequal distribution, both within and among nations, is a sine qua non of conservation in a world of growing populations. Waste and degradation of natural resources seem likely to become normal practice when the private, local incentive to conserve the carrying capacity disappears. If everyone owns or uses the resource, who is going to conserve it? And who will believe in scarcity (overpopulation) so long as anyone, anywhere, is better off and professes a commitment to share?

When ownership of a natural resource is ambiguous, or the resource is inadequate, the consumption and loss of natural capital are inevitable. Thus in an overpopulated world, a redistribution ethic is inappropriate. The challenge is to develop a policy and ethic which recognizes that a modicum of distributional equity is probably a luxury sustainable only within relatively rich nations that have stationary populations. Given the speed of global environmental deterioration, hard thinking seems in order.

References

Abernethy, V. 1979. *Population Pressure and Cultural Adjustment.* New York: Human Sciences Press.

Brooks, G. 1989. "Lavish U.S. food aid to Egypt has bought peace but little else," *Wall Street Journal*, 3 April, pp. 1 and 8.

Bruce, J. W., and L. Fortmann. 1989. "Agroforestry: Tenure and incentives," Land Tenure Center Paper No. 35. Madison: Land Tenure Center, University of Wisconsin.

Business Week. 1989. "Can this flight be grounded?," 10 April, p. 74.

Cohen, R. 1989. "Amazon tug-of-war reaches fever pitch," *Wall Street Journal*, 7 April, p. A6.

Fletcher, J. 1976. "Feeding the hungry: An ethical appraisal," in *Lifeboat Ethics: The Moral Dilemmas of World Hunger,* ed. George L. Lucas, Jr. and Thomas W. Ogletree. New York: Harper and Row.

Hardin, G. 1968. "The tragedy of the commons," *Science* 162 (13 December): 1243–1248.

Harper's Index. 1989. *Harper's Magazine,* March, p. 17.

Haub, C. 1988. "A billion more each decade: The population crisis lives," *International Herald Tribune,* 29 July.

Hernandez, M., and S. Braun. 1988. "Negatives cited in *Times* poll on immigrants," *Los Angeles Times,* 19 September.

Marlowe, L. 1989. "A five-star exit," *This World,* 2 April, pp. 18–19.

McConnell, S. 1988. "The new battle over immigration," *Fortune,* 9 May, pp. 89–102.

Micklin, P. O. 1988. "Dessication of the Aral Sea: A water management disaster in the Soviet Union," *Science* 241 (2 September): 1170–1176.

Pittsburgh Press. 1988. "Poll reveals U.S. fear of global population," 19 September p. 2.

Russell, W. M. S. 1988. "Population, swidden farming and the tropical environment," *Population and Environment* 10, no.2: 77–94.

Willis, D. K. 1984. "Overcrowding: The impact and the risks," *The Christian Science Monitor,* 8 August, pp. 21–22.

Comment: Adverse Environmental Consequences of the Green Revolution

DAVID PIMENTEL
MARCIA PIMENTEL

THE NEW AGRICULTURAL TECHNOLOGIES, energy inputs, and crop varieties that together are known as the Green Revolution are widely accepted as a resounding success in raising agricultural yields in much of the Third World. The Green Revolution seemingly banished what had been projected as imminent food shortages in many countries as populations continued to grow at annual rates of 2 to 3 percent. Optimists could envisage increases in yields continuing indefinitely, as agricultural production was put on a sound technological footing supported by a modern research and development infrastructure. Early fears of labor displacement were shown to be misplaced: the crop regime required as much or more labor as before.

Implicit in such rosy scenarios, however, is the assumption that the Green Revolution does not have adverse side effects on the environment—on the immediate physical bases of production and on the broader physical setting in which the rural population lives. That assumption, we argue, is false. This comment briefly examines the environmental impacts of the Green Revolution and suggests that they call into question the long-run sustainability, let alone the long-run further growth, of high agricultural yields. In some instances they are potentially damaging to public health. We conclude that this technological route cannot be seen as an alternative to urgent action to stem population growth.

Focused mainly on enhanced yield, the Consultative Group on International Agricultural Research that developed the crop plant improvement for the Green Revolution paid little or no attention to how this new technology would affect the quality of the environment (Baum, 1987). Pesticide use in Green Revolution rice production, for example, was reported to increase sevenfold over levels used in traditional rice production (Subramanian et al., 1973). Despite this increased use of insecticides there is no proof that losses due to insects in rice have been reduced; rather, at best such losses have remained around 27 percent (Oka, 1987). One reason for this is that more insect-susceptible varieties of rice have been planted. Further, the use of 2,4-D herbicide has increased the level of attack of insects on rice. One investigation documented that the rice stem-borer grew 45 percent larger in size on 2,4-D–treated rice and as a result, the pest consumed 45 percent more rice (Pimentel, 1971).

Perhaps the most serious problem associated with pesticide use is human poisonings. The World Health Organization (1981) estimates that annually there are 500,000 human pesticide poisonings and about 10,000 fatalities worldwide (see also Loevinsohn, 1987). In addition, heavy application of pesticides causes numerous other environmental problems. For example, beneficial natural enemies of pests are killed and in some cases this may lead to new pest outbreaks. In Indonesia in the early 1980s, when the Ministry of Agriculture encouraged farmers to use more insecticide on rice, the brown planthopper pest increased in numbers because of the destruction of its natural enemies; the result was a significant decline in Indonesian rice production during the mid-1980s (Oka, 1987). The situation became so desperate that in March 1985 President Suharto banned 56 of 57 insecticides used on rice in Indonesia. This drastic action helped rice yields to return to the high levels farmers were achieving before the heavy use of insecticides.

Pesticides have also reduced fish and shrimp populations in the paddy fields that provide an important food source for poor people (Oka, 1987). The pesticides lower the quantity of fish and shrimp that can be harvested and contaminate the harvest, posing a serious threat to public health (ICAITI, 1977).

Another major problem associated with the treatment of aquatic environments, either intentionally as with rice or unintentionally (by drift) as with dryland crops, is the contamination of aquatic ecosystems with insecticides. The spread of insecticides into aquatic environments has contributed to the increased resistance observed in mosquito populations, resulting in the spread of malaria in Asia, Africa, and Latin America (ICAITI, 1977). Research on pesticide use on cotton in Central America revealed that malaria increased threefold during a two-year period, principally due to this practice (ibid.).

In addition to the heavy reliance on pesticides, the Green Revolution made necessary increased fertilizer requirements, in some cases by 20- to 30-fold (Wen and Pimentel, 1984; Wittwer et al., 1987). Fertilizer washed and leached into lakes and streams enriches the aquatic system and may result in heavy algal growths that kill fish, shrimp, and other beneficial organisms (Pimentel, 1989). This eutrophication is a serious problem in industrialized countries where fertilizer use is very heavy, and it can be expected to grow in developing nations. Higher levels of fertilizer use, especially nitrogen, also has increased the susceptibility of rice to more intense insect and disease attack. It is common knowledge that when the nutrient level of crops is increased, insect and disease populations also increase (Pimentel, 1977).

As with all agriculture, mismanagement of soils and water results in diminishing yields, lack of future sustainability, and increased costs of production. Thus in the vast areas where the Green Revolution predominates, soil erosion and water runoff are ever-present problems. In India, for example, the average rate of erosion is 30 tonnes/hectare/year (Pimentel et al., 1987). There the amount of fertilizer nutrients lost with the eroded soil is about equal to the total amount of commercial fertilizer applied each year (Khoshoo and Tejwani, 1989). The loss of water associated with erosion (Pimentel et al., 1987) reduces crop productivity even more than does the loss of nutrients. The reduced productivity requires added fertilizer, irrigation, and pesticides to offset soil and water degradation. This starts a cycle of greater agricultural chemical use, increased reliance on energy (especially fossil-based), and further increases the production costs the farmer must bear. Poorer farmers are finding it difficult to afford the fertilizers and pesticides needed to sustain yields of their Green Revolution crops.

We conclude that considering the Green Revolution the answer to providing adequate food supplies for the ever-expanding human population is shortsighted. Unless the basic resources of agriculture, such as arable land, pure and adequate water supplies, and use of chemicals, are better managed, agricultural technology of the sort represented by the Green Revolution will be unable to meet the challenge.

References

Baum, W. C. (with the collaboration of Michael L. Lejeune). 1987. *Partners Against Hunger.* Published for the Consultative Group on International Agricultural Research. Washington, D.C.: The World Bank.

ICAITI. 1977. *An Environmental and Economic Study of the Consequences of Pesticide Use in Central American Cotton Production.* Guatemala City: Instituto Centro Americano de Investigación y Tecnología Industrial.

Khoshoo, T. N., and K. G. Tejwani. 1989. "Soil erosion and conservation in India (status and policies)," *World Soil Erosion and Conservation.* Gland, Switzerland: International Union for the Conservation of Nature.

Loevinsohn, M. E. 1987. "Insecticide use and increased mortality in rural Central Luzon, Philippines," *The Lancet* 8546 (13 June): 1350–1362.

Oka, I. N. 1987. Personal communication, Bogor Research Institute for Food Crops, Indonesia.

Pimentel, D. 1971. *Ecological Effects of Pesticides on Non-Target Species.* Washington, D.C.: US Government Printing Office.

_____. 1977. "Ecological basis of insect pest, pathogen and weed problems," in *The Origins of Pest, Parasite, Disease and Weed Problems,* ed. J. M. Cherrett and G. R. Sagar. Oxford: Blackwell Scientific Publishers, pp. 3–31.

———, et al. 1987. "World agriculture and soil erosion," *BioScience* 37: 277–283.

Pimentel, M. 1989. "Food as a resource," in *Food and Natural Resources,* ed. D. Pimentel and C. W. Hall. New York: Academic Press, pp. 409–437.

Subramanian, S. R., K. Ramamoorthy, and S. Varadarajan. 1973. "Economics of I. R. 8 paddy—a case study," *Madras Agricultural Journal* 60: 192–195.

Troeh, F. R., J. A. Hobbs, and R. L. Donahue. 1980. *Soil and Water Conservation for Productivity and Environmental Protection.* Englewood Cliffs, N.J.: Prentice Hall.

Wen, D., and D. Pimentel. 1984. "Energy inputs in agricultural systems of China," *Agriculture, Ecosystems and Environment* 11: 29–35.

World Health Organization. 1981. "Pesticide deaths: What's the toll?" *Ecoforum* 6: 10.

Wittwer, S., et al. 1987. *Feeding a Billion.* East Lansing: Michigan State University Press.

The Wealth of Nations and the Environment

MIKHAIL S. BERNSTAM

DOES ECONOMIC GROWTH CONTINUOUSLY AND UNIVERSALLY increase environmental disruption? Virtually all the relevant literature answers in the affirmative (e.g., Kneese, Ayres, and d'Arge, 1970; Holdren and Ehrlich, 1974; Kneese, 1977: 64–71, 84–89; Simon, 1981: 241; Slade, 1987: 339). This answer is damning for the wealth of nations, especially for low-income countries.

Yet, growing evidence shows that high levels of economic development and continuing economic growth in one small part of the world, namely open competitive market economies, have recently reversed the relationship between expansion and pollution from positive to negative (data in United Nations Environment Programme, 1987; OECD, 1989). Smil and Kuz (1976) and Slade (1987: 353–356) found a similar reversal in the case of energy consumption per capita with respect to gross national product per capita. Winiecki (1983; 1987: 16–26) showed that this reversal applies only to market economies, while in socialist countries energy use continuously increases with or without economic growth.

This article will venture to show how, and explain why, the long-term relationship between economic growth and pollution may be concave and decreasing. Simply put, as economies grow, discharges to the environment increase rapidly, then decelerate, and eventually decline. I will also analyze why this relationship is effective for market economies while the trend in socialist economies is monotonically concave and ever-increasing; it may be backward-bending at the end.

The framework

The first section surveys the evidence across nations with different economic systems. The second section discusses the distinct forces of resource through-put. The changes in these forces and the ensuing trends in pollution lie in a different dimension from the growth or decline of national incomes. In short, economic growth can be attributable to nonresource sectors (agriculture and services) and it can be attributable to technological progress that may either increase or reduce the input of resources and the emission of pollutants. By the law of conservation of mass, the weight of residuals discharged into the environment (including outputs that are used up over time) equals the mass of resource inputs (Kneese, Ayres, and d'Arge, 1970; Kneese, 1977; James, 1985). I discuss the trend in resource use as the race between growing (and then declining) resource-containing output and productivity of resource inputs in the production of this output. The outcome of this race, not economic growth, determines whether the total resource input and environmental discharges increase or decline.

The third section shows that the resulting trend in resource use and pollution ultimately depends on economic systems. The two extreme systems, open competitive markets and regulated state monopolies, create different patterns of resource use (Kornai, 1979, 1980, 1982, 1986; Winiecki, 1983, 1987). I characterize these patterns as, respectively, cost minimization and input maximization. It is this systemic difference in resource use that splits environmental trends in market and socialist economies. The fourth section puts this divergence in the context of global economic development. Arithmetically, the future of the environment depends on the race between population growth and an improvement in the throughput of resources within the finite ecological niche. I provide rough estimates of future environmental conditions according to different scenarios of the global choice of economic system.

The tale of two industrial developments

In the 1970s and 1980s, an amazing bifurcation took place in the trends in resource use and pollution within the developed industrial world. This divergence between Western market economies and socialist economies of the Soviet Union and Eastern Europe went virtually unnoticed. Yet, if it is not a medium-term fluke, it may signify the most important reversal in economic and environmental history since the Industrial Revolution. Tables 1–6 and Figure 1 summarize these trends across economic systems. The amounts of throughput of major resources and the ensuing discharges of air, water, and soil pollution began to decline rapidly across nations with competitive market economies. This is despite, or rather because of, further economic growth in Western market countries. During the same two decades, throughput of resources and environmental disruption were rapidly increasing in the Soviet Union and European socialist countries despite an economic slowdown and subsequent stagnation (Gzovskii, 1985, pointed out this apparent paradox). Only a small fraction of the evidence can be surveyed here. The sources cited contain more data; I have also compiled some 600 obscure Soviet sources, which are available for examination.

The recent environmental split

Table 1 shows emissions of major air pollutants in the United States in selected years from 1940 to 1986. Table 2 provides air pollution data for seven
Western market countries for 1970–85. All emissions are broken down by
sources, mainly transportation and stationary units. The latter consist of discharges from fuel combustion and industrial processes. One can observe a
very rapid decline in pollution in the 1970s and the 1980s, ranging from 12
percent to 33 percent depending on the country. The decline was so significant that, in the United States, emissions of 127.7 million metric tons in
1986 were 13.2 percent lower than in 1940, although the US population rose
by 82.4 percent and the real gross national product increased by 381.5 percent during the same period. Annual amounts of emissions decreased so
steeply in the United States that even absolute levels of accumulated concentration of pollutants in the air began to decline after 1977 (US Bureau of the
Census, 1989: 7, 421, 200).

   In addition to spectacular magnitudes, seven features stand out from
these and later tables. First, the recent decline in pollution occurred in many
developed market economies of Europe and North America. The data for
Japan are too sketchy but point in the same direction. One can reasonably
conclude that the downward trend runs across the economic system. Second, the decline of emissions occurred in both transportation and stationary
sources; therefore, a hypothesis that the decline was due solely to a higher
fuel efficiency of cars does not stand scrutiny. Third, declines in pollution
occurred across most physico-chemical substances, not only those originating from fossil fuels. Therefore, the energy crisis of the 1970s and the 1980s
cannot be given credit as the sole cause. Fourth, the extent of government
environmental regulation and environmentalist movements across countries
does not correlate with the steepness of pollution declines. If anything, there
is a slight negative correlation. Fifth, the decline in pollution in the United
States was faster in the 1980s than in the 1970s, while economic growth was
about the same (US Bureau of the Census, 1989: 421, Table 1). Sixth, in the
United States economic growth was roughly the same as in Western Europe
in the 1970s but about twice as high in the 1980s (US President, 1987: 368).
But the United States experienced a more rapid decrease in pollution than
most Western European countries. The latter two points suggest that the
newly emerging negative relationship between economic growth and pollution may be accelerating. I would predict such acceleration in the long term.

   The final, seventh point will be examined later with the help of the
data. This concerns the question of whether pollution-abatement efforts in
market countries were mainly responsible for the decline of emissions in the
1970s and 1980s. A different hypothesis will emphasize a secular increase in
the productivity of resource use in Western market economies, which eventually produced absolute declines in resource throughput and pollution.
These hypotheses are complementary in the high-income economies, but I

TABLE 1 Air pollutant emissions, by source and type of pollutant, in million metric tons: United States, selected years, 1940–86

Year	Total	Source		Source of discharge				Lead (thousand tons)
		Transportation	Stationary[a]	Particulate matter	Sulfur oxides	Nitrogen oxides	Carbon monoxide	
1940	147.1	n.a.	n.a.	22.8	17.5	6.8	81.6	n.a.
1960	165.4	n.a.	n.a.	21.1	19.5	12.8	88.4	n.a.
1970	191.4	93.8	76.0	18.5	28.4	18.1	98.7	203.8
1975	159.6	83.1	63.7	10.6	26.0	19.1	81.0	147.0
1980	151.9	72.3	64.6	8.5	23.9	20.3	76.1	70.6
1986	127.7	59.9	57.1	6.8	21.2	19.3	60.9	8.6

NOTES: The figures for sources of discharge do not add to the total in Table 1 because emissions from solid wastes and miscellaneous uncontrolled sources are not included. Table 2, by contrast, calculates the data from OECD, which uses a (perhaps illegitimate) broad definition of stationary sources inclusive of solid wastes and miscellaneous sources.

[a] Stationary fuel combustion and industrial processes.

n.a. = not available.

SOURCES: US Bureau of the Census, *Statistical Abstract of the United States, 1988* (Washington, D.C.: US Government Printing Office, 1987), p. 192; US National Center for Health Statistics, *Health, United States, 1988* (Washington, D.C.: US Government Printing Office, 1989), p. 103.

want to emphasize the second phenomenon, which is ignored in environmental analysis.

The decline in air pollution is part of a larger picture. It was accompanied in many market countries by similar noticeable improvements in water quality (US Bureau of the Census, 1989: 191; United Nations Environment Programme, 1987: 37, 52, 56–59; OECD, 1989: 61–67) and reductions in pesticide residues in food, water, and human bodies. There even were decreases in solid wastes, especially industrial wastes dumped at sea (United Nations Environment Programme, 1987: 279, 284–289). Table 3 shows major reductions in pesticide residue in human tissue in the United Kingdom over 1963–83 and especially in the United States over 1970–83. Leaping to a later attribution of such trends to growing productivity of inputs and their decreasing absolute use, one can consult the data on the trend in pesticide consumption. Since the mid-1970s, this consumption has significantly declined in the United States, Japan, and the Scandinavian countries, but only for one type of pesticide in the United Kingdom (US Bureau of the Census, 1989: 203; OECD, 1989: 299). The improvements in human exposure probably resulted from both the decrease in total use of pesticides and changes in the mix and impact of chemicals. Table 3 also compares human exposure to pesticides in 1979–82 across several Western market countries and in China and India, where pesticide residues in human milk are much higher while agricultural output per capita is much lower.

In contrast with the rapid decline in pollution in market economies, environmental disruption significantly increased in the 1970s and the 1980s in socialist countries. In this volume, Li documents such trends for China (see also Smil, 1984), and Carlson and I do so for the Soviet Union and Eastern Europe. Rapid environmental degradation includes rising air pollution and increases in water pollution and soil erosion (e.g., USSR Supreme Soviet, 1989; Iablokov, 1989; USSR State Committee on Statistics, 1989a; Samsonov, 1989; Voloshin, 1990). Discharges of polluted water increased in the Soviet Union from 35 billion cubic meters in 1970 to 150 billion in 1988; the abatement efforts are 60–80 percent ineffective (Lukianenko, 1989).

Two specific observations are relevant for relating trends in pollution to the analysis of economic systems. First, in 1985, the new Soviet administration began to change the economic system. Some of the most polluting plants were shut down. Air pollution dropped by about 10 percent during the last several years (USSR State Committee on Statistics, 1989a: 7, 83). Second, international data document increases in emissions and concentration of pollutants in Poland, Hungary, and Czechoslovakia, but, curiously, the trends are mixed in Yugoslavia (United Nations Environment Programme, 1987: 13, 15; OECD, 1989: 21, 61–63). Yugoslavia modified its socialist economic system, and its monopolistic enterprises do not need to maximize inputs in order to maximize profits, justify price increases, and relax output quotas.

TABLE 2 Trends in emissions of air pollutants in market economies, by source, selected countries, 1970–85, in thousand metric tons

Country	1970			1975			1980		
	Transportation	Stationary	Total	Transportation	Stationary	Total	Transportation	Stationary	Total
Canada	10078	12068	22146	10619	11089	21708	9975	10552	20527
United States	93600	96700	190300	83100	76400	159500	72200	79600	151800
West Germany	11189	12858	24047	12802	9427	22229	11822	9190	21012
France	5451	7889	13340	5805	8184	13989	6472	7976	14448
United Kingdom	4395	11435	15830	4942	9547	14489	5722	8908	14630
Sweden	1997	1397	3394	1853	1139	2992	1690	960	2650
Netherlands	2096	1822	3918	2097	1342	3439	1673	1447	3120
Quinquennial index for seven countries (in percent)	n.a.	n.a.	n.a.	94.1	81.2	87.3	90.4	101.3	95.7

Country	1985			Ratio: 1985/1970 (in percent)		
	Transportation	Stationary	Total	Transportation	Stationary	Total
Canada	9340	10260	19600	92.7	85.0	88.5
United States	63000	70000	133000	67.3	72.4	69.9
West Germany	9379	7641	17020	83.8	59.4	70.8
France	6882[a]	4830[a]	11712[a]	126.3[a]	61.2[a]	87.8[a]
United Kingdom	5636	7574	13210	128.2	66.2	83.4
Sweden	1921	1021	2942	96.2	73.1	86.7
Netherlands	1417	1280	2697	67.6	70.3	68.8
Quinquennial index for seven countries (in percent)	89.1	86.5	87.7	75.8[b]	71.2[b]	73.3[b]

NOTES: In some cases, the data on emissions from one of the five major emission sources are missing for a given year. The data for a previous or subsequent year were then added, assuming no change for a given source of emissions over a five-year period. The figures for sources of discharges do not add to the total in Table 1 because emissions from solid wastes and miscellaneous uncontrolled sources are not included. Table 2, by contrast, calculates the data from OECD, which uses a (perhaps illegitimate) broad definition of stationary sources inclusive of solid wastes and miscellaneous sources.

n.a. = not applicable

[a] 1987

[b] The 1985/1970 ratio

SOURCES: Calculated from OECD, *OECD Environmental Data Compendium, 1989* (Paris: OECD, 1989), pp. 21–29.

TABLE 3   Pesticide residue levels in human adipose tissue and human milk, selected countries, 1963–83, in mg per kg

	DDE	DDT	HCH (BHC)	Dieldrin
Human tissue				
United Kingdom				
1963–64	2.2	1.20	n.a.	0.27
1965–67	2.2	0.83	0.28	0.23
1969–71	1.9	0.54	0.27	0.16
1976–77	2.1	0.20	0.30	0.11
1982–83	1.3	0.01	0.24	0.07
United States				
1970	7.95[a]		0.37	0.16
1973	5.96[a]		0.25	0.17
1976	4.34[a]		0.18	0.09
1979	3.10[a]		0.15	0.08
1981	2.38[a]		0.10	0.05
1983	1.63[a]		0.08	0.06
Human milk				
United States, 1979	2.0	0.10	0.05	n.a.
Japan, 1980–81	1.8	0.21	2.30	n.a.
West Germany, 1981	1.2	0.28	0.30	n.a.
Sweden, 1981	0.96	0.10	0.09	n.a.
Belgium, 1982	1.0	0.13	0.20	n.a.
Israel, 1981–82	2.4	0.26	0.37	n.a.
China, 1982	4.4	1.80	6.70	n.a.
India, 1982	5.4	1.20	4.70	n.a.

[a]Combined data for DDE and DDT
n.a. = not available
SOURCE: UN Environment Programme, *Environmental Data Report* (London: Basil Blackwell, 1987), pp. 100–101.

Estimates of emissions of air pollutants in socialist countries are deficient because about 76–80 percent of discharges from stationary sources are assumed to be abated according to nominal technical capabilities of scrubbers and precipitators. But actual abatement does not exceed 30 percent (compare USSR State Committee on Statistics, 1989b: 249, with Lisovenko and Trach, 1989; Tsaturov, 1989; and Simmons, 1990). Due to this uncertainty about the data, I assume as the upper and lower bounds of emissions in socialist countries the amounts after 30 percent and 77 percent of abatement of pollution from stationary sources.

No adjustments are made for air pollution from transportation. In the Soviet Union in 1988, emissions from transportation amounted to 35.8 million metric tons (MMT) (Valentei, 1990) as against 59.9 MMT in the United States in 1986. There were 71 land vehicles of all types per thousand persons in the Soviet Union and 723 in the United States (calculated from US Bureau

TABLE 4   Pollutant emissions from stationary sources, United States, 1986 and Soviet Union, 1987, in million metric tons

	United States	Soviet Union
Total	57.1	64.1
Particulate matter	4.3	15.6
Sulfur oxides	20.3	18.6
Nitrogen oxides	10.6	4.5
Carbon monoxide	11.7	15.5
Volatile organic compounds	10.2	9.9

SOURCES: United States: US National Center for Health Statistics, *Health, United States, 1988* (Washington, D.C.: US Government Printing Office, 1989), p. 103; Soviet Union: USSR State Committee on Statistics, *Narodnoe Khoziaistvo SSSR v 1987 Godu* (Moscow, 1988), p. 571.

of the Census, 1989: 825). Given the differences in population size, emissions per vehicle were five times higher in the Soviet Union than in the United States; the gap would widen if airplanes were included. Soviet air is thus protected by their small automotive capacity.

Table 4 compares US and Soviet emissions of air pollutants from stationary sources in the mid-1980s. Soviet data are presented at the lower bound. Even at this bound, Soviet levels of emissions are higher than American. The higher bound of Soviet emissions of air pollutants from stationary sources can be estimated for 1987 as 275.7 MMT (USSR State Committee on Statistics, 1989b: 249). This is 4.8 times higher than in the United States at a level of gross national product that is less than half as high. Using the above numbers and the OECD data from Table 2 and related sources for two groups of countries, I roughly estimated air pollution from both transportation and stationary sources in market and socialist economies. At the lower bound, the amount of discharges of air pollutants per capita in socialist countries is approximately the same as in Western market economies, about 350 kilograms (kg) per year. This is at the level of GNP per capita in socialist countries about 40 percent of that in Western market economies (Illarionov, 1990: 6–7). At the higher bound, the socialist average is 800 kg per capita, that is, 2.3 times higher than in market economies. The ratios per US$1000 of GNP in socialist versus market economies are much higher: 2.5 times at the lower bound and 5.8 times at the higher bound.

Comparative trends in resource use

My explanation of the environmental split within the developed industrial world is simple. It is the split in resource trends. First, resource use per unit of output is much higher in socialist than in market economies. On a per capita basis, resource use in socialist countries is as high as or higher than in the West, although socialist GNP per capita is about 40 percent of that in West market countries (new semi-official Soviet estimates of GNP per capita are in Illarionov, 1990). Second, inputs of basic resources declined in Western market economies at the recent stage of economic growth and technological progress. These inputs continuously increased in socialist economies with or without economic growth.

Tables 5 and 6 and Figure 1 present comparative trends in resource inputs, with special emphasis on energy. This emphasis here and throughout the article is warranted because in industrial societies energy conversion constitutes about 50 percent of total resource use (Haveman, 1974: 103). Table 5 and Figure 1 show that in terms of energy consumption per capita the Soviet Union has been converging with the United States, and socialist economies in general have been converging with market economies in general. They have been converging because the trends have been diverging: the downward trend in market economies and the upward trend in socialist economies. Per capita energy consumption in the United States and Canada in the 1980s was only slightly higher than in 1960. In the 1970s and 1980s, energy consumption per capita declined in most Western economies. In absolute terms, which are ultimately important for environmental discharges, total consumption of energy declined in the 1980s in the United States, Canada, West Germany, France, and Belgium, and remained stable in Japan, Italy, Sweden, the Netherlands, Denmark, and Austria. At the same time, total energy consumption significantly increased in the Soviet Union (by about 25 percent) and most other socialist countries (OECD, 1989: 235; US Bureau of the Census, 1989: 833–834; United Nations Environment Programme, 1987: 256–289).

Similar divergent trends led to the widening of the gap in per capita steel consumption in market and socialist economies in the 1970s and 1980s (Table 5). In terms of both energy and steel, the ratio of inputs per $1000 GNP in socialist and market economies increased from about 2.5:1 in the second half of the 1970s to about 3:1 in the mid-1980s. The gap is wider between the Soviet Union and the United States. Given low population growth in Western countries, one can readily infer from Table 5 that steel consumption declined there in absolute terms. The same is true for many other primary metals. Note that Table 5 allows us to compare East Germany with West Germany and North Korea with South Korea. In both cases, the differences in resource use per $1000 of GNP and per capita were either the same or even more pronounced than between the two groups of countries on the average.

Table 6 provides a broader picture comparing the resource throughput in the Soviet Union and the United States in 1960, 1970, and 1987 over the production cycle. Note that the decline in domestic production of resources and materials in the United States as presented in Table 6 is generally larger

TABLE 5 Consumption of energy and steel per capita and per $1000 of GNP, selected countries, 1975, 1980, and 1985–86

| | Energy (in kilograms of coal equivalent) | | | | Steel (in metric tons) | | | |
| | Per capita | | Per $1000 of GNP[a] | | Per capita | | Per $1000 of GNP[a] | |
	1980	1986	1980	1986	1975	1985	1975	1985
Market economies								
United States	10386	9489	690	590	541	448	40	28
Canada	10547	9694	840	740	581	471	51	35
Japan	3726	3625	410	330	580	553	78	51
United Kingdom	4850	5363	670	680	376	254	56	32
West Germany	5829	5672	600	550	489	481	60	47
France	4409	3881	500	430	365	258	48	29
Belgium	5997	5577	780	710	314	275	48	36
Switzerland	3636	3990	250	260	n.a.	n.a.	n.a.	n.a.
Austria	4058	4024	500	460	284	235	44	27
Denmark	5254	5331	340	290	n.a.	n.a.	n.a.	n.a.
Sweden	5376	4893	500	430	773	384	75	34
South Korea	1373	1625	870	790	52	198[b]	42	93[b]
Unweighted average	5450	5260	580	520	436	356	54	41
Socialist economies								
Soviet Union	5549	6389	1130	1250	554	557	124	121
Bulgaria	5254	5780	1310	1590	252	336	64	80
Czechoslovakia	6364	6258	1160	1100	731	709	144	124
East Germany	7276	7944	1150	1920	566	574	101	82
Hungary	3787	3735	800	760	n.a.	n.a.	n.a.	n.a.
Poland	4935	4700	1150	1100	524	409	120	95
Romania	4505	4483	1340	1260	463	480	159	133
North Korea	2713	2771	2490	2450	186	413	177	356
Unweighted average	5048	5260	1320	1430	468	497	127	142

[a]In constant 1984 dollars. Estimates per $1000 of GNP in socialist countries are corrected assuming average GNP per capita in these countries is equal to 40 percent of that in Western market economies (for recent semi-official Soviet estimates see A. Illarionov, "Paradoksy Statistiki," *Argumenty i Fakty*, no. 3 [1990]: 6–7). No corrections were made for North Korea due to lack of data.

[b]1984

n.a. = not available.
SOURCE: US Bureau of the Census, *Statistical Abstract of the United States, 1989* (Washington, D.C.: US Government Printing Office, 1989), pp. 822, 832–834.

FIGURE 1   Energy consumption per capita: Selected world regions, 1960–84

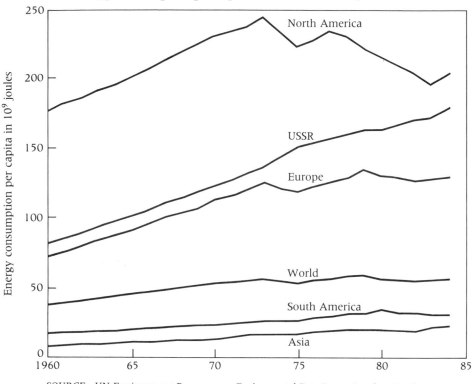

SOURCE: UN Environment Programme, *Environmental Data Report* (London: Basil Blackwell, 1987), p. 247.

than the decline in their consumption, which includes imports. The direction of both trends is the same, however (see US Bureau of the Census, 1989: 679–680, 686, 740–741; see also Table 5 and Figure 1). For environmental analysis, total consumption of energy is more relevant than domestic production, but domestic production of metals is as relevant as final consumption.

Table 6 shows a very dramatic decline in the throughput of many physical resources in the United States between 1970 and 1987 after a significant increase in the 1960s. This encompasses oil and gas, iron ore and iron-originated materials and outputs, and the stock of farm animals. This reversing trend closely corresponds to a similar reversal in the trend in pollution presented in Table 1. This suggests that the decline in discharges was not due solely to abatement efforts. The effect was largely produced by the decline of resource and material inputs per unit of output over the production cycle (e.g., more meat was produced while there were fewer heads of livestock and less feed grain; fewer tractors and combines were produced out of less steel from less pig iron out of less iron ore). This reduced the discharge of residuals.

TABLE 6 Comparable data on trends in productive activities, United States and Soviet Union, 1960, 1970, 1987

	United States			Soviet Union		
	1960	1970	1987	1960	1970	1987
Oil and gas condensate (million tons)	348	475	415	148	353	624
Natural gas (billion cubic meters)	n.a.	521	480	n.a.	200	678
Coal (million tons)	400	542	820	371	577	680
Electricity (trillion W/hr)	892	1730	2750	292	740	1665
Electricity for industrial use (trillion W/hr)	n.a.	730	870	n.a.	488	957
Iron ore (million tons)[a]	89	90.7	36	106	195	251
Pig iron (million tons)[a]	n.a.	83.3	44	n.a.	85.9	114
Steel (million tons)[a]	92	122	81	65	116	162
Cement (million tons)[a]	56.1	66.5	81.6	45.5	95.2	137
Chemicals (thousand tons)	774	2250	4100	211	623	1517
Synthetics and plastics (million tons)	2.9	n.a.	25.5	0.29	n.a.	4.5
Tractors (thousands)	n.a.	224	93	n.a.	459	567
Grain combines (thousands)	n.a.	24.0	8.3	n.a.	99.2	96.2
Mineral fertilizers (million nutrient tons)	7.6	14.9	20.0	3.3	13.1	36.3
Pesticides (thousand tons of active mass)[b]	n.a.	342	236	n.a.	264	328
Grain (million tons)	147.6[c]	168.2[c]	280.9[c]	125.5[d]	186.7[d]	211.4[d]
Cattle (million head)	97.7	112.4	102.0	75.8	95.1	120.9
Hogs and pigs (million head)	59.0	57.0	51.0	58.7	56.1	79.5
Meat, carcass weight (million tons)	18.6	23.8	28.9	8.7[d]	12.3[d]	18.9[d]
Milk cows (million head)	19.5	13.3	10.5	34.8	40.5	42.4
Milk per cow (tons)	2.9	4.4	6.0	1.8	2.1	2.7

[a] Domestic production. Net of exports and imports. domestic consumption of iron ore in 1986 was 51 8 million metric tons (MMT) in the United States and 214.0 MMT in the Soviet Union. Consumption of pig iron was 48.5 MMT and 108.5 MMT, respectively. Consumption of steel was 99.2 MMT and 160 6 MMT, respectively.

[b] Annual averages for 1976–80 and 1981–85 are presented in columns for 1970 and 1987. respectively. The definition in the Soviet source (and thus the measurement) is not clear; US sources provide different numbers but for the United States only; the data are presented here only for comparative purpose.

[c] Sorghum, barley, and rice are not included. The totals are about 12 percent higher if the preceding are included.

[d] To convert to international definitions, this gross amount should be reduced by at least 15 percent.

n.a. = not available.

SOURCES: USSR Central Statistical Department. *Narodnoe Khoziaistvo SSSR v 1970 godu. Statisticheskii Ezhegodnik* (Moscow, 1971), pp. 94–97. 352. 367; USSR State Committee on Statistics, *Narodnoe Khoziaistvo SSSR v 1987 godu. Statisticheskii Ezhegodnik* (Moscow, 1988), pp. 123–124. 126, 213, 226, 603–604. 63ว–645; US Government Printing Office. *Statistical Abstract of the United States, 1961* (Washington, D.C.: US Government Printing Office, 1961), pp. 651–652. 676–677. 681; *Statistical Abstract of the United States, 1981* (Washington, D.C.: US Government Printing Office, 1981), pp. 686, 688–689, 693; *Statistical Abstract of the United States, 1988* (Washington, D.C.: US Government Printing Office, 1987), pp. 633–635; *Statistical Abstract of the United States, 1989* (Washington, D.C.: US Government Printing Office, 1989), pp. 643. 686, 740–741. 832. Pesticides: Boris Cherniakov. "Khimiia ili Zhizn," *Moscow News*, no. 25 (June 1985). p. 10.

In the 1970s and 1980s, the production of both coal and electricity continued to increase in the United States, but productivity of electricity with respect to coal increased even more. The share of electricity for industrial use in total consumption of electricity declined by about 25 percent (Table 6).

Table 6 also shows that the Soviet trends have been the opposite of the American. All major physical resource-containing inputs and outputs have expanded in the 1970s and 1980s in continuation of the trend of the 1960s. With the exception of coal, all Soviet inputs either expanded much faster than in the United States or rapidly increased when analogous production in the United States declined sharply. Soviet production of oil, gas, steel, cement, fertilizers and pesticides, agricultural machinery, and the number of cattle and swine, often starting from levels lower than those in the United States in 1960, exceeded that of the United States by 1987—with little positive result for the consumer economy and with dire environmental costs.

Even the advantage of economic backwardness, when a nation can easily leap upward from low output levels by using proven Western technology, does not seem to help in the Soviet case. Consider milk yield per cow. It obviously has some biological limits, and there must be diminishing increases with rising yield. Yet, it doubled in the United States in 27 years from a level in 1960 that the USSR had not achieved in 1987, while the Soviet increase over the same period was only 50 percent. Over the entire production cycle in the USSR, there were continuous increases in resource throughput, which explains the continuously rising environmental damage. Table 5 and other related evidence suggest that this conclusion applies to all socialist countries and their economic system.

The race between productivity of resources and population growth

The tale of two industrial developments showed that economic growth and environmental disruption are not twins. They are not prisoners of progress tied together. Depending on the economic system, pollution can decline or increase when the economy grows and it can increase when the economy does not grow. The following section presents a simple accounting mechanism that explains these relationships.

Introducing the race between resource productivity and resource output

Consider both separate and overlapping systems of economic and material accounting sketched in Figure 2. According to the law of conservation of mass, the total amount of discharges of residuals to the environment (including outputs that are used up over time) is equal to the weight of inputs of

FIGURE 2   Systems of economic and material accounting

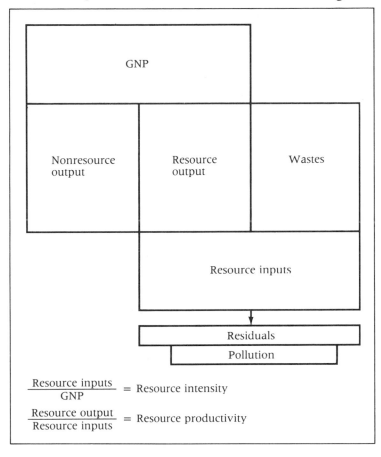

resources (including oxygen derived from the atmosphere and alloyed during processing—Ayres and Kneese, 1969: 284–285). This is shown at the bottom left of Figure 2. The amount of pollution is smaller than the weight of residuals. Not all residuals are pollutants, and some potential pollutants are abated and/or recycled. Note, however, that weight is not the only parameter of pollution. Highly toxic pollutants (e.g., radiation) need not weigh much to significantly affect the environment and people. This damaging capability per unit of weight needs special measurement, which will be discussed later. At the moment, we need to separate, distinguish, and disaggregate economic and material balances on the top and in the center of Figure 2.

The gross national product consists of both resource-originated output and nonresource output such as agricultural products of photosynthesis and various services, including engineering. The material throughput of the economy has total resource inputs (or total resource use) at the beginning of production and two types of production at the end. One type is the resource-originated output, which has economic value and is identical with the resource part of the GNP. The other type is everything else that derives from resources, has no economic value, and/or serves no useful purpose. These are uselessly processed resources, or wastes (in economic, not in physical sense; "waste" in physical sense usually denotes all residuals, including outputs that are used up). Resource output plus resource wastes are the total resource use. The previous three sentences hold the key to the entire argument of this article and, if this argument is correct, to the entire relationship between economic growth and environmental disruption.

For it is the change in the amount of these wastefully used resources that determines the relationship between economic growth and pollution. Wastes are economically useless production: scrap, spills, slag, discards, refuses, and other processing losses (Ayres and Kneese, 1969: 283–285; Kneese, Ayres, d'Arge, 1970: 9). Wastes also include destroyed primary resources (e.g., Amazonian rain forests felled and burned in order to clear pasture land for livestock production) and losses of intermediary and final output in transportation and storage (e.g., losses of agricultural output, which range from 20 percent to 40 percent in the Soviet Union according to the USSR State Committee on Statistics, 1989c: 13). According to estimates made at the USSR Central Institute of Mathematical Economics, about 33 percent of industrial production is economically useless output, mostly unnecessary and unutilized producer goods and various primary and intermediary outputs involved in the production of this machinery (Uliukaev, 1989: 84).

When technical efficiency of resource use grows, wastes and input/output ratios decline over the production cycle. Inversely, productivity of resources, defined as the ratio of economically useful resource outputs to total resource inputs, increases. If productivity of resources increases faster (that is, if the amount of resource wastes declines faster) than resource output increases, then the total amount of resource inputs declines. Resource output may grow, as it has ever since the Industrial Revolution, and thus make the GNP grow, but resource use and pollution may decline. Economic growth and pollution decline occur simultaneously. This becomes possible for the same technological reason: the growth in resource productivity in excess of the growth of resource output.

One can conduct a visual experiment and imagine these changes on Figure 2. Simply increase resource output and thus the GNP by a square unit but reduce wastes by, say, 1.5 square units. Resource inputs and pollution are reduced by 0.5 square units, while the GNP is increased by one square unit. The growth in resource productivity outpaced the growth in resource output. The race is won, and pollution declined. Economic growth actually reduced pollution. This is what happened in Western market economies in the 1970s and 1980s.

Figure 2 also shows that nonpolluting economic growth can be attributable to the nonresource sector. In this case, resource intensity (inputs per unit of GNP) declines and resource use and pollution remain unchanged. Pollution and resource inputs decline only if resource intensity declines faster than GNP grows, that is, if the above-described efficiency improvements take place in the resource sector. The decisive race is the race against wastes, the race between resource output and resource productivity. There is also one more participant in the race, on which the absolute amount of resource output depends: population.

Environmental damage as the outcome of the race between productivity and population

At each given level of resource output per capita and resource productivity, the size of population determines the absolute amount of resource use and eventual discharges to the environment. All other things being equal, more people mean more resource use, and higher productivity of resources means lower resource use. Therefore, the ultimate race is between population growth and the growth of resource productivity.

Holdren and Ehrlich (1974) proposed a measure of environmental damage that is the product of three multipliers: population size, consumption per capita, and environmental damage per unit of consumption. The idea of the multiplicative nature of pollution, with special emphasis on the degree of pollution per unit of resources, is instructive. Including consumption per capita as a central multiplier is fallacious, however, unless consumption is defined as the total resource use—that is, including all production and excluding all nonresource consumption. Otherwise, the Holdren–Ehrlich formula violates the law of conservation of mass. From the wrong definition of the central multiplier and from the extension of the static accounting formula to a dynamic relationship, the standard inference is drawn that economic growth increases pollution.

Here I will present different formulas that are congruent with the law of conservation of mass. I separate industrial production from household wastes. The quantity of the latter is not dependent on technological progress, although its unit damage may be. In addition, my approach disaggregates by individual resources and individual countries. This allows us to capture major damages embodied in small quantities of some discharges and to avoid the typical fallacy of global averages.

Total environmental damage can be measured as:

$$\dot{D} = \sum_1^N P_i \left[\left(\sum_0^J R_{ji}^P d_{ji}^R \right) + H_i^P d_i^H \right],$$ (1)

$$i = 1, 2, \ldots, N \quad j = 1, 2, \ldots, J$$

$$\dot{D} = \sum_1^N P_i \left\{ \left[\sum_0^J (O_{ji}^P + W_{ji}^P) \, d_{ji}^{O,W} \right] + H_i^P d_i^H \right\},$$ (2)

$$i = 1, 2, \ldots, N \quad j = 1, 2, \ldots, J$$

and

$$\dot{D} = \sum_1^N P_i \left[\left(\sum_0^J O_{ji}^P R_{ji}^O d_{ji}^R \right) + H_i^P d_i^H \right],$$ (3)

$$i = 1, 2, \ldots, N \quad j = 1, 2, \ldots, J$$

where $\dot{D}$ is the total flow of environmental damages from processing of all resources j in all countries i. P_i is the population of each country i. R_{ji}^P represents resource inputs per capita for each resource j in each country i. O_{ji}^P is economic (useful) output per capita originated in each resource j in each country i; and W_{ji}^P is economic waste per capita for j and i. H_i^P is household waste per capita in each country. One can define this as biological waste only, or also include trash and recreational waste; if not included in household waste, the latter two must be included in O_i^P and W_i^j as their used-up residuals. $d_{ji}^{O,W}$ is environmental damage per unit of resource-originated output, both economic and wasteful, in each j and i. d_{ji}^R is damage per unit of mass of j's resource input processing over the production cycle in i's country. d_i^H is a similar damage measure of household waste. R_{ji}^O in equation 3 is the total input/useful output ratio. This is the inverse of the productivity of resources. By definition,

$$R_{ji}^O = R_{ji}^P / O_{ji}^P.$$

Equations 1 and 2 are equal by the law of conservation of mass and by the identity of the total environmental damage. The proof of equation 3 is trivial. It simply modifies the term for resource inputs in equation 1 as the product of useful output and the input/useful output ratio. The implications are not so trivial.

The formulas rigorously show that, holding unit damages constant, total environmental damage is the outcome of the race between population growth and resource use per capita, which is dependent on productivity of resources. Resource output per capita, as one component of the level of economic well-being, cannot solely determine the level and the course of pollution. Even less so can the level of income per capita, which is outside the material balance. The direct dynamic inference is that economic growth can increase pollution if it increases the resource output of the economy; and economic growth can reduce pollution if it increases productivity of resources (that is, reduces wastes) faster than both resource output and population grow.

From hunting and gathering to agriculture to industry, output included more and more products originated in natural resources. Many new resources were involved in production. The productivity of new resources, be they livestock or fossil fuels or metals, is initially low. The average resource productivity thus declines while the amount of both resource outputs and wastes grows. New resources bring to the scene new resource-specific environmental damages and increase the average unit damage. Even without population growth, agricultural and especially industrial development increases environmental damage multifold. Population growth merely magnifies this. This proliferation of resources, rather than economic growth per se, is at the core of the damage explosion of the industrial era.

Then the process decelerates. Productivity of resources and resource output per capita compete. As long as the latter outpaces the former, which was characteristic of industrial development until the recent reversal in Western market economies, total resource use, its total residuals, and their pollution increase. The latter three increase more and more slowly as the growth of productivity of resources catches up with the growth of resource output. Again, population growth magnifies the increase in residuals. Later, population growth cancels in absolute terms the improvements on a per capita basis when productivity of resources outpaces the growth of useful output per capita, and the resource use per capita declines. The process decelerates more and more until resource output per capita grows more slowly than resource productivity or not at all, while resource productivity grows faster than population. Then the concave curve of pollution goes down as was documented earlier.

Damage per unit of mass of resources is another participant in this multivariate race. Total damage depends, among other things, on resource mix. Additions of new resources to processing at early industrial stages worsen the mix in environmental terms. Further substitution of new materials (e.g., fiber optics for copper) reduces both the mass of inputs per unit of output and environmental damage per unit of mass. Improvements in resource mix are a powerful reducer of pollution. Abatement efforts also reduce unit damage.

There are probably many interdependencies between multipliers of the formulas. Population growth is influenced by growth of output per capita and resources per capita; productivity of resources is influenced by population growth, and so on. Even without these interdependent influences, population is not a mere multiplier in the economic–environmental relationship as the standard literature sees it. Population is a participant in the multivariate race with offsetting economic forces. Even if population did not influence these economic forces, population growth could be compensated for by improvements in resource productivity.

The simplest example is livestock, which greatly affects water and air quality and other sanitary conditions. It is well known that the human population exceeds 5 billion. It is less well known that the domesticated animal population of the Earth also exceeds 5 billion. In 1987, there were over 4 billion farm animals (think for a moment about almost one billion pigs; or 1.5 billion cows—those environmental beasts that produce methane by chewing grass). Their annual average growth rate was about 1 percent in the 1980s. Growth rate was minus 2.5 percent in the United States and most market economies and plus 1.3–1.5 percent in socialist and developing countries (UN Food and Agriculture Organization, 1988: 241–249). According to Soviet experience, biological and poisonous waste to water and air from a typical semi-modern large farm with 108,000 pigs is equal to that of an industrial city with 300,000 people (Lemeshev, 1985: 89). A simple calculation shows that improvements in livestock yield in socialist and developing countries toward the levels of Western market economies, and the consequent liberation from the excessive livestock herd, are capable of compensating for many impacts of world population growth. The tradeoff between people and pigs or between people and cows may not be a bad deal in a world where an alternative proposition is the tradeoff between people and their standard of living.

De-industrialization: Compression of resources over the production cycle

But how much can productivity of resources increase? Ayres (1978: 50) warned against an immediate technological fallacy that improvements in efficiency of particular processes are unbounded. One cannot reach output/ input ratios in excess of unity for each material process. Lovins (in this volume) shows that energy consumption seems to be one area where actual and potential efficiency improvements are large. This is important because this concerns more than half of all resource inputs.

The above formulas and accumulated evidence open up an additional perspective beyond immediate technological progress in resource processing. This perspective is the compression of producer goods relative to final household goods in market economies. Many specific resource outputs over which the formulas are integrated are actually inputs in final production. The reduction in input/output ratios compresses the amount of these intermediary outputs over the production cycle. Thus an increase in resource productivity changes the other multiplier, resource output. The latter is not an independent multiplier in the race with resource productivity. It is also a variable that is itself dependent on resource productivity. Increases in resource productivity extend the race into resource output. There the reduction in input/output ratios continues as the race between producer outputs and final consumer outputs. This means that increases in resource productivity not only outpace increases in resource output but also, eventually, reduce resource output itself. This is the major reason why both total resource inputs and pollution decline in Western market economies.

For example, higher fuel efficiency is achieved by better automotive carburators. It is also achieved by the elimination of carburators altogether and the substitution of fuel injection needles. This saves more petroleum but also saves steel and aluminum and reduces the stock of machine tools, which, in turn, saves steel. There are many ripple effects over the production cycle from such substitutions. Consider improved livestock breeding. It increases meat and milk yield per livestock head and prompts a reduction in herd size. This saves feed grains and reduces cultivation. This, in turn, reduces the demand for fertilizers, pesticides, tractors, combines, construction materials, and the like. This extends to petrochemicals, steel, and other fabricated metals. Eventually, improved breeding saves primary metals, ores, and fossil energy. One can consider many second and higher order effects of improvements in seeds and in the substitution of fiber optics for copper and of plastics for metals.

The compression of resources and producer goods over the production cycle in the United States and other Western market economies is already apparent. While extensive input/output tables (including the data on net trade in relevant producer and consumer goods) are necessary for documenting this, a few simple observations can be made here. Table 5 showed that steel consumption per capita declined in the United States and other Western market countries from 1975 to 1985 at about 2 percent per year. Given low population growth, absolute consumption of steel and its products also declined significantly (US Bureau of the Census, 1989: 832). At the same time, production of final consumer goods increased at or higher than the rate of real GNP growth (e.g., about 3 percent per year in the United States). This suggests the compression of many machine tools and other producer goods originated in steel.

The United States is a net exporter of both agricultural machinery and grains (US Bureau of the Census, 1989: 787, 793–797). Table 6 shows that the domestic US production of tractors and combines greatly decreased from 1970 to 1987 while grain production increased. Similar simple illustrations concern other industries and products where final household goods increased, while their domestic producer goods increased at a lower rate. At the same time, these producer goods were either exported or net imports are very recent and small. These producer goods in the United States in the 1970s and 1980s were, in broad categories, fabricated metal products, machinery (except electrical), and instruments and tools (for trade data see US Bureau of the Census, 1989: 797).

Table 7 shows that the growth of the physical volumes of these products consistently declined in the 1960s, 1970s, and 1980s. The rate of growth of fabricated metals was lower than that of GNP in the 1970s and 1980s. The

TABLE 7   Decadal indexes of real gross national product and physical volume of industrial production,[a] United States, 1950–87

	1960/50	1970/60	1980/70	1987/80
Real gross national product	1.38	1.45	1.32	1.21
Industrial production (manufacturing, mining, utilities)	n.a.	n.a.	1.38	1.19
Manufacturing (durable and nondurable goods)	1.44	1.62	1.43[b]	1.35
Durable goods	1.43	1.62	1.40	1.22
Primary metals	1.04	1.45	0.95	0.90
Fabricated metal products	1.26	1.51	1.24	1.09
Machinery except electrical	n.a.	1.79	1.69	1.24
Mining	1.21[c]	1.42	1.13	0.90
Utilities	n.a.	n.a.	1.32	1.03

NOTE: The underlined numbers are at or below the GNP index.
[a] Federal Reserve Board Series
[b] Corrected: the source contains an obvious typographical error
[c] 1960/53
n.a. = not available.
SOURCES: GNP, 1950–87 and production, 1970–87: US Bureau of the Census, *Statistical Abstract of the United States, 1989* (Washington, D.C.: US Government Printing Office, 1989), pp. 421, 730; production, 1950–70: US Bureau of the Census, *Historical Statistics of the United States, Colonial Times to 1970* (Washington, D.C.: US Government Printing Office, 1975), Pt. 1, p. 585, Pt. 2, p. 667.

growth of fabricated metals was slower than overall industrial production, slower than the entire manufacturing sector (which includes both durable and nondurable goods), slower than durable goods in general, and slower than nonelectrical machinery. The growth of machinery (except electrical) significantly decelerated and was slower in the 1980s than growth in the entire manufacturing sector. Machinery growth was roughly at the rate of growth of GNP and durable goods in general. Given that primary metals and fabricated metal products grew even more slowly, this suggests that many final durable and nondurable consumer products increased more rapidly than their producer goods. These trends in fabricated metals and machinery indicate both a general increase in resource productivity and the compression of producer goods relative to consumer goods. To reiterate, the data are not influenced by changes in imports and exports. Table 7 also shows that the production of primary metals and products of mining underwent an absolute decline and that the physical volume of utilities virtually ceased to grow.

A similar overall pattern emerged in the 1980s in most Western market economies. The following table compares indexes of the physical volume of industrial production (including manufacturing, mining, and utilities) and real GNP in the largest market economies and Western Europe as a whole from 1980 to 1987 (OECD, 1989: 267; US Bureau of the Census, 1989: 823):

	Industrial production	Real GNP
United States	1.19	1.21
Japan	1.22	1.29
West Germany	1.05	1.11
United Kingdom	1.14	1.18
France	1.02	1.12
Italy	1.03	1.14
Netherlands	1.07	1.09
Australia	1.04	1.24
OECD Europe	1.08	1.13

Whether these are countries whose economies have a large mining sector (e.g., Australia, Great Britain) or little mining at all (e.g., Japan), whether they are net exporters (e.g., Japan and West Germany) or net importers (e.g., the United States) of manufacturing products, the pattern is the same. In all these countries, in the 1980s the physical volume of industrial production grew more slowly than in the 1970s and more slowly than the growth of real GNP.

This and earlier evidence suggests that the compression of resources over the production cycle, especially the slowdown in producer goods relative to final consumer goods, is a major factor in declining resource use and diminishing pollution. It can eventually lead to absolute reductions in the total physical volume of resource-originated outputs, although the volume of final consumer goods will increase. If population growth becomes zero or negative, consumer goods and nonresource outputs may become the only two growing components in market economies.

In the 1980s, a new term emerged in Western vernacular: de-industrialization. From both economic and environmental perspectives, I do not see anything wrong with this term, nor with the trend it describes.

Cost minimization under competitive markets and input maximization under regulated state monopolies

Most readers have probably already deduced from the previous discussion that something akin to the Invisible Environmental Hand is at work in market economies. Competitive firms in trying to maximize their profits have to, among other things, minimize their costs. They increase productivity through the use of capital stock and energy at early industrial stages when these both substitute for, and complement, labor. However, resources involved in energy conversion, materials processing, and the employment of machinery represent costs. All these costs continue to be minimized. The growth in resource productivity then outpaces the growth of resource output and eventually compresses the producer goods' part in the latter. Environmental disruption slows down after the initial rise and then declines at an increasing rate. This result was not a design of participants of open competitive markets. They were driven by profit motives to eventual environmental ends with no intention of their own.

The relationship between economic growth and pollution under competitive markets can also be put in this context. Long-term economic growth is impossible without technological progress. The latter eventually reduces resource use and environmental discharges. Paradoxically, then, long-term economic growth is impossible without environmental improvements. The Invisible Hand stretches out over two centuries and takes care of this.

Proliferation of (the waste of) resources over the production cycle

Under the alternative economic system of regulated socialist monopolies, the proliferation of resources over the production cycle never ceases. Recall Tables 5 and 6 and Figure 1. One can make a general comparison of the production cycle in the United States and the Soviet Union. In the second half of the 1980s, consuming about 1.6 times as much steel as the United States, the Soviet Union produced about 0.75–0.80 as much physical volume of metal-originated machinery and other producer goods (Kheinman, 1989:67). With these 75–80 percent of producer goods, the Soviet Union made less than 33 percent of final consumer goods relative to the United States (estimated from 40 percent of GNP per capita in the USSR compared with the United States; about 50 percent share of consumption in the Soviet GNP and 77 percent in the US GNP; and 18 percent larger population in the Soviet Union). The socialist economy can be thought of as a bottom-heavy pyramid with spreading slopes of resources, a gigantic corpus of producer goods, and a thin top of final consumer goods. I find it a suggestive coincidence that a roughly estimated overall ratio of resource inputs to final outputs and the total amount of pollution from stationary sources at the higher bound are both about 4.5–4.8 times higher in the Soviet Union than in the United States (the overall input/output ratio made allowances for the difference in population size and final output per capita).

Figures 3 and 4 present evidence for the two largest socialist economies, the Soviet Union and China, since 1940 and 1950, respectively. In both countries the gap widened between the production of energy (oil), primary and fabricated metals (pig iron and steel), and final household goods (fabrics and shoes) made with the use of resources and producer goods. The trends in production indexes are remarkably similar, although the Chinese economy has been fully independent of the Soviet economy at least since the

FIGURE 3   Indexes of industrial production, resources, and final goods, USSR, 1940–86

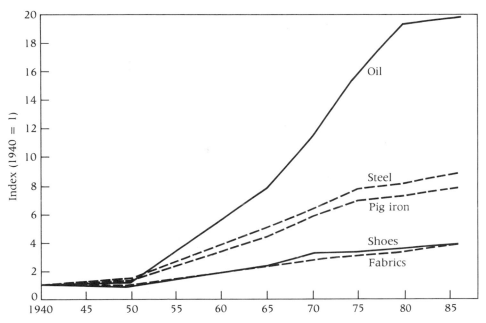

SOURCE: USSR State Committee on Statistics, "Razvitie Promyshlennosti SSSR," *Vestnik Statistiki*, no. 5 (1987), pp. 63–64.

late 1950s. This similarity in the proliferation of resources and intermediary inputs over the production cycle thus represents a systemic feature. The widening of the gap between the amount of resource inputs and final household outputs over decades cannot be simply attributed to low technological levels. Technology improves over the course of economic development, but this is overpowered by the systemic factors to which I now turn.

To emphasize the growth of producer goods relative to household goods consider, in addition to Table 6, some general trends. The share of final consumer goods in Soviet industrial production declined from 60.5 percent in 1928 to 39.0 percent in 1940, 31.2 percent in 1950, 27.5 percent in 1960, 26.6 percent in 1970, 26.2 percent in 1980, and 24.9 percent in 1987, and the share of producer goods increased accordingly (Kostin, 1989:12). At the same time, as I mentioned earlier, about 33 percent of the total Soviet industrial production in the 1980s, chiefly producer goods, are considered economically useless outputs, or wastes (Uliukaev, 1989:84). In the Soviet economy as a whole, the share of capital investment in the GNP grew in real terms from 24.2 percent in 1960 to 28.2 percent in 1970 to 33.0 percent in 1980, against about half as much in Western market economies (Ofer, 1987:1788, 1806). This simply means that machines produce other ma-

FIGURE 4   Indexes of industrial production, resources, and final goods, China, 1950–85

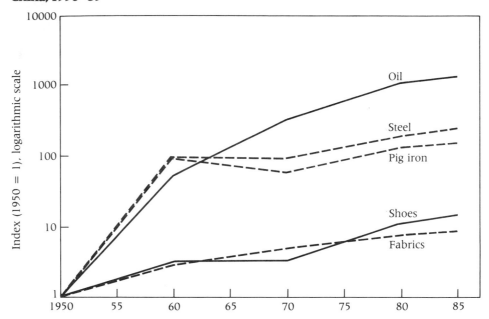

SOURCE: USSR State Committee on Statistics, "Kitaiskoi Narodnoi Respublike 40 Let," *Vestnik Statistiki*, no. 10 (1989), p. 58.

chines in order to produce other machines, which extract additional resources in order to produce more machines. Seliunin (1988:158–159) called this "a cannibalistic economy," "the self-feeding and self-devouring industrialized economy."

Figure 5 shows where this proliferation of wastes of resources over the production cycle eventually leads. The figure presents Soviet estimates of how much energy it takes and will take to produce energy over the period 1975–2035. In 1975, energy inputs (including energy used to produce equipment for energy extraction) constituted about 22 percent of energy output of natural gas. This fraction grew to 28 percent in 1980 and 32 percent in 1985 and 1990, and it is projected to increase to 46 percent in 1995, 58 percent in 2000, and so on, until it reaches 100 percent in 2030 and exceeds 100 percent thereafter. Net energy output grew in absolute terms until 1989 and began to decline thereafter. Absolute declines of gross output are projected after 2005. Inputs have grown faster than output, and this pattern applies to most economic activities. Moreover, inputs have grown faster than output at an increasing rate. Eventually, the relationship becomes backward-bending, that is, inputs continue to grow while output declines.

FIGURE 5 **Gross output, energy input, and net output of natural gas extraction, USSR, 1975–2035 (reported and officially projected)**

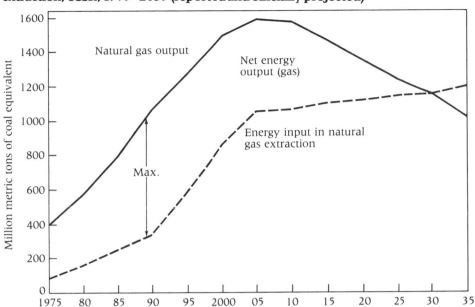

NOTE: Energy from 1 million metric tons of coal equivalent is equal to energy derived from 789 million cubic meters of natural gas.
SOURCE: D. Aksenov, "Strategiia Chistoi Energii," *Ekonomicheskaia Gazeta*, no. 16 (April 1989), p. 5.

Input maximization under regulated state monopolies

The remaining question is the causes of this pattern in socialist economies. I can offer a simple and quick proximate explanation of the proliferation of the waste of resources over the production cycle. At least in the last few decades, supply prices of most outputs are cost-based and enterprise profits are proportional to costs. If one does not believe that enterprise managers are loyal agents of the state but rather assumes that they are normal human beings who maximize enterprise profits for the sake of managerial bonuses, housing allocations for managers and workers, and other articles of wealth and power, a simple conclusion follows. In order to maximize profits, producers maximize inputs. It pays to maximize costs and wastes over the production cycle (see, e.g., Gorbachev, 1985:1–2; Valovoi, 1990:3).

This is a proximate explanation. Readers who find it sufficient can skip the rest of this section and go directly to the concluding section, which offers a global summary and future estimates of pollution under different scenarios. Others may consider the new theory of the socialist economy proposed by Kornai (1979, 1980, 1982, 1986) from which I will draw heavily and which I will also modify. The pre-Kornai literature, from Soviet economists of the 1920s to Western textbooks of the 1980s, emphasizes the demander-state in the absence of open competitive markets. The literature does not use this simple concept, though, but rather describes it via such familiar terms as central planning, the command economy, central management, and the like. The demander-state means that the government takes upon itself the determination of production in terms of both quantities and prices.

But the new theory implies that the demander-state is itself only an outcome of the supplier-state. The supplier-state is really at the core of the system in which the government maximizes power over individuals by economic means (and also maximizes its share of national income and its total revenues via suppressed wages). The supplier-state provides producer firms with inputs (resources, labor, and capital in terms of both money and producer goods) and provides households with consumer goods. In order to provide, the state needs to set up producer firms and to make them produce. The owner-state and the demander-state follow from this. Another implication is that the supplier-state that wants to maximize its supplier role must close the market entry and set up agencies and/or large producer firms that are product monopolies. Indeed, in the Soviet Union in the mid-1980s, the entire industrial production was divided between 46,000 firms (USSR State Committee on Statistics, 1989b:330). Compare this with 1,401,000 industrial establishments with payroll and 2,741,000 tax-paying industrial proprietorships and corporations in the United States (US Bureau of the Census, 1989:523, 517). In the Soviet Union, single corporations controlled by federal agencies produce from 74 percent to 94 percent of the volume of particular outputs, and the remainder of product markets belongs to local monopolies (e.g., Kholodkov, 1989; Volkov and Matiukhin, 1989).

Since the supplier-state is also the demander-state, these monopolistic producers are regulated state monopolies on which demand output quotas are imposed. In order to provide, the state has to maintain and expand production of its enterprises, and in order to secure production, the state has to maintain and expand provision of inputs. The state must increase output of resources and producer goods in order to supply its firms with inputs. Output maximization becomes the objective function of the supplier-state and the demander-state. The race between inputs and outputs becomes circular. Thus the state and its own monopolistic firms are locked in a mutually dependent relationship of inputs and outputs. Like any large functioning body, the supplier-state becomes dependent on its own parts.

The tournament between the interdependent state and its regulated monopolistic firms also becomes circular. Inputs cannot be provided by independent competitive firms since the latter do not exist. Output maximization renders the supplier-state more and more dependent on its own producer firms. But these corporations have their own natural interests, they are not loyal agents of the state, and they do not oblige with output maximization. Their interests are actually opposite to those of the state. The deman-der-state wishes more output at lower prices and with fewer inputs, while monopolistic firms wish to produce less output at higher prices and with more inputs. In the words of Kornai (1986:55), this is the central issue over which the well-known phenomenon of "plan bargaining" takes place. Iron-ically, the state, like any other consumer in a monopoly setting, has to suc-cumb to the producer's power and live with both shortages and high prices. Wassily Leontief, during his recent trip to the Soviet Union, made an appo-site remark. He said that shortages exist not simply due to the excessive de-mand for, and use of, resources and other products (as Kornai's theory implies), but because there are economic agents interested in shortages.

As in any other monopoly, the socialist firms raise prices and max-imize their rents from output reductions and price-raising, instead of maxi-mizing profits from output volume and cost reductions (see Tullock, 1967; Krueger, 1974; Wenders, 1987). This alone leads to low productivity of in-puts, the failure to adopt advanced technology, and a perpetual excessive use of resources. But the system absorbs inputs much beyond that. Unlike unregulated monopolies in many developing countries, where the govern-ment is not responsible for providing inputs and exerting outputs, socialist regulated monopolies cannot raise prices without the government's consent. They have to bargain with the government, justifying why prices should be raised and output underproduced.

From this follows a central point missing in Kornai's theory. The the-ory does not explain why firms would not economize their inputs. Why are the firms themselves interested in the excessive use of resources, which goes much beyond a mere waste of free or subsidized goods? Consider that al-though the enterprises do not have an effective budget constraint, they hit the supply constraint. Not everything can be obtained for money. Why, then, do they not use inputs more efficiently?

The interdependence of the state and the firms and the resulting inter-dependence of output maximization and input maximization provide an ex-planation. Like a bad and resisting secretary who receives less work from his/her boss than a good secretary, the regulated monopolistic firms are do-ing well by doing badly. They raise costs, fail new technology, waste re-sources, hoard producer goods, and otherwise maximize inputs in order to both justify the cost-based price increases and sabotage the state-imposed demand quotas for output. By maximizing inputs, the regulated monopolis-tic firms exert higher prices and higher profits while producing less. Enter-prises effectively show the state how many additional scarce inputs it will take to produce additional output at an even higher price—and the state stops the pressure and pays the price at a mutually agreeable level.

Input maximization is thus the best profit-maximizing behavior of reg-ulated state monopolies. Cost-based prices and cost-proportional profits that directly create input maximization have emerged in the interests of state monopolistic producers. This does not mean that the government is myopic, let alone blind, in allowing and even inviting these input-maximizing arrangements. Far from this, the government is fully aware that its producer firms will in any event raise prices, contract output, and maximize inputs as a means to achieve these aims. Cost-based prices and cost-proportional profits are then in the interest of the government as much so as they are in the interests of corporations. These are government monitoring devices, which provide negotiating ground where input–output and input–price agreements are reached between the demander-state and producers. Kornai (1986:viii) pointed out that some socialist arrangements are reminiscent of Western military industries. I relegate to the Appendix a more detailed and technical discussion of input maximization.

Input maximization on the enterprise level leads to the main paradox of the socialist economic system. The supplier-state strives for output maximization, but its own producer firms maximize profits via input maximization. Since the state economy is simply an aggregation of its producer firms over the production cycle, the entire system adopts the mode of input maximization. The state actually maximizes the production of inputs under the appearance of the maximization of output. As long as economic growth continues and the government collects revenues via suppressed wages and residual enterprise profits (after subtracting management bonuses, housing, and other direct allocations to enterprises, etc.), the government is content. When input maximization eventually impedes economic growth and inputs exceed outputs, the government revolts against its own system.

The special function of the waste of resources in input maximization

In the contest between the demander-state and its monopolistic producer firms, inputs of physical resources become a special weapon. Enterprises deliberately waste them in order to make the costs of additional production prohibitively steep for the government. Consider that producers make life difficult for the demanding government, not for their buying firms or consumers. The commercial buyers, that is other corporations, are willing to pay higher prices for additional output because they pass their costs via higher prices onto their own buyers at the next state of the production cycle. Consumers are also willing to pay, given the shortages—at least some consumers. The demand is price inelastic, as the Appendix illustrates. The pressure of all these buyers on the government for inputs and/or outputs is transmitted by the state to the producers of inputs. The pressure is circular over the production cycle. Collusion between firms for reducing demand pressures is not often feasible because few producers form a mutual input–output cycle.

Resource inputs and producer goods, unlike monetary inputs, are a physical constraint, and even the all-owning government cannot give more than it has. Therefore, maximization of resources, of all inputs, is the optimal means for producers to raise prices and reduce the demand output quotas. High input/output ratios and outright waste of resources and producer goods in production processes are the optimal means to increase profits. Socialist enterprises are interested in the waste of resources. In the Soviet Union, each five-year plan since the 1950s dictated final consumer goods to grow relative to producer goods, and each five-year period of actual economic performance ended the other way around. This is one of the fallouts of the system that the government could never control and has long since given up trying.

Which path of economic development?

Table 8 and Figure 6 summarize the long-term relationship between GNP per capita and energy use per capita, given the economic system. Recall that trends in environmental damage closely correspond to trends in resource use per capita; that energy use constitutes about one-half of total resource use; and that trends in energy use and total resource use per capita by economic system are very close over time. Hence, in the absence of other data of similar scope, the energy analysis in Table 8 and Figure 6 should be representative of the long-term trends in overall resource use and pollution per capita by economic system.

Following and modifying the original tests by Slade (1987:353–356), Table 8 analyzes the relationship between GNP per capita and energy use per capita in 1982 in 49 countries with different economic systems. There are four nested ordinary least squares regressions. The functional form is linear but I equalized the means so that coefficients represent elasticities. I added to Slade's tests a dummy variable called "statism" for socialist countries, both developed and developing (e.g., China, Cuba, Ethiopia), but not for Yugoslavia. Enterprises in Yugoslavia are more independent of the demander-state, and they do not need to practice input maximization.

In the first three equations, energy consumption per capita is regressed on GNP per capita, the quadratic term of GNP per capita, the type of economic system, and some other variables. Among them, equation 3 includes the shares of the labor force in industry and services. Resource use per capita is predicted to have a positive relationship with the former and a negative one with the latter. The number of observations is reduced in this equation due to lack of data.

The quadratic form of GNP per capita is added to the set of exogenous variables in all equations for the following reason. The predicted sign of the GNP–energy relationship in the overall sample of 49 developed market, de-

TABLE 8 Cross-national regressions of energy use per capita on GNP per capita and population size in nonlinear models, 1982

Equation number	1	2	3	4
Dependent variables	Energy consumption per capita			Total energy consumption
Independent variables				
Constant	−0.56** (2.96)	−1.48** (9.75)	−1.42** (5.58)	−5.52** (2.98)
GNP per capita	1.56** (5.97)	1.70*** (8.85)	1.40** (3.09)	2.35** (3.94)
GNP-per-capita squared	−0.45** (2.72)	−0.64** (4.86)	−0.44* (1.67)	−0.99*** (3.02)
United States and Canada		0.97*** (12.54)	1.25** (5.44)	2.98** (1.54)
Statism	0.46** (3.75)	0.45** (4.33)	0.25** (2.26)	0.98** (2.68)
Industry			0.46** (2.64)	
Service			−0.50 * (1.68)	
Population size				2.05** (2.96)
Population size squared				−0.85*** (2.78)
$\bar{R}^2$	0.74	0.86	0.89	0.66
F-statistic	47.36	75.63	45.77	16.86
N	49	49	33	49

NOTE: All estimates are heteroskedastic-consistent. t-statistics are in parentheses.
** Significant at 1 percent level
* Significant at 5 percent level

SOURCE: Margaret E. Slade, "Natural resources, population growth, and economic well-being," in D. Gale Johnson and Ronald D. Lee (eds.), *Population Growth and Economic Development: Issues and Evidence* (Madison: University of Wisconsin Press, 1987), p. 355. All estimates are mine.

FIGURE 6   Relationship between energy use per capita and GNP per capita under different economic systems, 1982

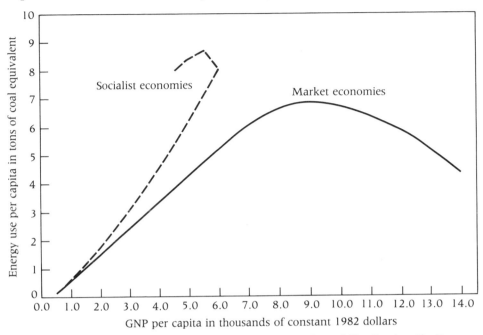

SOURCE: Derived from Jan Winiecki, *Economic Prospects—East and West* (London: The Centre for Research into Communist Economies, 1987), p. 25; and from Figure 1, Tables 5 and 8, and their sources.

veloped socialist, and various developing countries is positive. But the prediction is that the long-term relationship becomes negative in market economies and that the earlier positive relationship gradually lowers its slope over the course of economic growth. The quadratic form of GNP per capita tests the prediction that resource use per capita increases at a decreasing rate and then declines. In other words, the predicted sign of the coefficient of the GNP-per-capita squared is negative.

The fourth equation regresses total energy consumption on the same set of variables plus population size and the quadratic form of population size. The rationale for the latter is similar to using the quadratic form of GNP per capita. Following Slade (1987), a dummy variable for the United States and Canada (where per capita use of energy is higher than in other countries) was added in three of the four equations. This sharpens the performance of the regressions but does not change the nature of the findings (compare equations 1 and 2).

All the coefficients in all four equations have predicted signs and are statistically significant at the 1 percent or 5 percent level. The tests show that the currently prevailing relationship between resource use per capita and GNP per capita is positive but that the overall shape of this relationship is nonlinear. The shape of the curve is nonmonotonically concave and decreasing: as GNP per capita grows, resource use per capita decelerates and then declines. Interestingly, the relationship between population size and resource use has the same shape. The industrial share of the economy is positively and the share of services is negatively related to resource use per capita at each given level of GNP per capita. The principal finding concerns the role of statism. It is positively and statistically significantly related to resource use in all four equations.

Figure 6 depicts the actual shapes of the relationships between energy use per capita and GNP per capita in 1982 for the subsamples of market and socialist economies. The data are combined from Slade (1987: 355), Winecki (1987: 25), Figure 1, and Tables 5 and 8. This figure effectively summarizes the ideas and evidence of this article. It shows the split in the trends in resource use over the course of economic growth between market and socialist economies. In competitive market countries, the relationship between GNP per capita and resource use is initially positive; resource use increases at a decreasing rate in response to economic growth, until the level of development achieved some time in the 1970s turns the relationship into an increasingly negative one. In socialist countries, resource use per capita grows continuously over the course of economic growth, even after the economies begin to decline. Eventually, in accordance with Figure 5, resource use may decline as the economies decline further. The curve thus becomes backward-bending.

As I suggested above, the nonmonotonically concave and decreasing curve in market economies applies also to the long-term trends in pollution: over the course of their economic growth, pollution first increases at a decreasing rate and then declines. The case of socialist economies was simpler (i.e., ever-increasing pollution with or without economic growth), until economic crisis prompted both economic reform and environmental action.

Table 9 summarizes the range of the current state of emissions of traditional air pollutants by three groups of economies. Emissions include carbon monoxide, sulphur oxide, nitrogen oxide, particulate matter, volatile organic compounds, and lead. Table 9 also projects the increases in global pollution under different scenarios. In other words, how many times will the per capita amount of emissions increase if one or another of the current systems of production is adopted by the entire world. These estimates and projections are as tentative and rough as the current state of ignorance can provide. This is especially true for developed socialist countries, for which this article is a first attempt to estimate the lower and higher bounds of overall air pollution as discussed above. For less developed and newly industrialized countries, which constitute over three-fourths of the world population, estimates made by international agencies are taken as the lower bound. These agencies imply that about 100 MMT of air pollutants are emitted per

TABLE 9   Estimates of emissions of air pollutants in relation to population and economic development in three groups of economies, by three scenarios, ca. 1986

Panel A   Emissions of air pollutants

	Per capita (kilograms)	Per $1000 of GNP (kilograms)
Western market economies	350	30
Developed socialist economies (DSEs)		
Lower bound	350	75
Higher bound	800	175
Less developed and newly industrialized countries	50 (100)	75 (150)

Panel B   Percent of world's population, GNP, and air pollution

	Popula-tion	GNP	Air pollution Lower bound for DSEs	Air pollution Higher bound for DSEs
Western market economies	15.2	68.9	45.0	35.0 (28.0)
Developed socialist economies	7.5	13.7	22.3	40.0 (32.0)
Less developed and newly industrialized countries	77.3	17.4	32.7	25.0 (40.0)

Panel C   If the entire world assumes the parameters of a given economic setting, global emission of air pollutants will multiply as follows

With the parameters of	Multiplier for global pollution Per capita	Multiplier for global pollution Per $1000 of GNP
Western market economies		
Lower bound for DSEs	3.0	0.65
Higher bound for DSEs	2.3 (1.9)	0.50 (0.41)
Developed socialist economies		
Lower bound for DSEs	3.0	1.63
Higher bound for DSEs	5.3 (4.3)	2.92 (2.34)
Less developed and newly industrialized countries		
Lower bound for DSEs	0.4	1.88
Higher bound for DSEs	0.3 (0.5)	1.44 (2.30)

NOTES: The lower bound assumes a 77 percent rate of success in abatement of air pollution from stationary sources in developed socialist economies. The higher bound assumes a 30 percent rate. The numbers in parentheses refer to higher pollution estimates for less developed countries. Note that the *OECD Environmental Data Compendium* implies the amount of polluting discharges in all less developed and newly industrialized countries as about 100 million metric tons per year. This amount is almost certainly underestimated. Doubling the amount of discharges per $1000 of GNP and per capita in these countries in Panel A would alter the multipliers in Panel C. For the higher bound for DSEs, global pollution would increase 1.9 times under global market economies, 4.3 times under global socialist economies, and 0.5 times under global adoption of current economic parameters (including the standard of living) of less developed countries.
SOURCES: Population and GNP: Calculated from World Bank, *World Development Report 1988* (New York: Oxford University Press, 1988), pp. 187, 222–223. The average GNP per capita in developed socialist countries in 1986 is estimated as $5200, that is, 40 percent of that in Western market economies. Emission of air pollutants: Calculated from OECD, *OECD Environmental Data Compendium, 1989* (Paris: OECD, 1989), pp. 17–19. Pollution in socialist economies is estimated by the author. See the first and fourth sections of the text for discussion of estimates.

year in this part of the world. Since this number cannot be verified, I put in parentheses some estimates of what may happen if the true number is twice as high. These parentheses do not imply a preference for one or another bound.

Panel A of Table 9 simply points out that in 1986 the total global emissions of air pollutants was 577.1 MMT if pollution in both socialist and developing countries is calculated at the respective lower bounds. Global pollution was 742.4 MMT at the higher bound for socialist and at the lower bound for developing countries. And it was 931.5 MMT at the higher bound for both latter groups. On a per capita basis, pollution was 350 kg in market countries, from 350 kg to 800 kg in developed socialist countries (DSEs), and from 50 to 100 kg in less developed and newly industrialized countries. Interestingly, at both lower and higher bounds, pollution per $1000 of GNP was roughly the same in DSEs and developing countries. This alone shows that the higher technological level in DSEs could not overpower the systemic impact of input maximization and deliberately wasteful practices of resource use.

Panel B shows that Western market economies produce a smaller fraction of global pollution than their share of global GNP, while socialist countries produce a higher fraction. Both economies, of course, produce a higher fraction of world pollution than their share of world population. At the higher bound of pollution estimates, socialist countries produce a higher share of global pollution (from 32 percent to 40 percent) than Western market economies, although the latter have twice the share of world population and five times the share of global GNP.

Panel C provides multipliers of global pollution increases under different scenarios. These multipliers do not take into account future population growth because estimates are made only per $1000 of GNP and per capita. Also, they project future pollution per capita in terms of global averages. This actually means that only the areas with pollution lower than the chosen standard will increase environmental disruption (and much of this increase will be local). Panel C shows that in the unlikely case of the entire world moving to levels of GNP per capita and pollution per capita of the average developing country, global pollution per capita will decline from one-third to one-half of its present level. Given world population growth, present total amounts of emissions will not decline much under this scenario, and the total economic sacrifice may not be worth considering even from the extreme environmental standpoint.

The worst possible range of future pollution is provided by a global socialist scenario. Environmental damage will increase from 3.0 to 5.3 times per capita under global transition to socialist economic parameters, and twice that much given world population growth. The scenario of global economic development along the lines of Western market economies promises increases in air pollution per capita in the world from 1.9 to 3.0 times. Again, increases will be additionally doubled given world population growth. The picture may improve significantly if present trends in the reduction of pollution continue and accelerate over the course of economic growth in market economies. To conclude, the future of the world environment depends to a significant extent on the choice of economic system in developing countries.

Since economic development of currently less developed countries will increase local and global pollution under any conceivable scenario, two compensatory factors acquire special significance. One is the economic transition from regulated state monopolies to open competitive markets in socialist countries, especially in the Soviet Union and China. The other factor is continuous economic growth in Western market economies. Both these developments will be accompanied by major, continuous, and accelerating increases in resource productivity and reductions in resource use and pollution. These two compensatory factors may be large enough to offset global (but not local) impacts of economic development in less developed countries. These conclusions are either paradoxical or plain wrong from the standpoint of the standard literature. They are correct if the race between population growth and resource productivity is the driving force of economic development and if resource productivity is winning in the long term under market economies. At least, these conclusions offer some livable perspective for the world by reconciling economic development and the environment. And what do standard literature and standard policies offer on the global scope? Economic stagnation and elaborate international controls.

Appendix: A model of input maximization

Figure A-1 shows two combinations of quantities and prices on an inelastic demand curve *DD*. These two combinations reproduce the rent-seeking model of Tullock (1967; see elaboration in Wenders, 1987). Once product monopoly is obtained and the supply is inelastic in the absence of competitive markets, the demand also becomes inelastic. On an inelastic (vertically sloped) demand curve, it is more gainful for a monopolistic producer to sell the quantity Q_R at the price P_R than the quantity Q_C at the price P_C. The associated parallelograms drawn with broken and solid lines, respectively, show this.

If the monopoly is unregulated, there is no need to increase production costs. Higher prices can be charged and rents extracted, subject to the demand curve and the highest profitable combination of prices and quantities, irrespective of costs. These unit costs are shown on the marginal cost curve *MC*. Even in the absence of competition and downward price pressures, it is profitable for

FIGURE A-1   Rent-seeking and input maximization under unregulated and regulated monopolies

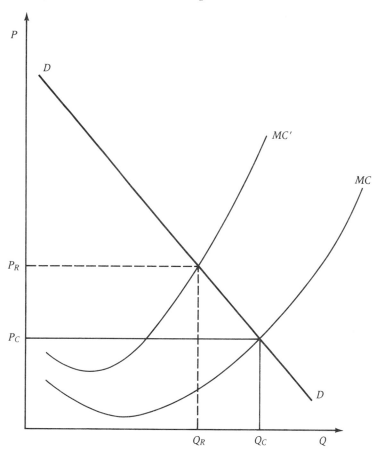

producers to reduce marginal costs, although they do not have as strong an incentive to do this as under competitive markets. But if the monopoly is state-owned and -regulated and the tournament takes place between the government and the producer over the combination of prices and quantities, this is a different game.

In order to reduce quantities to Q_R and raise prices to P_R, and to justify this most profitable combination, the regulated monopolistic firms have to uplift and reshape their marginal cost curves. The government has to face the impossibility of additional production beyond the point Q_R unless the demand curve is moved outward, capacity is increased, supplies of inputs are increased, and prices even higher than P_R are paid. Since the demander-state is simultaneously the supplier-state, the given demand curve signifies also the supply constraints of inputs (not only money, but also labor, capacity, resources, and producer goods). Raising production costs under the supplier-state means demanding more inputs. The uplifting of the marginal cost curve from *MC* to *MC'* by monopolistic producers puts the government at the edge. The combination of P_R and Q_R has to be accepted. The above logic also suggests that the new marginal cost curve *MC'* has to be steeper than *MC*.

Alternatively, the government has to enforce lower marginal costs. This can be done either by terrorizing enterprise management, or by using forced labor with few producer goods, or by confiscating output at nominal prices and not providing inputs. The third option is most suitable for agriculture where people have to produce for their own subsistence and where both subsistence output and inputs of seed and feed grains can be confiscated in lieu of salable outputs. This option, however, cannot be repeated for long and does not provide for necessary expansion of the supplier-state. The second option yields low productivity, and the first option was rejected by the managerial class when it became more powerful. The uplifting of the marginal cost curve then becomes the prevailing and winning game.

One needs to emphasize that under the supplier-state, raising production costs from *MC* to *MC'* means predominantly increasing physical inputs of resources and producer goods. These are the inputs whose maximization is the most powerful weapon for enterprises against the supplier-state. Input maximization is circular over the production cycle and is ever-growing. The supplier-state has to demand outputs that become inputs that are being maximized. This game of output maximization and input maximization is repeated over and over, until the system cannot be sustained.

References

Ayres, Robert U. 1978. *Resources, Environment, and Economics: Applications of the Materials/Energy Balance Principle.* New York: John Wiley and Sons.

———, and Allen V. Kneese. 1969. "Production, consumption, and externalities," *The American Economic Review* 59, no. 2: 282–297.

Gorbachev, M.S. 1985. "O sozyve ocherednogo XXVII sezda KPSS i zadachakh po ego podgotovke i organizatsii," *Pravda*, 24 April, pp. 1–5.

Gzovskii, V. 1985. "Sotsialnye problemy okhrany okruzhaiushchei sredy v stranakh SEV," *Voprosy Ekonomiki*, no. 12: 99–108.

Haveman, Robert H. 1974. "On estimating environmental damage: A survey of recent research in the United States," in OECD, *Environmental Damage Costs.* Paris: OECD, pp. 101–131.

Holdren, John P., and Paul R. Ehrlich. 1974. "Human population and the global environment," *American Scientist* 62: 282–292.

Iablokov, A. 1989. "Spasenie prirody i zakon," *Izvestiia*, 8 October, p. 2.

Illarionov, A. 1990. "Paradoksy statistiki," *Argumenty i Fakty*, no. 3: 6–7.

James, David. 1985. "Environmental economics, industrial process models, and Regional-Residuals Management models," in Allen V. Kneese and James L. Sweeney (eds.), *Handbook of Natural Resource and Energy Economics*, vol. 1. Amsterdam: North-Holland, pp. 271–324.

Kheinman, S. 1989. "O problemakh nauchno-tekhnicheskoi politiki," *Voprosy Ekonomiki*, no. 3: 65–74.

⭏⭏⭏⭏⭏⭏⭏⭏⭏⭏⭏

Kholodkov, V. 1989. "Diktat proizvoditelia i rynok," *Ekonomicheskaia Gazeta,* no. 22: 16.

Kneese, Allen V. 1977. *Economics and the Environment.* New York: Penguin Books.

———, Robert U. Ayres, and Ralph C. d'Arge. 1970. *Economics and the Environment: A Materials Balance Approach.* Baltimore: The John Hopkins Press for Resources for the Future.

Kornai, Janos. 1979. "Resource-constrained versus demand-constrained systems," *Econometrica* 47, no. 4: 801–819.

———. 1980. *Economics of Shortage,* vols. 1–2. Amsterdam: North-Holland.

———. 1982. *Growth, Shortage and Efficiency: A Macrodynamic Model of the Socialist Economy.* Berkeley: University of California Press.

———. 1986. *Contradictions and Dilemmas: Studies on the Socialist Economy and Society.* Cambridge, Mass.: MIT Press.

Kostin, L. 1989. "Litsom k cheloveku," *Agitator,* no. 15: 12–15.

Krueger, Anne. 1974. "The political economy of the rent-seeking society," *The American Economic Review* 64, no. 3: 291–303.

Lemeshev, M. Ia. 1985. "Prodovolstvennaia programma i okhrana okruzhaiushchei sredy," *Voprosy Ekonomiki,* no. 12: 79–89.

Lisovenko N., and V. Trach. 1989. "Protivogaz dlia goroda," *Izvestiia,* 5 October, p. 3.

Lukianenko, V. 1989. "Drama vody," *Pravda,* 11 August, p. 2.

OECD. 1989. *OECD Environmental Data Compendium, 1989.* Paris: OECD.

Ofer, Gur. 1987. "Soviet economic growth: 1928–1985," *The Journal of Economic Literature* 25, no. 4: 1767–1833.

Samsonov, E. 1989. "Tsena zemli," *Pravitelstvennyi Vestnik,* no. 19: 11.

Seliunin, Vasilii. 1988. "Glubokaia reforma ili revansh biurokratii?" *Znamia,* no. 7: 155–167.

Simon, Julian L. 1981. *The Ultimate Resource.* Princeton: Princeton University Press.

Simons, Marlise. 1990. "Pollution's toll in Eastern Europe: Stumps where great trees once grew," *The New York Times,* 19 March, p. 9.

Slade, Margaret E. 1987. "Natural resources, population growth, and economic well-being," in *Population Growth and Economic Development: Issues and Evidence,* ed. D. Gale Johnson and Ronald D. Lee. Madison: University of Wisconsin Press, pp. 331–369.

Smil, Vaclav. 1984. *The Bad Earth: Environmental Degradation in China.* New York: M. E. Sharpe.

———, and T. Kuz. 1976. "A new look at energy and GDP correlation," *Energy International* 13, no. 1: 31–34.

Tsaturov, Iu. S. 1989. "Kto dast nam shans," *Nedelia,* no. 33: 13.

Tullock, Gordon. 1967. "The welfare costs of tariffs, monopolies and theft," *Western Economic Journal* 5, no. 2: 224–232.

Uliukaev, A. 1989. "Novaia istoriia gammelnskogo dudochnika," *Kommunist,* no. 18: 78–86.

United Nations Environment Programme. 1987. *Environmental Data Report.* Oxford: Basil Blackwell.

UN Food and Agriculture Organization. 1988. *FAO Yearbook. Production. 1987,* vol. 41. Rome.

US Bureau of the Census. 1989. *Statistical Abstract of the United States. 1989.* Washington, D.C.: US Government Printing Office.

US President. 1987. *Economic Report of the President, 1987.* Washington, D.C.: US Government Printing Office.

USSR State Committee on Statistics. 1989a. *Okhrana Okruzhaiushchei Sredy i Ratsionalnoe Ispolzovanie Prirodnykh Resursov SSSR.* Moscow: Finansy i Statistika.

———. 1989b. *Narodnoe Khoziaistvo SSSR v 1988 Godu. Statisticheskii Ezhegodnik.* Moscow: Finansy i Statistika.

———. 1989c. "Selskoe khoziaistvo," *Politicheskoe Obrazovanie,* no. 6: 13–14.

USSR Supreme Soviet. 1989. "O neotlozhnykh merakh ekologicheskogo obnovleniia strany," *Pravda,* 3 December, pp. 1–2.

Valentei, A. 1990. "Ob ekologii bez prikras," *Ekonomika i Zhizn,* no. 3: 24.

Valovoi, D. 1990. "Plata za rastochitelstvo," *Pravda,* 2 March, p. 3.

Volkov, N., and G. Matiukhin. 1989. "Konkurentsiia i monopolii," *Pravda,* 29 June, p. 4.

Voloshin, V. 1990. "Kakuiu vodu my piem," *Okhrana Truda i Sotsialnoe Strakhovanie*, no. 1: 2–7.

Wenders, John T. 1987. "On perfect rent dissipation," *The American Economic Review* 77, no. 3: 456–459.

Winiecki, Jan. 1983. "Resource constraints and East European foreign trade structures," *Intereconomics: Review of International Trade and Development* 18, no. 3: 125–129.

_____ . 1987. *Economic Prospects—East and West.* London: The Centre for Research into Communist Economies.

Population and Resources under the Socialist Economic System

Elwood Carlson
Mikhail S. Bernstam

THE RECENT EXPERIENCE OF DEVELOPED SOCIALIST COUNTRIES calls for a revision of the standard view of the relationship between population growth, economic expansion, and natural resources. The standard approach (e.g., Holdren and Ehrlich, 1974) is to view resource depletion and environmental degradation as a function of population growth and economic growth. The experience of the Soviet Union and Eastern Europe since the 1970s suggests a more complicated relationship.

This recent development in socialist countries suggests that resource depletion, environmental disruption, and their impacts on rising mortality can occur virtually without growth in population and the economy. Recent literature suggests that a steady long-term depletion of energy resources in socialist countries is a direct result of an overall economic decline rather than economic expansion (e.g., Aksenov, 1989). Adverse environmental and demographic effects may even increase with the decline in growth of both population and the economy, and especially with the latter's absolute decline (see, e.g., Gzovskii, 1985). Neither population growth nor economic expansion thus seems to qualify as a necessary condition of modern environmental crises. At the same time, as the present essay will discuss, the socialist economic system may provide a sufficient (although not necessary) condition for environmental and demographic problems.

We will try to show that the socialist economy has system-specific mortality impacts, both related to and independent of environmental hazards. The most conspicuous of these impacts is relatively high and (until very recently) rising mortality in the prime working ages. It can in part be attributed to the high incidence of industrial accidents under the state-owned monopolistic production system. Other instances of mortality increase can be attributed to localized environmental degradation (e.g., deterioration of water quality) in areas of large-scale development projects.

There is, however, one case in the developed socialist world, that of Soviet Central Asia, where rapid population growth in rural areas coincided with growing pollution of water supplies and rising infant and overall mortality. Yet, these adverse effects are caused by an external factor—namely the USSR government policy of the expansion of cotton plantations in climatically suitable areas, with the excessive use of fresh water and pesticides—rather than by internal population pressure on resources.

Our discussion starts with a brief description of economic and environmental features of the socialist system. The next sections provide a detailed analysis of mortality in Hungary, Czechoslovakia, and the Soviet Union, using demographic and econometric methods.

The power of monopolistic producers and the environmental and demographic implications

Among widely discussed generic characteristics of socialist economies are high resource intensity, high volume of inputs per unit of output, and relatively low productivity of resources and other factors of production (Bergson, 1978, 1987; Kornai, 1979, 1980, 1982; Winiecki, 1987; see also Bernstam in this volume). The high volume of resource inputs in processing over the production cycle entails high emission of polluting residuals and potentially high adverse impacts on human health.

One can compare socialist and market economies in this context. In 1986 the Soviet Union produced more than twice as much emission of air pollutants as the United States: 273.3 and 127.7 million metric tons, respectively (USSR State Committee on Statistics, 1988a: 571; and US Bureau of the Census, 1989: 200). Dollar estimates of Soviet gross national product are currently uncertain. If Soviet GNP is about half the size of the US GNP (as US official estimates maintained before a 90 percent devaluation of the ruble in late 1989), the USSR/US ratio of pollution per $1 of GNP is 4:1. The ruble devaluation suggests that real Soviet GNP must be lower and the relative Soviet–US pollution ratio per $1 of GNP must be higher. Winiecki (1987: 77) estimated that East Germany produces more than four times as much air pollution per capita as West Germany at half the level of gross domestic product per capita. The resulting ratio of pollution per one DM of GDP is 8:1.

These physical outcomes can be put in the context of systemic economic features. Modern theoretical work views socialist economies as "supply constrained," while their individual enterprises are not effectively constrained by demand, prices, and costs (Kornai, 1979, 1980, 1982, 1986). The state owns resources and enterprises, provides for economic inputs and consumption, and, at least on paper, controls production. When this system of centralized state control began, a true command economy (enforced by terror against managers and workers) insured planned output quotas and redistributional restraint. To the extent this overt coercion has been abandoned, the system must turn to alternate means of enforcing output quotas, typically including subsidies to producer firms—resource provisions, credits, price allowances, wage and bonus increases above productivity, and high unearned profits. In the socialist system the idea of centralized state control of production has become a mask for the monopoly power of producer firms controlling most of the economy (Aven and Shironin, 1987). Aganbegian (1987: 2) suggests that "by subsidies the state created a harmful development, the power of monopolistic producers." Gorbachev (1985: 1) found that

> [T]he management of many economic branches and enterprises strives to beat out of the state as much capital investment, tools and equipment, energy, and resources as possible. They use these irresponsibly and do not work to full productive capacity.

The degree of monopolization of specific types of industrial output by large individual corporations in the Soviet Union is reported to range from 74 percent to 85 percent depending on the industry, while product-specific government agencies command 100 percent of their respective product markets (Kholodkov, 1989: 16; Volkov and Matiukhin, 1989; Nikerov, 1990: 2). Pressure from monopolistic firms for state-supplied inputs reinforced the state's pressure on producer firms for output quotas. This in turn generated upward pressure on prices and subsidies. Soviet estimates show that in the 1960s, 1970s, and 1980s, average productivity of the machine tool industry's output rose by about one-third of the price increases. For a 25–50 percent improvement in productivity of metal-cutting tools, producers triple and quadruple their prices. Extractive equipment prices increased 10–15 percent per year without any positive change in productivity (Gelvanovskii, 1989: 18; Shmelev and Popov, 1989: 42; Ericson, 1988). This cost/inputs maximization led to a mutually reinforcing web of price increases and resource pumping. Shatalin (1987: 57) argues that:

> There is not another economy in the world in which resources were free to users in such abundance. . . . Labor resources, natural resources, new capital investment, old capital stock, and what not.

The monopoly power of heavily subsidized producers generates a unique cycle of economic development in the socialist system, with direct implications for resource use and pollution control. Producer firms maximize inputs and prices, resist risks associated with new technology or organizational change, and minimize outputs. This generates a low-productivity, high input/low output economy.

The production cycle from natural resources to consumer goods becomes a steep pyramid deriving from the dependence of the state on producer firms—a hierarchical system with the power to insulate itself from real
costs and competition, a system that eventually begins to consume itself.
Socialist economic development becomes characterized by growing inputs
and declining productivity.

Due to consolidation and overlap of political and economic decisionmaking, economic monopoly and position in the production process translate into political leverage and a disproportionate claim on resources and
subsidies. Over time, the entire production process becomes increasingly
concentrated at the lowest stages, and the ratio of outputs to inputs inexo-
rably declines until a point of excess inputs dependence is reached (in the
mid-1970s in the Soviet Union, for example) at which the rate of growth of
inputs begins to exceed the rate of growth of outputs (see Ofer, 1987;
Khanin, 1988).

A combination of high resource intensity and the monopolistic power
of producers in the socialist economy has significant environmental and
demographic consequences. We have already mentioned high environmental disruption per capita and per unit of national product. The monopolistic
power of state-owned noncompetitive producer firms leads to adverse environmental impacts not only via high resource intensity of production but
also directly. The government is effectively dependent on the output of pro
ducer firms to provide both inputs to other producer firms and products to
consumers. In this setting, production takes priority over environmental
conditions and their impacts on population. Environmental externalities are
either discounted by the government or defiantly produced by enterprises
regardless of government intentions.

A typical case pending before the USSR Supreme Court concerns a synthetic rubber plant in the city of Voronezh in the south of Central Russia.
Over the course of 20 years, this plant generated emissions of air pollutants
of 511,000 metric tons per annum. This is an amount only marginally lower
than that produced by entire small industrial countries such as Ireland and
New Zealand (OECD, 1989: 17). The same plant discharged 14.6 million cubic meters of polluted water, which is comparable to discharges registered in
the mouth of the Seine, one of the major European rivers (United Nations
Environment Programme, 1987: 54). For 20 years, economic agencies of the
central and local government could not restrain this plant until, under the
economic reform, the USSR Attorney's Office closed down one of the plant's
shops in 1988. The Attorney's Office reports that morbidity in the area surrounding the plant increased by 20 percent from 1967 to 1987 due to air and
especially water pollution (USSR Attorney's Office, 1989: 19).

This situation was possible because large industrial corporations exercise both economic power and effective political power over other institu-

tions and over population. About 35 percent of the Soviet population, more than 100 million people, live in one-company towns where the entire infrastructure, local government, and living conditions are commanded by factory management (Nikiforov, 1986: 116).

Special environmental and demographic pressures also emerge when the government implements large-scale development projects such as oil industry expansion in the Soviet North and cotton plantation expansion in Soviet Central Asia and Azerbaijan. The power of industrial and agricultural management over natural, environmental, and human resources in such areas can be predicted to be especially significant. We should expect to find specific impacts on human mortality in such areas during periods of major development projects. Later in this essay we test this prediction using environmental and mortality evidence.

In addition to affecting mortality and morbidity via environmental deterioration, the monopolistic power of producers has a direct demographic impact. In the absence of free market entry and given minimal employment opportunities outside the socialized sector, the monopolistic enterprises have monopsony power with respect to labor. This monopsony power is greatly enhanced at the local and factory level by reduced opportunities for labor mobility due to residence restrictions and absence of a free housing market. Thus, while the government to a significant extent guarantees employment, working conditions and housing allocation are in the hands of individual enterprise management. It is not really possible for the government to enforce work safety even when it intends to. Numerous safety regulations remain largely a bureaucratic issue unrelated to real economic interests (Shishenkov, 1986; Sorokin, 1989a; Arutiunian, 1989; Volin, 1989). According to the USSR Council of Trade Unions survey, over 75 percent of Soviet laborers work under conditions that are classified as dangerous, hazardous, or both (USSR Council of Trade Unions, 1989; Volin, 1989: 10).

Work safety and general maintenance of working conditions interfere with management's production priorities. There are no independent insurance markets or other economic devices for workers' protection. Trade unions were, until very recently, subordinate to management. Whereas improving work safety increases production costs on which management cannot capitalize in order to raise output prices, paying compensation for injuries and hiring compensatory labor does help producers to increase the wage fund and pass the costs on to higher prices. Thus, as the USSR Council of Trade Unions recently found, industrial accidents are actually in the direct economic interest of enterprises (Sukhoruchenkova, 1989; see also Volkov and Matiukhin, 1989).

Another implication of the monopolistic power of producers for work safety and mortality is the quality of producer goods. In noncompetitive product markets, buyers cannot demand and control safety of producer goods. Accordingly, the USSR Council of Trade Unions found that only 8 percent of Soviet machine tools and related equipment meet government safety regulations (USSR Council of Trade Unions, 1989; Sorokin, 1989b: 3; Volin, 1989: 10). In addition, workers themselves have incentives to sacrifice safety for productivity. While the government guarantees employment and while persistent labor shortages create full employment by default, it would not be possible to monitor and enforce workers' performance if wages were simply set per hour. Productivity under this system cannot be enforced by potential layoffs. Therefore, the government and enterprises set a complex wage structure under which individual wages are based on a mix of formal credentials and actual productivity. Productivity-based wages make workers themselves disregard safety (Vorobievskii, 1989 and references cited therein).

We have surveyed five aspects of the socialist economic system relevant to demographic conditions, especially to working-age mortality: (1) high and growing resource intensity; (2) the monopoly power of state-owned enterprises over environmental and other living conditions; (3) the monopsony power of management over labor and working conditions; (4) the monopoly power of producers over the quality of their output; and (5) the productivity-based wages under guaranteed employment. We expect these factors to contribute significantly to the high and rising mortality in socialist countries. Later we test whether this reasoning finds support in the data.

Environmental signature of the socialist system

Each economic system displays a characteristic environmental "fingerprint" based on its intrinsic dynamic of resource use and disposal of residuals and waste. Under socialism, state ownership of natural resources actually means reduced environmental costs impinging on producer firms (McIntyre and Thornton, 1978), resulting from their leverage as monopoly suppliers to the next level of production. Despite political insulation for such monopolistic producer firms against environmental (extraction and disposal) costs, however, what seemed from a static perspective to be an abundance of resources in fact produced scarcity.

The gradual deterioration of the ratio of output produced to resources consumed, inherent in the institutional structure of the socialist system, leads to additional pressure on resources. The economy responds wherever possible by substituting greater resource consumption, intensifying the environmental effects already described. Admittedly, substitution between resources on the one hand and labor and capital on the other is limited. But there are cases in which substitution of resources and rudimentary capital for labor and technology is possible, such as excessive application of pesticides on plantations and excessive use of fuels instead of insulation in industrial and residential construction.

At the other end of the economic process, controls on disposal of wastes reflect the same growing dependency on inputs, the same increasingly bottom-heavy economic structure, and the same insulation of firms from the environmental costs of their actions. These features of the socialist system largely explain the fact, for example, that if the amount of sulphur dioxide emitted per unit of gross domestic product is set at an index of 100 for West Germany, then the comparable figure for East Germany is 490, for Czechoslovakia 485, for Hungary 386, for Poland 332, for Romania 279, for Bulgaria 229, and the USSR 236. Comparisons of nitric oxide emissions are equally unfavorable (Slama, 1986). Water pollution presents a similar picture, particularly in Poland where even in 1980 about 45 percent of all sewage from industrial and municipal sources was completely unpurified upon emission, and most of the remainder received only mechanical treatment incapable of removing soluble wastes.

> The purification of municipal sewage is especially inadequate. Over 450 cities, including 20 cities with over 50,000 residents (among them, Krakow, Lodz, and Warsaw) still lack municipal treatment facilities; Warsaw is one of only two national capitals in Europe without such facilities. (Kramer, 1987: 154)

Not all pollution indicators are uniformly worse in the socialist system. Policies directly related to the systemic goal of centralized control and management (for example, decisions to develop mass transit and suppress private automobile use) reduce pollution generated by autonomous individual activities disproportionately. This reinforces the impression of a characteristic pattern of waste disposal as well as resource use in the socialist system, distinct from the overall level of economic development achieved. Of course, one must consider potentially confounding natural conditions. Thus environmental problems have been judged to be worse in Eastern Europe, in particular the northernmost states (Poland, East Germany, Czechoslovakia, and Hungary) than in the Soviet Union and most of Western Europe (Oldberg, 1985). This situation results from a combination of different mixes of terrain, population density, and development. Oldberg's view is tempered by recognition of such variations in the countries singled out for attention. One important illustration might be the dominant role of coal as a fuel, which has made the area from Polish Silesia across Bohemia to Saxony and Thuringia the most polluted in Europe (Oldberg, 1985: 295).

Quite apart from natural conditions as factors to be controlled, highly centralized economic management and fusion of institutional subsystems (political, economic, legal, and so on) produce clear and distinctive environmental outcomes. On the economic side, the distinctiveness stems from growth of the bottom-heavy pyramid of monopoly producer firms. On the political side, the same consolidation and centralization mean the system has no mechanism for adjusting to consumer and citizen influence. These facts argue against the notion of convergence in environmental disruptions from different societal systems (Goldman, 1970; Dahmen, 1971; Hanson, 1971; McIntyre and Thornton, 1974, 1978; Ziegler, 1980).

Demographic signature of the socialist system

Just as a distinctive pattern of resource extraction and waste disposal is a predictable outcome of the socialist system, so are certain demographic outcomes. One such outcome is decline to quite low levels of fertility.

Socialist societies share the fertility profile of other developed welfare states, but the socialist system also exhibits special demographic characteristics. Economic effects already outlined simply carry over into the realm of demographic processes. Dependence of economic growth on inputs rather than productivity eventually hits a demographic restraint in the form of a finite labor force. However, such feedback effects are largely denied any influence upon the consolidated mechanism for making plans and decisions. Instead, families face a chronic quantitative and qualitative inadequacy of consumer products in general, and more particularly of housing and household amenities. Housing shortages are reinforced by residence and mobility restrictions. Decisionmakers must then resort to episodic, imperative pronatalist plans and commands. This characteristic approach of the socialist system's command structure to the demographic externalities it produces in its own internal environment gives rise to certain distinctive features of fertility —notably, an earlier and more universal entry into marriage and/or parenthood, followed by a compensatory restriction of completed family size.

The demographic signature of the socialist system also encompasses distinctive mortality patterns. Large-scale government projects to improve labor productivity through universal education and massive public health programs met with dramatic early successes in all developed socialist countries. However, a slowdown of economic growth weakened all these efforts.

The last 25 years have seen the advent of a more pernicious demographic pattern. Death rates for working-age men began to increase in the early or mid-1960s in the Soviet Union and most of the countries of Eastern Europe (Valkovics, 1984; Bourgeois-Pichat, 1985; Jozan, 1986a; Okolski, 1987). While much remains to be learned about this trend, it is already clear that the age pattern of the rising death rates (Giersdorf and Schuler, 1984; Valkovics, 1984; Carlson and Watson, 1988), the causes of death involved (Okolski and Pulaska, 1983; Scholz et al., 1984; Strnad and Kopecky, 1985; Jozan, 1986b), and even the concentration of the increase in certain population strata (Carlson and Watson, 1988; Carlson, 1989) all point to a clear and distinctive influence of social structure on patterns of death. Although this impact appears to different degrees and in varying forms in different countries in the region, in each case the underlying effect centered on men in the working ages and was characterized by a similar cause structure of mortality. We turn now to an empirical analysis of these trends and their possible causes. We will try to separate direct environmental impacts from the above-postulated systemic economic impacts, which influence mortality either via environmental conditions or via working and living conditions.

Direct environmental and systemic economic impacts on mortality

The burden placed on water and sewage systems by massive population influx to cities, or the effects of air and water pollution on human life and health, do not depend on the economic or political system.

Pollutants introduced into the air have clear demographic effects, as demonstrated on a local scale, for example, by seasonal variation in carbon monoxide poisoning in urban Korea, caused by burning coal for domestic heat (Kim, 1985). Balarajan (1983) asserts a relationship between malignant lymphomas and exhaust fumes inhaled by transport workers in Britain. On a larger, societal scale, debate continues about the widespread health and mortality effects of air pollution (Chappie and Lave, 1982; Lipfert, 1984; Selvin et al., 1984). One of the studies that did find a link between air pollution and mortality concerned the city of Cracow in Poland and specified the clearest effects for men, especially in interaction with smoking (Krzyzanowski and Wojtyniak, 1982).

A dramatic example of water pollution was the so-called minimata disease observed as a result of industrial effluent poisoning in Japan (Tamashiro et al., 1986). Epidemiologic evidence of increased mortality has also been demonstrated for insecticides used in agriculture in the Philippines (Loevinsohn, 1987).

Environmental damage is a public bad on a large scale. It should affect all ages and both sexes, given heterogeneity of most settlements. Increasing death rates in socialist countries, however, show remarkable unanimity in their concentration among men rather than women, and in their concentration at certain ages.

Eastern European nations experienced rising death rates at young adult and working ages, while the phenomenon does not appear in Western Europe. The pattern was universal throughout Eastern Europe and is strikingly similar to Soviet mortality trends discussed later. The fact that vulnerable groups in Eastern Europe such as children and old people have been largely immune to increasing death rates makes it unlikely that any generalized, direct environmental cause is responsible for the increase.

Information on causes of death reinforces this conclusion. Tables 1 and 2 show probabilities of dying from selected causes in Hungary and Czechoslovakia for 1965 and 1985, spanning the period in which death rates were

**TABLE 1   Independent probabilities of dying by sex and age group
for major causes of death: Hungary, 1965, 1985, and ratio 1985/1965**

	Ages 30–59			Ages 60–84		
	1965	1985	Ratio: 1985/65	1965	1985	Ratio: 1985/65
Males						
All causes	.16657	.27287	1.64	.86439	.87365	1.01
Neoplasms	.04208	.06741	1.60	.28034	.34771	1.24
Heart disease	.04364	.08028	1.84	.48801	.44383	0.91
Stroke	.01340	.02770	2.07	.31414	.30237	0.96
Pneumonia	.00134	.00257	1.86	.02615	.01077	0.41
Cirrhosis	.00416	.02730	6.56	.01518	.04086	2.69
Bronchitis, emphysema, and asthma	.00131	.00874	6.67	.01720	.12082	7.03
Motor vehicles	.00566	.00815	1.44	.00510	.01197	2.35
Suicide	.01763	.02914	1.65	.02461	.03621	1.47
Other external	.01045	.02248	2.15	.03898	.06244	1.60
Remainder	.03947	.03687	0.93	.38952	.32964	0.85
Females						
All causes	.10542	.12589	1.19	.78737	.73964	0.94
Neoplasms	.03982	.04311	1.08	.19592	.20400	1.04
Heart disease	.02448	.02639	1.08	.43389	.33726	0.78
Stroke	.01131	.01469	1.30	.27623	.24729	0.90
Pneumonia	.00072	.00090	1.25	.01903	.00686	0.36
Cirrhosis	.00162	.01003	6.18	.00842	.01344	1.60
Bronchitis, emphysema, and asthma	.00032	.00327	10.19	.00772	.04143	5.37
Motor vehicles	.00077	.00222	2.85	.00187	.00529	2.84
Suicide	.00650	.00805	1.24	.01077	.01354	1.26
Other external	.00189	.00486	2.58	.03964	.05297	1.34
Remainder	.02250	.01931	0.86	.29485	.24875	0.84

NOTES: Mortality rates converted to cumulative force of mortality (Kenneth Manton and Erik Stallard, *Recent Trends in Mortality Analysis*, Orlando: Academic Press, 1984). Probabilities of dying shown are antilogs of age-cumulated force of mortality figures. Probability of surviving (unity minus probability of dying) for all causes equals the cumulative product of survival probabilities for all cause-of-death categories.
SOURCES: Five-year central mortality rates and deaths by age, sex, and cause taken from Hungarian Central Statistical Office, *Demographic Yearbook 1965* and *Demographic Yearbook 1985* (Budapest, 1966 and 1986, respectively).

rising in Eastern Europe as a whole. These probabilities of dying are calculated from age-specific death rates for five-year groups, as published by the
Hungarian and Czechoslovak statistical agencies. The probability of surviving all causes of death (unity minus the probability of dying shown for "all

TABLE 2   Independent probabilities of dying by sex and age group for major causes of death: Czechoslovakia, 1965, 1985, and ratio 1985/1965

	Ages 30–59			Ages 60–84		
	1965	1985	Ratio: 1985/65	1965	1985	Ratio: 1985/65
Males						
All causes	.17515	.22129	1.26	.86719	.88594	1.02
Neoplasms	.04924	.06774	1.38	.32841	.34503	1.05
Heart disease	.05321	.06123	1.15	.43557	.45804	1.05
Stroke	.00894	.01737	1.94	.24348	.31529	1.29
Pneumonia	.00201	.00509	2.53	.06548	.07890	1.20
Cirrhosis	.00418	.01177	2.82	.01829	.02538	1.39
Bronchitis, emphysema, and asthma	.00617	.00532	0.86	.12673	.10270	0.81
Motor vehicles	.00771	.02057	2.67	.01000	.05525	5.53
Suicide	.01298	.01316	1.01	.02092	.01870	0.89
Other external	.01382	.01561	1.13	.03762	.04709	1.25
Remainder	.03079	.02684	0.87	.38031	.34055	0.90
Females						
All causes	.09788	.09426	0.96	.76467	.74834	0.98
Neoplasms	.03918	.03849	0.98	.19935	.18664	0.94
Heart disease	.02192	.01584	0.72	.36253	.31276	0.86
Stroke	.00639	.00895	1.40	.21663	.26887	1.24
Pneumonia	.00123	.00163	1.33	.04678	.05242	1.12
Cirrhosis	.00124	.00302	2.44	.01087	.00914	0.84
Bronchitis, emphysema, and asthma	.00158	.00176	1.11	.04946	.02749	0.56
Motor vehicles	.00127	.00416	3.28	.00362	.05213	14.40
Suicide	.00434	.00307	0.76	.00723	.00650	0.90
Other external	.00308	.00318	1.03	.03948	.04989	1.26
Remainder	.02147	.01781	0.83	.30880	.24628	0.80

NOTES: See Table 1.
SOURCES: Five-year central mortality rates and deaths by age, sex, and cause taken from Czechoslovak Central Statistical Office, *Statistical Yearbook 1965* and *Statistical Yearbook 1985* (Prague, 1966 and 1986, respectively).

causes") is equal to the cumulative product of probabilities of surviving for each cause category shown (one minus the probability of dying for each cause category). Figures are presented separately for males and females, and for working ages (30 to 59 years) and retirement ages (60 to 84 years).

Hungary represents the extreme case of such increases, while Czechoslovakia represents a more moderated rise in death rates for middle-aged men. In Hungary, little if any possible direct environmental causation can be inferred from cause-of-death statistics. To the contrary, the largest increases occurred for causes of death associated with self-administered toxins, such as smoking and drinking, and for stroke. The respiratory diseases that might indicate air pollution problems (bronchitis, emphysema, and asthma) actually showed the greatest increases in rural areas with the smallest populations (Hungarian Central Statistical Office, 1987), so the serious pollution problems of cities may be overbalanced by rural exposure to airborne particulate residues from heavy fertilizer and pesticide use. In Czechoslovakia, only working-age men exhibited clearly increasing death rates, although for certain causes such as cirrhosis of the liver and motor vehicle accidents, dramatic increases were observed among women and in old age as well. For working-age men these were the fastest-rising causes of death, with the increase in cirrhosis deaths actually matching the increase for heart disease even in absolute terms. In all age and sex groups in Czechoslovakia, pneumonia deaths also increased noticeably, perhaps indicating growing problems of health care delivery, but this does not represent a direct environmental impact so much as an outcome of social organization. The case of East Germany is even more important because, although levels of pollution there are higher than in most other areas in Europe, death rates have shown less increase there than anywhere else in Eastern Europe.

The main trends in Soviet mortality in the 1960s, 1970s, and early 1980s show patterns remarkably similar to the Eastern European patterns. Soviet trends are presented in Figures 1–4 and Tables 3–6. Data in Figures 1–4 are expressed as age-specific probabilities of dying, that is, life table's $q_x s$ in 1958–59, 1964–65, 1969–70, and 1984–85 (relative over time, female relative to male, and rural relative to urban). This is the most comprehensive data set on Soviet mortality change over the last 30 years available to date. Numerical values associated with these diagrams are not available, and we thus reproduce the data as presented in the source.

Provided these newly released official data are accurate, the Soviet Union clearly experienced significant mortality increases during this period, especially in the second half of the 1960s and in the 1970s and early 1980s. It is clear that these increases were not universal, which makes one skeptical in evaluating a hypothesis of direct overall environmental deterioration as the cause. Mortality increases over several time intervals in the period 1958/59– 1984/85 are specific to ages, such as infant mortality and death rates at working-age adult and old ages. Mortality increased among females in the 1970s and 1980s only at ages over 45. This is also confirmed by the data disaggregated by urban–rural residence. Female mortality declined among both urban and rural females, except for rural females under age five (see Table 3 and USSR State Committee on Statistics, 1988b: 384–399). Males experienced rising mortality only at ages over 20, but especially at ages 20–

**FIGURE 1   Indexes of age-specific probabilities of dying: USSR males,
1964–65, 1969–70, 1984–85 (1958–59 = 100)**

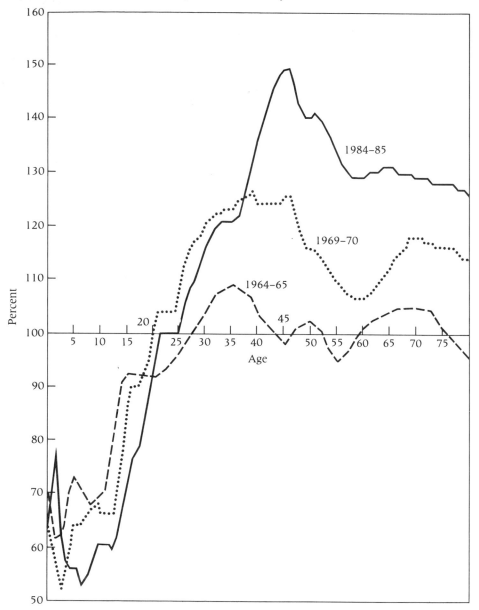

SOURCE: R. Dmitrieva and E. Andreev, "O srednei prodolzhitel'nosti zhizni
naseleniia SSSR," *Vestnik Statistiki,* no. 12 (1987), p. 34.

45. At ages under five, only rural male mortality increased between 1970
and 1980 (USSR State Committee on Statistics, 1988b: 384–399; see also Figure 4 for rural males and females combined).

FIGURE 2   Indexes of age-specific probabilities of dying: USSR females, 1964–65, 1969–70, 1984–85 (1958–59 = 100)

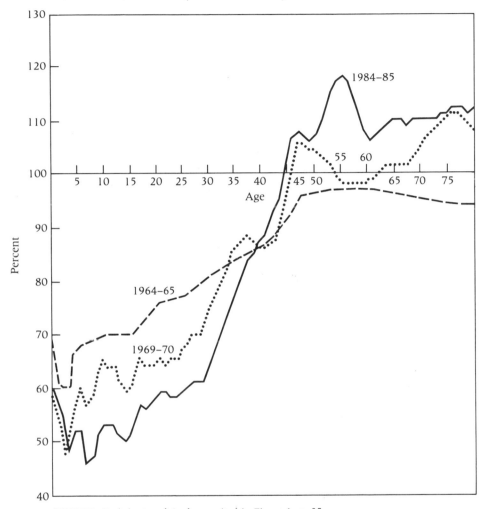

SOURCE: Dmitrieva and Andreev, cited in Figure 1, p. 35.

The most significant mortality increases at working and other ages took place among the rural population (Figure 4 and Table 3). This also makes one skeptical with regard to the direct environmental hypothesis. Environmental impacts on urban populations should be stronger due to a higher concentration of harmful materials in urban industries, unless the most telling damage is done by pesticides and poisoning of water supplies in the rural areas. There is evidence that such environmental effects did indeed occur, but, as in any water pollution, they were regional and thus localized by their very nature.

For the USSR as a whole, deterioration of water quality in the countryside does not seem to have produced a significant mortality effect. The inci-

**FIGURE 3   Indexes of age-specific probabilities of dying: USSR males
relative to females, 1958–59, 1969–70, 1984–85 (female $_{x+n}q_x$ = 100)**

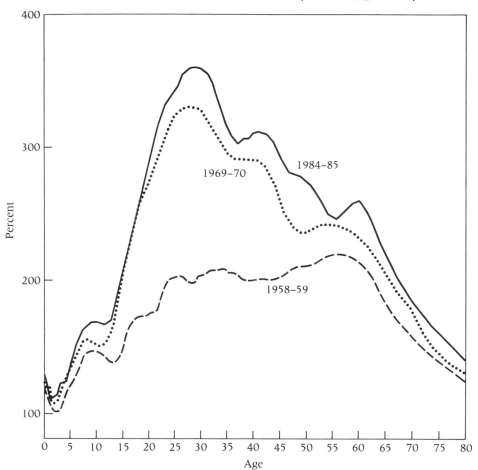

SOURCE: Dmitrieva and Andreev, cited in Figure 1, p. 37.

dence of infectious hepatitis, which is caused largely by water pollution,
more than doubled between 1970 and 1985 (USSR State Committee on Statistics, 1988a: 549), but deaths from hepatitis constituted only 0.2 percent of
all USSR deaths (USSR State Committee on Statistics, 1988b: 361). Table 3
and its source imply that for all ages combined and at specific ages for the
USSR as a whole, the residual of all listed causes of death, which may include infectious diseases, is very small.

Regional impacts of water pollution may, however, be significant in
the areas with expanded cotton plantations. Deaths from infectious diseases
were the largest cause of infant mortality in the Tadzhik Republic and the
second largest in the Uzbek, Azerbaijan, Kirghiz, and Turkmen Republics in
1984–86, while this was a minor cause in the rest of the USSR. Compare, for
example, 20.0 infant deaths from infectious diseases per thousand live

**FIGURE 4   Indexes of age-specific probabilities of dying: USSR
rural population relative to urban, 1958–59, 1969–70, 1984–85
'urban $_{x+n}q_x$ = 100)**

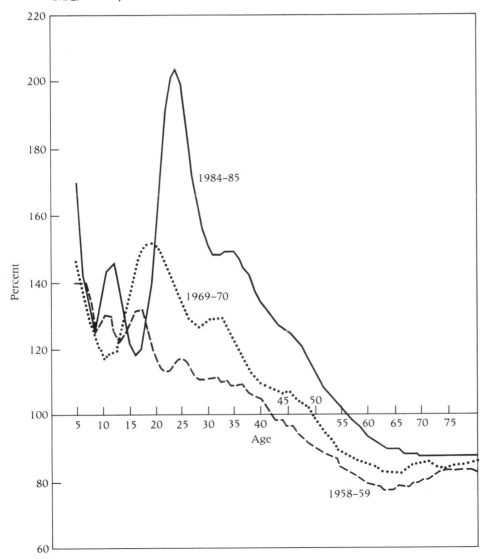

SOURCE: Dmitrieva and Andreev, cited in Figure 1, p. 38.

births in the Tadzhik Republic with 0.7 in the Estonian Republic in 1984
(USSR State Committee on Statistics, 1988b: 400–407). According to the Soviet Red Cross, in especially exposed areas around the Aral Sea with the
most severe clean water shortages, infant mortality increased from 44.7 per
thousand live births in 1965 to 71.5 in 1986. (However, underregistration of
Soviet infant mortality is still very high, and the real rates in Central Asian
rural areas may be twice as high as recorded [USSR State Committee on Sta-

TABLE 3 Mortality rates by sex, selected age groups, urban–rural residence, and major causes of death: USSR, 1970 and 1980 (per 100,000 population)

	Males						Females					
	Total		Urban		Rural		Total		Urban		Rural	
	1970	1980	1970	1980	1970	1980	1970	1980	1970	1980	1970	1980
All ages												
All causes	890.9	1111.7	828.1	1017.2	972.8	1271.1	765.5	967.5	701.8	868.2	846.6	1134.7
Cardiovascular diseases	331.6	467.6	299.5	419.0	373.3	549.6	430.8	609.8	390.6	539.0	482.2	728.9
Neoplasms	140.1	159.0	152.1	169.6	124.5	141.1	121.0	127.7	137.4	143.4	100.0	101.2
Lung and respiratory diseases	119.5	130.8	84.8	90.9	164.8	198.1	92.0	91.4	59.4	54.8	133.5	153.1
Accidents, injuries, and poisoning	175.9	221.3	176.8	211.7	174.8	237.5	42.7	56.8	42.8	54.6	42.4	60.4
Ages 25–29												
All causes	340.7	369.4	311.4	333.3	395.0	453.5	104.9	98.7	88.4	84.3	134.0	135.0
Cardiovascular diseases	23.4	27.9	20.4	23.9	29.1	37.2	14.7	12.8	11.2	8.6	20.9	23.5
Neoplasms	16.7	14.9	16.8	14.5	16.7	15.7	16.0	14.4	15.9	13.9	16.1	15.8
Lung and respiratory diseases	7.5	9.2	6.0	7.8	10.1	12.6	4.7	5.3	3.1	4.0	7.4	8.6
Accidents, injuries, and poisoning	247.5	275.9	232.3	250.9	275.8	334.0	31.6	37.8	31.4	35.6	31.8	43.5
Ages 45–49												
All causes	939.1	1215.2	921.0	1186.0	964.3	1262.2	372.9	422.8	366.3	405.7	382.2	451.2
Cardiovascular diseases	246.8	362.3	260.5	367.0	277.8	354.7	103.2	129.8	100.8	119.3	106.5	147.2
Neoplasms	182.2	201.8	190.5	206.9	170.6	193.4	134.5	123.5	140.9	131.2	125.6	110.8
Lung and respiratory diseases	66.0	87.4	54.8	75.0	81.6	107.4	18.7	22.0	15.2	17.4	23.7	29.5
Accidents, injuries, and poisoning	281.9	400.8	265.7	379.0	304.5	436.1	57.7	84.9	56.9	80.1	58.9	92.9

NOTES: Figures may not add to totals due to incomplete list of causes.
SOURCE: USSR State Committee on Statistics. *Naselenie SSSR: 1987. Statisticheskii Sbornik* (Moscow: Finansy i Statistika, 1988), pp. 384–399.

TABLE 4   Standardized mortality rates per thousand population of working ages,[a] by major causes of death: USSR, 1980–88 (selected years)

	1980	1984	1985	1986	1988
All causes	5.53	5.63	5.22	4.47	4.50
Cardiovascular diseases	1.61	1.70	1.62	1.43	1.43
Neoplasms	1.07	1.12	1.12	1.13	1.11
Lung and respiratory diseases	0.35	0.33	0.31	0.23	0.21
Accidents, injuries, and poisoning	1.75	1.70	1.44	1.07	1.18

[a] Men aged 16–59, women aged 16–54. The age structure for 1980 is apparently used as a standard.
NOTE: Figures may not add to totals due to incomplete list of causes.
SOURCES: USSR State Committee on Statistics, *Narodnoe Khoziaistvo SSSR v 1987 godu. Statisticheskii Ezhegodnik* (Moscow: Finansy i Statistika, 1988): 356; *Narodnoe Khoziaistvo SSSR v 1988 godu. Statisticheskii Ezhegodnik* (Moscow: Finansy i Statistika, 1989): 27.

tistics, 1989: 3].) Maternal mortality and overall mortality also increased sharply between 1965 and 1986. Over the period 1973–88, there were 36 epidemics of infectious diseases; the incidence of infectious hepatitis increased sevenfold and that of typhus increased 30 times (Amiridze and Samokhin, 1989).

In these rural areas, according to the USSR Ministers of Hydrometeorology, Irrigation, and Water Supplies and to the USSR Representative to UNESCO, steep mortality increases across all ages are directly attributable to water pollution. The high use of water resources on cotton plantations created water shortages for human use and lowered sanitary conditions. Drinking water there is discharged from the fields. The most important cause of water pollution is the use of pesticides, which is 20 to 30 times higher per hectare in these areas than in the Soviet countryside on average (Izrael, Vasiliev et al., 1988: 2; Vinogradov, 1989: 19). In the Tadzhik Republic, only an estimated 3 percent of the rural population has access to nonpolluted drinking water (Karpov and Tutorskaia, 1989).

There is growing evidence that this excessive use of highly poisonous pesticides on cotton plantations in Central Asia, parts of Kazakhstan and Azerbaijan, and tobacco plantations in the Moldavian Republic has direct effects on infant mortality and birth defects. The literature, however, emphasizes that adverse environmental effects are intertwined with adverse effects of industrial policies in the above areas, including child labor, work during pregnancy, and work while mothers are nursing (Kozhevnikova, 1987; Drutse, 1987; Oreshkin, 1988; Volkov, 1988; Treplev, 1988a, 1988b; Minkin, 1988a, 1988b; Asadulloev, 1988; Petrov, 1989; Ovchinnikova, 1989; Bakaev, 1989; USSR Children's Fund, 1989).

One must emphasize that the expansion of cotton growing in the Soviet southern tier, which was conducted with the excessive use of pesticides

TABLE 5   Changes in expectation of life at birth (in years) due to major causes of death, by sex: USSR, 1967–84 and 1985–87

	1967–84		1985–87	
	Males	**Females**	**Males**	**Females**
All causes	− 3.5	− 1.4	2.7	1.2
Cardiovascular diseases	− 2.2	− 1.7	0.6	0.6
Neoplasms	− 0.2	0.2	− 0.1	− 0.03
Lung and respiratory diseases	− 0.3	− 0.1	0.5	0.3
Infections and parasitic diseases	0.3	0.1	0.1	0.1
Accidents, injuries, and poisoning	− 1.0	− 0.3	1.4	0.3

NOTE: Figures may not add to totals due to incomplete list of causes.
SOURCE: USSR State Committee on Statistics, "Ozhidaemaia Prodolzhitelnost Zhizni," *Vestnik Statistiki,* no. 10 (1989): 63.

and overuse of water resources and which resulted in the destruction of water supplies and rising mortality, was the external policy of the central government. This policy was supported and implemented by regional governments whose members received high bonuses and amassed personal wealth, but the initiation and implementation of this policy were independent of rapid population growth in Central Asia. The destruction of the environment and ensuing mortality increases there do not derive from the direct pressures of rapidly growing population on resources.

Air pollution and other environmental deterioration should have affected mortality from neoplasms and lung and respiratory diseases in urban or rural areas, or both. Analysis of Table 3 shows that these causes made an insignificant contribution to Soviet mortality increases. At ages 25–29, the ages at which the sharpest increases of male mortality and rural mortality occurred (Figures 1, 3, 4), mortality from neoplasms actually declined and that from lung and respiratory diseases was steadily very low (Table 3). Some impact of regional air pollution may be suspected in the case of infant mortality in the above cotton-growing areas where death from respiratory diseases is very high. The latter, however, may also be attributed to the deterioration of health services in rural areas, to which we now turn. To conclude with respect to the environmental factors among the causes of rising Soviet mortality, they do not seem to be important outside of several particular regions. An econometric analysis later in the essay will support this conclusion.

A general phenomenon that probably contributed to the rise of rural mortality both in absolute terms and relative to urban mortality was the Soviet government's policy of induced rural resettlement from the late 1960s through the mid-1980s. This was a policy of closing down or destroying

TABLE 6 Standardized mortality rates per thousand population of working ages,[a] by major causes of death: USSR and Western market countries, 1987

	Males		Females	
	USSR	Western market countries [b]	USSR	Western market countries [b]
All causes	6.59	3.63	2.54	1.78
Cardiovascular diseases	2.17	1.09	0.82	0.38
Neoplasms	1.51	1.03	0.81	0.78
Lung and respiratory diseases	0.34	0.12	0.10	0.06
Accidents, injuries, and poisoning	1.78	0.79	0.38	0.25

[a] Men aged 16–59, women aged 16–54.
[b] United States, West Germany, France, Great Britain, Japan (source does not specify whether weighted or unweighted average is used).
NOTE: Apparently, the USSR age composition was used as the standard, but the source does not indicate this.
SOURCE: USSR State Committee on Statistics, "Ozhidaemaia Prodolzhitelnost Zhizni," *Vestnik Statistiki*, no. 10 (1989): 63.

small-sized villages (over 500,000 villages were affected in the Soviet Union) and resettling the population in aggregated large villages (CPSU Central Committee and USSR Council of Ministers, 1968). This policy is not peculiar to the Soviet Union but, rather, derives naturally from the functioning of the socialist economic system. A similar policy was initiated in 1989 in socialist Romania, whose government was independent of the Soviet Union. The extreme objective of the statist government can be assumed to lie in the elimination of economic independence of its subjects so that their employment, provision, and entire livelihood depend on the government. From this perspective, small villages where this objective is difficult to enforce must sooner or later be abolished. To persuade rural populations to leave small villages and move to aggregated agro-industrial settlements, the government closed down most medical, educational, child care, and trading facilities and other infrastructure. About 90 percent of rural medical facilities were eliminated. Resettlement was never completed, and the remaining small villages—some 60 to 75 percent of all villages, containing more than 40 million residents and more than 40 percent of the Soviet rural population—had virtually no access to medical care (Dementieva and Tutorskaia, 1987: 3; Vasiliev and Nikonov, 1989: 16; for detailed data and analysis see Bernstam and Carlson, 1988: 10–12).

We think the elimination of the rural health care system is the reason infant and child (under age five) mortality from respiratory diseases in the period 1970–80 increased by 53 percent in the rural areas while it declined by 10 percent in the urban areas (USSR State Committee on Statistics, 1988b: 394–395). We presented evidence elsewhere that the increase in deaths from

respiratory diseases at the postneonatal age was the main contributor to rising Soviet infant mortality in the 1970s (Bernstam and Carlson, 1988).

An additional factor in assessing the comparative trends in rural and
urban mortality is the self-selection of healthier rural migrants of working
ages to the cities. This consideration is fully consistent with the trends in
Figure 4; the only remaining question is whether this self-selection was a
strong enough factor to produce a change of significant magnitude (for example, doubling the increase in rural mortality relative to urban among
both sexes at ages 25–29 years between 1958–59 and 1984–85).

In addition, there is interesting, albeit sketchy evidence that deterioration of working conditions and work safety was especially pronounced in
the Soviet countryside relative to urban areas in the last two decades of
mechanization of agriculture (e.g., Kuznetsov and Vovk, 1989). Table 3
shows that increases in rural mortality relative to urban were to a significant
extent due to accidents, injuries, and poisoning, especially among males
and particularly among working-age males.

What stands out most clearly from Tables 3–6 is the importance of
mortality from accidents, injuries, and poisoning among causes of death
and mortality trends in the Soviet Union. From the 1960s to the mid-1980s,
this was the second largest cause of death among Soviet males (Table 3) and
the largest cause of death among both males and females of working age
(Tables 3 and 4). A spectacular decline in deaths from this cause after an
anti-alcohol campaign was initiated in 1985 contributed to about two-thirds
of the mortality decline at working ages for males and females combined
(Table 4) and to about half of the increase in male expectation of life at birth
(Table 5). Still, in 1987 an age-standardized comparison of Soviet male mortality at working ages with that in Western market countries shows a much
larger disparity in mortality from accidents and injuries than from most
other causes. The Soviet mortality rate from accidents, injuries, and poisoning among working-age males was 2.25 times as high as the Western rate in
1987 (Table 6) and can be estimated at about five times as high before 1985.

Table 5 shows that accidents, injuries, and poisoning contributed
significantly to the decline in male and female life expectancy in the Soviet
Union in the period 1967–84. Comparing both male and female mortality
increases at working ages in the 1970s in Figures 1, 2, and 3 and Table 3, one
can clearly conclude that deaths from injuries, accidents, and poisoning
constituted the principal contribution. This finding is crucial for testing our
prediction on the impact of the socialist economic system on mortality.

A statistical analysis of Soviet mortality

The trends in Soviet mortality from the 1960s to the 1980s do not show overall effects that can be directly and unambiguously associated with environ-

mental deterioration, with the exception of certain regions. This is so despite a large body of evidence that such deterioration indeed occurred and that some adverse health effects of worsening environmental conditions are real (evidence summarized in USSR Supreme Soviet, 1989). The lack of a direct and apparent association of rising Soviet mortality with environmental disruption is not conclusive, however, because environmental effects may be offset by other general factors (e.g., improvements in housing provision per capita, medical advancements, etc.). The issue can be resolved only by a more detailed, region- and period-specific statistical analysis in which various mortality measures are related to particular environmental indicators.

In this section, we analyze statistically the impacts of environmental conditions, work safety, housing conditions, socialist industrial development, and other socioeconomic factors on expectation of life at birth for Soviet males and females. We also approximate and quantitatively evaluate these and other environmental, demographic, and socioeconomic impacts on infant mortality. Tables 7 and 8 show results of two-stage log-linear least squares regressions in which male and female life expectancy and infant mortality are the dependent variables. The independent variables include an array of the aforementioned socioeconomic, demographic, and environmental factors. Their instrumental variables include various exogenous measures of systemic economic impacts, economic development, total fertility rates (in the case of infant mortality), and regional dummies. Among these instruments are also urban and rural wages, savings per capita, and other measures of wealth and amenities.

We pooled the officially published Soviet data for 15 Union Republics for the years 1969/70, 1979/80, and 1985/86 (1970, 1980, and 1986 in the case of infant mortality). Thus we have 45 observations. The data are limited in scope and the quality is often poor. Still, this is the first such statistical analysis in the literature on Soviet demographic trends.

In the equations of Table 7 where life expectancy at birth is the dependent variable, we control for infant mortality. Thus other independent variables could actually show their influence on life expectancy at age one. Since the variation in child and adolescent mortality at the moderately high levels of life expectancy found in the Soviet Union is not high among various regions, the above specification can probably allow measurement of the impacts on adult mortality.

Note that life expectancy is a "good" dependent variable (Table 7) while infant mortality is a "bad" dependent variable (Table 8). Therefore, we would predict opposite signs of influence on the part of main independent variables. For example, wealth per capita and housing per capita should be positively related to life expectancy (Table 7) and negatively related to infant mortality (Table 8). More importantly from the perspective of our theory, some measures of socialist industrial expansion may have a negative

TABLE 7 Two-stage regressions of male and female expectation of life at birth: USSR republics, 1969/70, 1979/80, 1985/86

Equation number	1		2		3		4		5		6	
Dependent variables	Log of male life expectancy						Log of female life expectancy					
Independent variables (in logs)												
Constant	3.72**	(29.78)	4.07**	(23.14)	3.40**	(28.53)	4.43**	(33.58)	4.61**	(25.08)	3.84**	(32.39)
Infant mortality[a]	−0.05**	(5.52)	−0.06**	(5.72)	−0.07**	(8.76)	−0.05**	(5.59)	−0.07**	(5.74)	−0.07**	(7.13)
Urban housing stock per capita [b]	0.07**	(2.87)	0.06**	(2.76)	0.05*	(2.24)	0.02	(0.92)	0.01	(0.76)	0.06*	(2.31)
New housing construction per capita per year	0.04**	(4.38)	0.04**	(3.61)	0.03**	(3.03)	0.03**	(3.56)	0.03*	(2.38)	0.02	(1.26)
Capital stock per worker	−0.09**	(8.12)	−0.08**	(7.33)	−0.10**	(6.42)	−0.03*	(2.24)	−0.03**	(2.79)	−0.06**	(3.83)
Regional industrial development			0.01	(0.01)					−0.01*	(1.94)		
Industrial fatalities and injuries proxy	−0.05**	(3.01)	−0.04**	(2.44)	−0.14**	(7.92)	0.04**	(2.63)	0.03*	(1.99)	−0.08**	(4.79)
Deaths from alcohol per 1000	−0.02**	(10.12)	−0.02**	(5.17)	−0.01	(1.46)	−0.02*	(5.59)	−0.01**	(4.24)	0.01	(0.74)
Hospital beds per 1000			−0.06**	(2.85)					−0.02	(0.84)		
Air pollution per sq. km			−0.01	(0.02)					−0.01	(1.59)		
Water pollution per sq. km			−0.01	(0.48)					0.01	(0.24)		
Regional dummies (R2 thru R15) [c]					R2 • • • • • R15						R2 • • • • • R15	
1980 year dummy	0.01	(1.08)	0.01	(1.84)	0.01	(0.41)	0.01	(0.99)	0.01*	(1.78)	−0.01	(0.05)
1986 year dummy	0.02*	(2.21)	0.03**	(3.06)	0.03**	(2.52)	0.01	(0.60)	0.01	(1.20)	0.01	(0.96)
$\bar{R}^2$	0.88		0.89		0.96		0.83		0.84		0.94	
F-statistic	43.11		30.15		45.39		28.60		19.74		34.40	
N	45		45		45		45		45		45	

NOTES: All estimates are heteroskedastic-consistent. t-statistics are in parentheses.

** = Significant at 1 percent level.

* = Significant at 5 percent level.

[a] Endogenous and estimated by instrumental variables (IV): total fertility rates, female employment ratio, female collective farm participation, cotton fields per female farmer.

[b] IV: urban and rural wages, savings per capita, auto roads per sq. km.

[c] Included only in equations 3 and 6 and not reproduced here for brevity.

SOURCES: USSR State Committee on Statistics. *Naselenie SSSR. 1987. Statisticheskii Sbornik* (Moscow: Finansy i Statistika. 1988); *Narodnoe Khoziaistvo SSSR. 1917–1987. Statisticheskii Ezhegodnik* (Moscow: Finansy i Statistika. 1987); *Narodnoe Khoziaistvo SSSR v 1987 Godu. Statisticheskii Ezhegodnik* (Moscow: Finansy i Statistika, 1988); Soviet statistical yearbooks similar to the above, various years; *Vestnik Statistiki*, various issues; USSR State Committee on Statistics, "Smertnost naseleniia ot prichin, neposredstvenno sviazannykh s alkogolizmom," *Sotsiologicheskie Issledovaniia,* no. 1 (1988): 119.

relationship with life expectancy and, when applicable, a positive relationship with infant mortality. Relevant environmental factors, which are complementary (and endogenous) to specific industrial policies, can also be adversely related to life expectancy (Table 7) and have a positive sign with respect to infant mortality (Table 8).

In Table 8, the total fertility rates, and not the rates of natural increase, were chosen to approximate the independent force of population growth. This is done to avoid an overlap: mortality is the dependent variable here, and mortality is a partial determinant of population growth.

The tests in Tables 7 and 8 suggest that several independent variables exert a consistent and statistically significant influence on all our measures of mortality and that this influence is in accordance with the predictions of the theory. The coefficients have the above-predicted signs; however, most coefficients are low. At most, a 10 percent increase in the industrial fatalities variable can reduce male life expectancy by 1.4 percent, and a 10 percent increase in capital stock per worker lowers male life expectancy by 1.0 percent (equation 3, Table 7). A 10 percent expansion of cotton fields, with its implied water pollution, increases infant mortality by 1.8 percent (equation 4, Table 8). The two variables with large coefficients in the infant mortality equations are urban housing stock per capita and female employment. A 10 percent increase in the former lowers, and a 10 percent increase in the latter increases infant mortality by more than 10 percent (Table 8). We expected to see similar magnitudes in the influence of housing on life expectancy in Table 7, but the small size of the coefficients there (about 0.5 percent increase in response to a 10 percent increase) is disappointing.

The variable that stands out in Table 7 as a negative force behind life expectancy is a proxy for industrial fatalities and injuries. This is the proportion of persons on survival and disability pensions (as a percent of the total population of a given republic in a given year). By official definition, these are either industrial invalids or members of families who have lost a breadwinner as a result of industrial fatalities. The term "industry" here, as in the usual economic context, includes agriculture and all types of economic activity. This variable is our best available approximation of the mortality impact of the industrial expansion under the socialist economic system. It is negatively and statistically significantly related to male life expectancy in all equations and to female life expectancy in the best-specified equation 6. This variable also has a much higher statistical significance for males than for females, which is consistent with the age-specific/sex-specific mortality trends observed in Figures 1–3 and Tables 3 and 5.

Another key feature of socialist economic development that also has environmental implications is the independent influence of housing on mortality, even holding other determinants constant. Housing in the Soviet Union is primarily distributed by the government and by enterprise management. It represents one of the most important power mechanisms of the provider-state and its managerial elite. The average family waits in the housing queue from 10 to 20 years (USSR Academy of Sciences, 1987: 106). Still, some 23 percent of Soviet households, at least 70 million people, live in substandard housing that qualifies them for a public housing queue (USSR State Committee on Statistics, 1988a: 471). Over 100 million Soviet people, 35 percent of the entire population, live in one-industry company towns (Nikiforov, 1986: 116). In such settlements, all jobs, incomes, housing provision, food distribution, schooling, individual opportunities, health care, legal conditions, and personal safety depend on the producer firms' management. The factory director is king. Given a virtually one-time housing provision over the life cycle and an extremely high shadow price, housing also represents the main Soviet asset. Also, housing space per capita is, generally speaking, an environmental measure of the amenities of daily life. The variable evaluates crowdedness and congestion: on the margin, housing space per capita literally means the difference between life and death. And this is what our results show. The impact of housing space is especially significant in the case of infant mortality and male life expectancy—negative on the former and positive on the latter. In the case of female life expectancy, at least one of the two housing variables is statistically significant, and both have the predicted positive sign. These findings are consistent with the declining female and especially male life expectancy from the late 1960s through the mid-1980s when housing conditions deteriorated for young workers and other groups of the Soviet population.

The variables that approximate measures of population growth show no consistent influence on mortality. The total fertility rates are positively related to infant mortality, but are not statistically significant when the regional dummies are held constant.

Among environmental variables, three showed consistently interesting results. Air pollution (normalized by territory) exerted little influence on either male or female life expectancy, or on infant mortality. Water pollution does not seem to affect these variables either. Note, however, that the latter variable evaluates the combined impact of industrial and agricultural water pollution, and thus its variation may not reflect a variation in rural water shortages and pesticide poisoning by regions. It is thus more important to control for the expansion of cotton plantations in these regressions.

The infant mortality equations (Table 8) show a positive and highly statistically significant impact of the measure of the expansion of cotton fields (the hectarage sown for cotton normalized by the number of female farmers, who are the most vulnerable and most relevant for analyzing infant mortality). According to a number of Soviet sources cited above, this expansion of cotton crops in several regions, with extremely high use of pesticides and overuse of fresh water, was a crucial factor in rising Soviet infant mortal-

TABLE 8 Two-stage regressions of infant mortality: USSR republics, 1970, 1980, 1986

Equation number	1		2		3		4	
Dependent variable			Log of infant mortality					
Independent variables (in logs)								
Constant	8.21**	(8.34)	5.52**	(4.14)	7.00**	(2.75)	11.33**	(6.31)
Total fertility rate [a]			1.21**	(5.61)	0.86**	(3.09)	0.20	(0.80)
Savings per capita			-0.20*	(2.15)	-0.15	(1.66)	-0.54**	(4.69)
Urban housing stock per capita [b]	-1.55**	(7.38)	-0.11	(0.42)	0.24	(0.75)	-1.90**	(2.69)
Auto roads per sq. km					-0.15**	(3.06)		
Female employment ratio [c]			1.37**	(3.64)	1.31**	(4.68)	1.02*	(2.38)
Female collective farm participation [d]					0.06	(0.13)		
Cotton fields per female farmer	0.02*	(2.41)	0.01	(1.20)	0.02*	(2.36)	0.18**	(3.59)
Obstetric beds per newborn	-0.32	(1.64)	-0.48*	(2.24)	-0.96**	(4.01)	-0.40*	(1.79)
Mineral fertilizers per farmer [e]	-0.36**	(4.34)	-0.45**	(4.84)				
Air pollution per sq. km					0.03	(0.94)		
Water pollution per sq. km					-0.01	(0.26)		
Regional dummies (R2 thru R15) [f]							R2 • • • • • R15	
1980 year dummy	0.25**	(3.07)	0.41**	(3.52)	0.31**	(2.84)	0.75**	(6.38)
1986 year dummy	0.28**	(3.24)	0.40**	(2.97)	0.27*	(2.32)	0.94**	(5.58)
$\bar{R}^2$	0.75		0.87		0.89		0.91	
F-statistic	27.73		32.48		28.50		21.70	
N	45		45		45		45	

NOTES: All estimates are heteroskedastic-consistent. t-statistics are in parentheses.

** = Significant at 1 percent level.

* = Significant at 5 percent level.

[a] Endogenous and estimated by instrumental variables (IV): regional dummies and regional industrial development expressed as a percent of indigenous labor force employed in industry.

[b] IV: new housing construction per capita per year.

[c] IV: urban wages, female education, capital stock per worker.

[d] IV: rural wages.

[e] IV: agricultural development proxy (irrigation per sq. km of arable land).

[f] Included only in equation 4 and not reproduced here for brevity.

SOURCES: See Table 7.

ity in the 1970s and 1980s. Our tests support this hypothesis in principle, but the coefficients of the cotton fields variable are low.

As we discussed earlier, the environmental variables that exert a statistically recognizable negative impact on human survival (e.g., water pollution in areas of cotton plantations) are precisely those that both depend on systemic economic factors and function in conjunction with such factors. Again, the socialist economic setting is at the heart of the matter.

We end our empirical section with perhaps the most dramatic demographic outcome of socialist industrial development of the last two decades. Several ethnic groups of Soviet Eskimos have experienced unprecedented declines in life expectancy and population contraction. In 1987–88, the average expectation of life at birth among Soviet Eskimos was 45 years for males and 55 years for females (Pika and Prokhorov, 1988). According to another source, the decline in life expectancy of Soviet Eskimos from the mid-1960s to the mid-1980s was from 59 to 44 years among males and from 67 to 54 years among females (Arifdzhanov, 1988). Specific examples include the Khanty and Mansi ethnic groups, whose life expectancy declined by about 20 years to 43 years for males and 45 years for females (Sangi, 1988a; Sangi and Dmitrieva, 1989: 17), and the Evenki ethnic group, whose life expectancy for both sexes fell to 40 years—the level of the least developed African nations (Sokolov, 1988). While oil and gas development has produced environmental damage in the regions inhabited by these groups (Gamov, 1988), the actual mortality effect has been indirect. Oil and gas extraction expanded into the tundra and to the Arctic shores and destroyed the natural habitat of these people. Fuel pipes warmed the tundra, destroying food sources for reindeer herds. About 20 million hectares of reindeer pasture were eliminated, and the number of reindeer declined fivefold (Sangi, 1989: 26; Sangi and Dmitrieva, 1989: 17). Oil spills produced water pollution, which reduced fish stocks. Subsistence settlements of the indigenous population then deteriorated to slums, and the resulting mortality increase was concentrated in high infant mortality, tuberculosis, and alcohol-related deaths (Sangi, 1988b, 1989; Shestalov, 1988; Sokolov, 1988; Pika and Prokhorov, 1988; Arifdzhanov, 1988; Silin, 1989).

The meaning of autonomy from the environment

The general conclusion from this analysis seems clear. The socialist system has demonstrated that population growth, economic development, and environmental impact are three distinct outcomes of the way human societies organize life. Each outcome must be understood as independent in important ways from the others.

In evaluating problems of environmental degradation, scientists stress the fact that human intervention in the general ecological system of the

planet must respect the inter-connectedness and dynamic balance of that
system.

> We cannot manage the biosphere in detail. It manages itself, and in an ideal
> world we would preserve the circumstances in which that self-management
> can continue with no cost to the human enterprise. (Woodwell, 1985: 63)

An ecological perspective on humanity as part of the biosphere stresses
that a system, whether life in a pond, organs in a body, or economic and
political institutions in a society, is *not* controlled by some centralized power.

The difficulty with the socialist system rested precisely on this matter
of centralized command. In the language of systems analysis (Bennett and
Chorley, 1978), plan-control as distinct from feedback-control is appropriate
only where all external influences on the system are understood and subject
to manipulation. In the context of our uncontrollable natural environment,
closed command systems are ecologically unsound. Their unresponsiveness
leads to environmental accumulation of problems—resource and pollution
problems in the natural environment, and demographic problems in the social environment. By contrast, the sensitivity of an open system to its environment requires that external influences can find their way into and be
acted upon by the system. This is what Hayek (1944) meant when he suggested that goals are not made, but rather evolve or emerge.

Much of the current thinking about pollution control and environmental protection starts from a radically different and ecologically unsound
premise—that only a more perfectly hierarchical control of the entire production process, including extraction of resources and disposition of wastes
as activities to be managed from above, can successfully defend the environment:

> Effective and truly efficient remediation of environmental malfunctions in
> both market and non-market industrial economies will require a large bu-
> reaucratic body and control apparatus similar in many ways to the arch-
> typical Soviet planning organization. (McIntyre and Thornton, 1978: 175)

This perspective, that social coordination must be organized from
above and maintained by supervision and regulation, has been at the heart
of the socialist system. Such a command perspective dictates, in fact, that
the adaptive complexity of society be reduced by fusing previously differen-
tiated, autonomous subsystems (such as the legal, political, and economic
subsystems) into a unified hierarchy of control. Suppressing the differentiation of church from state, of the economy from the political bureaucracy, or
even of law from politics, always reduces the complexity of the system and
destroys some of its autonomy with respect to the environment (Luhmann,
1982). We have tried to present theoretical reasoning and empirical evidence

from developed socialist countries in this regard. To resolve population–resource imbalances, an ecological understanding of autonomy as an intrinsic feature of differentiation must extend not only to the interface with our natural environment, but also into the internal organization of society. Sustainable openness and responsiveness to the natural environment will be a mirror-image of the openness and responsiveness achieved in the complex institutional structure of human social life.

References

The translated titles appear in the originals. Where no translation was provided, none is given below.

Aganbegian, Abel G. 1987. "Otstupat nekuda," *Izvestiia* (25 August): 2.

Aksenov, D. 1989. "Strategiia chistoi energii," *Ekonomicheskaia Gazeta*, no. 16: 5.

Amiridze, S., and A. Samokhin. 1989. "Zona ekologicheskogo bedstviia," *Argumenty i Fakty*, no. 51: 4–5.

Arifdzhanov, Rustam. 1988. "Liudi na kraiu," *Sobesednik*, no. 42: 10–11.

Arutiunian, T. V. 1989. "Prodaetsia zdorovie," *Ekonomika i Organizatsiia Promyshlennogo Proizvodstva*, no. 8: 81–86.

Asadulloev, Nasrullo. 1988. "Pod nikotinovym udarom nakhodiatsia zhenshchiny i deti selskhikh raionov Tadzhikistana," *Literaturnaia Gazeta*, no. 12: 13.

Aven, P. O., and V. M. Shironin. 1987. "Reforma ekonomicheskogo mekhanizma," *Izvestiia Sibirskogo Otdeleniia Akademii Nauk SSSR, Seriia Ekonomiki i Prikladnoi Sotsiologii 3*, no. 13: 32–41.

Bakaev, K. 1989. "Deti na poliakh," *Pravda Vostoka* (7 July): 1.

Balarajan, A. 1983. "Malignant lymphomas in road transport workers," *Journal of Epidemiology and Community Health 37*, no. 4: 279–280.

Bennett, Robert, and Richard Chorley. 1978. *Environmental Systems: Philosophy, Analysis and Control*. Princeton: Princeton University Press.

Bergson, Abram. 1978. *Productivity and the Social System*. Cambridge, Mass.: Harvard University Press.

––––––. 1987. "Comparative productivity: The USSR, Eastern Europe, and the West," *The American Economic Review 77*, no. 3: 342–357.

Bernstam, Mikhail S., and Elwood Carlson. 1988. "Neonatal and postneonatal components of Soviet infant mortality trends: A note on bureaucratic irrelevance," *Hoover Institution Working Papers in International Studies*, no. 9.

Bourgeois-Pichat, Jean. 1985. "Recent changes in mortality in industrialized countries," in *Health Policy, Social Policy and Mortality Prospects*, ed. J. Vallin and A. Lopez. Liège: Ordina-IUSSP.

Carlson, Elwood. 1989. "Concentration of rising Hungarian mortality among manual workers," *Sociology and Social Research 73*, no. 3: 119–128.

––––––, and Mary Watson, 1988. "Rising Hungarian death rates, the family, and the state," paper presented at the International Sociological Association seminar on kinship and aging, Zamardi, Hungary.

Chappie, Michael, and Lester Lave. 1982. "The health effects of air pollution: A reanalysis," *Journal of Urban Economics 12*: 346–376.

CPSU Central Committee and the USSR Council of Ministers. 1968. "Ob uporiadochenii stroitelstva na sele," *Pravda* (2 October): 1.

Dahmen, E. 1971. "Environmental control and economic systems," in *The Economics of the Environment*, ed. P. Bohm and A. Kneese. London: St. Martin's.

Dementieva, I., and S. Tutorskaia. 1987. "Plius polsanitarki, minus akusherka," *Izvestiia* (7 May): 3.

Drutse, Ion. 1987. "Zelenyi list, voda i znaki prepinaniia," *Literaturnaia Gazeta*, no. 31: 12.

Ericson, Richard E. 1988. "The Soviet statistical debate: Khanin vs. the TsSU," paper presented at the Rand Corporation conference on the Soviet economy, Stanford, California, March.

Gamov. A. 1988. "Kak zdorovie, severiane?" *Sovetskaia Rossia* (28 July): 2.

Gelvanovskii, M. 1989. "Reforma tsenoobrazovaniia v SSSR," *Voprosy Ekonomiki*, no. 8: 14–25.

Giersdorf, P., and H. Schuler. 1984. "Tendenzen der mortalitat mannlicher personen im mittleren alter" [Trends in the mortality of middle-aged males], *Zeitschrift für Ärtzliche Fortbildung* 78, no. 3: 83–87.

Goldman, Marshall. 1970. "The convergence of environmental disruption," *Science* 170, no. 3953: 37–42.

Gorbachev, Mikhail S. 1985. "O sozyve ocherednogo XXVII s'ezda KPSS 1 zadachakh po ego podgotovke i organizatsii," *Pravda* (24 April): 1–5.

Gzovskii, V. 1985. "Sotsialnye problemy okhrany okruzhaiushchei sredy v stranakh SEV," *Voprosy Ekonomiki*, no. 12: 99–108.

Hanson, Philip. 1971. "East–West comparisons and comparative economic systems," *Soviet Studies* 22, no. 3: 327–343.

Hayek, Friedrich. 1944. *The Road to Serfdom*. London: Routledge and Kegan Paul.

Holdren, John P., and Paul R. Ehrlich. 1974. "Human population and the global environment," *American Scientist* 62: 282–292.

Hungarian Central Statistical Office. 1966. *Demografiai Evkonyv 1965* [Demographic Yearbook 1965]. Budapest.

———. 1986. *Demografiai Evkonyv 1985* [Demographic Yearbook 1985]. Budapest.

———. 1987. "Mortality differentials by causes of death and by the population size of settlements," *Studies in Mortality Differentials*, Series 2, Part 14. Budapest.

Izrael, Iu.A., N. F. Vasiliev et al. 1988. "Aral i Priaralie: Trevoga vsenarodnaia," *Pravda Vostoka* (12 October): 2.

Jozan, Peter. 1986a. "Recent mortality trends in Eastern Europe," paper presented at the UN/WHO/CICRED conference on socioeconomic differentials in mortality in industrialized countries, Zamardi, Hungary.

———. 1986b. "A Budapesti halandosagi kulonbsegek okologiai vizsgalata 1980-1983" [An ecological study on the mortality differentials in Budapest], *Demografia* 29, nos. 2–3: 193–240.

Karpov, A., and S. Tutorskaia. 1989. "Legko li byt malenkim. Kak boriutsia s detskoi smertnostiu v Tadhikistane," *Izvestiia* (2 January): 3.

Khanin, G. 1988. "Ekonomicheskii rost: Alternativnaia otsenka,"*Kommunist*, no. 17: 78–88.

Kheinman, S. 1989. "O problemakh nauchno-tekhnicheskoi politiki," *Voprosy Eknomiki*, no. 3: 65–74.

Kholodkov, V. 1989. "Diktat proizvoditelia i ryok," *Ekonomicheskaia Gazeta*, no. 22: 16.

Kim, Yoon Shin. 1985. "Seasonal variation in carbon monoxide poisoning in urban Korea," *Journal of Epidemiology and Community Health* 39, no. 1: 79–81.

Kornai, Janos. 1979."Resource-constrained versus demand-constrained systems," *Econometrica* 47, no. 4: 801–819.

———. 1980. *Economics of Shortage*, 2 vols. Amsterdam: North Holland.

———. 1982. *Growth, Shortage, and Efficiency*. Berkeley: University of California Press.

———. 1986. "The Hungarian reform process: Visions, hopes, reality," *Journal of Economic Literature* 24, no. 4: 1687–1737.

Kozhevnikova, Kapitolina. 1987. "Krik zemli," *Literaturnaia Gazeta*, no. 31: 13.

Kramer, John M. 1987. "Environmental crisis in Poland," in *Environmental Problems in the Soviet Union and Eastern Europe*, ed. Fred Singleton. Boulder: Lynne Rienner, pp. 149–168.

Krzyzanowski, Michal, and Bogdan Wojtyniak. 1982. "Ten-year mortality in a sample of an adult population in relation to air pollution," *Epidemiology and Community Health* 36, no. 4: 262–268.

Kuznetsov, M. N., and A. N. Vovk. 1989. "Pokushenie na zhizn i zdorovie," *Okrana Truda i Sotsialnoe Strakhovanie*, no. 1: 6–7, 19.

Lipfert, Frederick. 1984. "Air pollution and mortality: Specification searches using SMSA-based data," *Journal of Environmental Economics and Management* 11, no. 3: 208–243.

Loevinsohn, Michael. 1987. "Insecticide use and increased mortality in rural central Luzon, Philippines," *The Lancet*, no. 8546: 1359–1362.

Luhmann, Niklas. 1982. *The Differentiation of Society*. New York: Columbia University Press.

McIntyre, Robert, and James Thornton. 1974. "Environmental divergence: Air pollution in the USSR," *Journal of Environmental Economics and Management* 1, no. 2: 109–120.

――――. 1978. "On the environmental efficiency of economic systems," *Soviet Studies* 30, no. 2: 153–172.

Minkin, Aleksandr. 1988a. "Zaraza ubiistvennaia," *Ogonek*, no. 13: 26–27.

――――. 1988b. "Posledstviia zarazy," *Ogonek*, no. 33: 25.

Nikerov, G. 1990. "Ot gigantomanii k konkurentsii," *Argumenty i Fakty*, no. 1: 2.

Nikiforov, V. 1986. "Poselok," *Sibirskie Ogni*, no. 3: 104–120.

OECD. 1989. *OECD Environmental Data Compendium 1989*. Paris.

Ofer, Gur. 1987. "Soviet economic growth: 1928–1985," *The Journal of Economic Literature* 25, no. 4: 1767–1833.

Okolski, Marek. 1987. "Umieralnosc mezczyan w Europie Wschodniej i w Europie Zachodniej" [Male mortality trends in Eastern and Western Europe], *Studia Demograficzne* 87, no. 3: 3–28.

――――, and B. Pulaska. 1983. "Umieralnosc w Polsce w okresie powojennym wedlug przyczyn zgonow" [Mortality in Poland in the postwar years by cause of death], *Studia Demograficzne* 73, no. 3: 3–26.

Oldberg, Ingmar. 1985. "Planned economy and environmental problems: Eastern Europe from a comparative perspective," in *Environmental History: Critical Issues in Comparative Perspective*, ed. K. Bailes. Lanham, Md.: University Press of America.

Oreshkin, A. 1988. "Deti v pole," *Pravda Vostoka* (6 October): 1.

Ovchinnikova, I. 1989. "Khlopkovaia chetvert," *Izvestiia* (12 July): 3.

Petrov, S. 1989. "Nikotinovoe detstvo," *Pravda* (12 August): 2.

Pika, A., and B. Prokhorov. 1988. "Bolshie problemy malykh narodov," *Kommunist*, no. 16: 76–83.

Sangi, Vladimir. 1988a. "Otchuzhdenie," *Sovetskaia Rossiia* (11 September): 2.

――――. 1988b. "Kolichestvo prishlogo naseleniia . . .," in "Perestroika i Publitsistika," *Literaturnaia Rossiia*, no. 52: 6.

――――. 1989. "Chtob ne ostalas pustota," *Sovetskii Voin*, no. 14: 26–27, 70–71.

――――, and A. Dmitrieva. 1989. "Spasti narodnosti Severa, sokhranit ikh kulturu," *Voprosy Literatury*, no. 3: 3–29.

Scholz, D., et al. 1984. "Zur methodik von todesursachentafeln und deren anwendung zur beurteilung der sterblichkeits-verhaltnisse der DDR-bevolkerung im langsschnittvergleich" [Methodology of tables on causes of death and their use for assessing mortality relationships of the population of the GDR in a longitudinal comparison], *Santé Publique* 27, no. 1: 31–44.

Selvin, S., et al. 1984. "Ecologic regression analysis and the study of the influence of air quality on mortality," *Environmental Health Perspectives* 54: 333-340.

Shatalin, S. S. 1987. "Vmesto fondirovaniia," *Ekonomika i Organizatisiia Promyshlennogo Proizvodstva*, no. 6: 22–59.

Shestalov, Iu. 1988. "Byt ili ne byt narodam Severa," in "Perestroika i Publitsistika," *Literaturnaia Rossiia*, no. 52: 9–10.

Shishenkov, Iuri. 1986. "Predupredit by," *Novyi Mir*, no. 6: 89–122.

Shmelev, N. P., and V. V. Popov. 1989. *Na Perelome. Ekonomicheskaia Perestroika v SSSR*. Moscow: APN.

Silin, A. N. 1989. "Tiumenskii Sever ne koloniia," *Ekonomika i Organizatsiia Promyshlennogo Proizvodstva*, no. 7: 69–76.

Slama, Jiry. 1986. "An international comparison of sulfur dioxide emissions," *Journal of Comparative Economics* 10: 277–292.

Sokolov, Mikhail. 1988. "Evenkiia: Konets vechnosti," *Sobesednik*, no. 49: 4–5.

Sorokin, Iu. 1989a. "U semi nianenk ditia," *Argumenty i Fakty*, no. 19: 4–5.

_____. 1989b. "Kto ostanovit stanki-ubiitsy," *Pravda* (8 September): 3.

Strnad, L. and L. Kopecky. 1985. "Vliv nekterych zavaznych nemoci na stredni delku zivota obyvatel CSSR" [The effect of serious diseases on the average life span of the population in Czechoslovakia], *Ceskoslovenske Zdravotnictvi* 33, no. 1: 1–8.

Sukhoruchenkova, G. 1989. "Kak realno pomoch zhenshchine," *Argumenty i Fakty*, no. 9: 1.

Tamashiro, Hidehiko, et al. 1986. "Methylmercury exposure and mortality in southern Japan: A close look at causes of death," *Journal of Epidemiology and Community Health* 40, no. 2: 181–185.

Treplev, Aleksandr. 1988a. "Khlopkorab," *Ogonek*, no. 43: 36.

_____. 1988b. "Do i posle aplodismentov," *Ogonek*, no. 50: 36–37.

United Nations Environment Programme. 1987. *Environmental Data Report*. London: Basil Blackwell.

United States Bureau of the Census. 1989. *Statistical Abstract of the United States. 1989*. Washington, D.C.: US Government Printing Office.

USSR Academy of Sciences. 1987. *Ekonomika i Organizatsiia Promyshlennogo Proizvodstva*, no. 2: 106.

USSR Attorney's Office. 1989. "Nuzhny realnye rezultaty," *Sotsialisticheskaia Zakonnost*, no. 6: 19.

USSR Children's Fund. 1989. "Desant-89. No. 9. Uzbekskaia SSR. No. 10. Kirgizskaia SSR," *Sem'ia*, no. 40: 4.

USSR Council of Trade Unions. 1989. "Stanki-ubiitsy," *Okhrana Truda i Sotsialnoe Strakhovanie*, no. 2: 1–11.

USSR State Committee on Statistics. 1988a. *Narodnoe Khoziaistvo SSSR V 1987 godu. Statisticheskii Ezhegodnik*. Moscow: Finansy i Statistika.

_____. 1988b. *Naselenie SSSR. 1987. Statisticheskii Sbornik*. Moscow: Finansy i Statistika.

_____. 1989. "Mladenshecskaia smertnost v SSSR," *Argumenty i Fakty*, no. 45: 3.

USSR Supreme Soviet. 1989. "O neotlozhnykh merakh ekologicheskogo ozdorovleniia strany," *Pravda* (3 December): 1, 3.

Valkovics, E. 1984. "L'evolution recente de la mortalite dans les pays de l'Est: Essai d'explication a partir de l'exemple hongrois," *Espace, Populations, Societes* 10, no. 3: 141–168.

Vasiliev, I., and A. Nikonov. 1989. "Tsentr Rossii: Chelovek i zemlia," *Kommunist*, no. 9: 15–20.

Vinogradov, B. 1989. "Vernut Aralu status moria," *Ekonomicheskaia Gazeta*, no. 35: 19.

Volin, V. 1989. "A question of work safety," *Moscow News*, no. 35: 10.

Volkov, M. 1988. "Khlopkovyi molokh prodolzhaet pozhirat vremia, sily, zdorovie detei," *Pravda* (24 November): 2.

_____, and I. Totskii. 1989. "Usnuvshaia sovest," *Pravda* (12 February): 8.

Volkov, N., and G. Matiukhin. 1989. "Konkurentsiia i monopolii," *Pravda* (29 June): 4.

Vorobievskii, Iu. 1989. "Vpered k avarii," *Zhurnalist*, no. 11: 15–17.

Winiecki, Jan. 1987. *Economic Prospects: East and West*. London: The Centre for Research into Communist Economies.

Woodwell, George. 1985. "On the limits of nature," in *The Global Possible: Resources, Development and the New Century*, ed. R. Repetto. New Haven: Yale University Press, pp. 47–65.

Ziegler, Charles. 1980. "Soviet environmental policy and Soviet central planning: A reply to McIntyre and Thornton," *Soviet Studies* 32, no. 1: 124–134.

Tradeoffs Between Human Numbers and Material Standards of Living

PAUL DEMENY

NATURE EXISTS WITHOUT HUMAN PRESENCE, as it did before Homo Sapiens appeared on Earth, or as it does on Mars where inhabitants from a neighboring planet have yet to set foot. Environment, in contrast, is nature seen through the eyes of humans, experienced by them, and evaluated by human criteria. Humans are dependent on a biophysical environment that permits survival and reproduction. Improved human welfare requires success in shaping this environment and in using its renewable and nonrenewable resources, so as to better satisfy human material and spiritual aspirations. These aspirations have meaning only if seen as lodged in persons now alive: in members of present human societies. Values persons hold, however, incorporate a regard for the interests of future generations. Such values may also be sensitive to the perceived interests of nonhuman sentient beings.

A coherent perspective on the impact of population on the environment presupposes clarity about the identity of the evaluator. In God's eyes, presumably, plutonium and oxygen are just two of many elements, an eagle is no more beautiful than a mosquito, and the climate of the Moon is no less agreeable than that of Tuscany. Humans make more biased judgments. To point out this distinction is important, since there is a strong current in the contemporary discussion of environmental issues that, albeit with varying consistency, rejects the validity of the anthropocentric approach. In what follows, in line with standard utilitarian doctrine, I will assume that the criterion of environmental preservation is subordinate to the criterion of improved human welfare at large.

Human valuations concerning either of these desiderata—*environment*, defined in a narrow sense as the agreeableness of people's physical surroundings and their capacity to satisfy human wants, or *welfare*, defined in a comprehensive fashion, balancing environmental goods and values against all other human needs and values—are apt to differ. If such differences affected only the immediate actors, the legitimate public policy interest they could elicit would be nil. How tidy one's neighbor's living room is nobody's business but the neighbor's. But humans live in society, not in isolation, and the sphere of strictly private behavior—private in the sense that no significant external effects are attached to a person's acts—is narrow. All too commonly, the interests of individuals and of their various social groupings in transforming and exploiting the environment are in conflict. Reconciling these differences so as to attain a development path that is socially optimal— that best serves the separate interests of the individual members that compose society—is the task of human institutional design and public policy.

In shaping institutions and adopting public policies that aim at enhancing human welfare, the size and composition of a society's membership list are of eminent interest. The intuitively obvious existence of tradeoffs between human numbers and material welfare is easily envisaged by making extreme assumptions—picturing, say, Japan with a population size equal to that of China or, alternatively, to that of Iceland. Such extremes suggest the putative existence of an optimum population size—a point (or a more or less narrow size-band) somewhere in between: neither too large nor too small. But a search for such an optimum is rather pointless. Population size in a given polity at a given time is inherited from history. Social interest in aggregate human numbers therefore is naturally focused on *change:* on the rules that ultimately govern the rate at which population is growing or decreasing. This brief essay discusses some of the considerations concerning the human environment and bearing on policy decisions related to demographic growth. Do they provide arguments that would justify attempts to influence aggregate change in population numbers through deliberate collective action? The scope of the discussion is narrowed somewhat by a focus on situations characterized by rapid population growth—growth at the historically unprecedented rates of change that still prevail in most contemporary developing countries.

Population and the environment

Sheer human presence and all human activities modify the environment. The extent of the impact tends to be strongly related to human numbers, the scope and intensity of their exertions, and the technology at their disposal. Significant and lasting impact presupposes fairly large numbers and a technology advanced at least beyond that employed by hunter-gatherers. A simple classification of the impacts on the environment distinguishes between outcomes that were the intended fruits of deliberate human action, and those that were necessary, if typically unintended and often unwelcome or unforeseen, byproducts of such action. The notion of "environmental impact," by convention, focuses not on the purposeful achievement but on its undesired side effects—not on the goods created but on the "bads"; not on the cathedral but on the marred hillside from which the stone for building it was quarried.

The potential importance and pervasiveness of such "negative goods" amply justify interest in environmental impacts defined in that narrow sense. The demise of a number of ancient civilizations—for example those of Mesopotamia and Greece—can be traced, at least in part, to ecological damage wrought by human activities, resulting in the exhaustion of some critical resource upon which those civilizations depended. Neither modern industrial economies nor technologically backward contemporary societies with unfavorable population–resource ratios and rapidly growing populations can consider themselves safely exempt from analogous ecological ambushes.

As a generalized example of negative environmental impacts, consider "pollution." In a formulation first suggested by Paul Ehrlich, pollution, at a given time period and defined for the appropriate spatial unit, may be thought of as the combined product of population size, income per capita, and the pollution-intensity of income. The following equation expresses a definitional identity:

$$\text{Pollution} = \text{Population} \times \frac{\text{Income}}{\text{Population}} \times \frac{\text{Pollution}}{\text{Income}}$$

The formula is applicable for consideration of numerous specific environmental impacts. Thus, for example, use of a nonrenewable resource, say oil, can be factored as:

$$\text{Resource use} = \text{Population} \times \frac{\text{Income}}{\text{Population}} \times \frac{\text{Resource use}}{\text{Income}}$$

The formula is readily extended to characterize changes in environmental impact over time. Thus, if income per capita and the pollution-intensity (or the resource use-intensity) of income are held constant, the size of the environmental impact will change in direct proportion to change in population size. Other things equal, and as a first approximation, doubling population size will double pollution and resource use.

The assumption of independence between the three factors in the right-hand side of the equations above is, however, invalid. For example, changes in population size and changes in income per capita may be partly compensating. In particular, slower population growth may be accompanied by more rapid increase in income per capita. The interaction of each of these two terms with the third term, the resource intensity of income use, may be even more important. The latter is affected by the state of the technology characterizing the production and consumption of income. It is also affected by the individual and collective choices that govern the particular uses through which income is expended. Both of these factors are strongly affected by the level of income per capita and, more relevant in the present context, by the relation of population size to the environment and by the rate of population growth. A significant change in the demographic parameters is bound to cause shifts in these relationships, sometimes compensating and sometimes reinforcing the environmental impact a given demographic change in and by itself could be expected to generate. In particular, over time, nonlinearities to scale may appear. Quantitative increases can generate qualitative changes; thresholds separating, for example, tolerable levels of pollution from levels that generate unacceptable risks for human health may be crossed. Up to a certain level, damage to a renewable resource, such as a forest ecosystem, may be corrected by a spontaneous and relatively rapid biological process; beyond that level the damage may be irreparable, or the natural recovery or the human-engineered repair of the ecosystem in question may require a very long time or entail exorbitant cost. Thus, a doubling of population size, even if the other terms on the right-hand side of the equation remain constant, could more than double the environmental impact. In some other instances, scale economies would make the effect less than proportionate.

Simple applications of the formulas above, nevertheless, are broadly suggestive of plausible orders of magnitude of environmental impacts and of the relative importance of the different factors identified in the equations. They explicate and confirm the intuitively obvious: for example, that rapid demographic growth since mid-century (which between 1950 and the late 1980s doubled the world's population) must have been a major contributor to the introduction of pollutants into the human environment and to the use of nonrenewable resources.

This is not to discount the importance of the second and third terms in the equations above. Their impacts on the environment and on nonrenewable resource use were highly important during recent decades. From mid-century to the late 1980s, global income per capita increased approximately two-and-a-half-fold. Rapid technological change, while beneficial in contributing to the increase in labor productivity that permitted such rapid income growth, entailed the adoption of industrial processes that introduced a new range of toxic chemicals and noxious byproducts into the environment. Thus, deleterious environmental effects can be observed even if demographic growth is moderate or nil. For example, the especially severe environmental deterioration in Eastern Europe during recent decades, which is now being documented in increasing detail, seems largely unrelated to rapid demographic growth (although not unrelated to changes in the spatial distribution of the population). Between 1950 and 1990, Eastern Europe's population increased by only 28 percent, and, in some of the environmentally worst affected countries, much more slowly than that. The lion's share of the explanation in this instance appears to be attributable to the drastic rise in the pollution- and resource use-intensities of income that accompanied rapid industrialization in the region. But to ignore the effects of population growth because of such examples is clearly illogical. The examples merely serve as a reminder that situations differ depending on demographic characteristics.

Contrasting demographic–economic patterns

With an admittedly heroic abstraction from the multiplicity of intermediate situations, two contrasting patterns of demographic–economic characteristics may be usefully identified, patterns that are also distinguished by greatly differing significance of population growth for the human environment. The distinction corresponds to the conventional division of countries as belonging to the "developed" (DC) or the "developing" (LDC) world.

In the aggregate, the DC group is characterized by an absolute population size that is large by historical standards—roughly equivalent to the population of the entire globe around the middle of the nineteenth century—even if this population of 1.2 billion (in 1990) constitutes just 23 percent of the world's total. The rate of population growth in the developed countries as a whole is low: currently .5 percent per year and declining. On the assumption that DC fertility rates will reverse the steady downward trend exhibited during the last four decades and will actually increase somewhat from 1990 to 2025, the United Nations population projections (medium variant) anticipate an average annual growth of .33 percent during that period. (The assumption of a future fertility increase is less than convincing. Actual population growth rates may well turn out to be much closer to zero than is projected.) The population of the developed countries in 2025 thus would exceed its 1990 level by 12 percent. In that year, it would constitute 16 percent of the global population.

Further characteristics of the DC group include a per capita income that is extraordinarily high by historical standards. Based on World Bank estimates (with modest extension to countries not covered by the Bank's statistics), gross national product per capita in DCs in 1987 was slightly over $10,000, measured in 1987 dollars. Production of that income (which during the last quarter century has been increasing at an annual rate of over 2 percent per capita) is facilitated by the use of science-based modern technology that is dependent on heavy use of energy derived primarily from fossil fuels, but also and increasingly from nuclear fission; on modes of transportation and communication permitting rapid and low-cost movement of materials, people, and information over large distances; on extensive use of machinery, including machinery capable of markedly changing surface vegetation and topographic features of the land; and on industry producing or making use of an ever-widening array of chemicals and toxic materials.

Conditions in the LDCs are markedly different. In 1990, the aggregate population in these countries was 4 billion: twice as large as the entire global population around 1930. The current rate of expansion of the population exceeds 2 percent per annum. The United Nations projections assume that fertility rates in the developing countries as a whole during the next 35 years will drop by 40 percent. Although, again, this assumption is less than compelling (actual growth rates may be higher than projected because in a number of countries the assumed generalized fertility decline is not yet supported by observed evidence), it would still lead (in combination with moderate assumptions as to the further decrease of mortality) to a 2025 LDC population of 7.1 billion, or an increase of 74 percent over its current level. At that time, population increase in these countries would still exceed 1.1 percent, or nearly 80 million persons per annum. The share of the population of the countries now classified as less developed will have risen from its present 77 percent to 84 percent of the global total.

These demographic characteristics of the LDCs are at present accompanied by per capita income levels markedly lower than in the DCs. Based again on World Bank estimates, average GNP per capita in 1987 was $780, or less than 8 percent of the estimated GNP per capita in the DCs. Certainly, this implied 1:13 ratio between average per capita incomes in LDCs and DCs cannot be taken as an accurate estimate of differences in material levels of welfare. A correction of the estimated figures, making them more closely reflect purchasing-power parities, would appreciably narrow the income gap. Nevertheless, the striking contrast between LDCs and DCs with respect to income per capita would remain after any statistically defensible adjustment. The low income levels, in turn, reflect a state of the LDC economies characterized by only a shallow and partial spread of the advanced technology applied in DCs. The economic structure of most LDCs remains numerically dominated by technologically backward and highly labor-intensive agriculture and by low-productivity handicraft and service sectors. Average per capita use of energy sources dominant in modern industrial economies is still low in LDCs, with use of fuelwood representing a significant fraction of total energy use.

Abstracting from the significant complications introduced by differences in technology between DCs and LDCs with respect to the pollution- and resource use-intensity of income, the current levels of population-related environmental impacts in these two categories of countries may be approximately characterized by the comparative product of the first two terms in the above equations: population size times income per capita.

Using the relevant estimates noted in the preceding paragraphs, the gross world product (GWP) in 1987 can be put at $15 trillion. Eighty percent of this sum, $12 trillion, was income produced in the OECD countries, which, in combination, represent somewhat less than 15 percent of the world's population. OECD income per capita in 1987 was $14,700, or nearly 20 times the corresponding overall LDC figure. Within the latter group, the countries classified by the World Bank as "low income" comprised 56 percent of the world's population, had an average annual income of $290 (or one-fiftieth of the OECD average), and produced less than 6 percent of GWP. Even allowing for significant error in these figures, the estimated composition of GWP by country of origin provides a strong presumptive identification of the DCs as the dominant current source of whatever deleterious environmental impact is attendant upon economic activity. Apart from differences in the ways in which income is produced and expended (differences that partly reinforce, partly weaken this presumption), two considerations modify the portent of the claim. The first concerns change over time, the main topic of the present discussion. The second consideration is related to the geographic–political unit within which environmental impact is experienced: most of the impact is not global but is contained within national boundaries, indeed, within subnational units. In what follows, these two points will be discussed briefly.

The present size of the world population is a given, as are the differing levels of economic development associated with its component parts. The status quo is effectively beyond the reach of policy: deliberate human action can hold sway only over the future. The striking DC–LDC contrasts in anticipated demographic dynamics were noted above. They suggest that population growth per se during the coming decades, and most likely beyond, will virtually cease contributing to changing environmental impact in the DCs. Virtually all such change in these countries will be due to the dynamics of income per capita and the technology applied in producing and expending it.

Demographic growth, in contrast, will continue to be rapid in LDCs. But, as noted above, such growth is currently lightly weighted by income per capita, thus moderating the potential environmental impact. The low incomes now prevailing in LDCs, however, should be seen as anomalous and, it is to be hoped, temporary. Certainly, they do not reflect the aspirations of the LDCs themselves, nor their determination to narrow and eventually to close the gap that separates them from the level of affluence now enjoyed by the developed countries. The populations of the less developed world made no vow of permanent poverty—indeed, their economic policies are oriented toward maximum feasible material growth. Should LDC income per head rise in a rapid and sustained fashion (as has been spectacularly the case in a number of successful LDCs in recent decades), these countries would not only generate virtually all environmental impact attendant upon future demographic growth, but the massive demographic weight of their expanding populations would eventually dominate the global economic picture, including the environmental impact of GWP. Assessment of the size and character of such impact thus crucially depends on expectations about the prospects of LDCs for increasing levels of material welfare. Further considerations that enter into such assessment concern the anticipated feedback of development on demographic change—might it modify the scenario incorporated in the standard UN projections?—and, of course, on judgment about the severity and intractability of the deleterious environmental impact associated with increasing per capita income.

On each of these issues, informed opinion continues to reflect startlingly wide disagreement. It is difficult to avoid concluding that the fields of study bearing on the subject remain in a pre-scientific state, with experts defending positions and making forecasts that are often diametrically opposed. Signs of convergence between conflicting interpretations of empirical evidence or between contending theoretical constructs are largely absent. For the sake of mnemonic convenience and brevity, although with some injustice to disciplinary labels, two salient and conflicting perspectives may be distinguished. They may be characterized as "ecological" and "economic."

Ecological perspectives

In the ecological perspective, the dominant tone in discussing the impact of demographic and economic growth (and of modern technology) on the environment tends to be deeply pessimistic. There is a vast and rapidly expanding literature identifying and documenting damage generated by such growth upon terrestrial and aquatic ecosystems and their various specific components, and demonstrating growing atmospheric pollution. Indeed, a plausible discussion of the impact of rapid demographic change could be offered by reporting salient findings culled from the literature discussing changes in the human environment—as is done, in fact, albeit in non–population-centered contexts, in numerous specialized reports. Accounts of environmental issues in the mass media also largely consist of retailing such findings.

But, at least for practitioners of the social sciences, and especially for economists and historians, the accumulation of ecological studies resists such use. For all their scientific underpinnings and admirable empirical bent, the findings in the ecological literature thus far lend themselves poorly to generalizations that would aid understanding of overall developmental trends. Reflecting, no doubt, the vast complexity of ecosystems susceptible to damage from economic activity and the great variety of means through which such damage can be inflicted, the findings offered tend to be episodic, often plainly focused on the untypical and the extreme, and often simply eclectic or even merely anecdotal. The list of documented dire ecological consequences attendant upon human activity, each more or less loosely linked or linkable to population growth, seems, at least to the nonexpert, endless. Loss of topsoil, desertification, deforestation, toxic poisoning of drinking water, oceanic pollution, shrinking wetlands, overgrazing, species loss, shortage of firewood, exhaustion of oil reserves and of various mineral resources, siltation in rivers and estuaries, encroachment of human habitat on arable land, dropping water tables, erosion of the ozone layer, loss of wilderness areas, global warming, rising sea levels, nuclear wastes, acid rain—these and many other problems cover the range from the dubiously conjectural through the plainly marginal to the disturbing but evidently exceptional all the way to the potentially cataclysmic. These catalogues of man-inflicted damages are seldom relieved by reports of agreeable ecological–environmental change, thus arousing lay suspicion that their muster is directed to support a preconceived analytic conclusion and a political agenda: that sustained material growth is impossible, or rather that it necessarily leads to decay, deterioration, and ultimately to ecological collapse. These latter propositions, qua long-run propositions, are universally accepted, as indeed they are self-evident. But findings about ecological changes, to be relevant for shaping public policy, would need to be fitted into broader conceptual models that can plausibly accommodate and organize disparate facts, including human behavioral responses, and provide adequate parametrization for identifying time scales and for assessing relative importance of deleterious effects—issues critical for taking corrective action. In the absence of this, the findings poorly support the sweeping policy conclusion that is not only hostile to demographic growth but often explicitly urges responses that would be apt to drastically slow or even preclude future economic growth.

Economic perspectives

Economists' interpretations of salient issues of population change, development, and the environment, despite the notable divergences in detail and emphasis between expert positions, differ significantly from those derived from the ecological perspective. While economists recognize that, other things equal, sustained population growth would lead to an ultimate low-level Malthusian equilibrium or, alternatively, to systemic collapse, with few exceptions (more vocal in the 1960s and 1970s than in the 1980s) economists see such outcomes as sufficiently remote in time so as not to qualify as a guide for prediction or ground for policy intervention in the near and medium-term future. Even with no further progress in state-of-the-art technology, including organizational skills, economists see large hidden reserves for growth in the existing inefficiencies with which production is carried out in LDCs, and in the extent of unused technological knowledge. Tapping these reserves by adopting the institutional arrangements and production practices of the most successful economies should permit substantial material improvement in virtually all LDCs even if they have to accommodate further major population increases.

This expectation is reinforced in the light of historical experience, which suggests that assuming cessation of technological–organizational progress is plainly unrealistic. Indeed, most economists tend to read the lessons of the past as ground for optimism concerning the overall direction of world economic development. Taking measured changes in average material conditions over long periods of time as the criterion of welfare improvement, the last 200 years, and especially the last 40 years, can be fairly described as an historically unprecedented success story in material progress. This claim is not contradicted by the recognition that the rate of advance has been uneven, both geographically and between social strata within countries. Nor is it necessarily negated by the fact that, along with rapidly increasing total population size, the absolute number of people in poverty may have also been increasing. The relevant measures of success are the decreasing proportion of the poor and progress toward material improvement among those who are still in poverty. In a process of secular transition, widening relative differentials of income are an expected concomitant of the differing time of entry, by country and by social strata, in the process of modern economic growth—a process characterized by the adoption of institutions and policies permitting the increasing application of science, technology, and physical and human capital in expanding society's capacity to satisfy human wants. As that process spreads, geographically and between social strata, the rate of material progress among the highest-income population segments slows down and the latecomers eventually are able to catch up with them. As to demographic growth, its initial acceleration is a natural byproduct of such economic transformation since, predictably, the fruits of economic improvement are in part used for obtaining better health and lowered mortality. Malthusian outcomes, however, need not be the inevitable result of rapid population growth. Such growth is transitory: given economic success, the spontaneous onset of "demographic transition" can be confidently expected. Pressures built into the reward mechanisms of modern industrial society induce behavioral changes that eventually lead to low fertility, hence to low or no population growth.

The economic perspective also offers a more benign and optimistic interpretation of environmental changes. This holds both for past trends and for anticipated future developments. Improving environmental quality and securing the best possible environmental outcome are objectives that people pursue not single-mindedly but in competition and along with other desirable goals. They seek an overall welfare optimum, rather than maximize satisfaction in particular domains without regard to cost in terms of opportunities foregone. Their choices are constrained by their income within a set of preferences, and are conditioned by their knowledge, access to information, and cultural background.

Environmental choices

The environmental choices of individuals or individual families that do not significantly affect other persons are instructive in this regard. They show wide variations in their environment-affecting practice, even at given levels of income and knowledge. There are individuals who are tidy and highly safety-conscious; and there are individuals who are not. But both types are optimizers according to their best lights, rather than maximizers of any particular component within their preference sets: even in Swiss households pianos may not be dusted-off twice a day. Depending on tastes, environmental choices may vary considerably, yet make equally good sense. When incomes also differ, optimal tradeoffs between environmental and other objectives will naturally differ as well. Someone with modest means will rationally choose to live in an environment of lower quality than a rich person, and accept greater risks to his safety and health. Such tradeoffs also shift with increasing knowledge about the true environmental risks and qualities attached to available options. Some environmental actions are not highly knowledge-intensive. Thus, garden-variety household pests are easily recognized, eliciting the correct remedies, for example, the acquiring of a cat. But detecting radon gas is not possible without scientific instruments, and acting upon relevant findings requires sophisticated understanding of possible dangers.

The homey examples just cited intimate the essential nature of environmental choices and their crucial dependence on income levels, knowledge, and preferences. But they deal with problems whose solution entails costs and benefits that affect essentially the person or persons who decide how to deal with the problem. The most difficult, and often the most important, environmental issues arise from individual and group actions whose benefits accrue to the actors but whose costs are borne, entirely or disproportionately, by someone else. To seek to privatize the benefits of one's actions and transfer the costs of those actions to the rest of society is a universal human tendency. In modern societies and under conditions of rapid economic development, this tendency, as a rule, is too weakly kept in check by social norms and moral precepts alone. When such is the case, the damage generated by environmental "externalities" may get out of hand, with grave consequences for human welfare. Solution of the problem calls for recourse to social technologies: the adoption or development of institutional frameworks permitting efficient negotiation and effective enforcement of mutually acceptable standards and modes of behavior. In a complex society, the difficulties of devising appropriate institutional arrangements—low-cost mechanisms for reaching and enforcing private contracts, tort laws, taxes and bounties discouraging undesirable patterns of consumption and promoting desirable modes of conduct, government regulations limiting or prohibiting socially disapproved behavior, collective action aimed at producing or protecting public environmental amenities, and so on—are enormous. So are the potential environmental and general welfare benefits which success in that endeavor can secure for the members of a society. But seeking solutions to environmental problems through institutional changes and legal–political arrangements is itself a potentially error-prone process, with great opportunities for social mischief.

Population growth and material progress

It follows from the above discussion that three major factors will largely determine future environmental trends. Each is a potentially powerful lever for ameliorative intervention through appropriate public policies, especially in LDCs. The first factor is economic growth. Higher incomes would broaden the range of available choices and permit satisfaction of needs beyond basic necessities. The income elasticity of demand for environmental quality is high. Economic growth and environmental improvement are not enemies. To the contrary, they go hand in hand: controlling pollution and purchasing improved environmental quality are value-producing charges on income. Only reasonably affluent societies can afford adequate levels of such spending. In low-income countries rapid economic growth is especially indispensable for creating a capacity that would permit protecting and improving the environment.

The second factor is knowledge, embodied in a widely diffused form in the citizenry at large, accumulated in public agencies, and concentrated at the state-of-the-art level in well-established scientific and educational institutions. Better monitoring of environmental changes and clearer understanding of environmental options, risks, and benefits permit more enlightened and efficient choices both by private individuals and by public bodies.

The third factor is least easily measured but by all evidence is the most important. It involves social technology: improved institutions and related socio-political arrangements capable of generating efficient, coordinated responses to recognized social problems. Preventing environmental problems from getting out of hand and devising ways of acquiring and protecting the level and quality of environmental amenities best suited to citizens' preferences are crucial tasks for the public agenda.

The brief enumeration above of the factors playing the most influential roles in setting future environmental trends brings us back to the issue of rapid population growth in LDCs. As was noted above, according to mainline economic thinking rapid population growth, given reasonably enlightened economic and social policies in the countries experiencing such growth, need not be inconsistent with continuing economic improvement. Contemporary LDCs also have a special asset: they can exploit the advantages of being latecomers to modern economic growth. They can adopt, at relatively low cost, technologies developed elsewhere, bypass technological detours pioneers unwittingly had to follow, learn from other countries' policy mistakes, attract foreign capital and expertise, relieve domestic natural resource constraints through access to foreign markets, and so on. Thus, most LDCs should be able to attain rates of economic growth that are faster than their rates of population growth, hence increase their incomes per capita. Only egregiously misguided public policies could bar this avenue of steady material improvement. As in earlier development experience, economic growth would eventually bring about the onset of fertility decline. Where fertility is already decreasing, continued economic growth would in due course bring the demographic transition to its ultimate conclusion.

But avoiding disaster and making slow improvement may fall far short of what should be not only a desirable but also an attainable rate of material progress. Countries experiencing rapid population growth are necessarily forced to devote a disproportionate share of their economic and social efforts to keeping pace with sheer demographic expansion. There is a long list of problems whose solution is rendered more difficult and more onerous under conditions of rapid population growth. The central task of development—the structural transformation of the traditional economy into a high-productivity modern industrial economy—will require far greater investments and take more time than would be the case with slower demographic growth. The absorption of large youth cohorts that seek entry into the labor force will be more difficult, as will be lowering the existing levels of unemployment and underemployment. Urbanization will be a greater burden as cities grow faster, and economies of scale will be exhausted earlier than would be the case with slower population growth. In many LDCs with relatively unfavorable land–population ratios, attainment of self-sufficiency in food, even if strongly desired, is likely to be delayed or rendered technically unfeasible. With rapidly increasing absolute numbers, a country's capacity to finance its development through exports drawing on the domestic natural resource-base is bound to be lowered. These and similar problems would tend to slow economic development in terms of income growth per capita. Thus, when population growth is rapid, countries' ability, both on private and on public account, to address environmental problems is weakened, and private and collective spending on positive environmental improvements receives low priority. Progress toward greater knowledge and sophistication in handling environmental problems is hindered due to countries' impaired capacity to provide good-quality education to all young persons and to support a strong state-of-the-art scientific base that is needed to accurately assess and successfully address environmental issues. Finally, rapid population growth further overloads the typically weak administrative-political structures found in LDCs, and makes reform of institutional arrangements affecting the efficacy of environmental and other development-related policies more difficult.

Developing countries with rapid population growth, and international organizations that seek to assist the development efforts of such countries, including their efforts to improve the environment, thus can ill afford to ignore the issue of population change. In particular, the timing of the onset of fertility decline and the tempo of that decline are unlikely to be optimal under a laissez faire national fertility policy. Exceptional situations apart, the demographic predicament in LDCs during the next few decades is not the inability of these countries to upgrade economic performance and to effect environmental improvements if population growth remains rapid and fertility declines but slowly. The problem, rather, is the likelihood of an increasing demographic saturation that is successfully accommodated, but that locks LDCs into a long-term development path which is distinctly inferior in terms of standards of material welfare and its environmental component to what would be attainable with a rapid decline of fertility to replacement level or, temporarily, even below it.

The welfare and environmental consequences of a failure to achieve effective social control of fertility at present are still largely contained within individual countries. For this reason, the tradeoffs that must be made between continuing population growth and gains in material progress are primarily for each country to decide, in light of their own preferences. Population-generated spillovers crossing international borders, however, are increasing in importance and this trend is bound to continue in the future, particularly as growing LDC populations achieve higher levels of income per capita. Assessing such tradeoffs and acting upon the findings will have to move increasingly also to the international political and economic agenda.

VIRGINIA ABERNETHY is Professor of Psychiatry, School of Medicine, Vanderbilt University, Nashville, Tennessee, and Editor, *Population and Environment.*

MEINRAT O. ANDREAE is Professor and Director, Biogeochemistry Department, Max Planck Institute for Chemistry, Mainz, Germany.

RICHARD ELLIOT BENEDICK is on leave from the US Department of State as Senior Fellow of The Conservation Foundation, World Wildlife Fund, Washington, D.C.

MIKHAIL S. BERNSTAM is Senior Research Fellow, Hoover Institution, Stanford University.

RICHARD E. BILSBORROW is Research Professor, Department of Biostatistics, and Fellow, Carolina Population Center, University of North Carolina, Chapel Hill.

ELWOOD CARLSON is Professor of Sociology, Department of Sociology, University of South Carolina, Columbia.

ELLIS B. COWLING is Associate Dean for Research, College of Forest Resources, and University Professor at Large, North Carolina State University, Raleigh.

HERMAN E. DALY is Senior Economist, Environment Department, The World Bank, Washington, D.C.

KINGSLEY DAVIS is Senior Research Fellow, Hoover Institution, Stanford University, and Distinguished Professor of Sociology, University of Southern California.

PAMELA F. DeLARGY is Research Associate, Carolina Population Center, University of North Carolina, Chapel Hill.

PAUL DEMENY is Distinguished Scholar, The Population Council, New York.

MALIN FALKENMARK is Professor of International Hydrology, Swedish Natural Science Research Council, Stockholm, Sweden.

GRIFFITH FEENEY is Research Associate, Population Institute, East-West Center, Honolulu, Hawaii.

MICHAEL H. GLANTZ is Head, Environmental and Societal Impacts Group, National Center for Atmospheric Research, Boulder, Colorado.

EDWARD D. GOLDBERG is Professor of Chemistry, Scripps Institution of Oceanography, San Diego, La Jolla, California.

NATHAN KEYFITZ is Head, Population Program, International Institute for Applied Systems Analysis, Laxenburg, Austria.

RONALD D. LEE is Professor of Demography and Economics, Graduate Group in Demography, University of California, Berkeley.

JING-NENG LI is Professor and Director, Institute of Population and Development Research, Nankai University, Tianjin, China.

AMORY B. LOVINS is Director of Research, Rocky Mountain Institute, Old Snowmass, Colorado.

IRA S. LOWRY is a Consultant in Housing and Development, Pacific Palisades, California.

NORMAN MYERS is a Consultant in Environment and Development, Oxford, England.

DAVID PIMENTEL is Professor, College of Agriculture and Life Sciences, Cornell University, Ithaca, New York.

MARCIA PIMENTEL is Senior Lecturer, Division of Nutritional Sciences, Cornell University, Ithaca, New York.

PETER H. RAVEN is Director, Missouri Botanical Garden, St. Louis.

KENNETH W. WACHTER is Professor, Graduate Group in Demography, University of California, Berkeley.

EUGENE ZAVARIN is Professor, Forest Products Laboratory, College of Natural Resources, University of California, Richmond.